Lecture Notes in Computer Science 581
Edited by G. Goos and J. Hartmanis

J.-C. Raoult (Ed.)

CAAP '92

17th Colloquium on Trees in Algebra and Programming
Rennes, France, February 26–28, 1992
Proceedings

Springer-Verlag
Berlin Heidelberg New York
London Paris Tokyo
Hong Kong Barcelona
Budapest

Series Editors

Gerhard Goos
Universität Karlsruhe
Postfach 69 80
Vincenz-Priessnitz-Straße 1
W-7500 Karlsruhe, FRG

Juris Hartmanis
Department of Computer Science
Cornell University
5148 Upson Hall
Ithaca, NY 14853, USA

Volume Editor

Jean-Claude Raoult
IRISA, University of Rennes
Campus Universitaire de Beaulieu, Avenue du Général Leclerc
35042 Rennes Cedex, France

CR Subject Classification (1991): D.1, E.1, F

ISBN 3-540-55251-0 Springer-Verlag Berlin Heidelberg New York
ISBN 0-387-55251-0 Springer-Verlag New York Berlin Heidelberg

Printed in Germany

Typesetting: Camera ready by author
Printing and binding: Druckhaus Beltz, Hemsbach/Bergstr.
45/3140-543210 - Printed on acid-free paper

Preface

This seventeenth Colloquium on Trees in Algebra and Programming was held jointly with the European Symposium on Programming, in Rennes, February 26-28, 1992. The previous colloquia were held in France, Italy, Germany, Spain, Denmark and England. Every even year, as in 1992, it is held jointly with ESOP; every other year, it is part of TAPSOFT (Theory And Practice of SOFTware development). The proceedings of ESOP appear in an accompanying volume of Lecture Notes in Computer Science.

In the beginning, CAAP was devoted to algebraic and combinatorial properties of trees, and to their role in various fields of computer science. As the reader will notice, the scope of CAAP has been extended to other discrete structures, like graphs, equations and transformations of graphs, and their links with logical theories. The programme committee received 40 submissions (one being too late), from which 18 were selected.

ESOP addresses fundamental issues and important developments in the specification and implementation of programming languages and systems. It continues lines begun in France and Germany under the names "Colloque sur la Programmation" and the GI workshop on "Programmiersprachen und Programmentwicklung". The programme committee received 71 submissions, from which 26 were selected.

Programme Committee for

CAAP	ESOP
A. Arnold (Bordeaux)	E. Astesiano (Genova)
A. Bertoni (Milano)	G. Cousineau (Paris)
P. Darondeau (Rennes)	O.-J. Dahl (Oslo)
M. Dauchet (Lille)	H. Kirchner (Nancy)
R. De Nicola (Pisa)	B. Krieg-Brückner (Bremen)*
M. Dezani-Ciancaglini (Torino)	T. Maibaum (London)
J.W. Klop (Amsterdam)	P. Mosses (Aarhus)
M. Nivat (Paris)	B. Nordström (Göteborg)
A. Poigné (St. Augustin)	F. Orejas (Barcelona)
J.-C. Raoult (Rennes)*	D. Sannella (Edinburgh)
M. Steinby (Turku)	P. Wadler (Glasgow)
C. Stirling (Edinburgh)	R. Wilhelm (Saarbrücken)
W. Thomas (Kiel)	
J. Tiuryn (Warsaw)	

(*chairmen)

Invited Speakers for

CAAP	ESOP
Bruno Courcelle (Paris)	Ole-Johan Dahl (Oslo)
Harald Ganzinger (Saarbrücken)	Andrezj Tarlecki (Warsaw)

The colloquium was sponsored by INRIA, CNRS, and the University of Rennes, and supported by GI, the University of Bremen, and the township of Rennes.

I wish to express my gratitude to all the members of the programme committees, as well as the referees listed below for their care in reviewing the submitted papers; I also thank Elisabeth Lebret, who took care efficiently of many details of the local organization.

Rennes, January 1992 Jean-Claude Raoult

List of Referees for CAAP 1992

André Arnold
Egidio Astesiano
Alberto Bertoni
M.A. Bonuccelli
Ahmed Bouajjani
Gérard Boudol
J.C.Bradfield
Manfred Broy
Danilo Bruschi
Felice Cardone
Didier Caucal
Mario Coppo
Philippe Darondeau
Max Dauchet
Mariangiola Dezani-Ciancaglini
Frank Drewes
Hartmut Ehrig
D. Frutos Escrig
G. Faglia
Boubakar Gamatié
S. Gnesi
Annegret Habel
Furio Honsell
Ullrich Hustadt
P. Inverardi
Claude Jard
Jean-Pierre Jouannaud
Richard Kennaway
A.J. Kfoury
Jan Willem Klop
Hans-Jörg Kreowski
Michel Latteux
Ugo de 'Liguoro
Michael Löwe
G. Mauri
E. Moggi
Fritz Müller
David Murphy
Rocco De Nicola
D. Niwinski
J.G. Penaud
Michele Pinna
V. van Oostrom
G. Pighizzini
Ramon Pino Perez
Adolfo Piperno
Detlef Plump
Axel Poigné
Andreas Potthoff
E. Rachini
Jean-Claude Raoult
Ronchi Della Rocca
Kay Salomaa
Davide Sangiorgi
S. Seibert
Magnus Steinby
Colin Stirling
Wolfgang Thomas
Sophie Tison
Jerzy Tiuryn
Pawel Urzyczyn
E. Valkema
Fer-Jan de Vries
R.C. de Vrijer
Wand
Th. Wilke
M. Zacchi
W. Zielonka

Contents

A Constructive Valuation Interpretation for Classical Logic and its Use in Witness Extraction

Franco Barbanera, Stefano Berardi
Dipartimento di Informatica
Corso Svizzera, 185 10149 Torino (Italy)
barba,stefano@di.unito.it

Abstract A constructive interpretation of classical arithmetic in terms of a Kripke-like valuation semantics of proofs is presented. We use this interpretation for motivating a constructive procedure, based on reduction rules, for extracting witnesses from proofs of Σ_1^0 sentences in classical arithmetic.

Introduction.

It is an old result that from a proof of a Σ_1^0 sentence (i.e. a sentence of the form $\exists$n.P(n) for a decidable predicate) in classical arithmetic we may effectively extract a *witness*, i.e. an integer n such that P(n) holds (see [Kre], [Fried]). Several procedures of witness extraction are known. However, all known procedures are *very* involved. Even on simple examples it is difficult to apply them "by hand", or to foresee their behaviour if we implement them.
Such a situation is similar to the first attempts to implement program extraction from proofs in intuitionistic logic thirty years ago. The development of typed functional languages was then greatly helped by the use of Heyting constructive semantics for intuitionistic proofs. By analogy, we suppose that now it is so difficult to deal with witness extraction procedures because we lack a constructive semantics for classical proofs. We consider this paper a first step in this direction.

We first introduce a Kripke-like semantics for First Order Classical Arithmetic. "Possible worlds" are interpreted by partial valuations, a familiar concept in Classical Logic (see [Schü]). Then we consider a witness extraction procedure defined in [BB] and inspired by [Pra 2]. This procedure makes use of reductions on an extension of typed λ-calculus, with a double negation connective, called PVS. These reductions can be nicely justified by means of our semantics. The normalization process for PVS is interpreted as a process which extracts a finite inconsistent valuation from an infinite inconsistent one.

How can we make sense of a normalization procedure in a semantics of classical proofs? Consider again the well-known example of Heyting semantics for intuitionistic proofs. Such a semantics perfectly interprets the β-reduction rule, as follows. In Heyting semantics, a function a |-> b[a], from the proofs of A to the proofs of B, is considered to be a proof of A$\rightarrow$B. Such proof is denoted by λx:A.b. The β-rule: (λx:A.b)(a) -> b[a] can be justified *extensionally* because (λx:A.b)(a) and b[a] have the same interpretation, and *intensionally* because it makes explicit the intended meaning of (λx:A.b)(a). We want to find a similar "justification" for the reduction rules we use for witness extraction in Classical Logic.

In the classical case Heyting's semantics cannot be applied. Let us explain why. Heyting's interpretation of the intuitionistic falsehood ($\bot$) is empty. Therefore if the interpretation of A is inhabited then the interpretation of $\neg A$ ($\equiv A\rightarrow\bot$) is empty; and if the interpretation of A is empty then the interpretation of $\neg A$ consists of the unique function from the empty set to the empty set. In particular, the interpretation of $\neg\neg A$ ($\equiv \neg A\rightarrow\bot$) consists of at most one element. Any function from a set with at most one element is constant. Thus the double negation axiom: $\neg\neg A\rightarrow A$ of Classical Logic should be constructively interpreted as a *constant* function from (the interpretation of) $\neg\neg A$ to (the interpretation of) A, i.e. as *an effective way to pick an element of a non-empty A, uniformly on A*. But one can easily see that such a choice function cannot be constructive.

It is then clear that a constructive interpretation of Classical Logic must give to the classical falsehood $\bot$ a different meaning. Instead, the connectives $\rightarrow$, $\wedge$, $\forall$ may be interpreted as in Heyting semantics, and the connectives $\neg$, $\vee$, $\exists$ may be defined from those, given the constructive interpretation of $\bot$.
Hence the main problem is to find a constructive interpretation of the classical $\bot$.
What is the rôle of $\bot$ in classical proofs?
When we have a proof

$$\begin{array}{c} A \\ \vdots \\ \bot, \end{array}$$

we do not record how we get $\bot$ from a proof of A. This accounts for the empty interpretation of $\bot$. In the Σ^0_1 (or Π^0_2) fragment of classical logic, exactly this "missed-out" information that we disregarded can account for the constructive meaning of $\bot$. Hence to interpret $\bot$ we have to interpret even the information we used to obtain it. In other words, we have to introduce an indexed $\bot$ (i.e. $\bot_v$)[1]. The index v, that, as we shall see, has to be extended to each formula in the proof, behaves like a memory location where some of the information contained in the proof is stored, to be retrieved when necessary.

We describe now our solution. Following ideas contained in [Ber] we interpret v as any partial valuation (a set of "judgments" about the truth or falsity of atomic formulas) which forces A to be true. Then we interpret $\bot_v$ as the statement "v forces $\bot$", i.e. "v is inconsistent". By a compactness argument, a proof of $\bot_v$ (a proof that v is inconsistent) must really use only a finite subset v_0 of v. *v_0 is now a positive information associated to the classical $\bot$.* Such positive information accounts for the constructive meaning of Σ^0_1 (and Π^0_2) classical formulas, and also allows an informal semantics interpretation of Prawitz's reductions and of the witness extraction procedure described in [BB].

The above program is carried out in several steps.
In section 1, we extend the "partial valuation interpretation" to any proof in Peano Arithmetic. We add indexes of the shape $v\models t.\dots$, $v\models f.\dots$ to the formulas in classical proofs expanding any proof p of "if $A_1,\dots, A_n$ then A" to a proof of "if $v_1\models t.A_1,\dots,v_n\models t.A_n$ ($v_1,\dots,v_n$ force $A_1,\dots, A_n$) then $\Sigma^n_{j=1}v_j\models t.A$ (the union of $v_1,\dots,v_n$ forces A)". The formulas in logical rules are expanded as well to take care of partial valuations. *No changes are instead required on the tree structure of the proof.* For instance, double negation rule:

---

[1] One could object that indeed $\bot$ has already an index, namely its proof, but we want to interpret $\bot$ as a connective, independently from its proofs.

$$\frac{\begin{array}{c}\neg A \\ \vdots \\ \bot\end{array}}{A}$$

becomes:

$$\frac{\begin{array}{c}[v\models \mathbf{f}.A] \\ \vdots \\ \mathbf{inc}(v+vt)\end{array}}{vt\models \mathbf{t}.A}$$

where vt is a "valuation term" and v a "valuation variable" bound in the proof.
For each logical connective and rule we outline a constructive interpretation in term of partial valuations.

In section 2 we introduce Prawitz's reduction rules for Peano Arithmetic in our partial valuation setting. We call the resulting system PVS. Then we show that each reduction rule makes explicit the constructive meaning of *classical* logical connectives in the partial valuation semantics; exactly as β-rule makes explicit the constructive meaning of the *intuitionistic* connective "→" in Heyting semantics. All this is used to interpret the whole extraction procedure.

In section 3 a proof of strong normalization for Prawitz's reductions is given, alternative to the proofs given in [Pra 2] and [BB]. We obtain here the strong normalization by means of a "reduction-preserving" translation of our system in a strongly normalizing system (a variant of Gödel's system T).

1. The Valuation System for Peano Arithmetic.

This section will be devoted to the presentation of our valuation system for Peano Arithmetic (PA). This valuation system is a sort of semantic enrichment of the usual natural deduction calculus, exploiting ideas similar to Kripke forcing semantics. The basis of such a system are the notions of judgment and valuation. It can then be viewed as a formal system to reason about judgments and (abstract) valuations and yields a natural constructive interpretation for Peano Arithmetic.

Let us first recall what are the terms of PA and its formulas.

PA-terms

The *PA-terms* are defined inductively in the following way :

- the constant 0 is a term
- a variable $n,m,n_1,\ldots$ is a term
- if u is a term then s(u) is a term
- if u, f, t are terms and n,m are variables, then $Rec_{n,m}(u,f,t)$ is a term

We shall omit the subscripts n,m in $Rec_{n,m}(u,f,t)$ when it is not strictly necessary.
In the following these terms will be referred to simply as *terms* if no confusion arises.
If f is a term, we shall denote with f(n) the fact n is a variable in f.

The *atomic formulas* are all the expressions of the form t = u , where t and u are terms.

We shall use $\neg$, $\wedge$ and $\forall$ as primitive logical connectives. All the other usual connectives can be defined in the the traditional way for classical logic:
$A\vee B =_{df} \neg(\neg A\wedge\neg B)$ $A\rightarrow B =_{df} \neg(A\wedge\neg B)$ $\exists n.A =_{df} \neg\forall n.\neg A$.

We are now ready to formally define the notion of judgment and valuation.

Judgments.
A *judgment* is an expression of the form **t**.A or of the form **f**.A, with A a formula. (Intuitively the expressions **t**.A and **f**.A stand for "A is true" and "A is false" respectively).

In what follows γ will be a variable ranging over the set $\{\mathbf{t},\mathbf{f}\}$. $\bar{\gamma}$ is defined in the following way

$$\bar{\gamma} = \begin{cases} \mathbf{f} & \text{if } \gamma=\mathbf{t} \\ \mathbf{t} & \text{if } \gamma=\mathbf{f} \end{cases}$$

We define now a notion of canonical form of judgments. The operation of putting a judgment in canonical form is nothing else but the usual elimination of two consecutive negations in calssical formulas.
Formally, a judgment $\gamma'.A'$ is the *canonical form* of $\gamma.A$ <u>iff</u>
1. A" is obtained from A by eliminating all consecutive double negations
2. if $A'' \equiv \neg A\hat{}$ then $\gamma' \equiv \bar{\gamma}$ and $A' \equiv A\hat{}$, else $\gamma' \equiv \gamma$ and $A' \equiv A''$

For instance, the canonical form of $\mathbf{t}.\neg\neg\neg(\neg\neg A_1\wedge\neg\neg\neg A_2)$ is $\mathbf{f}.A_1\wedge\neg A_2$.

We define a relation " ~ " among judgments in the following way :
$\gamma.A \sim \gamma'.A'$ <u>iff</u> there exist $\underline{A}$ and $\underline{A'}$ such that :
- A and A' are obtained from $\underline{A}$ and $\underline{A'}$ by substituting equal PA-terms;
- $\gamma.\underline{A}$ and $\gamma'.\underline{A'}$ have the same canonical form.

From now on, we shall implicitely identify judgements having the same canonical form.

A judgment is called *conjunctive* (*disjunctive*) if its canonical form has one of the following shapes :
t(**f**).P (with P a propositional variable); $\mathbf{t}(\mathbf{f}).A_1\wedge A_2$; $\mathbf{t}(\mathbf{f}).\forall n.A$.

Judgments for atomic formulas will be referred to as *atomic* judgments.

Valuations.
A *(partial) valuation* is a set of judgments.
The terms of the formal system we are defining (*valuation-terms*) are terms denoting valuations. Let us define them formally.
- Φ is a valuation-term (intuitively the "empty" valuation).
- $v,w,v_1,w_1,...$ are valuation-terms (valuation variables).
- vt+vt' is a valuation-term if vt and vt' are so (intuitively the "union" of the valuations).
- $\{\gamma.P \mid n_1,..,n_m\}$ is a valuation-term, provided that $n_1,..,n_m$= FV(P) and P is atomic. (intuitively the partial valuation consisting in the set of all possible *closed* instances of γ.P). If P is closed we shall use the notation $\{\gamma.P\}$.

In a valuation-term $\{\gamma.P \mid n_1,..,n_m\}$ one has to list all the variables of P since we need to order them.

In the following, in order not to use a too cumbersome notation, we shall not distinguish between a valuation term and the partial valuation it denotes (we have not been formal in specifying the partial valuation denoted by a valuation-term since it is quite clear from the syntax and the informal explanations given).

Let us define now some operations on valuation terms which define the notion of subterm for valuation-terms.
Let vt be a valuation-term.
$\boldsymbol{C}$ (vt) = $\{ vt_i \mid vt = \Sigma_{i=1}^{n} vt_i$ and $vt_i \neq \Phi \}$ ($\boldsymbol{C}$ stands for "components")
$\boldsymbol{I}$ (vt) =
$\{\{\gamma.P(t_1,..,t_m)\} \mid \{\gamma.P \mid n_1,..,n_m\} \in \boldsymbol{C}$ (vt) and $P(t_1,..,t_n)$ is an instance (possibly open) of P$\}$
($\boldsymbol{I}$ stands for "instances").

In the following it will be necessary to have a relation on valuation-terms that equates those valuation-terms denoting the same partial valuation. We then define such an equivalence relation in the following way : vt = vt' <u>iff</u> $\boldsymbol{C}$ (vt) = $\boldsymbol{C}$ (vt').
Of course this relation can be also axiomatized as follows:

vt = vt	vt+vt' = vt'+vt	Φ + vt = vt
vt + vt = vt	vt+(vt'+vt") = (vt+vt')+vt".	

With all the ingredients at hand we are now ready to define the valuation system for Peano arithmetic.

The Valuation System.

Above we have just defined the terms of our valuation system : the valuation-terms.
In the valuation system there is a predicate on valuations : **inc**(-).
Intuitively **inc**(vt) means that vt denotes a valuation inconsistent with the atomic rules of PA (not that the valuation denotes all the possible judgments, but that from it is possible to derive all the possible judgments).
As it will be clarified later in the procedure for witness extraction, if we manage to derive **inc**(vt) from an empty set of assumptions then it will be *effectively* possible to "find out" a (finite) subset $vt_o \subseteq vt$ together with an argument in PA for the inconsistency of vt_o (note that we have made no distinction between valuation-terms and partial valuations denoted by them).

The formulas of the system are of the form **inc**(v) or vt $\models \gamma$.A.

vt $\models$ **t**(**f**).A means intuitively that A is true(false) in the valuation vt.

The axioms and rules of the valuation system are the following:

- <u>*Axioms and (atomic) rules for Peano arithmetic*</u>

$$(PA_1)\ \frac{}{vt \models \mathbf{t}.n = n} \quad \text{for any vt.} \qquad\qquad (PA_2)\ \frac{vt \models \mathbf{t}.n = m}{vt \models \mathbf{t}.m = n}$$

$$(PA_3)\ \frac{vt_1 \models t.n = m \quad vt_2 \models t.m = z}{vt_1+vt_2 \models t.n = z} \qquad (PA_4)\ \frac{vt \models t.s(0)=0}{\mathbf{inc}(vt)}$$

$$(PA_5)\ \frac{vt \models t.n = m}{vt \models t.f[n] = f[m]} \text{ for any term f.} \qquad (PA_6)\ \frac{}{vt \models t.Rec(0,f,t) = t} \text{ for any vt.}$$

$$(PA_7)\ \frac{}{vt \models t.Rec_{n,m}(s(u),f,t) = f[n:=u,m:=Rec_{n,m}(u,f,t)]}$$

- *Rules for valuations*

$$\frac{\mathbf{inc}(vt)}{\mathbf{inc}(vt+vt')} \text{ for any vt'.}$$

$$\frac{}{vt \models \gamma.P(t_1,..,t_n)} \text{ if } \gamma.P(t_1,..,t_m) \in \mathit{I}\,(vt)$$

- *Logical rules*

$$\frac{\begin{array}{c}[v \models \gamma.A] \\ \vdots \\ \mathbf{inc}(v+vt)\end{array}}{vt \models \gamma.A}\ (*) \qquad \frac{vt \models \gamma.A \quad vt' \models \gamma.A}{\mathbf{inc}(vt+vt')}$$

$$\frac{vt \models t.A_1 \quad vt \models t.A_2}{vt \models t.A_1 \wedge A_2} \qquad \frac{vt \models t.A_1 \wedge A_2}{vt \models t.A_i}\ i=1,2$$

$$\frac{vt \models t.A}{vt \models t.\forall n.A}\ (\overset{*}{*}) \qquad \frac{vt \models t.\forall n.A}{vt \models t.A(u)}$$

$$\frac{vt \models t.A(0) \quad vt \models t.\forall n.(A(n) \rightarrow A(s(n)))}{vt \models t.A(u)}$$

(*) it is possible to discharge only assumptions with valuation terms consisting of a single variable; besides, the valuation-variable v does not occur free in the assumptions on which **inc**(v+vt) depends but [v⊨ γ.A].

($\overset{*}{*}$) n not free in the judgments of the assumptions on which vt⊨ t.A depends.

In this sytem if we have two equal valuation terms, two judgments with the same canonical form or two equal PA-terms, then we can always substitute one for the other.

Axioms (PA_6) and (PA_7) can indeed be viewed as computation rules on terms. We do not define now formally what we mean by *computation* and by "the term u computes to the term u'", since it is quite clear. We just recall that all the computations on PA-terms terminate.

Remark.1 We have given rules for conjunction and universal quantification only for the case of judgments beginning with **t**. The rules dealing with conjunction and universal quantification in the other case, namely

$$\frac{vt \models \mathbf{f}.A_i}{vt \models \mathbf{f}.A_1 \wedge A_2}\ i=1,2 \qquad \text{and} \qquad \frac{vt \models \mathbf{f}.A}{vt \models \mathbf{f}.\forall m.A},$$

are useless. They correspond to rules for disjunction and existential quantification and, since we are in a classical context, they are derivable:

$$\frac{\dfrac{\dfrac{[w \models \mathbf{t}.A_1 \wedge A_2]}{w \models \mathbf{t}.A_i} \quad v \models \mathbf{f}.A_i}{\mathbf{inc}(v+w)}}{v \models \mathbf{f}.A_1 \wedge A_2} \qquad \frac{\dfrac{\dfrac{[w \models \mathbf{t}.\forall m.A]}{w \models \mathbf{t}.A} \quad v \models \mathbf{f}.A}{\mathbf{inc}(v+w)}}{v \models \mathbf{f}.\forall m.A}$$

In the following we shall use the first two rules of the above remark as abbreviations of their derivations.

Constructive interpretation of the rules

We discuss here briefly the constructive interpretation of the rules given above. This interpretation is quite natural, given the interpretation of classical falsehood in terms of inconsistent valuations.
Let us start with the rule

$$\frac{\begin{array}{c}[v \models \bar{\gamma}.A]\\ \vdots\\ \mathbf{inc}(v+vt)\end{array}}{vt \models \gamma.A}.$$

This rule indeed consists of two different rules according to what is actually γ. If $\gamma \equiv \mathbf{f}$ it is the equivalent to the classical rule of double negation elimination, otherwise it is the equivalent to the introduction of the negation.
It can be interpreted *functionally* . A proof of $vt \models \gamma.A$ can be viewed as a "function" that, given a proof of $vt' \models \bar{\gamma}.A$, returns a proof of the inconsistency of vt'+vt (a proof of **inc**(vt) consists in a *finite* valuation included in vt and a proof of its inconsistency).

The rules for introducing $\wedge$ and $\forall$ have a Heyting-like interpretation.

The rule

$$\frac{vt \models \gamma.A \qquad vt' \models \bar{\gamma}.A}{\mathbf{inc}(vt+vt')}$$

is the equivalent, in our interpretation, to the rule of modus ponens in intuitionistic logic, which has an interpretetion, in Heyting's semantics, in terms of application of a function to its argument. Since our rule is completely symmetric, by the fact that $\gamma.A$ is equivalent to $\bar{\gamma}.\neg A$, it can be interpreted as two different applications according to which one of the two subproofs is seen as the function.

The interpretation of the rules for the elimination of $\wedge$ and $\forall$ would be similar to Heyting's one if the only way to obtain a conjunction or a universal quantification were by means of the corresponding introduction rule. But in classical logic this is not the case. A proof of a conjunction, for instance, is not always a pair since we can obtain a conjunction also by an application of the double negation elimination. In such a situation however a justification, and a constructive interpretation of the rule of elimination of $\wedge$ can be given as follows. Suppose that a proof of vt$\models$ **t**.$A_1\wedge A_2$ be given by a function that, given a proof of vt'$\models$ **f**.$A_1\wedge A_2$, returns a proof of **inc**(vt'+vt). We want to obtain two proofs of vt$\models$ **t**.A_1 and vt$\models$ **t**.A_2. Let i=1,2; by our functional interpretation of double negation, it is enough to define a function that takes a proof of vt'$\models$ **f**.A_i and returns a proof of **inc**(vt'+vt). We already remarked that from vt'$\models$ **f**.A_i we can prove vt'$\models$ **f**.$A_1\wedge A_2$. From it and vt$\models$ **t**.$A_1\wedge A_2$ we can get **inc**(vt'+vt) as wished. The interpretation of the elimination of $\forall$ can be given similarly.

It is possible to prove that a formula D is derivable in Peano arithmetic from assumptions $G_1,..,G_n$ <u>iff</u> under the assumptions $w_1\models$**t**.$G_1,..,w_1\models$**t**.G_n ($w_1,..,w_n$ valuation-variables), $\Sigma_{j=1}^{n} w_j\models$**t**.D is provable.

The System PVS

We define now a typed system such that there exists a formulae-as-types correspondence with our valuation system. Of course we could have chosen to deal directly with proofs in the valuation system, but it is no doubt easier to "handle" terms rather then proofs.

Let us first define what the types of our system are.
The types are the formulas of our valuation system, i.e. the set of types of PVS is defined by the following grammar :

T ::= **inc**(vt) | [vt $\models$ γ.A] where vt is a valuation-term and A a formula of PA.

The system PVS is based on a set of pseudo-terms $\boldsymbol{M}$ defined by the following grammar :

$\boldsymbol{M}$ ::= $PA_j(t_1,..,t_k,\boldsymbol{M_1},..,\boldsymbol{M_n})$ | $\gamma.P(t_1,..,t_m)$ | **x** | $\aleph$x:[v $\models$ γ.A].$\boldsymbol{M}$ | Cut($\boldsymbol{M},\boldsymbol{M}$) | <$\boldsymbol{M},\boldsymbol{M}$> | $\pi_i(\boldsymbol{M})$ | λn.$\boldsymbol{M}$ | $\pi_u(\boldsymbol{M})$ | Ind(u,$\boldsymbol{M},\boldsymbol{M}$)
where **x** is the category of variables, P ranges over atomic formulas of PA, A over formulas of PA, j=1,..,8 , $1\leq k\leq 3$, $0\leq n\leq 2$, $m\geq 0$, i=1,2 , t_i and u range over terms of PA and $\gamma.P(t_1,..,t_m)$ is a judgment.

A *statement* is an expression of the form M:T where M is a pseudo-term and T a type. M is called the *subject* of the statement.
A *declaration* is a statement where M is a variable.
A *basis* is a set of declarations.
If B is a basis we shall denote with B,x:T the basis B$\cup${x:T}.
It will be clear from the context if by FV(B) we mean the term variables forming the subjects of the statements of B, the valuation-variables or the PA-term variables in B.
A pseudo-term M is a *term* in the basis B with type T if we manage to derive B$\vdash$ M:T by means of the following term rules.

With respect to the system of valuation, in the present system we formalize better (by means of rule (eq) below) the possibility of replacing (when possible) a judgment, valuation term or PA-term for another.

Ax) $B,x{:}T \vdash x{:}T$ T a type

$$\text{PA}_j)\ \frac{B\vdash M_1{:}[vt_1\models t.P_1] \ldots\ldots B\vdash M_{n_j}{:}[vt_{n_j}\models t.P_{n_j}]}{B\vdash PA_j(t_1,..,t_{k_j},M_1,..,M_{n_j}) : [\Sigma_{i=1}^{n_j} vt_i \models t.P^j]}\ (*)\quad j\neq 4$$

(*) if $\frac{vt_1\models t.P_1 \ldots\ldots vt_{n_j}\models t.P_{n_j}}{\Sigma_{i=1}^{n_j} vt_i \models t.P^j}$ is the instance of axiom (PA_j) of the valuation calculus obtained by replacing $t_1,..,t_{k_j}$ for its free variables.

$$\text{PA}_4)\ \frac{B\vdash M{:}[vt\models t.s(0)=0]}{B\vdash PA_4(M) : \mathbf{inc}(vt)}$$

$$\text{I})\ \frac{}{B \vdash \gamma.P(u_1,..,u_m) : [vt \models \gamma.P(u_1,..,u_m)]}\quad \text{if } \{\gamma.P(u_1,..,u_m)\}\in \mathit{I}\ (vt)$$

$$\mathcal{N})\ \frac{B,x{:}[v\models \gamma.A]\vdash M : \mathbf{inc}(v+vt)}{B\vdash \mathcal{N}x{:}[v\models \gamma.A].M : [vt\models \gamma.A]}\quad \text{if } x\notin B \text{ and } v\notin B$$

$$\text{Cut})\ \frac{B\vdash M : [vt\models \gamma.A] \quad B\vdash N : [vt'\models \gamma.A]}{B\vdash Cut(M,N) : \mathbf{inc}(vt+vt')}$$

$$\langle\_,\_\rangle)\ \frac{B\vdash M_1 : [vt\models t.A_1] \quad B\vdash M_2 : [vt\models t.A_2]}{B\vdash \langle M_1,M_2\rangle : [vt\models t.A_1\wedge A_2]}$$

$$\pi_i)\ \frac{B\vdash M : [vt\models t.A_1\wedge A_2]}{B\vdash \pi_i(M) : [vt\models t.A_i]}\quad i=1,2$$

$$\lambda)\ \frac{B\vdash M : [vt\models t.A]}{B\vdash \lambda n.M : [vt\models t.\forall n.A]}\quad \text{if } n\notin FV(B)$$

$$\pi_u)\ \frac{B\vdash M : [vt\models t.\forall n.A]}{B\vdash \pi_u(M) : [vt\models t.A(u)]}$$

$$\text{Ind})\ \frac{B\vdash N : [vt\models t.A(0)] \quad B\vdash M : [vt\models t.\forall n.(A(n)\rightarrow A(s(n)))]}{B\vdash Ind(u,N,M) : [vt\models t.A(u)]}$$

$$\text{eq})\ \frac{B\vdash M : [vt\models \gamma.A] \quad \gamma.A \sim \gamma'.A' \quad vt \subseteq vt'}{B\vdash M : [vt'\models \gamma'.A']}$$

In rule (eq) $vt \subseteq vt'$ stands for $vt = vt'$ or $\mathcal{C}(vt) \subseteq \mathcal{C}(vt')$ (set-theoretically).
Note that, because of the presence of rule (eq), the rules given above are not really term formation rules, but define indeed a system of *type inference* . Rule (eq) is necessary since we want to take into account the rule that allows to infer **inc**(vt+vt') from **inc**(vt). Moreover we

want that, when one uses the reductions that we shall define below, the type of a term is preserved. It would have been possible to avoid rule (eq) only by considering the judgments modulo "~".[2]

It is straightforward to check that the terms corresponding to the derived rules of Remark 1 are the following : $\mathcal{N}x:[w\models \mathbf{t}.A_1\wedge A_2].Cut(\pi_i(x),M)$ (: $[v\models \mathbf{f}.A_1\wedge A_2]$)
$\mathcal{N}x:[w\models \mathbf{t}.\forall m.A'].Cut(\pi_u(x),M)$ (: $[v\models \mathbf{f}.\forall m.A']$)
We shall use in the following the abbreviations $\sigma_i(M)$ and $\sigma_u(M)$ for the first and second term above respectively.

In the following, when we state B⊢ M:T we mean that *it is possible to derive* B⊢ M:T in system PVS .

A PVS-term is called *closed* if it has no free term variables. It is called *PA-closed* if it does not contain free PA-variables and *valuation-closed* if it does not contain free valuation variables.

We define Terms(PVS) = {M | B⊢ M:T for some basis B and some type T }

A type is called conjunctive(disjunctive) if it is of the form $v \models \gamma.A$ with $\gamma.A$ conjunctive(disjunctive). A term is called conjunctive(disjunctive) if its type is so.

It is not difficult to prove that there is a "minimal" type of a term up to "~" for judgments, and up to "=" for valuations.

We state now the formal equivalence between our valuation calculus and Peano arithmetic in natural deduction style.

Theorem 1.1 (*Validity Theorem*)
A formula D is derivable in Peano arithmetic from assumptions $G_1,..,G_n$ <u>iff</u> for a term M $w_1\models \mathbf{t}.G_1,..,w_n\models \mathbf{t}.G_n \vdash M : [\Sigma_{j=1}^{n} w_j\models \mathbf{t}.D]$ is derivable in system PVS .
Proof
By induction on the derivations. □

Reductions for Terms of System PVS.

We define and justify now a set of reductions on terms of system PVS, similar to the ones defined by Prawitz in [Pra2]. These reductions will be used by our witness extraction procedure.

Ind. $\begin{cases} Ind(0,N,M) \rightarrow N \\ Ind(s(u),N,M) \rightarrow \mathcal{N}y:[v \models \mathbf{f}.A(s(u))].Cut(<Ind(u,N,M),y>,\pi_u(M)) \end{cases}$

Comp. $u \rightarrow u'$ iff u is a PA-term which computes to u'.

[2] What would be possible to do it is also to introduce two types of atomic formulas : P and P', the latter standing for the negation of the former. In such a way negation it is no more a primitive connective, rule (eq) can be avoided (or at least simplified) and even some proofs can be shortened. We have restrained however to make such a choice in order not to have too many defined notions.

disj.-$\mathcal{N}$. if $\gamma.A$ is a *conjunctive* -judgment then

$$\mathrm{Cut}(\mathcal{N}x{:}[v \models \gamma.A].M,N) \;\rightarrow\; M[x{:=}N,v{:=}vt]$$

where the type of N is $[vt \models \gamma.A]$.

disj.-$\mathcal{N}'$. if $\gamma.A$ is a *conjunctive* -judgment then

$$\mathrm{Cut}(N,\mathcal{N}x{:}[v \models \gamma.A].M) \;\rightarrow\; M[x{:=}N,v{:=}vt]$$

where the type of N is $[vt \models \gamma.A]$.

conj.-$\mathcal{N}$. $\mathcal{N}x{:}[v\models\gamma.A].M \;\rightarrow\; \langle\mathcal{N}x{:}[v\models\mathbf{f}.A_1].M[x{:=}\sigma_1(x)],\mathcal{N}x{:}[v\models\mathbf{f}.A_2].M[x{:=}\sigma_2(x)]\rangle$

if $cf(\gamma.A) = \mathbf{f}.A_1\wedge A_2$

where $\sigma_i(N) = \mathcal{N}x{:}[w\models\mathbf{t}.A_1\wedge A_2].\mathrm{Cut}(\pi_i(x),N)$ (: $[v\models \mathbf{f}.A_1\wedge A_2]$)

conj$\forall$-$\mathcal{N}$. $\mathcal{N}x{:}[v\models\gamma.A].M \;\rightarrow\; \lambda m.\mathcal{N}x{:}[v\models\mathbf{f}.A'].M[x{:=}\sigma_m(x)]$

if $cf(\gamma.A) = \mathbf{f}.\forall m.A'$

where $\sigma_u(N) = \mathcal{N}x{:}[w\models\mathbf{t}.\forall m.A'].\mathrm{Cut}(\pi_u(x),N)$ (: $[v\models \mathbf{f}.\forall m.A']$)

π. $\pi_i(\langle M_1,M_2\rangle) \;\rightarrow\; M_i \quad i=1,2$

β. $\pi_u(\lambda n.M) \;\rightarrow\; M[n{:=}u]$

Each of these reductions clearly corresponds to a reduction of a proof in the valuation system. The second of the rules Ind looks rather messy just because we do not consider the implication as a primitive connective. This leads to the fact that, if we have Ind(u,N,M) which proves $vt\models \mathbf{t}.A(u)$ and M which proves $vt\models\mathbf{t}.\forall n.\neg(A(n)\wedge\neg A(s(n)))$ (recall that $A\rightarrow B =_{def}\neg(A\wedge\neg B)$) we can obtain a proof of $vt\models \mathbf{t}.A(s(u))$ in the following way

$$\dfrac{\dfrac{\genfrac{}{}{0pt}{}{\Pi}{vt\models \mathbf{t}.A(u)} \quad \dfrac{v\models \mathbf{f}.A(s(u))}{v\models \mathbf{t}.\neg A(s(u))}}{v+vt\models \mathbf{t}.(A(u)\wedge\neg A(s(u)))} \qquad \dfrac{\genfrac{}{}{0pt}{}{\Pi'}{vt\models \mathbf{t}.\forall n.\neg(A(n)\wedge\neg A(s(n)))}}{vt\models \mathbf{f}.(A(u)\wedge\neg A(s(u)))}}{\genfrac{}{}{0pt}{}{}{vt\models \mathbf{t}.A(s(u))}}\;\mathbf{inc}(v+vt)$$

To avoid such sorts of cumbersome terms we of course could have presented the implication as a primitive connective. We wish to stress however that we made this choice in order to have always clear throughout the paper the fact that we are working in a *classical* context, a context where the connectives $\neg$, $\wedge$ and $\forall$ are enough.

The reduction rules described above have a precise computational meaning in terms of the interpretation of the rules of the valuation system outlined before. In particular, the reduction rules makes explicit the constructive meaning of the *classical* logical connectives in the partial valuation semantics; exactly as the β-rule makes explicit the constructive meaning of the *intuitionistic* connective "$\rightarrow$" in Heyting semantics. This "computational rôle" of the reduction rules is now briefly discussed.

We have seen that the rule for the introduction of Cut can be viewed, in our interpretation, as an application (two different simmetric applications indeed).
Rules disj.-$\mathcal{N}$ and disj.-$\mathcal{N}'$ clearly exploit this interpretation. The actual shape of this rules is not the only possible. We chose it in order to have a neat correspondence with Prawitz's reduction rules and to simplify the proof of strong normalization.

For conj.$\mathcal{N}$ and conj.$\forall$-$\mathcal{N}$ let us see first see what they look like in the valuation system.

Rule conj.-$\mathcal{N}$.

$$\dfrac{\begin{array}{c}[v\models f.A_1\wedge A_2]\\ \vdots\\ \mathbf{inc}(v+vt)\end{array}}{vt\models t.A_1\wedge A_2} \quad \rightarrow \quad \dfrac{\dfrac{\begin{array}{c}\dfrac{v\models f.A_1}{v\models f.A_1\wedge A_2}\\ \vdots\\ \mathbf{inc}(v+vt)\end{array}}{vt\models t.A_1} \qquad \dfrac{\begin{array}{c}\dfrac{v\models f.A_2}{v\models f.A_1\wedge A_2}\\ \vdots\\ \mathbf{inc}(v+vt)\end{array}}{vt\models t.A_2}}{vt\models t.A_1\wedge A_2}$$

Rule conj$\forall$-$\mathcal{N}$.

$$\dfrac{\begin{array}{c}[v\models f.\forall m.A]\\ \vdots\\ \mathbf{inc}(v+vt)\end{array}}{vt\models t.\forall m.A} \quad \rightarrow \quad \dfrac{\dfrac{\begin{array}{c}\dfrac{[v\models f.A]}{v\models f.\forall m.A}\\ \vdots\\ \mathbf{inc}(v+vt)\end{array}}{vt\models t.A}}{vt\models t.\forall m.A}$$

It is not always true in classical logic that, when we have a proof for a conjunction or a universal quantification, this proof is reducible respectively to a pair or an abstraction : we could have obtained it by means of a double negation.
However, as remarked previously, our interpretation of a proof of $vt\models \gamma.A$ as a "function" that, given a proof of $vt'\models \overline{\gamma}.A$, returns a proof of the inconsistency of vt'+vt, allows us to give, even in such a case, a constructive meaning to the proofs. In fact we can look at proofs of conjunctions or universal quantification obtained by double negation as pairs of functions and abstractions respectively. This constructive meaning of conjunction and universal quantification obtained by double negation is exactly what rules conj.$\mathcal{N}$ and conj.$\forall$-$\mathcal{N}$ express.

The rôle of rules Ind and Comp does not need further explanation, being quite clear; as well as rules π and β, whose existence is motivated as in Heyting's semantics of proofs.

All the terms of system PVS are strongly normalizable with respect to the reductions defined above.

Theorem 1.2 (*Strong Normalization Theorem*)
Let M$\in$Terms(PVS). Then M is strongly normalizable.

The proof of this theorem will be the subject of Section 3.

All the strong normalization theorems for natural deduction calculi allow one to have theorems about the form of normalized proofs. This is also our case. The theorem on the form of terms in normal form, given below, will be crucial for our witness extraction procedure.

The symbols <->, λ, $\mathcal{N}$, 0 and s will be called *introduction symbols* since they are the main symbols of introduction rules.
The symbols π_i, π_u, Cut (when Cut is not applied to terms with types that are not atomic), Ind and $Rec_{n,m}$ will be called *elimination symbols* since they are the main symbols of elimination rules.

The free variables, the component $\gamma.P(u_1,..,u_m)$ of a term, PA_j's and Cut (when Cut is applied to terms with atomic types) will be called, "par abuse de langage", *atomic symbols* .

Theorem 1.3 (*Form of Normal Terms*)
Let M∈Terms(PVS) and let M be in normal form.
If the first symbol of M is an elimination symbol then $FV(M) \neq \Phi$.
Proof
By induction on the structure of M.
If the first symbol of M is an elimination symbol then there is no discharging of variables by means of this symbol. Hence if an immediate subterm of M begins with an elimination symbol the thesis follows by the induction hypothesisis. If an immediate subterm of M is a variable the thesis follows easily. Let us assume that all the immediate subterms of M begin with an introduction symbol or an atomic symbol and show that this leads to a contradiction. Let us consider different cases according to the first symbol s of M.

- $s = \pi_i$

if the the first symbol of an immediate subterm is an introduction symbol it has necessarily to be <-> or $\mathcal{N}$. In both cases this would imply that the term is not in normal form. In fact in the first case we could apply the reduction π_i and in the second one the reduction conj-$\mathcal{N}$.

- $s = \pi_u$

if the the first symbol of an immediate subterm is an introduction symbol it has necessarily to be λ or $\mathcal{N}$. In both cases this would imply that term is not in normal form. In fact in the first case we could apply rule β and in the second one rule conj$\forall$-$\mathcal{N}$.

- s = Cut

in such a case (since by hypothesis the Cut is not atomic) we have necessarily that the immediate subterms of M do not have an atomic type and that the second symbols of one of them is $\mathcal{N}$, because there exist no other introduction symbols for a non-atomic disjunctive term. It would then be possible to apply the reduction disj-$\mathcal{N}$ or disj-$\mathcal{N}$' to M.

- s = Ind

in such a case the second symbol has necessarily to be Rec since if it is s or 0 we could apply reduction Ind to M. Then if there is no free variable we could apply rule Comp. □

Corollary 1.4
Let M∈Term(PVS), M in normal form, closed and PA-closed.
Then the symbol it begins with is *either* an introduction symbol *or* an atomic symbol.
Proof
Easy, since, by hypothesis and Theorem 1.3, M cannot begin with an elimination symbol . □

Corollary 1.5
Let M∈Term(PVS), M closed and PA-closed with type **inc**(vt) or vt $\models \gamma.P$ with $\gamma.P$ atomic.
Then M is formed only by atomic symbols, atomic cuts and $\mathcal{N}$ for disjunctive atomic judgments.
Proof
Easy from Corollary 1.4. □

2. Extracting Constructive Content from Classical Proofs.

We are interested in extracting the constructive content from (closed) proofs of Σ^0_1 formulas (and then from Π^0_1 formulas, by allowing free variables) in Peano arithmetic.

As mentioned in the introduction, we wish to use our partial valuation semantics to interpret (a variant of) a witness extraction procedure devised in [BB] for Peano arithmetic[3]. In the previous section we have interpreted the reduction rules of system PVS. They are used in [Pra 1][Pra 2] to give proofs of consistency for various logics and in [BB] to extract a witness.

It is possible to look at the witness-extraction procedure used in [BB] as a *counterexample-destructor* procedure.
An interpretation one could give to constructive proofs is that they provide examples of what they prove, i.e. if we prove $\forall x.\exists y.P(x,y)$, the proof provides us with a function ϕ such that, for all x, $P(x,\phi(x))$ holds. In classical logic instead, a point of view from which one could look at proofs is that of considering them as non-counterexamples, i.e. if we prove classically a sentence A its proof is, in a sense, something that, when it is given a counterexample of A, destroys it by showing that it leads to an inconsistency. Kreisel's result ([Kre]) that the sets of Π^0_2 sentences provable in classical and intuitionistic logics coincide, can be viewed as the fact that in classical logic non-counterexamples and examples coincide.

In the witness extraction procedure we start with a closed proof of a formula $\exists n.f(n)=0$ (it is possible to show that a quantifier-free formula in Peano arithmetic can always be replaced by an atomic formula of the form $f(n)=0$, where f is a PA-term for a primitive recursive function).
From this proof it is possible to obtain, by Theorem 1.1, a term $M : [\Phi \models \mathbf{t}.\exists n.f(n)=0]$.
Of course this term can act as non-countrexample only if we *offer* to it a counterexample to destroy. In our context a counterexample is nothing else but a valuation which falsifies our existential statement, leading to an inconsistency. Destroying the counterexample will then consist in producing a ground and finite instance of the counterexample-valuation that generates the inconsistency.

Let us define formally the counterexample-valuation $vt_{\neg\exists n.f(n)=0}$ which falsifies the given Σ^0_1 formula $\exists n.f(n)=0$.

$$vt_{\neg\exists n.f(n)=0} =_{Def} \{\mathbf{f}.f(n)=0 \mid n\}.$$

In our valuation system it is possible to have a closed proof of $vt_{\neg\exists n.f(n)=0} \models \mathbf{f}.\exists n.f(n)=0$. Let us give the derivation of the corresponding term in system PVS :

$$\cfrac{\cfrac{\cfrac{\cfrac{}{\vdash c(n) : [vt_{\neg\exists n.f(n)=0} \models \mathbf{f}.f(n)=0]}\,(I)}{\vdash c(n) : [vt_{\neg\exists n.f(n)=0} \models \mathbf{t}.\neg f(n)=0]}\,(eq)}{\vdash \lambda n.c(n) : [vt_{\neg\exists n.f(n)=0} \models \mathbf{t}.\forall n.\neg f(n)=0]}\,(\lambda)}{\vdash \lambda n.c(n) : [vt_{\neg\exists n.f(n)=0} \models \mathbf{f}.\neg\forall n.\neg f(n)=0\ (\equiv \mathbf{f}.\exists n.f(n)=0)]}\,(eq)$$

where $c(n) \equiv \mathbf{f}.f(n)=0$.

---

[3] It is worth to point out that the procedure for witness extraction from *classical* proofs in [BB] works also for higher order Peano arithmetic and, moreover, it needs not necessarily to be restricted to proofs in PA. Indeed we could treat in the same way any extentions of PA with rules for Horn sequents, i.e. atomic rules that in the valuation system would become :

$$\frac{vt_1 \models \mathbf{t}.P_1 \ldots\ldots vt_k \models \mathbf{t}.P_k}{\Sigma_{i=1}^{k} vt_i \models P} \qquad \frac{vt_1 \models \mathbf{t}.P_1 \ldots\ldots vt_k \models \mathbf{t}.P_k}{inc(\Sigma_{i=1}^{k} vt_i)} \qquad n \geq 0 \quad P_i, P, Q \ \text{ atomic}$$

Then, given the term M : $[\Phi \models t.\exists n.f(n)=0]$ and using the term $\lambda n.(\mathbf{f}.f(n)=0)$, it is straightforward to get a closed term of type **inc**$(vt_{\neg\exists n.f(n)=0})$ i.e.

$$Cut(M,\lambda n.(\mathbf{f}.f(n)=0)) : \mathbf{inc}(vt_{\neg\exists n.f(n)=0})$$

We shall call *extr-f(n)* the PVS-term so obtained.

The task of what we have naively called "counterexample destruction" is performed on the term *extr-f(n)* by the reductions defined in the previous section.

By the Strong Normalization Theorem we can (strongly) normalize *extr-f(n)* .
The theorem on the form of normal terms allows us to get important informations from the normal form of *extr-f(n)*, mainly deriving by the fact that in terms in normal form the double-negation rule is used only on closed atomic judgments. How to get this informations and what they consist of is made explicit in the following definition and Lemma.

Definition 2.1 (*Finite valuations and vt-ext* (M))
- A valuation term vt is called *finite* iff $\mathcal{C}$ (vt) = $\{vt_i \mid 1 \le i \le n\}$ with $vt_i \equiv \{\gamma.P_i\}$ for all $1 \le i \le n$.
- Let M∈Terms(PVS). *vt-ext* (M) is the valuation defined as follows:
vt-ext (M) = $\Sigma_{i\in I} \{\gamma.P_i(u_1,..,u_{mi}) \mid n_1,..,n_{pi}\}$ ($n_1,..,n_{pi} = FV(P_i(u_1,..,u_{mi}))$)
where $\{\gamma.P_i(u_1,..,u_{mi}) \mid i\in I\}$ is the set of subterms of M of the shape $\gamma.P(t_1,..,t_l)$.

Lemma 2.2
Let M∈Terms(PVS), M normal, closed and PA-closed and M with type **inc**(vt) or vt $\models \gamma.P$ with $\gamma.P$ atomic .
Then it is also possible to derive for M the type **inc**(vt') or vt' $\models \gamma.P$ with vt'=*vt-ext* (M).
Moreover *vt-ext* (M) is finite.
Proof
To prove this lemma we indeed prove a stronger property, i.e. that if M has free variables of type $w_j \models \gamma.P$ (w_j valuation variable, j∈J and $\gamma.P$ disjunctive) and M has type **inc**($\Sigma_{k\in K}\, w_k$ +vt)
or $\Sigma_{k\in K}\, w_k$ +vt $\models \gamma.P$ then it is possible to derive for M also the type
inc($\Sigma_{k\in K}\, w_k$ +vt') or $\Sigma_{k\in K}\, w_k$ +vt' $\models \gamma.P$ with vt'=*vt-ext* (M).
By induction on the derivation of M.
By Corollary 1.5 we need to consider only few cases.

- Ax) $B,x:[w_k \models \gamma.P] \vdash x : [w_k \models \gamma.P]$

trivial

- PA$_j$)

$$\frac{B\vdash M_1:[\Sigma_{k\in K1}\, w_{1k} + vt_1 \models \mathbf{t}.P_1] \ldots\ldots B\vdash M_{nj}:[\Sigma_{k\in Knj}\, w_{njk} + vt_{nj} \models \mathbf{t}.P_{nj}]}{B\vdash PA_j(t_1,..,t_{hj},M_1,..,M_{nj}) : [\Sigma_{i=1}^{nj}(\Sigma_{k\in Ki}\, w_{ik} + vt_i) \models \mathbf{t}.P^j]}$$

Easy by induction hypothesis

- I)

$$\frac{}{B \vdash \gamma.P(u_1,..,u_m) : [vt \models \gamma.P(u_1,..,u_m)]} \quad \text{if } \gamma.P(t_1,..,t_m) \in I \text{ (vt)}$$

It is easy to see that it has necessarily to be $P(t_1,..,t_m)$ PA-closed, otherwise, since M is PA closed, the free PA-variables in $P(t_1,..,t_m)$ should have been closed by some application of rule (λ) contradicting corollary 1.5.
Then it is possible to have
$B \vdash \gamma.P(t_1,..,t_m) : [vt' \models \gamma.P(t_1,..,t_m)]$ with $vt' = \{\gamma.P(t_1,..,t_m)\} = \mathit{vt\text{-}ext}\ (\gamma.P(t_1,..,t_m))$.

- $\mathcal{N}$)

$$\frac{B, x:[w \models \gamma.A] \vdash M : \mathbf{inc}(w + \Sigma_{k\in K}\, w_k + vt)}{B \vdash \mathcal{N} x:[w \models \gamma.A].M : [\Sigma_{k\in K}\, w_k + vt \models \gamma.A]} \quad \text{with } cf(\gamma.A) \text{ atomic}$$

Easy by induction hypothesis.

- Cut)

$$\frac{B \vdash M : [\Sigma_{k\in K}\, w_k + vt \models \gamma.A] \qquad B \vdash N : [\Sigma_{h\in H}\, w_h + vt' \models \gamma.A]}{B \vdash Cut(M,N) : \mathbf{inc}(\Sigma_{k\in K}\, w_k + \Sigma_{h\in H}\, w_h + vt + vt')}$$

By Corollary 1.5 we have that this Cut is atomic. The thesis follows easily from induction hypothesis.
It is easy to check that if M is closed and PA-closed then *vt-ext* (M) is finite. □

Then in the normal form of *extr-f(n)* only a finite number of closed instances of $vt_{\neg\exists n.f(n)=0}$ (i.e.$\mathcal{C}$ (*vt-ext* (*extr-f(n)*))) is used . If *vt-ext* (*extr-f(n)*) $=\{f.f(u_1)=0\}+...+\{f.f(u_k)=0\}$ then a witness of the inconsistency is exactly one of the elements $u_1,..,u_h$ since, by having derived an inconsistency, for at least one of them, say u_k, $t.f(u_k)=0$ must hold.

This looks like the end of the story but, as it is easy to see, a last problem is left to us. In fact in *vt-ext* (*extr-f(n)*) we can have many judgments, without knowing which of them are real witnesses of the inconsistency.
In such a case it is impossible to find out *directly* a term witnessing for the formula $\exists n.f(n)=0$. (We have used the word "directly" since a possible way to find out the real witnesses is, taken the numerals $u_1,..,u_k$ from *vt-ext* (*extr-f(n)*), to check which of them satisfies $f(u_i)=0$, since $f(n)=0$ is a decidable predicate. This is not what we want. We are looking for a method enabling us to extract the witness without having to perform computations).
We shall prove in the following that this problem can be solved by introducing a new sort of reduction on terms. Before doing this let us give an example where this problem arises. In the example we shall not be too formal, since we want just to give the "flavour" of the problem. In order to have a clear example, we shall not use a formula of the form $\exists n.f(n)=0$, but a different one for which there is no loss of generality for the procedure. Moreover, to simplify the notation, we shall present the example directly in the valuation system.

Let be $\phi(n)$ a PA-term representing a certain recursive function. In PA, if we manage to prove that $\phi(1)+\phi(2)+\phi(3) = 30$, it possible to prove also $\exists n.\phi(n) \geq 10$. The proof of this fact in our system of valuation will then look like as follows

$$\dfrac{\dfrac{\dfrac{\dfrac{[v\models \mathbf{t}.\forall n.\phi(n) < 10]}{v\models \mathbf{t}.\phi(1) < 10}\quad \dfrac{[v\models \mathbf{t}.\forall n.\phi(n) < 10]}{v\models \mathbf{t}.\phi(2) < 10}\quad \dfrac{[v\models \mathbf{t}.\forall n.\phi(n) < 10]}{v\models \mathbf{t}.\phi(3) < 10}}{v\models \mathbf{t}.\phi(1)+\phi(2)+\phi(3) < 30}\qquad \begin{matrix}\vdots\\ \models \mathbf{t}.\phi(1)+\phi(2)+\phi(3) = 30\end{matrix}}{\mathbf{inc}(v)}}{\models \mathbf{t}.\exists n.\phi(n) \geq 10}$$

Notice that $\mathbf{t}.\phi(1)+\phi(2)+\phi(3) = 30$ can be proved in the empty valuation.

It is easy to see now that using the valuation $\{\mathbf{f}.\phi(n) \geq 10 \mid n\}$ we can get

$$\dfrac{\dfrac{}{\{\mathbf{f}.\phi(n) \geq 10 \mid n\}\models \mathbf{f}.\phi(n) \geq 10}}{\{\mathbf{f}.\phi(n) \geq 10 \mid n\}\models \mathbf{f}.\exists n.\phi(n) \geq 10}$$

and then from the derivation above we can get

$$\dfrac{\begin{matrix}\vdots\\ \models \mathbf{t}.\exists n.\phi(n) \geq 10\end{matrix}\qquad \dfrac{\dfrac{}{\{\mathbf{f}.\phi(n) \geq 10 \mid n\}\models \mathbf{f}.\phi(n) \geq 10}}{\{\mathbf{f}.\phi(n) \geq 10 \mid n\}\models \mathbf{f}.\exists n.\phi(n) \geq 10}}{\mathbf{inc}(\{\mathbf{f}.\phi(n) \geq 10 \mid n\})}$$

We can now apply the reduction disj-$\mathcal{N}$ to the obtained derivation.

$$\dfrac{\dfrac{\dfrac{\dfrac{\dfrac{}{vt'\models \mathbf{t}.\phi(n) < 10}}{vt'\models \mathbf{t}.\forall n.\phi(n) < 10}}{vt'\models \mathbf{t}.\phi(1) < 10}\quad \dfrac{\dfrac{\dfrac{}{vt'\models \mathbf{t}.\phi(n) < 10}}{vt'\models \mathbf{t}.\forall n.\phi(n) < 10}}{vt'\models \mathbf{t}.\phi(2) < 10}\quad \dfrac{\dfrac{\dfrac{}{vt'\models \mathbf{t}.\phi(n) < 10}}{vt'\models \mathbf{t}.\forall n.\phi(n) < 10}}{vt'\models \mathbf{t}.\phi(3) < 10}}{vt'\models \mathbf{t}.\phi(1)+\phi(2)+\phi(3) < 30}\qquad \begin{matrix}\vdots\\ \models \mathbf{t}.\phi(1)+\phi(2)+\phi(3) = 30\end{matrix}}{\mathbf{inc}(vt')}$$

where $vt' = \{\mathbf{f}.\phi(n) \geq 10 \mid n\}$.

Then applying rule (β) we get

$$\dfrac{\dfrac{vt'\models \mathbf{t}.\phi(1) < 10\quad vt'\models \mathbf{t}.\phi(2) < 10\quad vt'\models \mathbf{t}.\phi(3) < 10}{vt'\models \mathbf{t}.\phi(1)+\phi(2)+\phi(3) < 30}\qquad \begin{matrix}\vdots\\ \models \mathbf{t}.\phi(1)+\phi(2)+\phi(3) = 30\end{matrix}}{\mathbf{inc}(vt')}$$

By normalizing also the derivation of $\models \mathbf{t}.\phi(1)+\phi(2)+\phi(3) = 30$ we get a proof of **inc**(vt') in normal form. It is easy to see that from this proof we can get a finite valuation term witnessing the inconsistency, namely $\{\mathbf{t}.\phi(1) < 10\}+\{\mathbf{t}.\phi(2) < 10\}+\{\mathbf{t}.\phi(3) < 10\}$.
We now know that the term witnessing the formula $\exists n.\phi(n) \geq 10$ is 1, 2 or 3 but we still do not know precisely which one it is. This information is contained in the derivation of $\models \mathbf{t}.\phi(1)+\phi(2)+\phi(3)=30$.

To pick one of the right witnesses among the numerals $u_1,..,u_h$ that it is possible to get after normalizing *extr-f(n)* we use a reduction similar to the one used by Prawitz in [Pra2] and which he dubbed "trivial reduction". This sort of reduction, which will be defined shortly, performs a sort of "choice" (a nondeterministic choice indeed) among the possible witnesses. We have not included it in the ones defined above since it is possible to use it only at the end of the normalization process. Of course, as it will be clear later, performing this sort of reduction not only at the end of the normalization process, would "speed-up" the extraction procedure. This improvement however would complicate the exposition and the strong normalization proof and therefore, since we are not concerned here with problems of efficiency , we shall not deal with it.

Prawitz's trivial reduction is informally defined as follows : if we have a proof of a formula containing a subdeduction proving the same formula and using a subset of set of assumptions of the proof we have, then we can replace the whole proof by this subdeduction (it is now easy to understand why the adjective *trivial* is used).
For our purposes the use of trivial reductions can be limited to closed and normal proofs of inconsistency.

Definition 2.3 (*Trivial Reductions*)
Let M∈ Terms(PVS), M closed, normal and with type **inc**(vt). Besides, let M contain a subterm N with type **inc**(vt'). Then a *trivial reduction* of M is the following : $M \rightarrow_{triv} N$.

It is straightforward to check that the trivial reduction, used alone, is strongly normalizing.

The use of trivial reductions for extracting a witness is explained by the following theorem.

Theorem 2.4 (*Witness Extraction via Trivial Deductions*)
Let M∈ Terms(PVS), M normal, closed, PA-closed, of type **inc**(vt) and obtained by normalizing a *extr-f(n)* term. Let M' be the normal form of M with respect to the reduction $\rightarrow_{triv}$.
Then
(i) the subterms of M' of the form ℵx.Q are such that either x∉ FV(Q) or Q ≡ Cut(Q',x) (Cut(x,Q')) and x∉ FV(Q') with x of disjunctive type.
(ii) if Q is a subterm of M' and FV(Q) ≠ ϕ then either Q ≡ Cut(Q',x) (Cut(x,Q')) or Q is a variable of disjunctive type.
(iii) *vt-ext* (M') is of the form {**f**.f(t)=0} with t closed and moreover M'≡ Cut(**f**.f(t)=0,Q) (Cut(Q,**f**.f(t)=0)) with no term of the form **f**.f(t')=0 in Q (t' closed normal).
Proof
(i) Let us assume, to a contradiction, that there exists a subterm ℵx.Q of M' such that Q is not Cut(Q',x) with x∉ FV(Q') but nonetheless x∈ FV(Q). Then it is possible to choose a subterm ℵx.Q minimal among the ones with the property above mentioned. Therefore, if a certain ℵy.P is in ℵx.Q then either y∉ FV(P) or P≡Cut(P',y) (Cut(y,P') with y∉ FV(P'). Now, since x∈ FV(Q) and x has a disjunctive type, x must occur in subterms of Q of the form Cut(x,S) (Cut(S,x)). Let us choose a minimal Cut(x,S) (Cut(S,x)). Then x∉ FV(S) and moreover, since for all the ℵy.P in ℵx.Q we have that x∉ FV(P) or P≡Cut(P',y) (Cut(y,P') with y∉ FV(P'), no free variable in S is bound in Q. Hence FV(Q) ⊇ FV(S) and Q reduces to Cut(x,S) (Cut(S,x)) since, by hypothesis Q≠Cut(x,S) if x∉ FV(S) (i.e. since Cut(x,S) is a proper subterm of Q). Then M is not in normal form : contradiction.
(ii) By (i) in M' a bound variable x can occur only in some ℵx.Cut(Q,x) with x∉ FV(Q).
(iii) All the terms of the form **f**.f(t')=0 are disjunctive and can occur only in expressions of the form Cut(Q,**f**.f(t')=0) (Cut(**f**.f(t')=0,Q)). Q has to be conjunctive and then, by (ii) is closed. Then to avoid M'→Cut(Q,**f**.f(t')=0) it has necessarily to be M'≡Cut(Q,**f**.f(t')=0)

(Cut(f.f(t')=0,Q)). By the same argument no f.f(t')=0 can occur in Q (otherwise Cut(Q,f.f(t')=0)→Cut(Q',f.f(t')=0)).
The derivation tree of M' then has necessarily to be of the following form :

$$
(\mathrm{Cut})\frac{\dfrac{\Pi}{\vdash \mathrm{N} : [vt' \models \mathbf{f}.f(t)=0]} \qquad (\mathrm{I})\dfrac{}{\vdash \mathbf{f}.f(t)=0 : [vt'' \models \mathbf{f}.f(t)=0]}}{\mathbf{inc}(vt'+vt'')}
$$

and *vt-ext* (M') = {**f**.f(t)=0}. □

To summarize, if we have a closed proof of a Σ_1^0 sentence : *extr-f(n)* we can get from its normal form a finite valuation containing at least one witness for our formula and possibly even non-witnesses : *vt-ext* (*extr-f(n)*). To extract exactly one of possible witnesses we normalize *extr-f(n)* using the trivial reduction, obtaining a term *R(extr-f(n))*. Theorem 2.4 assures us that *vt-ext* (*R(extr-f(n))*) is of the form {**f**.f(t)=0}. t is the witness we were looking for.

3. Strong Normalization for System PVS.

We now want to prove the Strong Normalizability property for terms of system PVS. To this purpose we shall define a "reduction-preserving" translation from terms of PVS to terms of a strongly normalizable simply typed λ-calculus with pairs. The technique of proving Strong Normalizability of a calculus by means of a reduction-preserving translation into another calculus is quite common [HHP][GN]. A different proof could be obtained by translating system PVS in the classical natural deduction calculus for Peano arithmetic equipped with Prawitz's reduction rules. The translation to this calculus would preserve all the reductions but Comp, which would be transformed in the identity. The Strong Normalizazion of system PVS would follow in this case from (a variation of) the result of Strong Normalization obtained by Prawitz [Pra1][Pra2].

Firstly let us define the calculus in which we shall translate the terms of system PVS.
The system we define can be seen as a variant of Gödel's system T.

Definition 3.1 (*The System* $\lambda^{\times\mathrm{Ind}}$)
The system $\lambda^{\times\mathrm{Ind}}$ is a simply typed λ-calculus with pairs, defined in the following way
(i) *Types*
- Int, Atoms ∈ Types($\lambda^{\times\mathrm{Ind}}$)
- $\alpha,\beta \in$ Types($\lambda^{\times\mathrm{Ind}}$) ⇒ $\alpha\to\beta$, $\alpha\times\beta \in$ Types($\lambda^{\times\mathrm{Ind}}$)

(ii) *Terms*
The set of pre-terms of $\lambda^{\times\mathrm{Ind}}$ is

$$\mathbf{T} ::= \mathbf{x} \mid \mathbf{T}(\mathbf{T}) \mid \lambda\mathbf{x}{:}\mathit{Types}\,.\mathbf{T} \mid \langle\mathbf{T},\mathbf{T}\rangle \mid \pi_i(\mathbf{T}) \mid 0 \mid s(\mathbf{T}) \mid \mathrm{Ind}(\mathbf{T},\mathbf{T},\mathbf{T}) \mid \mathrm{PA}_j$$

with i=1,2, j = 1,..7.
The term formation rules are the following

(Ax-$\lambda^{\times\mathrm{Ind}}$) $\quad B,x{:}\alpha \vdash x{:}\alpha$
$\quad B \vdash 0 : \mathrm{Int}$
$\quad B \vdash \mathbf{s} : \mathrm{Int} \to \mathrm{Int}$

(Ax-$\lambda^{\times\mathrm{Ind}}$-$\mathrm{PA}_j$) $\quad B \vdash \mathrm{PA}_j : \mathrm{Atoms} \to_{.n_j.}\to \mathrm{Atoms} \to \mathrm{Int} \to_{.k_j.}\to \mathrm{Int} \to \mathrm{Atoms}$ (*)
$\quad$ j=1,..,7

(*) n_j is the number of premises of axiom (PA_j) and k_j the number of its free variables.

$$(\lambda^{\times Ind}\text{-}\rightarrow\text{-I})\ \frac{B, x:\alpha \vdash Q : \beta}{B \vdash \lambda x:\alpha.Q : \alpha\rightarrow\beta} \qquad (\lambda^{\times Ind}\text{-}\rightarrow\text{-E})\ \frac{B \vdash Q : \alpha\rightarrow\beta \quad B \vdash S : \alpha}{B \vdash QS : \beta}$$

$$(\lambda^{\times Ind}\text{-}\langle\text{-}\rangle)\ \frac{B \vdash Q : \alpha \quad B \vdash S : \beta}{B \vdash \langle Q,S\rangle : \alpha\times\beta} \qquad (\lambda^{\times Ind}\text{-}\pi_i)\ \frac{B \vdash Q : \alpha_1\times\alpha_2}{B \vdash \pi_i(Q) : \alpha_i}\ \ i=1,2$$

$$(\lambda^{\times Ind}\text{-Ind})\ \frac{B \vdash S : \mathsf{Int} \quad B \vdash P : \alpha \quad B \vdash Q : \mathsf{Int}\rightarrow\alpha\rightarrow\alpha}{B \vdash \mathrm{Ind}(S,P,Q) : \alpha}$$

(iii) *Reductions*

β) $(\lambda x.Q)S \rightarrow Q[x:=S]$

π_i) $\pi_i(\langle Q_1,Q_2\rangle) \rightarrow Q_i$

Ind) $\begin{cases} \mathrm{Ind}(0,P,Q) \rightarrow P \\ \mathrm{Ind}(\mathbf{s}(S),P,Q) \rightarrow Q(S)(\mathrm{Ind}(S,P,Q)) \end{cases}$

In the sequel a *numeral term* of $\lambda^{\times Ind}$ will be a term of the form s(s(..s(0)..)).

$[\![-]\!]_J$ is the translation from judgments to the types of $\lambda^{\times Ind}$ defined inductively as follows :

$[\![-]\!]_J$: Judgments $\rightarrow$ Types($\lambda^{\times Ind}$)

(i) $[\![t.P]\!]_J = \mathsf{Atoms}$

(ii) $[\![\gamma.A]\!]_J = [\![\bar{\gamma}.A]\!]_J \rightarrow \mathsf{Atoms}$ if $\gamma.A$ is disjunctive

(iii) $[\![\gamma.\neg A]\!]_J = [\![\bar{\gamma}.A]\!]_J$

(iv) $[\![t.A_1\wedge A_2]\!]_J = [\![t.A_1]\!]_J \times [\![t.A_2]\!]_J$

(v) $[\![t.\forall n.A]\!]_J = \mathsf{Int} \rightarrow [\![t.A]\!]_J$

It is easy to check that $\gamma.A \sim \gamma'.A' \Rightarrow [\![\gamma.A]\!]_J = [\![\gamma'.A']\!]_J$

τ is the translation from types of system PVS to types of $\lambda^{\times Ind}$ defined inductively as follows:

τ : Types(PVS) $\rightarrow$ Types($\lambda^{\times Ind}$)

$\tau(\mathbf{inc}(vt)) = \mathsf{Atoms}$

$\tau(v\models\gamma.A) = [\![\gamma.A]\!]_J$

We now easily extend τ to a map from contexts for realizer to contexts for $\lambda^{\times Ind}$.

- $\tau(x: T) = ax : \mathsf{Atoms}, x : \tau(T)$
- $\tau(x:T,B) = \tau(x:T),\tau(B)$

Recall that $\sigma_i(M)$ stands for the term $\mathbf{N}x:[v\models\mathbf{t}.A_1\wedge A_2].\mathrm{Cut}(\pi_i(x),M)$.

Having defined $[\![-]\!]_J$ and τ we can now define the translation $[\![-]\!]$ from system PVS to $\lambda^{\times Ind}$.

$[\![-]\!]$: Terms(PVS) $\rightarrow$ Terms($\lambda^{\times ind}$)

(i) $[\![x]\!] = x$

(ii) $[\![PA_j(t_1,..,t_{k_j},M_1,..,M_{n_j})]\!] = PA_j u_1..u_{k_j}[\![M_1]\!]..[\![M_{n_j}]\!]$ where the term t_i computes to u_i

(iii) $[\![\mathbf{t}.P(t_1,..,t_m)]\!] = ax$ (ax is a distinguished variable of type Atoms)

(iv) $[\![\mathbf{f}.P(t_1,..,t_m)]\!] = id_{At}$ (id_{At} denotes the term $\lambda x:\mathsf{Atoms}.x$)

(v) $[\![\langle M_1,M_2\rangle]\!] = \langle[\![M_1]\!],[\![M_2]\!]\rangle$

(vi) $[\![\pi_i(M)]\!] = \pi_i([\![M]\!])$

(vii) $[\![\lambda n.M]\!] = \lambda n:\mathsf{Int}.[\![M]\!]$

(viii) $[\![\pi_u(M)]\!] = [\![M]\!](u')$ where u computes to u'.

(ix) $[\![\text{Cut}(M,N)]\!] = \begin{cases} [\![M]\!]([\![N]\!]) & \text{if M is disjunctive and N conjunctive} \\ [\![N]\!]([\![M]\!]) & \text{if M is conjunctive and N disjunctive} \end{cases}$

(x) $[\![\mathcal{N}x{:}[v{\models}\gamma.A].M]\!] = \lambda x{:}[\![\gamma.A]\!]_J.[\![M]\!]$ if $\gamma.A$ is conjunctive

(xi) $[\![\mathcal{N}x{:}[v{\models}\gamma.A].M]\!] = [\![M]\!][x{:=}id_{At}]$ if $cf(\gamma.A) = \mathbf{f}.P$

(xii) $[\![\mathcal{N}x{:}[v{\models}\gamma.A].M]\!] = <[\![\mathcal{N}x{:}[v{\models}\mathbf{f}.A_1].M[x{:=}\sigma_1(x)]]\!],[\![\mathcal{N}x{:}[v{\models}\mathbf{f}.A_2].M[x{:=}\sigma_2(x)]]\!]>$ if $cf(\gamma.A) = \mathbf{f}.A_1 \wedge A_2$

(xiii) $[\![\mathcal{N}x{:}[v{\models}\gamma.A].M]\!] = \lambda m{:}\mathsf{Int}.[\![\mathcal{N}x{:}[v{\models}\mathbf{f}.A'].M[x{:=}\sigma_m(x)]]\!]$ if $cf(\gamma.A) = \mathbf{f}.\forall m.A'$

(xiv) $[\![\text{Ind}(t,N,M)]\!] = \text{Ind}(u,[\![N]\!], F)$ where t computes to u and
$F = \lambda n{:}\mathsf{Int}.\lambda\theta{:}[\![t.A]\!]_J.[\![\mathcal{N}x{:}[v \models \mathbf{f}.A(s(n))].\text{Cut}(\pi_n(M),<\theta,x>)]\!]$

The correctnes of the definition of $[\![-]\!]$ can be proved by three fold induction : the number of Ind's, the sum of the lenghts of disjunctive γ.A's and the lenght of the term.

Notice that the clause (ix) for $[\![\text{Cut}(M,N)]\!]$ is well defined since, if Cut(M,N) is a correct term, it has been necessarily formed by rule (Cut) and then it has necessarily to be that M is conjunctive and N disjunctive or the other way around.

Remark. We could have defined a translation not in $\lambda^{\times\text{Ind}}$ but in the simply typed λ-calculus. The choice of $\lambda^{\times\text{Ind}}$ has been done in order not to have sequences of λ-terms, multiabstraction and multiapplication, and then not to have a too cumbersome notation.

Lemma 3.2 (*Interpretation Correctness*)
$B\vdash M : T \quad \Rightarrow \quad \tau(B) \vdash [\![M]\!] : \tau(T)$

Proof
By induction on a suitable ordinal associated to the derivation of $B\vdash M{:}T$. □

We can now prove that the translation defined is "reduction preserving". From this property, since system $\lambda^{\times\text{Ind}}$ is strongly normalizing, the strong normalizability of system PVS easily follows.

Lemma 3.3 (*Reduction Preservation*)
Let M,M'∈ Terms(PVS).

$M \to M' \quad \Rightarrow \quad [\![M]\!] \to^+ [\![M']\!]$ if $\to$ is neither $\to_{conj.\mathcal{N}}$ nor $\to_{conj\forall\mathcal{N}}$
otherwise $[\![M]\!] \equiv [\![M']\!]$.

Proof
By induction on a suitable ordinal associated to the derivation for M. □

Definition 3.4
Let M∈ Terms(PVS) and P∈ Terms($\lambda^{\times\text{Ind}}$).
$Num_{b\lambda}(M)$ = number of "<",">" and "λ" in M.
$Num_{b\lambda}(P)$ = number of "<",">" and "λ" in P.

Lemma 3.5
Let M∈ Terms(PVS) and $M \to_{conj\text{-}\mathcal{N}} M'$ or $M \to_{conj\forall\mathcal{N}} M'$.
(i) $Num_{b\lambda}(M) \le Num_{b\lambda}([\![M]\!])$
(ii) $Num_{b\lambda}(M) < Num_{b\lambda}(M')$.

Proof
(i) By cases on the reductions.
(ii) Easy by checking rule conj-$\mathcal{N}$. □

Theorem 3.6
Let $M \in$ Terms(PVS). Then M is strongly normalizable.
Proof
Let us associate to each term M the following ordinal :

$\omega^2 \cdot hred\,(M) + \omega \cdot (Num_{b\lambda}([\![M]\!]) - Num_{b\lambda}(M)) + \Sigma_{u \in PA\,(M)}\, hred\,(u)$,

where *PA* (M) is the number of PA-terms in M and *hred*(M) and *hred*(u) with u PA-term are the height of the reduction trees of M and u respectively.
Given a term M it strongly normalizes since for each reduction the ordinal defined strictly decreases. If the reduction is not conj.$\mathcal{N}$, conj$\forall$.$\mathcal{N}$ or Comp it is the index of ω^2 which decreases. If the reduction is conj.$\mathcal{N}$, conj$\forall$.$\mathcal{N}$ then the index of ω (which is correct by Lemma 3.5(i)) decreases by the Reduction Preservation Lemma and Lemma 3.5(ii). If the reduction is Comp it is the last index that obviously decreases; the second is not altered. Possibly it is the first that could decrease. □

Acknowledgements
We are grateful to Mariangiola Dezani for her gentle guidance and helpful comments and to Furio Honsell for many useful discussions.
The first author wishes to thank also Julia Caldarini for her encouragement and support.

References

[BB] Barbanera F., Berardi S. Witness extraction in classical logic through normalization, Technical Report Dipartimento di Informatica Universita' di Torino, 1991.

[Ber] Berardi S. A semantic purely intuitionistic proof of Takeuti's conjecture. *Rendiconti del Seminario Matematico Univers. Politecn. Torino* , vol.46, 59-89, 1988.

[FFKD] Felleisen M., Friedman D., Kohlbeker E., Duba B. Reasoning with continuations. In *Proceedings of the First Annual Symposium on Logic in Computer Science,* 131-141, 1986.

[Fried] Friedman H. Classically and intuitionistically provable recursive functions. In Scott D.S. and Muller G.H. editors, *Higher Set Theory,* vol.699 of *Lecture Notes in Mathematics,* 21-28, Springer Verlag, 1978.

[GN] Geuvers H., Nederhof M.J. A simple modular proof of the strong normalization for the Calculus of Construction. To appear in *Journal of functional Programming*.

[Gir] Girard J.-Y. Une extension de l'interpretation de Gödel a l'analyse, et son application a l'elimination des coupures dans l'analyse et la theorie des types. In *Proceedings of the second Scandivian Logic Symposium,* eds.J.E.Fenstad, Amsterdam, North-Holland, 63-92, 1971.

[Griff] Griffin T.G. A formulae as types notion of control. In *Conference Record of the Seventeenth Annual ACM Symposium on Principle of Programming Languages,* 1990.

[HHP] Harper R., Honsell F., Plotkin G. A framework for defining logics. *Proceedings of the symposium on Logic in Computer Science* . Ithaca, New York, IEEE, Washington D.C. 1987.

[Kre] Kreisel G. Mathematical significance of consistency proofs. *Journal of Symbolic Logic,* 23:155-182, 1958.

[Plot] Plotkin G. Call-by-name, call-by-value and the λ-calculus. *Theoretical Computer Science,* 125-159, 1975.

[Pra 1] Prawitz D. Natural deduction, a proof theoretical study. Stockolm, Almqvist and Winskell, 1965.

[Pra 2] Prawitz D. Validity and normalizability of proofs in 1-st and 2-nd order classical and intuitionistic logic. In *Atti del I Congresso Italiano di Logica,* Napoli, Bibliopolis, 11-36, 1981.

[Schü] Schütte K. Proof Theory. Springer Verlag, 1977.

VARIETIES OF INCREASING TREES

François Bergeron
LACIM
Université du Québec à Montréal
Case Postale 8888, Succursale A
Montréal, Québec H3C3P8
Canada

Philippe Flajolet
Algorithms Project
INRIA Rocquencourt
78153 Le Chesnay
France

Bruno Salvy
Algorithms Project
INRIA Rocquencourt
78153 Le Chesnay
France

Abstract

An increasing tree is a labelled rooted tree in which labels along any branch from the root go in increasing order. Under various guises, such trees have surfaced as tree representations of permutations, as data structures in computer science, and as probabilistic models in diverse applications.

We present a unified generating function approach to the enumeration of parameters on such trees. The counting generating functions for several basic parameters are shown to be related to a simple ordinary differential equation,

$$\frac{d}{dz}Y(z) = \phi(Y(z)),$$

which is non linear and autonomous.

Singularity analysis applied to the intervening generating functions then permits to analyze asymptotically a number of parameters of the trees, like: root degree, number of leaves, path length, and level of nodes. In this way it is found that various models share common features: path length is $O(n \log n)$, the distribution of node levels and number of leaves are asymptotically normal, etc.

Introduction

A *labelled tree* of size n is a rooted tree comprising n nodes that are labelled by distinct integers of the set $\{1, \ldots, n\}$. An *increasing tree* is a labelled tree such that the sequence of labels along any branch starting at the root is increasing.

The enumeration of trees is a major branch of combinatorial analysis. A classical result due to Arthur Cayley in 1889 states that the number of labelled non-plane trees with n nodes is n^{n-1}. For plane trees, the corresponding count is $(n-1)!\binom{2n-2}{n-1}$ since the number of unlabelled plane trees is the Catalan number $\frac{1}{n}\binom{2n-2}{n-1}$ and there are $n!$ possible labellings given a fixed traversal order of trees, e.g., preorder. On this and other standard combinatorial analysis results, we refer the reader to the treatises of Comtet [6], Goulden and Jackson [19], or Bergeron *et al.* [3].

This paper concerns the enumeration of parameters on various families of increasing trees. The families to be considered are of two types: (i) *non-plane* trees, which are taken in the graph theoretic sense so that subtrees stemming from a node are not ordered between themselves; (ii) *plane trees*, where a plane embedding is specified so that subtrees stemming from a node are ordered between themselves. Rather arbitrary conditions can be imposed on the node degrees that are allowed.

Definition 1 Let $\{s_r\}_{r=0}^{\infty}$ be a sequence of non negative integers, such that $s_0 \neq 0$ and $s_r \neq 0$ for some $r \geq 2$. The *variety of trees* associated to $\{s_r\}$ and the specification of an element of

{Plane, Non-plane} is the collection of all increasing trees (plane or non plane depending on the specification) with s_r sorts of nodes of outdegree (arity) r for all r.

The *degree function* of a variety of trees associated with $\{s_r\}$ is defined as follows.

In the plane case: $$\phi(w) := \sum_{r\geq 0} s_r w^r.$$

In the non-plane case: $$\phi(w) := \sum_{r\geq 0} s_r \frac{w^r}{r!}.$$

The degree function condenses all the information needed for the analysis of tree parameters considered in this paper. We denote the coefficients of the degree function $\phi(w)$ by ϕ_r, so that $\phi(w) = \sum_{r=0}^{\infty} \phi_r w^r$, with $\phi_r = s_r$ in the plane case, while $\phi_r = s_r/r!$ in the non plane case. Whenever the collection of node types allowed is finite, $\phi(w)$ is a polynomial. In that case we call the variety a *polynomial variety* and let d denote the degree of $\phi(w)$; the integer d is then the maximum node degree allowed in the variety, and we call it the *degree* of the variety.

Our treatment is directed towards asymptotic estimates via generating functions (GF's). It aims at global results applicable across varieties of increasing trees. In that sense, it can be viewed as a transposition to increasing trees of a programme carried out by Meir and Moon who extensively studied so-called *simple families of trees*, see for instance [32]. However, due to the constraint of increasing labels, we are typically facing *algebraic differential equations* rather than plain algebraic equations. The key analytic method employed here is that of singularity analysis, developed by Flajolet and Odlyzko [11], though Darboux's method [6, p. 277] could have been employed instead in a few places at perhaps the expense of a little more work.

As a byproduct, the generating function approach sometimes provides explicit form for various tree counting problems, in the case of *exactly solvable models*. In this way we are able to unify several results that have appeared scattered in the literature.

For combinatorial counting purposes, we appeal to *exponential generating functions*: let $\{f_n\}_{n\geq 0}$ be a sequence of numbers; the exponential generating function (EGF) of the sequence is defined as

$$f(z) = \sum_{n\geq 0} f_n \frac{z^n}{n!}. \tag{1}$$

(Note that we use the same letters for a sequence and its EGF. We shall henceforth adhere to this convention, except for a few explicitly indicated situations where we have to resort to different types of generating functions.)

Our main results are as follows. Fix a variety of trees $\mathcal{Y}$, i.e., the degree function $\phi(w)$. Let Y_n be the number of trees of size n in the variety. The EGF of the variety of trees,

$$Y(z) = \sum_{n=1}^{\infty} Y_n \frac{z^n}{n!}, \tag{2}$$

is defined implicitly by

$$\int_0^{Y(z)} \frac{dw}{\phi(w)} = z. \tag{3}$$

The inversion problem is solvable in terms of special functions in a few particular cases of interest and we then call the corresponding models *solvable.*

Under fairly general conditions—most notably whenever $\phi(w)$ is a polynomial, which means a finite set of allowed degrees—the equation (3) can be analyzed near its dominant singularity. For polynomial varieties, this leads to an asymptotic counting result of the form

$$\frac{Y_n}{n!} \sim K \cdot \left(\frac{1}{\rho}\right)^n \cdot n^{-(d-2)/(d-1)} \qquad \text{with} \qquad \rho = \int_0^{\infty} \frac{dw}{\phi(w)}, \tag{4}$$

where $K = K_\phi$ is a constant that depends on ϕ alone, and d is the degree of the variety. The quantity ρ appears to be always a logarithmic form in algebraic numbers.

(Technically, this approach is analogous to the analytic method used by Meir and Moon in [33], where the authors enumerate recursive trees without unary nodes.)

Let $s[.]$ be a tree function that admits an inductive definition. Path length or the number of leaves in the tree are typical examples, and the precise meaning is explained below. Let $S(z)$ be the associated EGF,

$$S(z) = \sum_{t \in \mathcal{Y}} s[t] \frac{z^{|t|}}{|t|!},$$

where as usual $|t|$ represents the size of t. Then it is found that $S(z)$ is expressible as a sort of integral transform

$$S(z) = Y'(z) \int_0^z \left(\frac{d}{dt} F(t) \right) \cdot \frac{dt}{Y'(t)}. \tag{5}$$

The fact that this transform is determined by the variety $\mathcal{Y}$ under consideration is materialized by the occurrences of Y', while F reflects in a direct manner the inductive definition of the parameter $s[.]$ under consideration.

In solvable models where $Y(z)$ admits an explicit expression, the transform (5) is itself explicit. For instance, for binary increasing trees, and an inductive parameter

$$s[t] = f_{|t|} + s[t_{\text{left}}] + s[t_{\text{right}}],$$

it becomes

$$S(z) = \frac{1}{(1-z)^2} \left[f_0 + \int_0^z \left(\frac{d}{dt} F(t) \right) \cdot (1-t)^2 \, dt \right], \tag{6}$$

where $F(t)$ is in this particular case the ordinary generating function of the number sequence $\{f_n\}$, $F(t) = \sum_n f_n t^n$. In this way, for solvable models, we can get exact EGF's for parameters like path length, number of leaves, and so forth, on the trees.

However, in general, the solution is *asymptotic* rather than exact. It consists in viewing Eq. (5) as a "singularity transformer". We find, for finite families and for the other classical families, that path length is on average $\lambda n \log n$, that the expected number of leaves is asymptotic to αn, for some constants λ, α dependent upon ϕ.

A variation of this scheme in line with Bender's work [2] and with [12, 13] leads to limit distributions. For instance, the distribution of nodes in strata of a tree or the number of leaves both asymptotically conform to a Gaussian law.

Most existing works (with the notable exception of Meir and Moon's studies [32, 33]) appeal to special recurrence relation, often based on the insertion of a new node, and to the existence of closed–form solutions. In contrast, in this work, we resort to a combination of algebraic and analytic generating function methods which is versatile and widely applicable. In this way, it becomes possible to cast into a unifying framework a number of existing analyses concerning increasing trees and also to vastly extend the range of problems and models amenable to asymptotic analysis.

1 Classical Tree Models

We review here some of the models arising from diverse areas that constitute varieties of increasing trees.

Binary increasing trees. Any permutation σ of n elements can be written as a word σ whose ith letter is $\sigma(i)$; if $\min(\sigma)$ is the minimal element of σ, then, as a word, σ can be decomposed into $\sigma_{\text{left}} \cdot \min(\sigma) \cdot \sigma_{\text{right}}$, where σ_{left} (σ_{right}) designates the factors that appear to the left (resp. right) of the minimal element. One can construct a binary tree, $\mathbf{T}(\sigma)$, by repeated use of this decomposition:

> The root of the tree $\mathbf{T}(\sigma)$ is $\min(\sigma)$, with the left and right root subtrees being constructed recursively as $\mathbf{T}(\sigma_{\text{left}})$ and $\mathbf{T}(\sigma_{\text{right}})$; the tree associated to the empty permutation is the empty tree.

In this way, we associate bijectively to each permutation of $\{1, 2, \ldots, n\}$ a labelled tree with n labelled internal nodes and $n+1$ unlabelled external nodes.

Equivalently, by eliminating the unlabelled external nodes, we obtain a labelled unary–binary tree with two sorts of unary nodes, the left branching nodes and the right branching nodes. Thus, the binary increasing trees associated to permutations correspond to a plane family defined by $s_0 = 1, s_1 = 2, s_2 = 1$, so that $\phi(w) = 1 + 2w + w^2$. From the correspondence, there results in particular that the number of binary increasing trees of size n is $n!$.

This construction is recalled in Stanley's book [35, pp. 23–41] who attributes it "to the French". Here, we refer to Françon's work (see [15] and references therein) which is based in part on earlier methods developed by Foata and Schützenberger and in part on a pioneering paper [4] written by Burge in 1972.

Now, a number of classical permutation parameters have direct translations into basic tree parameters. For instance, the distribution of the number of nodes on the leftmost branch of the tree (i.e., the number of left–to–right minima in the permutation) is given by the Stirling numbers of the first kind; the distribution of the number of nodes with a left son in the tree (the descents in the permutation) is given by the Eulerian numbers, etc. Some of these classical results appear here as corollaries in Section 5

Binary increasing trees (under the alternative names of heap ordered trees or tournament trees) can also be used as a data structure to represent mergeable priority queues, with algorithms that can be precisely analyzed, see especially Burge's paper and Vuillemin's survey in [39], or [18, 38] for an overview. Finally, this model is of special importance since it is isomorphic to the analytic models of standard *binary search tree* and the *Quicksort algorithm*, see, e.g., [4, 9, 15, 21, 24, 29, 38, 39]. There, the model is equivalent to a splitting process in which n elements are split into a "root" and into two subgroups of cardinalities K and $n-1-K$, with the distribution of the random variable K being uniform over its range, $\Pr\{K = k\} = 1/n$ for all $k \in \{0, \ldots, n-1\}$.

Strict binary increasing trees. They correspond to binary increasing trees in which each node has either 0 or 2 sons, so that $\phi(w) = 1 + w^2$. By the standard correspondence with permutations described above, these trees give rise to *alternating permutations*, also called up-and-down, that are of the form $\sigma = \sigma_1\sigma_2\ldots\sigma_n$ with $\sigma_1 > \sigma_2 < \sigma_3 > \sigma_4 \cdots$. By implicitly using such a construction, Desiré André obtained in 1881 that the number of such trees over $2n+1$ nodes is equal the Taylor coefficient[1] $(2n+1)!\,[z^{2n+1}]\tan(z)$. (This number is known as a tangent number or Euler number.) The use of this principle in enumerating alternating permutations is detailed for instance in [19, p. 169].

Recursive trees. Meir and Moon [32] define recursive trees as the variety of non-plane increasing trees such that all node degrees are allowed. Thus, the degree function is $\phi(w) = \exp(w)$.

---

[1] As usual, $[z^n]f(z)$ denotes the coefficient of z^n in the expansion of $f(z)$ into powers of z, see [20, §5.4].

This model lies at the basis of Burge's sorting method of [4]. It was proposed as a statistical model in philology for problems related to the identification of terminal copies of manuscripts [34]; it has also been used for the legal assessment of chain letters and pyramids [17]. Its basic property for applications is that it can be generated by successive insertions of nodes, where at each stage each node is taken with equal likelihood as the father of the new node inserted.

All authors have noticed a close connection between recursive trees and permutations, the number of increasing trees of size n being $(n-1)!$. It is however a little less known (though it is already explicit in [4]) that this model is equivalent to that of binary increasing trees by the following remarks.

> *1).* Take a recursive tree of size n. *2).* Make it into a special plane increasing tree by ordering brother subtrees at each place in the tree from left to right according to increasing values of their roots. *3).* Chop off the root of the tree and apply the classical rotation correspondence [23, Sec. 2.3.2] that transforms a forest into a binary tree. The resulting tree is isomorphic to a binary increasing tree labelled on $\{2,\ldots,n\}$, itself isomorphic to a similar tree canonically labelled on $\{1,\ldots,n-1\}$.

From this correspondence and the observations above regarding binary increasing trees, one gets directly that the distribution of root degrees is given by Stirling numbers of the first kind, that the distribution of the number of leaves is Eulerian, and that path length is on average $\sim n\log n$. We rederive these and other properties in Section 5.

Plane recursive trees. This is a model introduced by Szymański [36] and further developed by Mahmoud *et al.* [30, 31]. In our terminologyit corresponds exactly to a variety of plane trees with degree set $\Omega = \{0,1,2,3,\ldots\}$, so that $\phi(w) = 1/(1-w)$. It also admits a construction by successive insertions, where at each stage each insertion slot is taken with equal likelihood. Alternatively, each node is selected as an insertion node with a probability proportional to its degree. As picturesquely described by Mahmoud, this is a propagation model in which "success brings success". (Footnote: Some of our results of Section 5 regarding plane recursive trees have also been independently obtained by Wen–Chin Chen and Wen–Chun Ni [5].)

2 Exact Enumeration of Varieties

We express here the basic counting problem for varieties of trees in terms of generating functions. This leads to a few cases of interest—the solvable models—where the generating functions are expressible in terms of standard functions. The definition of the generating function of a variety $\mathcal{Y}$ has been given in the introduction, see (2). The following result is a folk theorem. Fascinating combinatorial variations around it form the subject of a series of papers by Leroux and Viennot [26, 27] regarding the combinatorics of elementary calculus.

Theorem 1 *The exponential generating function $Y(z)$ of a variety of trees defined by the degree function ϕ is given implicitly by*

$$\int_0^{Y(z)} \frac{dw}{\phi(w)} = z. \tag{7}$$

Proof. This can be obtained from standard counting lemmas [19, 35, 40]. (Alternatively, the reader could return to underlying recurrences.) In terms of EGFs, forming a forest of k trees enumerated by $Y(z)$ corresponds to the EGF $Y^k(z)$ if the forest is ordered (plane case) and to $Y^k(z)/k!$ if it is unordered (non plane case). Appending a root with a minimal label to a forest

Name	Diff. eqn.	Explicit solution	ρ
Plane d–ary	$y' = (1+y)^d$	$y(z) = -1 + [1-(d-1)z]^{-1/(d-1)}$	$\frac{1}{d-1}$
Plane Strict d–ary	$y' = 1 + y^d$	$d=2$ $y(z) = \tan z$ $d>2$ —	$\frac{\pi}{d}\frac{1}{\sin\frac{\pi}{d}}$
Non plane Strict d–ary	$y' = 1 + \frac{y^d}{d!}$	$d=2$ $y(z) = \sqrt{2}\tan\frac{z}{\sqrt{2}}$ $d>2$ —	$\frac{\pi}{d}\frac{(d!)^{1/d}}{\sin\frac{\pi}{d}}$
Plane unary-binary	$y' = 1 + y + y^2$	$y(z) = \frac{\sqrt{3}}{2}\tan\left(\frac{\sqrt{3}}{2}z + \frac{\pi}{6}\right) - \frac{1}{2}$	$\frac{2\pi\sqrt{3}}{9}$
Non plane unary-binary	$y' = 1 + y + y^2/2$	$y(z) = \tan\left(\frac{z}{2} + \frac{\pi}{4}\right) - 1$	$\frac{\pi}{2}$
Plane "Recursive"	$y' = \frac{1}{1-y}$	$y(z) = 1 - \sqrt{1-2z}$	$\frac{1}{2}$
(Non plane) "Recursive"	$y' = \exp(y)$	$y = \log\frac{1}{1-z}$	1

Table 1: Some varieties of increasing trees and solvable models. For each type, we have listed the differential equation of the EGF, the explicit forms available, and the radius of convergence which dictates the exponential growth, ρ^{-n}, of the family.

enumerated by $W(z)$ corresponds to the EGF $\int_0^z W(t)\,dt$. Thus, with $\phi(w) = \sum_{r=0}^{\infty} \phi_r u^r$, we obtain

$$Y(z) = \int_0^z \left(\sum_{r=0}^{\infty} \phi_r Y^r(t)\right) dt.$$

From there, we derive

$$Y'(z) = \phi(Y(z)), \quad Y(0) = 0 \quad \text{or} \quad \frac{Y'(z)}{\phi(Y(z))} = 1, \tag{8}$$

and the result follows by integration. □

From Theorem 1, there results an explicit expression for the EGF of a variety of trees provided the integral $\int dw/\phi(w)$ is expressible in terms of special functions *and* its inverse is reducible to special functions. This is notably the case for the classical tree varieties described in the previous section.

Corollary 1 *(i) For binary trees, $\phi(w) = (1+w)^2$, we have*

$$Y(z) = \frac{z}{1-z}, \qquad Y_n = n!.$$

(ii) For strict binary trees, $\phi(w) = 1 + w^2$,

$$Y(z) = \tan(z), \qquad Y_{2n+1} = (2n+1)!\,[z^{2n+1}]\tan(z).$$

(iii) For recursive trees, $\phi(w) = \exp(w)$,

$$Y(z) = \log\frac{1}{1-z}, \qquad Y_n = (n-1)!.$$

(iv) For plane recursive trees, $\phi(w) = (1-w)^{-1}$,

$$Y(z) = 1 - \sqrt{1-2z}, \qquad Y_n = 1\cdot 3\cdot 5\cdots(2n-3) = \frac{(n-1)!}{2^{n-1}}\binom{2n-2}{n-1}.$$

Proof. It only involves elementary integration.

$$\begin{aligned} \int_0^y \frac{dw}{(1+w)^2} &= \frac{y}{1+y}, & \int_0^y \frac{dw}{1+w^2} &= \arctan(y), \\ \int_0^y \frac{dw}{\exp(w)} &= 1 - e^{-y}, & \int_0^y \frac{dw}{(1-w)^{-1}} &= y - \frac{y^2}{2}, \end{aligned}$$

and all the inverse functions are explicitly computable. □

The results of Corollary 1 are each well known under one guise or another. See, *e.g.*, [3, 19, 32, 36, 39].

A collection of explicit results is summarized in Table 1. An interesting solvable model whose asymptotic behaviour is characteristic of polynomial families is given below.

EXAMPLE 1. *d–ary trees.* The class of d–ary increasing trees corresponds to $\phi(w) = (1+w)^d$. (It can be viewed as d-ary trees in which only internal nodes are labelled.) We have

$$\int_0^y \frac{dw}{(1+w)^d} = \frac{1}{d-1}\left[1 - \frac{1}{(1+y)^{d-1}}\right] \qquad \text{and} \qquad Y(z) = -1 + [1-(d-1)z]^{-1/(d-1)}, \tag{9}$$

so that

$$Y_n = \delta^{1-n}(1+\delta)\cdot(2+\delta)\cdots(n-1+\delta) \qquad \text{where} \qquad \delta = \frac{1}{d-1}, \qquad \text{whence}$$

$$\frac{Y_n}{n!} \sim \frac{1}{\Gamma(\delta)}\delta^{-n} n^{-1+\delta}.$$

□

EXAMPLE 2. *Special ternary trees.* This is a rather artificial example just meant to demonstrate that explicit EGF's may arise in unexpected contexts. Take $\phi(w) = w^3 + 6w^2 + 11w + 6$, which corresponds to a variety of plane ternary trees with six sorts of leaves, eleven sorts of unary nodes, six sorts of binary nodes, and one sort of ternary node. We find

$$Y(z) = -2 + \frac{2}{\sqrt{4-3e^{2z}}} = 6\,z + 66\,\frac{z^2}{2!} + 1158\,\frac{z^3}{3!} + 28290\,\frac{z^4}{4!} + 887046\,\frac{z^5}{5!} + \&c.$$

□

3 Asymptotic Enumeration of Polynomial Varieties

In general, no exact form is available and we have to resort to asymptotic analysis. Our discussion at this point focuses on *polynomial varieties.*

A preliminary observation regarding periodicity phenomena is in order here. If $\phi(w)$ is a function of w^p for some $p \geq 2$, so that $\phi(w) = \psi(w^p)$ for some power series ψ;, we say that $\phi(w)$ is *periodic* and the maximum possible p is called its *period.* Otherwise, $\phi(w)$ is said to be aperiodic (and we take $p = 1$). For strict binary trees the period is $p = 2$, but for unary-binary trees $p = 1$. For period $p \geq 2$, we have $Y(z) = zY^*(z^p)$, for some power series Y^*; accordingly, the non–zero coefficients Y_n are those whose index satisfies the congruence condition $n \equiv 1 \pmod{p}$. In subsequent statements, this restriction $n \equiv 1 \pmod{p}$ is implicitly assumed in all periodic cases.

Theorem 2 *Let $\mathcal{Y}$ be a polynomial variety associated with the degree function $\phi(w) = \phi_d w^d + \cdots + \phi_0$. The number Y_n of elements of $\mathcal{Y}$ with size n satisfies*[2] *for $d > 3$*

$$\frac{Y_n}{n!} = \frac{p}{\eta\Gamma(\delta)}\left(\frac{1}{\rho}\right)^n n^{-1+\delta} + \frac{ph_2\eta}{\Gamma(-\delta)}\rho^{-n}n^{-1-\delta} + O(n^{-1-2\delta}). \tag{10}$$

where

$$\rho = \int_0^\infty \frac{dw}{\phi(w)}, \quad \delta = \frac{1}{d-1}, \quad \eta = \left(\frac{\phi_d \rho}{\delta}\right)^\delta,$$

p is the period of ϕ, and h_2 is as defined in Lemma 2 below. In particular, if ϕ has distinct roots, then

$$\rho = -\sum_{j=1}^{d} \frac{1}{\phi'(\zeta_j)} \log(-\zeta_j),$$

where the ζ_j are the roots of ϕ and the principal determination of the logarithm is taken.

Proof. We first determine the radius of convergence ρ of $Y(z)$; next we analyze $Y(z)$ in the vicinity of $z = \rho$; finally we translate the behaviour of $Y(z)$ into asymptotics of the coefficients Y_n by means of the method of singularity analysis, see [11].

Recall that a *dominant singularity* is one of smallest modulus. By Pringsheim's theorem [37, §7.21] we know that one of the dominant singularities is real positive, and this singularity is equal to the radius of convergence of $Y(z)$.

Lemma 1 *Given a degree function $\phi(w)$ that is polynomial or entire, the dominant real positive singularity of the function $Y(z)$, solution to $Y' = \phi(Y)$ and $Y(0) = 0$, is*

$$\rho = \int_0^\infty \frac{dy}{\phi(y)}.$$

Furthermore, if ϕ is non periodic, then ρ is the only dominant singularity of $Y(z)$. If ϕ has period $p \geq 2$, then $Y(z) = zY^*(z^p)$, where Y^* has a unique dominant singularity at $\rho^{1/p}$.

Proof. The integral is clearly defined since $\phi(w)$ does not vanish on the positive real axis and increases at least like w^2 at infinity. For any y with $0 < y < +\infty$, the integral $\int_0^y dw/\phi(w)$ is an analytic function of y with a non zero derivative; it is therefore invertible. Thus we find that $Y(z)$ is analytic at least for all real z, with $0 < z < \rho$. Clearly $Y(z)$ becomes infinite as $z \to \rho^-$, so that ρ is an actual singular point of $Y(z)$.

Let $z_0 = r_0 \exp(i\theta)$, with $r_0 < \rho$. Since Y has positive Taylor coefficients, we have $|Y(z_0)| \leq Y(r_0)$ by the triangular inequality. By a well known lemma, equality $|Y(z_0)| = Y(r_0)$ is possible for $\theta \neq 0$ only if $Y(z) = z^a Y^*(z^p)$ for some integers a, p with $p \geq 2$, in which case $\theta = 2m\pi/p$. (This in turn implies that $\phi(w)$ is periodic.)

Assume first that we are in the non periodic case. Thus $|Y(z_0)| < Y(r_0)$. Let r_1 be a positive real such that $|Y(z_0)| = Y(r_1)$; we have $r_1 < r_0$ by growth of $Y(z)$ on the positive real axis. Consider the function ψ solution to $\psi'(z) = \phi(\psi(z))$, with $\psi(r_0) = Y(r_1)$. Then ψ and Y are related by $\psi(z) = Y(z - r_0 + r_1)$ since the system is autonomous (i.e., there is no explicit dependency of z). From the positivity of the problem (i.e., ϕ), we then have $|Y(z)| \leq \psi(|z|)$. Thus the modulus of the solution $Y(z)$ is upper bounded by $Y(|z| - r_0 + r_1)$. In plain words a delay in the growth of $Y(z)$ along a non real ray "propagates" along that ray. In particular, $Y(z)$ exists along the ray of angle θ for $|z| < \rho - r_0 + r_1$, and it is analytic there.

[2] For $d = 2$, the term containing $n^{-1-\delta}$ disappears and the error after the first term is exponentially small; for $d = 3$, the form of h_2 given in Eq. (10) has to be modified.

In the periodic case, a suitable amended form of the argument applies, with the exceptional angles being simply the multiples of π/p. □

Lemma 2 *Let $\phi(w) = \phi_0 + \cdots + \phi_d w^d$ be a polynomial degree function with degree $d \geq 2$. Then, in a complex neighbourhood of ρ, the solution $Y(z)$ of (7) is of the form*

$$Y(z) = \frac{1}{\Delta(z)} \cdot H(\Delta(z)) \qquad \text{where} \qquad \Delta(z) = \eta(1 - z/\rho)^{\delta}, \tag{11}$$

and $H(w) = \sum_{m=0}^{\infty} h_m w^m$ is analytic at $w = 0$,

$$h_0 = 1, \quad h_1 = -\frac{\phi_{d-1}}{d\phi_d}, \quad h_2 = -\frac{2d\phi_d\phi_{d-2} - (d-1)\phi_{d-1}^2}{2d(d+1)\phi_d^2}.$$

Proof. We start with the expansion of $1/\phi$ as $w \to +\infty$,

$$\frac{1}{\phi(w)} = \frac{1}{\phi_d w^d} - \frac{\phi_{d-1}}{\phi_d^2 w^{d+1}} + \frac{\phi_{d-1}^2 - \phi_d\phi_{d-2}}{\phi_d^3 w^{d+2}} + \cdots.$$

By integration, we find as $Y \to +\infty$,

$$\int_Y^{\infty} \frac{dw}{\phi(w)} = \frac{\delta}{\phi_d} Y^{-d+1} - \frac{\phi_{d-1}}{d\phi_d^2} Y^{-d} + \cdots. \tag{12}$$

But from

$$\int_0^{Y(z)} \frac{dw}{\phi(w)} = z \quad \text{and} \quad \int_0^{\infty} \frac{dw}{\phi(w)} = \rho,$$

we have

$$\rho - z = \int_{Y(z)}^{\infty} \frac{dw}{\phi(w)}. \tag{13}$$

Therefore, by comparing (12) and (13), we get

$$\frac{\delta}{\phi_d} Y^{1-d} - \cdots = (\rho - z).$$

Inverting this relation, leads to the singular expansion of $Y(z)$ as a function of $(\rho - z)^{1/(d-1)}$.

This process is purely formal. The analytic character of the resulting series $H(w)$ is easily established by means of the method of majorizing series or by observing that $1/\phi(w)$ and derived functions are analytic at ∞. □

We return to the proof of Theorem 2. The bare principle of singularity analysis consists in applying the following rules,

$$\begin{aligned} Y(z) &= (1 - z/\rho)^{\alpha} & &\Longrightarrow & [z^n]Y(z) &\sim \rho^{-n}\frac{n^{-\alpha-1}}{\Gamma(-\alpha)}(1 + O(\frac{1}{n}) \\ Y(z) &= O((1 - z/\rho)^{\alpha}) & &\Longrightarrow & [z^n]Y(z) &= O(\rho^{-n}n^{-\alpha-1}), \end{aligned}$$

inside the local asymptotic expansion of a function which is singular at $z = \rho$. These two rules are applied to the expansion (11) of $Y(z)$.

Validity of the process in the aperiodic case is ensured because $Y(z)$ exists in a domain larger than the disk of convergence as guaranteed by the two lemmas (see [11]). In the periodic case, contributions from the p dominant singularities must be added, which accounts for the extra factor of p.

This concludes the proof of Theorem 2. □

EXAMPLE 3. *Strict ternary trees.* For the variety of strict ternary trees, we have $\phi(w) = 1+w^3$. Thus, $Y(z)$ satisfies

$$\frac{1}{3}\log(1+Y) - \frac{1}{6}\log(1-Y+Y^2) + \frac{1}{\sqrt{3}}\arctan(\frac{2Y-1}{\sqrt{3}}) + \frac{\pi}{6\sqrt{3}} = z.$$

This relation is *not* explicitly solvable for $Y(z)$. However, the singularity is easily determined to be $\rho = 2\pi\sqrt{3}/9$, and

$$Y(z) = \frac{1}{\sqrt{2}\sqrt{\frac{2\pi\sqrt{3}}{9} - z}} + h_2(1 - z/\rho) + O((1 - z/\rho)^{5/2})$$

so that

$$\frac{Y_n}{n!} = \frac{1}{\sqrt{2\pi}}\left(\frac{2\pi\sqrt{3}}{9}\right)^{-n-1/2} n^{-1/2}\,[1 - \frac{1}{8n} + \frac{1}{128n^2} + O(n^{-3})].$$

Full expansions are readily obtained. □

4 Inductive Parameters

We show here how a fairly general theory of cost measures on varieties of trees can be developed, based on the algebraic and analytic methods used for basic tree enumerations. In order not to obscure the line of reasoning too much we have limited the discussion to "inductive maps" defined below, and to a particular "elementary" subclass with interesting analytic properties.

4.1 Exact Generating Functions.

Definition 2 A function from trees to complex numbers is called an *inductive map* if it is definable by a relation

$$s[t] = f_{|t|} + \sum_{\tau \propto t} s[\tau],$$

for some number sequence $\{f_n\}$, where the sum is over all root subtrees τ of t (noted $\tau \propto t$).

Given a tree function $s[.]$ and a variety $\mathcal{Y}$, the generating function of $s[.]$ (over $\mathcal{Y}$) is

$$S(z) = \sum_{t \in \mathcal{Y}} s[t] \frac{z^{|t|}}{|t|!}.$$

Typical examples of inductive maps are tree size ($f_n = 1$), number of leaves ($f_n = \delta_{n,1}$) and path length ($f_n = n$). The GF $S(z)$ is an EGF of cumulated values since $n![z^n]S(z) = \sum_{|t|=n} s[t]$.

Theorem 3 *Let $s[t]$ be an inductive map,*

$$s[t] = f_{|t|} + \sum_{\tau \propto t} s[\tau].$$

The generating function of $s[t]$, on a variety $\mathcal{Y}$, is computable by

$$S(z) = Y'(z) \int_0^z \left(\frac{d}{dt}F(t)\right) \frac{dt}{Y'(t)}, \tag{14}$$

where $F(z)$ is defined from $\{f_n\}$ and $\mathcal{Y}$ by

$$F(z) = \sum_{n \geq 0} f_n Y_n \frac{z^n}{n!}. \tag{15}$$

Proof. The bivariate generating function

$$Y(z,u) = \sum_{t \in \mathcal{Y}} u^{s[t]} z^{|t|}$$

is easily seen to satisfy

$$\begin{aligned} Y(z,u) &= \textstyle\sum_n Y_n u^{f_n} \frac{z^n}{n!} + \int_0^z \sum_{r=1}^{\infty} \phi_r Y^r(t,u)\,dt \\ &= \textstyle\sum_n Y_n u^{f_n} \frac{z^n}{n!} + \int_0^z \phi(Y(t,u))\,dt. \end{aligned} \tag{16}$$

The argument is of the same type as that used for equation (7): the contribution to $Y(z,u)$ comes either from the root (the first sum), or—when the root has degree r—from one of the r root subtrees with multiplicity ϕ_r.

From equation (16) and the fact that $Y(z,1) = Y(z)$ and $\partial Y/\partial u(z,1) = S(z)$, we obtain by differentiation

$$S(z) = F(z) + \int_0^z S(t)\phi'(Y(t))\,dt. \tag{17}$$

Eq. (17) next translates into a linear differential equation

$$S'(z) = F'(z) + S(z)\phi'(Y(z)), \quad S(0) = 0.$$

First solve the associated homogeneous equation, which yields $S(z) = CY'(z)$. Then solve the inhomogeneous equation by the variation-of-parameter method, which gives

$$S(z) = Y'(z) \int_0^z \frac{F'(t)}{Y'(t)}\,dt. \tag{18}$$

□

4.2 Asymptotic Estimates.

Definition 3 An inductive map $s[.]$ is called *elementary* when the associated number sequence $\{f_n\}$ is of the form

$$f_n = Cn^\alpha \log^r n,$$

for some real C, α and non-negative r. The triple (C, α, r) is called the *parameter* of the map.

Theorem 4 *Let s be an elementary map with parameter (C, α, r) defined on a polynomial variety $\mathcal{Y}$. Then the average value $\overline{S_n}$ of s on the elements of $\mathcal{Y}$ with size n satisfies asymptotically:*

1. *if $\alpha < 1$, then*

$$\overline{S_n} \sim \lambda n \qquad \textit{with} \qquad \lambda = \frac{1}{\rho} \int_0^\rho \frac{F'(t)}{Y'(t)}\,dt;$$

2. *if $\alpha = 1$, then*

$$\overline{S_n} \sim \lambda n \log^{r+1} n \qquad \textit{with} \qquad \lambda = \frac{C(\delta+1)}{r+1};$$

3. *if $\alpha > 1$, then*

$$\overline{S_n} \sim \lambda n^\alpha \log^r n \qquad \textit{with} \qquad \lambda = \frac{C}{\alpha - 1}(\alpha + \delta).$$

Proof. The result follows from singularity analysis and from the analysis of $Y(z)$ already effected in the proof of Theorem 2. We assume without loss of generality that $\mathcal{Y}$ is non periodic. The major steps are as follows.

A. It is *a priori* clear from growth conditions, namely $S_n = O(Y_n n^{\alpha+2}) = O(\rho^{-n} n^{\alpha+1/2})$, that $S(z)$ has $z = \rho$ as a dominant singularity. We must therefore analyse $S(z)$ locally there.

B. The modified generating function $F(z) = \sum f_n Y_n z^n$ is a Hadamard product (a "termwise" product) of $Y(z)$ with the ordinary generating function $\mathcal{F} = \sum_{n=1}^{\infty} f_n z^n$. With the standard notation of Hadamard products ($\odot$), we have

$$F(z) = \mathcal{F}(z) \odot Y(z).$$

The analysis of $F(z)$ associated with $f_n = Cn^{\alpha} \log^r n$ is then effected by the following steps.

> $\mathcal{F}(z)$ is analytically continuable and has the expected asymptotic expansion—it has an algebraic–logarithmic singularity—when $z \to 1$ in the complex plane. This results from classical complex integral representations, see for instance Ford's book [14] or Evgrafov [8, p. 165].
>
> Hadamard products preserve analytic continuation. (This is Hadamard's celebrated theorem on composition of singularities by Hadamard products.)
>
> Hadamard products preserve algebraic–logarithmic singularities. This theorem is due to Pólya, see [41] for a discussion relevant to our goals.

C. Once the singular behaviour of F is known, the corresponding analysis for S is done mechanically using rules for differentiation, integration, and usual Cauchy products. The necessary expansions are summarized by the following lemma.

Lemma 3 *If s has parameter (C, α, r) then the singular expansion of $S(z)$ near ρ is given by*

$$S(z) \sim \lambda(1 - z/\rho)^{-1-\delta}\psi(z), \quad z \to \rho,$$

where λ is a constant and

$$\psi(z) = \begin{cases} 1 & \text{if } \alpha < 1, \\ \log^{r+1} \frac{1}{1-z/\rho} & \text{if } \alpha = 1, \\ (1 - z/\rho)^{1-\alpha} \log^r \frac{1}{1-z/\rho} & \text{if } \alpha > 1. \end{cases}$$

Proof. First, $\mathcal{F}$ has an isolated singularity at $z = 1$ as follows from integral representations [14, 8]. Next, F has an algebraic–logarithmic singularity at $z = \rho$: by Theorem 2, its coefficients grow as

$$\frac{C}{\eta\Gamma(\delta)} \rho^{-n} n^{\alpha-1+\delta} \log^r n,$$

and by the closure theorems discussed by Wilson [41], $F(z)$ has the corresponding singularity. Then,

$$F'(t) \sim \lambda_0 (1 - t/\rho)^{-\alpha-1-\delta} \log^r \frac{1}{1 - t/\rho} \quad (t \to \rho) \text{ with } \lambda_0 = \frac{C}{\eta\rho} \frac{\Gamma(\alpha + \delta + 1)}{\Gamma(\delta)}.$$

Thus, the integrand in (14) grows like

$$\lambda_0 \frac{\eta\rho}{\delta} (1 - t/\rho)^{-\alpha} \log^r \frac{1}{1 - t/\rho}, \quad t \to \rho,$$

and several cases need to be distinguished.

1. If $\alpha < 1$, then the integral is convergent and we get the statement of the lemma with
$$\lambda = \frac{\delta}{\eta\rho}\int_0^\rho \left(\frac{d}{dt}F(t)\right)\frac{dt}{Y'(t)};$$
2. if $\alpha = 1$, then integrating by parts, we get the statement with $\lambda = \lambda_0\rho/(r+1)$;
3. if $\alpha > 1$, then again integrating by parts, we get the statement with $\lambda = \lambda_0\rho/(\alpha-1)$.

This completes the evaluation of $S(z)$ near ρ and the lemma is established. □

From the last lemma and singularity analysis applied to $S(z)$, the proof of Theorem 4 is in turn completed. □

Theorem 4 admits a number of extensions. For instance, the same methodology accommodates exponentially decaying f_n like $\theta^n n^\alpha$, with $\theta < 1$, boundary condition terms like $\delta_{n,0}$ or $\delta_{n,1}$, and any finite linear combinations. In all these cases, and more generally whenever the generating function $\mathcal{F}(z)$ is analytic in a disk that properly contains the unit disk, the formula of case 1 of Theorem 4 applies. Quantities f_n that are asymptotically equivalent (rather than equal) to $n^\alpha \log^r n$ are also amenable to these methods.

5 Characteristics of Increasing Trees

The estimates presented here illustrate direct consequences of the theorems and methods introduced in the last section, when specialized to a few classical tree parameters. This concerns statistics on path length, mean number of leaves, and root degree.

In addition, extensions of the method lead to asymptotic probability distributions for levels and number of leaves, which are proved to be Gaussian in the limit.

5.1 Path length

Path length of a tree t is by definition the sum of the distances of all nodes in t to the root of t, distances being measured by number of nodes[3] on the connecting branch. An alternative inductive definition is thus
$$s[t] = |t| + \sum_{\tau \propto t} s[\tau].$$
Path length is directly amenable to techniques of the last section, and in this case, function F introduced in Theorem 3 takes the explicit form $F(z) = zY'(z)$.

Theorem 5 *Let the variety of trees $\mathcal{Y}$ be defined by the degree function ϕ. The generating function of path length $S(z)$ is given by*
$$S(z) = Y'(z)\int_0^z \frac{Y'(t)+tY''(t)}{Y'(t)}\,dt.$$
Asymptotically, for a polynomial variety of degree d, we have
$$\overline{S_n} = \frac{S_n}{Y_n} = (\delta+1)n\log n + Cn + O\left(\frac{\log n}{n^{\min(0,2\delta-1)}}\right),$$
with
$$C = -1 - \psi(\delta) + \frac{1}{\rho}\int_0^\rho \left[1 + t\frac{Y''(t)}{Y'(t)} - \frac{\delta+1}{1-t/\rho}\right] dt,$$
where ψ is the logarithmic derivative of Euler's Γ function.

[3] Path length is sometimes defined by measuring the distance to the root as the number of connecting edges. This variant of path length, $s^*[t]$ satisfies $s^*[t] = s[t] - |t|$, so that $\overline{S_n^*} = \overline{S_n} - n$.

Proof. A direct application of Theorem 4 to the case $f_n = n$, plus some extra care for the subdominant terms. □

Corollary 2 *(i) For binary trees, $\phi(w) = (1+w)^2$, we have*

$$\overline{S_n} = 2n\log n + (2\gamma - 3)n + 2\log n + 2\gamma + 1 + O(1/n).$$

(ii) For strict binary trees, $\phi(w) = 1 + w^2$,

$$\overline{S_n} = 2n\log n + (2\gamma + 3 + \frac{\pi^2}{36} + \frac{\pi^4}{7200})n + 2\log n + (2\gamma + 1 - \frac{\pi^2}{36} - \frac{\pi^4}{7200}) + O(1/n).$$

(iii) For recursive trees, $\phi(w) = \exp(w)$,

$$\overline{S_n} = n\log n + \gamma n + \frac{1}{2} + O(1/n).$$

(iv) For plane recursive trees, $\phi(w) = (1-w)^{-1}$,

$$Y_n = \frac{1}{2}n\log n + (\log 2 + \frac{\gamma+1}{2})n - \frac{1}{4}\log n - \frac{2\log 2 + \gamma}{4} + O(1/n).$$

Proof. The GF $S(z)$ is determined by integration, and we find the four expressions:

$$\frac{2\log(1-z)^{-1} - z}{(1-z)^2}, \quad \frac{1}{\cos^2 z}\int_0^z (1 + 2t\tan t)\,dt, \quad \frac{\log(1-z)^{-1}}{(1-z)}, \quad \frac{2z + \log(1-2z)^{-1}}{4(1-2z)^{1/2}}.$$

This corresponds to more or less complicated explicit forms, e.g. $\overline{S_n} = nH_n$ for recursive trees and the asymptotic forms follow by singularity analysis. □

Variance. From equation (16), we can compute the variance of a general inductive map by

$$\sigma^2 = \frac{[z^n]\frac{\partial^2}{\partial u^2}Y(z,1)}{Y_n} + \overline{S_n} - \overline{S_n}^2.$$

The second derivative is obtained in a way similar to the first one,

$$\frac{\partial^2}{\partial u^2}Y(z,1) = Y'(z)\int_0^z \frac{H'(t) + \phi''(Y(t))S^2(t)}{Y'(t)}dt,$$

where

$$H(z) = \sum_n Y_n f_n(f_n - 1)\frac{z^n}{n!} = Y(z)\odot(\mathcal{F}(z)\odot\mathcal{F}(z) - \mathcal{F}(z)).$$

From this equation, using the same arguments as in the proof of Theorem 4, it is possible to attain a classification of the possible variances in the polynomial case, and a similar but complicated process would yield moments of higher order.

In the particular case of path length, we have $f_n = n$, and

$$H(z) = \sum_{n\geq 0} n(n-1)Y_n\frac{z^n}{n!} = z^2Y''(z),$$

so that $\frac{\partial^2 Y}{\partial u^2}(z,1)$ reduces to

$$Y'(z)\int_0^z \frac{2tY''(t) + t^2Y'''(t) + \phi''(Y(t))S^2(t)}{Y'(t)}dt.$$

This has a singularity at ρ, and in the polynomial case, the local behaviour yields the following.

Corollary 3 *The variance of path length on a polynomial variety $\mathcal{Y}$ is asymptotic to λn^2, with*

$$\lambda = \psi(\delta+1)(\delta+1)(2\delta+4-\frac{2C}{\rho}) - \psi'(\delta+1)(\delta+1)^2 + 2(\delta+1)(\delta+2) - \frac{4C}{\rho} + \frac{\delta+2}{\rho^2},$$

and C as in Theorem 5.

This result is well known in the case of quicksort and path length in binary search trees for which $\lambda = 7 - 2\frac{\pi^2}{3}$.

5.2 Node Sorts

The next example shows a parameter that does not strictly speaking falls in the general category treated by Theorem 4, though exactly the same method of proof applies.

Theorem 6 *Let $s[t]$ be the number of nodes of outdegree i in a random tree t of size n from a variety defined by $\phi(w)$. With $\phi_i = [w^i]\phi(w)$, the generating function of $s[.]$ is*

$$S(z) = \phi_i Y'(z) \int_0^z \frac{Y^i(t)}{Y'(t)}\, dt. \tag{19}$$

For a polynomial family, the mean number of i–nodes is

$$\overline{S_n} = \lambda_i n[1 + O(n^{-\delta})] \qquad \text{where} \qquad \lambda_i = \frac{\phi_i}{\rho} \int_0^\rho \frac{Y^i(t)}{Y'(t)}\, dt.$$

Proof. The parameter $s[t]$ which represents the number of nodes of degree i satisfies

$$s[t] = \mathbf{1}_{\text{degree}(\text{root}(t))=i} + \sum_{u \propto t} s[u].$$

Hence, the integral equation for the EGF $S(z)$:

$$S(z) = \phi_i \int_0^z Y^i(t)\, dt + \int_0^z S(t)\phi'(Y(t))\, dt,$$

whose solution is

$$S(z) = \phi_i Y'(z) \int_0^z \frac{Y^i(t)}{Y'(t)}\, dt.$$

The dominant singularities of S are therefore those of Y, and the singular behaviour at ρ is

$$\frac{\phi_i \delta}{\eta\rho}(1 - z/\rho)^{-1-\delta} \int_0^\rho \frac{Y^i(t)}{Y'(t)} dt,$$

the integral being convergent. From there we get the coefficients via singularity analysis. □

Corollary 4 *(i) For binary trees, $\phi(w) = (1+w)^2$, the expected numbers of nodes of degrees* $0, 1, 2$ *are* equal *to*

$$\frac{n+1}{3}, \frac{n+1}{3}, \frac{n-2}{3}.$$

(ii) For recursive trees, $\phi(w) = \exp(w)$, the expected number of nodes of outdegree i is asymptotic to

$$\lambda_i n \qquad \text{where} \qquad \lambda_i = \frac{1}{2^{i+1}}.$$

(iii) For plane recursive trees, $\phi(w) = (1-w)^{-1}$, the expected number of nodes of outdegree i is asymptotic to

$$\lambda_i n \qquad \text{where} \qquad \lambda_i = \frac{2}{(i+1)(i+2)(i+3)}.$$

Proof. For binary trees, the result follows by elementary integration. (For strict binary trees, the problem is degenerate!) For the other two cases, one estimates simultaneously all the λ_i by means of their ordinary generating function, $\Lambda(x) = \sum_i \lambda_i x^i$.

For recursive trees, we find

$$\begin{aligned}\Lambda(x) &= \sum_{i=0}^{\infty} \frac{x^i}{i!} \int_0^1 (1-t) \log^i \frac{1}{1-t}\, dt \\ &= \int_0^1 \frac{(1-t)}{(1-t)^x}\, dt = \left[\frac{T^{2-x}}{2-x}\right]_0^1 = \frac{1}{2-x}.\end{aligned}$$

For plane recursive trees, we find

$$\begin{aligned}\Lambda(x) &= \int_0^{1/2} \frac{\sqrt{1-2t}}{1-x(1-\sqrt{1-2t})}\, dt \\ &= \frac{(1-x)^2}{x^3} \log \frac{1}{1-x} + \frac{3x-2}{2x^2}.\end{aligned}$$

□

The result for binary trees is of course classical. For recursive trees, the result appears in [1, Thm 3.3] in the combinatorial literature but seems to have been first noted by Gastwirth [16].

5.3 Root degree

Let $r[t]$ denote the root degree of tree t. Then the EGF of trees with root degree j is clearly

$$\phi_j \int_0^z Y^j(t)\, dt. \qquad (20)$$

The bivariate generating function for the distribution of root degree in trees in a variety $\mathcal{Y}$ is defined by

$$R(z,u) = \sum_{t \in \mathcal{Y}} u^{r[t]} \frac{z^{|t|}}{|t|\,!}.$$

Theorem 7 *The bivariate generating function of root degrees, $R(z,u)$, is given by*

$$R(z,u) = \int_0^z \phi(uY(t))\, dt.$$

Let $S(z) = R_u(z,1)$ and $T(z) = R_{uu}(z,1)$ be the generating functions of the first and second factorial moments of root degree. Then

$$\begin{aligned}\tfrac{d}{dz} S(z) &= Y(z) \tfrac{d}{dz} \log Y'(z) \\ \tfrac{d}{dz} T(z) &= \tfrac{Y^2(z)}{Y'(z)} \tfrac{d^2}{dz^2} \log Y'(z)\end{aligned} \qquad (21)$$

For a polynomial variety of degree d, almost all trees of size n have root degree equal to d. The probability π_{nj} that a tree of size n has root degree j, with $1 \le j \le d$, is

$$\pi_{nj} \sim \alpha_j n^{-1+(j-1)\delta} \qquad \textit{with} \qquad \alpha_j = \frac{\rho\phi_j}{\eta^{j-1}} \frac{\Gamma(\delta)}{\Gamma(j\delta)}.$$

Proof. The bivariate generating function follows from (20). For computational purposes, it is advantageous to deal with $\frac{\partial}{\partial z}R(z,u)$ from which the forms of S and T follow.

The case of polynomial varieties results immediately from singularity analysis. □

Corollary 5 *(i) For recursive trees, $\phi(w) = \exp(w)$, the number of trees with size n and root degree k is $s_{n-1,k}$. The mean root degree is H_{n-1}.*

(ii) For plane recursive trees, $\phi(w) = (1-w)^{-1}$, the number of trees with size n and root degree k is

$$\frac{(2n-3-k)!}{2^{n-1-k}(n-1-k)!}.$$

The mean root degree is $\sqrt{\pi n} + O(1)$.

Proof. The theorem provides the generating functions

$$\frac{(1-z)^{1-u}-1}{u-1} \quad \text{and} \quad \frac{1-\sqrt{1-2z}}{u} + \frac{1-u}{u^2}\log(1-u+u\sqrt{1-2z}),$$

from which the results are deduced. □

The result for recursive trees is classical, at least under equivalent formulations (see the section on models). The mean for plane recursive trees constitutes Thm 1 of Mahmoud *et al.*'s paper [31]. The distribution result appears to be new and the expression is related to ballot numbers.

5.4 Profiles of trees

Consider the quantity L_{nk} representing the expected number of nodes at depth k on all trees of a variety $\mathcal{Y}$ with size n. (By convention the depth of the root is taken to be 0.) For fixed n, the sequence $\{L_{n,k}\}_{k=0}^{n}$ describes the mean "profile" of trees in the variety (see [32]). Let $L(z,u)$ be the bivariate generating function,

$$L(z,u) = \sum_{n,k\geq 0} L_{nk}\frac{z^n}{n!}u^k,$$

Theorem 8 *The bivariate generating function $L(z,u)$ of node levels satisfies*

$$L(z,u) = (Y'(z))^u \int_0^z (Y'(t))^{1-u}\, dt. \tag{22}$$

Let Ω_n be the depth of a random node in a random tree of $\mathcal{Y}$ with size n, i.e.,

$$Pr(\Omega_n = k) = \frac{L_{nk}}{\sum_k L_{nk}}.$$

For a polynomial variety of degree d, the mean μ_n and the variance σ_n^2 of Ω_n satisfy

$$\mu_n = (\delta+1)\log n + O(1) \quad \text{and} \quad \sigma_n^2 = (\delta+1)\log n + O(1).$$

The distribution of Ω_n is asymptotically normal,

$$(\Omega_n - \mu_n)/\sigma_n \to \mathcal{N}(0;1),$$

in the sense of convergence in distribution.

Proof. Define $s[t]$, the level polynomial of a tree t, to be the sum $\sum_\nu u^{\mathrm{depth}(\nu)}$ taken over all nodes ν of t. Then $s[t]$ is inductively defined by

$$s[t] = \begin{cases} 1 & \text{if } |t| = 1 \\ u \sum_{\tau \propto t} s[\tau] & \text{otherwise.} \end{cases}$$

Algebraically, the generating polynomial $L_n(u) = \sum_k L_{nk} u^k$ behaves like the expectation of an inductive parameter. Using the same reasoning as for counting trees in Section 2 or for inductive maps, we get the equation

$$L(z,u) = Y(z) + u \int_0^z L(t,u)\phi'(Y(t))\,dt,$$

which translates into a linear differential equation

$$\frac{\partial}{\partial z} L(z,u) = Y'(z) + uL(z,u)\frac{\phi'(Y(z))Y'(z)}{\phi(Y(z))}, \quad L(0,u) = 1.$$

Integrating the homogeneous equation first, we get the solution

$$\exp(u \log Y'(z)) = (Y'(z))^u.$$

The integral form of $L(z,u)$ is then obtained by the variation–of–parameter method.

In the case of a polynomial ϕ, using Lemma 2, we determine

$$\log Y'(z) = (\delta+1)\log\frac{1}{1-z/\rho} + C + O[(1-z/\rho)^{2\delta}].$$

A theorem of Flajolet and Soria [12] states that a bivariate scheme of the form $\exp(uL(z))$ for some function $L(z)$ with a dominant logarithmic singularity induces Gaussian distributions in the asymptotic limit. It applies here to $(Y'(z))^u = \exp(u \log Y'(z))$.

In the case of $L(z,u)$ in Eq. (22), the integral is convergent for u in a complex neighbourhood of 1 and $|z| \le \rho$ so that it plays the role of an unessential perturbation. A simply amended form of the main result of [12] then applies. □

The result for μ_n is also consistent with the estimate of expected path length which is precisely $n\mu_n + n$.

Corollary 6 *(i) For binary trees, $\phi(w) = (1+w)^2$, we have*

$$L(z,u) = \frac{(1-z)^{-2u} - (1-z)^{-1}}{2u-1},$$

$$\mu_n = 2\log n + 2\gamma - 4 + O(\log n/n), \quad \sigma_n^2 = 2\log n + 4 + 2\gamma - \frac{2\pi^2}{3} + O(\log^2 n/n).$$

(ii) For recursive trees, $\phi(w) = \exp(w)$,

$$L(z,u) = \frac{(1-z)^{-u} - 1}{u},$$

$$\mu_n = \log n + \gamma - 1 + O(1/n), \quad \sigma_n^2 = \log n + \gamma - \frac{\pi^2}{6} + O(1/n).$$

(iii) For plane recursive trees, $\phi(w) = (1-w)^{-1}$,

$$L(z,u) = \frac{(1-2z)^{-u/2} - (1-2z)^{1/2}}{1+u},$$

$$\mu_n = \frac{1}{2}\log n + \frac{\gamma}{2} + \log 2 - \frac{1}{2} + O(\log n/n), \quad \sigma_n^2 = \frac{1}{2}\log n + \frac{\gamma}{2} + \log 2 - \frac{1}{4} - \frac{\pi^2}{8} + O(\log^2 n/n).$$

For binary trees, the distribution has been given by a number of authors independently in the 1980's, see [28]; for recursive trees, it was found by Devroye [7] using the theory of records. Both explicit forms and limit distributions are derivable from these GF's. For recursive trees we find the coefficients $s_{n,k+1}$, while the two other ones give rise to convolution of Stirling numbers of the first kind. (We recall that the Stirling number of the first kind, s_{nk} is defined as $[u^k]\, u(u+1)(u+2)\cdots(u+n-1)$; Stirling numbers are ubiquitous in this category of problems.)

5.5 Distribution of the number of leaves

In order to approach the distribution of the number of leaves and more generally of nodes by sorts, we introduce

$$\phi(\mathbf{u}; y) = \sum_{r=0}^{\infty} \phi_r u_r y^r,$$

a series involving in general infinitely many indeterminates, (u_r). Let $N(n_0, n_1, \ldots)$ be the number of trees of size n (in the variety defined by ϕ) that have n_0 leaves, n_1 nodes of degree 1, etc. The multivariate GF

$$Y(\mathbf{u}; z) = \sum_{n_0, n_1, \ldots} N(n_0, n_1, \ldots) u_0^{n_0} u_1^{n_1} \cdots \frac{z^{n_0+n_1+\cdots}}{(n_0+n_1+\cdots)!}$$

satisfies

$$\int_0^{Y(\mathbf{u};z)} \frac{dt}{\phi(\mathbf{u}; t)} = z.$$

This function condenses all the distribution information of all node sorts in a variety. In particular, it specializes to the bivariate GF for the distribution of the number of leaves, $Y(u; z) = Y(u, 1, 1, \ldots; z)$.

Theorem 9 *The bivariate generating function for leaves $Y(u;z)$ is defined implicitly by*

$$\int_0^{Y} \frac{dt}{(u-1)\phi_0 + \phi(t)} = z.$$

For random trees of size n in a polynomial variety, the number of leaves tends to a Gaussian limit (in the sense of convergence in distribution).

Proof. (Sketch) The argument for the Gaussian limit is based on analyzing the "perturbation" caused by the variable u in the non linear differential equation $Y' = \phi(Y)$, with u near 1. We consider some fixed u close enough to 1.

First, the radius of convergence of $Y(u; z)$ is

$$\rho(u) = \int_0^{\infty} \frac{dt}{(u-1)\phi_0 + \phi(t)}.$$

We have

$$\begin{aligned}\rho(u) - \rho(1) &= \int_0^\infty \frac{dt}{\phi(t)} \left(\frac{1}{1 + \phi_0 \frac{u-1}{\phi(t)}} - 1 \right) \\ &= -(u-1)\phi_0 \int_0^\infty \frac{dt}{\phi^2(t)} + (u-1)^2 \phi_0^2 \int_0^\infty \frac{dt}{\phi^3(t)} - \cdots . \end{aligned} \tag{23}$$

The singular exponent of $Y(u; z)$ is still δ, and we have

$$Y(u; z) = H_0(u)(1 - z/\rho(u))^{-\delta} + H_1(u) + etc.$$

By a suitable use of majorizing series arguments, a uniform version of this expansion is established, when u lies in a real neighbourhood of 1. It is known from Bender's work that similar analytic schemas lead to Gaussian laws [2]. Here, we use a slightly stronger form of Bender's theorem discussed in [13]. In this way, the result is established. □

Let $Y_{n,k}$ denote the number of trees of size n having k leaves in variety $\mathcal{Y}$.

Corollary 7 *(i). For binary trees, $\phi(w) = (1 + w)^2$, $Y_{n,k}$ is a pseudo-Eulerian number,*

$$Y_{n,k} = n![u^k z^n] Y(u; z) \qquad \textit{where } Y(u; z) = \xi \frac{\xi \tan(\xi z) + 1}{\xi - \tan(\xi z)} - 1 \textit{ and } \xi = (u-1)^{1/2}.$$

(ii). For recursive trees, $Y_{n,k}$ is a shifted Eulerian number,

$$Y_{n,k} = A_{n-1,k} = (n-1)![u^k z^{n-1}] \left(u - 1 + \frac{1-u}{1 - ue^{z(1-u)}}\right).$$

(iii). For plane recursive trees, $Y_{n,k}$ is a second order Eulerian number,

$$Y_{n,k} = n![u^k z^n] \frac{C(ue^{-u} e^{z(u-1)^2}) - C(ue^{-u})}{u-1}, \qquad \textit{where} \qquad C(z) = \sum_{n=1}^{\infty} n^{n-1} \frac{z^n}{n!}$$

is Cayley's function.

In all three cases, the distribution is Gaussian in the limit.

Proof. The generating functions follow from straight integration. In the case of recursive trees, we get a modified GF for the Eulerian numbers in the form

$$Y(u; z) = \log \frac{1-u}{1 - ue^{z(1-u)}}.$$

For plane recursive trees, we arrive at second order Eulerian numbers (for a definition, see [20, p. 256]). Cayley's function arises through inversion of $Ce^C = z$. □

The result for binary trees is classical. The one for recursive trees was found independently by several authors, an early reference being [34]. Mahmoud *et al.* [31] discovered the connection with second order Eulerian numbers. The EGF given above does not seem to have appeared in the literature however. The Gaussian law in this case is in [31] where it is derived from limit theorems on Pólya urn models.

Similar limit distribution results hold for other sorts of nodes, like i–nodes.

6 Extensions

Results in this paper can be extended in various directions. On the algebraic side, variants of our basic algebraic schemes may be considered. On the analytic side, we may treat varieties defined by degree functions that are either entire or have singularities at a finite distance.

6.1 Algebraic Schemes

The basic scheme of Thm. 1,

$$Y(z) = \int_0^z \phi(Y(t))\, dt,$$

arises with ϕ being rather generally the GF of a "species" of structures in the sense of Joyal [3, 22]. For instance, we can fit into our algebraic framework, the cases of

$$\phi(w) = 1 + \log \frac{1}{1-w}, \quad \phi(w) = \tan(w).$$

The first case corresponds to "mobiles" where subtrees dangling from a node are arranged in cyclic order and thus constitute a freely rotating cycle. The second case corresponds to "festoon" trees in which labels of the sons of a node go up an down, forming an alternating permutation. (Of course the increasing tree property is still assumed in these constructions.)

The algebra of such series is indistinguishable from that of increasing trees varieties considered earlier. The analysis, as we discuss below, can be treated along similar lines.

6.2 Analytic Schemes

The principles of analysis employed generalize to either entire functions or functions with singularities at a finite distance. The argument runs as follows.

> *The singular behaviour of $Y(z)$ is obtained by inverting the singular expansion of $\int dw/\phi(w)$ near its smallest positive singularity. The asymptotic form of the coefficients of $Y(z)$ derives from that singular behaviour by means of singularity analysis.*

Assume that $\phi(w)$ which has positive coefficients becomes singular at $\sigma > 0$. We have either $\sigma = +\infty$ or $\sigma < \infty$ depending on whether ϕ is entire or not. In both cases, however, the argument employed in the proof of Thm. 2 generalizes, and the radius of convergence of $Y(z)$ is

$$\rho = \int_0^\sigma \frac{dw}{\phi(w)}. \tag{24}$$

Eq. (24) is consistent with what we have found (see Cor. 1) for recursive trees, where $\phi(w) = \exp(w)$ so that $\sigma = +\infty$, and for plane recursive trees where $\phi(w) = (1-w)^{-1}$ so that $\sigma = 1$. In these two cases, we have

$$\rho = \int_0^{+\infty} e^{-w}\, dw = 1 \quad \text{and} \quad \rho = \int_0^1 (1-w)\, dw = \frac{1}{2}.$$

Singularity at a finite distance. Consider the typical case of

$$\phi(Y) = \frac{1}{P(Y)},$$

with P a polynomial. In this case, the equation $P(Y)Y' = 1$ has the integral $Q(Y) = z$, with $Q' = P$ and $Q(0) = 0$. Thus Y is an algebraic function and its coefficients are *a priori* of the asymptotic form $C\rho^{-n}n^{p/q}$ for some rational p/q. The singularity of $Y(z)$ is at

$$\rho = \int_0^\sigma P(y)\,dy = Q(\sigma),$$

where σ is the smallest positive root of P. The singular expansion of Y is then found by inverting

$$\rho - z = \int_{Y(z)}^\sigma P(y)\,dy = Q(\sigma) - Q(Y(z)).$$

In the generic case, $P'(\sigma) \neq 0$, and we obtain the singular expansion

$$Y(z) = \sigma - \sqrt{\frac{2(\rho - z)}{|P'(\sigma)|}} + O(\rho - z), \quad z \to \rho,$$

from which we deduce

$$\frac{Y_n}{n!} = \sqrt{\frac{\rho}{\pi |P'(\sigma)|}}\rho^{-n}n^{-3/2}[1 + O(1/n)].$$

Thus the particular explicit form obtained for plane recursive trees is indeed attached to a fairly general scheme.

EXAMPLE 4. *Special plane trees and festoon trees.* As an illustration, consider plane recursive trees in which nodes degrees are all multiples of a fixed integer t, so that $\phi(w) = (1 - w^t)^{-1}$. In this case, the equation for Y, which is $Y'(1 - Y^t) = 1$ leads to

$$Y - \frac{Y^{t+1}}{t+1} = z.$$

The trinomial equation is solvable by Lagrange inversion, from which we find

$$Y_{nt+1} = \frac{(nt)!}{(t+1)^n}\binom{n(t+1)}{n},$$

a formula that generalizes that of plane recursive trees and is also in agreement with the asymptotic estimates above.

Festoon trees already discussed correspond to $\phi(w) = \tan(w)$, so that $\sigma = \frac{\pi}{2}$. We find $\rho = \frac{\pi}{4}$, and asymptotically, by a direct extension of the situation of rational functions, $Y_n/n! \sim C(4/\pi)^n n^{-3/2}$, for some $C > 0$. □

EXAMPLE 5. *Mobile trees.* They correspond to $\phi(w) = 1 + \log(1 - w)^{-1}$. The asymptotic analysis takes us a little out of beaten tracks. The radius of convergence ρ is

$$\rho = \int_0^\infty \frac{e^{-t}}{1+t}\,dt = 1! - 2! + 3! - 4! + \cdots = -e\gamma + e\sum_{n=1}^\infty \frac{(-1)^{n-1}}{n \cdot n!} \approx 0.59634\,73623.$$

The local expansion of $Y(z)$ is provided by inverting the famous divergent series of Euler,

$$Y(z) = 1 - (\rho - z)\log\frac{1}{1 - z/\rho} + (\rho - z)\log\log\frac{1}{1 - z/\rho} + O(\frac{(\rho - z)(\log\log(1 - z/\rho)^{-1})^2}{\log(1 - z/\rho)}).$$

This type of singular expansion itself necessitates the full power of singularity analysis, and we find

$$Y_n = \rho^{1-n}\left[\frac{1}{n^2} - \frac{1}{n^2\log n} + O(\frac{1}{n^2\log^2 n})\right].$$

□

Entire functions. The same principles apply. If $\phi(w) \sim Kw^m e^w$, for some constant K and integer m, when $w \to +\infty$, then

$$\rho - z = \int_Y^\infty \frac{dw}{\phi(w)} \sim \frac{1}{Ke^Y Y^m},$$

so that $Y(z)$ is dominated by a logarithmic term at $z = \rho$, and

$$\frac{Y_n}{n!} \sim \rho^{-n} n^{-1}. \tag{25}$$

EXAMPLE 6. *Even and Odd Trees.* Non plane even trees have all their nodes of even degree, so that $\phi(w) = \cosh(w)$. Odd trees have all their non leaf nodes of odd degree, so that $\phi(w) = 1 + \sinh(w)$. The EGF's are explicitly computable in both cases, and we find:

$$Y^{\text{even}}(z) = \log \tan\left(\frac{z}{2} + \frac{\pi}{4}\right), \quad Y^{\text{odd}} = \log\left[\frac{(\sqrt{2}+1)(e^{\sqrt{2}z}+1)}{3 + 2\sqrt{2} - e^{\sqrt{2}z}}\right].$$

The corresponding singularities are at

$$\rho^{\text{even}} = \frac{\pi}{2}, \quad \rho^{\text{odd}} = \frac{\sqrt{2}}{2}\log(3 + 2\sqrt{2}).$$

The coefficients obey Eq. (25). □

The example of $\phi(w) = e^w - w$ is treated in full detail by Meir and Moon [33]. Their main result,

$$\frac{Y_n}{n!} \sim \rho^{-n} n^{-1}, \quad \rho = \int_0^\infty \frac{dw}{e^w - w},$$

which is Thm. 3 of [33], also matches with our Eq. (25).

7 Conclusion

We have demonstrated here a fairly general approach to the analysis of tree parameters where a basic equation for trees is studied from the point of view of its singularities. Here, we have been dealing with a non linear autonomous differential equation or order 1, $Y' = \phi(Y)$.

Major characteristic parameters of trees have GF's that are expressible in terms of the basic GF $Y(z)$ by means of transformations (here integrals). Once we view these expressions as "singularity transformers", it becomes possible to study a large number of statistical problems in a unified manner. In this context, composition theorems for singularities of analytic functions prove especially valuable.

The techniques developed here are not restricted to varieties of increasing trees. Notably, Knuth and Pittel's results regarding union–find trees [25] are amenable to analytic techniques based on singularity analysis instead of recurrences, this being done along the very same steps as in this paper.

The perturbation techniques used here in order to derive limit distributions by means of bivariate analytic schemes of a general nature certainly deserve further attention. For instance, some counterparts in linear cases have already proved useful in analyzing distributions of quadtrees [10]. Quite clearly general bivariate analytic schemes on differential equations are conducive to Gaussian laws under quite a wide range of conditions.

Acknowledgements. This work was supported in part by the Basic Research Action of the E. C. under contract No. 3075 (Project ALCOM).

The authors are grateful to Hosam Mahmoud for communicating many bibliographical pointers and preprints.

References

[1] BALIŃSKA, K. T., QUINTAS, L. V., AND SZYMANSKY, J. Random recursive forests. Preprint, August 1991.

[2] BENDER, E. A. Central and local limit theorems applied to asymptotic enumeration. *Journal of Combinatorial Theory 15* (1973), 91–111.

[3] BERGERON, F., LABELLE, G., AND LEROUX, P. Computation of the expected number of leaves in a tree having a given automorphism, and related topics. preliminary version, 1991.

[4] BURGE, W. H. An analysis of a tree sorting method and some properties of a set of trees. In *First USA-JAPAN Computer Conference Proceedings* (October 1972), AFIPS and IPSJ, pp. 372–378.

[5] CHEN, W., AND NI, W. Heap ordered trees. Personal communication, October 1991. Based on Wen–Chun Ni's Master Thesis, National Taiwan University.

[6] COMTET, L. *Advanced Combinatorics.* Reidel, Dordrecht, 1974.

[7] DEVROYE, L. Applications of the theory of records in the study of random trees. *Acta Informatica 26* (1988), 123–130.

[8] EVGRAFOV, M. A. *Analytic Functions.* Dover, New York, 1966.

[9] FLAJOLET, P. Random tree models in the analysis of algorithms. In *PERFORMANCE'87* (1988), P.-J. Courtois and G. Latouche, Eds., Elsevier Science Publishers (North Holland), pp. 171–187. (Invited lecture).

[10] FLAJOLET, P., GONNET, G., PUECH, C., AND ROBSON, J. M. Analytic variations on quadtrees. *Algorithmica* (1992). 24 pages, to appear.

[11] FLAJOLET, P., AND ODLYZKO, A. M. Singularity analysis of generating functions. *SIAM Journal on Discrete Mathematics 3*, 2 (1990), 216–240.

[12] FLAJOLET, P., AND SORIA, M. Gaussian limiting distributions for the number of components in combinatorial structures. *Journal of Combinatorial Theory,* Series A *53* (1990), 165–182.

[13] FLAJOLET, P., AND SORIA, M. General combinatorial schemas: Gaussian limit distributions and exponential tails. *Discrete Mathematics* (1991). To appear in the Special Issue on *Combinatorics and Algorithms,* A. S. Fraenkel Editor. Available as Research Report 632, LRI, Université Paris-Sud, January 1991. 21 pages.

[14] FORD, W. B. *Studies on divergent series and summability and the asymptotic developments of functions defined by Maclaurin series,* 3rd ed. Chelsea Publishing Company, New York, 1960.

[15] FRANÇON, J. Arbres binaires de recherche : Propriétés combinatoires et applications. *RAIRO Informatique Théorique 10,* 12 (Dec. 1976), 35–50.

[16] GASTWIRTH, J. L. A probability model of a pyramid scheme. *American Statistician 31* (1977), 79–82.

[17] GASTWIRTH, J. L., AND BHATTACHARYA, P. K. Two probability models of pyramid or chain letter schemes demonstrating that their promotional claims are unreliable. *Operations Research 32,* 3 (May-June 1984), 527–536.

[18] GONNET, G. H., AND BAEZA-YATES, R. *Handbook of Algorithms and Data Structures: in Pascal and C,* second ed. Addison–Wesley, 1991.

[19] GOULDEN, I. P., AND JACKSON, D. M. *Combinatorial Enumeration.* John Wiley, New York, 1983.

[20] GRAHAM, R., KNUTH, D., AND PATASHNIK, O. *Concrete Mathematics.* Addison Wesley, 1989.

[21] HENNEQUIN, P. Combinatorial analysis of quicksort algorithm. *RAIRO Theoretical Informatics and Applications 23*, 3 (1989), 317–333.

[22] JOYAL, A. Une théorie combinatoire des séries formelles. *Advances in Mathematics 42*, 1 (1981), 1–82.

[23] KNUTH, D. E. *The Art of Computer Programming*, vol. 1: Fundamental Algorithms. Addison-Wesley, 1968. Second edition, 1973.

[24] KNUTH, D. E. *The Art of Computer Programming*, vol. 3: Sorting and Searching. Addison-Wesley, 1973.

[25] KNUTH, D. E., AND PITTEL, B. A recurrence related to trees. *Proceedings of the American Mathematical Society 105*, 2 (Feb. 1989), 335–349.

[26] LEROUX, P., AND VIENNOT, G. X. Combinatorial resolution of systems of differential equations I: Ordinary differential equations. In *Combinatoire Énumérative* (1986), G. Labelle and P. Leroux, Eds., no. 1234 in Lecture Notes in Mathematics, Springer-Verlag, pp. 210–245.

[27] LEROUX, P., AND VIENNOT, X. G. Combinatorial resolution of systems of differential equations. IV. separation of variables. *Discrete Mathematics 72* (1988), 237–250.

[28] LOUCHARD, G. Exact and asymptotic distributions in digital and binary search trees. *RAIRO Theoretical Informatics and Applications 21*, 4 (1987), 479–495.

[29] MAHMOUD, H. *Evolution of Random Search Trees.* John Wiley, New York, 1991. In press.

[30] MAHMOUD, H. M. Distances in random plane-oriented recursive trees, 1991. Preprint. To appear in the *Journal of Applied and Computational Mathematics*, special issue on asymptotic analysis in discrete mathematics.

[31] MAHMOUD, H. M., SMYTHE, R. T., AND SZYMAŃSKI, J. On the structure of random plane-oriented recursive trees and their branches, 1991. Preprint.

[32] MEIR, A., AND MOON, J. W. On the altitude of nodes in random trees. *Canadian Journal of Mathematics 30* (1978), 997–1015.

[33] MEIR, A., AND MOON, J. W. Recursive trees with no nodes of out-degree one. *Congressus Numerantium 66* (1988), 49–62.

[34] NAJOCK, D., AND HEYDE, C. C. On the number of terminal vertices in certain random trees with an application to stemma constructions in philology. *Journal of Applied Probability 19* (1982), 675–680.

[35] STANLEY, R. P. *Enumerative Combinatorics*, vol. I. Wadsworth & Brooks/Cole, 1986.

[36] SZYMAŃSKI, J. On a non-uniform random recursive tree. In *Random Graphs '85*, M. Karoński and Z. Palka, Eds., vol. 33 of *Annals of Discrete Mathematics*. North-Holland, 1987, pp. 297–306.

[37] TITCHMARSH, E. C. *The Theory of Functions*, second ed. Oxford University Press, 1939.

[38] VITTER, J. S., AND FLAJOLET, P. Analysis of algorithms and data structures. In *Handbook of Theoretical Computer Science*, J. van Leeuwen, Ed., vol. A: Algorithms and Complexity. North Holland, 1990, ch. 9, pp. 431–524.

[39] VUILLEMIN, J. A unifying look at data structures. *Communications of the ACM 23*, 4 (Apr. 1980), 229–239.

[40] WILF, H. S. *Generatingfunctionology*. Academic Press, 1990.

[41] WILSON, R. Functions with dominant singularities of the generalized algebraic-logarithmic type (II): On the order of the Hadamard product. *Proceedings of the London Mathematical Society*, Series 2 *43*, 2190 (1937), 417–438.

Origin Functions in λ-calculus and Term Rewriting Systems

Yves Bertot
INRIA Sophia-Antipolis
e-mail: bertot@mirsa.inria.fr

We use *Origin functions* to describe the notions of descendance and residuals in reduction systems such as the λ-calculus and linear term rewriting systems. We compare the origin functions for the λ-calculus and for term rewriting systems that implement this calculus, $\lambda\sigma$ and λEnv. We show that the notions of origin do not correspond exactly, but we describe an extension of the notion of origin that permits the correct computation of λ-calculus origins for derivations of λEnv. We show that this extension is not sufficient to give the same result for $\lambda\sigma$ and we give another extension for that system. This work is interesting as it provides a distinction between the two term rewriting systems. This work has applications in the debugging of languages based on the λ-calculus or environments.

1. Introduction.

1.1. *Motivation and Related Work.*

The main motivation of this work is source-level debugging of programming languages, focusing especially on functional languages, based on the λ-calculus, and their implementation by term rewriting systems. To implement source-level debugging, one needs to establish a relation between the current state of an execution machine and a position in the source program. In reduction systems this facility is usually provided by the notions of descendance and residuals [Morris68], [Lévy78], [Klop80].

Recent work from Hardin and Lévy [Hardin&Lévy89] and from Abadi, Cardelli, Curien, and Lévy [ACCL90] described term rewriting systems that permit to represent completely the λ-calculus. these results are significant in that previous rewriting systems like CL [Hindley&Seldin86] described only part of the λ-calculus, namely weak reductions. Whereas the papers [Hardin&Lévy89] and [ACCL90] only compare term rewriting systems derivations and λ-calculus derivations in terms of initial and final value, the present work studies these derivations with respect to the notion of residuals.

That a rewriting system implements the λ-calculus means that for any λ-calculus derivation we can find a rewriting system derivation that performs the same computations. We want to see if the two derivations also give the same notion of residuals, that is, if the same sub-expressions of the final term are residuals of an expression of the initial term in both settings. In this respect, we show that the two rewriting systems λEnv [Hardin&Lévy89] and $\lambda\sigma$ [ACCL90], which we study, do not represent the λ-calculus faithfully. We show that a simple extension of the notion of residual permits to overcome this difficulty for one of the systems, λEnv and that a more complicated

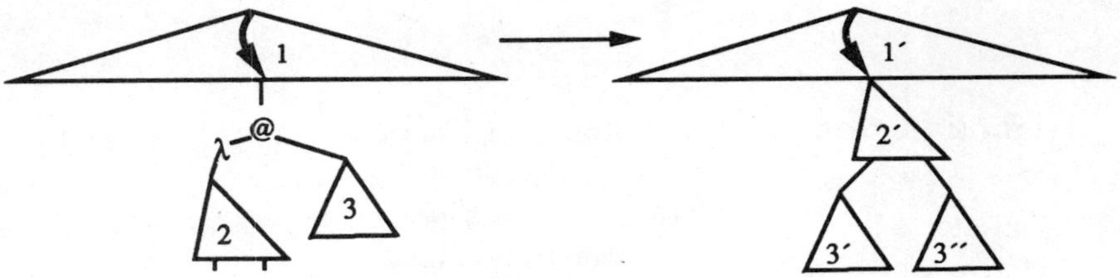

Figure 1. A schematic β-reduction.
(*The stubs below area 2 represent occurrences of the substituted variable*)

extension permits to have the same result for $\lambda\sigma$. this result provides a way to compare the two systems, that can be added to the investigation provided in work from Curien, Hardin, and Lévy [CHL91].

The descendance relation or residual relation associated to a reduction system is usually studied using labeled or marked systems, as in [Morris68], [Lévy78], [Klop80], or [Field90]. We prefer to use a simple notion of *origin functions* that permits to concentrate on the key aspects of the notions of descendance and residuals which may be hidden by marked derivations: an expression is residual of at most one expression in the initial term, and the residual relation does not depend on the set of names used to mark terms. However, we reuse results that have previously been established using marking terms, for instance [Field90]. Another advantage of origin functions over marked reduction systems is that marks can only give an extensional representation of descendance, whereas one is free to implement origin functions with an intensional representation, as in [Bertot91a]. This may mean significant economies in memory consumption.

1.2. *Origins in the λ-calculus and Term Rewriting Systems.*

We consider the $\lambda\beta$-calculus, in its de Bruijn representation [de Bruijn72]. It is based on the following rule, also called the β-rule.

$$(\lambda M)N \to M[1\backslash N]$$

In this representation variable names are replaced by indices which represent the distance between the variables and their binders. The substitution mechanism represented by the notation $M[1\backslash N]$ requires non-trivial manipulation of these indices, since the distance between a variable and its binder may change in the process. A schematic β-reduction is represented in figure 1.

For the descendance relation, it is obvious that a node at any position in area $1'$ descends from the node at the same position in area 1, whereas a node in area $2'$ descends from the node at the same position in area 2 (note that the position in the entire term changes, since area 2 moves during the β-reduction), and the nodes that are at a same position relative to areas $3'$ and $3''$ descend from the node that at the same position in area 3.

We remark that the relation of descendance is simply a relation between occurrences in the final term and occurrences in the initial term. We also notice that the converse of this descendance relation is a function. We call this function an *origin function.*

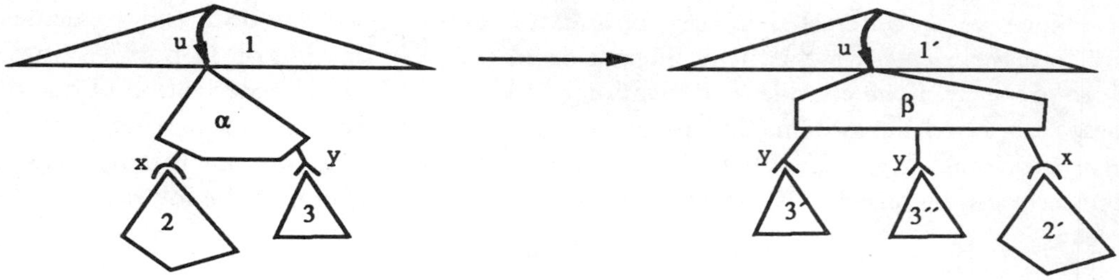

Figure 2. A schematic term rewriting.

For multi-step derivations, the origin functions are quite simple to understand. The origin function for an empty derivation is the identity function and the origin of the concatenation of two derivations D and D' is the composition of the two origin functions $f \circ f'$. This simply means that if position u comes from a node position v by the derivation D' (expressed by $v = f'(u)$) and v comes from w by D (expressed by $w = f(v)$) then u comes from w by the concatenated derivation $D; D'$ (expressed by $w = f(f'(u)) = f \circ f'(u)$).

The same notion of descendance also appears in linear term rewriting systems. Such systems are sets of couples of patterns $\alpha \to \beta$, with the constraint that every variable appearing in β also appears in α and no variable appears more than once in α. Computing with such rewriting systems means replacing instances of the pattern α by the corresponding instances of the pattern β. A schematic reduction is represented in figure 2.

As far as origin of nodes are concerned, area $1'$ has its origins in area 1 as for the λ-calculus, area $2'$ has its origins in area 2, areas $3'$ and $3''$ have their origins in area 3. The choice of origin for areas $2'$, $3'$, and $3''$ is done using the variables in the patterns α and β: the area under a given variable has its origins in the area that is under the same variable in α. This definition is not ambiguous, since we are dealing with linear systems. The nodes in the pattern β do not have any origin; they are "created" by the reduction. Conversely, the nodes inside the pattern α are consumed by the rewriting and do not have any descendants.

1.3. *Relations between Origin Functions.*

Since the discovery of λ-calculus, various attempts have been made to represent it using term rewriting systems, mostly with combinators as in [Curry&Feys58], [Hindley&Seldin86], [Curien86]. These attempts were all incomplete in the sense that they only presented a part of λ-calculus computations, mostly known as weak computations. Only lately, rewriting systems have been proposed that exactly describe the λ-calculus. These rewriting systems are $\lambda\sigma$ [ACCL90] and λEnv [Hardin&Lévy89], [CHL91].

The main idea in these rewriting systems is to add operators to the λ-calculus to represent "substitution in the making". These operators permit to delay and compose substitution operations, stacking them in environments. As such, these rewriting systems provide a nice tool to study in a common setting both the λ-calculus and its implementation on environment machines (see, for example [Field90], [Maranget91]).

Since we are interested in origins, and this notion exists for both the λ-calculus and term rewriting systems, it is interesting to compare this notion in both settings. More precisely, if we consider a derivation of the λ-calculus and a derivation of one of these term rewriting systems that performs the same computations, do these derivations have the same origin function? The answer is negative and we can rapidly give a counterexample, based on the fact that both $\lambda\sigma$ and λEnv contain the following three rules:

Beta	$(\lambda M)N \to M[N \cdot id]$
App	$(MN)[s] \to M[s]N[s]$
FVar	$1[M \cdot s] \to M$

Counterexample 1. *The origin of the following two derivations differ, if D_1 is a λ-calculus derivation and D_2 is a $\lambda\sigma$ or λEnv derivation (a is any λ-term).*

$$D_1 : \qquad (\lambda(1\ 1))\ a \xrightarrow{\varepsilon} a\ a$$

$$\begin{aligned} D_2 : \qquad (\lambda(1\ 1))\ a &\overset{(\varepsilon,Beta)}{\to} (1\ 1)[a \cdot id] \\ &\overset{(\varepsilon,App)}{\to} (1[a \cdot id]\ 1[a \cdot id]) \\ &\overset{(1,Fvar)}{\to} a\ 1[a \cdot id] \\ &\overset{(2,Fvar)}{\to} a\ a \end{aligned}$$

Let f_1 be the origin function for D_1 and f_2 be the one for D_2. From the informal definition of origins given above, we infer $f_1(\varepsilon) = 1.1$ (the empty occurrence, ε, designates the top of a term, whereas 1.1 designates the first child of the first child) and $f_2(\varepsilon)$ is not defined, because the application node at the top of the resulting term was created during the second rewriting (rule App).

The analysis of this counterexample shows that the application operator in the resulting term is created by the second reduction step of D_2, whereas the application operator that appears inside the λ-abstraction in the initial term is consumed by the same step. This leads to the following suggestion: why not extend origin functions for term rewritings so that created nodes (inside β in Figure 2) descend from consumed nodes (inside α)? We call such extensions of origin functions *marking functions.*

The main result of this paper is that these extensions are sufficient to represent λ-calculus origins for λEnv, but not for $\lambda\sigma$. The main difference between the two systems lies in the treatment of substitution inside a λ-abstraction. Both introduce an extra operator to express that the variables in the substituent will need some updating, but only λEnv introduces an extra operator to express that the variables bound by the

λ-abstraction must be protected from the substitution. The system λEnv contains the following two rules:

Lambda $\quad (\lambda M)[s] \rightarrow \lambda(M[\Uparrow(s)])$

FVarLift1 $\quad 1[\Uparrow(s)] \rightarrow 1$

Whereas the system $\lambda\sigma$ gets away with the following trick, using substitution (rule *FVar*) to recover the correct value for the bound variable:

Lambda' $\quad (\lambda M)[s] \rightarrow \lambda(M[1 \cdot (s \circ \uparrow)])$

Thus, in $\lambda\sigma$, the bound variable is protected because it receives the same value when the substitution is applied. However, the origins are all mixed up, since a substitution actually took place. The problem of computing correctly λ-calculus origins can still be solved, with more complicated extension of origin functions, which we describe in section 4.

2. Definitions.

2.1. *The λ-calculus.*

We denote $\mathcal{N}_+$ the set of strictly positive integers. The set Λ of λ-terms is the set defined by the following syntax:

$$\Lambda ::= \lambda\Lambda \mid \Lambda\Lambda \mid n$$

where n is an element of $\mathcal{N}_+$. We note @ the head operator of a term of the form MN and λ the head operator of a term of the form λM. Thus, Λ is the set of terms built from the operators of $Op_\lambda = \{@, \lambda\} \cup \mathcal{N}_+$.

We use occurrences to denote positions in terms. The set of occurrences $\mathcal{O}$ is the set of words of $\mathcal{N}_+$. We denote the concatenation of occurrences u and v as $u.v$ and the empty occurrence as ε. We note $u \leq v$ whenever there exists an occurrence w such that $v = u.w$ (we note $u < v$ if $u \leq v$ and $u \neq v$) and we denote $|u|$ the length of the occurrence u. The notation M/u denotes the subterm of M at occurrence u, $op(u, M)$ denotes its head operator, and $M[u \leftarrow N]$ denotes M where the subterm at occurrence u is replaced by N. For any term T, the set of occurrences u such that T/u is defined is called its *domain* and is noted $\mathcal{D}(T)$. We also denote $depth(u, M)$ the number $card\{v \mid v < u \quad op(v, M) = \lambda\}$, that is the number of λ operators in M on the path represented by the occurrence u.

Examples. $((MN)P)/1.2 = N$, $op(\varepsilon, (\lambda M)N) = @$, $op(1, (\lambda M)N) = \lambda$, $depth(1.1.2, (\lambda(1\ 2)N)) = 1$.

We note $T \xrightarrow{u} T'$ the β-reduction (or elementary λ-derivation) of T at occurrence u. This means that there exist two terms M and N such that $T/u = (\lambda M)N$ and $T' = T[u \leftarrow M[1\backslash N]]$. We denote

$$T \overset{u_1;\cdots;u_n}{\twoheadrightarrow} T' = T \xrightarrow{u_1} \cdots \xrightarrow{u_n} T'$$

and more generally we denote $T \overset{S}{\twoheadrightarrow} T'$ any derivation of the λ-calculus, where S is a list of occurrences. We use ";" to represent the concatenation of lists of occurrences, and we denote the empty list as $\emptyset$. If D and D' are the two derivations $D = T \overset{S}{\twoheadrightarrow} T'$ and $D' = T' \overset{S'}{\twoheadrightarrow} T''$, we note $D; D'$ the derivation $D; D' = T \overset{S;S'}{\twoheadrightarrow} T'$, thus overloading the operator ";". Also, we denote $u.S$ the list of occurrences $u.u_1; \cdots; u.u_n$ when S is the list of occurrences $u_1; \cdots; u_n$.

2.2. *The system λEnv.*

Linear term rewriting systems have already been presented earlier. We denote $T \overset{(u,r)}{\rightarrow} T'$ the rewriting of T at occurrence u using rule $r = \alpha \rightarrow \beta$ to the term T'. This means that there exists a substitution σ such that $T/u = \sigma(\alpha)$ and $T' = T[u \leftarrow \sigma(\beta)]$. We note $T \overset{S}{\twoheadrightarrow} T'$ a derivation of the term rewriting system, where S is a list of couples of the form (u, r) in which u is an occurrence and r is a rule. As for the λ-calculus, we note $D; D'$ the concatenation of two derivations and $\emptyset$ the empty derivation.

The rewriting system λEnv works with the language ΛEnv defined by the following syntax:

$$M ::= \lambda M \mid MM \mid n \mid M[s]$$
$$s ::= s \circ s \mid M \cdot s \mid id \mid \Uparrow(s) \mid \uparrow$$

Thus, ΛEnv is obtained from Λ by adding new operators $[]$, $\circ$, $\cdot$, $\Uparrow$, id, and $\uparrow$. The term rewriting system contains 24 rules that are given in the appendix. One of these rules, *Beta*, is used to represent the β-rule:

Beta $$(\lambda M)N \rightarrow M[N \cdot id]$$

Informally, the right-hand side of this rule represents the application of the substitution $N \cdot id$ to the term M. The substitution $N \cdot id$ itself represents the operation of replacing the variable index 1 by N and any other variable index n by $n - 1$. All the other rules describe how to compute with substitutions. We note $SEnv$ the system obtained by removing rule *Beta* from λEnv.

2.3. *Origin Functions.*

The origin functions for the λ-calculus are given by an origin mapping Ω that maps λ-calculus derivations to functions over occurrences. This mapping is defined by the following properties:

1. For any derivation $D = T \overset{S}{\twoheadrightarrow} T'$, one has $dom(\Omega(D)) = \mathcal{D}(T')$ and $codom(\Omega(D)) = \mathcal{D}(T)$.
2. For any derivations D and D', one has $\Omega(D; D') = \Omega(D) \circ \Omega(D')$. For any derivation D of the form $D = T \overset{\emptyset}{\rightarrow} T$, one has $\Omega(D) = 1_{\mathcal{D}(T)}$.
3. For any derivation $D = T \overset{S}{\twoheadrightarrow} T'$ such that $\Omega(D) = \omega$ and for any term M such that $M/u = T$, the function $\omega' = \Omega(D')$ where D' is the embedded derivation $D' = M \overset{u.S}{\twoheadrightarrow} M[u \leftarrow T']$ verifies the following properties:
   a. For any occurrence v such that $u \not\leq v$, one has $\omega'(v) = v$,
   b. For any occurrence $v \in \mathcal{D}(T')$, one has $\omega'(u.v) = u.\omega(v)$.

4. For any elementary derivation $D = (\lambda M)N \xrightarrow{\varepsilon} M[1\backslash N]$, the function $\omega = \Omega(D)$ is defined by the following properties:
   a. For any occurrence $u \in \mathcal{D}(M)$ which is not an occurrence of the substituted variable, one has $\omega(u) = 1.1.u$,
   b. For any occurrence $u \in M[1\backslash N]$ such that $u = v.w$ where v is an occurrence of the substituted variable in M and w is an occurrence in $\mathcal{D}(N)$, one has $\omega(u) = 2.w$.

The origin functions for linear term rewriting systems are also given by a mapping Ω_{trs}. To handle the fact that origin functions are only partial functions, we add an element *nil* to $\mathcal{O}$ that represents the lack of origin for some occurrences. Thus, the images of derivations by Ω_{trs} are functions over $\mathcal{O} \cup \{nil\}$ that map *nil* to *nil*. The mapping Ω_{trs} is defined by the same properties 1, 2, 3 as those used for Ω and by the property 4′ given below:

4′. For any elementary derivation $D = T \overset{(\varepsilon,r)}{\rightarrow} T'$ where r is a rule of the form $\alpha \rightarrow \beta$, the function $\omega = \Omega_{trs}(D)$ is the function defined by the following properties:
   a. For any occurrence $v_x \in \mathcal{D}(\beta)$ such $\beta/v_x = x$ is a variable and for any occurrence w and v such that $w = v_x.v \in T'$, one has $\omega(w) = u_x.v$ where u_x is the only occurrence of x in α (remember that we are working with a linear term rewriting system).
   b. For any occurrence $v \in \mathcal{D}(\beta)$ which is not an occurrence of variable, one has $\omega(v) = nil$.

2.4. *Markings as extensions of Origins.*

A ***marking*** $\mathcal{M}$ is a function that maps the derivations of a linear term rewriting system to functions over $\mathcal{O} \cup \{nil\}$. It is defined by the same properties as the origin mapping Ω_{trs} for term rewriting systems, except that constraint 4′ is replaced by the following one:

4″. For any elementary derivation $D = T \overset{(\varepsilon,r)}{\rightarrow} T'$ where $r = \alpha \rightarrow \beta$, the function $f = \mathcal{M}(D)$ is the function defined by the following properties:
a. *same as* 4′.*a, replacing* ω *by* f.
b. For any occurrence v such that $v \in \mathcal{D}(\beta)$, we have $f(v) = f_r(v)$ where $f_r = \mathcal{M}(D_r)$ and $D_r = \alpha \overset{(\varepsilon,r)}{\rightarrow} \beta$.

Note that a marking is entirely specified by the values of all the functions f_r for the rules in the term rewriting system. The properties of markings given above make that we do not need to know the initial and final terms of a derivation to compute the marking function, we only need to know the sequence of elementary steps and the domain of the final term. Also, Ω_{trs} simply appears as a special kind of marking.

3. Correct Markings for λEnv.

In this section, we first describe constraints on markings for the term rewriting system λEnv such that marking functions associated to derivations of λEnv represent correctly the origin functions associated to the λ-calculus derivations they represent, and we then sketch a proof that these constraints are sufficient (this proof is detailed in [Bertot91b]).

3.1. *A class of Correct Markings.*

The rules of $SEnv$ can be classified in two subsets. Some rules describe the interaction of the substitution mechanism with the operators of the λ-calculus (***App***, ***Lambda***, ***FVar***, ***RVar***, ***VarShift1***, ***VarShift2***, ***FVarLift1***, ***FVarLift2***, ***RVarLift1***, ***RVarLift2***); the others describe the interaction of the substitutions with substitutions.

For the rules of the first subset, the left hand side always has the substitution operator $\cdot[\cdot]$ as head operator, the head operator of the first subterm is an operator from Op_λ, and it is the only occurrence of such an operator in the left hand side. In the right hand side, an operator of Op_λ may or may not occur. For the rules of the second subset, no operator of Op_λ occurs.

We consider the markings verifying the extra constraint that for every rule of the first set $r = \alpha \rightarrow \beta$ and any occurrence u such that $op(u, \beta) \in Op_\lambda$, one has $f_r(u) = 1$. Since r is in the first set, one has $op(1, \alpha) \in Op_\lambda$.

From now on, $\mathcal{M}$ will be a marking that verifies this constraint. We prove in the following that the marking functions associated to derivations of λEnv represent correctly the origin functions of the λ-calculus.

3.2. *Proof of Correctness.*

To prove that λEnv implements the λ-calculus, the authors of [Hardin&Lévy89] have to prove that for every derivation of the λ-calculus there exists a coinitial and cofinal derivation of λEnv and conversely that for any derivation of λEnv whose initial and final terms are in Λ there also exists a coinitial and cofinal λ-calculus derivation. We have to be more careful because two coinitial and cofinal λ-calculus derivations may have different origin functions, as is shown by the derivations D_1 and D_2 below:

$$D_1 \qquad (\lambda 1)((\lambda 1)(\lambda 1)) \xrightarrow{\varepsilon} (\lambda 1)(\lambda 1)$$

$$D_2 \qquad (\lambda 1)((\lambda 1)(\lambda 1)) \xrightarrow{2} (\lambda 1)(\lambda 1)$$

The origin functions f_1 and f_2 for these two derivations are different. For example, one has $f_1(\varepsilon) = 2$ and $f_2(\varepsilon) = \varepsilon$. It is obviously useless to try to compare the marking function associated to a λEnv derivation that implements D_2 with the origin function of D_1.

To turn around this problem, we prefer to state our result using the following two theorems.

Theorem 1.*For any derivation Δ of the λ-calculus, there exists a derivation D of λEnv, that has the same initial and final term as Δ and such that $\mathcal{M}(D) = \Omega(\Delta)$.*

Theorem 2.*For any derivation D of λEnv whose initial and final terms are both in Λ, there exists a derivation Δ of the λ-calculus that has the same initial and final term as D and such that $\mathcal{M}(D) = \Omega(\Delta)$.*

Theorem 1 is rather easy to establish but its proof is long and tedious. We only sketch this proof here, the exact detail can be found in [Bertot91b]. Basically, to find a derivation of the term rewriting system that performs the same computation as derivation of the λ-calculus, one can simply perform one beta reduction at a time. The

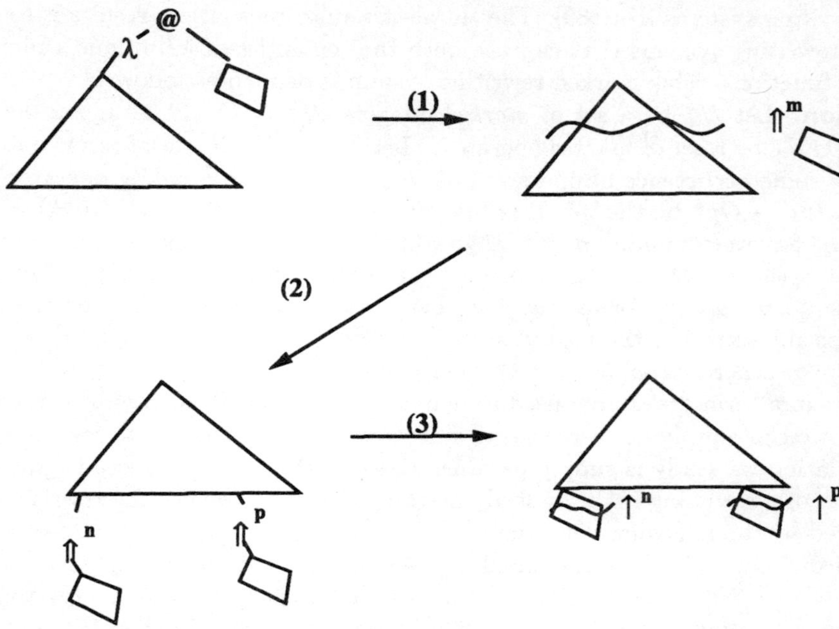

Figure 3. Computation of a β-reduction using a Term Rewriting System.

computation in that case can be roughly described as in figure 3. It contains three main stages:

(1) One creates a substitution replacing the variable bound in the β-redex by the argument.

(2) One traverses the body of the function part of the β-redex with the substitution, updating this substitution with the $\Uparrow$ operator each time one traverses a λ (rules *App* and *Lambda*). The constraints we have put on the marking ensures that instances of the operators @ and λ in the body are given a correct origin. Variable indexes that do not correspond to the bound variable are either decremented if they are free (rule *RVar*) in the body or restored to their value (rule *FVarLift1*). Here again the constraints put on the marking ensure that these variables are given a correct origin.

(3) On the leaves that correspond the bound variable, the substitution is actually performed, but some updating of the variable indexes corresponding to variables that are free in the argument has to be performed. This updating uses a substitution constructed with the operator $\uparrow$ by the rules *RVarLift1* and *RVarLift2*. We have a second traversal of a term. The constraints put on the marking ensure the origin function restricted to these arguments is the identity function.

Origins for λEnv derivations that perform the same computation as a non elementary λ-calculus derivation are then simply deduced from the fact that origin function of non-elementary derivations are defined the same way for the λ-calculus and for term rewriting systems.

The proof of theorem 2 is simply a proof of confluence, where the confluence has to be extended to origin functions. Problems of confluence have been best studied for term rewriting systems [Huet80]. The simplest way to reuse these results is to define a marked rewriting systems that capture both the semantics of λEnv and the notion of marking functions. This marked rewriting system is defined as follows:

Definition. Let $\mathcal{N}_+^*$ be a set of *marked* integers, $\mathcal{N}_+^* = \{1^*, 2^*, \ldots\}$, and let $Op_\lambda^* = \{@^*, \lambda^*\} \cup \mathcal{N}_+^*$ be a set of *marked* operators. Let ΛEnv^* be the set of terms obtained by replacing some occurrence of operators of Op_λ by the corresponding operator of Op_λ^*. Let $m : Op_\lambda \to Op_\lambda^*$ be the marking bijection such that $m(@) = @^*$, $m(\lambda) = \lambda^*$, and $m(n) = n^*$ for every number n. For any term $t \in \Lambda Env^*$, and any occurrence $u \in \mathcal{D}(t)$ such that $op(u,t) \in Op_\lambda$, we note $m(t,u)$ the term t' such that $op(u,t') = m(op(u,t))$ and $op(w,t') = op(w,t)$ for any $w \neq u$. Let *erase* : $\Lambda Env^* \to \Lambda Env$ be the function that maps any term t to the term t' such that $op(u,t') = op(u,t)$, if $op(u,t') \notin Op_\lambda^*$ and $op(u,t') = op$ where $m(op) = op(u,t)$ otherwise.

Stars in a term are simply used to denote occurrences. To compute a descendance relation, we can simply use a rewriting system working on marked terms. The descendance relation we study is simply parameterized by the way we choose to put stars on both sides of a rewriting rule. To study marking functions, we use the rewriting system introduced by the following definition:

Definition. Let λEnv^* be the smallest rewriting system containing λEnv and such that if $r = \alpha \to \beta$ is a rule in λEnv^*, u is an occurrence such that $\alpha/u \in Op_\lambda$ and v is the occurrence such that $\beta/v \in Op_\lambda$, $\alpha' = m(u,\alpha)$ and $\beta' = m(v,\beta)$ then the rule $\alpha' \to \beta'$ is also in λEnv^*. The function *erase* introduced in the previous definition extends naturally to rules of λEnv^*. For any derivation $D = M \overset{(u,r)}{\to} N$ in λEnv, and any term M' such that $erase(M') = M$, we denote $lift(D, M')$ the derivation $D' = M' \overset{(u,r')}{\to} N'$ where r' is the only rule in λEnv^* such that $erase(r') = r$ and D' is a valid derivation. This function *lift* extends naturally to non-elementary derivations by concatenation. We denote $\mathcal{S}Env^*$ the subset of λEnv^* that contains any rule r such that $erase(r) \in \mathcal{S}Env$ and $Beta^*$ the system $\lambda Env^* - \mathcal{S}Env^*$.

Example. For instance, λEnv^* contains the following rules, where the first two are obtained from App and the last two are obtained from $FVar$:

$$(ab)[s] \to (a[s]b[s])$$
$$(ab)^*[s] \to (a[s]b[s])^*$$
$$1[a \cdot s] \to a$$
$$1^*[a \cdot s] \to a$$

The following lemma shows that λEnv^* enables us to directly use rewriting for studying marking functions.

Lemma 1. *Let $D = M \twoheadrightarrow N$ be a derivation of λEnv, and f be the function $f = \mathcal{M}(D)$. For any occurrences $v \in \mathcal{D}(N)$ and $u \in \mathcal{D}(M)$ such that $op(u,M) \in Op_\lambda$ and $op(v,M) \in Op_\lambda$, and for any terms M' and N' in ΛEnv^* we have the following property:*

$$lift(D, m(M,u)) = M' \twoheadrightarrow N' \quad \Rightarrow \quad op(v,N') \in Op_\lambda^* \Leftrightarrow u = f(v)$$

Proof. By induction on the length of D.

- If D is a derivation of length 0, then the result is trivial.
- If $D = D'; D''$ where D'' is of the form $P \overset{(w,r)}{\to} N$, let f' and f'' be the function

such that $f' = \mathcal{M}(D')$ and $f'' = \mathcal{M}(D'')$ Let P' be the term of $\mathcal{S}Env^*$ such that $lift(D', m(M,u))$. If we have $v = w.v'$ where $v' \in \mathcal{D}(\beta)$ and β/v' is not a variable, then $op(v, N') \in Op^*_\lambda$ if and only if $op(f''(v), P') \in Op^*_\lambda$, from the definition of $\mathcal{S}Env^*$. By induction hypothesis, $op(f''(v), P') \in Op^*_\lambda$ if an only if $f'(f''(v)) = u$. If $v \neq w.v'$ where $v' \in \mathcal{D}(\beta)$ and β/v' is not a variable, then we have directly $op(v, N') = op(f''(v), P')$ and the induction hypothesis also gives the result. □

Property P1. *The rewriting system $\mathcal{S}Env^*$ is noetherian and confluent.*

Proof. This rewriting system is locally confluent, as can be checked automatically using the algorithm of Knuth and Bendix [Knuth&Bendix70], and it is also noetherian, since $\mathcal{S}Env$ is noetherian [Hardin&Lévy89] and any derivation of $\mathcal{S}Env^*$ is mapped to a derivation of $\mathcal{S}Env$ of same length by the function *erase*. Therefore, it is confluent [Huet80]. □

Corollary 1. *If M and N are elements of Λ, then all the normalizing derivations for $\mathcal{S}Env$ starting from $M[N \cdot id]$ have a marking function equal to the origin function of the corresponding β-reduction.*

In the following, we shall write $Sim\beta^*$ the set of derivations in λEnv^* that perform first a reduction using one of the rules in $Beta^*$ then a $\mathcal{S}Env^*$ normalization, then a $Beta^*$ reduction, etc. Corollary 1 simply indicates that derivations in $Sim\beta^*$ have the property needed in theorem 2.

Lemma 2. *any derivation of λEnv^* whose initial and final terms are in Λ^* has the same initial and final term as a derivation in $Sim\beta^*$.*

The proof of this lemma is rather long and technical, and we do not give it here. The precise proof can be found in [Bertot91b]. The following example helps understanding the inherent complication of this proof.

Example. Let us consider the following λEnv^* derivation:

1 $(\lambda(11)^*)((\lambda 1)1) \to (11)^*[((\lambda 1)1^*) \cdot id]$
2 $\to (11)^*[1^* \cdot id]$
3 $\to (1[1^* \cdot id]1[1^* \cdot id])$
4 $\to (1^*1[1^* \cdot id])$
5 $\to (1^*1^*)$

This derivation has the same initial and final term as the following one, which actually is a $Sim\beta^*$ derivation:

1 $(\lambda(11)^*)((\lambda 1)1) \to (11)^*[((\lambda 1)1^*) \cdot id]$
2 $\to (1[((\lambda 1)1^*) \cdot id]1[((\lambda 1)1^*) \cdot id])$
3 $\to (((\lambda 1)1^*)1[((\lambda 1)1^*) \cdot id])$
4 $\to (((\lambda 1)1^*)((\lambda 1)1^*))$
5 $\to (1[1^* \cdot id]((\lambda 1)1^*))$
6 $\to (1^*((\lambda 1)1^*))$
7 $\to (1^*1[1^* \cdot id])$
8 $\to (1^*1^*)$

The second derivation is actually longer than the first one, for various reasons. This makes it difficult to use arguments such as "induction on the length of the derivation" to establish the result. One way to turn around this is to use the notion of parallel derivation of non-overlapping redexes as is already done in [Hardin&Lévy89] to extend the result of confluence from $\mathcal{S}Env^*$ to λEnv^*. This is also the method we use in

[Bertot91b] where the exact proof of lemma 2 is presented. by simple transitivity of equality, lemma 2 and corollary 1 give us theorem 2.

4. Computing Origins for $\lambda\sigma$.

The rewriting system $\lambda\sigma$ is presented in the appendix. We call σ the subsystem obtained by removing rule ***Beta***. the set of terms on which $\lambda\sigma$ works is the subset $\Lambda\sigma$ of ΛEnv that contains all the terms constructed without the operator $\Uparrow$. As we saw in the introduction, $\lambda\sigma$ uses the rule *FVar* both to perform actual substitutions and to protect bound variables from substitution. With respect to origin computations the two usages should be distinguished. We recall the form of this rule:

FVar $\qquad 1[M \cdot id] \rightarrow M$

When an actual substitution is performed, we agree that the origins of nodes in the result M are actually in the subterm M of the left hand side, but when the reduction corresponds to protecting a bound variable, M is actually a term that derives to a number n and we want the origin of the result to be in the subterm 1 of the left hand side. Thus, we have to choose between two possible marking functions for a derivation of the form $T \stackrel{(u,FVar)}{\rightarrow} T'$, as is shown in the following example.

Example. *Let us consider the two following derivations, where we have used mark to describe origins:*

$$
\begin{array}{lrl}
1 & (\lambda(\lambda 1^*))1) & \rightarrow (\lambda 1)[1 \cdot id] \\
2 & & \rightarrow \lambda(1^*[1 \cdots ((1 \cdot id) \circ \uparrow)]) \\
3 & & \rightarrow \lambda(1^*)
\end{array}
$$

and

$$
\begin{array}{lrl}
1' & (\lambda 1)1^* & \rightarrow 1[1^* \cdot id] \\
2' & & 1^*
\end{array}
$$

The steps 3 and 2′ both use the rule FVar. In the first case, the origin of the result is taken in the variable part of the redex, whereas for the second case, this origin is taken in the value part of the redex.

When computing the marking function for a non-elementary derivation, we need to find a way to choose which function to use each time the rule *FVar* is used.

4.1. *A Correct Mapping for $\lambda\sigma$.*

The solution we propose is a mapping $\mathcal{M}_\sigma$ working only for derivations that start from a term of Λ, constructed recursively using the following rules. In these rules we note (u *or* v) the occurrence w such that $w = u$ if $u \neq nil$ and $w = v$ otherwise (*or* behaves like a sequential or).

1. For any term $M \in \Lambda$, if D is the derivation $D = M \stackrel{\emptyset}{\rightarrow} M$ then $\mathcal{M}_\sigma(D) = 1_{\mathcal{D}(M)}$.
2. If D, D', and D'' are derivations such that $D = T \stackrel{S}{\rightarrow} T'$, $D' = T \stackrel{S;(u,r)}{\rightarrow} T''$, and $D'' = T' \stackrel{(u,r)}{\rightarrow} T''$ then the function $f' = \mathcal{M}_\sigma(D')$ is defined from the function $f = \mathcal{M}_\sigma(D)$ by $f' = f \circ f''$ where f'' is given as follows:
   a. If the rule r is ***Beta***, ***app***, ***IdL***, ***ShiftId***, ***Shift***, ***AssEnv***, or ***MapEnv***, then $f'' = \mathcal{M}(D'')$ where $\mathcal{M}$ is a mapping verifying the constraints defined previously for

λEnv. In all the other cases we have $f'' = \Omega_{trs}(D'')$, almost everywhere, with the following exceptions:

b. If the rule r is *Lambda'*, then we have $f(u) = f(u.1)$. We recall that rule *Lambda'* has the following form:

$$\textit{Lambda}' \qquad (\lambda M)[s] \rightarrow \lambda(M[1 \cdot (s \circ \uparrow)])$$

Note that this definition does not give any origin to the index in the right hand side.

c. If r is the rule $r = FVar$, we have $f(u) = f'(u.2.1)$ *or* $\big(f'(u.1)$ *or* $f'(u)\big)$.
d. If r is the rule $r = Closure$, we have $f(u.1) = f'(u.1.1)$ *or* $\big(f'(u.1)$ *or* $f'(u)\big)$.
e. If r is *VarShift2* or *RVar*, we have $f(u.1) = f'(u.1)$ *or* $f'(u)$.
f. If r is *VarShift1* or *VarId*, we have $f(u) = f'(u.1)$ *or* $f'(u)$.

4.2. *Proof of Correctness.*

With this mapping $\mathcal{M}_\sigma$ we have the same results for $\lambda\sigma$ as we had earlier for λEnv, that is, we have the following two theorems:

Theorem 3. *For any derivation Δ of the λ-calculus, there exists a derivation D of $\lambda\sigma$, that has the same initial and final term as Δ and such that $\mathcal{M}_\sigma(D) = \Omega(\Delta)$.*

Theorem 4. *For any derivation D of $\lambda\sigma$ whose initial and final terms are both in Λ, there exists a derivation Δ of the λ-calculus that has the same initial and final term as D and such that $\mathcal{M}_\sigma(D) = \Omega(\Delta)$.*

the proof of theorem 3 is very similar to the proof of theorem 1. We first show that elementary reductions of the λ-calculus and their origin functions can be faithfully represented by derivations of $\lambda\sigma$ and their marking functions. Of course, we have to take care of the two possible uses of the rule *FVar*, but the different cases for the rules *Closure*, *VarShift2*, *RVar*, *VarShift1*, and *VarId* do not appear. The proof of theorem 3 is detailed in [Bertot91b]. Proving theorem 4 can be obtained using a confluence argument identical to the one used for theorem 2. to establish this result we use a more elaborate labeled rewriting system than before. This rewriting system is based on the following language of labels.

Definition. Given an infinite set $\mathcal{A}$, we consider the language L constructed from $\mathcal{A} \cup \{nil, or\}$ where *nil* and the elements of $\mathcal{A}$ have a null arity and *or* has arity two. Let *or* and *nil* have the following properties, for every x, y, and z in L.

$$x \textit{ or } nil = nil \textit{ or } x = x \qquad\qquad (x \textit{ or } y) \textit{ or } z = x \textit{ or } (y \textit{ or } z)$$

$$x \textit{ or } y = x \qquad \text{if } x \neq nil$$

We consider the set $\Lambda\sigma^L$ of terms $\Lambda\sigma$ labeled with elements of L. We assimilate unlabeled terms with labeled terms where all the nodes are labeled with *nil*. Given a term $M \in \Lambda\sigma$, and a function $\mathcal{L} : \mathcal{D}(M) \rightarrow L$, we note $\langle M, \mathcal{L}\rangle$ the labeled term $M' \in \Lambda\sigma^L$ that carries the label $\mathcal{L}(u)$ at occurrence u, for any ocurrence $u \in \mathcal{D}(M)$. We also note $M = erase(M')$ and $\mathcal{L} = labels(M')$. labeled terms are represented by writing the label as exponent. For example, if P is the term $P = (\lambda(M)^l N)^m$ and $\mathcal{L} = labels(P)$ we have $\mathcal{L}(\varepsilon) = m$ and $\mathcal{L}(1) = l$. We allow ourselves to add a label l to a term M by writing M^l, with the convention that $(M^l)^m = M^{l \textit{ or } m}$.

The basic idea behind this labeling is the same as in [Lévy78], [Klop80], [Field90], and [Maranget91]. However, the language of labels is much simpler.

Definition. The labeled rewriting system $\lambda\sigma^L$ is given in appendix. The function *erase* introduced in the previous definition extends naturally to rules of $\lambda\sigma^L$. For any derivation $D = M \overset{(u,r)}{\rightarrow} N$ of $\lambda\sigma$ and any labeling function $\mathcal{L} : \mathcal{D}(M) \rightarrow L$ we note $lift_L(D, \mathcal{L})$ the derivation $D' = \langle M, \mathcal{L}\rangle \overset{(u,r')}{\rightarrow} N'$ such that $erase(r') = r$ (in the following, $erase(r')$ and r will always be noted with the same name, the ambiguity being always solved by the context). As for the function *lift*, this function $lift_L$ extends naturally to non-elementary derivations. We note σ^L the sub-system $\lambda\sigma^L - \{Beta\}$.

Example. *The following derivation is an example derivation of the system $\lambda\sigma^L$:*

1 $(\lambda^b(\lambda^d(1^f2^g)^e1^h)^c1^i)^a \rightarrow (\lambda^d(1^f2^g)^e1^h)^c[1^i \cdot id]$
2 $\rightarrow (\lambda^d(1^f2^g)^e[1^i \cdot id]1^h[1^i \cdot id])^c$
3 $\rightarrow (\lambda^d((1^f2^g)^e[1 \cdot ((1^i \cdot id) \circ \uparrow)])1^h[1^i \cdot id])^c$
4 $\rightarrow (\lambda^d(1^f[1 \cdot ((1^i \cdot id) \circ \uparrow)]2^g[1 \cdot ((1^i \cdot id) \circ \uparrow)])^e1^h[1^i \cdot id]$
5 $\rightarrow (\lambda^d(1^f2^g[1 \cdot ((1^i \cdot id) \circ \uparrow)])^e1^h[1^i \cdot id])^c$
6 $\rightarrow (\lambda^d(1^f1^g[(1^i \cdot id) \circ \uparrow])^e1^h[1^i \cdot id])^c$
7 $\rightarrow (\lambda^d(1^f1^g[1^i[\uparrow] \cdot (id \circ \uparrow)])^e1^h[1^i \cdot id])^c$
8 $\rightarrow (\lambda^d(1^f(1^i[\uparrow])^g)^e1^h[1^i \cdot id])^c$
9 $\rightarrow (\lambda^d(1^f2^i)^e1^h[1^i \cdot id])^c$
10 $\rightarrow (\lambda^d(1^f2^i)^e1^i)^c$

Note how the meaning attached to the operator or affects the way labels are transmitted in reduction steps 5, 8, 9, and 10.

This labeled rewriting system permits to represent computations of origins for $\lambda\sigma$ exactly as λEnv^* did λEnv. We formally express this property with the following lemma, whose detailed proof is given in [Bertot91b].

Lemma 3. *For any term $M \in \Lambda$, for any labeling function $\mathcal{L} : \mathcal{D}(M) \rightarrow \mathcal{A}$, for any derivation $D = M \twoheadrightarrow N$ of $\lambda\sigma$, if $\mathcal{L}'$ is the labeling function such that $lift_L(D, \mathcal{L}) = \langle M, \mathcal{L}\rangle \twoheadrightarrow \langle N, \mathcal{L}'\rangle$, and if f is the function $f = \mathcal{M}_\sigma(D)$, then we have:*

$$\forall v \in \mathcal{D}(N) \quad \mathcal{L}(f(v)) = \mathcal{L}'(v)$$

As for the proof of theorem 2, we need a confluence property to establish theorem 4. Such a property can be found, although it is weaker than for λEnv^*.

Definition. A term of $\Lambda\sigma^L$ is *well labeled* if it contains no occurrence of an unlabeled operator of Op_λ.

Property P2. *The rewriting system σ^L is confluent on well labeled ground terms.*

Most critical pairs of the system are simply confluent. For the others, a simple analysis by cases on variable instances generally gives the result.

We then have the following lemma, that mimics lemma 2 for the rewriting system $\lambda\sigma^L$. This lemma uses a set of derivations $Sim\beta^L$ that corresponds to the set $Sim\beta^*$ used for λEnv^*.

Lemma 4. *Any derivation of $\lambda\sigma^L$ that begins and finishes on terms of Λ^L has the same initial and final term as a derivation of $Sim\beta^L$.*

To prove this result, we have to examine the critical pair introduced by adding the rule *Beta* to σ^L. The problems encountered can be sketched as follows.

We examine the problem of proving that the critical pair between *Beta* and *App* is confluent on ground terms. We recall that these rules have the following form:

Beta	$((\lambda a)^u b)^v \rightarrow a[b \cdot id]$
App	$((ab)^u[s])^v \rightarrow (a[s]b[s])^{u \text{ or } v}$

The critical pair appears when reducing the term $(((\lambda a)^u b)^v[s])^w$. The two completely reduced outcomes are the terms $a^w[b[s] \cdot s]$ and $a[b[s] \cdot (s \circ id)]$. To establish a confluence result, we have to express that the label w on top of a in the first term will not be used in the final term of σ^L-normalizing derivation and second that $(s \circ id)$ and s are equivalent substitutions. The first statement comes from a lemma given in [Bertot91b] that expresses that any derivation starting with a well labeled term finishes in a well labeled term. For this reason the term a can be normalized in a term a'. Since this term σ^L-normal, its head operator is in Op_λ and since it is well labeled, we have $a'^w = a'$. The second statement can be proved a case analysis on the head operator using a lemma expressing that for any term t, $t[id]$ and t reduce to a same value; this lemma can be proved by induction on the size of t.

Lemma 4 has consequences for $\lambda\sigma^L$ that are equivalent to the consequences of lemma 2 for λEnv^*, and among them comes theorem 4.

5. Conclusion.

The concept of origin functions we have used in this paper seems a good tool to study the notion of descendance in reduction systems, with a good separation between descendance and other aspects of reduction. With the concept of marking functions, we have extended this notion of descendance in a way that proves fruitful when studying the λ-calculus and the system λEnv.

The difference between λEnv and $\lambda\sigma$, mainly that the former is confluent on all terms whereas the latter is confluent only on ground terms, is studied in detail in [CHL91], along with conditional variants of these systems. Our result shows another difference between the two systems. It would be interesting to understand whether the problem of computing origins and the problem of confluence are related.

On the side of programming language study and implementation, it would be interesting to extend this kind of result to graph rewriting systems, as many new implementations of functional programming languages use graph rewriting.

References.

[ACCL90] M. Abadi, L. Cardelli, P.-L. Curien, J.-J. Lévy, "Explicit Substitutions", *Proceedings of the 17th Annual Symposium on the Principles of Programming Languages*, San Francisco, California, January 1990, pp. 31–46.

[Bertot91a] Y. Bertot, *Une Automatisation du Calcul des Résidus en Sémantique Naturelle*, PhD thesis, University of Nice, France, June 1991.

[Boudol85] G. Boudol, "Computational Semantics of Term Rewriting Systems", *Algebraic Methods in Semantics*, M. Nivat, J. C. Reynolds (editors), Cambridge University Press, 1985.

[**de Bruijn72**] N. DE BRUIJN, "Lambda-Calculus Notation with Nameless Dummies, a Tool for Automatic Formula Manipulation, with Application to the Church-Rosser Theorem", Indag. Math. 34,5, 1972, pp. 381–392.

[**CHL91**] P.-L. CURIEN, T. HARDIN, J.-J. LÉVY, "Confluence Properties of Weak and Strong Calculi of Explicit Substitutions", Personal communication, July 1991.

[**Curien86**] P.-L. CURIEN, *Categorical Combinators, Sequential Algorithms and Functional Programming*, Pitman, London, 1986.

[**Curry&Feys58**] H. CURRY, R. FEYS, *Combinatory Logic, Vol. I*, North-Holland, 1958.

[**Field90**] J. FIELD, "On Laziness and Optimality in Lambda Interpreters: Tools for Specification and Analysis", *Proceedings of the 17th ACM Symposium on Principles of Programming Languages*, San Francisco, California, January 1990, pp. 1–15.

[**Hardin&Lévy89**] T. HARDIN, J.-J. LÉVY, "A Confluent Calculus of Substitutions", *Proceedings of the France Japan Artificial Intelligence and Computer Science Symposium*, Izu, Japan, November 89.

[**Hindley&Seldin86**] J. HINDLEY, J. SELDIN, *Introduction to Combinators and λ-calculus*, London Mathematical Society Student Texts, Cambridge University Press, 1986.

[**Huet80**] G. HUET, "Confluent reductions: abstract properties and applications to term rewriting systems", Journal of the ACM, 27, 4, pp. 797–821, 1980.

[**Klop80**] J. W. KLOP, *Combinatory Reduction Systems*, PhD Thesis, Mathematisch Centrum Amsterdam, 1980.

[**Knuth&Bendix70**] KNUTH, D. E., BENDIX P. B., "Simple Word Problems in Universal Algebras", *Computational Problems in Abstract Algebra*, J. Leech (editor), Pergamon Press, 1970.

[**Lévy78**] J.-J. LÉVY, *Réductions Correctes et Optimales dans le Lambda Calcul*, PhD Thesis, Université de Paris VII, 1978.

[**Maranget91**] L. MARANGET, "Optimal Derivations in Weak Lambda-Calculi and in Orthogonal Terms Rewriting Systems", *Proceeding of the 18th ACM Symposium on Principles of Programming Languages*, Orlando, Florida, January1991, pp. 255–269.

[**Morris68**] J. MORRIS, *Lambda Calculus Models of Programming Languages*, PhD Thesis, MIT, Cambridge, Massachusetts, 1968.

[**Tolmach&Appel90**] A. P. TOLMACH, A. W. APPEL, "Debugging Standard ML without Reverse Engineering", *Proceedings of the 1990 ACM Conference on Lisp and Functional Programming*, Nice, France, June 1990, pp. 1–12.

Appendix: The Rewriting Systems λEnv and $\lambda\sigma$

(Beta)	$(\lambda a)b$	$\rightarrow$	$a[b \cdot id]$				
(App)	$(ab)[s]$	$\rightarrow$	$a[s]b[s]$	*(Lambda)*	$(\lambda a)[s]$	$\rightarrow$	$\lambda(a[\Uparrow(s)])$
(Closure)	$(a[s])[t]$	$\rightarrow$	$a[s \circ t]$	*(VarShift1)*	$n[\uparrow]$	$\rightarrow$	$n+1$
(VarShift2)	$n[\uparrow \circ s]$	$\rightarrow$	$n+1[s]$	*(FVar)*	$1[a \cdot s]$	$\rightarrow$	a
(FVarLift1)	$1[\Uparrow(s)]$	$\rightarrow$	1	*(FVarLift2)*	$1[\Uparrow(s) \circ t]$	$\rightarrow$	$1[t]$
(RVar)	$n+1[a \cdot s]$	$\rightarrow$	$n[s]$	*(RVarLift1)*	$n+1[\Uparrow(s)]$	$\rightarrow$	$n[s \circ \uparrow]$
(RVarLift2)	$n+1[\Uparrow(s) \circ t]$	$\rightarrow$	$n[s \circ (\uparrow \circ t)]$	*(AssEnv)*	$(s \circ t) \circ u$	$\rightarrow$	$s \circ (t \circ u)$
(MapEnv)	$(a \cdot s) \circ t$	$\rightarrow$	$a[t] \cdot (s \circ t)$	*(Shift)*	$\uparrow \circ (a \cdot s)$	$\rightarrow$	s
(ShiftLift1)	$\uparrow \circ \Uparrow(s)$	$\rightarrow$	$s \circ \uparrow$	*(ShiftLift2)*	$\uparrow \circ (\Uparrow(s) \circ t)$	$\rightarrow$	$s \circ (\uparrow \circ t)$
(Lift1)	$\Uparrow(s) \circ \Uparrow(t)$	$\rightarrow$	$\Uparrow(s \circ t)$	*(Lift2)*	$\Uparrow(s) \circ (\Uparrow(t) \circ u)$	$\rightarrow$	$\Uparrow(s \circ t) \circ u$
(LiftEnv)	$\Uparrow(s) \circ (a \cdot t)$	$\rightarrow$	$a \cdot (s \circ t)$	*(IdL)*	$id \circ s$	$\rightarrow$	s
(IdR)	$s \circ id$	$\rightarrow$	s	*(LiftId)*	$\Uparrow(id)$	$\rightarrow$	id
(IdEnv)	$a[id]$	$\rightarrow$	a				

The rewriting system λEnv.

(Beta)	$(\lambda a)b$	$\rightarrow$	$a[b \cdot id]$				
(App)	$(ab)[s]$	$\rightarrow$	$(a[s]\ b[s])$	*(VarId)*	$n[id]$	$\rightarrow$	n
(FVar)	$1[a \cdot s]$	$\rightarrow$	a	*(Closure)*	$a[s][t]$	$\rightarrow$	$a[s \circ t]$
(Lambda')	$(\lambda a)[s]$	$\rightarrow$	$\lambda(a[1 \cdot (s \circ \uparrow)])$	*(IdL)*	$id \circ s$	$\rightarrow$	s
(ShiftId)	$\uparrow \circ id$	$\rightarrow$	$\uparrow$	*(Shift)*	$\uparrow \circ (a \cdot s)$	$\rightarrow$	s
(AssEnv)	$(s_1 \circ s_2) \circ s_3$	$\rightarrow$	$s_1 \circ (s_2 \circ s_3)$	*(MapEnv)*	$(a \cdot s) \circ t$	$\rightarrow$	$a[t] \cdot (s \circ t)$
(VarShift1)	$n[\uparrow]$	$\rightarrow$	$n+1$	*(VarShift2)*	$n[\uparrow \circ s]$	$\rightarrow$	$n+1[s]$
(RVar)	$n+1[a \cdot s]$	$\rightarrow$	$n[s]$				

The rewriting system $\lambda\sigma$.

(Beta)	$((\lambda a)^u b)^v$	$\rightarrow$	$a[b \cdot id]$				
(App)	$((ab)^u[s])^v$	$\rightarrow$	$(a[s]\ b[s])^{u \text{ or } v}$	*(VarId)*	$(n^u[id])^v$	$\rightarrow$	$n^{u \text{ or } v}$
(FVar)	$(1^u[a \cdot s])^v$	$\rightarrow$	$a^{u \text{ or } v}$	*(Closure)*	$((a[s])^u[t])^v$	$\rightarrow$	$a^{u \text{ or } v}[s \circ t]$
(Lambda')	$((\lambda a)^u[s])^v$	$\rightarrow$	$\lambda(a[1 \cdot (s \circ \uparrow)])^{u \text{ or } v}$	*(IdL)*	$id \circ s$	$\rightarrow$	s
(ShiftId)	$\uparrow \circ id$	$\rightarrow$	$\uparrow$	*(Shift)*	$\uparrow \circ (a \cdot s)$	$\rightarrow$	s
(AssEnv)	$(s_1 \circ s_2) \circ s_3$	$\rightarrow$	$s_1 \circ (s_2 \circ s_3)$	*(MapEnv)*	$(a \cdot s) \circ t$	$\rightarrow$	$a[t] \cdot (s \circ t)$
(VarShift1)	$(n^u[\uparrow])^v$	$\rightarrow$	$n+1^{u \text{ or } v}$	*(VarShift2)*	$(n^u[\uparrow \circ s])^v$	$\rightarrow$	$n+1^{u \text{ or } v}[s]$
(RVar)	$n+1^u[a \cdot s]^v$	$\rightarrow$	$n^{u \text{ or } v}[s]$				

The labeled rewriting system $\lambda\sigma^L$.

An algebraic approach to the interpretation of recursive types

FELICE CARDONE
Dipartimento di Scienze dell'Informazione
Università di Milano
Via Comelico, 39/41
I-20135 MILANO

Abstract

We present an algebraic framework for the interpretation of type systems including type recursion, where types are interpreted as *partial equivalence relations* over a Scott domain. We use the notion of *iterative algebra*, introduced by J. Tiuryn [26] as a counterpart to the categorical notion of *iterative algebraic theory* by C.C. Elgot [15]. We show that a suitable collection of partial equivalence relations is closed under type constructors and forms an iterative algebra. The existence of type interpretations follows from the initiality, in the class of iterative algebras, of the algebra of regular infinite trees obtained by infinitely unfolding recursive types.

1 Introduction

There are by now several techniques available for interpreting recursive types for functional languages in such a way that the mixed variance of the function type constructor is preserved ([21], [12]). This means that if $\leq$ stands for a (formal) subtyping relation, and we assume that the conditions $\sigma' \leq \sigma$ and $\tau \leq \tau'$ hold, then $(\sigma \to \tau) \leq (\sigma' \to \tau')$ also holds in these interpretations. The soundness of this subtyping rule is important when modelling type systems for object-oriented programming languages built along the lines of [8] or [9]. For the semantics of such systems it turns out to be convenient to look at types as suitably structured collections of values from a domain providing denotations to untyped terms, taking as interpretation of the subtyping relation plain set-theoretic inclusion of such collections. So, when a type system is presented as a set of rules of type inference for terms of an untyped λ-calculus with constants, and the equational theory for typed terms is inherited from that of the untyped language, it is common to interpret types as *ideals* over a Scott domain D (*i.e.* non empty closed sets in the Scott topology over D) which is a model of the term language. Subtyping is modelled by set-theoretic inclusion of ideals, and the interpretation of recursive types is performed by a construction that exploits, in the case of [21], a complete metric space structure which can be defined on the set of ideals over D. The observation that all definable non-trivial type constructors are interpreted as *contractive mappings* over ideals permits an application of Banach's fixed point theorem in order to find the interpretation of a recursive type. In [12] every ideal is represented as a kind of limit of a denumerable chain of "approximations," and the interpretation of a recursive type expression is built as the limit of its inductively defined approximations. These techniques can be extended to provide semantics to strongly typed systems in which function application satisfies an extensionality rule. Types are then interpreted as partial equivalence relations over an untyped domain D, *i.e.* symmetric and transitive relations which are reflexive only on their field, generally a proper subset of D (see [6]). The requirement of closure under type recursion makes it necessary to impose further conditions on partial equivalence relations, based on the structure of D: these define the class of *complete* and *uniform* partial equivalence relations of [2], [10] and [1].

An advantage of the technique introduced in [12] (and further extended in [11], [2], [10]) over the metric approach consists in its ability to deal with type constructors which do not define contractive mappings over the collection of types, exploiting properties of the domain D which follow directly from its construction as the solution of a recursive domain equation (as described, for example, in [25]). On the other hand, although a powerful proof principle is suggested by looking at the interpretation of a type as completely determined by a denumerable sequence of approximate interpretations, the process of explicit construction of such an interpretation remains quite involved. It is customary to look at interpretation mappings as homomorphisms from the free Σ-algebra over a set of variables, for some signature Σ: given a mapping η assigning values to variables, there is a *unique* Σ-homomorphism which extends η to the set of Σ-terms (with variables). In the present paper we suggest how this principle can be applied to type interpretations, for a set of types defined by the rules:

$$\sigma ::= t \mid \mathsf{I} \mid \sigma_\perp \mid \sigma \oplus \sigma \mid \sigma \otimes \sigma \mid \sigma \times \sigma \mid \sigma \to \sigma \mid \mu t.\sigma$$

where the type constructors correspond to domain constructors used in the denotational semantics of programming languages (see [20]). On the syntactical side, a useful observation is that although some finitary notation for recursive types is needed in type systems, it is often better both on practical and theoretical grounds to consider a type expression of the form $\mu t.\sigma$ as the (usually) infinite tree arising from the infinite unfolding of the recursion, and to identify recursive types with the same associated tree. These are the *regular* trees (as defined, for example, in [13]), which can be given the structure of an *iterative algebra*. Iterative algebras have been introduced by Tiuryn [26] as a counterpart to the categorical notion of *iterative algebraic theory* by [15] (see also [16]): their main property for the purpose of this paper is that the algebra of regular trees over a signature Σ is the initial iterative Σ-algebra [26]. We show that the collection of complete and uniform partial equivalence relations over a suitably chosen domain D forms an iterative algebra (Section 4) after developing in some detail the theory of what we call *cpo's with a notion of approximation* in Sections 3.2, 3.3. Finally we can exploit the freeness of the iterative algebra of regular trees over a set of variables in order to obtain, for any type environment η mapping type variables to complete and uniform partial equivalence relations, a unique type interpretation extending η.

Although this is a simple example of situations where we have both recursive types and subtyping ([6],[2],[10]), yet we believe that our viewpoint may contribute to a more thorough understanding of the principles underlying the techniques of both [21] and [12].

2 Trees

It is convenient to introduce an equivalent way of looking at recursive types, *viz.* by considering the infinite trees arising from the process of unwinding their recursive definitions. We shall only consider (possibly infinite) trees labeled by symbols from a signature Σ consisting of a unary (postfix) function symbol $(.)_\perp$, binary function symbols $\oplus, \otimes, \times, \rightarrow$ and of the constant symbol I.

Let 2^* be the set of finite words over the alphabet {0,1}. A **Σ-tree** α is a partial function $\alpha : 2^* \longrightarrow \Sigma$ satisfying the following conditions:

- if $uv \in \mathbf{Dom}(\alpha)$, then also $u \in \mathbf{Dom}(\alpha)$;
- if $u1 \in \mathbf{Dom}(\alpha)$, then also $u0 \in \mathbf{Dom}(\alpha)$;
- if $\alpha(u) = (.)_\perp$, then $u0 \in \mathbf{Dom}(\alpha)$; if $\alpha(u) = \oplus, \otimes, \times, \rightarrow$ then $u0, u1 \in \mathbf{Dom}(\alpha)$; if $\alpha(u) = \mathsf{I}$ then $ui \notin \mathbf{Dom}(\alpha)$, for $i \in \{0,1\}$.

The set of Σ-trees will be denoted by T^∞_Σ or simply by T^∞ leaving the signature unspecified, and its elements shall be ranged over by small Greek letters $\alpha, \beta, \gamma, \ldots, \zeta, \ldots$. T_Σ is the set of *finite* trees over Σ, ranged over by $\sigma, \tau, \ldots$.

Among infinite Σ-trees, trees having a certain periodic structure, allowing to look at them as solutions of (systems of) equations of the form $\xi = \sigma[\xi]$, are especially interesting from the present viewpoint. These are the *regular trees*:

Definition 1 (Regular trees) *Given a tree α and a word $w \in \mathbf{Dom}(\alpha)$, let $\alpha|w$ be the tree defined by the conditions:*

- $\mathbf{Dom}(\alpha|w) = \{u \in 2^* : wu \in \mathbf{Dom}(\alpha)\}$;
- $(\alpha|w)(u) = \alpha(wu)$, *for all* $u \in \mathbf{Dom}(\alpha|w)$.

A tree is **regular** *if the set $\{\alpha|w : w \in \mathbf{Dom}(\alpha)\}$ is finite. The set of regular trees is denoted by R_Σ.* □

In many cases it is useful to exploit a partial order that can be defined over T^∞: in this partially ordered set, an infinite tree turns out to be the least upper bound of the finite trees below it. For this purpose, the signature Σ is expanded with a new constant symbol Ω: the new signature is denoted by Σ_Ω and the set of Σ_Ω-trees by T^∞_Ω. In a similar way is defined the set R_Ω. Given $\alpha, \beta \in T^\infty_\Omega$, set

$$\alpha \preceq \beta \Leftrightarrow \begin{cases} \mathbf{Dom}(\alpha) \subseteq \mathbf{Dom}(\beta) \\ \forall w \in \mathbf{Dom}(\alpha). \alpha(w) \neq \Omega \Rightarrow \alpha(w) = \beta(w) \end{cases}$$

Clearly Ω is the least element of the partially ordered set $\langle T_\Omega^\infty, \preceq\rangle$, and every increasing sequence of the form $\alpha_0, \alpha_1, \alpha_2, \ldots$ has a least upper bound $\bigvee_{n\in\omega} \alpha_n$.

In the following we shall only consider trees in which may appear *variables* from a fixed countable set V: these are defined as $\Sigma_\Omega(V)$-trees, where the signature $\Sigma_\Omega(V)$ is the signature Σ_Ω expanded with the symbols in V as new constants. The notations $T_\Omega^\infty(V)$ and $R_\Omega(V)$ will be used to indicate the sets of infinite and regular Σ_Ω-trees with variables from V, respectively. A **substitution** (resp. **regular substitution**) is a function $S : V \longrightarrow T_\Omega^\infty(V)$ (resp. $S : V \longrightarrow R_\Omega(V)$). For a substitution S define $S^\sharp$ as the set of all $t \in V$ such that $S(t) \neq t$. A substitution S can be extended to a function defined over the set T_Ω^∞. If $S^\sharp = \{t_1, \ldots, t_n\}$ and $S(t_i) = \zeta_i$ for $i = 1, \ldots, n$, we write

$$\alpha[t_1 := \zeta_1, \ldots, t_n := \zeta_n]$$

instead of $S(\alpha)$.

The following property exploits the cpo structure of $\langle T_\Omega^\infty(V), \preceq\rangle$:

Proposition 1 *The function $\lambda\zeta \in T_\Omega^\infty(V).\alpha[t := \zeta]$ is continuous, for every $\alpha \in T_\Omega^\infty(V)$. Furthermore, if $\alpha \in R_\Omega(V)$ then also*

$$\mathbf{fix}(\lambda\zeta \in T_\Omega^\infty(V).\alpha[t := \zeta])$$

is an element of $R_\Omega(V)$, where **fix** *is the least fixed point operator.* □

The proof of this proposition and of other relevant facts about regular trees can be found in [13]. The interest of regular trees in the present context lies in the fact that they correspond precisely to unfoldings of recursive types, defined as follows:

Definition 2 (Recursive types) *The set T_μ of* **recursive types** *is the smallest set satisfying the conditions:*

- *$V \subseteq T_\mu$;*
- *$\mathsf{I} \in T_\mu$;*
- *if $\sigma, \tau \in T_\mu$ then $\sigma_\perp, \sigma \oplus \tau, \sigma \otimes \tau, \sigma \times \tau, \sigma \to \tau \in T_\mu$;*
- *if $\sigma \in T_\mu$ then also $\mu t.\sigma \in T_\mu$ for any variable $t \in V$.*

□

Indeed, we can give a (surjective) translation of recursive types into regular trees, as a function $(.)^* : T_\mu \longrightarrow R_\Omega(V)$ defined by induction on the structure of recursive type expressions:

- $t^* = t$, for all $t \in V$;
- $\mathsf{I}^* = \mathsf{I}$;
- $(\sigma_\perp)^* = (\sigma^*)_\perp$;
- $(\sigma \oplus \tau)^* = \sigma^* \oplus \tau^*$;

- $(\sigma \otimes \tau)^* = \sigma^* \otimes \tau^*$;
- $(\sigma \times \tau)^* = \sigma^* \times \tau^*$;
- $(\sigma \to \tau)^* = \sigma^* \to \tau^*$;
- $(\mu t.\sigma)^* = \mathbf{fix}(\lambda\zeta \in T_\Omega^\infty(V).\sigma^*[t := \zeta])$.

Observe that $(\mu t.\sigma)^* = \sigma^*[t := (\mu t.\sigma)^*]$, and also that $(\mu t_1 \ldots t_n.t_i)^* = \Omega$ for $i = 1, \ldots, n$. We shall consider recursive types up to equality of their unfoldings, by factoring T_μ through the equivalence relation defined by

$$\sigma \approx \tau \text{ iff } \sigma^* = \tau^*$$

(see [11], in which this approach is followed systematically).

Another simple but fundamental observation is that the structure

$$\langle T_{\Sigma_\Omega}, \mathsf{I}, (.)_\perp, \oplus, \otimes, \times, \to\rangle$$

is the initial Σ_Ω-algebra [17]. A consequence of this fact is that any function

$$\eta : V \longrightarrow \mathbf{A}$$

from V to an arbitrary Σ_Ω-algebra $\mathbf{A}$ extends uniquely to a Σ_Ω-homomorphism

$$[\![.]\!]\eta : T_{\Sigma_\Omega}(V) \longrightarrow \mathbf{A}.$$

If $\sigma \in T_{\Sigma_\Omega}(V)$ contains variables $t_1, \ldots, t_n, s_1, \ldots, s_k$ then it defines a *derived operator* (equivalently, a *polynomial*) $\sigma_{\eta,\mathbf{A}}(t_1, \ldots, t_n; s_1, \ldots, s_k) : \mathbf{A}^n \longrightarrow \mathbf{A}$ for each k-tuple of values assigned by η to the k parameters $s_1, \ldots, s_k$, by setting:

$$\sigma_{\eta,\mathbf{A}}(t_1, \ldots, t_n; s_1, \ldots, s_k)(A_1, \ldots, A_n) = [\![\sigma]\!]\eta[t_1 \mapsto A_1, \ldots, t_n \mapsto A_n].$$

A polynomial of this form is a **Greibach polynomial** if σ is not a variable.

The preceding notions are instrumental in defining a class of Σ_Ω-algebras containing R_Ω as the initial algebra; the notion is due to J. Tiuryn, building on previous work by C. Elgot and others on *iterative algebraic theories* [15,4,16]. A Σ_Ω-algebra $\mathbf{A}$ is an **iterative algebra** whenever the following conditions hold:

- For every function $\eta : V \longrightarrow \mathbf{A}$ and every n-tuple of Greibach polynomials $\sigma_1, \ldots, \sigma_n$ in the n variables $t_1, \ldots, t_n$ and parameters $s_1, \ldots, s_k$, the system:

$$\begin{aligned} X_1 &= [\![\sigma_1]\!]\eta[t_1 \mapsto X_1, \ldots, t_n \mapsto X_n] \\ &\;\;\vdots \\ X_n &= [\![\sigma_n]\!]\eta[t_1 \mapsto X_1, \ldots, t_n \mapsto X_n] \end{aligned}$$

  has a unique solution.

- The function of the k parameters $s_1, \ldots, s_k$, $f : \mathbf{A}^k \longrightarrow \mathbf{A}^n$, defined by the solution of the system is such that for some k-tuple $\langle Y_1, \ldots, Y_k \rangle$, the first coordinate of $f(\langle Y_1, \ldots, Y_k \rangle)$ is different from Y_1.

Theorem 1 (Tiuryn [26], Thms. 3.3.3; 3.3.4) *1. R_Ω is the initial iterative Σ_Ω-algebra.*

2. For every set V, every iterative algebra $\mathbf{A}$ and every function $\eta : V \longrightarrow \mathbf{A}$ there exists exactly one Σ_Ω-homomorphism $[\![.]\!]\eta : R_\Omega(V) \longrightarrow \mathbf{A}$ extending η.

□

3 Domains and their approximations

From the semantical viewpoint, types will be considered as suitably structured collections of elements from a domain which provides the meanings of the untyped terms of the language, the structure to be defined over such collections depending closely on properties of the domain. Before examining such properties we briefly recall some definitions and notational conventions: they are mostly standard, and more details can be found in the monograph [20], whose notations we shall generally follow.

3.1 Domains

A **domain** is a bounded complete cpo whose finite elements form a countable basis. If D, E are cpo's, a **continuous function** $f : D \longrightarrow E$ is a monotonic function which preserves the least upper bounds of directed subsets of D. A continuous function is **strict** if it preserves the least element. Continuous functions $e : D \longrightarrow E$ and $p : E \longrightarrow D$ such that $p \circ e = 1_D$ and $e \circ p \sqsubseteq 1_E$ form an **embedding-projection pair**, p being the projection (of E onto D) and e the embedding (of D into E). Embeddings and projections are always strict functions. Often a **projection** is taken to be a continuous function $p : D \longrightarrow D$ such that $p \circ p = p \sqsubseteq 1_D$: this is justified by the fact that $p(D)$ is a cpo and the inclusion mapping $p(D) \hookrightarrow D$ provides the (unique) embedding associated with $p : D \longrightarrow p(D)$. Conversely, an embedding-projection pair $\langle e, p \rangle$ defines a projection $e \circ p : E \longrightarrow E$ in the latter sense. A projection $p : D \longrightarrow D$, where D is a domain, is **finitary** if $p(D) = \{p(d) : d \in D\}$ is a domain. The collection of finitary projections over a domain D forms a cpo $\mathsf{Fp}(D)$.

The domain I consists of a single point $\bot$: it is the terminal object in the cartesian closed category of domains and continuous functions. We obtain other domains by applying the domain constructors familiar from denotational semantics:

- For a domain D, its **lifting** $D_\bot$ is obtained from D by adding a new least element $\bot$. It comes equipped with two continuous functions $\mathsf{down} : D_\bot \longrightarrow D$ and $\mathsf{up} : D \longrightarrow D_\bot$ with the property that

$$\begin{aligned} \mathsf{down} \circ \mathsf{up} &= 1_D \\ \mathsf{up} \circ \mathsf{down} &\sqsupseteq 1_{D_\bot}. \end{aligned}$$

The action of this functor on a continuous function $f : D \longrightarrow E$ yields a strict and continuous function

$$f_\perp : D_\perp \longrightarrow E_\perp.$$

- If D, E are domains, their **coalesced sum** $D \oplus E$ is the disjoint union of the partially ordered sets $D - \{\perp_D\}$ and $E - \{\perp_E\}$ with a new least element $\perp_{D\oplus E}$. There are strict continuous injections $\mathsf{inl} : D \longrightarrow (D \oplus E)$, $\mathsf{inr} : E \longrightarrow (D \oplus E)$ and for strict continuous $f : D \longrightarrow C, g : E \longrightarrow C$ a unique strict continuous function $[f, g] : (D \oplus E) \longrightarrow C$ such that $[f, g] \circ \mathsf{inl} = f$ and $[f, g] \circ \mathsf{inr} = g$. The coalesced sum of strict continuous $f : D \longrightarrow D', g : E \longrightarrow E'$ is $f \oplus g : (D \oplus E) \longrightarrow (D' \oplus E')$ defined as $[\mathsf{inl} \circ f, \mathsf{inr} \circ g]$.

- If D, E are domains, their **product** $D \times E$ is their cartesian product ordered coordinatewise, with projections $\mathsf{fst} : (D \times E) \longrightarrow D$ and $\mathsf{snd} : (D \times E) \longrightarrow E$. Given continuous $f : C \longrightarrow D, g : C \longrightarrow E$ there is a unique continuous function $\langle f, g \rangle : C \longrightarrow (D \times E)$ such that $\mathsf{fst} \circ \langle f, g \rangle = f$ and $\mathsf{snd} \circ \langle f, g \rangle = g$. The continuous function $f \times g : (D \times E) \longrightarrow (D' \times E')$ for $f : D \longrightarrow D', g : E \longrightarrow E'$ is $\langle f \circ \mathsf{fst}, g \circ \mathsf{snd} \rangle$.

- If D, E are domains, their **smash product** $D \otimes E$ is the collection of all pairs $\langle d, e \rangle$ such that $d \neq \perp_D, e \neq \perp_E$, ordered coordinatewise, with a new least element $\perp_{D\otimes E}$. There are continuous functions $\mathsf{smash} : (D \times E) \longrightarrow (D \otimes E)$ and $\mathsf{unsmash} : (D \otimes E) \longrightarrow (D \times E)$ and for strict continuous $f : D \longrightarrow D', g : E \longrightarrow E'$ define $f \otimes g$ as $\mathsf{smash} \circ (f \times g) \circ \mathsf{unsmash}$.

- If D, E are domains, their **exponential** $[D \to E]$ is the domain of all continuous functions $D \longrightarrow E$ ordered pointwise. For continuous $f : D' \longrightarrow D, g : E \longrightarrow E'$, define $f \to g : [D \to E] \longrightarrow [D' \to E']$ as $\lambda h \in [D \to E].g \circ h \circ f$.

All these functors preserve finitary projections: this is the key fact in the method we shall follow for finding solutions of recursive domain equations.

3.2 Domain equations

The solution of the recursive domain equation

$$D \cong \mathsf{I} \oplus D_\perp \oplus [D \oplus D] \oplus [D \otimes D] \oplus [D \times D] \oplus [D \to D]$$

exploits the existence of a domain U, the *universal domain*, with the property that for every domain D there exists a projection $\Phi_\mathsf{U} : \mathsf{U} \longrightarrow D$ and an embedding $\Psi_\mathsf{U} : D \longrightarrow \mathsf{U}$ such that the set of fixed points of the finitary projection $\Psi_\mathsf{U} \circ \Phi_\mathsf{U}$ is isomorphic to D. Accordingly, every domain will be identified with a finitary projection, and the solution of the above equation becomes the least fixed point of the continuous function

$$\lambda p \in \mathsf{Fp}(\mathsf{U}).\mathsf{I} \oplus p_\perp \oplus [p \oplus p] \oplus [p \otimes p] \oplus [p \times p] \oplus [p \to p]$$

from the cpo $\mathsf{Fp}(\mathsf{U})$ of finitary projections of U to itself, writing $u \in p$ when $u \in \mathsf{U}$ satisfies $p(u) = u$. The usual construction of fixed points of continuous functions determines this as the least upper bound of an increasing sequence of finitary projections $D_n : \mathsf{U} \longrightarrow \mathsf{U}$:

$$\begin{cases} D_0 = & \bot_{\mathsf{Fp(U)}} \\ D_{n+1} = & \mathsf{I} \oplus (D_n)_\bot \oplus [D_n \oplus D_n] \oplus [D_n \otimes D_n] \oplus [D_n \times D_n] \oplus [D_n \to D_n] \end{cases}$$

These induce an increasing sequence of projections over (the image of) D:

$$\{(.)_n : D \longrightarrow D\}_{n \in \omega}$$

by defining d_n as $D_n(d)$, such that the following properties hold, for $d \in D$ and $n \in \omega$:

$$d_0 = \bot_D \tag{1}$$

$$(d_n)_m = d_{\min(n,m)} \tag{2}$$

$$d = \bigsqcup_{n \in \omega} d_n. \tag{3}$$

For the construction of type interpretations we need a more detailed analysis of the action of projections on the summands of D: the following facts are based on the observation that D_{n+1} is determined by D_n and the definitions of domain constructors. We give the proof of the first of them only, the others being similar.

- If $d \in D_\bot$ and $e \in D$, define $\downarrow d$ as $\mathsf{down}(\Phi_\bot(d))$ and $\uparrow d = \Psi_\bot(\mathsf{up}(d))$, where $\Phi_\bot : \mathsf{U} \longrightarrow \mathsf{U}_\bot$ and $\Psi_\bot : \mathsf{U}_\bot \longrightarrow \mathsf{U}$ exist by universality of U. Observe that either $d = \bot$ or $d = \uparrow e$ for some $e \in D$. Then:

$$\downarrow (d_n) = (\downarrow d)_{n-1}. \tag{4}$$

  Infact, if $d = \bot$, then $\mathsf{down}(\Phi_\bot(d)) = \bot$ by strictness of the functions down and $\Phi_\bot$. Otherwise $\downarrow d = \downarrow (\uparrow e) = \mathsf{down}(\mathsf{up}(e)) = e$, and

$$\begin{aligned} \downarrow (D_n(d)) &= \mathsf{down}(\Phi_\bot(D_n(d))) \\ &= \mathsf{down}(\Phi_\bot(\Psi_\bot((D_{n-1})_\bot(\Phi_\bot(d))))) \\ &= \mathsf{down}((D_{n-1})_\bot(\Phi_\bot(d))) \\ &= \mathsf{down}((D_{n-1})_\bot(\mathsf{up}(e))) \\ &= \mathsf{down}(\mathsf{up}(D_{n-1}(e))) \\ &= D_{n-1}(e) \\ &= D_{n-1}(\downarrow d). \end{aligned}$$

- If $d \in D$, define $\mathsf{left}(d)$ as $\Psi_\oplus(\mathsf{inl}(d))$ and $\mathsf{right}(d)$ as $\Psi_\oplus(\mathsf{inr}(d))$, where $\Psi_\oplus : \mathsf{U} \oplus \mathsf{U} \longrightarrow \mathsf{U}$ exists by universality of U. Then:

$$(\mathsf{left}(d))_{n+1} = \mathsf{left}(d_n) \tag{5}$$

$$(\mathsf{right}(d))_{n+1} = \mathsf{right}(d_n). \tag{6}$$

- If $d \in D \otimes D$, then either $d = \perp$ or $d = (d', d'')$ where $d' \neq \perp, d'' \neq \perp$,

$$\begin{aligned} d' &= D(\mathsf{fst}(\mathsf{unsmash}(\Phi_{\otimes}(d)))) \\ d'' &= D(\mathsf{snd}(\mathsf{unsmash}(\Phi_{\otimes}(d)))) \end{aligned}$$

and (d', d'') is defined as $\Psi_{\otimes}(\mathsf{smash}(\langle d', d'' \rangle))$, where $\Phi_{\otimes} : \mathsf{U} \longrightarrow \mathsf{U} \otimes \mathsf{U}$, $\Psi_{\otimes} : \mathsf{U} \otimes \mathsf{U} \longrightarrow \mathsf{U}$. In the latter case we have:

$$d_{n+1} = (d'_n, d''_n). \tag{7}$$

- If $d \in D \times D$, then d can be written as

$$(\mathsf{first}(d), \mathsf{second}(d))$$

defined as

$$\Psi_{\times}(\langle \mathsf{first}(d), \mathsf{second}(d) \rangle),$$

where

$$\begin{aligned} \mathsf{first}(d) &= D(\mathsf{fst}(\Phi_{\times}(d))) \\ \mathsf{second}(d) &= D(\mathsf{snd}(\Phi_{\times}(d))) \end{aligned}$$

and $\Phi_{\times} : \mathsf{U} \longrightarrow \mathsf{U} \times \mathsf{U}$, $\Psi_{\times} : \mathsf{U} \times \mathsf{U} \longrightarrow \mathsf{U}$. Then:

$$d_{n+1} = (\mathsf{first}(d_n), \mathsf{second}(d_n)) \tag{8}$$

- For $d, e \in D$ define

$$d \cdot e = (\Phi_{\rightarrow}(d))(e),$$

where $\Phi_{\rightarrow} : \mathsf{U} \longrightarrow [\mathsf{U} \rightarrow \mathsf{U}]$ exists by universality of U. If $f \in [D \rightarrow D]$ and $d \in D$, then:

$$n \leq k \Rightarrow f_{n+1} \cdot d_k = f_{n+1} \cdot d_n \tag{9}$$

$$n \leq k \Rightarrow (f_{k+1} \cdot d_n)_n = f_{n+1} \cdot d_n \tag{10}$$

$$f_{n+1} \cdot d_n = f_{n+1} \cdot d = (f \cdot d_n)_n \tag{11}$$

$$f = f_{n+1} \Leftrightarrow \forall d \in D. f \cdot d = (f \cdot d_n)_n \tag{12}$$

$$f \cdot d = \bigsqcup_{n \in \omega} (f_{n+1} \cdot d_n). \tag{13}$$

3.3 Cpo's with a notion of approximation

The above properties concerning the relationships between compound values and approximations of D define a special case of what we shall call a *notion of approximation* over D. The general framework we shall work in is summarized as follows:

Definition 3 (Cpo with a notion of approximation) *Given a cpo $\langle D, \sqsubseteq \rangle$, a* **notion of approximation** *over D is a denumerable family of continuous endofunctions $\pi_n : D \longrightarrow D$ such that, for all $n, m \in \omega$:*

$$\begin{aligned} \pi_n &\sqsubseteq \pi_{n+1} && (14) \\ \pi_n \circ \pi_m &= \pi_m \circ \pi_n \\ &= \pi_{\min(n,m)} && (15) \\ \bigsqcup_{n \in \omega} \pi_n &= 1_D && (16) \\ \pi_0 &= \bot_{[D \to D]}. && (17) \end{aligned}$$

□

Often we shall write d_n instead of $\pi_n(d)$ for $d \in D$, and take $d_\infty = d$ for every $d \in D$. The *rank* of an element d of D, $\mathbf{rk}(d)$, is the least $n \in \omega \cup \{\infty\}$ such that $d = d_n$.

If D is a cpo with a notion of approximation, set:

$$d \lhd_n e \Leftrightarrow d = e_n$$

for $d, e \in D$ and $n \in \omega \cup \{\infty\}$, and define:

$$d \lhd e \Leftrightarrow d \lhd_n e, \text{ for some } n \in \omega \cup \{\infty\}.$$

Proposition 2 *The structure $\langle D, \lhd \rangle$ is a partially ordered set with least element $\bot_D$.*
□

Observe that the relation $\lhd$ is in a sense orthogonal to the cpo ordering $\sqsubseteq$: $d \lhd e$ implies $d \sqsubseteq e$ but the converse fails in general. The structure $\langle D, \lhd \rangle$ will turn out to be a cpo with the property that if each of the functions π_n has finite image (*i.e.* D is a *profinite domain* in the sense of [19]) then $\langle D, \lhd \rangle$ has a countable basis of finite elements.

Proposition 3 *If $X \subseteq D$ has an upper bound with respect to $\lhd$ or is $\lhd$-directed, then it is a countable chain.*

Proof: If $x, y \in X$, then $x \lhd z$ and $y \lhd z$ for any upper bound z of X. So, for some $n, m \in \omega \cup \{\infty\}$ we have $x = z_n$ and $y = z_m$ and it is immediate to check that either $x \lhd y$ or $y \lhd x$ using equation (15), showing that X is a chain. The same argument applies when X is a $\lhd$-directed subset of D. For every $n \in \omega$, X contains at most one element of rank n: infact, if $x, y \in X$ and $\mathbf{rk}(x) = \mathbf{rk}(y) = n$ we have $x = z_n = y$ for the upper bound z of x and y, thus X is countable. □

Proposition 4 *Let $\{d^{(i)}\}_{i \in \omega} \subseteq D$ be a sequence of elements of D such that*

$$d^{(0)} \lhd d^{(1)} \lhd d^{(2)} \lhd \ldots \lhd d^{(i)} \lhd d^{(i+1)} \lhd \ldots$$

If $n \leq \mathbf{rk}(d^{(j)})$ for some element $d^{(j)}$ in the sequence, then $\{(d^{(i)})_n\}_{i \in \omega}$ stabilizes at $(d^{(j)})_n$.

Proof: There exists a function

$$k : \omega \longrightarrow (\omega \cup \{\infty\})$$

such that

$$d^{(0)} \lhd_{k(0)} d^{(1)} \lhd_{k(1)} d^{(2)} \lhd_{k(2)} \cdots \lhd_{k(i-1)} d^{(i)} \lhd_{k(i)} d^{(i+1)} \lhd_{k(i+1)} \cdots$$

For every $m \geq 0$:

$$d^{(j)} = (d^{(j+m)})_{\min(k(j),k(j+1),\ldots,k(j+m))} \tag{18}$$

holds by definition, yielding

$$(d^{(j)})_n = (d^{(j+m)})_{\min(n,k(j),k(j+1),\ldots,k(j+m))}. \tag{19}$$

Equation (18) entails that $k(j+l) \geq n$ for $0 \leq l \leq m$, so we finally have

$$(d^{(j)})_n = (d^{(j+m)})_n$$

which proves the conclusion. □

Given an (infinite) directed subset of $\langle D, \lhd \rangle$, we know that it can be written as:

$$d^{(0)} \lhd d^{(1)} \lhd d^{(2)} \lhd \ldots \lhd d^{(i)} \lhd d^{(i+1)} \lhd \ldots$$

and also that, for all $i \in \omega$, $d^{(i)} \sqsubseteq d^{(i+1)}$. So we can define:

$$\bigvee_{i \in \omega} d^{(i)} = \bigsqcup_{i \in \omega} d^{(i)}.$$

Proposition 5 *$\bigvee_{i\in\omega} d^{(i)}$ is the least upper bound of $\{d^{(i)}\}_{i\in\omega}$ in $\langle D, \lhd \rangle$.*

Proof: Given $i \in \omega$, let $n = \mathbf{rk}(d^{(i)})$. It follows from continuity of approximation mappings and the preceding Proposition that:

$$(\bigvee_{i\in\omega} d^{(i)})_n = (\bigsqcup_{i\in\omega} d^{(i)})_n = \bigsqcup_{i\in\omega} (d^{(i)})_n = d^{(i)},$$

so $d^{(i)} \lhd \bigvee_{i\in\omega} d^{(i)}$ for all $i \in \omega$ and $\bigvee_{i\in\omega} d^{(i)}$ is an upper bound of the sequence. In order to prove that it is the least such, assume that $d^{(i)} \lhd e$ for all $i \in \omega$. Then $d^{(i)} = e_{k(i)}$ for some function $k : \omega \longrightarrow (\omega \cup \{\infty\})$. The only interesting case is when the sequence $\{\mathbf{rk}(d^{(i)})\}$ is unbounded, and $\forall i \in \omega.\mathbf{rk}(d^{(i)}) < \infty$: we show that in this case $\bigvee_{i\in\omega} d^{(i)} = e$. Otherwise there would exist $n \in \omega$ such that

$$(\bigvee_{i\in\omega} d^{(i)})_n \neq e_n$$

and $(\bigvee_{i\in\omega} d^{(i)})_n = (d^{(j)})_n$, where j is the least index for which $\mathbf{rk}(d^{(j)}) \geq n$, by the preceding Proposition. It is sufficient now to observe that $d^{(j)} = e_{k(j)}$, so $(d^{(j)})_n = e_{\min(k(j),n)}$. If $k(j) < n$ then $\mathbf{rk}(d^{(j)}) < n$, contradicting the assumption on j, and if $n \leq k(j)$ then we get $e_n \neq e_n$, thus giving the desired conclusion. □

Let $D^{<\omega} = \{d | d = d_n, \text{ for some } n \in \omega\}$. Denoting by $K(D)$ the set of finite (= isolated = compact) elements of the domain D we have the following formula:

Proposition 6 $K(\langle D, \lhd \rangle) = D^{<\omega}$.

Proof: ($\subseteq$) It is sufficient to check that if for every increasing $\lhd$-chain $\{d^{(i)}\}$ we have

$$(d \lhd \bigvee_{i \in \omega} d^{(i)}) \Rightarrow (\exists k \in \omega . d \lhd d^{(k)}),$$

then $d \in D^{<\omega}$. Consider the chain $\{d^{(i)}\}_{i\in\omega}$ where $d^{(i)} = d_i$. Of course $d \lhd \bigvee_{i\in\omega} d_i$. If $d \lhd d_n$ for some $n \in \omega$ then $d = (d_n)_m$ for some m, so d has the form d_k where $k = \min(n, m)$, and finally $d \in D^{<\omega}$.
($\supseteq$) If $d_n \lhd \bigvee_{i\in\omega} d^{(i)}$ then $d_n = (d^{(j)})_m$ for some $j \in \omega$ and $m \in \omega \cup \infty$, and $(d^{(j)})_m \lhd d^{(j)}$, so the finiteness condition (with respect to $\lhd$) is satisfied. □

Observe that if $\mathbf{card}(\pi_n(D)) < \aleph_0$ for each $n \in \omega$ then $K(D)$ is a countable set, so in this case $\langle D, \lhd \rangle$ is an ω-algebraic cpo. Summarising the preceding discussion we obtain:

Proposition 7 *The structure $\langle D, \lhd \rangle$ is a Scott domain. If*

$$\forall n \in \omega . \mathbf{card}(\pi_n(D)) < \aleph_0$$

then $\langle D, \lhd \rangle$ has a countable basis. □

There is more to the approximation structure of a cpo D with a notion of approximation than the existence of a domain of the form $\langle D, \lhd \rangle$: it permits the definition of a class of functions on D with properties that will turn out to be essential for showing the existence of type interpretations in the next section. Explicitly, we shall call a **Greibach function** any function from D to itself satisfying:

$$\pi_{n+1} \circ f \circ \pi_n = \pi_{n+1} \circ f.$$

Proposition 8 *Let $\{d^{(i)}\}_{i\in\omega}$ be a sequence of elements of D such that for every $n \in \omega$ the condition*

$$\pi_n(d^{(n+1)}) = d^{(n)} \tag{20}$$

is satisfied. Then, for all $m > n$, $\pi_n(d^{(m)}) = d^{(n)}$.

Proof: By induction on $m - n$. The basis is true by assumption, while for the induction step we calculate: $d^{(n)} = \pi_n(d^{(m)}) = (\pi_n \circ \pi_m)(d^{(m+1)}) = \pi_n(d^{(m+1)})$, using the induction hypothesis. □

Proposition 9 *Assume that the sequence $\{d^{(i)}\}_{i\in\omega}$ satisfies (20). Then $\pi_n(\bigsqcup_{i\in\omega} d^{(i)}) = d^{(n)}$ for all $n \in \omega$.*

Proof: In the first place observe that the set is indeed an increasing $\sqsubseteq$-chain, because $d^{(n)} = \pi_n(d^{(n+1)}) \sqsubseteq d^{(n+1)}$, for all $n \in \omega$. So the element $\bigsqcup_{i\in\omega} d^{(i)}$ exists and it is sufficient to calculate:

$$\begin{aligned} \pi_n(\bigsqcup_{i\in\omega} d^{(i)}) &= \\ &= \bigsqcup_{i\in\omega}(\pi_n(d^{(i)})) \\ &= \bigsqcup_{i\geq n}(\pi_n(d^{(i)})) \\ &= d^{(n)}. \end{aligned}$$

□

Proposition 10 *Every Greibach function over a cpo D with a notion of approximation has a unique fixed point.*

Proof: Define a sequence of elements of D as follows:

$$\begin{aligned} x_0 &= \bot_D \\ x_{(n+1)} &= \pi_{n+1}(f(x_{(n)})). \end{aligned}$$

An inductive argument shows that the sequence $\{x_{(n)}\}_{n\in\omega}$ satisfies (20): the basis is obvious from property (17) of the notion of approximation. If $n > 0$ we have:

$$\begin{aligned} \pi_n(x_{(n+1)}) &= \pi_n(\pi_{n+1}(f(x_{(n)}))) \\ &= \pi_n(f(x_{(n)})) \\ &= \pi_n(f(\pi_{n-1}(x_{(n)}))) \\ &= \pi_n(f(x_{(n-1)})). \end{aligned}$$

Also, the sequence $\{x_{(n)}\}_{n\in\omega}$ is increasing:

$$\begin{aligned} x_{(n)} &= \pi_n(f(x_{(n-1)})) \\ &= \pi_n(f(\pi_{n-1}(x_{(n)}))) \\ &= \pi_n(f(x_{(n)})) \\ &\sqsubseteq \pi_{n+1}(f(x_{(n)})) \\ &= x_{(n+1)}. \end{aligned}$$

Set now $x = \bigsqcup_{n\in\omega} x_{(n)}$, and observe that, by the preceding Proposition, $\pi_n(x) = x_{(n)}$. By induction we check that x is a fixed point of f, that is we verify that, for all $n \in \omega$, $\pi_n(f(x)) = \pi_n(x)$. Infact $\pi_n(f(x)) = \pi_n(f(\pi_{n-1}(x))) = \pi_n(f(x_{(n-1)})) = x_{(n)} = \pi_n(x)$. Once more by induction on n we prove that the fixed point of f is unique: if $f(y) = y$ for some $y \in D$, then $\pi_n(x) = \pi_n(f(x)) = \pi_n(f(\pi_{n-1}(x))) = \pi_n(f(\pi_{n-1}(y))) = \pi_n(f(y)) = \pi_n(y)$, concluding the proof. □

A weaker version of this theorem, needing the assumption of continuity of the Greibach function $f : D \longrightarrow D$, for domains D satisfying conditions similar to those defining a notion of approximation over them, is attributed to S. Eilenberg in [24], p. 61.

4 Type interpretations

Having analyzed in some detail the structure of the domain we use for the interpretation of (untyped) terms we proceed now to single out a class of structured collections of values from D which is closed with respect to the type forming operations of the language, as introduced in Definition 2. While for type inference systems it turns out (see [21], [11]) that one such class is that of *ideals* of D, *i.e.* the non empty closed subsets of D in the Scott topology, in the present context we need further constraints in order to obtain an extensional, strongly typed structure for the language. Extensionality is achieved by moving from subsets of D to *partial equivalence relations* (*per*'s) over D. General per's are not closed under recursive definitions: for this we have to restrict this class to those partial equivalence relations that respect both the cpo and the approximation structures of D.

Definition 4 (Complete uniform per's) *A nonempty partial equivalence relation R over D is* **complete** *and* **uniform** *if the following two conditions are satisfied:*

Completeness *If $\{d^{(i)}\}_{i\in\omega}$ and $\{e^{(i)}\}_{i\in\omega}$ are increasing chains in D such that, for all $i \in \omega$, $d^{(i)}Re^{(i)}$, then also*

$$(\bigsqcup_{i\in\omega} d^{(i)})R(\bigsqcup_{i\in\omega} e^{(i)}).$$

Uniformity *If dRe then, for all $n \in \omega$, d_nRe_n.*

□

This class has been introduced in [2], [10]. The terminology has been modified according to [1]. Denoting by $\mathcal{R}(D)$ the collection of complete and uniform per's over D, we observe that $\mathcal{R}(D)$ is closed under arbitrary intersections, hence it is a complete lattice and, in particular a cpo whose least element is the per I, defined by the condition

$$d \,\mathsf{I}\, e \Leftrightarrow d = e = \bot_D.$$

It is clearly complete and uniform, and indeed it is the least such, remembering that for all $d \in D$, $d_0 = \bot_D$. If $R \in \mathcal{R}(D)$, define the complete and uniform per R_n for all $n \in \omega$ by the condition:

$$R_n = \{\langle d_n, e_n\rangle : \langle d, e\rangle \in R\}.$$

This is easily shown to provide a notion of approximation over the cpo $\langle \mathcal{R}(D), \subseteq \rangle$:

Proposition 11 *For every $\mathcal{X} \subseteq \mathcal{R}(D)$:*

$$(\bigsqcup_{R\in\mathcal{X}} R)_n = \bigsqcup_{R\in\mathcal{X}} R_n$$

where $\bigsqcup \mathcal{X} = \bigcap\{S \in \mathcal{R}(D) \mid S \supseteq \mathcal{X}\}$.

Proof: Define, for $T \in \mathcal{R}(D)$ and $n \in \omega$, $T^{-n} = \{\langle d, e\rangle \mid \langle d_n, e_n\rangle \in T\}$. It is readily seen that $T^{-n} \in \mathcal{R}(D)$ and that $T \supseteq R_n$ if and only if $T^{-n} \supseteq R$. Now, if $\langle d, e\rangle \in (\bigcap\{S \in \mathcal{R}(D) \mid S \supseteq \mathcal{X}\})_n$ then $\langle a, b\rangle \in S$ for all $S \supseteq \mathcal{X}$, where a, b are such that $a_n = d, b_n = e$. If $T \supseteq R_n$ for all $R \in \mathcal{X}$ then $T^{-n} \supseteq R$ for all $R \in \mathcal{X}$ and $\langle a, b\rangle \in T^{-n}$, so $\langle d, e\rangle \in T$, and, as T is arbitrary, $\langle d, e\rangle \in \bigsqcup_{R\in\mathcal{X}} R_n$. Conversely, if $\langle d, e\rangle \in R_n$ for some $R \in \mathcal{X}$ then $\langle d, e\rangle \in R$ for some $R \in \mathcal{X}$, so $\langle d, e\rangle \in S$ for all $S \supseteq \mathcal{X}$. Then $\langle d, e\rangle \in \bigsqcup_{R\in\mathcal{X}} R$ and $\langle d_n, e_n\rangle = \langle d, e\rangle \in (\bigsqcup_{R\in\mathcal{X}} R)_n$. This shows that $(\bigsqcup_{R\in\mathcal{X}} R)_n$ is an upper bound of the family $\{R_n\}_{R\in\mathcal{X}}$, concluding the proof. □

4.1 Type constructors

The domain constructors involved in the definition of the domain D can be lifted to operations on the class of complete uniform per's, providing the interpretations of type constructors.

- If $R \in \mathcal{R}(D)$ and $d, e \in D_\bot$, define

$$dR_\bot e \Leftrightarrow (\downarrow d)R(\downarrow e); \tag{21}$$

- If $R, S \in \mathcal{R}(D)$ and $d, e \in [D \oplus D]$, define

$$\begin{aligned} d(R \oplus S)e \quad \Leftrightarrow \quad & d = \mathsf{left}(a), e = \mathsf{left}(b) \text{ and } aRb, \text{ for some } a, b \in D \\ & \text{or} \\ & d = \mathsf{right}(a), e = \mathsf{right}(b) \text{ and } aRb, \text{ for } a, b \in D \\ & \text{or} \\ & d = e = \bot_D; \end{aligned} \tag{22}$$

- If $R, S \in \mathcal{R}(D)$ and $d, e \in [D \otimes D]$, define

$$d(R \otimes S)e \Leftrightarrow d'Re' \text{ and } d''Se''; \tag{23}$$

- If $R, S \in \mathcal{R}(D)$ and $d, e \in [D \times D]$, define

$$\begin{aligned} d(R \times S)e \quad \Leftrightarrow \quad & \mathsf{first}(d)\ R\ \mathsf{first}(e) \\ & \text{and} \\ & \mathsf{second}(d)\ S\ \mathsf{second}(e); \end{aligned} \tag{24}$$

- If $R, S \in \mathcal{R}(D)$ and $d, e \in [D \to D]$, define

$$d(R \to S)e \Leftrightarrow (aRb \Rightarrow (d \cdot a)S(e \cdot b)). \tag{25}$$

The next proposition provides the clue to interpreting types as complete and uniform per's: it states that type constructors are Greibach functions over the cpo $\langle \mathcal{R}(D), \subseteq \rangle$.

Proposition 12 *1. If $R, S \in \mathcal{R}(D)$ then also $R_\bot, R \oplus S, R \otimes S, R \times S, R \to S \in \mathcal{R}(D)$.*

2. For all $R, S \in \mathcal{R}(D)$ we have, for all $n \in \omega$:

$$\mathsf{I}_n = \mathsf{I} \tag{26}$$
$$(R_\bot)_{n+1} = ((R_n)_\bot)_{n+1} \tag{27}$$
$$(R \oplus S)_{n+1} = (R_n \oplus S_n)_{n+1} \tag{28}$$
$$(R \otimes S)_{n+1} = (R_n \otimes S_n)_{n+1} \tag{29}$$
$$(R \times S)_{n+1} = (R_n \times S_n)_{n+1} \tag{30}$$
$$(R \to S)_{n+1} = (R_n \to S_n)_{n+1} \tag{31}$$

Proof: Easy, using the properties 4, 6, 7, 8, 9, 10, 11, 13 of the notion of approximation on D. □

4.2 Interpretation of types

Recursive types will be considered as notations for their regular unfoldings in the set $R_\Omega(V)$: for every type $\sigma \in T_\mu$ its interpretation $[\![\sigma]\!]\eta$, relative to a *type environment* η assigning complete uniform per's to type variables, shall be defined as

$$[\![\sigma]\!]\eta = \mathcal{R}[\![\sigma^*]\!]\eta$$

where

$$\mathcal{R}[\![.]\!]\eta : R_\Omega(V) \longrightarrow \mathcal{R}(D)$$

satisfies the conditions:

- $\mathcal{R}[\![t]\!]\eta = \eta(t)$
- $\mathcal{R}[\![\mathsf{I}]\!]\eta = \mathsf{I}$
- $\mathcal{R}[\![\sigma_\perp]\!]\eta = (\mathcal{R}[\![\sigma]\!])_\perp$
- $\mathcal{R}[\![\sigma \oplus \tau]\!]\eta = \mathcal{R}[\![\sigma]\!]\eta \oplus \mathcal{R}[\![\tau]\!]\eta$
- $\mathcal{R}[\![\sigma \otimes \tau]\!]\eta = \mathcal{R}[\![\sigma]\!]\eta \otimes \mathcal{R}[\![\tau]\!]\eta$
- $\mathcal{R}[\![\sigma \times \tau]\!]\eta = \mathcal{R}[\![\sigma]\!]\eta \times \mathcal{R}[\![\tau]\!]\eta$
- $\mathcal{R}[\![\sigma \rightarrow \tau]\!]\eta = \mathcal{R}[\![\sigma]\!]\eta \rightarrow \mathcal{R}[\![\tau]\!]\eta$.

Observe that then

$$[\![\mu t.\sigma]\!]\eta = [\![\sigma]\!]\eta[t \mapsto [\![\mu t.\sigma]\!]\eta].$$

While for types in $T_{\Sigma_\Omega}(V)$ the preceding clauses *define* a unique extension of the type environment, this does not happen when the types involved are regular, and an independent justification is needed in such a case. However, according to Theorem 1, in order to find an interpretation for regular types as complete uniform per's it will suffice to endow $\mathcal{R}(D)$ with an iterative Σ_Ω- algebra structure. The constant Ω will be interpreted as the per consisting of the only element $\langle \perp_D, \perp_D \rangle$, but it should be emphasized that this is by no means necessary: actually, Ω can be interpreted as an arbitrary per (see [11], where this remark is made in the context of an ideal model for a type inference system and the ideal which interprets Ω is taken as an additional parameter to the interpretation function. This may also be seen as a consequence of results in [4,5]).

Lemma 1 *Given a type environment η, let η_n be any environment possibly differing from η in that $\eta_n(t) = (\eta(t))_n$ for some type variable t. Then:*

1. *For every finite type σ, every type environment η and every $m \geq n$:*

$$(\mathcal{R}[\![\sigma]\!]\eta)_n = (\mathcal{R}[\![\sigma]\!]\eta_m)_n.$$

2. *For every finite type $\sigma \notin V$, every type environment η and every $n \in \omega$:*

$$(\mathcal{R}[\![\sigma]\!]\eta)_{n+1} = (\mathcal{R}[\![\sigma]\!]\eta_n)_{n+1}.$$

Proof: The two parts are both proved by induction on σ. The first is clear, while for the second it is sufficient to use properties 26, 27, 28, 29, 30, 31. For example, when $\sigma = \sigma_1 \rightarrow \sigma_2$:

$$\begin{aligned}(\mathcal{R}[\![\sigma]\!]\eta_n)_{n+1} &= (\mathcal{R}[\![\sigma_1 \rightarrow \sigma_2]\!]\eta_n)_{n+1} \\ &= (\mathcal{R}[\![\sigma_1]\!]\eta_n \rightarrow \mathcal{R}[\![\sigma_2]\!]\eta_n)_{n+1} \\ &= ((\mathcal{R}[\![\sigma_1]\!]\eta_n)_n \rightarrow (\mathcal{R}[\![\sigma_2]\!]\eta_n)_n)_{n+1} \\ &= ((\mathcal{R}[\![\sigma_1]\!]\eta)_n \rightarrow (\mathcal{R}[\![\sigma_2]\!]\eta)_n)_{n+1} \\ &= (\mathcal{R}[\![\sigma_1]\!]\eta \rightarrow \mathcal{R}[\![\sigma_2]\!]\eta)_{n+1} \\ &= (\mathcal{R}[\![\sigma]\!]\eta)_{n+1}\end{aligned}$$

all other cases being similar. □

We now show that every Greibach system defines a Greibach function from a cartesian power of $\mathcal{R}(D)$ to itself.

Lemma 2 *For every $k \geq 1$, every k-tuple of types $\sigma_1, \ldots, \sigma_k \in T_\Sigma(V)$ such that no σ_i is a variable, and every type environment η the function $f : \mathcal{R}(D)^k \longrightarrow \mathcal{R}(D)^k$ defined by the assignment:*

$$\langle X^{(i)}\rangle_{1\leq i\leq k} \longmapsto \langle \mathcal{R}[\![\sigma_i]\!]\eta[t_1 \mapsto X^{(1)}, \ldots, t_k \mapsto X^{(k)}]\rangle_{1\leq i\leq k}$$

satisfies the condition:

$$\forall X^{(1)}, \ldots, X^{(k)} \in \mathcal{R}(D)^k.(f\langle X^{(1)}, \ldots, X^{(k)}\rangle)_{n+1} = (f((\langle X^{(1)}, \ldots, X^{(k)}\rangle)_n)_{n+1}$$

where $\mathcal{R}(D)^k$ is the kth power of $\mathcal{R}(D)$ and the notion of approximation over $\mathcal{R}(D)^k$ is defined coordinatewise by the condition:

$$(\langle X^{(1)}, \ldots, X^{(k)}\rangle)_n = \langle X^{(1)}_n, \ldots, X^{(k)}_n\rangle$$

for all $n \in \omega$.

Proof: A straightforward consequence of Lemma 1. □

Using the unique fixed point property of Greibach functions over cpo's with a notion of approximation, we may then conclude:

Theorem 2 *The structure $\langle \mathcal{R}(D), \mathsf{I}, (.)_\perp, \oplus, \otimes, \times, \rightarrow\rangle$ is an iterative algebra.* □

Corollary 1 *For any type environment $\eta : V \longrightarrow \mathcal{R}(D)$ there exists a unique type interpretation extending η.* □

Clearly, the type interpretations obtained satisfy the subtyping rule for function types mentioned in the Introduction, namely:

$$\frac{\sigma' \leq \sigma \quad \tau \leq \tau'}{\sigma \rightarrow \tau \leq \sigma' \rightarrow \tau'}$$

where a type environment η satisfies a subtyping statement $\sigma \leq \tau$ whenever $\mathcal{R}[\![\sigma]\!]\eta \subseteq \mathcal{R}[\![\tau]\!]\eta$.

Although we have not specified the set of terms of the language whose type system we are considering, it is however important to remark that the interpretation of typed terms can be defined straightforwardly given the interpretation of types as partial equivalence relations over D. Infact, given a typed term $e : \sigma$ we can take its (typed) meaning to be the equivalence class of its interpretation in D modulo the per that interprets σ, after showing that this element of D belongs to the field of the relation by a standard inductive argument on the construction of the typed term as in [23], [10].

5 Conclusions

A first remark on the above ideas concerns their relationship with the metric approach. Indeed, a metrics can be defined on every cpo D with a notion of approximation, in such a way that D becomes a complete metric space. Greibach functions are easily seen to be contractive mappings over it, so that the existence and uniqueness of fixed points for such functions is a consequence of Banach's theorem. Interestingly, a closer examination of the processes of construction of fixed points in the two approaches shows that they coincide also in a strong intensional sense. Yet we believe an advantage of the present formulation to be on one side its emphasis on the algebraic aspects of the mechanisms underlying the interpretation, on the other the avoidance of any reference to structure not explicitly carried by the sets involved.

Another point of interest is to find out to what extent the present framework can be helpful for the interpretation of higher order type systems including polymorphism and kinds. A comparison with independent results by Bruce and Mitchell [7] shows the possibility of further generalizing the present approach in order to deal with the semantics of such systems as well. Indeed, the *rank-ordered sets* used in [7] as a structuring concept of which the class of complete and uniform per's is an instance, form a cartesian closed category, a key property for the interpretation of kinds. It turns out that the formalisms of rank-ordered sets and cpo's with a notion of approximation are equivalent, and structures in both classes are instances of the *complete projection spaces* studied in [14], [18] and motivated by an attempt to define algebraic specifications for process algebras in the sense of Bergstra and Klop (see, for example, [3]).

Finally, an interesting open question is to investigate the relationship of the model of the metalanguage for denotational semantics presented in this paper with the ordinary, domain-theoretic model. This shall involve also an analysis of the issues of *(complete) adequacy* discussed in [22].

Acknowledgements

The ideas discussed in this paper found their motivations in uncountably many discussions with Mario Coppo on recursive types. Jan Willem Klop brought to my attention the close similarity between cpo's with a notion of approximation and the projection spaces of [14], [18], and the referees made useful comments on a previous version of this paper.

The research was supported by 40% MURST.

References

[1] M. Abadi and G.D. Plotkin. A per model of polymorphism and recursive types. In *Proc. Symposium on Logic and Computer Science*, pages 355–365. IEEE, 1990.

[2] R. Amadio. Recursion over realizability structures. *Information and Computation*, 91(1):55–85, 1991.

[3] J.A. Bergstra and J.W. Klop. A convergence theorem in process algebra. Technical Report CS-R8733, CWI, Amsterdam, 1987.

[4] S.L. Bloom, C.C. Elgot, and J.B. Wright. Solutions of the iteration equation and extensions of the scalar iteration operation. *SIAM Journal on Computing*, 9(1):25–45, 1980.

[5] S.L. Bloom, C.C. Elgot, and J.B. Wright. Vector iteration in pointed iterative theories. *SIAM Journal on Computing*, 9(3):525–540, 1980.

[6] K. Bruce and G. Longo. A modest model of records, inheritance and bounded quantification. In *Proc. Symposium on Logic and Computer Science*, pages 38–50. IEEE, 1988.

[7] K. Bruce and J.C. Mitchell. PER models of subtyping recursive types and higher-order polymorphism. 1991. To appear, POPL 1992.

[8] L. Cardelli. A semantics of multiple inheritance. *Information and Computation*, 76:138–164, 1988.

[9] L. Cardelli and P. Wegner. On understanding types, data abstraction and polymorphism. *ACM Computing Surveys*, 17:471–522, 1985.

[10] F. Cardone. Recursive types for Fun. *Theoretical Computer Science*, 83:29–56, 1991.

[11] F. Cardone and M. Coppo. Type inference with recursive types. Syntax and Semantics. *Information and Computation*, 92(1):48–80, 1991.

[12] M. Coppo. A completeness theorem for recursively defined types. In W. Brauer, editor, *Proc. 12th International Colloquium on Automata, Languages and Programming, LNCS 194*, pages 120–129. Springer, 1985.

[13] B. Courcelle. Fundamental properties of infinite trees. *Theoretical Computer Science*, 25:95–169, 1983.

[14] H. Ehrig, F. Parisi-Presicce, P. Boehm, C. Rieckhoff, C. Dimitrovici, and M. Grosse-Rhode. Algebraic data type and process specification based on projection spaces. In *Recent trends in data type specification, LNCS 332*, pages 23–43. Springer, 1988.

[15] C.C. Elgot. Monadic computation and iterative algebraic theories. In H.E.Rose and J.C.Shepherdson, editors, *Logic Colloquium 73*, pages 175–318, Amsterdam, 1975. North Holland.

[16] C.C. Elgot, S.L. Bloom, and R. Tindell. The algebraic structure of rooted trees. *Journal of Computer and System Sciences*, 16(3):362–399, 1978.

[17] J. Goguen, J.W. Thatcher, E.G. Wagner, and J.B. Wright. Initial algebra semantics and continuous algebras. *Journal of the ACM*, 24:68–95, 1977.

[18] M. Grosse-Rhode and H. Ehrig. Transformation of combined data type and process specifications using projection algebras. In *Stepwise refinement of distributed systems, LNCS 430*, pages 301–339. Springer, 1989.

[19] C. Gunter. Universal profinite domains. *Information and Computation*, 72:1–30, 1987.

[20] C.A. Gunter and D.S. Scott. Semantic domains. In J. van Leeuwen, editor, *Handbook of Theoretical Computer Science, Volume B*, pages 633–674, Amsterdam, 1990. North Holland.

[21] D. MacQueen, G.D. Plotkin, and R. Sethi. An ideal model for recursive polymorphic types. *Information and Control*, 71((1/2)):95–130, 1986.

[22] A.R. Meyer. Semantical paradigms: Notes for an invited lecture, with two appendices by Stavros S. Cosmadakis. In *3rd Symposium on Logic in Computer Science*, pages 236–255. IEEE, 1988.

[23] J.C. Mitchell. A type inference approach to reduction properties and semantics of polymorphic expressions. In *Proc. ACM Conference on LISP and Functional Programming*, pages 308–319, 1986.

[24] D.S. Scott. Lectures on a mathematical theory of computation. Lecture notes, Merton College, Oxford, Michaelmas Term, 1980.

[25] M. Smyth and G.D. Plotkin. The category-theoretic solution of recursive domain equations. *SIAM Journal of Computing*, 11:761–783, 1982.

[26] J. Tiuryn. Unique fixed points *vs.* least fixed points. *Theoretical Computer Science*, 12:229–254, 1980.

Decidability of reachability and disjoint union of term rewriting systems

Anne-Cécile CARON *
Laboratoire d'Informatique Fondamentale de Lille
UFR IEEA. UA 369 CNRS.
Université des Sciences et Techniques de Lille I
59655 Villeneuve d'Ascq Cedex. FRANCE.
email: caronc@lifl.lifl.fr

Abstract

The reachability problem for term rewriting systems is to decide whether, given a system S and two terms t and t', t can be reduced in t' with rules of S. We study the disjoint union of term rewriting systems whose reachability problem is decidable and give sufficient conditions for obtaining the modularity of decidability of this problem.

1 Introduction

If $\mathcal{F}_1$ and $\mathcal{F}_2$ are two disjoint finite alphabets, and if $(\mathcal{F}_1, \mathcal{R}_1)$ and $(\mathcal{F}_2, \mathcal{R}_2)$ are two term rewriting systems on $\mathcal{F}_1$ and $\mathcal{F}_2$, the disjoint union $\mathcal{R}_1 \oplus \mathcal{R}_2$ of $(\mathcal{F}_1, \mathcal{R}_1)$ and $(\mathcal{F}_2, \mathcal{R}_2)$ is the term rewriting system $(\mathcal{F}_1 \cup \mathcal{F}_2, \mathcal{R}_1 \cup \mathcal{R}_2)$. A property of term rewriting system is modular if it is preserved under disjoint union.

In programming, modularity permits to decompose a problem into simpler problems easier to solve. For inferring properties of term rewriting systems (like confluence or termination) several methods are known but they have the greatest chance of succeeding if the systems concerned have few rewrite rules. Therefore, it is interesting to have results at our disposal which state that a term rewriting system has a certain property P if it can be partitioned into smaller term rewriting systems which all have the property P

Starting with Toyama, several authors studied modular properties. Toyama [Toy87b] showed that confluence is preserved under disjoint union. In [Toy87a], he found a counterexample for modularity of termination (also called strong-normalization). Rusinowitch [Rus87] and Middeldorp [Mid89b] give sufficient conditions for the termination of the disjoint union of terminating term rewriting systems. Kurihara and Ohuchi [KO90] showed that termination is a modular property of term rewriting systems whose termination can be shown by a simplification ordering. Barendregt and Klop in [Toy87a] and Drosten

*This work was supported in part by PRC-Mathématique et Informatique and by ESPRIT2-working group ASMICS.

[Dro89] gave counterexamples of modularity of completeness (confluence + termination). Toyama, Klop and Barendregt [TKB89] showed that the restriction to left-linear TRS's is sufficient for obtaining the modularity of completeness. Middeldorp [Mid89a] showed that the property of having unique normal forms is modular for general TRS's. He gives a survey of modular aspects of TRS's in [Mid90] and studied more particularly conditional TRS's [Mid91].
In this paper, we study the property of decidability of reachability. The reachability problem for term rewriting systems is to decide whether, given a system S and two terms t and t', t can be reduced in t' with rules of S. Reachability is generally undecidable. But in particular it is decidable for quasi-ground rewrite systems [Oya86] or monadic systems (see [BJW82] and [GB85] for a survey of monadic systems). First, we prove that decidability of reachability is modular for left-linear TRS's without collapsing rules, or for linear TRS's with possibly collapsing rules. In particular, we study the complexity of our algorithm of decidability when the two systems are string rewriting systems. In a second section, we prove that decidability of reachability is not preserved under disjoint union if the two systems are not left-linear. Eventually, we show that decidability of ground reachability is not a modular property, even for linear TRS's without collapsing rules.

2 Preliminaries

Most of the following definitions originate from Toyama [Toy87b] and Middeldorp [Mid90]. Let $\mathcal{V}$ be a countably infinite set of *variables*. A *signature* or an *alphabet* is a set $\mathcal{F}$ of *function symbols*. Associated with every $F \in \mathcal{F}$ is a natural number denoted its *arity*. Function symbols of arity 0 are called *constants*. The set of *terms* $\mathcal{T}(\mathcal{F},\mathcal{V})$ built from a signature $\mathcal{F}$ and a countably infinite set of variables $\mathcal{V}$ with $\mathcal{F}\cap\mathcal{V}=\emptyset$ is the smallest set such that $\mathcal{V}\subset\mathcal{T}(\mathcal{F},\mathcal{V})$ and if $F\in\mathcal{F}$ is an n-ary function symbol and $t_1,\cdots,t_n\in\mathcal{T}(\mathcal{F},\mathcal{V})$ then $F(t_1,\cdots,t_n)\in\mathcal{T}(\mathcal{F},\mathcal{V})$. The set of *ground terms* is the set of terms without variables. Identity of terms is denoted by $\equiv$.
A *term rewriting system* (TRS for short) is a pair $(\mathcal{F},\mathcal{R})$ consisting of a signature $\mathcal{F}$ and a set $\mathcal{R}\subset\mathcal{T}(\mathcal{F},\mathcal{V})\times\mathcal{T}(\mathcal{F},\mathcal{V})$ of *rewrite rules*. Every rule (l,r) satisfies the following two constraints: the left-hand side l is not a variable and the variables which occur in the right-hand side r also occur in l.
A *context* $C[,...,]$ is a 'term' which contains at least one occurrence of a special constant $\Box$. If $C[,...,]$ is a context with n occurrences of $\Box$ and $t_1,\cdots,t_n$ are terms then $C[t_1,\cdots,t_n]$ is the result of replacing from the left to the right the occurrences of $\Box$ by $t_1,\cdots,t_n$. A context containing precisely one occurrence of $\Box$ is denoted by $C[\,]$. A term s is a subterm of a term t if there exists a context $C[\,]$ such that $t\equiv C[s]$.
The *rewrite relation* $\rightarrow_{\mathcal{R}}$ is defined as follows: $s\rightarrow_{\mathcal{R}} t$ if there exists a rewrite rule $l\rightarrow r$ in $\mathcal{R}$ a substitution σ and a context $C[\,]$ such that $s\equiv C[l^\sigma]$ and $t\equiv C[r^\sigma]$. The transitive-reflexive closure of $\rightarrow_{\mathcal{R}}$ is denoted by $\xrightarrow{*}_{\mathcal{R}}$. If $s\xrightarrow{*}_{\mathcal{R}} t$ we say that *s reduces to t*. Two terms t_1 and t_2 are *joinable*, notation $t_1\downarrow_{\mathcal{R}} t_2$, if there exists a term t_3 such that $t_1\xrightarrow{*}_{\mathcal{R}} t_3$ and $t_2\xrightarrow{*}_{\mathcal{R}} t_3$. Such a term t_3 is called *common reduct* of t_1 and t_2.
Let $(\mathcal{F}_1,\mathcal{R}_1)$ and $(\mathcal{F}_2,\mathcal{R}_2)$ two TRS's such that $\mathcal{F}_1\cap\mathcal{F}_2=\emptyset$. The *disjoint union* $\mathcal{R}_1\oplus\mathcal{R}_2$ of $(\mathcal{F}_1,\mathcal{R}_1)$ and $(\mathcal{F}_2,\mathcal{R}_2)$ is the TRS $(\mathcal{F}_1\cup\mathcal{F}_2,\mathcal{R}_1\cup\mathcal{R}_2)$. A property P is *modular* if: ($\mathcal{R}_1\oplus\mathcal{R}_2$ has the property $P\Leftrightarrow(\mathcal{F}_1,\mathcal{R}_1)$ and $(\mathcal{F}_2,\mathcal{R}_2)$ have the property P).

Let $(\mathcal{F}_1, \mathcal{R}_1)$ and $(\mathcal{F}_2, \mathcal{R}_2)$ be disjoint TRS's. Every term $t \in \mathcal{T}(\mathcal{F}_1 \cup \mathcal{F}_2, \mathcal{V})$ can be decomposed into $\mathcal{F}_1$-parts and $\mathcal{F}_2$-parts:

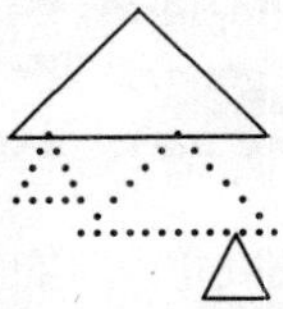

NOTATION: We abbreviate $\mathcal{F}_1 \cup \mathcal{F}_2$ to $\mathcal{F}_\oplus$ and $\mathcal{T}(\mathcal{F}_\oplus, \mathcal{V})$ in $\mathcal{T}_\oplus$. We write $\mathcal{T}_i$ instead of $\mathcal{T}(\mathcal{F}_i, \mathcal{V})$ for $i = 1, 2$. The following definitions give a formalism to the structure of terms of $\mathcal{T}_\oplus$.

- the *root symbol* of a term $t \in \mathcal{T}_\oplus$, denoted root(t), is defined by

$$\begin{cases} \text{root}(t) = F & \text{if } t \equiv F(t_1, \cdots, t_n) \\ \text{root}(t) = t & \text{if } t \in \mathcal{V} \end{cases}$$

- Let $t \equiv C[t_1, \cdots, t_n]$ with $C[,...,] \not\equiv \Box$. We write $t \equiv C[\![t_1, \cdots, t_n]\!]$ if $C[,\cdots,] \in \mathcal{T}(\mathcal{F}_a \cup \{\Box\}, \mathcal{V})$ and root(t_1),...,root$(t_n) \in \mathcal{F}_b$ for some $a, b \in \{1, 2\}$ with $a \neq b$. The t_i's are the *principal subterms* of t.

- The *rank* of a term $t \in \mathcal{T}_\oplus$ is defined by

$$\begin{cases} \text{rank}(t) = 1 & \text{if } t \in \mathcal{T}_1 \cup \mathcal{T}_2 \\ \text{rank}(t) = 1 + \max\{\text{rank}(t_i), 1 \leq i \leq n\} & \text{if } t = C[\![t_1, \cdots, t_n]\!] \end{cases}$$

  REMARK: If $s \xrightarrow{*}_{\mathcal{R}_1 \oplus \mathcal{R}_2} t$ then rank$(s) \geq$ rank(t).

- The multiset $S(t)$ of *special subterms* of a term $t \in \mathcal{T}_\oplus$ is defined as follows:

$$\begin{cases} S_1(t) & = < t > \\ S_{n+1}(t) & = < > \text{ if rank}(t) = 1 \\ & = S_n(t_1) \cup \cdots \cup S_n(t_m) \text{ if } t \equiv C[\![t_1, \cdots, t_m]\!] \end{cases}$$

  $S(t) = \bigcup_{i \geq 1} S_i(t)$

- The *topmost homogeneous part* of a term $t \in \mathcal{T}_\oplus$, notation top(t), is the result of replacing all the principal subterms of t by $\Box$, i.e.

$$\begin{cases} \text{top}(t) & = t \text{ if rank}(t) = 1 \\ & = C[,...,] \text{ if } t \equiv C[\![t_1, \cdots, t_n]\!] \end{cases}$$

- We define top'(t) by:

  – if rank$(t) = 1$ then top'$(t) = t$.

  – else, top'(t) is obtained from top(t) by replacing the p occurrences $\Box$ in top(t) by p distinct variables $x_1, \cdots, x_p$ such that for all $i \in [1, p]$, x_i does not occur in top(t).

  (top'(t) is defined only up to α-conversion).

- The multiset $P(t)$ of *parts* of a term $t \in \mathcal{T}_\oplus$ is defined by

$$P(t) = \{\text{top}'(s) | s \in S(t)\} = \text{top}'(S(t))$$

- The multiset $E(t)$ of *erasable parts* of a term $t \in \mathcal{T}_\oplus$ is defined by
$$E(t) = P(t) - (\mathcal{T}(\mathcal{F}_1, \emptyset) \cup \mathcal{T}(\mathcal{F}_2, \emptyset))$$
i.e. $E(t)$ is the multiset of non ground trees of $P(t)$.

EXAMPLE: We consider the following term t:

$$\{F, G, A, B\} \subseteq \mathcal{F}_1$$
$$\{e, f, c\} \subseteq \mathcal{F}_2$$
$$x \in \mathcal{V}$$

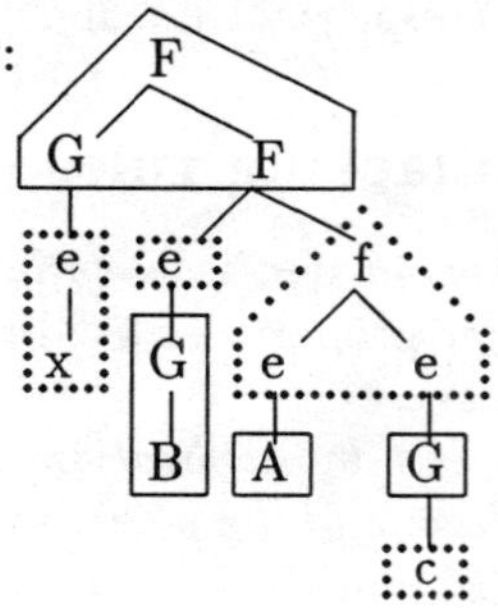

– The rank of t is 4.
– $t \equiv C[\![t_1, t_2, t_3]\!]$ with $C \equiv F(G(\square), F(\square, \square))$,
$t_1 \equiv e(x)$, $t_2 \equiv e(G(B))$, $t_3 \equiv f(e(A), e(G(c)))$.
– special subterms of t :
$S_1(t) =< t >$
$S_2(t) =< e(x),\ e(G(B)),\ f(e(A), e(G(c))) >$
$S_3(t) =< G(B),\ A,\ G(c) >$
$S_4(t) =< c >$
$S(t) = S_1(t) \cup S_2(t) \cup S_3(t) \cup S_4(t)$
– parts of t and erasable parts of t :
$E(t) =< F(G(x), F(y, z)),\ e(x),\ e(x),\ f(e(x), e(y)),\ G(x) >$
$P(t) = E(t) \cup < G(B),\ A,\ c >$

Let s be a term of $\mathcal{T}_\oplus$ and let $e_1, \cdots, e_k \in E(s)$. $\mathcal{R}_1$ and $\mathcal{R}_2$ are left-linear rewrite systems. We say that s' is obtained from s collapsing the erasable parts $e_1, \cdots, e_k$ if there exist k variables $x_1, \cdots, x_k$ respectively in $e_1, \cdots, e_k$ such that for all i in $[1, k]$, $e_i \xrightarrow{*}_{\mathcal{R}_1} x_i$ or $e_i \xrightarrow{*}_{\mathcal{R}_2} x_i$ and s' is built from s rewriting the e_i to x_i.
EXAMPLE: We consider the term t given in the previous example. The term t' built from t collapsing the erasable part $f(e(x), e(y))$ with the rule $f(e(x), e(y)) \xrightarrow{*}_{\mathcal{R}_2} x$ is $t' \equiv F(G(e(x)),\ F(e(G(B)),\ A))$.

In the following sections, we study the modularity of decidability of the reachability problem for TRS.

- Given a TRS $(\mathcal{F}, \mathcal{R})$ and two terms t_1 and t_2 in $\mathcal{T}(\mathcal{F}, \mathcal{V})$, the *reachability problem* for $(\mathcal{F}, \mathcal{R})$, t_1 and t_2 is to decide whether $t_1 \xrightarrow{*}_{\mathcal{R}} t_2$.

- We say that reachability is decidable for a class of TRS's if there exists an algorithm which can solve every reachability problem of this class.

- The problem of *ground reachability* is the reachability problem restricted to ground terms (i.e. without variables).

3 Left-linear TRS

A rewrite rule $l \to r$ is *left-linear* (resp. *right-linear*) if l (resp. r) does not contain multiple occurrences of the same variable. A TRS is left-linear (resp. right-linear) if all its rules are left-linear (resp. right-linear).

3.1 Without collapsing rules

A rule $l \to r$ is *collapsing* if r is a variable. We want to show that decidability of reachability is a modular property of left-linear TRS's without collapsing rules.

Definition 3.1 *Let $s \to t$ by application of a rewrite rule $l \to r$. We write $s \to^{\mathrm{i}} t$ if $l \to r$ is being applied in one of the principal subterms of s and we write $s \to^{\mathrm{o}} t$ otherwise. The relation $\to^{\mathrm{i}}$ is called* inner *reduction and $\to^{\mathrm{o}}$ is called* outer *reduction.*

Proposition 3.2 (Middeldorp) *Let $(\mathcal{F}_1, \mathcal{R}_1)$ and $(\mathcal{F}_2, \mathcal{R}_2)$ be disjoint left-linear TRS's without collapsing rules. For every reduction sequence $s \xrightarrow{*}_{\mathcal{R}_1 \oplus \mathcal{R}_2} t$ there exists a term s' such that $s \xrightarrow{*}^{\mathrm{o}} s' \xrightarrow{*}^{\mathrm{i}} t$*

Proposition 3.3 *Decidability of reachability is a modular property for left-linear TRS's without collapsing rules.*

Proof: Let $(\mathcal{F}_1, \mathcal{R}_1)$ and $(\mathcal{F}_2, \mathcal{R}_2)$ be two left-linear TRS's without collapsing rules. We suppose that reachability is decidable for $(\mathcal{F}_1, \mathcal{R}_1)$ and $(\mathcal{F}_2, \mathcal{R}_2)$.

1. We show that, if $s \xrightarrow{*}_{\mathcal{R}_1 \oplus \mathcal{R}_2} t$ then $s \equiv C[\![s_1, \cdots, s_n]\!]$ and $t \equiv C'[\![t_1, \cdots, t_p]\!]$ for some n and p non negative, C and C' contexts on the same alphabet F_a, $(a \in \{1, 2\})$.

   If $s \xrightarrow{*}_{\mathcal{R}_1 \oplus \mathcal{R}_2} t$ then there exists s' such that $s \xrightarrow{*}^{\mathrm{o}} s' \xrightarrow{*}^{\mathrm{i}} t$, from the proposition 3.2. Therefore $s \equiv C[\![s_1, \cdots, s_n]\!] \xrightarrow{*}^{\mathrm{o}} s' \equiv C'[\![s_{i_1}, \cdots, s_{i_p}]\!] \xrightarrow{*}^{\mathrm{i}} t \equiv C'[\![t_1, \cdots, t_p]\!]$, $\{s_{i_1}, \cdots, s_{i_p}\} \subset \{s_1, \cdots, s_n\}$. So C and C' are contexts on the same alphabet $\mathcal{F}_a$ for $a \in [1, 2]$ and there exists n new variables $x_1, \cdots, x_n$ such that $C[x_1, \cdots, x_n] \xrightarrow{*}_{\mathcal{R}_a} C'[x_{i_1}, \cdots, x_{i_p}]$ and $s_{i_j} \xrightarrow{*}_{\mathcal{R}_1 \oplus \mathcal{R}_2} t_j\ \forall j \in [1, p]$. C' is a context non equal to $\Box$ because $\mathcal{R}_a$ is a TRS without collapsing rules.

2. We prove by induction on rank(s) that the reachability problem $s \xrightarrow{*}_{\mathcal{R}_1 \oplus \mathcal{R}_2} t$ is decidable.

   a) Suppose $s \xrightarrow{*}_{\mathcal{R}_1 \oplus \mathcal{R}_2} t$ with rank(s) = 1. Reachability is decidable because rank(s) = rank(t) = 1 and reachability is decidable for $(\mathcal{F}_1, \mathcal{R}_1)$ or $(\mathcal{F}_2, \mathcal{R}_2)$.

   b) Suppose that, for some k, reachability is decidable for rank(s) $< k$. We prove that it remains decidable if rank(s) $= k$. The problem is to answer to the question: $s \xrightarrow{*}_{\mathcal{R}_1 \oplus \mathcal{R}_2} t$? with $s \equiv C[\![s_1, \cdots, s_n]\!]$ and $t \equiv C'[\![t_1, \cdots, t_p]\!]$

   – If C and C' are contexts on different alphabets, the answer is NO.

   – Otherwise, $C, C' \in \mathcal{T}(\mathcal{F}_a \cup \{\Box\}, \mathcal{V})$ for some $a \in \{1, 2\}$.

   $s \xrightarrow{*}_{\mathcal{R}_1 \oplus \mathcal{R}_2} t \Leftrightarrow \exists s'\ s \xrightarrow{*}^{\mathrm{o}} s' \xrightarrow{*}^{\mathrm{i}} t$ with $s' \equiv C'[\![s_{i_1}, \cdots, s_{i_p}]\!]$ for some $\{s_{i_1}, \cdots, s_{i_p}\} \subset \{s_1, \cdots, s_n\}$. To find the term s', we choose p variables not necessarily distinct in the set $\{x_1, \cdots, x_n\}$ of distinct new variables. There is a finite number of cases. If $C[x_1, \cdots, x_n] \xrightarrow{*}_{\mathcal{R}_a} C'[x_{i_1}, \cdots, x_{i_p}]$ then we say that $< x_{i_1}, \cdots, x_{i_p} >$ is a multiset solution.

Finally, $s \xrightarrow{*}_{\mathcal{R}_1 \oplus \mathcal{R}_2} t$ if and only if there exists a multiset solution $< x_{i_1}, \cdots, x_{i_p} >$ such that $s_{i_j} \xrightarrow{*}_{\mathcal{R}_1 \oplus \mathcal{R}_2} t_j \; \forall j \in [1,p]$. Since $\text{rank}(s_{i_j}) < \text{rank}(s)$ for all j, the problems $s_{i_j} \xrightarrow{*}_{\mathcal{R}_1 \oplus \mathcal{R}_2} t_j$ are decidable by induction hypothesis.

□

We define a set of inference rules operating on pairs $(P; A)$. P is a set of reachability problems and A is a partial answer $(A \in \{T, F\})$.

INFERENCE RULES:

- **Simplify:** $(\{s \xrightarrow{?} s\} \cup P; A) \Rightarrow (P; T)$
- **Check:** $(\{C[\![s_1, \cdots, s_n]\!] \xrightarrow{?} C'[\![t_1, \cdots, t_p]\!]\} \cup P; A) \Rightarrow (\emptyset; F)$
  If C context on $\mathcal{F}_a$ and C' context on $\mathcal{F}_{3-a}$, $a \in \{1, 2\}$.
- **Fail:** $(\{C[\![s_1, \cdots, s_n]\!] \xrightarrow{?} C'[\![t_1, \cdots, t_p]\!]\} \cup P; A) \Rightarrow (\emptyset; F)$
  If C and C' contexts on $\mathcal{F}_a$ and there does not exist a multiset $< x_{i_1}, \cdots, x_{i_p} >, i_j \in [1,n]$ such that $C[x_1, \cdots, x_n] \xrightarrow{*}_{\mathcal{R}_a} C'[x_{i_1}, \cdots, x_{i_p}]$
- **Decompose:** $(\{C[\![s_1, \cdots, s_n]\!] \xrightarrow{?} C'[\![t_1, \cdots, t_p]\!]\} \cup P; A)$
  $$\Rightarrow (\{s_{i_1} \xrightarrow{?} t_1\} \cup \cdots \cup \{s_{i_p} \xrightarrow{?} t_p\} \cup P; T)$$
  If C and C' contexts on $\mathcal{F}_a$ and if $< x_{i_1}, \cdots, x_{i_p} >, i_j \in [1,n]$ is a multiset such that $C[x_1, \cdots, x_n] \xrightarrow{*}_{\mathcal{R}_a} C'[x_{i_1}, \cdots, x_{i_p}]$

This set of rules is such that $s \xrightarrow{*}_{\mathcal{R}_1 \oplus \mathcal{R}_2} t$ if and only if, starting with $(\{s \xrightarrow{?} t\}; T)$ and using the inference rules repeatedly until none is applicable, there exists a sequence which gives the result $(\emptyset; T)$. Note that for every s and t, there is a finite number of sequences starting from $(\{s \xrightarrow{?} t\}; T)$.

3.2 With collapsing rules and linearity

A TRS is linear if it is both left-linear and right-linear. Now, we consider linear TRS's with possibly collapsing rules.

Proposition 3.4 *Decidability of reachability is a modular property of linear TRS's with possibly collapsing rules.*

To prove this proposition, we need four lemmas.

Lemma 3.5 *Let $(\mathcal{F}_1, \mathcal{R}_1)$ and $(\mathcal{F}_2, \mathcal{R}_2)$ be two left-linear TRS's. Suppose $s \xrightarrow{*}_{\mathcal{R}_1 \oplus \mathcal{R}_2} t$ without collapsing erasable parts. Then, there exists a term s' such that $s \xrightarrow{*}^{o} s' \xrightarrow{*}^{i} t$*

PROOF : It is an extension of proposition 3.2. □

Lemma 3.6 *Let $(\mathcal{F}_1, \mathcal{R}_1)$ and $(\mathcal{F}_2, \mathcal{R}_2)$ be two linear TRS's. Let s be a term with n parts, arbitrarily numerated. If $s \xrightarrow{*}_{\mathcal{R}_1 \oplus \mathcal{R}_2} t$ without collapsing erasable parts then there exist $s_1, \cdots, s_{n-1}$ such that:*
$s \xrightarrow{*}_{\mathcal{R}_1 \oplus \mathcal{R}_2} s_1$ reducing only the part 1.
$s_1 \xrightarrow{*}_{\mathcal{R}_1 \oplus \mathcal{R}_2} s_2$ reducing only the part 2.
...
$s_{n-1} \xrightarrow{*}_{\mathcal{R}_1 \oplus \mathcal{R}_2} t$ reducing only the part n.

PROOF :
When we reduce a part p, we can delete some parts under the part p, but such parts cannot be duplicated because $\mathcal{R}_1 \oplus \mathcal{R}_2$ is linear. $N(t)$ is the set of the numbers of the parts of t. When a part p is reduced to the part p' then we assume that (the number of p) = (the number of p'). Therefore the reduction-step $t \rightarrow_{\mathcal{R}_1 \oplus \mathcal{R}_2} t'$ transforms the set $N(t)$ to the set $N(t')$ such that $N(t') \subset N(t)$.
We show that we can reduce parts of t in any order.
- We consider two parts p_1 and p_2 such that p_1 is under p_2. To rewrite p_1 and p_2, we can either reduce p_1 and p_2 simultaneously, or reduce only p_1 and after reduce only p_2, or reduce only p_2 and after reduce only p_1 if p_1 is not collapsed by the reduction of p_2. If p_1 is collapsed, we say that we reduce p_1 with an empty reduction.
- We consider two parts p_1 and p_2 such that p_1 is not under p_2 and p_2 is not under p_1. It is obvious that in this case, we can reduce p_1 and p_2 independently. □

Lemma 3.7 *Let $(\mathcal{F}_1, \mathcal{R}_1)$ and $(\mathcal{F}_2, \mathcal{R}_2)$ be two linear TRS's. Suppose that $s \xrightarrow{*}_{\mathcal{R}_1 \oplus \mathcal{R}_2} t$ is a reduction sequence collapsing exactly one erasable part $e \in E(s)$. Then there exists a term s' such that $s \xrightarrow{*}_{\mathcal{R}_1 \oplus \mathcal{R}_2} s' \xrightarrow{*}_{\mathcal{R}_1 \oplus \mathcal{R}_2} t$ with $s \xrightarrow{*}_{\mathcal{R}_1 \oplus \mathcal{R}_2} s'$ reduction which reduces only e and collapses it and $s' \xrightarrow{*}_{\mathcal{R}_1 \oplus \mathcal{R}_2} t$ reduction which does not collapse erasable part.*

PROOF :
Suppose that s is a term with n parts arbitrarily numerated. Suppose that $s \xrightarrow{*}_{\mathcal{R}_1 \oplus \mathcal{R}_2} t$ collapsing the erasable part which has the number j, $j \in [1, n]$.
There exist two terms s' and s'' such that $s \xrightarrow{*}_{\mathcal{R}_1 \oplus \mathcal{R}_2} s' \rightarrow_{\mathcal{R}_1 \oplus \mathcal{R}_2} s'' \xrightarrow{*}_{\mathcal{R}_1 \oplus \mathcal{R}_2} t$ with $s \xrightarrow{*}_{\mathcal{R}_1 \oplus \mathcal{R}_2} s'$ without collapsing erasable part, $s' \rightarrow_{\mathcal{R}_1 \oplus \mathcal{R}_2} s''$ collapsing the part j and $s'' \xrightarrow{*}_{\mathcal{R}_1 \oplus \mathcal{R}_2} t$ without collapsing erasable part.
From the lemma 3.6, we can reduce $s \xrightarrow{*}_{\mathcal{R}_1 \oplus \mathcal{R}_2} s'$ ending with the reduction steps reducing the part j. So there exists s''' such that $s \xrightarrow{*}_{\mathcal{R}_1 \oplus \mathcal{R}_2} s''' \xrightarrow{*}_{\mathcal{R}_1 \oplus \mathcal{R}_2} s'$ with $s \xrightarrow{*}_{\mathcal{R}_1 \oplus \mathcal{R}_2} s'''$ reducing all except the part j, and $s''' \xrightarrow{*}_{\mathcal{R}_1 \oplus \mathcal{R}_2} s'$ reducing only the part j.
We obtain $s \xrightarrow{*}_{\mathcal{R}_1 \oplus \mathcal{R}_2} s''' \xrightarrow{*}_{\mathcal{R}_1 \oplus \mathcal{R}_2} s' \rightarrow_{\mathcal{R}_1 \oplus \mathcal{R}_2} s'' \xrightarrow{*}_{\mathcal{R}_1 \oplus \mathcal{R}_2} t$.
The reductions done in $s \xrightarrow{*}_{\mathcal{R}_1 \oplus \mathcal{R}_2} s'''$ can be done after reducing the part j : Each step $a \rightarrow b$ on a part k in the reduction $s \xrightarrow{*}_{\mathcal{R}_1 \oplus \mathcal{R}_2} s'''$ can be either done after reducing the part j if the part k is not collapsed by the rewriting of the part j, or be suppressed if the part k is collapsed by the reduction of the part j.
Therefore, there exist t' and t'' such that $s \xrightarrow{*}_{\mathcal{R}_1 \oplus \mathcal{R}_2} t' \rightarrow_{\mathcal{R}_1 \oplus \mathcal{R}_2} t'' \xrightarrow{*}_{\mathcal{R}_1 \oplus \mathcal{R}_2} t$ with $s \xrightarrow{*}_{\mathcal{R}_1 \oplus \mathcal{R}_2} t'$ reducing the part j, $t' \rightarrow_{\mathcal{R}_1 \oplus \mathcal{R}_2} t''$ collapsing the part j and $t'' \xrightarrow{*}_{\mathcal{R}_1 \oplus \mathcal{R}_2} t$ without collapsing erasable parts. □

Lemma 3.8 *Let* $(\mathcal{F}_1, \mathcal{R}_1)$ *and* $(\mathcal{F}_2, \mathcal{R}_2)$ *be two linear TRS's. If* $s \xrightarrow{*}_{\mathcal{R}_1 \oplus \mathcal{R}_2} t$ *collapsing* k *erasable parts* $e_1, \cdots, e_k$ *in this order, then there exist* k *terms* $s_1, \cdots, s_k$ *such that*
$s \xrightarrow{*}_{\mathcal{R}_1 \oplus \mathcal{R}_2} s_1 \xrightarrow{*}_{\mathcal{R}_1 \oplus \mathcal{R}_2} s_2 \cdots \xrightarrow{*}_{\mathcal{R}_1 \oplus \mathcal{R}_2} s_k \xrightarrow{*}_{\mathcal{R}_1 \oplus \mathcal{R}_2} t$ *with*
$s \xrightarrow{*}_{\mathcal{R}_1 \oplus \mathcal{R}_2} s_1$ *reducing and collapsing* e_1
$s_1 \xrightarrow{*}_{\mathcal{R}_1 \oplus \mathcal{R}_2} s_2$ *reducing and collapsing* e_2
...
$s_k \xrightarrow{*}_{\mathcal{R}_1 \oplus \mathcal{R}_2} t$ *without collapsing erasable parts.*

PROOF :
We prove this lemma by induction on $k \geq 0$.
• If $k = 0$ the lemma holds.
• Suppose the lemma holds for a fixed $k \geq 0$. Let s and t be two terms such that $s \xrightarrow{*}_{\mathcal{R}_1 \oplus \mathcal{R}_2} t$ collapsing $k + 1$ erasable parts. Then there exists a term s_1 such that $s \xrightarrow{*}_{\mathcal{R}_1 \oplus \mathcal{R}_2} s_1 \xrightarrow{*}_{\mathcal{R}_1 \oplus \mathcal{R}_2} t$ where $s \xrightarrow{*}_{\mathcal{R}_1 \oplus \mathcal{R}_2} s_1$ is a reduction collapsing one erasable part e. Therefore, from the lemma 3.7, there exists s'_1 such that $s \xrightarrow{*}_{\mathcal{R}_1 \oplus \mathcal{R}_2} s'_1 \xrightarrow{*}_{\mathcal{R}_1 \oplus \mathcal{R}_2} s_1$ with $s \xrightarrow{*}_{\mathcal{R}_1 \oplus \mathcal{R}_2} s'_1$ reducing and collapsing the part e. Therefore $s \xrightarrow{*}_{\mathcal{R}_1 \oplus \mathcal{R}_2} s'_1 \xrightarrow{*}_{\mathcal{R}_1 \oplus \mathcal{R}_2} s_1 \xrightarrow{*}_{\mathcal{R}_1 \oplus \mathcal{R}_2} t$ with $s'_1 \xrightarrow{*}_{\mathcal{R}_1 \oplus \mathcal{R}_2} t$ reduction collapsing k erasable parts.
We deduce the lemma by the induction hypothesis. □

PROOF OF THE PROPOSITION :
Let $(\mathcal{F}_1, \mathcal{R}_1)$ and $(\mathcal{F}_2, \mathcal{R}_2)$ be two linear TRS's. We suppose that reachability is decidable for $(\mathcal{F}_1, \mathcal{R}_1)$ and for $(\mathcal{F}_2, \mathcal{R}_2)$ and we prove that it remains decidable for $\mathcal{R}_1 \oplus \mathcal{R}_2$. Let s and t be two terms. We want to solve the reachability problem $s \xrightarrow{*}_{\mathcal{R}_1 \oplus \mathcal{R}_2} t$.
If $s \xrightarrow{*}_{\mathcal{R}_1 \oplus \mathcal{R}_2} t$ then either no erasable part has been collapsed, or this reduction has collapsed erasable parts.
• First case: We search to solve the problem without collapsing erasable part. From lemma 3.5, $s \xrightarrow{*}_{\mathcal{R}_1 \oplus \mathcal{R}_2} t$ if and only if there exists a term s' such that $s \xrightarrow{*}^{o} s' \xrightarrow{*}^{i} t$ Therefore, we prove that reachability is decidable for $\mathcal{R}_1 \oplus \mathcal{R}_2$ with a proof similar to proposition 3.3.
• Second case: We solve the problem $s \xrightarrow{*}_{\mathcal{R}_1 \oplus \mathcal{R}_2} t$ collapsing erasable part.
It means that there exists $k \in [1, n]$ with n the number of erasable parts of s such that $s \xrightarrow{*}_{\mathcal{R}_1 \oplus \mathcal{R}_2} t$ collapsing k erasable parts. So there exist $e_1, \cdots, e_k$ in $E(s)$ such that $s \xrightarrow{*}_{\mathcal{R}_1 \oplus \mathcal{R}_2} t$ collapsing the parts $e_1, \cdots, e_k$ in this order. From the lemma 3.8, there exists $s_1, \cdots, s_k$ such that $s \xrightarrow{*}_{\mathcal{R}_1 \oplus \mathcal{R}_2} s_1 \xrightarrow{*}_{\mathcal{R}_1 \oplus \mathcal{R}_2} s_2 \cdots \xrightarrow{*}_{\mathcal{R}_1 \oplus \mathcal{R}_2} s_k \xrightarrow{*}_{\mathcal{R}_1 \oplus \mathcal{R}_2} t$ with
$s \xrightarrow{*}_{\mathcal{R}_1 \oplus \mathcal{R}_2} s_1$ reducing and collapsing e_1
$s_1 \xrightarrow{*}_{\mathcal{R}_1 \oplus \mathcal{R}_2} s_2$ reducing and collapsing e_2
...
$s_k \xrightarrow{*}_{\mathcal{R}_1 \oplus \mathcal{R}_2} t$ without collapsing erasable parts.
There is a finite number of cases, i.e. a finite number of k and for each k a finite number of k-uple $e_1, \cdots, e_k$. For each case, we can decide if every e_i can be collapsed because these are reachability problems on $(\mathcal{F}_1, \mathcal{R}_1)$ or on $(\mathcal{F}_2, \mathcal{R}_2)$. If every e_i can be collapsed, we obtain the term s_k and we have to solve the problem $s_k \xrightarrow{*}_{\mathcal{R}_1 \oplus \mathcal{R}_2} t$ without collapsing erasable parts. From the first part of this proof, the problem $s_k \xrightarrow{*}_{\mathcal{R}_1 \oplus \mathcal{R}_2} t$ is decidable. □

The following set of inference rules gives a decision algorithm of reachability on $\mathcal{R}_1 \oplus \mathcal{R}_2$, supposing $(\mathcal{F}_1, \mathcal{R}_1)$ and $(\mathcal{F}_2, \mathcal{R}_2)$ are two linear TRS's whose reachability is decidable.

These inference rules operate on 4-uples (P_1;P_2;P_3;A). P_1 contains a reachability problem. P_2 is a set of reachability problems of the form $s \stackrel{?}{\rightarrow} t$ that we have to solve without collapsing erasable parts. P_3 is a set of collapsing problems, i.e. reachability problems of the form $s \stackrel{?}{\rightarrow} x$ with x variable occuring in s. A is a partial answer to the problem P_1 ($A \in \{T, F\}$).

INFERENCE RULES :

1. $(\{s \stackrel{?}{\rightarrow} t\}; \emptyset; \emptyset; A) \Rightarrow (\emptyset; \{s \stackrel{?}{\rightarrow} t\}; \emptyset; A)$
2. $(\{s \stackrel{?}{\rightarrow} t\}; \emptyset; \emptyset; A) \Rightarrow (\{s' \stackrel{?}{\rightarrow} t\}; \emptyset; \{s_1[x_1] \stackrel{?}{\rightarrow} x_1\} \cup \cdots \cup \{s_k[x_k] \stackrel{?}{\rightarrow} x_k\}; A)$
   If s' is obtained from s collapsing $s_1[x_1], \cdots, s_k[x_k]$ with $1 \leq k \leq \mathrm{Card}(E(s))$.
3. $(\emptyset; \{s \stackrel{?}{\rightarrow} s\} \cup P_2; P_3; A) \Rightarrow (\emptyset; P_2; P_3; T)$
4. $(\emptyset; \{C[\![s_1, \cdots, s_n]\!] \stackrel{?}{\rightarrow} C'[\![t_1, \cdots, t_p]\!]\} \cup P_2; P_3; A) \Rightarrow (\emptyset; \emptyset; \emptyset; F)$
   If C context on $\mathcal{F}_a$ and C' context on $\mathcal{F}_{3-a}$, $a \in \{1, 2\}$.
5. $(\emptyset; \{C[\![s_1, \cdots, s_n]\!] \stackrel{?}{\rightarrow} C'[\![t_1, \cdots, t_p]\!]\} \cup P_2; P_3; A) \Rightarrow (\emptyset; \emptyset; \emptyset; F)$
   If C and C' contexts on $\mathcal{F}_a$ and there does not exist some multiset $< x_{i_1}, \cdots, x_{i_p} >$ $i_j \in [1, n]$ such that $C[x_1, \cdots, x_n] \stackrel{*}{\rightarrow}_{\mathcal{R}_a} C'[x_{i_1}, \cdots, x_{i_p}]$
6. $(\emptyset; \{C[\![s_1, \cdots, s_n]\!] \stackrel{?}{\rightarrow} C'[\![t_1, \cdots, t_p]\!]\} \cup P_2; P_3; A)$
   $$\Rightarrow (\emptyset; \{s_{i_1} \stackrel{?}{\rightarrow} t_1\} \cup \cdots \cup \{s_{i_p} \stackrel{?}{\rightarrow} t_p\} \cup P_2; P_3; T)$$
   if C and C' contexts on $\mathcal{F}_a$ and if $< x_{i_1}, \cdots, x_{i_p} >, i_j \in [1, n]$ is a multiset such that $C[x_1, \cdots, x_n] \stackrel{*}{\rightarrow}_{\mathcal{R}_a} C'[x_{i_1}, \cdots, x_{i_p}]$
7. $(\emptyset; P_2; \{s[x] \stackrel{?}{\rightarrow} x\} \cup P_3; A) \Rightarrow (\emptyset; P_2; P_3; T)$
   If $s[x]$ is a term of $\mathcal{T}_a$ and $s[x] \stackrel{*}{\rightarrow}_{\mathcal{R}_a} x$
8. $(\emptyset; P_2; \{s[x] \stackrel{?}{\rightarrow} x\} \cup P_3; A) \Rightarrow (\emptyset; \emptyset; \emptyset; F)$
   If $s[x]$ is a term of $\mathcal{T}_a$ and we do not obtain $s[x] \stackrel{*}{\rightarrow}_{\mathcal{R}_a} x$

- With the rule 1, we choose to solve the problem without collapsing erasable parts.
- With the rule 2, we collapse k erasable parts and we obtain the term s'. We have to solve k collapsing problems, and a new reachability problem $s' \stackrel{?}{\rightarrow} t$.
- The rules 3, 4, 5, 6 permit to solve the problem without collapsing erasable parts. These rules are similar to the inference rules defined in the previous section.
- The rules 7 and 8 permit to solve the collapsing problems.

This set of rules is such that $s \stackrel{*}{\rightarrow}_{\mathcal{R}_1 \oplus \mathcal{R}_2} t$ if and only if there exists an inference sequence starting from $(\{s \stackrel{?}{\rightarrow} t\}; \emptyset; \emptyset; T)$ and using the inference rules repeatedly until none is applicable, which gives the result $(\emptyset, \emptyset; \emptyset; T)$. Note that there is a finite number of inference sequences starting from $(\{s \stackrel{?}{\rightarrow} t\}; \emptyset; \emptyset; T)$.

To complete our study of left-linear TRS's, it misses the case of left-linear TRS's with collapsing rules and without right-linearity. In this case, we cannot apply the algorithm seen in this section. The following example explains the problem:

EXAMPLE :
$\mathcal{F}_1 = \{b(,),\ a(),\ \$\}$, $\mathcal{R}_1 = \{b(x,\$) \to x\ ,\ a(x) \to b(x,x)\}$
$\mathcal{F}_2 = \{F()\}$, $\mathcal{R}_2 = \{F(x) \to x\}$
We get $a(F(\$)) \xrightarrow{*}_{\mathcal{R}_1 \oplus \mathcal{R}_2} F(\$)$ by the reduction sequence:
$a(F(\$)) \to_{R_1} b(F(\$), F(\$)) \to_{R_2} b(F(\$), \$) \to_{R_1} F(\$)$

We conjecture that decidability of reachability is not a modular property of left-linear TRS's with collapsing rules.

3.3 Complexity in the word case

In the case of term rewriting systems, it is clear that our algorithm has an exponential complexity, even in the case of left-linear TRS's without collapsing rules. (It is easy to prove that it is NP-hard in this case). Indeed, when we have to solve a reachability problem of the form $C[\![s_1,\cdots,s_n]\!] \xrightarrow{*} C'[\![t_1,\cdots,t_p]\!]$ we have to find the multisets $< x_{i_1},\cdots,x_{i_p} >$ such that $C[\![x_1,\cdots,x_n]\!] \xrightarrow{*}_{\mathcal{R}_a} C'[\![x_{i_1},\cdots,x_{i_p}]\!]$ (if C and C' contexts on $\mathcal{F}_a$). Therefore, there are n^p possible cases, thus n^p reachability problems on $(\mathcal{F}_a, \mathcal{R}_a)$ to examine. Moreover, for each multiset solution, we have to treat p new reachability problems on $\mathcal{R}_1 \oplus \mathcal{R}_2$: $s_{i_j} \xrightarrow{*} t_j,\ j \in [1,p]$.

We study in this section the complexity of our algorithms in the particular case of string rewriting systems. We consider two systems $(\mathcal{F}_1, \mathcal{R}_1)$ and $(\mathcal{F}_2, \mathcal{R}_2)$ where rules of $\mathcal{R}_1$ and $\mathcal{R}_2$ have the form $m_1 \to m_2$ with m_1 and m_2 words. We represent the empty word by the symbol ϵ. We compute the number of calls to the procedure which solve the reachability problem on $(\mathcal{F}_1, \mathcal{R}_1)$ and $(\mathcal{F}_2, \mathcal{R}_2)$. Therefore, the complexity we obtain has to be multiply by the complexity of this procedure.

FIRST CASE : If there is no collapsing rules, i.e. no rules $m_1 \to \epsilon$, the decision algorithm of the reachability problem $m \xrightarrow{*}_{\mathcal{R}_1 \oplus \mathcal{R}_2} m'$ has a linear complexity depending on the rank of m. Indeed:

- if $m \equiv \epsilon$ then $m \xrightarrow{*}_{\mathcal{R}_1 \oplus \mathcal{R}_2} m' \Leftrightarrow m' \equiv \epsilon$
- Suppose that m begins by a letter of $\mathcal{F}_a$, $a \in \{1,2\}$. Then m is written $m \equiv u_1 u_2 \cdots u_n$, $n \geq 1$, with u_i word of $\mathcal{F}_a^*$ if i is odd and u_i word of $\mathcal{F}_{3-a}^*$ otherwise.

  – If m' begins by a letter of $\mathcal{F}_{3-a}$ then the answer to the reachability problem is NO.

  – Otherwise, $m' \equiv v_1 v_2 \cdots v_p$, $p \geq 0$, with v_i word of $\mathcal{F}_a^*$ if i is odd and v_i word of $\mathcal{F}_{3-a}^*$ otherwise. We get $(m \xrightarrow{*}_{\mathcal{R}_1 \oplus \mathcal{R}_2} m' \Leftrightarrow (p = n)$ and $u_i \xrightarrow{*}_{\mathcal{R}_1 \oplus \mathcal{R}_2} v_i\ \forall i \in \{1,\ldots,n\})$. Each reachability problem $u_i \to v_i$ is a problem on $(\mathcal{F}_1, \mathcal{R}_1)$ or $(\mathcal{F}_2, \mathcal{R}_2)$. Thus, there are n "simple" reachability problems to solve, with n the rank of m. So the complexity of our algorithm is linear depending on the rank of m.

SECOND CASE : If there are some collapsing rules, the complexity becomes exponential.

- if $m \equiv \epsilon$, then $m \xrightarrow{*}_{\mathcal{R}_1 \oplus \mathcal{R}_2} m' \Leftrightarrow m' \equiv \epsilon$

- Suppose that $m \equiv u_1 u_2 \cdots u_n$, $n \geq 1$ with u_i word of $\mathcal{F}_a^*$ if i is odd and u_i word of $\mathcal{F}_{3-a}^*$ otherwise ($a \in \{1,2\}$). Moreover, we suppose that $m' \equiv v_1 v_2 \cdots v_p$, $p \geq 0$, with v_i word of $\mathcal{F}_b^*$ if i is odd and v_i word of $\mathcal{F}_{3-b}^*$ otherwise, for $b \in \{1,2\}$.

  – if $n = p$, we are in the previous case, so the complexity is linear.

  – if $n < p$ then the answer to the reachability problem is NO.

  – if $n > p$ then we have to choose $n - p$ words to collapse between n words. The order is important, and the words are not necessarily distincts so there are n^{n-p} cases to consider. For each case, there are n "simple" reachability problems to solve. Indeed, there are $n - p$ problems of the form $u_i \to \epsilon$ and p problems of the form $u_i \to v_j$. Therefore, in the worst case, the complexity of the algorithm $m \xrightarrow{*}_{\mathcal{R}_1 \oplus \mathcal{R}_2} m'$ is $\mathcal{O}(n^{n-p+1})$ if we suppose that the complexity of decision algorithm on $(\mathcal{F}_1, \mathcal{R}_1)$ and $(\mathcal{F}_2, \mathcal{R}_2)$ is constant. So the complexity of the algorithm $m \xrightarrow{*}_{\mathcal{R}_1 \oplus \mathcal{R}_2} m'$ is exponential depending on the ranks of m and m'.

4 Non left-linear term rewriting systems

Proposition 4.1 *Decidability of reachability is not a modular property of non left-linear TRS's.*

To prove this proposition, we build two TRS's on disjoint alphabets. Reachability is decidable for these systems and we prove that reachability on $\mathcal{R}_1 \oplus \mathcal{R}_2$ is equivalent to the Post Correspondence Problem.

Definition 4.2 *The* Post Correspondence Problem $P(\phi, \psi)$ *over an alphabet* F *is given by two morphisms* ϕ *and* ψ *from* I^* *to* F^*. $P(\phi, \psi)$ *has a solution if and only if there exists* m_I *in* I^+ *such that* $\phi(m_I) = \psi(m_I)$.

The Post Correspondence Problem is well-known undecidable.

We consider the system $\mathcal{R}_1$ on the alphabet $\mathcal{F}_1 = \{\mathrm{f}(,), \clubsuit\}$. f is a letter of arity 2 and $\clubsuit$ is a constant. $\mathcal{R}_1$ contains only one rule:

f → ♣
x x

$\mathcal{R}_1$ is not left-linear.

Lemma 4.3 *Reachability is decidable for* $(\mathcal{F}_1, \mathcal{R}_1)$.

Proof : $(\mathcal{F}_1, \mathcal{R}_1)$ is strictly decreasing, so reachability is decidable. □

We consider now a finite ranked alphabet Σ. Each letter of Σ has the arity 1. Let $\mathcal{F}_2 = \{\#(), \phi(), \psi(), \$\} \cup \Sigma$, with $\{\#(), \phi(), \psi(), \$\}$ and Σ disjoint alphabets.
Let ϕ and ψ be two morphisms from Σ to Σ^*. $(\mathcal{F}_2, \mathcal{R}_2)$ is a left-linear TRS defined with ϕ and ψ. $\mathcal{R}_2$ is the set of rules :

For all $i \in \Sigma$:

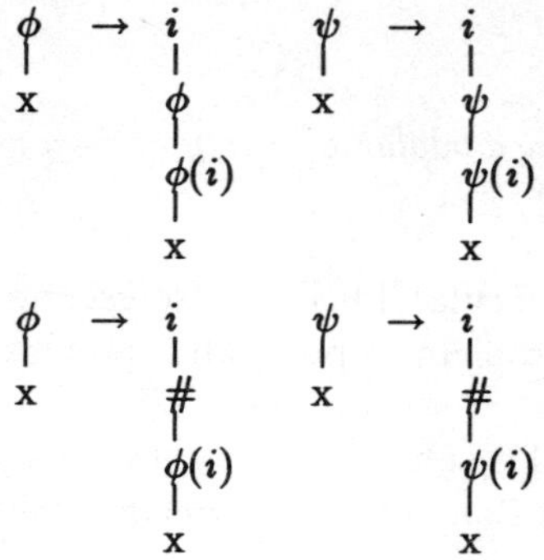

Lemma 4.4 *Reachability is decidable for $(\mathcal{F}_2, \mathcal{R}_2)$.*

PROOF :
We consider the reachability problem $t \xrightarrow{*}_{\mathcal{R}_2} t'$ for t and t' terms of $\mathcal{T}_2$. Let n be the depth of t'. There is a finite number of derivations from t giving a term of depth n, because Σ is a finite alphabet. Therefore reachability is decidable for $(\mathcal{F}_2, \mathcal{R}_2)$. □

Lemma 4.5 *The reachability problem*

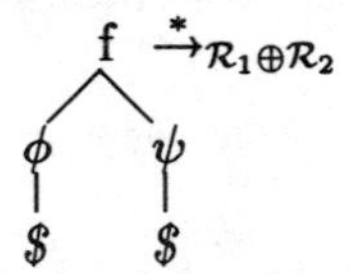

is equivalent to the Post Correspondence Problem for ϕ and ψ.

PROOF :
This problem is equivalent to prove that $\phi(\$)$ and $\psi(\$)$ have a common reduct.
From $\phi(\$)$ the system can generate all the terms of the form:

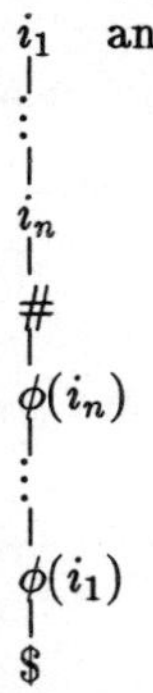

and all the terms

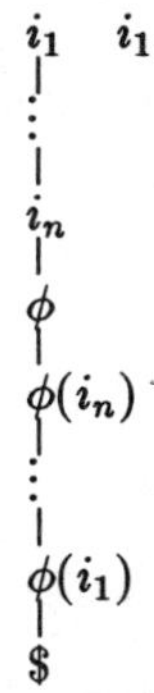

$i_1, \cdots, i_n \in \Sigma$, $n \geq 0$

It is the same thing for $\psi(\$)$. Therefore $\phi(\$)$ and $\psi(\$)$ have a common reduct if and only if there exists a solution to the Post Correspondence Problem for ϕ and ψ. □

PROOF OF THE PROPOSITION : The Post Correspondence Problem is undecidable. Therefore, from the previous lemma, reachability is undecidable for $\mathcal{R}_1 \oplus \mathcal{R}_2$. But it was decidable for $(\mathcal{F}_1, \mathcal{R}_1)$ and for $(\mathcal{F}_2, \mathcal{R}_2)$. Thus decidability of reachability is not a modular property of non left-linear term rewriting systems. □

REMARK : $(\mathcal{F}_1, \mathcal{R}_1)$ and $(\mathcal{F}_2, \mathcal{R}_2)$ are both right-linear and contain no collapsing rules. Nevertheless, reachability is not modular.

5 Ground reachability

Proposition 5.1 *Ground reachability is not a modular property of linear TRS's without collapsing rules.*

For the proof of this proposition, we build particular TRS's whose ground reachability is decidable and use the Post Correspondence Problem to prove that ground reachability is undecidable for their disjoint union .
Let $\mathcal{F}_1 = \{\alpha(),\ 0\}$ (α is a letter of arity 1 and 0 is a constant). We consider a first TRS $(\mathcal{F}_1, \mathcal{R}_1)$. $\mathcal{R}_1$ contains no rules so it is obvious that reachability is decidable for $(\mathcal{F}_1, \mathcal{R}_1)$.

Let I be a monadic alphabet, disjoint from $\mathcal{F}_1$.
Let $\mathcal{F}_2 = \{\mathrm{c}(,,),\ \mathrm{c}'(,,),\ \mathrm{c}''(,,),\ \mathrm{a}(),\ \mathrm{a}'(),\ \mathrm{a}''(),\ \#\}$ (c, c′ and c″ are letters of arity 3 , a, a′ and a″ are letters of arity 1 and # is a constant). $\mathcal{F}_2$ and $\mathcal{F}_1$ are disjoints. $\mathcal{G}_1$ is the set of ground terms on the alphabet $\mathcal{F}_1$ and $\mathcal{G}_2$ is the set of ground terms on the alphabet $\mathcal{F}_2$. With every pair (ϕ, ψ) of morphisms from I to $\{\mathrm{a}, \mathrm{a}'\}^*$ we associate a TRS $(\mathcal{F}_2, \mathcal{R}_2)$.

- $\mathcal{R}_2$ contains rules which permit to reduce a ground term of $\mathcal{G}_2$ to #.

$$\mathrm{a}(\#) \xrightarrow{1} \# \qquad \mathrm{a}'(\#) \xrightarrow{2} \# \qquad \mathrm{a}''(\#) \xrightarrow{3} \#$$

$$\mathrm{c}(\#,\#,\#) \xrightarrow{4} \# \qquad \mathrm{c}'(\#,\#,\#) \xrightarrow{5} \# \qquad \mathrm{c}''(\#,\#,\#) \xrightarrow{6} \#$$

- $\mathcal{R}_2$ contains all the rules which permit to generate every ground term of $\mathcal{G}_2$ from #.

$$\# \xrightarrow{7} \mathrm{a}(\#) \qquad \# \xrightarrow{8} \mathrm{a}'(\#) \qquad \# \xrightarrow{9} \mathrm{a}''(\#)$$

$$\# \xrightarrow{10} \mathrm{c}(\#,\#,\#) \qquad \# \xrightarrow{11} \mathrm{c}'(\#,\#,\#) \qquad \# \xrightarrow{12} \mathrm{c}''(\#,\#,\#)$$

  Therefore, we get for all ground terms t and t', $t \xrightarrow{*}_{\mathcal{R}_2} \# \xrightarrow{*}_{\mathcal{R}_2} t'$.
  Thus ground reachability is decidable for $(\mathcal{F}_2, \mathcal{R}_2)$.

- Eventually, $\mathcal{R}_2$ contains rules associated with the Post Correspondence Problem for ϕ and ψ. (adding these rules do not change the ground rewrite relation).

for all i in I

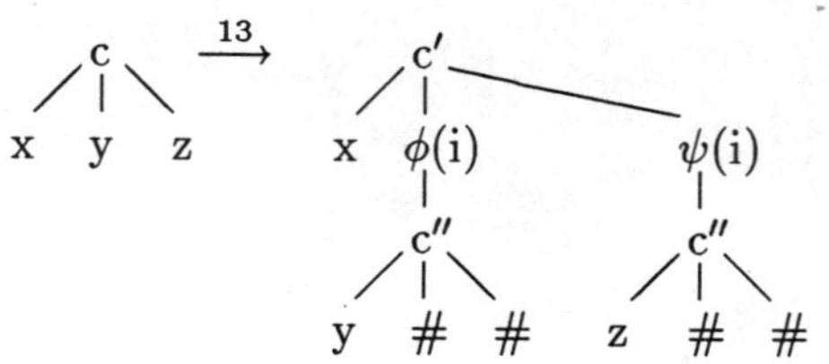

and

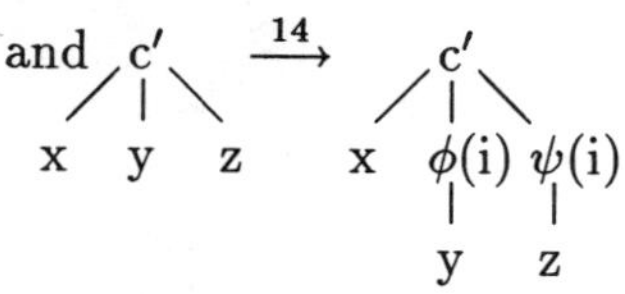

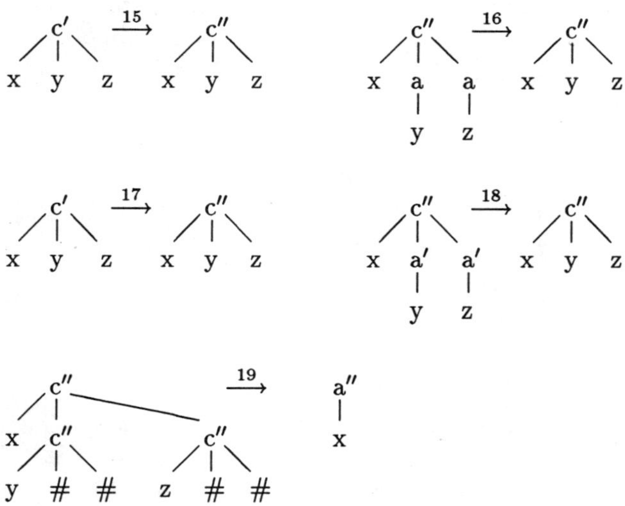

$\mathcal{R}_2$ is a linear TRS, without collapsing rules.

Lemma 5.2 *The ground reachability problem*

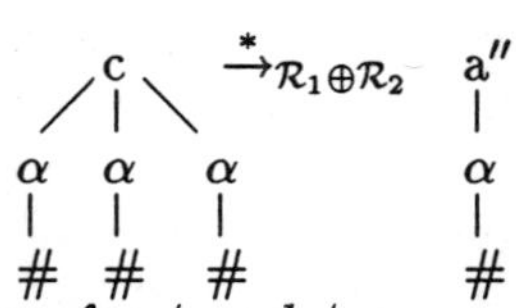

is equivalent to the Post Correspondence Problem for ϕ *and* ψ.

PROOF :

We are interested in the reachability problem: $t \equiv$

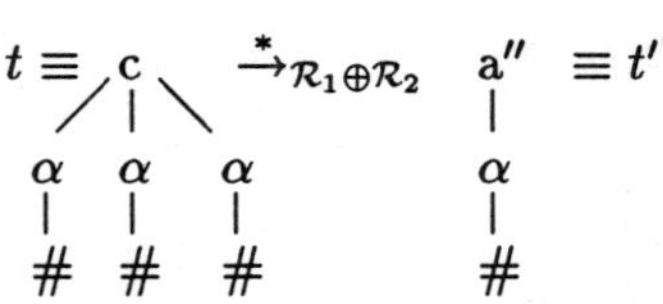

The two systems do not contain collapsing rules, so from lemma 3.6 we can decompose the reachability problem : $t \xrightarrow{*}_{\mathcal{R}_1 \oplus \mathcal{R}_2} t'$ if and only if we have applied the rule 19, i.e. there exist two terms t_1 and t_2 such that

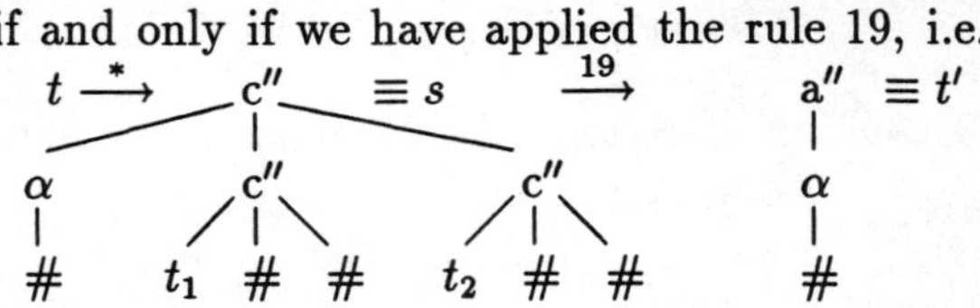

Thus we study the new reachability problem $t \xrightarrow{*} s$. But $t \xrightarrow{*} s$ if and only if $t_1 \equiv t_2 \equiv \alpha(\#)$ and there exist $i_1, \cdots, i_n, n \geq 1$ such that

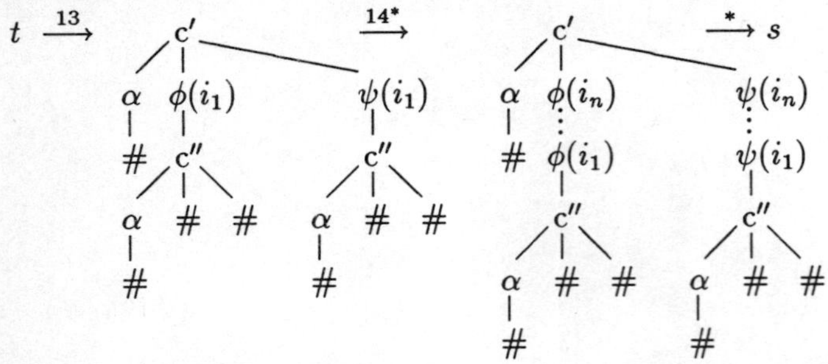

Note that, because of the symbols α, we cannot apply rules which permit to reduce a term of root c, c$'$ or c$''$ to #. s is a term of root c$''$. But we rewrite a term of root c$'$ to a term of root c$''$ applying the rule 15 or the rule 17. Thus $t \xrightarrow{*} s$ if and only if there exists $m = i_n \cdots i_1$ $(n \geq 1)$ such that

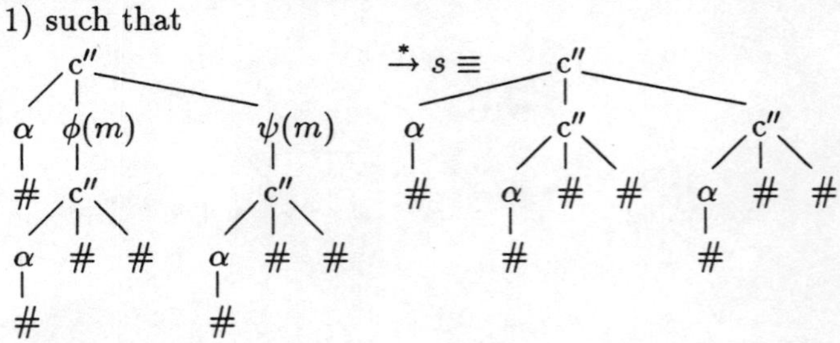

We delete the letters of $\phi(m)$ and of $\psi(m)$ with the rules 16 or 18. Thus $t \xrightarrow{*} s$ if and only if there exists $m = i_n \cdots i_1 (n \geq 1)$ such that $\phi(m) = \psi(m)$. Therefore $t \xrightarrow{*} t' \Leftrightarrow t \xrightarrow{*} s \Leftrightarrow$ the Post Correspondence Problem for ϕ and ψ has a solution. Thus the reachability problem $t \xrightarrow{*} t'$ is undecidable. □

Proof of the proposition : Let ϕ and ψ be two morphisms from I to $\{a,a'\}^*$. $(\mathcal{F}_2, \mathcal{R}_2)$ is the TRS associated with ϕ and ψ. Ground reachability is decidable for $(\mathcal{F}_1, \mathcal{R}_1)$ and for $(\mathcal{F}_2, \mathcal{R}_2)$. But from the previous lemma, ground reachability is undecidable for $\mathcal{R}_1 \oplus \mathcal{R}_2$. Therefore decidability of ground reachability is not a modular property of linear TRS's without collapsing rules. □

I am grateful for my referees for their useful remarks.

References

[BJW82] R.V. Book, M. Jantzen, and C. Wrathall. Monadic Thue systems. *Theoretical Computer Science*, 19(3):231–252, 1982.

[Dro89] K. Drosten. Termersetzungssysteme. Informatik-Fachberichte 210, Springer, Germany, 1989.

[GB85] J.H. Gallier and R.V. Book. Reductions in tree replacement systems. *Theoretical Computer Science*, 37(2):123–150, 1985.

[KO90] M. Kurihara and A. Ohuchi. Modularity of simple termination of term rewriting systems. *Journal of IPS Japan*, 31(5):633–642, 1990.

[Mid89a] A. Middeldorp. Modular aspects of properties of term rewriting systems related to normal forms. In *Lecture Notes in Computer Science Vol 355*, pages 263–277, Chapel Hill, 1989. 3rd International Conference on Rewriting Techniques and Applications. Full version: Report IR-164, Vrije Universiteit, Amsterdam, 1988.

[Mid89b] A. Middeldorp. A sufficient condition for the termination of the direct sum of term rewriting systems. In *Proceeding of the 4th IEEE Symposium on Logic in Computer Science*, pages 396–401, Pacific Grove, 1989.

[Mid90] A. Middeldorp. *Modular Properties of Term Rewriting Systems.* PhD thesis, Vrije Universiteit, Amsterdam, 1990.

[Mid91] A. Middeldorp. Modular properties of conditional term rewriting systems. Report CS R9105, Centre for Mathematics and Computer Science, Amsterdam, 1991.

[Oya86] M. Oyamaguchi. The reachability problem for quasi-ground term rewriting systems. *Journal of Information Processing*, pages 9–4, 1986.

[Rus87] M. Rusinowitch. On termination of the direct sum of term rewriting systems. *Information Processing Letters*, 26:65–70, 1987.

[TKB89] Y. Toyama, J.W. Klop, and H.P. Barendregt. Termination for the direct sum of left-linear term rewriting systems. In *Lecture Notes in Computer Science Vol 355*, pages 477–491, Chapel Hill, 1989. 3rd International Conference on Rewriting Techniques and Applications.

[Toy87a] Y. Toyama. Counterexamples to termination for the direct sum of term rewriting systems. *Information Processing Letters*, 25:141–143, 1987.

[Toy87b] Y. Toyama. On the Church-Rosser property for the direct sum of term rewriting systems. *Journal of the ACM*, 34(1):128–143, 1987.

A complete type inference algorithm for simple intersection types [1]

M . Coppo - P. Giannini
Dipartimento di Informatica
Universita' di Torino
C. Svizzera 185- 10100 TORINO
ITALY

Abstract

In this paper we present a decidable restriction of the intersection type discipline, obtained by combining intersection and universal quantification over types. The system, which has a notion of principal type, is a proper extension of the ML type system. A sound and complete type checking algorithm is presented and proved correct.

1. Introduction

One of the most interesting notions of type constraint for functional programming languages is the one derived from Curry's *Functionality Theory* [Curry, Feys, 1958], which suggested the type disciplines incorporated in some programming languages of recent design, notably ML [Gordon, Milner, Wadsworth, 1979] and Miranda [Turner, 1985]. In this approach types are assigned to terms of the λ–calculus according to a set of formal rules which can be effectively checked at compile time. Types describe the functional behaviour of terms in such a way that, in general, the same term can be assigned infinitely many types depending on the particular program context in which it occurs. This causes a natural notion of *implicit* polymorphism to be introduced, where *type schemes* are assigned to terms and they may be instantiated to match the types required by the surrounding program context. Several features make this sort of polymorphism particularly attractive both from the practical and the theoretical point of view. The type inference algorithm is complete, due to the existence of *principal type schemes*, [Hindley, 1969] and [Milner, 1978] which fully characterize the set of types assignable to each

[1] Work partially supported by MPI 60% funding.

term. Moreover natural properties of typed terms can be easily proven like the property of strong normalization and the fact that types are preserved by reduction. An important consequence of this property is, for example, that terms having a type cannot produce run time errors during their evaluation.

In spite of that, considerable effort has been done recently to find stronger type systems that, while retaining the basic good properties of the ML type system (decidability, completeness, strong normalization, etc..) could overcome its weakness. In ML, in fact, not all meaningful terms have a proper type, even when they are used in a consistent way. Take for instance the operators **twice**=λf.λx.f(f x) and **K**=λx.λy.x. The type given to **twice** by the ML type checker is such that the term (**twice K**) has no type whreas (**twice K**) β-reduces to λx.λu.λv.x which is well typed. In ML, however, we can assign a type to the term **let** f=K **in** λx.f(f x). Here the body of **twice** must be typed, in the **let** construct, using explicitly the fact that f is **K**. That means that any other use of **twice** requires a different type checking. This is contrary to the functional style of programming in which a function is typechecked once and for all, and all its uses require only its type specification.

Several extensions of the ML type system have been proposed. One of the most interesting is characterized by the introduction (in a type inference context) of the notion of (second-order) universal quantification over types taken from Girard's system F [Girard 1972]. It is not known, however, whether typability in the second-order type assignment system is decidable . Moreover, no notion of principal type seems to exist in this system

A number of restrictions of the second-order type assignment system have been studied. The restriction to rank two has been proved to be decidable [Kfoury, Tyurin, 1990], but it turns out to be essentially equivalent to the ML type system (with the **let** operator). At rank three, instead, the second-order type assignment system is undecidable [Kfoury, Tyurin, 1990]. Another approach to overcome the intrinsic complexity of the second-order type inference is taken in [Giannini, Ronchi, 1991] where a complete stratification of the second-order type discipline is introduced. Such stratification is decidable. In this system, however, type inference is not compositional. The typing properties of a term are represented by a set of equations that can have many uncomparable solutions.

Also related to the second-order type inference system is the recursively polymorphic extension of ML [Mycroft, 1984], which has been proven to be undecidable [Kfoury, et al., 1989]. In this system, moreover, the extension of ML is limited to the use of recursion over polymorphic functions, which is not so usual in the functional programming practice.

In this paper we introduce a type assignment system based on a combination of the notions of rank two polymorphism and intersection . Intersection types, which have been introduced in [Coppo, Dezani, 1980] (see also [Barendregt, Coppo, Dezani, 1983]), allow to assign types to all strongly normalizable terms . As a consequence of this, however, the typechecking in systems with intersection types is undecidable, even if a notion of principal type exists [Ronchi, Venneri, 1984]. Indeed, intersection types in their full generality are more suitable to study semantic properties of λ-terms. This is also supported by the fact that it is possible to define models in which the interpretation of a term is given by the set of its types [Barendregt, Coppo, Dezani, 1983].

In this paper the notion of intersection is used in a limited way, to allow a term variable to have different types in its different occurrences. When a variable is abstracted, instead of unify all the types of its uses, as in ML, we take the intersection of all such types (represented by a finite set of types). In this way we do not commit to a specific representative for all the types. Intersections can be generated also by instantiation of a (universally quantified) type scheme, in the style of the ML type system. So we get an inference system which is substantially stronger than the ML type system (all pure normal form, for instance, have a type). We prove that a notion of principal type exists for such a system and give a complete type inference algorithm. Owing to the finite nature of intersection, it turns out that a term has, in general, a finite set of principal types and not only one as in ML. Each of such types, however, is "more general" than the ML principal type. Terms having more than one principal type, however, are rather pathological (we will show one in section 4). Indeed all terms that arise in the programming practice have only one principal type.

The type assignment system with its properties is introduced in section 2. In section 3 we introduce another system with labelled quantifiers which represents a sort of meta-system in which the type checking properties will be studied. Finally the type checking algorithm is presented in section 4.

2 The type assignment system and its properties

We introduce the type assignment system $\vdash_\wedge$ we will be dealing with. As remarked in the introduction our system is a variant of the intersection type system of [Coppo, et al., 1980]. As in [Coppo, et al., 1980] we avoid the explicit use of intersection by denoting with $\{\alpha_1;...;\alpha_n\}$ the intersection $\alpha_1\wedge...\wedge\alpha_n$ (in the notation of [Barendregt, Coppo, Dezani, 1983]). Moreover we consider also type schemes (in the sense of [Damas, Milner, 1982]) that can generate intersections by (multiple) instantiations.

Therefore, in describing the syntax of types we use three categories of objects : the *types*, the *intersections of types*, and the *schemes*. These categories are kept separate to emphasize their different role in the type assignment system. Types are the ultimate result of our type assignment system. Indeed they express the functionality of the terms we want to characterize. Intersections of types allow to delay the commitment (unification) to a specific type in the multiple use of variables (see rules (VAR) and ($\rightarrow$I)). So they appear in the left-hand-side of an arrow constructor (we do not allow intersections in the right-hand-side of an arrow). Finally schemes are descriptions of (infinite) sets of types. They express, through the use of universal quantification over generic type variables, the polymorphism intrinsic in terms (see rule ($\forall$I) and ($\forall$E)). The fact that schemes are not components of types emphasize their metatheoretical nature. (This is also the view taken in [Damas, Milner, 1982].)

We will study type assignment for a standard core language which consists of the basic λ–calculus with constants, whose terms are defined from a a set of basic constants and a set of terms variables by the operations of application and abstraction.

Definition 2.1. (i) The sets T of *types* and Q of *intersections of types* are defined from a set K of basic types and a set V of type variables by:

- $V, K \subseteq T$
- $\{\alpha_1;...;\alpha_n\} \in Q$ whenever $\alpha_1,...,\alpha_n \in T$. ($\{\} \in Q$ is the empty intersection)
- $\xi \rightarrow \beta \in T$ whenever $\xi \in Q$, $\beta \in T$.

(ii) The set S of *schemes* is defined by

- $\forall \underline{t}.\alpha \in S$ whenever $\alpha \in T$ and $\underline{t}$ is a (possibly empty) sequence of type variables. □

α, β, γ, and δ range over types, ξ, χ over intersections and σ, τ over schemes. Variables are ranged over by t, u, v ... $\underline{t}$, $\underline{u}$, ... denote finite sequences of type variables, and $\underline{\alpha}$, $\underline{\beta}$, $\underline{\gamma}$, etc. denote sequences of types. ε denotes the empty sequence.

When explicitly mentioned α can also be used to denote objects that belong to more than one syntactic category.

Note that, for technical reasons, schemes are obtained from types by the use of a unique universal quantification over a sequence of variables. Intersections and sequences of variables may be seen, respectively, as finite sets of type or type variables and are considered equal modulo permutations and repetitions of the same element.

A substitution is a function $s:V \rightarrow T$. For substitutions we use the standard notations for finite functions. $[t_1:=\alpha_1, \ldots, t_n:=\alpha_n]$ ($n \geq 0$) denotes the substitution assigning α_1 to t_1, ..., α_n to t_n. $s[t_1:=\alpha_1, \ldots, t_n:=\alpha_n]$ is the function that coincides with s on all the variables except t_1, ..., t_n, and is such that $s(t_i)=\alpha_i$ ($1 \leq i \leq n$). Substitutions can be extended to $T \cup Q \cup S$ in the standard way. We use the same notatin to denote explicit substitution. So $\alpha[t:=\beta]$ is the same as $[t:=\beta](\alpha)$.

Types, intersections and schemes are closed under substitution, i.e. if α is a type (intersection, scheme) $s(\alpha)$ is a type (intersection, scheme).

The type assignment system $\vdash_\wedge$ is given as a set of formal rules in natural deduction.

Definition 2.2. (i) A basis B is a set of statements $x:\alpha$ where α is a type. Define $B/x = B - \{x:\alpha \mid x:\alpha \in B\}$.

(ii) A type assignment statement is an expression $B \vdash_\wedge M:\alpha$ where B is a basis and α is a type, an intersection or a scheme. The rules for type assignment are the following.

(VAR) $\{x:\alpha\} \vdash_\wedge x:\alpha$

$$(\rightarrow I)\ \frac{B/x \cup \{x:\alpha_1,...,x:\alpha_n\} \vdash_\wedge M:\beta}{B/x \vdash_\wedge \lambda x.M:\{\alpha_1;...;\alpha_n\} \rightarrow \beta}$$

$$(\rightarrow E)\ \frac{B_1 \vdash_\wedge M:\xi \rightarrow \beta \qquad B_2 \vdash_\wedge N:\xi}{B_1 \cup B_2 \vdash_\wedge (MN):\beta}$$

$$(\forall I)\ \frac{B \vdash_\wedge M:\alpha}{B \vdash_\wedge M:\forall \underline{t}.\alpha} \qquad \text{(the variables in } \underline{t} \text{ are not free for M in B)}$$

$$(\forall E)\ \frac{B\vdash_{\wedge} M:\forall \underline{t}\,\alpha}{B\vdash_{\wedge} M:\{\alpha[\underline{t}:=\underline{\beta}_1];\ldots;\alpha[\underline{t}:=\underline{\beta}_n]\}}\quad (n\geq 0)\quad (\text{where } \underline{\beta}_1,\ldots,\underline{\beta}_n\in T^*)\qquad \square$$

It is immediate to see that deductions are closed under substitution, i.e. if $B\vdash_{\wedge} M:\alpha$, then $s(B)\vdash_{\wedge} M:s(\alpha)$, where α is a type, an intersection or a schema.

Remark 2.3. (i) If $B\vdash_{\wedge} M:\alpha$ then B contains assumptions on all and only the free variables of M, and for each variable x there are at most as many different assumptions as occurrences of x in M. In the conclusion of ($\to$I) if x is not a free variable of M we have $B\vdash_{\wedge} \lambda x.M:\{\,\}\to\beta$.
(ii) The only way we can derive an intersection for M is by an application of ($\forall$E). Therefore only intersections whose elements are instances of a same type are derivable for a term M.
(iii) From $B\vdash_{\wedge} M:\alpha$ we can always derive, by ($\forall$I), $B\vdash_{\wedge} M:\forall\varepsilon.\alpha$ (where ε is the empty string) and, by ($\forall$E), then $B\vdash_{\wedge} M:\{\alpha\}$. So the following rule is derivable.

$$(\text{INT})\ \frac{B\vdash_{\wedge} M:\alpha}{B\vdash_{\wedge} M:\{\alpha\}}$$

This rule is useful since the minor premise of ($\to$E) must be an intersection.
(iv) An instance of ($\forall$I) followed by an instance of ($\forall$E) with n=0 produces the following derived rule

$$(\{\}\text{-I})\ \frac{B\vdash_{\wedge} M:\alpha}{B\vdash_{\wedge} M:\{\,\}}$$

That is, we can derive the empty intersection for M if and only if we can derive a type for M. Note the difference between {} and ω of [Coppo, et. al., 1980]. In that case ω is always derivable for a term. □

Example 2.4. (i) We show a derivation of type $\{v\}\to v$ for $(\lambda x.xx)(\lambda y.y)$.
Let Δ be $\lambda x.xx$, $\mathbf{D}_\Delta$ is the following derivation of a type for Δ

$$(\to I)\ \frac{(\to E)\ \dfrac{\{x:\{t\}\to u\}\vdash_{\wedge} x:\{t\}\to u \qquad (\text{INT})\dfrac{\{x:t\}\vdash_{\wedge} x:t}{\{x:t\}\vdash_{\wedge} x:\{t\}}}{\{x:\{t\}\to u,\ x:t\}\vdash_{\wedge} (xx):u}}{\varnothing\vdash_{\wedge} \lambda x.(xx):\{t;\{t\}\to u\}\to u}$$

Observe that two different types are assigned to the two occurrences of x. Note that $\lambda x.(xx)$ has not type in the ML type system.
(ii) Let $\mathbf{D}_1$ be the following derivation of an intersection for the identity :

$$(\forall E)\ \frac{(\forall I)\ \dfrac{(\to I)\ \dfrac{\{y:t\}\vdash_{\wedge} y:t}{\varnothing\vdash_{\wedge} \lambda y.y:\{t\}\to t}}{\varnothing\vdash_{\wedge} \lambda y.y:\forall t.\{t\}\to t}}{\varnothing\vdash_{\wedge} \lambda y.y:\{\{v\}\to v;\{\{v\}\to v\}\to\{v\}\to v\}}$$

The intersection assigned to $\lambda y.y$ is generated by two different instances of $\{t\}\to t$ obtained by ($\forall$E).

(iii) Let $\mathbf{D}_2 = \mathbf{D}_\Delta[t,u:=\{v\}\to v]$ be a proof of

$\emptyset\vdash_\wedge \lambda x.(xx):\{\{v\}\to v;\{\{v\}\to v\}\to\{v\}\to v\}\to\{v\}\to v\}.$

Combinig $\mathbf{D}_2$ and $\mathbf{D}_1$ by ($\to$E) we get a derivation of $\emptyset\vdash_\wedge(\lambda x.(xx))(\lambda y.y):\{v\}\to v$. □

Also terms which have a type in ML can be assigned "more informative" types in $\vdash_\wedge$. Take, for instance, the term **twice** = $\lambda f.\lambda x.\ f\ (f\ x)$ whose principal type scheme in ML is $(t\to t)\to t\to t$. **twice** represents a combinator which applies twice a function f to an argument x. In $\vdash_\wedge$ we can assign to **twice** type $\{\{t\}\to u;\{u\}\to v\}\to\{t\}\to v$ (where t, u, v are type variables). The meaning of this type can be informally explained saying that, if f is a function that maps both t into u and u into v then $f\circ f$ maps t into v . Now, referring to a more extended set of types containing a "list" type constructor (as ML, but lists can be represented in the pure λ-calculus as well), let F be a term of type $\{t\}\to$t-list (for example, F could be a polymorphic function mapping an object x of an arbitrary type t into the list containing x as the unique element). Then , using ($\forall$I) and ($\forall$E) we can deduce

$\vdash_\wedge$**twice**: $\{\{t\}\to$t-list ;$\{$t-list$\}\to$t-list-list$\}\to\{t\}\to$t-list-list and

$\vdash_\wedge$(**twice** F):$\{t\}\to$t-list-list

while no type could be assigned to (**twice** F) in ML.

In the following we establish the property of subject reduction for the system $\vdash_\wedge$. Subject reduction tells us that types are preserved by computations. An immediate consequence of subject reduction is the well-known property that "typed terms cannot go wrong", i.e. the fact that no type-incorrect application (like, for instance, (3 3)) can appear reducing a well-typed term.

Theorem 2.5 (*Subject reduction*). If $B\vdash_\wedge M:\alpha$ and $M\to^*_{\beta\eta}N$, then $B'\vdash_\wedge N:\alpha$ for some $B'\subseteq B$, where α is a type, an intersection or a scheme. □

The reason for which, in general, we have only $B'\subseteq B$ is that, in a reduction step $(\lambda x.M)N\to_\beta M[x:=N]$, if x does not occur in M, $M[x:=N]$ can have less free variables than $(\lambda x.M)N$.

Two main properties of the system are the strong normalization property and the fact that each term in normal form without occurrences of constants has a type. The condition that there be no occurrences of constants is necessary since terms like (3 3), although being in normal form, cannot be typed. Indeed any term in normal form that has not a type in $\vdash_\wedge$ contains some incorrect application and is semantically meaningless.

Strong normalization follows from the strong normalization theorem for the system with unrestricted intersection and universal quantification proved in [Leivant, 1986] of which $\vdash_\wedge$ is a proper subsystem.

Property 2.6. If If $B\vdash_\wedge M:\alpha$ for some B and α then M is strongly normalizable. □

Property 2.7. If M is a term in β-normal form then there exists a basis B and a type α such that $B \vdash_{\wedge} M{:}\alpha$.

Proof. By induction on M. We have four possible cases.

If $M \equiv x$ is a variable take $\{x{:}t\} \vdash_{\wedge} x{:}t$ where t is a type variable.

If $M \equiv \lambda x.M'$ then, by induction hypothesis, we have $B' \vdash_{\wedge} M'{:}\alpha$ for some B', α. There are two possible cases:

- If x occurs in M' then let $B' = B/x \cup \{x{:}\beta_1,...,x{:}\beta_n\}$. By an application of ($\rightarrow$I), we get $B/x \vdash_{\wedge} \lambda x.M'{:}\{\beta_1;...;\beta_n\} \rightarrow \alpha$.
- If x does not occur in M' then $B = B/x$ and we get $B \vdash_{\wedge} \lambda x.M'{:}\{\} \rightarrow \alpha$.

If $M \equiv (xM_1...M_n)$ $(n \geq 1)$ then by induction hypotheses there are B_i, α_i $(1 \leq i \leq n)$ such that $B_i \vdash_{\wedge} M_i{:}\alpha_i$. Now let $B = B_1 \cup ... \cup B_n$ and $\sigma \equiv \{\alpha_1\} \rightarrow ... \rightarrow \{\alpha_n\} \rightarrow t$ where t is a new type variable. By applying n times ($\rightarrow$E) we get $B \cup \{x{:}\sigma\} \vdash_{\wedge} M{:}t$. □

The type assigned to the normal form M in the proof of 2.7 corresponds in some sense to its principal type, as it will be remarked in section 4.

We end this section with a result about the relations between $\vdash_{\wedge}$ and the ML type assignment system. Such a system is an extension of the basic Curry's type assignment system for λ-terms [Curry, Feys, 1958] in which the new syntactic form **let** has been added to the pure λ-calculus. The form **let** is the only operator that allows to exploit the notion of scheme.

The ML terms are defined by the same syntax of the λ-calculus with constants with the addition of the clause that **let** x = N **in** M is a term whenever M and N are terms. Operationally this term is equivalent to $(\lambda x.M)N$, but not from the point of view of typechecking. The set T_{ML} of *ML-types* is defined from K (the set of basic types) and V (the set of type variables) by the rule

- $\alpha \rightarrow \beta$ is a type whenever α, β are types

The set S_{ML} of ML-*type schemes* is defined from T_{ML} as in Def. 2.1(ii). Then T_{ML} and S_{ML} are, respectively, isomorphic to a subset of T and S. The type assignment rules are given following [Damas, Milner, 1982], but keeping our syntax.

Definition 2.8. (i) An ML-basis B is a set $\{x_i{:}\alpha_i \mid i \in I\}$, where x_i are term variables and α_i are ML-types or ML-schemes, such that for each variable x_i there is at most one premise in B.

(ii) The type assignment rules are the following, where α, β denote ML-types and σ a ML-scheme:

(VAR) $B \vdash_{ML} x{:}\alpha$ if $x{:}\alpha \in B$ where α is a type or a scheme.

$$(\rightarrow I) \quad \frac{B/x \cup \{x{:}\alpha\} \vdash_{ML} M{:}\beta}{B/x \vdash_{ML} \lambda x.M{:}\alpha \rightarrow \beta}$$

$$(\rightarrow E) \quad \frac{B \vdash_{ML} M{:}\alpha \rightarrow \beta \qquad B \vdash_{ML} N{:}\alpha}{B \vdash_{ML} (MN){:}\beta}$$

$$(\forall I)\quad \frac{B\vdash_{ML} M:\alpha}{B\vdash_{ML} M:\forall \underline{t}.\alpha}\qquad \text{(if all variables in } \underline{t} \text{ do not occur free in B)}$$

$$(\forall E)\quad \frac{B\vdash_{ML} M:\forall \underline{t}.\alpha}{B\vdash_{ML} M:\alpha[\underline{t}:=\underline{\beta}]}\qquad (\text{where } \underline{\beta}\in T_{ML})$$

$$(LET)\quad \frac{B/x\cup\{x:\sigma\}\vdash_{ML} M:\alpha \qquad B/x\vdash_{ML} N:\sigma}{B\vdash_{ML} (\mathbf{let}\ x=N\ \mathbf{in}\ M):\alpha}\qquad \square$$

Note that in rule (→E) we are forced to consider the same basis in both premises, since any variable x must occur at most once in B, and the assumption for x must be the same in both deductions. The (LET) rule is essential in ML since a term **let** x = N **in** M can have a type while (λx.M)N, although operationally equivalent, may not. We shall see that the **let** form is useless (as far as typechecking is concerned) in $\vdash_\wedge$. Moreover $\vdash_\wedge$ is more powerful than $\vdash_{ML}$, since there are terms that have a type in $\vdash_\wedge$ and have none in $\vdash_{ML}$, even using **let** instead of application whenever possible (like, for instance, λx.xx).

To make more formal the relation between $\vdash_{ML}$ and $\vdash_\wedge$ we define a formal translation from the set of ML types and schemes into our language. Let $()^*:T_{ML}\cup S_{ML}\to T\cup S$ be defined by:

- $t^* = t$ - $c^*=c$ where t is type variable and c a basic type.
- $(\alpha\to\beta)^*=\{\alpha^*\}\to\beta^*$
- $(\forall\underline{t}.\alpha)^*=\forall\underline{t}.\alpha^*$

Since schemes cannot be assigned to variables in $\vdash_\wedge$ we must translate an assumption $x:\sigma$ in $\vdash_{ML}$ to a set of assumptions $\{x:\alpha_1,\dots,x:\alpha_n\}$. So if B is an ML basis we define

$$B^*=\left\{ B' \;\middle|\; \begin{array}{l} x:\sigma\in B \Rightarrow x:\alpha_1\dots x:\alpha_n\in B' \text{ for some instances } \alpha_1\dots\alpha_n \text{ of } \sigma^* \ (n\geq 0) \\ x:\alpha\in B \Rightarrow \text{ either } x:\alpha^*\in B' \text{ or } x \text{ does not occur in } B' \end{array} \right\}.$$

B^* is the set of all bases that could correspond to B translating a deduction in $\vdash_{ML}$ to one in $\vdash_\wedge$.

Finally let M be an ML-term. Define M^* as the pure λ-term obtained by replacing in M each occurrence of **let** x=N **in** M by (λx.M)N. The following property can be easily proved by induction on derivations in $\vdash_{ML}$.

Property 2.9. If $B\vdash_{ML} M:\alpha$ then there exist $B'\in B^*$ such that $B'\vdash_\wedge M^*:\alpha^*$. □

In [Kfoury, Tyurin, 1990] it has been proved that $\vdash_{ML}$ is essentially equivalent to the (type inference version of the) polymorphic (or second-order) typed λ-calculus limited at rank 2, i.e., in which the ∀ operator may occur only in the left scope of not more than one arrow. Then by the previous property in $\vdash_\wedge$ we can assign a type to more terms that in the polymorphic typed λ-calculus of rank 2 even though, as for ML, the types can be different.

In $\vdash_\wedge$ we can give a type also to terms which cannot be typed in the full polymorphic λ-calculus, like the term ((λy.λx.y(x(λz.z))(x(λu.λv.u))) Δ) (see [Giannini, Ronchi, 1988] for the proof that this term cannot be typed in the second-order calculus). We leave as an exercise to find a type for this term in $\vdash_\wedge$. On the other side there are terms which have a type in the second-order λ-calculus (even limited at rank 3) for which we can not infer a type in our system. An example is given by ((λx.xΔx)(Δ **twice**)) which in the second-order type assignment system at rank three has type $\forall t.(t\to t)\to t\to t$ while it has no type in $\vdash_\wedge$.

As already remarked the present system is a restriction of the intersection type system $\vdash_{int}$ of [Coppo, Dezani, 1980] (see also [Van Bakel, 1991] for a more detailed description and properties). In particular in $\vdash_{int}$ there is a rule of intersection introduction of the kind

$$(\wedge I)\ \frac{B\vdash_{int}M:\alpha_1 \ \dots \ B\vdash_{int}M:\alpha_n}{B\vdash_{int}M:\{\alpha_1;\dots;\alpha_n\}}$$

which allows to assign to a term M an intersection of types whose deductions can have a quite different structure. In our system, instead, we can assign to M only intersection obtained by generic instance of a unique type. The system $\vdash_{int}$ is very strong (it allows to give a type to all strongly normalizable terms) but its type assignment is undecidable [van Bakel, 1991], as for the case of the intersection type system of [Barendregt, Coppo, Dezani, 1983] (see also [Ronchi, Venneri, 1984]).

An interesting restriction of $\vdash_{int}$ is that of allowing only intersections at rank two. That is intersections may occur either at top level or in the left scope of only one arrow. Also in this system (let call it $\vdash_{int,2}$) we can give type to (the translation in the pure λ-calculus of) all ML-terms which have a type in the ML type system [Leivant, 1983]. $\vdash_{int,2}$, moreover, has the principal type scheme property and its typechecking is decidable. The set of terms that can be typed in $\vdash_{int,2}$ and $\vdash_\wedge$ are, however, incomparable. There are terms that can be typed in $\vdash_\wedge$ but not in $\vdash_{int,2}$. Not all normal forms, for instance, can be typed in $\vdash_{int,2}$ and conversely, there are terms that can be typed in $\vdash_{int,2}$ but not in $\vdash_\wedge$. The main reason for this is that in $\vdash_\wedge$ we cannot assign an intersection to a variable in a basis, while this would be necessary to type terms like $\Delta'=\lambda y.\Delta\ y$. In fact we should assign $\{t;\{t\}\to u\}$ to y (see example 2.4) to give a type to Δ', and this can be done in $\vdash_{int,2}$ but not in $\vdash_\wedge$.

More generally the terms that can be typed in $\vdash_{int,2}$ and not in $\vdash_\wedge$ have at least a subterm of the shape (M x) where x is a variable and M is a term that would not have a type in ML. Instead terms of the kind (f M) where M is a term that can have intersections in its type are typed in $\vdash_\wedge$ but not in $\vdash_{int,2}$.

3. The system $\vdash_L$.

Now we turn to the problrm of authomatic inference of types for the system $\vdash_\wedge$. In particular we want to establish a dependency between all different derivations for the same term via a notion of principal type and principal deduction [Hindley, Seldin, 1986]. To this aim we will introduce a "more informative" system $\vdash_L$ in which deductions are (informally speaking) schemes which represent a class of deductions in the original system $\vdash_\wedge$. In fact $\vdash_L$ turns out to be equivalent to $\vdash_\wedge$. The main feature of $\vdash_L$ is the introduction of a notion of labelled universal quantifier. A labelled quantifier is a syntactic tool used to represent a class of intersections, namely all these that could be obtained by (∀E) from a given scheme. Let us consider the following examples.

Let $\mathbf{D_I}$ be the following deduction, where I is λx.x.

$$\mathbf{D_I}: \quad (\to I)\ \frac{\{x:t\}\vdash_\wedge x:t}{\varnothing\vdash_\wedge \lambda x.x:\{t\}\to t}$$

If we want to assign a type to a term λx.xI the most obvious deduction seems to be the following:

$$\mathbf{D_2}: \quad (\to I)\ \frac{(\to E)\ \dfrac{\{x:\{\{t\}\to t\}\to u\}\vdash_\wedge x:\{\{t\}\to t\}\to u \qquad (INT)\ \dfrac{\mathbf{D_I}}{\varnothing\vdash_\wedge \lambda x.x:\{\{t\}\to t\}}}{\{x:\{\{t\}\to t\}\to u\}\vdash_\wedge (xI):u}}{\varnothing\vdash_\wedge \lambda x.(xI):\{\{\{t\}\to t\}\to u\}\to u}$$

This deduction scheme is good if we want to apply, for instance, λx.xI to I (we have just to make an instance of it replacing u by $\{t\}\to t$, observing that $\{\{t\}\to t\}\to\{t\}\to t$ is a type for I.

However, if we want to apply λx.xI to Δ, which has type $\{t;\{t\}\to u\}\to u$ (and, obviously, all its substitution instances), we cannot use any deduction for λx.xI which is a substitution instance of $\mathbf{D_1}$. Instead we have to use the following deduction for λx.xI.

$$\mathbf{D_2}: \quad (\to I)\ \frac{(\to E)\ \dfrac{\{x:\alpha\}\vdash_\wedge x:\alpha \qquad (\forall E)\ \dfrac{(\forall I)\ \dfrac{\mathbf{D_I}}{\varnothing\vdash_\wedge \lambda x.x:\forall t.\{t\}\to t}}{\varnothing\vdash_\wedge I:\{\{t\}\to t;\{\{t\}\to t\}\to\{t\}\to t\}}}{\{x:\alpha\}\vdash_\wedge xI:\{t\}\to t}}{\varnothing\vdash_\wedge \lambda x.xI:\{\alpha\}\to\{t\}\to t}$$

where $\alpha=\{\{t\}\to t;\{\{t\}\to t\}\to\{t\}\to t\}\to\{t\}\to t$. In fact α is a type for Δ, being an instance of $\{t;\{t\}\to u\}\to u$ (replace simultaneously t and u by $\{t\}\to t$).

Note that $\mathbf{D_2}$ (and any of its substitution instances) whould not be useful to type ((λx.xI) I) since no type of the form $\{\alpha;\beta\}\to\gamma$ can be assigned to I.

We can see, on the contrary, that any derivation of a type for I (or Δ) can be obtained by substitution from $\mathbf{D_I}$ (or $\mathbf{D_\Delta}$) (adding, possibly, an application of (∀I)-(∀E) at the end), so we could claim that $\{t\}\to t$ and $\{\{t\}\to u;t\}\to u$ are, respectively, the principal types for I and Δ. However, in the case of λx.xI we have not, in $\vdash_\wedge$ any good candidate to be its principal type.

We now introduce a new system in which we can represent a potential intersection using the notion of "labelled" universal quantifier. In this system, for instance, the principal type of λx.xI is a type $\forall u.\ \{(\overset{1}{\forall} t.\{t\}\to t\ )\to u\}\to u$ where the internal quantified type $\overset{1}{\forall} t.\{t\}\to t$ does indeed represent all the possible intersections that can be obtained from it by (∀E), thus allowing a unified treatement of deductions like $\mathbf{D_1}$ and $\mathbf{D_2}$. We remark, however, that a labelled quantifier is not intended to be a universal quantifier as in the second-order polymorphic lambda-calculus. In fact a second-order type $\forall t.\alpha$ can be instantiated, using (∀E), in different ways in each of its occurrences in a deduction while a labelled quantifier $\overset{1}{\forall} t.\alpha$ is a sort of intersection scheme that must be instantiated in the same way in all its possible occurrences in a deduction. This will force us to introduce a somewhat more complicated rule for ∀ elimination.

We now introduce formally the system $\vdash_L$ with labelled quantifiers. Labelled quantifiers can be considered both as a particular kind of intersections or as schemes. So they can occurr either in the left-hand-side of → or as the final result of a deduction.

Definition 3.1. (i) The sets T_L, Q_L of *labelled types* and *intersections* are defined inductively from K and V and a set L of *labels* in the following way:

- $V, K \subseteq T_L$
- $\{\alpha_1;...;\alpha_n\} \in Q_L$ whenever $\alpha_1,...,\alpha_n \in T_L$
- $\overset{l}{\forall}\underline{t}.\alpha \in Q_L$ whenever $\alpha \in T_L$ and $l \in L$ (l *is the label* of $\overset{l}{\forall}\underline{t}.\alpha$)
- $\xi \to \beta \in T_L$ whenever $\xi \in Q_L$, $\beta \in T_L$

with the constraint that all types with the same label must be α-equivalent (differ at most in the name of bound variables).

(ii) A *type context* $\alpha[-]$ is a type α with a missing subterm. □

Each labelled $\forall$ identifies indeed a type rather than simply a type operator. There are no two types $\overset{l}{\forall}\underline{t}.\alpha$, $\overset{l}{\forall}\underline{u}.\beta$ with the same label such that α is different from β (modulo a re-naming of bound type variables). In particular there cannot be two nested labelled $\forall$ with the same label.

A type context just represents the part of a type surrounding a given subtype. Owing to the previous condition there is in general no freedom in choosing the term that has to fill the hole, if this occurs in the scope of a labelled quantifier.

In order to handle labelled quantifiers we need the operation of expansion, which is crucial in the typechecking algorithm. This operation is defined relatively to a context represented by a set of types or type contexts.

Definition 3.2 (i) The *scope* of a label l occurring in $\overset{l}{\forall}\underline{t}.\alpha$ is α (by the above condition on labelled types α is unique).

(ii) A *environment* is a finite set of types, intersections and type contexts.

(iii) Let A be a environment. We say that a label l *directly dominates* another label m in A if:

1. m occurs in A only in the scope of l.
2. there is no other label l' which occur in the scope of l and such that m occurs in the scope of l'.

(iv) A label l *dominates* m in A if there are $m_1,...,m_k$ (k>2) such that $l=m_1$, $m=m_k$ and each m_i directly dominates m_{i+1}.

As remarked before the instantiation of a labelled quantifier must be performed simultaneously on all its occurrences in a given environment. This is achieved by the operation of expansion.

Definition 3.3. (i) Let A be a environment. A *simple expansion* in A is a partial function denoted $[\overset{l}{\forall}\underline{t}.\alpha:=\xi]$ where ξ can be

-1. an intersection $\{\alpha_1[\underline{t}:=\underline{\beta}_1]);...;\alpha_n[\underline{t}:=\underline{\beta}_n])\}$ (n>1) where $\underline{\beta}_1,...,\underline{\beta}_n \in T_L^*$ and α_i are obtained from α, respectively, by choosing an independent name (say $\overset{m_i}{\forall}$) for each labelled $\overset{m}{\forall}$ in α which is dominated by l in A. In this case we say that m_i is the label *corresponding* to m in α_i.

- 2. $\overset{m}{\forall}\underline{u}.\beta[\underline{\gamma}/\underline{t}]$ where $\underline{u}$ are variables which occur free in $\underline{\gamma}$ and not in β or A, and m is a new label not occurring in A.

(ii) A simple expansion $r = [\overset{l}{\forall}\underline{t}.\alpha:=\xi]$ can be extended to the set of all types and sequences by defining:

$r(\overset{l}{\forall}\underline{t}.\alpha) = \xi$

$r(\alpha\to\beta)= r(\alpha)\to r(\beta)$

$r(\{\alpha_1;\ldots;\alpha_n\}) = \{r(\alpha_1);\ldots;r(\alpha_n)\}$.

(iii) An *expansion* is a composition of simple expansions. □

Example 3.4. Let $A = \{(\overset{m}{\forall}u.\{(\overset{l}{\forall}\underline{t}.t\to t)\to u\}\to u\ )\to v,\ v\}$. An example of simple expansion in A is

$r=[\overset{m}{\forall}u.\{(\overset{l}{\forall}\underline{t}.t\to t)\to u\}\to u := \{\{(\overset{l_1}{\forall}\underline{t}.t\to t)\to\alpha\}\to\alpha\,;\{(\overset{l_2}{\forall}\underline{t}.t\to t)\to\beta\}\to\beta\}]$

where α,β are types. The result of applying r to A is the set

$\{\{\{(\overset{l_1}{\forall}\underline{t}.t\to t)\to\alpha\}\to\alpha;\ \{(\overset{l_2}{\forall}\underline{t}.t\to t)\to\beta\}\to\beta\}\to v,\ v\}.$

If we take instead

$r'=[\overset{l}{\forall}\underline{t}.t\to t:=\{\{v\}\to v;\{\{v\}\to v\}\to\{v\}\to v\}]$

the result of applying r' to A is

$\{(\overset{m}{\forall}u.\{\{\{v\}\to v\ ;\ \{\{v\}\to v\}\to\{v\}\to v\}\to u\}\to u)\to v,\ v\}.$ □

If B is a basis then $A_B = \{\beta \mid x{:}\beta\in B\}$. In the following we will often use B as a environment, identifying B and A_B.

We now introduce the type assignment system $\vdash_L$. The main differences over $\vdash_\wedge$ are the introduction of two new rules to handle labelled quantifiers.

Definition 3.5.(i) The type assignment system $\vdash_L$ is defined as $\vdash_\wedge$ by replacing ($\forall$I) and ($\forall$E) by the following rules ($\forall^L$I) and (EXP) .

$$(\forall^L I)\quad \frac{B\vdash_L M{:}\alpha}{B\vdash_L M{:}\overset{l}{\forall}\underline{t}.\alpha}$$

where α is type, l is any label and the variables in $\underline{t}$ do not occur in B.

$$(EXP)\quad \frac{B\vdash_L M{:}\alpha[\overset{l}{\forall}\underline{t}.\beta]}{B\vdash_L M{:}\alpha[\xi]}$$

where α is either a type or an intersection, l does not occur in B, $\alpha[]$ and ξ has been obtained by a simple expansion of $\overset{l}{\forall}\underline{t}.\beta$ in the environment $B\cup\{\alpha[]\}$. □

Note that a corresponding of rule ($\forall$E) can be obtained as a particular case of rule (EXP) where $\alpha[]$ is the empty context.

Example 3.6. We show a deduction of an intersection for $\lambda x.x(\lambda y.y)$ (indeed its principal deduction) in $\vdash_L$

$$(\forall^{L}I)\ \dfrac{(\to I)\ \dfrac{(\to E)\ \dfrac{(VAR)\ \{x:(\overset{m}{\forall}t.\{t\}\to t)\to u\}\vdash_L x:(\overset{m}{\forall}t.\{t\}\to t)\to u \qquad (\forall I)\ \dfrac{\mathbf{D}_I}{\emptyset\vdash_L \lambda y.y:(\overset{m}{\forall}t.\{t\}\to t)}}{\{x:(\overset{m}{\forall}t.\{t\}\to t)\to u\}\vdash_L x(\lambda y.y):u}}{\emptyset\vdash_L \lambda x.xI:((\overset{m}{\forall}t.\{t\}\to t)\to u)\to u}}{\emptyset\vdash_L \lambda x.xI:\overset{l}{\forall}u.\{(\overset{m}{\forall}t.\{t\}\to t)\to u\}\to u}$$

The present notion of expansion (with respect, in particular, to the relabelling of the internal labels in Definition 3.3(i)-1.) is needed in order to keep the maximum level of generality in the potential intersections represented by labelled $\forall$. Take for instance the statement

$\emptyset\vdash_L \lambda x.xI:\overset{l}{\forall}u.\{(\overset{m}{\forall}t.\{t\}\to t)\to u\}\to u.$

The informal meaning of $\overset{m}{\forall}t.\{t\}\to t$ is that we can deduce $\emptyset\vdash_L \lambda x.xI:\overset{l}{\forall}u.\{\xi\to u\}\to u$ where ξ is any intersection that can be obtained by (simple) expansion from $\overset{m}{\forall}t.\{t\}\to t$. Now observe that we are indeed able to deduce, for instance,

$\emptyset\vdash_\wedge \lambda x.xI:\{\{\xi_1\to u_1\}\to u_1;\ \{\xi_2\to u_2\}\to u_2\}$

where ξ_1, ξ_2 are any two expansions of $\overset{m}{\forall}t.\{t\}\to t$. In fact let $\xi_1=\{\alpha_1;...;\alpha_h\}$ and $\xi_2=\{\beta_1;...;\beta_k\}$ (where α_i and β_i are instances of $\{t\}\to t$) and let $p=\max(h,k)$. We can deduce

$\emptyset\vdash_\wedge \lambda x.xI:\{\{\{t_1\}\to t_1;...;\{t_p\}\to t_p\}\to u\}\to u$

applying ($\forall$I) and ($\forall$E) to the endstatement of $\mathbf{D}_I$ and assigning a suitable type to x. Then, assuming that $t_1,...,t_p$ do not occur elsewhere in the deduction, we have

$\emptyset\vdash_\wedge \lambda x.xI:\forall u t_1...t_p.\{\{\{t_1\}\to t_1;...;\{t_p\}\to t_p\}\to u\}\to u.$

Now we can get

$\emptyset\vdash_\wedge \lambda x.xI:\{\{\xi_1\to u_1\}\to u_1;\ \{\xi_2\to u_2\}\to u_2\}$

by ($\forall$E) replacing the sequence u $t_1...t_p$ in the two copies generated by ($\forall$E), respectively, by $\underline{\alpha}=u_1\ \alpha_1...\alpha_p$ and $\underline{\beta}=u_2\ \beta_1...\beta_p$. If $\underline{\alpha}$ or $\underline{\beta}$ have less than p+1 types it is enough to identify some of the types replaced for the variables in $\underline{t}=t_1...t_p$ in them (intersections are seen modulo repetitions of the same type). By expanding $\overset{l}{\forall}u.\{(\overset{m}{\forall}t.\{t\}\to t)\to u\}\to u$ in

$\{\{(\overset{m_1}{\forall}t.\{t\}\to t)\to u_1\}\to u_1;\{(\overset{m_2}{\forall}t.\{t\}\to t)\to u_2\}\to u_2\}$

we keep track of this possibility, that would be lost if we identify the labels m_1 and m_2 (recall that expansion is performed uniformly on all label occurrences). Obviously this construction is possible only if the variables $\underline{t}$ can be quantified, i.e. if they (or equivalently $\overset{m}{\forall}$) do not occur elsewhere outside the range of $\overset{l}{\forall}$.

The need for a rule (EXP) more powerful than ($\forall$E) is a consequence of the possibility of renaming internal labels allowed by expansion. Since we want deduction in $\vdash_L$ to be closed under expansion (this is essential to prove the correctness of the typechecking algorithm), we must be able to expand also the internal labels like m_1 and m_2. This would not be possible without (EXP) (m_1 and m_2 are created only after the expansion of the label l).

Lemma 3.7. Deductions in $\vdash_L$ are closed by expansion, i.e. if $B\vdash_L M:\alpha$ and B', α' are obtained from B, α by expansion in the environment $B\cup\{\alpha\}$ then $B'\vdash_L M:\alpha'$. □

It is obvious that if $B\vdash_{\wedge}M:\alpha$ then $B\vdash_{L}M:\alpha$ (the rules of $\vdash_{\wedge}$ are weaker than the rules of $\vdash_{L}$). To prove the converse we need to establish a correspondence between types and intersections in $\vdash_{\wedge}$ (sets T and Q) and the (possibly) labelled ones in $\vdash_{L}$ (sets T_L and Q_L). In particular a labelled quantification in $\vdash_{L}$ can always be replaced by an intersection in $\vdash_{\wedge}$.

Definition 3.8. Let A be a environment. An expansion r in A is a *terminal expansion* if, for all $\alpha \in A$, $r(\alpha) \in T \cup Q$, i.e. no labelled quantifier is left in α. □

The correspondence between types and derivations in $\vdash_{\wedge}$ and in $\vdash_{L}$ is given by the following result, which states that $\vdash_{L}$ is conservative with respect to $\vdash_{\wedge}$.

Lemma 3.9. Let $B\vdash_{L}M:\alpha$ $(\alpha \in T_L \cup Q_L)$. Then $B'\vdash_{\wedge}M:\alpha'$ where B', α' is any terminal expansion of B, α. □

4. Typechecking

In this section we will prove the existence of principal type schemes and of a complete type inference algorithm for the system $\vdash_{L}$. This implies also the existence of a complete type inference algorithm for $\vdash_{\wedge}$ by Lemma 3.9. As remarked in the introduction the finitary nature of intersections determines the fact that we will have a set of principal types instead of a unique principal type as in the case of the ML type system. However each of them will be "more general" than the ML principal type scheme.

The crucial step in the type inference algorithm which is defined by induction on the structure of the term is obviously the case of application of two terms. For this case a sort of unification procedure is defined via the notion of reduction of a system of equations. It is useful, to this purpose, to introduce a notion of transformation on types which is a combination of substitutions and expansions.

Let us define, following Definition 3.3, a *simple substitution* $[t:=\alpha]$ to be a partial map between type variables and types in T_L. Simple substitutions can be extended to $T_L \cup Q_L$ in the obvious way, assuming that $[t:=\alpha](v)=v$ if $v\neq t$. A *substitution* is then a composition of simple substitutions.

Definition 4.1. (i) A *transformation* in a environment A is a composition of substitutions and expansions in A. We will write down explicitly a transformation as

$$r = [t_1:=\alpha_1,\ldots,t_n:=\alpha_n, \forall^{l_1}\underline{t}_1.\beta_1:=\xi_1,\ldots,\forall^{l_m}\underline{t}_m.\beta_m:=\xi_m]$$

$\{t_1,\ldots,t_n,\forall^{l_1}\underline{t}_1.\beta_1,\ldots,\forall^{l_m}\underline{t}_m.\beta_m\}$ is the *domain* of r and $\{\alpha_1,\ldots,\alpha_n,\xi_1,\ldots,\xi_m\}$ its *range*. We assume, without loss of generality, that the set of free variables of the domain and the set of free variables of the range of a transformations are disjoint.

(ii) $r\leq r'$ if $r'=r''\circ r$ for some transformation r''. □

Note that if

$$r = [t_1:=\alpha_1,\ldots,t_n:=\alpha_n,\overset{l_1}{\forall}\underline{t}_1.\beta_1:=\xi_1,\ldots,\overset{l_m}{\forall}\underline{t}_m.\beta_m:=\xi_m]$$

and $s = [u:=\gamma]$ is, for instance, a simple substitution, then

$$s\circ r = [u:=\gamma,t_1:=s(\alpha_1),\ldots,t_n:=s(\alpha_n),\overset{l_1}{\forall}\underline{t}_1.\beta_1:=s(\xi_1),\ldots,\overset{l_m}{\forall}\underline{t}_m.\beta_m:=s(\xi_m)]$$

(where we assume that u is different from $t_1,\ldots,t_m$). The same property holds if s is a simple transformation.

We consider the identity Id as the "empty" transformation, i.e such that $Id(\alpha)=\alpha$ for all types and sequences α. Note that $Id\leq r$ for all transformations r. If $r\leq r'$ then each label occurring in the domain of r must occur in the domain of r'.

We can now formally define what we mean by system of equations.

Definition 4.2 Let A be a environment.
(i) A *system* S in contex A is a set $S = \{(\alpha_i,\beta_i) \mid i\in I\}$ where α_i, and β_i are either both labelled types or both labelled intersections. Let FV(S) be the set of all variables free in S. A system S is *solved* if $\alpha_i=\beta_i$ for all $i\in I$.
(ii) A *solution* of a system S in a environment A is a transformation r in A such that r(S) is solved.
(iii) A set of solutions $\{r_i \mid i\in I\}$ of a system S is a *principal set of solutions* if for all solutions r' of S there is $i\in I$ such that $r_i\leq r'$. □

It is clear that the empty system is solved and any transformation r is a solution for it.

We now give a constructive proof that any system S which has a solution has a principal set of solutions. This is obtained by reducing the complexity of S by a collection of formal reduction rules which generate, in the process of reducing S, a set of transformations. We then show that S has a solution if and only if it can be reduced to the empty set. In this case the set of transformations produced by the reduction process is a principal set of solutions for S. Since the reduction process does always terminate, the reduction rules define an algorithm to find the principal set of solutions for S.

In particular we introduce a relation $\Rightarrow_A$ which reduces, in a contex A, a system S producing a transformation r and a set of (simpler) systems $\{S_1,\ldots,S_n\}$. We then show that S has a solution r' if and only if $r'=r''\circ r$ for some r'', where r'' is a solution of S_i for some i $(1\leq i\leq n)$. That is the transformation r is really needed in the solution of S, and the result of applying r to S is S_i. In all cases except one we have n=1 (i.e. S is reduced to a unique system S_1). But in one case (corresponding to the attempting the unification of two intersections) we can make different choices which determine a set of (possibly) incomparable solutions. The solution algorithm can thus be described, as for Huet's higher order unification [Huet, 1976] , as the construction of an OR tree whose nodes and brances are labelled, respectively, by systems and by transformations. The leaves are either the empty system, corresponding to a success in the solution of the system, or a non empty irreducible system, with respect to $\Rightarrow_A$, corresponding to a failure. A solution of S can be found composing the transformations on a path from the root to a success node. In this way we find the set of principal solutions. Finally we prove that such set is always finite (the unification tree does not have infinite paths).

In defining the reduction $\Rightarrow_A$ some care must be taken in case the reduction is determined by the attempt of matching two quantified types (this may happen if there is a pair $(\overset{l}{\forall}\underline{t}.\alpha, \overset{m}{\forall}\underline{u}.\beta)$ in S). For this case we introduce an extension of transformations in which a labelled quantified type $\overset{l}{\forall}\underline{t}.\alpha$ can be associated with a type in T_L indexed by a sequence of variables,denoted $\gamma|_{\underline{w}}$. The variables that index a type are not affected by transformations, i.e. $[v:=\delta](\gamma|_{\underline{w}})=\gamma[v:=\delta]|_{\underline{w}}$ even if v occurs in $\underline{w}$. The indexed type $\gamma|_{\underline{w}}$ is temporarily used in the system reduction to indicate that γ in the final transformation must be quantified with respect to the variables $\underline{w}$. Such types will be replaced in the final solution of the system by the corresponding labelled quantified types.

Definition 4.3 Let S be a system and α, β types or intersections.
(i) I_S is the set $\{\alpha \mid \alpha \in T_L \cup Q_L$, and either $(\alpha,\beta) \in S$ or $(\beta,\alpha) \in S\}$ of all types or intersections occurring in pairs of S.
(ii) For $\alpha \in I_S$, $\Im_S(\alpha)$ is the equivalence class of α in S . I.e.

$\Im_S(\alpha)=\{\beta \mid \beta \equiv \alpha$ <u>or</u> for some $\beta' \in \Im_S(\alpha)$ either $(\beta',\beta) \in S$ or $(\beta,\beta') \in S\}$. □

Therefore $\Im_S = \{\Im_S(\alpha) \mid \alpha \in I_S\}$ is a partition of I_S.

We introduce a more technical definition to formally handle the matching of two intersections.

Definition 4.4. Let R be a relation on A×B. R is *surjective* if and only if the *domain* of R (the set $\{a \mid (a,b) \in R$ for some b$\}$) is A and the *range* of R (The set $\{b \mid (a,b) \in R$ for some a$\}$, is B. R is *minimally surjective* if for no $(a,b) \in R$, $R-\{(a,b)\}$ is a surjective relation. □

In the following definition we write S+S' to indicate the union of two disjoint sets of equations S (i.e. no pair of S' is in S and vice-versa).

Definition 4.5 (*System reduction*). (i) Let A be a environment. The relation $\Rightarrow_A$ between a system S and a pair consisting of a transformation r and a finite set of systems $\{S_1,\ldots,S_n\}$ in A, denoted by $S \Rightarrow_A \langle r,\{S_1,\ldots,S_n\}\rangle$), is defined by the following clauses.

1. $S+\{(\xi\to\alpha,\ \chi\to\beta)\} \Rightarrow_A \langle Id,\{S+\{(\xi,\ \chi),\ (\alpha,\ \beta)\}\}\rangle$;
2. $S+\{(\{\alpha_1;\ldots;\alpha_n\},\ \{\beta_1;\ldots;\beta_m\}))\} \Rightarrow_A$
   $\langle Id,\{S+R \mid R$ is a minimally surjective relation on $\{\alpha_1,\ldots,\alpha_n\}\times\{\beta_1,\ldots,\beta_m\}\}\rangle$;
3. $S+\{(\alpha,\ \alpha)\} \Rightarrow_A \langle Id,\{S\}\rangle$;
4. Let $S =\ S'+\{(t,\ \alpha_1),\ldots,(t,\ \alpha_n)\}$ where t does occur neither in α_i (for $1 \le i \le n$) nor in S. Then
   $S \Rightarrow_A \langle [t:=\alpha_1],\ \{S'+\{(\alpha_1,\ \alpha_2),\ldots,(\alpha_1,\alpha_n)\}\}\rangle$
5. Let $S = S'+\{(\overset{l}{\forall}\underline{t}.\beta,\{\alpha_1;\ldots;\alpha_n\}),(\overset{l}{\forall}\underline{t}.\beta,\xi_1),\ldots,(\overset{l}{\forall}\underline{t}.\beta,\xi_m)\}$ where $\overset{l}{\forall}$ does not occur in S', α_i $(1 \le i \le n)$ and ξ_j $(1 \le i \le m)$. Then
   $S \Rightarrow_A \langle [\overset{l}{\forall}\underline{t}.\beta:=\{\beta_1[\underline{u}_1/\underline{t}]),\ldots,\beta_n[\underline{u}_n/\underline{t}]\}],$
   $\{S+\{(\alpha_1,\beta_1[\underline{u}_1/\underline{t}]),\ldots,(\alpha_n,\beta_n[\underline{u}_n/\underline{t}]),(\{\alpha_1;\ldots;\alpha_n\},\xi_1),\ldots,(\{\alpha_1;\ldots;\alpha_n\},\xi_m)\}\}\rangle$

where $\underline{u}_1,\dots,\underline{u}_n$ are fresh variables and $\beta_1,\dots,\beta_n$ are obtained by renaming internal labels of β in the environment A according to Def. 3.3(i).

6. Let $S=S'+\{(\forall^{m_i}\underline{u}_i.\alpha_i, \forall^{m_j}\underline{u}_j.\alpha_j) \mid \langle i,j\rangle \in P\}$ where there is a finite set I of indices such that $\{\forall^{m_i}\underline{u}_i.\alpha_i \mid i\in I\}\in \Im_S$ (i.e. is an equivalence class), $P\subseteq I\times I$ and for all $i\in I$ $\forall^{m_i}$ does not occur neither in S' nor in any α_j (for $j\in I$, $j\neq i$). Then

$$S\Rightarrow_A\langle[\forall^{m_i}\underline{u}_i.\alpha_i:=\alpha_i[\underline{u}'_i/\underline{u}_i]|_{\underline{w}} \mid i\in I],\ \{S'+\{(\alpha_i[\underline{u}'_i/\underline{u}_i],\alpha_j[\underline{u}'_j/\underline{u}_j]) \mid \langle i,j\rangle\in P\}\}\rangle$$

where $\underline{w}=\bigcup_{i\in I}\underline{u}'_i$ and $\underline{u}'_i$ (for $i\in I$) are fresh variables.

(ii) A system is *irreducible* if neither of the previous rules can be applied (i.e. if $\Rightarrow_A$ is not defined on S). □

Note that the six cases exhaust all the possible kinds of pairs (type,type) or (sequence,sequence). Rule 2 is the only one in which a set of systems containing more than one element is generated. This introduces an OR branch on the solution tree. All the other rules generate only one system . Rules 1, 2, and 3, moreover, generate a trivial transformation (the identity). They only simplify the system whereas the other rules solve one or more pairs.

Even though at any step there are many reductions that can be applied, the order in which the reductions are applied does not influence the final transformation produced by the system. The fact that many independent solutions can be found is due uniquely to rule 2.

In rule 2 we formalize the fact that a transformation, r, that solves $(\{\alpha_1;\dots;\alpha_n\}, \{\beta_1;\dots;\beta_m\})$ $(n,m\geq 1)$ must be such that $r(\{\alpha_1;\dots;\alpha_n\})=r(\{\beta_1;\dots;\beta_m\})=\{\gamma_1;\dots;\gamma_j\}$ for some types $\gamma_1,\dots,\gamma_j$ $(1\leq j\leq \min(n,m))$. So some types in $r(\{\alpha_1;\dots;\alpha_n\})$ must be equal to some types in $r(\{\beta_1;\dots;\beta_m\})$ and must be equal to γ_1 and so on. There could be more than one independent solution of this pair. That is an r_1 and r_2 solving the pair and such that neither $r_1\leq r_2$ nor $r_2\leq r_1$. This is why a system can have a finite set (of cardinality bigger than one) of independent solutions.

A particular case of rule 2 (one intersection is empty) is

$$S+\{(\{\},\{\beta_1;\dots;\beta_m\}))\}\Rightarrow_A\langle Id,\{S\}\rangle.$$

Rules 5 and 6 are applied when we need to unify pairs containing a labelled type $\forall^{m}\underline{t}.\alpha$. There are two possibilities. If $\Im(\forall^{m}\underline{t}.\alpha)$ contains at least one explicit intersection $\{\alpha_1;\dots;\alpha_n\}$) there is a pair $(\forall^{1}\underline{t}.\beta,\{\alpha_1;\dots;\alpha_n\})$ in the system (case 5) where $\forall^{1}\underline{t}.\beta\in\Im(\forall^{m}\underline{t}.\alpha)$. Then the number of instances that must be obtained from $\forall^{1}\underline{t}.\beta$ must be (not more than) n and we are reduced to matching n instances of $\forall^{1}\underline{t}.\beta$ with $\alpha_1,\dots,\alpha_n$. Moreover we replace all other occurrences of $\forall^{1}\underline{t}.\beta$ with $\{\alpha_1;\dots;\alpha_n\}$, thus eliminating the label 1 from the system. On the other hand if $\Im(\forall^{m}\underline{t}.\alpha)$ contains only intersections which are quantified types (case 6) then there is no reason to fix the number of instances we have to do. We simply force the body of all the equivalent types to match. In the final transformation we will restore the labelled quantification with respect to all generic type variables which occur in the body. This corresponds to apply an expansion of the kind of Definition 3.3(i)-2.

A nonempty system cannot be reduced only if it has no solutions

Lemma 4.6 If $S\neq\emptyset$ and S is irreducible then S has no solution. □

The set of solutions of a system can be obtained by iterated reductions. The notion of (iterated) system reduction is based on the one-step reduction of Def. 4.5, but is defined as a relation between a system and a pair of a system and a tranformation.

Definition 4.7. Let S be a system. Define $S \Longrightarrow_A \langle r',S' \rangle$ (S produces S' and r) if $S \Rightarrow_A \langle r,\{S_1,\ldots,S_n\}\rangle$ and

either $r=r'$ and $S'=S_i$ for some $1 \le i \le n$

or $S_i \Longrightarrow_{r(A)} \langle r'',S' \rangle$ for some $1 \le i \le n$ and $r' = r'' \circ r$. □

Indexed types can be removed by transformations by means of the operation of closure. The *closure* of of a transformation r , Cl(r), is the transformation obtained by replacing each occurrence of an indexed type $\alpha|_{\underline{u}}$ in the range of r by $\overset{l}{\forall}\underline{u}'.\alpha$ where l is a fresh label and $\underline{u}'$ is the subset of the variables in $\underline{u}$ that are free in α. A transformation r is *closed* if it has no occurrences of indexed types.

By a simlpe transfinite induction on a suitable measure of the complexity of the system we can prove that the relation ==> is <u>strongly terminating</u>, i.e. that each possible reduction of a system S ends producing either ∅ or an irreducible system.

Lemma 4.8. $\Longrightarrow_A$ is strongly terminating, i.e. there cannot be an infinite chain of reductions. □

Definition 4.9. Let S be a system in a environment A. Define $\mathcal{R}(S,A)$ (the set of solutions of S in A) as

$$\mathcal{R}(S,A) = \{Cl(r) \mid S \Longrightarrow_A \langle r,\emptyset \rangle\}.\ \square$$

The correctness and completeness of the reduction procedure can then be proved by induction on the number of steps using the following Theorem. This also proves that any system S of equations that has a solution has a finite principal set of solutions.

Theorem 4.10 (i) Let $S \Rightarrow_A \langle r,\{S_1,\ldots,S_n\}\rangle$, r' is a solution of S if there is an integer i ($1 \le i \le n$) and a solution r'' of S_i such that $r' = Cl(r'' \circ r)$.

(ii) $\mathcal{R}(S,A)$ is a principal set of solutions of S in the environment A. □

The set $\mathcal{R}(S,A)$ can then be systematically produced using the following algorithm.

Definition 4.11 (*Solution Procedure*) Let S be the system to be solved in the environment A. Start up a tree with the root labelled by the pair <S,A>. Given any node, labelled by <S',A'>, there are two possibilities

1. the node is terminal in which case S' is

   either empty (indicating success),

   or an irreducile system (indicating failure):

2. let $S' \Rightarrow_{A'} \langle r,\{S_1,\ldots,S_n\}\rangle$. S' has n children labelled by $\langle S_1,r(A')\rangle,\ldots,\langle S_n,r(A')\rangle$, and the branches from $\langle S',A'\rangle$ to the $\langle S_i,A_i\rangle$ are labelled by r.

By lemma 4.8 this construction produces a finite tree. The solutions of the system can be found composing the transformations on paths from the root to success nodes. □

Example 4.12 Consider the solution of the following system $S_0=\{(\overset{1}{\forall}t.(\{t\}\to t)\to u, \{z;\{\{z\}\to v\}\to v\})\}$ in the environment $\varnothing$. This system must be solved to find the principal type of $((\lambda x.xI)\Delta)$. The tree we obtain is as follows (the environment is always empty and has been omitted):

$$\boxed{\{(\overset{1}{\forall}t.(\{t\}\to t)\to u,\ \{z;\{z\}\to v\}\to v)\}}$$
$$\downarrow \mathrm{Id}$$
$$\boxed{\{(\overset{1}{\forall}t.\{t\}\to t,\{z;\{z\}\to v\}),(u,v)\}}$$
$$\downarrow [\overset{1}{\forall}t.\{t\}\to t:=\{\{t_1\}\to t_1,\{t_2\}\to t_2\}]\ =r_1$$
$$\boxed{\{(\{t_1\}\to t_1,z),\ (\{t_2\}\to t_2,\{z\}\to v),\ (u,v)\}}$$
$$\downarrow \mathrm{Id}$$
$$\boxed{\{(\{t_1\}\to t_1,z),\ (\{t_2\},\{z\}),\ (t_2,v),\ (u,v)\}}$$
$$\downarrow [v:=u]\ =r_2$$
$$\boxed{\{(\{t_1\}\to t_1,z),\ (t_2,z),\ (t_2,u)\}}$$
$$\downarrow [t_2:=z]\ =r_3$$
$$\boxed{\{(\{t_1\}\to t_1,z),\ (z,u)\}}$$
$$\downarrow [z:=u]\ =r_4$$
$$\boxed{\{(\{t_1\}\to t_1,u)\}}$$
$$\downarrow [u:=\{t_1\}\to t_1]\ =r_5$$
$$\boxed{\varnothing}$$

Hence the principal set of solutions for S contains only one element, i.e.

$$\mathcal{R}(S_0,\varnothing) = \{r_5\circ r_4\circ r_3\circ r_2\circ r_1\}$$
$$= \{[u:=\{t_1\}\to t_1, z:=\{t_1\}\to t_1, t_2:=\{t_1\}\to t_1, v:=\{t_1\}\to t_1,$$
$$\overset{1}{\forall}t.\{t\}\to t:=\{\{t_1\}\to t_1;\{\{t_1\}\to t_1\}\to\{t_1\}\to t_1\}]\}.\ \square$$

Property 4.8(i) assure that the set of solutions found with the previous procedure is principal.

We now give the type-inference algorithm for the system $\vdash_L$. Let **B** denote the set of bases. We will define a function

$T:\Lambda\text{->}\mathcal{P}_F(\mathbf{B}\times T_L)$ (where $\mathcal{P}_F$ is the finite power domain)

which applied to a term M gives a finite set of pairs basis-type which is intended to be its set of principal pairs.

Definition 4.13. (*Type-inference Algorithm*). The function $\mathbf{T}:\Lambda\text{->}\mathbf{B}\times T_L$ is defined inductively on Λ in the following way.

- $\mathbf{T}(x) = \{<\{x:t\},t>$ where t is a fresh type variable
- $\mathbf{T}(\lambda x.M) = \{<B,\{\alpha_1;...;\alpha_n\}\to\beta> \mid \{<B\cup\{x:\alpha_1,...,x:\alpha_n\},\beta>\}\in \mathbf{T}(M)\}$.
- $\mathbf{T}(MN) =$ <u>for all</u> $<B_M, \alpha>\in \mathbf{T}(M)$

  <u>for all</u> $<B_N, \beta>\in \mathbf{T}(N)$

  <u>let</u> $\xi=\overset{l}{\forall}\underline{t}..\beta$ where $\underline{t}$ is the set of variables free in β and not in B_N and l is a new label

  <u>in</u>

  <u>if</u> $\alpha\equiv t$ <u>then</u> $\{<[t:=\xi\to u](B_M)\cup B_N , u >\}$ where u is a fresh variable

  <u>if</u> $\alpha\equiv\chi\to\gamma$ <u>then</u> $\{<r(B_M\cup B_N), r\{\gamma\}> \mid r\in \mathcal{R}(\{(\xi,\chi)\},B_M\cup B_N)\}$

  where $r(B) = \{x:r(\alpha) \mid x:\alpha\in B\}$. □

If $<B,\alpha>\in \mathbf{T}(M)$ we say that $<B,\alpha>$ is a *principal pair* for M, α is a *principal type* and B a *pricipal basis* for it.

For terms in normal form, for instance, the principal type is the one defined in the proof of Lemma 2.7 with the only difference that sequences of the shape $\{\alpha\}$ are replaced by $\overset{l}{\forall}\underline{t}.\alpha$ where l is a new label and $\underline{t}$ are all the type variables generic in α. The type checking algorithm is sound and complete for the system $\vdash_L$, in the following sense.

Lemma 4.14 (i) (*Soundness*) For all $<B,\alpha>\in \mathbf{T}(M)$, $B\vdash_L M:\alpha$.
(ii) (*Completeness*) If $B\vdash_L M:\gamma$ for some type γ, then there exists $<B_p,\alpha>\in \mathbf{T}(M)$ such that for some transformation r, $r(B_p)=B$ and $r(\alpha)=\gamma$. □

The previous soundness and completeness with respect to the system $\vdash_L$ immediately imply the result we are ultimately interested in, i.e. the existence of a sound a complete type inference algorithm for the system $\vdash_\wedge$. Each deduction $\vdash_\wedge$ in fact is also a deduction in $\vdash_L$. Indeed the system $\vdash_L$ has only been a tool to this end. But remark that principal types (and principal bases) for M are indeed types in T_L rather than in T.

Main Theorem. (i) (*Soundness*) For all $<B,\alpha>\in \mathbf{T}(M)$, $B'\vdash_\wedge M:\alpha'$ where B' and α' are any terminal expansion of B and α.
(ii) (*Completeness*) If $B\vdash_\wedge M:\gamma$ for some type γ, then there exists $<B_p,\alpha>\in \mathbf{T}(M)$ such that for some terminal transformation r, $r(B_p)=B$ and $r(\alpha)=\gamma$. □

As already mentioned when matching an intersection with an intersection we can get a finite number of principal solutions. This case however does not seem to occur often in the usual programming practice. An example of a term which has three principal types is the following.

Take **twice** = $\lambda f.\lambda x.f(f\ x)$ and **four** = $\lambda f.\lambda x.f(f(f(f\ x)))$ whose principal types are, respectctvely,

$\tau_{twice}=\{a_1\to b_1;b_1\to c_1\}\to\{a_1\}\to c_1$ and

$\tau_{four}=\{a_2\to b_2;b_2\to c_2;c_2\to d_2;d_2\to e_2\}\to\{a_2\}\to e_2$.

Consider the term $T=\lambda z.\lambda y.((\lambda x.y\ (x\ \mathbf{twice})\ (x\ \mathbf{four}))\ (N\ z))$ where $N=(\Delta\ \mathbf{twice})$.

The principal type of N is $\{\{t\}\to t\}\to\{t\}\to t$ while the (unique) type assigned to $(\lambda x.y\ (x\ \mathbf{twice})\ (x\ \mathbf{four}))$ by the type inference algorithm is $\{\xi_{twice}\to a;\xi_{four}\to b\}\to d$ (where $\xi_{twice} = \forall a_1b_1c_1.\tau_{twice}$ and $\xi_{four} = \forall a_2b_2c_2d_2e_2.\tau_{four}$) with respect to the basis $\{y{:}a\to b\to c,\ z{:}t\to t\}$. Now to apply $\lambda x.y\ (x\ \mathbf{twice})\ (x\ \mathbf{four})$ to (N z) (whose type is $\{t\}\to t$) we have to solve the system $\{(\{\xi_{twice}\to a;\ \xi_{four}\to b\},\ \{t\to t\})\}$. This requires the unification of τ_{twice} and τ_{four} which, in its turn, requires the unification of the pair $(\{a_1\to b_1;b_1\to c_1\},\{a_2\to b_2;b_2\to c_2;c_2\to d_2;d_2\to e_2\})$ which has three different unifiers (none of the intersections, in fact, has been obtained by ($\forall$E)). The three unifiers are

-$[c_1:=b_1,a_2:=a_1,b_2:=b_1,c_2:=b_1,d_2:=b_1,e_2:=b_1]$, which yields $\{a_1\to b_1;b_1\to b_1\}$,

-$[b_1:=a_1,a_2:=a_1,b_2:=a_1,c_2:=a_1,d_2:=a_1,e_2:=c_1]$, which yields $\{a_1\to a_1;a_1\to c_1\}$ and

-$[c_1:=a_1,a_2:=a_1,b_2:=b_1,c_2:=a_1,d_2:=b_1,e_2:=a_1]$ which yields $\{a_1\to b_1;b_1\to a_1\}$.

Note that none of the solutions is more general than the other.

The principal types of T are then $\{\{\tau_i\}\to\tau_i\}\to\{\{\tau_i\}\to\{\tau_i\}\to c\}\to c$ for i=1,2,3 where

- $\tau_1 = \{a_1\to b_1;b_1\to b_1\}\to\{a_1\}\to b_1$
- $\tau_2 = \{a_1\to a_1;a_1\to c_1\}\to\{a_1\}\to c_1$
- $\tau_i = \{a_1\to b_1;b_1\to b_1\}\to\{a_1\}\to b_1$

References

[Barendregt, Coppo, Dezani, 1983] Barendregt, H. P., Coppo, M., Dezani Ciancaglini, M.: A filter lambda model and the completeness of type assignment, Journal of Symbolic Logic, **48**, 1983, pp. 931 - 940

[Coppo, Dezani, 1980] Coppo M., Dezani-Ciancaglini M.: An extension of basic functionality theory for lambda-calculus, Notre Dame J. Formal Logic **21**(4), 685-693.

[Coppo et. al., 1980] Coppo M., Dezani-Ciancaglini M., Venneri B.: Principal type schemes and lambda calculus semantics, in To H.B.Curry: essays on combinatory logic, lambda-calculus and formalism, J. Seldin and R. Hindley eds., Academic Press 1980, 536-560.

[Coppo et al., 1981] Coppo M., Dezani-Ciancaglini M., Venneri B.: Functional characters of solvable terms, Zeit. Math. Logik und Grund. Math. **27**(1981) , 45-58.

[Curry, Feys, 1958] Curry, H.B.; Feys, R.: Combinatory Logic, I, North-Holland, Amsterdam, 1958.

[Damas, Milner, 1982] Damas,L.M.M.; Milner,R.: Principal type schemes for functional programs, 9th ACM Symposium on Principles of Programming Languages, ACM, 1982, pp. 207 - 212.

[Giannini, Ronchi, 1988] Giannini P., Ronchi della Rocca S. Characterization of typings in polymorphic type discipline. In Logic in Computer Science, 1988, pp.61 - 70.

[Giannini, Ronchi, 1991] Giannini P., Ronchi della Rocca S. Type inference in polymorphic type discipline. In Theoretical aspects of Computer Science 1991, LNCS 526, 18-37.

[Girard,1971] Girard, J.Y.: Interpretation fonctionelle et elimination des coupures dans l'arithmetique d'ordre superieur, These de Doctorat d'Etat, Paris VII 1971.

[Gordon,Milner,Wadsworth,1979] Gordon M.J.C.; Milner, R.; Wadsworth, C.P.: Edinburgh LCF, Springer LNCS **78**, 1979

[Hindley, 1969] Hindley,J.R.: The principal type scheme of an object in combinatory logic, Trans. American Math. Soc., **146**,1969, pp. 29 - 60.

[Hindley, Seldin (eds.),1980] Hindley R., Seldin, J. (eds.): To H.B. Curry: Essays in Combinatory Logic, Lambda calculus and formalism, Academic Press, 1980.

[Hindley,Seldin, 1986] Hindley,J.R.;Seldin,J.P.: Introduction to Combinators and λ-Calculus, London Mathematical Society Student Texts 1, Cambridge University Press, London,1986

[Huet, 1976] Huet, G.: Resolution d'equations dans les langages d' ordre 1, 2, . . .,ω, These d'Etat, Universite' Paris VII, 1976.

[Kfoury, et.al., 1989] Kfoury A. J., Tyurin J., Urzyczyn P.: Computational consequences and partial solutions of a generalized unification problem. In Logic in Computer Science, pp.98 - 105., 1989.

[Kfoury, Tyurin, 1990] Kfoury A. J., Tyurin J.: Type Reconstruction in finite-rank fragments of the polymorphic λ-calculus . In Proc. of Logic in Computer Science '90, pp. 2-11.

[Leivant, 1986] Leivant D. Typing and computational properties of lambda-expressions, Theoretical Computer Science, **44** (1986), pp. 51-68.

[Mycroft, 1984] Mycroft A.: Polymorphic type schemes and recursive defintions. In International Symposium on Programming, LNCS 167, pp. 217-228.

[Milner, 1978] Milner, R.: A theory of type polimorphism in programming, J. Comput. System Sci., **17**, 1978, pp. 348 - 375

[Ronchi , Venneri, 1984] Ronchi della Rocca S., Venneri B. Principal Type Schemes for an extended type Theory Theoretical Computer Science **28** (1984), pp. 151-169.

[Turner, 1985] Turner, D.A.: Miranda: a non-strict functional language with polymorphic types, Proceedings of the IFIP International Conference on Functional Programming Languages and Computer Architecture, Springer LNCS **201**, 1985, pp. 1-16.

[van Bakel, 1991] van Bakel, S.: Complete restrictions of the intersection type discipline, to appear in Theoretical Computer Science 99 (1992).

MONADIC SECOND-ORDER DEFINABLE GRAPH TRANSDUCTIONS(*)

Bruno COURCELLE

Université BORDEAUX-1,
Laboratoire d'Informatique(+)
351, Cours de la Libération
33405 TALENCE, FRANCE

ABSTRACT

Formulas of monadic second-order logic can be used to specify graph transductions, i.e., multivalued functions from graphs to graphs. We obtain in this way classes of graph transductions, called *monadic second-order definable graph transductions* (or more simply *definable transductions*) that are closed under composition and preserve the two known classes of context-free sets of graphs, namely the class of Hyperedge Replacement (HR) and the class of Vertex Replacement (VR) sets. These two classes can be characterized in terms of definable transductions and recognizable sets of finite trees. These characterizations are independent of the rewriting mechanisms used to define the HR and VR grammars. When restricted to words, the definable transductions are strictly more powerful than the rational transductions with finite image; they do not preserve context-free languages. We also describe the sets of discrete (edgeless) labeled graphs that are the images of HR and VR sets under definable transductions: this gives a version of Parikh's Theorem (i.e., the characterization of the commutative images of context-free languages) which extends the classical one and applies to HR and VR sets of graphs.

INTRODUCTION

The Theory of Formal Languages investigates finite devices defining sets of finite and countably infinite words and trees, compares their expressive powers, and investigates the solvability of the associated decision problems. These investigations make an essential use of transformations from words or trees to words or trees usually called *transductions*. Of special importance are rational transductions; they are closed under composition and inverse, and they preserve the families of recognizable and context-free languages. Tree transductions are more complicated, and there is no unique notion that can be considered as the analogue of that of a rational transduction. For each class of tree transductions, the

(*) Supported by the ESPRIT Basic -Research project 3299 ("Computing by graph transformations") and by the "Programme de Recherches Coordonnées: Mathématiques et Informatique".

(+) Unité associée au CNRS n° 1304, email : courcell@geocub.greco-prog.fr

closure under composition is a major concern, and so is the preservation of recognizability; we refer the reader to the survey by Raoult [Rao]. Another important transduction is **yield** that maps derivation trees of context-free grammars to the corresponding words. The context-free languages can be characterized as the images of the recognizable sets of (finite) trees under **yield** mappings.

The study of sets of finite and countably infinite graphs (and hypergraphs) by tools like grammars, systems of equations and logical formulas is a relatively recent development of the Theory of Formal Languages. The need for a manageable and powerful notion of graph transduction appears in constructions dealing with graph grammars and is of interest on its own.

This paper is a survey presenting the notion of a *monadic second-order definable graph transduction* (a *definable transduction* for short), which has been introduced more or less explicitely and sometimes in restricted forms in several papers [ALS, Cou5, Cou7-10, CE, Eng2]. We collect the main results and give references to their proofs.

We now introduce informally these transductions. The term "monadic second-order" refers to a logical language, the *monadic second-order logic*. We recall the rôle of logic for defining sets of graphs (or hypergraphs; all what we shall say concerning graphs applies to hypergraphs as well). Graphs can be described by relational structures, i.e., by logical structures with no function symbols. The domain of the structure representing a graph is the set of its vertices and edges put together; basic relations describe the incidence of vertices and edges and possible labellings. (This is actually not the only way to represent a graph; see Sections 1 and 4 for more details.) Hence, formulas of appropriate logical languages define properties of this graph. Monadic second-order logic is popular among logicians because of its expressive power and its decidability properties. (See Gurevich [Gu] for a survey.) For dealing with graphs, it is very useful because it can express many fundamental properties (like planarity, connectivity, k-colorability for fixed k) whereas several general decidability results hold. The sets of words (resp. of trees) characterized by a property expressible in monadic second-order logic are exactly the recognizable sets by the results of Büchi and Elgot [Bü, Elg], see [Tho, Thm 3.2] (resp. of Doner [Don], see [Tho, Thm 11.1]). Sets of graphs defined similarly by characteristic monadic second-order properties behave very much like recognizable sets of words and trees, in particular in constructions involving context-free graph grammars. Since no notion of finite-state graph automaton is known, monadic second-order formulas are essential in such constructions.

We now come to graph transductions. Since we have no good (general) notion of graph automaton, we have no chance to obtain a good notion of graph transduction based on a finite-state machine model. Alternatively, we propose to define transductions of graphs (or more generally of relational structures) by means of monadic second-order formulas. The idea is to transform a structure S into a structure T by defining T "inside" S by means of such formulas. This is nothing but the classical notion of *semantic interpretation* (see for instance [Rab]), appropriately extended. In particular, we define T inside the *disjoint union of k copies of S* (for some fixed k), which makes possible to construct T with a domain larger than that of S, (larger within the factor k).

The family of definable transductions is closed under composition, but not under inverse. These transductions preserve the so-called HR and VR sets of graphs (namely, the two known types of context-free sets of graphs), and yield grammar independent characterizations of these sets

This paper is organized as follows. Section 1 reviews relational structures, the way they represent graphs and hypergraphs, and monadic second-order logic; Section 2 introduces (monadic second-order) definable graph transductions and presents examples of such transductions dealing with words, trees and graphs; Section 3 gives the main properties of definable transductions of relational structures; Section 4 presents the relationships between definable transduction and the classes of VR and HR sets of graphs (and hypergraphs); Sections 5 compares definable transductions with known transductions of words and trees; Section 6 deals with definable transductions from graphs to commutative words and gives forms of Parikh's Theorem that apply to HR and VR graph grammars.

1 - Hypergraphs and Relational Structures

A binary relation $R \subseteq A \times B$ is also called a *transduction* from A to B. We write aRb for $(a,b) \in R$, and we consider every b such that aRb as *an image of* a *under* R. The *domain* of R is $\mathbf{Dom}(R) := \{a \in A \mid aRb \text{ for some b in B}\}$ and the *image* of R is $\mathbf{Im}(R) := \{b \in B \mid aRb \text{ for some a in A}\}$. For $L \subseteq A$, the *image of* L *under* R is $R(L) := \{b \in B \mid aRb \text{ for some a in L}\}$. The transduction $R^{-1} := \{(b,a) \mid (a,b) \in R\}$ is called the *inverse* of R. If L is a subset of B, then $R^{-1}(L)$ is the *inverse image of* L *under* R. We say that R is *functional* if **Card**(R({a})) $\leq$ 1 for every a in A. We identify functional relations $R \subseteq A{\times}B$ with partial functions $R : A \longrightarrow B$, and we write b = R(a) instead of $b \in R(a)$. The composition of two transductions $R \subseteq A{\times}B$ and $S \subseteq B{\times}C$ is the transduction from A to C, defined as $\{(a,c) \mid (a,b) \in R$ and $(b,c) \in S$ for some b in B$\}$. By a *mapping*, we shall mean a total function.

Hypergraphs with sources

We shall deal with labeled, directed hypergraphs equipped with a sequence of distinguished vertices (called the *sources*) as in [BC, Cou3-8]. The labels (intended to label hyperedges) are chosen in a finite ranked alphabet A. The rank mapping is $\rho : A \longrightarrow \mathbb{N}$. The rank of the label of a hyperedge must be equal to the length of its sequence of incident vertices. This rank may be 0, i.e., we allow hyperedges with no vertex. Graphs appear as a special case where all labels are of rank 2.

A *concrete n-hypergraph over* A is a quintuple G = $\langle \mathbf{V}_G, \mathbf{E}_G, \mathbf{lab}_G, \mathbf{vert}_G, \mathbf{src}_G \rangle$ where: $\mathbf{V}_G$ is the finite set of vertices; $\mathbf{E}_G$ is the finite set of (hyper)edges, disjoint with $\mathbf{V}_G$; its elements will be called hereafter *edges* for shortness sake; $\mathbf{lab}_G$ is a mapping: $\mathbf{E}_G \longrightarrow A$ that defines the *label* of an edge; $\mathbf{vert}_G$ is a mapping that associates with every edge e the *sequence of its vertices*; this sequence must be of length $\rho(e) := \rho(\mathbf{lab}_G(e))$ (called the *rank* of the edge) and its ith element is denoted by $\mathbf{vert}_G(e,i)$; $\mathbf{src}_G$ is a sequence of vertices of length n (or equivalently a mapping : $[n] \longrightarrow \mathbf{V}_G$), called the *sequence of sources*; we shall denote by $\mathbf{src}_G(i)$ the ith element of this sequence; if n=0, then G has no source.

The integer n is the *rank* of G, denoted by $\rho(G)$. A concrete hypergraph G is *simple* if, for all e, e' in $\mathbf{E}_G$, if $\mathbf{vert}_G(e) = \mathbf{vert}_G(e')$ and $\mathbf{lab}_G(e) = \mathbf{lab}_G(e')$, then e = e'. By a *hypergraph,* we mean the isomorphism class of a concrete hypergraph (possibly with sources). We denote by $\mathbf{HG}(A)_n$ the set of n-hypergraphs over A. We denote by **HG**(A) the set of hypergraphs over A of all ranks.

Operations on **HG**(A) have been defined in [BC, Cou3-5] that make possible to denote hypergraphs by well-formed algebraic expressions (called *hypergraph expressions*) written with symbols denoting these operations and nullary symbols denoting basic hypergraphs. Hence, finite hypergraph expressions denote finite hypergraphs. Infinite hypergraph expressions can also be defined (they are analogous to formal power series), and they denote countable hypergraphs (see

[Cou5-7]). The hypergraph denoted by an expression t is called its value, and is denoted by **val**(t). The operations are the following ones: a disjoint noncommutative union that concatenates the sequences of sources (it associates with G and G' a hypergraph of rank $\rho(G) + \rho(G')$); unary operations indexed by pairs of integers (the operation associated with a pair (i,j) transforms a hypergraph by fusing its ith and jth sources; the rank of the hypergraph is preserved) and unary operations indexed by mappings between integers (the operation associated with a mapping α from [n] to [p] transforms a hypergraph G of rank p into the hypergraph H of rank n such that $\mathbf{src}_H(i) = \mathbf{src}_G(\alpha(i))$ for all i in [n], all other components of H being as in G.

Monadic second-order logic

Let R be a finite ranked set of symbols where each element r in R has a rank $\rho(r)$ in $\mathbb{N}_+$. A symbol r in R is considered as a $\rho(r)$-ary relation symbol. An *R-(relational) structure* is a tuple $S = \langle \mathbf{D}_S, (r_S)_{r \in R} \rangle$ where $\mathbf{D}_S$ is a finite (possibly empty) set, called the *domain* of S, and r_S is a subset of $\mathbf{D}_S^{\rho(r)}$ for each r in R. We denote by $\mathcal{S}(R)$ the class of R-structures.

We review *monadic second-order logic* briefly. Its formulas (called *MS formulas* for short), intended to describe properties of structures S as above, are written with variables of two types, namely lowercase symbols x,x',y,... called *object variables*, denoting elements of $\mathbf{D}_S$, and uppercase symbols X,Y,Y',... called *set variables*, denoting subsets of $\mathbf{D}_S$. The atomic formulas are of the forms $x = y$, $r(x_1,...,x_n)$ (where r is in R and $n=\rho(r)$), and $x \in X$, and formulas are formed with propositional connectives and quantifications over the two kinds of variables. See [Cou2-Cou8] for more details. For every finite set W of object and set variables, we denote by $\mathcal{L}(R,W)$ the set of all formulas that are written with relational symbols from R and have their free variables in W; we also let $\mathcal{L}(R) := \mathcal{L}(R,\emptyset)$ denote the set of closed formulas.

Let S be an R-structure, let $\varphi \in \mathcal{L}(R,W)$, and let γ be a W-assignment in S, (i.e., $\gamma(X)$ is a subset of $\mathbf{D}_S$ for every set variable X in W, and $\gamma(x) \in \mathbf{D}_S$ for every object variable x in W; we write this $\gamma : W \longrightarrow S$ to be short). We write $(S,\gamma) \models \varphi$ iff φ holds in S for γ. We write $S \models \varphi$ in the case where φ has no free variable. A set of R-structures L is *definable* if there is a formula φ in $\mathcal{L}(R)$ such that L is the set of all R-structures S such that $S \models \varphi$.

A hypergraph G in $\mathbf{HG}(A)_n$ can be represented by an $\mathbf{R}_{A,n}$-structure, where $\mathbf{R}_{A,n} := \{\mathbf{edg_a} \mid a \in A\} \cup \{\mathbf{ps_i} \mid i \in [n]\}$ with $\rho(\mathbf{edg_a}) := \rho(a)+1$ and $\rho(\mathbf{ps_i}) := 1$. The structure representing G is $|G|_2 := <\mathbf{D}_G, (\mathbf{edg_{aG}})_{a \in A}, \mathbf{ps}_{1G}, \ldots, \mathbf{ps}_{nG}>$ where $\mathbf{D}_G := \mathbf{V}_G \cup \mathbf{E}_G$ (let us recall that $\mathbf{V}_G \cap \mathbf{E}_G = \emptyset$), $\mathbf{edg_{aG}}(x, y_1, \ldots, y_n) : \Leftrightarrow x \in \mathbf{E}_G$, $\mathbf{lab}_G(x) = a$, and $\mathbf{vert}_G(x) = (y_1, \ldots, y_n)$, $\mathbf{ps}_{iG}(x) : \Leftrightarrow x = \mathbf{src}_G(i)$.

Clearly $|G|_2$ is isomorphic to $|G'|_2$ as a relational structure iff G = G' (i.e., G is isomorphic to G'). We shall consider any two isomorphic structures as equal, like for hypergraphs.

A hypergraph G can be represented by another structure $|G|_1 := <\mathbf{V}_G, (\mathbf{edg'_{aG}})_{a \in A}, \mathbf{ps}_{1G}, \ldots, \mathbf{ps}_{nG}>$ where $\mathbf{edg'_{aG}}(y_1, \ldots, y_n)$ holds iff $\mathbf{lab}_G(e) = a$ and $\mathbf{vert}_G(e) = (y_1, \ldots, y_n)$ for some e in $\mathbf{E}_G$, and $\mathbf{ps}_{iG}$ is as in $|G|_2$. Clearly, two simple hypergraphs G and G' are equal iff $|G|_1$ is equal (isomorphic) to $|G'|_1$. Hence, simple hypergraphs are unambigously represented by these latter structures whereas arbitrary hypergraphs are not.

The representation of hypergraphs by logical structures makes it possible to express their properties by logical formulas. We shall say that a property P of the hypergraphs G of a class $\mathcal{C}$ can be *expressed by a logical formula* φ *via a representation* $|G|$ if, for every G in $\mathcal{C}$, then P(G) holds iff $|G| \models \varphi$.

A property of hypergraphs is *i-definable* (where i is 1 or 2), if it is expressible by a MS formula, relative to the representation $|\text{-}|_i$. To give an example, the following formula expresses that a graph G represented by the structure $|G|_1$ is connected:

$$\forall x \forall y \forall X\, [\forall u \forall v\, ((u \in X \wedge \text{"u-v"}) \Rightarrow v \in X) \wedge x \in X \Rightarrow y \in X\,]$$

where "u-v" stands for the formula expressing that u and v belong to some edge, namely, for the disjunction of the formulas $\mathbf{edg'_a}(u,v) \vee \mathbf{edg'_a}(v,u)$ extended to all labels a. (All labels are assumed to be of rank 2).

The structure $|G|_1$ is less expressive than $|G|_2$, for representing properties of a simple hypergraph G by MS formulas. (Note that G is unambigously represented by both structures). For instance, the existence of a Hamiltonian circuit in a graph is a 2-definable property that is not 1-definable. The results of

[Cou9] comparing the expressive powers of MS formulas in the two cases are recalled in Section 4.

2 - Monadic Second-order Definable Transductions

We first define *transductions of relational structures*. Let R and R' be two finite ranked sets of relation symbols. Let W be a finite set of set variables, called here the set of *parameters*. (It is not a loss of generality to assume that all parameters are set variables.) An (R',R)-*definition scheme* is a tuple of formulas of the form

$$\Delta = (\varphi, \psi_1, \ldots, \psi_k, (\theta_w)_{w \in R'*k})$$

where : $k > 0$, $R'*k := \{(r,j) \;/\; r \in R', j \in [k]^{\rho(r)}\}$,
$\varphi \in \mathcal{L}(R,W)$,
$\psi_i \in \mathcal{L}(R, W \cup \{x_1\})$ for $i=1,\ldots,k$,
$\theta_w \in \mathcal{L}(R, W \cup \{x_1,\ldots,x_{\rho(r)}\})$, for $w = (r, j) \in R'*k$.

Let $S \in \mathcal{S}(R)$, let γ be a W-assignment in S. An R'-structure S' with domain $\mathbf{D}_{S'} \subseteq \mathbf{D}_S \times [k]$ is *defined by* Δ *in* (S,γ) if :

(i) $(S,\gamma) \models \varphi$,
(ii) $\mathbf{D}_{S'} = \{(d,i) \;/\; d \in \mathbf{D}_S, i \in [k], (S,\gamma,d) \models \psi_i\}$
(iii) for each r in R' :
$r_{S'} = \{((d_1, i_1),\ldots,(d_t,i_t)) \;/\; (S,\gamma, d_1,\ldots,d_t) \models \theta_{(r,j)}\}$,
where $j=(i_1,\ldots,i_t)$ and $t = \rho(r)$.

(By $(S,\gamma,d_1,\ldots,d_t) \models \theta_{(r,j)}$, we mean $(S,\gamma') \models \theta_{(r,j)}$, where γ' is the assignment extending γ, such that $\gamma'(x_i)=d_i$ for all $i=1,\ldots,t$; a similar convention is used for $(S,\gamma,d) \models \psi_i$.) Since S' is associated in a unique way with S, γ and Δ whenever it is defined, i.e., whenever $(S,\gamma) \models \varphi$, we can use the functional notation $\mathbf{def}_\Delta(S,\gamma)$ for S'.

The *transduction defined by* Δ is the relation $\mathbf{def}_\Delta := \{(S, S') / S' = \mathbf{def}_\Delta(S,\gamma)$ for some W-assignment γ in S$\} \subseteq \mathcal{S}(R)\times\mathcal{S}(R')$. A transduction $f \subseteq \mathcal{S}(R)\times\mathcal{S}(R')$ is *definable* if it is equal to $\mathbf{def}_\Delta$ for some (R',R)-definition scheme Δ. In the case where $W = \emptyset$, we say that f is *definable without parameters* (note that it is functional).

(2.1) Fact: *If f is a definable transduction, there exists an integer k such that,* $\mathbf{Card}(\mathbf{D}_T) \leq k.\mathbf{Card}(\mathbf{D}_S)$ *whenever* T *belongs to* f(S).

(2.2) Fact : *The domain of a definable transduction is definable.*

Proof: Let Δ be a definition scheme as above with $W = \{X_1,\ldots,X_n\}$. Then $\mathbf{Dom}(\mathbf{def}_\Delta) = \{S \mid S \models \exists X_1,\ldots,\exists X_n\, \varphi\}$. □

These definitions apply to hypergraphs via their representation by relational structures as explained above. However, since we have two representations of hypergraphs by logical structures, we must be more precise. We say that a *hypergraph transduction*, i.e., a binary relation f on hypergraphs is *(i,j)-definable*, where i and j belong to {1,2} iff the transduction of structures $\{(|G|_i, |G'|_j) \mid (G,G') \in f\}$ is definable. We shall also use transductions from trees to hypergraphs. Since a tree t is a graph, it can be represented by either $|t|_1$ or $|t|_2$. However, both structures are equally powerful for expressing monadic second-order properties of trees, and definable transductions from trees to trees and from trees to graphs. (This follows from the results of [Cou9]; see Theorem (4.3) below). When we specify a transduction involving trees (or words which are special trees) as input or output we shall use the symbol * instead of the integers 1 and 2, in order to recall that the choice of representation is not important in these cases. We shall use *definable* for *(*,*)-definable*.

The next three propositions list examples of definable transductions.

(2.3) Proposition: *The following mappings are definable transductions: (1) word homomorphisms, (2) inverse nonerasing word homomorphisms, (3) gsm mappings, (4) the mirror-image mapping on words, (5) the mapping* $\lambda u.[u^n]$ *(where* u *is a word and* n *a fixed integer), (6) the mapping* **yield** *that maps a derivation tree relative to a fixed context-free grammar to the generated word, (7) linear root-to-frontier or frontier-to-root tree transductions.*

Proof: The proofs are easy to do. A *gsm mapping* is a transduction from words to words defined by a *generalized sequential machine*, i.e., a (possibly nondeterministic) transducer that reads at least one input symbol on each move. See Gecseg and Steinby [GS] or the survey by Raoult [Rao] for tree transductions. □

Fact (2.1) which limits the sizes of the output structures, shows that certain transductions are *not definable*. This is the case of inverse erasing word homomorphisms and of ground tree transducers except in degenerated cases (see Dauchet *et al.* [DHLT] or [Rao] on ground tree transducers).

(2.4) Proposition [Cou5] : *The mapping* ***val*** *that associates with a finite or infinite hypergraph expression the hypergraph it denotes is (*,2)-definable.*

In [Cou7], systems of equations are investigated, that define infinite *equational* hypergraphs. Each equational hypergraph has an infinite *syntax tree*, i.e., some appropriately defined infinite derivation tree, that is close to an infinite hypergraph expression. The mapping from the syntax trees of a fixed system to the corresponding equational graphs is (*,2)-definable, and its inverse is (*,2)-definable.

(2.5) Proposition: *The transductions that associate with a graph G: (1) its spanning forests, (2) its connected components, (3) the connected component of some designated vertex (for instance the first source), (4) its minors, (5) its subgraphs satisfying some fixed 2-definable property, (6) its maximal subgraphs satisfying some fixed 2-definable property (maximal for subgraph inclusion), (7) the graph consisting of the union of two disjoint copies of G, are all (2,2)-definable. The mapping associating with a graph its line graph is (2,1)-definable but not (2,2)-definable.*

Proof: See [Cou6] for minors. See [CE] for line graphs. All other assertions are easy consequences of the existence of a MS formula expressing that two given vertices are linked by some path. See [Cou3-5]. □

3 - Properties of Definable Transductions of Relational Structures

The following proposition is the basic fact behind the notion of semantic interpretation ([Rab]). It says that if S = $\mathbf{def}_\Delta(T,\mu)$ then the monadic second-order properties of S can be expressed as monadic second-order properties of (T,μ).

Let $\Delta = (\varphi, \psi_1, \ldots, \psi_k, (\theta_w)_{w \in R^*k})$ be a (R,R')-definition scheme, written with a set of parameters $\mathcal{W}$. Let $\mathcal{V}$ be a set of set variables disjoint from $\mathcal{W}$. For every variable X in $\mathcal{V}$, for every i=1,...,k, we let X_i be a new variable. We let $\overline{\mathcal{V}} = \{X_i \,/\, X \in \mathcal{V},\ i=1,\ldots,k\}$. For every $\eta : \overline{\mathcal{V}} \longrightarrow \mathcal{P}(D)$, we let $\nu : \mathcal{V} \longrightarrow \mathcal{P}(D\times[k])$ be defined by: $\nu(X) = \eta(X_1)\times\{1\} \cup \ldots \cup \eta(X_k)\times\{k\}$. With these notations we can state:

(3.1) Proposition [Cou8, Cou9]: *For every formula* β *in* $\mathcal{L}(R,\mathcal{V})$, *one can construct a formula* $\overline{\beta}$ *in* $\mathcal{L}(R',\overline{\mathcal{V}}\cup\mathcal{W})$ *such that, for every* T *in* $\mathcal{S}(R')$, *for every* $\mu : \mathcal{W} \longrightarrow T$, *for every* $\eta : \overline{\mathcal{V}} \longrightarrow T$, *we have* :

> **def**$_\Delta$(T,μ) *is defined (if it is, we denote it by* S),
> ν *is a* $\mathcal{V}$*-assignment in* S, *and* (S,ν) $\models \beta$

iff

> (T, $\eta\cup\mu$) $\models \overline{\beta}$.

From this proposition, we get easily:

(3.2) Proposition: *(1) The inverse image of a definable set of structures under a definable transduction is definable.*

(2) The composition of two definable transductions is definable.

We could define more powerful transductions by which a structure S would be constructed "inside" T×T instead of "inside" a structure formed of k disjoint copies of T for fixed k. However, with this variant, one could construct a *second-order* formula $\overline{\beta}$ as in Proposition (3.1) (with quantifications on binary relations), but not a *monadic* second-order one (at least in general). We wish to avoid (full) second-order logic because most constructions and decidability results (like those of [Cou4]) break down.

(3.3) Proposition: *The union of two definable transductions is definable. So is the intersection of a definable transduction with a transduction of the form A×B where A and B are definable sets.*

Proof : See [Cou9] for the first assertion and [Cou8] for the second. □

Here are now some negative properties.

(3.4) Proposition: *(1) The image of a definable set under a definable transduction is a set that is not definable in general.*

(2) The inverse of a definable transduction is a transduction that is not definable in general.

(3) The intersection of two definable transductions is a transduction that is not definable in general

Proof : (1) The transduction of words mapping a^n to $b^nc^nb^n$ for $n > 0$ is definable (easy construction like those of Proposition (2.3)). The image of the definable language a* is a language that is not regular (and even not context-free), hence not definable by the basic result of Büchi and Elgot ([Tho, Thm 3.2]) recalled in the introduction.

(2) The inverse of this transduction is not definable since, if it would be, its domain is would be definable (by Fact (2.2)), hence regular, which is not the case.

(3) The intersection of the definable transductions of words that map a^nb^m to c^n, and a^nb^m to c^m is the one that maps a^nb^n to c^n. It is not definable because its domain is not a definable language. □

4 - Definable Transductions and Context-Free Graph Grammars

There are two classes of context-free graph (and hypergraph) grammars, the class of HR (Hyperedge Replacement) and the class of VR (Vertex Replacement) grammars. *HR grammars* (which generate the *HR sets* of graphs and hypergraphs) are based on the replacement, in a hypergraph, of a hypergraph for a (hyper)edge of the same rank: the labels of edges play the rôle of terminal and nonterminal symbols in context-free grammars. These grammars can be also defined as systems of fixed point equations, written with set union and the operations on hypergraphs recalled in Section 1. (See [Cou1] for a general theory of such systems of equations). We refer the reader to [BC, Cou3, Hab, HK] for definitions and basic properties. HR grammars are context-free in the sense of [Cou2]. This means in particular that they are *confluent*, i.e., that independent derivation steps can be permuted and that the equivalence classes of derivation sequences w.r.t. permutations of independent steps can be characterized by derivation trees. Another characteristic property of context-free grammars is that the generated sets can be characterized as forming the least solutions of systems of equations canonically associated with the considered grammar.

The relations between HR grammars and definable transductions are collected in the following theorem.

(4.1) Theorem: *(1) The mapping* **yield** *that associates with a derivation tree of a (fixed) HR grammar the generated hypergraph is (*,2)-definable.*

(2) A set of hypergraphs is HR iff it is the image of a recognizable set of finite trees under a (,2)-definable transduction.*

(3) The class of HR sets of hypergraphs is closed under (2,2)-definable transductions.

Proof : (1) is proved in [Cou8]; the "if" part of (2) is a difficult theorem established in [CE], whereas the "only if" part follows immediately from (1); (3) follows immediately from (2) since the composition of a (*,2)-definable transduction from trees to hypergraphs and a (2,2)-definable transduction from hypergraphs to hypergraphs is (*,2)-definable. □

Let us say that a HR grammar is *linear* if each righthand side of a production rule has at most one nonterminal, and that a set of hypergraphs is *linear HR* if there exists a linear HR grammar generating it. From the constructions establishing Theorem (4.1), we get that a set of hypergraphs is linear HR iff it is the image of a recognizable language under a (*,2)-definable transduction, and that the class LIN-HR of linear HR sets of hypergraphs is closed under (2,2)-definable transductions.

We now come to the more complex class of *VR ("Vertex Replacement")* sets of *simple* graphs. A few words of history are in order because the definition of this class has emerged from a sequence of papers. It comes out of the NLC grammars introduced by Janssens and Rozenberg [JR]; (NLC means "Node Labeled Controlled"). Not all NLC grammars are context-free because they are not always confluent (independent derivation steps cannot in general be permuted). The BNLC ("Boundary" NLC) grammars form a restriction of the general case and are confluent ([RW]). Whereas NLC grammars generate undirected graphs with unlabeled edges, the more general edNCE grammars can generate directed labeled graphs, and edge labels can be modified during the rewriting. Only the confluent ones (the C-edNCE grammars) are context-free. Other types of grammars, the S-HH ("Separated Handle Hypergraph") grammars, that are always context-free, generate exactly the same sets of graphs as the C-edNCE grammars and give more easily equivalent systems of fixed point equations ([CER]). See also [ER2] for more details and references. A grammar independent characterization of C-edNCE sets of graphs, slightly weaker than Theorem (4.2.2) is given by Engelfriet in [Eng2]. A *VR set of graphs* is a set of directed or undirected graphs generated by either a C-edNCE or a S-HH grammar, or defined as a component of the least solution of a systems of fixed point equations written with certain appropriate operations (see [CER]). Actually, the simplest way to define them is by systems of equations (see also [Cou12-13] for these systems).

(4.2) Theorem : *(1) The mapping* **yield** *that maps a derivation tree of a fixed C-edNCE or S-HH grammar to the generated graph is (*,1)-definable.*

(2) A set of simple graphs is VR iff it is the image of a recognizable set of finite trees under a (,1)-definable transduction.*

(3) The class of VR sets of graphs is closed under (1,1)-definable transductions.

Proof : (1) See [Cou10] or [Eng2]; (2) The "if" part is proved in [Eng2] for a restricted notion of transduction; the full form is Theorem (3.2) of [CE]; an alternative proof is given in [Cou10]; (3) follows from (2) like do the corresponding assertions of Theorem (4.1). □

As consequences, one gets that the set of *line graphs* of the graphs of a HR set is VR, and that the set of *chordal graphs* (i.e., of graphs in which every cycle of length at least 4 has a chord) is not VR.

The *linear* VR sets of graphs, i.e., those defined by *linear* C-edNCE or S-HH grammars (with at most one nonterminal in each righthand side of a production) can be characterized as the images of recognizable languages under (*,1)-definable transductions, and their class (let us denote it by LIN-VR) is closed under (1,1)-definable transductions.

Every HR set of simple graphs is VR. Conditions ensuring that a VR set is HR are given in [CE] and in [Cou11]. In particular, a VR set is HR iff its members do not contain arbitrary large complete bipartite graphs as subgraphs, and this is decidable as a consequence of Theorem (6.1) below.

What about VR sets of simple *hypergraphs*? We *define* them as the images of recognizable sets of finite trees under (*, 1)-definable transductions. Theorem (4.6) of [Cou10] gives a characterization in terms of systems of fixed point equations built with appropriate operations. Let us mention that S-HH grammars generate VR sets of simple hypergraphs, but not all of them ([CER]).

Definable transductions as a tool for studying hypergraphs as relational structures

Transductions of structures can be used in particular for two purposes: (1) in order to compare several representations of a same object by relational structures, and (2) to formalize encodings of hypergraphs by graphs, or more generally, of combinatorial objects by others. We illustrate successively these two uses.

We have defined two relational structures, $|G|_1$ and $|G|_2$ able to represent unambigously simple hypergraphs. For every set $\mathcal{C}$ of simple hypergraphs, we let $\mathbf{tr}(\mathcal{C})$ be the transduction: $\mathbf{tr}(\mathcal{C}) = \{(|G|_1, |G|_2) / G \in \mathcal{C}\}$. It is functional since we are dealing with simple hypergraphs and any two isomorphic graphs or structures are equal. If $\mathcal{C}$ is the set of simple graphs without sources, then $\mathbf{tr}(\mathcal{C})$ is not definable (otherwise, by Theorems (4.1) and (4.2), the classes of HR and VR sets of graphs would be the same which is not the case).

The *tree-width* of a graph is an integer that characterizes how close it is to be a tree: forests have tree-width 1, the tree-width of a clique with n vertices is n. The graphs in a HR set have tree-width bounded by some integer computable from the HR grammar generating it (see [Cou6, Cou12]).

(4.3) Theorem: *Let* k *be an integer. Let* $\mathcal{C}$ *be either the set of simple graphs of degree at most* k *or that of graphs of tree-width at most* k. *The transduction* $\mathbf{tr}(\mathcal{C})$ *is definable.*

Proof: See [Cou9] and [CE, Lemma 3.8]. □

This theorem has consequences relevant to the comparison between HR and VR sets of graphs.

(4.4) Corollary : *If a VR set of graphs has bounded degree, bounded tree-width, or is a subset of some HR set, then it is HR.*

Proof : Immediate application of Theorems (4.1), (4.2) and (4.3), and the fact that a HR set of graphs has bounded tree-width. The case of sets of graphs of bounded degree is also known from [EH2] and [Bra]. □

We now consider encodings of hypergraphs by graphs, along the lines of [ER1]. For H in $\mathbf{HG}(A)_0$, we denote by **gra**(H) the graph G such that:

$\mathbf{V}_G = \mathbf{V}_H \cup \mathbf{E}_H$ (recall that $\mathbf{V}_H \cap \mathbf{E}_H = \emptyset$),

$\mathbf{E}_G = \{(e,i,v) \ / \ e \in \mathbf{E}_H, v \in \mathbf{V}_H, v = \mathbf{vert}_H(e,i)\}$

$\cup \{(e,a) \ / \ e \in \mathbf{E}_H \ , \mathbf{lab}_H(e) = a \} \cup \{(v,*) \ / \ v \in \mathbf{V}_H \}$,

$\mathbf{vert}_G((e,i,v)) = (e,v)$ and $\mathbf{lab}_G((e,i,v)) = i$,

$\mathbf{vert}_G((e,a)) = (e)$ and $\mathbf{lab}_G((e,a)) = a$, and,

$\mathbf{vert}_G((v,*)) = (v)$ and $\mathbf{lab}_G((v,*)) = *$.

Thus, **gra**(H) belongs to $\mathbf{HG}(A\cup[m]\cup\{*\})_0$ where m is the maximum rank of an element of A. In this graph, the vertices represent the vertices of H as well as the edges of H. If $\mathbf{vert}_H(e) = (v_1,...,v_n)$ then, in **gra**(H), there is an i-labeled edge from the vertex representing e to the one representing v_i. If $\mathbf{lab}_H(e) = b$, then the vertex representing e is incident with an edge of rank 1 having the label b in **gra**(H). The vertices of G representing vertices of H have the "new" label *. The following result from [CE] is a generalization of Theorem 1 of [ER1] and the given proof is independent of the original one. It shows that the C-edNCE grammars generate the same sets of hypergraphs (via the coding **gra**) as the HR grammars.

(4.5) Theorem: *(1) The transduction* **gra** *is (2,2)-definable and the transduction* $\mathbf{gra}^{-1}$ *is (1,2)-definable.*

(2) For every subset L *of* $\mathbf{HG}(A)_0$, **gra**(L) *is* VR *iff* L *is* HR

Proof: It is easy to verify that **gra** is (2,2)-definable. Hence, if L is HR, then **gra**(L) is HR, hence also VR. Conversely, the transduction $\mathbf{gra}^{-1}$ is (1,2)-definable. Hence, by Theorems (4.1) and (4.2), $\mathbf{gra}^{-1}$(L') is HR if L' is VR. Hence, if **gra**(L) is VR then L = $\mathbf{gra}^{-1}$(**gra**(L)) is HR. □

5 - Definable Transductions of Words and Trees.

We review some relations between definable transductions and classical notions in language theory. The following proposition shows that the class of definable transductions and that of rational transductions are incomparable.

(5.1) Proposition: *A rational transduction is definable iff the image of every word is a finite language.*

Proof: The "only if" part follows from Fact(2.1). Conversely, a rational transduction such that every word has a finite image is of the form $\lambda L.[h(k^{-1}(L)\cap K)]$ where K is a recognizable language, h and k are homomorphisms with k non erasing (i.e., the image of a letter is not the empty word): see [Ber, Exercise 7.2, p. 87]. It is thus definable by Propositions (2.3), (3.2) and (3.3). □

We have observed that **yield**, the transduction from a derivation tree relative some fixed context-free grammar to the generated word, is definable. Its inverse is not definable in general even if the grammar is unambigous (otherwise the set of Polish prefix notations of terms over a finite ranked alphabet would be the domain of a definable transduction and would be definable whence recognizable which is not the case).

For some (but not all) HR grammars Γ, there exists a (2,*)-definable transduction associating with every hypergraph G, a derivation tree of this graph relative to Γ whenever G belongs to the set generated by the Γ. Hence, for these grammars, the definable transduction **yield** has a definable inverse (see [Cou8]). However, these grammars, analogous to left-linear grammars, are less powerful than the general HR grammars.

The example used in the proof of Proposition (3.4) shows that the image of a context-free language under a definable transduction is not context-free. The following is more precise.

(5.2) Theorem: *(1) The following classes of languages are identical:*

(1.1) the sets of words defined by HR (or VR) grammars,

(1.2) the images of HR (resp. VR) sets by (2,)-definable (resp. (1,*)-definable) transductions from hypergraphs to words,*

(1.3) the output languages of deterministic tree-walking tree-to-word transducers.

(2) The following classes of languages are identical:

(2.1) the images of regular languages under definable transductions from words to words,

(2.2) the languages in LIN-HR (or in LIN-VR),

(2.3) the images of LIN-HR (resp. LIN-VR) sets by (2,)-definable (resp. (1,*)-definable) transductions, from hypergraphs to words*

(2.4) the output languages of deterministic 2-way gsm mappings.

Proof: That (1.1) = (1.2) follows from Theorems (4.1.3) and (4.2.3); that (1.1) = (1.3) is the main result of [EH1]; that (2.1) = (2.4) is proved in [EH1]; the other equalities follow from previous remarks.□

Open problems: What is the class of images of context-free languages under definable (word-to-word) transductions? It is in between classes (1) and (2) of Theorem (5.2), but is it *strictly in between*? It is closely related, perhaps identical, to the class of images of context-free languages under deterministic 2-way gsm mappings. This later class has been considered in [ERS] where it is proved (Corollary 4.10) that it equals the class of *context-free controlled ETOL systems of finite index*, also considered in [Lan]. It would also be interesting to have "machine" characterizations of definable word-to-word transductions (in terms of 2-way generalized sequential machines or of related devices) and of definable tree-to-word transductions.

6 - PARIKH'S THEOREM AND DEFINABLE TRANSDUCTIONS FROM GRAPHS TO COMMUTATIVE WORDS.

Let $A = \{a_1,...,a_n\}$ be an alphabet. A commutative word over A can be identified with the n-tuples of numbers of occurrences of letters $a_1,...,a_n$ in the word or with the edgeless graph with one vertex labeled by a_i for each occurrence of a_i in the word and for each $i = 1,...,n$. We shall denote by $A^\$$ the set of such words, tuples and graphs.

In Theorem (5.2), we have characterized the images of HR and VR sets of hypergraphs under definable transductions from hypergraphs to words. We do the same here for those from hypergraphs to commutative words.

A subset of $A^\$$ is *semilinear* if it is semilinear in the usual sense when considered as a set of tuples of numbers, i.e. if it is a finite union of sets of the form $\{w + \lambda_1 z_1 + ... + \lambda_k z_k \ / \ \lambda_1,..., \lambda_k \in \mathbb{N}\}$ where $w, z_1,..., z_k \in \mathbb{N}^n$.

From Corollary 3.2.7 of [ERS] saying that the commutative images of the languages of the class (1.3) of Theorem (5.2) are semilinear sets, we obtain the following result.

(6.1) Theorem: *The following classes of sets of commutative words are identical:*

(1) the class of semilinear sets

(2) the class of HR (or VR) sets of commutative words,

(3) the images of HR (resp. VR) sets under (2,)- (resp.(1,*)- definable transductions from hypergraphs to commutative words.*

A proof that does not rest on the constructions of [ERS] can be given with the help of the following lemma of independent interest. Let ϕ be a formula in $\mathcal{L}(R,\{X_1, \ldots, X_k\})$ for some ranked set R of relational symbols. Let S be an R-relational structure. We define $\mathbf{sat}(\phi,S) := \{ (X_1,\ldots, X_k) \ / \ (S, X_1,\ldots, X_k) \models \phi \}$. With ϕ and a n×k matrix B of nonnegative integers, we can form the transduction $f_{\phi,B}$ from R-structures to $A^{\$}$ (identified with $\mathbb{N}^n$) such that:

$$f_{\phi,B}(S) := \{(\mathbf{Card}(X_1), \ldots, \mathbf{Card}(X_k)).B \ / \ (X_1,\ldots, X_k) \in \mathbf{sat}(\phi,S)\}.$$

(6.2) Lemma: *A transduction from structures to commutative words is definable iff it is of the form* $f_{\phi,B}$ *for some* ϕ *and* B.

Theorem (6.1) provides us with an extension of Parikh's Theorem.

(6.3) Corollary: *Let* L *be a HR (resp. VR) set of hypergraphs. Let* L' *the associated set of structures (of type 2 or 1 respectively). Then* $f_{\phi,B}(L')$ *is semilinear.*

This result extends the version of Parikh's Theorem of [Hab] in the sense that it does not only count vertex or edge labels but cardinalities of sets satisfying MS formulas.

7 - Conclusion

Definable transductions form a quite powerful class of graph transformations, that is netherless manageable, as shown by the closure theorems we have stated above. We have no space to review algorithmic aspects. Let us only mention that they form a key tool in [ALS], and that for every input graph G of tree-width at most some k, an output graph (relative to a fixed definable transduction) can be constructed in time **O**(**size**(G)) by [CM].

Can they be extended so as to include all inverse graph homomorphisms? The answer is no if we wish them to preserve the classes HR and VR, because, roughly speaking, the set of all finite graphs is neither HR nor VR. This is a striking difference with the case of words (the set of all words over a finite alphabet is context-free): there is no hope to generalize everything from words (or trees) to graphs.

ACKNOWLEDGEMENTS: I thank J. Engelfriet for pointing out the relevance of [ERS] and [Lan] to this work. I also thank A. Arnold and M. Mosbah for their comments on a first version of this paper.

REFERENCES

L.N.C.S. means Lecture Notes in Computer Science, Springer Verlag, Heidelberg, Berlin, New-York.

[ALS] ARNBORG S., LAGERGREN J.,SEESE D., Problems easy for tree-decomposable graphs, J. of Algorithms 12 (1991) 308-340

[BC] BAUDERON M., COURCELLE B., Graph expressions and graph rewritings, Mathematical Systems Theory 20 (1987) 83-127

[Ber] BERSTEL J., Transductions and context-free languages, Teubner Verlag, Stuttgart, 1979

[Bra] BRANDENBURG F.-J., The equivalence of boundary and confluent graph grammars on graph languages with bounded degree, L.N.C.S. 488 (1991)

[Bü] BÜCHI J., Weak second-order logic and finite automata, Z. Math. Logik Grundlagen Math. 5 (1960)66-92

[Cou1] COURCELLE B., Equivalences and transformations of regular systems. Applications to recursive program schemes and grammars, Theoret. Comput. Sci. 42 (1986) 1-122

[Cou2] COURCELLE B., An axiomatic definition of context-free rewriting and its application to NLC graph grammars, Theoret. Comput. Sci. 55 (1987) 141-181

[Cou3] COURCELLE B., Graph rewriting : An algebraic and logic approach, in "Handbook of Theoretical Computer Science, Volume B", J. Van Leeuwen ed., Elsevier,1990, pp.193-242

[Cou4] COURCELLE B., The monadic second-order logic of graphs I: Recognizable sets of finite graphs. Information and Computation 85 (1990) 12-75

[Cou5] COURCELLE B., The monadic second-order logic of graphs II: Infinite graphs of bounded width, Mathematical Systems Theory, 21(1989)187-221

[Cou6] COURCELLE B., The monadic second-order logic of graphs III: Tree-decompositions, minors and complexity issues, RAIRO Informatique Théorique et Applications, to appear.

[Cou7] COURCELLE B., The monadic second-order logic of graphs IV: Definability properties of equational graphs, Annals Pure Applied Logic 49(1990)193-255

[Cou8] COURCELLE B., The monadic second-order logic of graphs V: On closing the gap between definability and recognizability, Theoret. Comput. Sci. 80 (1991) 153-202

[Cou9] COURCELLE B., The monadic second order logic of graphs VI: On several representations of graphs by relational structures, Report 89-99, Discrete Applied Mathematics, to appear (see also Logic in Computer Science 1990, Philadelphia)

[Cou10] COURCELLE B., The monadic second order logic of graphs VII: Graphs as relational structures, Theoret. Comput. Sci., in press, Research Report 91-40, short version in the proceedings of the 4th International Workshop on Graph Grammars, L.N.C.S.532 (1991) 238-252

[Cou11] COURCELLE B., On the structure of context-free sets of graphs generated by vertex replacement, Research Report, Bordeaux-1 University, to appear.

[Cou12] COURCELLE B., Graph grammars, monadic second-order logic and the theory of graph minors, Proccedings of the Graph Minors Conference, Seattle, June 1991, Contemporary Mathematics, American Mathematical Society, to appear.

[CE] COURCELLE B., ENGELFRIET J., A logical characterization of the sets of hypergraphs generated by hyperedge replacement grammars, Research Report 91-41, Bordeaux-1 University, 1991, submitted.

[CER] COURCELLE B., ENGELFRIET J., ROZENBERG G., Handle-rewriting hypergraph grammars, Report 90-84, Bordeaux-I University, to appear in J.C.S.S.;short version in the proceedings of the 4th International Workshop on Graph Grammars, L.N.C.S. 532, (1991) 253-268

[CM] COURCELLE B., MOSBAH M., Monadic second-order evaluations on tree-decomposable graphs, Research report 90-110, Bordeaux-1 University, to appear in Theoret.Comput. Sci., (extended abstract in the Proceedings of WG'91, L.N.C.S., to appear.)

[DHLT] DAUCHET M., HEUILLARD T., LESCANNE P., TISON S., Decidability of the confluence of finite ground term rewrite systems and of other related term rewrite systems, Information and Computation 88 (1990) 187-201

[Don] DONER J., Tree acceptors and some of their applications, J.Comput.Syst.Sci.4 (1970) 406-451

[Elg] ELGOT C., Decision problems of finite automata design and related arithmetics, Trans. A.M.S. 98 (1961)21-52

[Eng1] ENGELFRIET J., Context-free NCE graph grammars, Proc. FCT' 89, L.N.C.S. 380 (1989) 148-161

[Eng2] ENGELFRIET J., A characterization of context-free NCE graph languages by monadic second-order logic on trees, L.N.C.S. 532 (1991) 311-327

[EH1] ENGELFRIET J., HEYKER L., The string generating power of context-free hypergraph grammars, J. Comp. Syst. Sci. 43 (1991) 328-360

[EH2] ENGELFRIET J., HEYKER L., Hypergraph languages of bounded degree, report 91-01, Univ. Leiden, 1991

[ER1] ENGELFRIET J., ROZENBERG G., A comparison of boundary graph grammars and context-free hypergraph grammars, Information and Computation 84 (1990) 163-206

[ER2] ENGELFRIET J., ROZENBERG G., Graph grammars based on node rewriting: an introduction to NLC graph grammars, L.N.C.S. 532 (1991) 12-23

[ERS] ENGELFRIET J., ROZENBERG G., SLUTZKI G., Tree transducers, L systems and two-way machines, J. Comput. System Sci. 20 (1980) 150-202

[GS] GECSEG F., STEINBY M., Tree automata, Akademiai Kiado, Budapest, 1984

[Gu] GUREVICH Y., Monadic second-order theories, in J. Barwise and S. Feferman eds.,"Model theoretic logic", Springer, Berlin, 1985, pp. 479-506

[Hab] HABEL A., Hyperedge replacement: grammars and languages, Doctoral dissertation, Bremen 1989

[HK] HABEL A., KREOWSKI H.J., May we introduce to you: Hyperedge replacement?, Proceedings of the 3rd International Workshop on Graph Grammars, L.N.C.S. 291 (1987) 15-26

[JR] JANSSENS D., ROZENBERG G., A survey of NLC grammars, L.N.C.S. 159 (1983) 114-128

[Lan] LANGE K.-J., Context-free controlled ETOL systems, Proceedings of 10th ICALP, L.N.C.S. 154 (1980) 723-733

[Rab] RABIN M., A simple method for undecidability proofs and some applications, in "Logic, Methodology and Philosophy of Science II", Y. Bar-Hilleled., North-Holland, Amsterdam, 1965, pp.58-68

[Rab] RAOULT J.-C., A survey of tree transductions, INRIA report 1410, to appear in the proceedings of an ASMICS workshop held in LeTouquet, France,June 1990, M. Nivat and A. Podelski eds.

[RW] ROZENBERG G., WELZL E., Boundary NLC grammars, Basic definitions, normal forms and complexity, Information and Control 69 (1986) 136-167

[Tho] THOMAS W., Automata on infinite objects, same volume as [Cou3] pp.133-192

CTL* and ECTL* as fragments of the modal μ-calculus [1]

Mads Dam
Department of Computer Science
University of Edinburgh

1 Introduction

Due to its inherent combinatorial difficulties, concurrency is an area of computer science where formal and automated verification methods have proved themselves particularly valuable, for instance in detecting errors difficult or impossible to find by informal reasoning alone (c.f. Gries [16], Clarke and Mishra [7], Browne et al [3]). For programming errors to be exposed by exhibiting mismatch to formal properties, those properties must correctly reflect the intent of the programmer. The correctness of this representation may be obvious for a few very simple theories, but unfortunately the need for greater expressive power often seems to call for a corresponding sacrifice in transparency.

A case in point is the modal μ-calculus L_μ (Kozen [18]). This logic is obtained as an enrichment of a simple modal base logic, Hennessy-Milner logic (Hennessy, Milner [17]), by least and greatest fixpoints of formally monotone operators. The result is a very general branching-time temporal logic capable of expressing a wealth of properties related to for instance partial and total correctness, liveness, safety and fairness, that are of crucial importance in practical program verification (c.f. Bradfield, Stirling [2], Walker [30]). Indeed L_μ encompasses a great many well-known program logics such as PDL (Fischer, Ladner [14]), PDL-Δ (Streett [25]), linear-time temporal logic PTL (Gabbay et al [15]), CTL (Clarke, Emerson [5]), and CTL* (Emerson, Halpern [10]). This can be shown by providing constructive translations (c.f. Kozen [18], Emerson, Lei [12], Wolper [31]).

In fact the containment in all these cases is strict. A typical example of a property expressible in L_μ but not, for instance, in CTL* is a cyclic property such as "along any path, at all even moments, ϕ holds" (c.f. Wolper [32]). Properties such as these are necessary in general for modular reasoning (Lichtenstein et al [19]). Despite this additional expressive power, L_μ is decidable in deterministic exponential time, and thus essentially is not harder than PDL (Emerson,

[1] This work was supported by SERC Grant GR/F 32219.

Jutla [11], Fischer, Ladner [14]). Moreover, for closed formulas L_μ preserves the characterisation of bisimulation equivalence (Hennessy, Milner [17]) and thus provides a natural temporal logic for process calculi such as CCS (Stirling [23]). A model checker for checking L_μ-properties against finite-state (CCS) processes due to Stirling and Walker [24] has been implemented in the Edinburgh Concurrency Workbench (Cleaveland et al [8]) and used in several case-studies such as mutual exclusion algorithms (Walker [30]) and communication protocols (Bruns, Anderson [4]).

Impeding the widespread practical use of L_μ, however, is its lack of transparency: Already at the second level of alternation formulas can become highly unintelligible. And alternation is indeed needed to express for instance fairness properties. Consequently it is important to develop tools to aid users in manipulating, generating, and understanding L_μ-formulas. Constructive translations such as those referred to above can be very useful for these purposes. They can be machine implemented to provide syntactical sugaring of L_μ properties. Moreover they can help also in understanding L_μ itself, provided they, and the results they produce, are sufficiently simple and intuitive. Most of the translations succeed very well in this: A first step towards a working understanding of L_μ is certainly to understand why the CTL-formula EFX is translated into $\mu Y.X \vee \Diamond Y$.

In this respect CTL* (Emerson, Halpern [10]) is of particular interest. Beyond CTL, CTL* is capable of expressing properties such as $EGF\phi$ ("along some path ϕ holds infinitely often"), useful for dealing with fairness (Emerson, Halpern [10]), and in general arbitrary nestings and boolean combinations of linear and branching time connectives for which the task of finding equivalent L_μ-formulations may present considerable difficulties. The previously only known translation of CTL* into L_μ is, however, rather indirect and not very transparent. It is obtained by composing Wolper's unpublished translation of CTL* into PDL-Δ [31] with the translation of PDL-Δ into L_μ (c.f. Emerson, Lei [12]). It involves 5 stages: The first and second stages builds a tableau and derives from it a deterministic Muller automaton (c.f. Emerson and Sistla [13]). Third stage derives from this automaton an equivalent ω-regular expression (c.f. McNaughton [20]). As the fourth stage a PDL-Δ formula is obtained, and finally this formula is translated into L_μ.

In this paper we present a relatively simple and much more direct algorithm for translating CTL* into L_μ. The idea is to represent a tableau directly as an equivalent L_μ formula. The notion of tableau used is fairly standard and closely related to those of e.g. Ben-Ari et al [1] and Wolper [32]. Their role is to decompose formulas according to their structure, and to detect recursion in the natural way of terminating when a node is repeated. The problem is to use the connectives of L_μ as an external means of characterising tableaux, and in particular to use least and greatest fixpoints to classify loops. The solution involves an analysis of the admissible ways of "regenerating" nodes, using the terminology of Streett and Emerson [26].

An alternative way of allowing cyclic properties to be expressed, is to include in CTL* not only the linear-time modalities of PTL, but more generally all linear-time modalities expressible in Wolper's Extended Temporal Logic, ETL [32]. ETL extends PTL by allowing arbitrary finite automata on infinite words as temporal operators. In this way the full power of the ω-regular languages is obtained (Wolper et al [33]), whereas PTL is capable of describing only the star-free ω-regular languages (Gabbay et al [15], Thomas [27]). Several expressively equivalent versions of extended CTL*, ECTL*, have been proposed (Vardi, Wolper [29], Clarke et al [6], Thomas [28]). Here we follow the approach of Thomas, adding linear-time operators corresponding to Büchi automata on infinite words.

Also for ECTL* the translation involves the building of tableaux and the use of fixpoints to classify loops. The construction turns out to be simpler, however, than for CTL* for two reasons: First there is no need to consider the explicit nesting of linear-time connectives present in CTL*, and secondly the use of Büchi automata allows attention to be restricted to automata with a single accepting state.

The remainder of the paper is organised as follows: In sections 2 and 3, L_μ and CTL* are introduced, sections 4, 5 and 6 describes the translation from CTL*, sections 7 and 8 introduces ECTL* and describes its translation, and finally in section 9 we discuss issues such as efficiency and related work. Proofs of the two main theorems have been deferred to an appendix.

2 The modal μ-calculus

Formulas ϕ, ψ, γ of (1-letter) L_μ are built from propositional variables X, Y, boolean connectives $\neg$ and $\wedge$, the modal nextstate quantifier $\Diamond$, and the least fixpoint operator $\mu X.\phi$. The latter is subject to the formal monotonicity condition that all free occurrences of X in ϕ lie in the scope of an even number of negations. Other connectives are derived in the usual way, and in particular: $\Box\phi \triangleq \neg\Diamond\neg\phi$, $\nu X.\phi \triangleq \neg\mu X.\neg\phi[\neg X/X]$. We use σ as a metavariable ranging over $\{\mu, \nu\}$. Usually indexed modalities <a> are considered instead of the unindexed $\Diamond$. For the purpose of embedding CTL* and ECTL*, however, one program letter suffices.

For the semantics fix a transition system $T = (S, R)$ where S is a set of states and R a binary transition relation on S. The semantics of the formula ϕ relative to T and a valuation $\mathcal{V} : X \mapsto B \subseteq S$ is the set $\|\phi\|\mathcal{V} \subseteq S$ defined as follows:

$$\begin{aligned}
\|X\|\mathcal{V} &= \mathcal{V}(X) \\
\|\neg\phi\|\mathcal{V} &= \overline{\|\phi\|\mathcal{V}} \\
\|\phi \wedge \psi\|\mathcal{V} &= \|\phi\|\mathcal{V} \cap \|\psi\|\mathcal{V} \\
\|\Diamond\phi\|\mathcal{V} &= \{s \in S \mid \exists s' \in S.\ sRs' \text{ and } s' \in \|\phi\|\mathcal{V}\} \\
\|\mu X.\phi\|\mathcal{V} &= \bigcap\{B \subseteq S \mid \|\phi\|\mathcal{V}[X \mapsto B] \subseteq B\}
\end{aligned}$$

Here $\mathcal{V}[X \mapsto B]$ is the usual update $\mathcal{V}'$ of $\mathcal{V}$ which agrees with $\mathcal{V}$ except that $\mathcal{V}'(X) = B$. The expected clauses are obtained for the derived connectives. In particular for greatest fixpoints:

$$\|\nu X.\phi\|\mathcal{V} = \bigcup\{B \subseteq S \mid B \subseteq \|\phi\|\mathcal{V}[X \mapsto B]\}.$$

Intuitively, least fixed points are used for eventualities and greatest fixed points for invariant properties. This intuition can be brought out by characterisations of the relation of satisfaction $s \in \|\phi\|\mathcal{V}$ due in somewhat different settings to Streett and Emerson [26] and Bradfield and Stirling [2]. Such a characterisation is given in the appendix.

3 Computation Tree Logic, CTL*

Formulas of CTL* are built from propositional variables using boolean connectives $\neg$ and $\wedge$, the linear next-time and until-operators O and U, and the existential path-quantifier E. The dual of E is the universal path-quantifier defined by $A\phi \triangleq \neg E \neg \phi$. Other connectives are derived as usual. In particular $F\phi \triangleq \text{true}U\phi$ and $G\phi \triangleq \neg F \neg \phi$. Also we let $\phi_1 \neg U \phi_2 \triangleq \neg(\phi_1 U \phi_2)$.

Formulas denote properties of infinite paths through a transition system $T = (S, R)$ with valuation $\mathcal{V}$. Such a path is a mapping $\rho \in S^\omega$ such that for all $i \in \omega$, $\rho(i) R \rho(i+1)$. The i'th suffix of ρ is the path ρ^i given by $\rho^i(j) = \rho(i+j)$ for all $j \in \omega$. The relation R is *total* if for all $s \in S$ there is some $s' \in S$ such that sRs'. The assumption of totality allows attention to be restricted to infinite paths. The semantics is standard (c.f. Emerson and Halpern [10]):

$$\rho \models_{\mathcal{V}} X \text{ iff } \rho(i) \in \mathcal{V}(X)$$

$$\rho \models_{\mathcal{V}} \neg\phi \text{ iff } \rho \not\models_{\mathcal{V}} \phi$$

$$\rho \models_{\mathcal{V}} \phi_1 \wedge \phi_2 \text{ iff } \rho \models_{\mathcal{V}} \phi_1 \text{ and } \rho \models_{\mathcal{V}} \phi_2$$

$$\rho \models_{\mathcal{V}} O\phi \text{ iff } \rho^1 \models_{\mathcal{V}} \phi$$

$$\rho \models_{\mathcal{V}} \phi_1 U \phi_2 \text{ iff } \exists i \in \omega \text{ such that } \rho^i \models_{\mathcal{V}} \phi_2 \text{ and } \forall j : 0 \leq j < i.\ \rho^j \models_{\mathcal{V}} \phi_1$$

$$\rho \models_{\mathcal{V}} E\phi \text{ iff } \exists \rho' \text{ such that } \rho(0) = \rho'(0) \text{ and } \rho' \models_{\mathcal{V}} \phi$$

Let $s \models_{\mathcal{V}} \phi$ iff for all paths ρ such that $\rho(0) = s$, $\rho \models_{\mathcal{V}} \phi$. We are particularly interested in formulas that depend only on the current state in the sense that $\rho \models_{\mathcal{V}} \phi$ iff $\rho(0) \models_{\mathcal{V}} \phi$. This is true, in particular, for boolean combinations of formulas that are either propositional variables or contains an outermost occurrence of the existential path-quantifier. Such formulas are called *state formulas.*

4 Tableaux

The aim is to translate state formulas into semantically equivalent L_μ formulas. Substantial parts of this translation can be performed structurally (c.f. Wolper [31]). Variables can be translated into themselves, and boolean combinations of state formulas can be translated into boolean combinations of their translations. Furthermore substitutions of state formulas for variables can be preserved. More formally let $\phi \leadsto \psi$ mean that the state formula ϕ is translated into the L_μ-formula ψ, and assume that the translation is correct in the sense that ϕ and ψ are semantically equivalent. That is, for all transition systems T, for all $s \in S_T$ and all valuations $\mathcal{V}$ on T, $s \models_\mathcal{V} \phi$ iff $s \in \|\psi\|\mathcal{V}$. Then the following four rules are validated:

$$X \leadsto X \qquad \frac{\phi \leadsto \psi}{\neg\phi \leadsto \neg\psi} \qquad \frac{\phi_1 \leadsto \psi_1 \quad \phi_2 \leadsto \psi_2}{\phi_1 \wedge \phi_2 \leadsto \psi_1 \wedge \psi_2}$$

$$\frac{\phi_1 \leadsto \psi_1 \quad \cdots \quad \phi_n \leadsto \psi_n \qquad \phi \leadsto \psi}{\phi[\phi_1/X_1, \ldots, \phi_n/X_n] \leadsto \psi[\psi_1/X_1, \ldots, \psi_n/X_n]}$$

where $\gamma[\gamma_1/X_1, \ldots, \gamma_n/X_n]$ denotes the simultaneous substitution of the γ_i for X_i in γ. By means of these rules attention can be restricted to formulas of the form $E\phi$ where ϕ is a linear-time formula, i.e. ϕ does not contain occurrences of the existential path-quantifier E. For formulas of this form the translation uses tableaux as an intermediate representation. A tableau is a rooted, finite directed graph which is generated by applying exactly one of a small set of rules to each node that is not a leaf. Leaves are propositional variables or their negations. Other nodes are formulas of the form $E\Phi \triangleq E \bigwedge \Phi$ where Φ is a finite set of path-quantifier free formulas. The purpose of the tableaux rules is to analyse the state-related structure of formulas by means of the basic L_μ connectives $\wedge$, $\vee$ and $\Diamond$. To each rule is consequently associated one of these connectives, or possibly the identity operator I. The tableau rules are the following:

$$I\colon \frac{E(\Phi, \neg\neg\phi)}{E(\Phi, \phi)} \qquad \wedge\colon \frac{E(\Phi, X)}{E\Phi \quad X} \qquad \wedge\colon \frac{E(\Phi, \neg X)}{E\Phi \quad \neg X}$$

$$I\colon \frac{E(\Phi, \phi \wedge \psi)}{E(\Phi, \phi, \psi)} \qquad \vee\colon \frac{E(\Phi, \phi \vee \psi)}{E(\Phi, \phi) \quad E(\Phi, \psi)}$$

$$\vee\colon \frac{E(\Phi, \phi_1 U \phi_2)}{E(\Phi, \phi_2) \quad E(\Phi, \phi_1, O(\phi_1 U \phi_2))}$$

$$\vee\colon \frac{E(\Phi, \phi_1 \neg U \phi_2)}{E(\Phi, \neg\phi_1, \neg\phi_2) \quad E(\Phi, \neg\phi_2, O(\phi_1 \neg U \phi_2))}$$

$$\Diamond\colon \frac{E(O\phi_1, \ldots, O\phi_n)}{E(\phi_1, \ldots, \phi_n)}$$

For the operators F and G the following rules can be used instead of those derived from the "until"-based ones above:

$$I: \frac{E(\Phi, G\phi)}{E(\Phi, \phi, OG\phi)} \qquad \vee: \frac{E(\Phi, F\phi)}{E(\Phi, \phi) \quad E(\Phi, OF\phi)}$$

It is not difficult to see that tableaux are finite, and that all the tableau rules are forwards and backwards sound in the sense that if $\Omega : \frac{\phi}{\phi_1 \cdots \phi_n}$ is an instance of any of the above rules, then $s \models_{\mathcal{V}} \phi$ iff $s \models_{\mathcal{V}} \Omega(\phi_1, \ldots, \phi_n)$ where $\diamond$ is interpreted as EO.

5 Admissible paths

A key task is to isolate those infinite paths through a given tableau τ that are admissible in the sense, intuitively, that eventualities are eventually also satisfied. An *eventuality* is any formula of the form $\phi U\psi$ or $O(\phi U\psi)$, or $F\psi$ or $OF\psi$ if F is taken as primitive. For a set Φ, $Ev(\Phi)$ is the set of all eventualities in Φ. To get at the notion of eventual satisfaction, and thus of admissibility, we analyse the way individual formulas are regenerated. Let $E\Phi_1 \to E\Phi_2$ if there is an edge from $E\Phi_1$ to $E\Phi_2$ in τ. Each transition $E\Phi_1 \to E\Phi_2$ determines a *generation relation* $\rhd \subseteq \Phi_1 \times \Phi_2$. For instance for the rules for U and $\diamond$:

(i) The transition $E(\Phi, \phi U\psi) \to E(\Phi, \psi)$ determines the relation

$$\rhd = \{(\phi U\psi, \psi)\} \cup \{(\gamma, \gamma) \mid \gamma \in \Phi\}$$

(ii) The transition $E(\Phi, \phi U\psi) \to E(\Phi, \phi, O(\phi U\psi))$ determines the relation

$$\rhd = \{(\phi U\psi, \phi)\} \cup \{(\phi U\psi, O(\phi U\psi))\} \cup \{(\gamma, \gamma) \mid \gamma \in \Phi\}$$

(iii) The transition $E(O\phi_1, \ldots, O\phi_n) \to E(\phi_1, \ldots, \phi_n)$ determines the relation

$$\rhd = \{(O\phi_i, \phi_i) \mid 1 \le i \le n\}$$

For the remaining transitions the generation relation is determined similarly.

Example 5.1 Consider the transition $E(O(\phi U\psi), \phi U\psi) \to E(O(\phi U\psi), \psi)$. In this case $O(\phi U\psi) \rhd O(\phi U\psi)$ and $\phi U\psi \rhd \psi$, but *not* $\phi U\psi \rhd O(\phi U\psi)$, as relative to the given transition $O(\phi U\psi)$ is not generated by $\phi U\psi$.

We use Π for $\to$-paths and π for $\rhd$-paths, and write $\pi \in \Pi$ if Π and π are of equal length, and for each $i > 0$ for which $\Pi(i)$ is defined, $\pi(i-1) \rhd \pi(i)$ relative to the transition $\Pi(i-1) \to \Pi(i)$. Then an infinite $\to$-path Π is *admissible*, if for each $\pi \in \Pi$, whenever $\pi(i) = \phi U\psi$ or $\pi(i) = F\psi$ then for some $j > i$, $\pi(j) = \psi$. Suppose that Π visits the node $E\Phi$ infinitely often. Consider a segment $\Pi(i_0, i_k) \triangleq \Pi(i_0), \ldots, \Pi(i_k)$ of Π for which $\Pi(i_0) = \Pi(i_k) = E\Phi$ and let $\phi \in Ev(\Phi)$. Then ϕ is *regenerated along* $\Pi(i_0, i_k)$ if there is some $\pi \in \Pi(i_0, i_k)$ such that $\pi(0) = \pi(i_k - i_0) = \phi$.

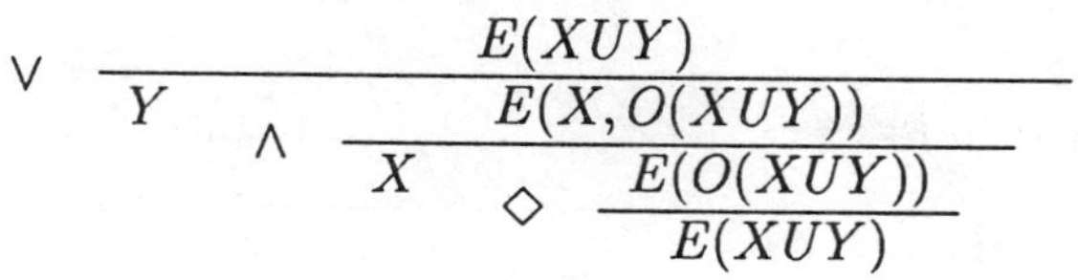

Figure 1: Tableau for $E(XUY)$

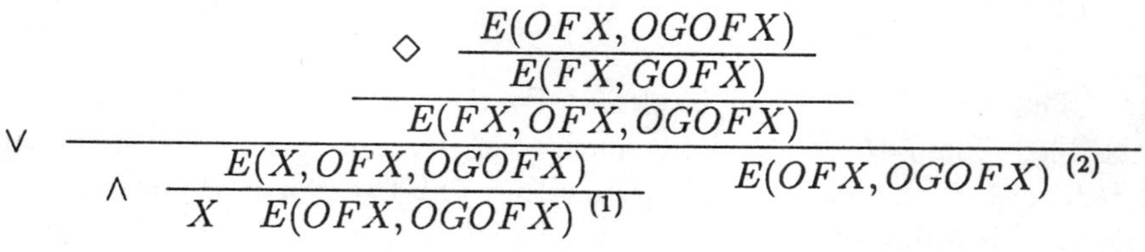

Figure 2: Tableau for $E(OFX, OGOFX)$

Example 5.2 Here and below we use a tree-like notation for tableaux, terminating the construction as soon as nodes are first repeated.

(i) Fig. 1 shows a tableau for $E(XUY)$. The eventuality XUY is regenerated along the $\rightarrow$-path from the root to its repetition.

(ii) Fig. 2 shows a tableau for the formula $\phi = E(OFX, OGOFX)$. This is semantically equivalent to the formula $EGFX$ expressing the fairness related property that X holds infinitely often along some path. No eventuality is regenerated along the $\rightarrow$-path from the root to its repetition labelled (1) whereas the eventuality OFX is regenerated along the $\rightarrow$-path to (2).

(iii) Similarly the formula $E\Phi$ of fig. 3 expresses that both X and Y holds infinitely often. In fig. 3 no eventuality is regenerated from the root to its repetition labelled (1), OFY is regenerated to (2), OFX is regenerated to (3) and both are regenerated to (4).

The following characterisation of the admissible $\rightarrow$-paths is of central importance to the translation procedure. Let a *simple node* be any node $E\Phi$ with the property that whenever $\phi U \psi \in \Phi$ ($F\phi \in \Phi$) then $O(\phi U \psi) \notin \Phi$ ($OF\phi \notin \Phi$). Clearly any infinite $\rightarrow$-path Π will infinitely often visit the same simple node. Consider for instance the set of all nodes visited by Π to which the $\Diamond$-rule applies.

Lemma 5.3 *Let Π be an infinite $\rightarrow$-path through a tableau τ, and let $i_0, i_1, \ldots$ be an infinite, strictly increasing sequence such that $\Pi(i_j)$ is the same simple node $E\Phi$ for all $j \in \omega$. Then Π is admissible iff for each $\phi \in Ev(\Phi)$ there are infinitely many $j \in \omega$ such that ϕ is not regenerated along the segment $\Pi(i_j, i_{j+1})$.*

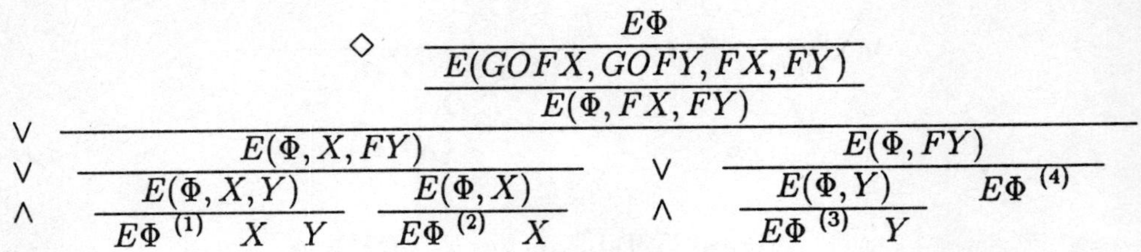

Figure 3: Tableau with $\Phi = \{OGOFX, OGOFY, OFX, OFY\}$.

PROOF: The only if direction is clear. For the if direction suppose that Π is inadmissible. Then there is an $\multimap$-path $\pi \in \Pi$, a $k \in \omega$, and an eventuality $\phi = \phi_1 U \phi_2$, say, such that for all $k' \geq k$, either $\pi(k') = \phi$ or $\pi(k') = O\phi$. As $E\Phi$ is a simple node it follows that either for all j such that $i_j \geq k$, $\pi(i_j) = \phi$, or for all j with $i_j \geq k$, $\pi(i_j) = O\phi$. In any case either ϕ is regenerated along every segment $\Pi(i_j, i_{j+1})$ for which $i_j \geq k$, or else $O\phi$ is. □

The restriction to simple nodes in Lemma 5.3 is indeed necessary. To see this let Π_1 be the $\rightarrow$-path

$$\begin{aligned} E(OGFX, FX, OFX, OGOFX) &\rightarrow E(OGFX, OFX, OGOFX) \\ &\rightarrow E(GFX, FX, GOFX) \\ &\rightarrow E(GFX, OFX, GOFX) \\ &\rightarrow E(OGFX, FX, OFX, GOFX) \\ &\rightarrow E(OGFX, FX, OFX, OGOFX) \end{aligned}$$

and let Π_2 be the $\rightarrow$-path

$$\begin{aligned} E(OGFX, FX, OFX, OGOFX) &\rightarrow E(OGFX, OFX, OGOFX) \\ &\rightarrow E(GFX, FX, GOFX) \\ &\rightarrow E(GFX, FX, OFX, OGOFX) \\ &\rightarrow E(OGFX, FX, OFX, OGOFX) \end{aligned}$$

Notice that FX is not regenerated along Π_1, and that OFX is not regenerated along Π_2. Consider the infinite $\rightarrow$-path $\Pi = (\Pi_1 \cdot \Pi_2)^\omega$ obtained by alternating between Π_1 and Π_2 ad infinitum, and pick as the sequence $i_0, i_1, \ldots$ the largest sequence such that $\Pi(i_j) = E(OGFX, FX, OFX, OGOFX)$. Clearly Π is not admissible, but both eventualities FX and OFX fails to be regenerated along infinitely many segments $\Pi(i_j, i_{j+1})$.

6 Translating CTL*

The structure of the translation is determined by the labelling of rule instances, and least or greatest fixpoints are used to characterise the admissible $\rightarrow$-paths.

The translation procedure passes each node ϕ at most twice. The interesting case is when ϕ is a simple node. In this case a suitable context is built up in the first pass of ϕ, using the label information together with fixpoint quantifiers to bind propositional variables. These variables are then used in the second pass, if it applies. Let $\phi = E\Phi$. First, if $Ev(\Phi) = \emptyset$ any infinite $\rightarrow$-path Π that visits ϕ infinitely often is admissible. A suitable scheme for the translation of ϕ in this case is consequently

$$\nu X_\Phi.\psi(X_\Phi)$$

where ϕ in the second pass is translated into X_Φ. In general, however, by Lemma 5.3, each $\phi \in Ev(\Phi)$ must infinitely often be prevented from being regenerated between subsequent visits to ϕ by Π. This suggests

$$\nu X_\Phi.\bigwedge_{\phi\in Ev(\Phi)}\mu Y_{\phi,\Phi}.\psi(X_\Phi, Y_{\phi,\Phi})$$

as a general scheme for the translation of ϕ where in the second pass ϕ is translated into $Y_{\phi,\Phi}$ if ϕ is regenerated along the path segment traversed since the first pass, and as X_Φ otherwise.

To make the notion of pass and segment traversal precise the translation of a node ϕ is really relativised to a path segment $\Pi = \phi_0, \ldots, \phi_n$ for which $\phi_n \rightarrow \phi$. We write $\Pi \vdash \phi$ for the relativisation of ϕ to Π. In addition as the translation progresses an environment ε is carried along which when $\phi = E\Phi$ and $Ev(\Phi)$ is nonempty choses an element $\varepsilon(\Phi) \in Ev(\Phi)$ intended to be significant when considering the regeneration of eventualities as above. Relative to Π and ε the node ϕ is translated into $tr(\Pi \vdash \phi)\varepsilon$. When the segment Π is understood from the context we often abbreviate $tr(\Pi \vdash \phi)\varepsilon$ as $tr(\phi)\varepsilon$. For leaves the translation is trivial:

$$tr(\Pi \vdash (\neg)X)\varepsilon = (\neg)X. \tag{1}$$

Let then $\phi = E\Phi$. Suppose first that $\Pi(i) = \phi$ for some $i : 1 \leq i \leq n$ so that ϕ is currently being passed the second time. If either $\varepsilon(\Phi)$ is undefined (because $Ev(\Phi) = \emptyset$), or $\varepsilon(\Phi)$ is not regenerated along the segment $\Pi(i), \ldots, \Pi(n), \phi$ let

$$tr(\Pi \vdash \phi)\varepsilon = X_\Phi \tag{2}$$

and otherwise let

$$tr(\Pi \vdash \phi)\varepsilon = Y_{\varepsilon(\Phi),\Phi}. \tag{3}$$

Assume then that $\Pi(i) \neq \phi$ for all $i : 1 \leq i \leq n$, and let the rule instance applied to ϕ be $\Omega : \frac{\phi}{\phi_1,\ldots,\phi_m}$. First, if ϕ is not a simple node or ϕ is not reachable from any of the nodes $\phi_1, \ldots, \phi_m$ let

$$tr(\Pi \vdash \phi)\varepsilon = \Omega(tr(\Pi, \phi \vdash \phi_1)\varepsilon, \ldots, tr(\Pi, \phi \vdash \phi_m)\varepsilon). \tag{4}$$

Secondly, if $Ev(\Phi) = \emptyset$ let

$$tr(\Pi \vdash \phi)\varepsilon = \nu X_\Phi.\Omega(tr(\Pi, \phi \vdash \phi_1)\varepsilon, \ldots, tr(\Pi, \phi \vdash \phi_m)\varepsilon). \tag{5}$$

Finally, in any other case,

$$tr(\Pi \vdash \phi)\varepsilon = \nu X_\Phi . \bigwedge_{\psi \in Ev(\Phi)} \mu Y_{\psi,\Phi} . \\ \Omega(tr(\Pi, \phi \vdash \phi_1)\varepsilon[\Phi \mapsto \psi], \ldots, tr(\Pi, \phi \vdash \phi_m)\varepsilon[\Phi \mapsto \psi]). \quad (6)$$

For the root node ϕ_0 let then $\phi_0 \rightsquigarrow \psi_0$ if for some tableau rooted in ϕ_0, $\psi_0 = tr(\phi_0)()$ where () is the empty environment, and ϕ_0 is relativised to the empty path segment.

Example 6.1 (i) From the tableau of fig. 1 the expected translation obtains:

$$E(XUY) \rightsquigarrow \mu Y'.Y \vee (X \wedge \Diamond Y').$$

(ii) For the tableau of fig. 2:

$$E(OFX, OGOFX) \rightsquigarrow \nu X'. \mu Y'. \Diamond((X \wedge X') \vee Y').$$

The example serves to illustrate why the translation schema uses ν-μ-alternation. For comparison two possible translations of the (equivalent) formula $EGFX$ are $\nu X'. \mu Y'. (X \wedge \Diamond X') \vee \Diamond Y'$ and $\nu X'. (X \wedge \Diamond X') \vee \mu Y'. \Diamond((X \wedge X') \vee (X \wedge Y') \vee Y')$.

(iii) Similarly the tableau of fig. 3 illustrates why the conjunction of μ-formulas of (6) is in general necessary. It is translated thus:

$$\begin{aligned} E\Phi \rightsquigarrow\ & \nu X'.(\mu Y'.\Diamond(X' \wedge X \wedge Y) \vee (Y' \wedge X) \vee (X' \wedge Y) \vee Y') \\ & \wedge(\mu Y'.\Diamond(X' \wedge X \wedge Y) \vee (X' \wedge X) \vee (Y' \wedge Y) \vee Y'). \end{aligned}$$

The translation function tr can be optimised in several respects. For instance we avoid generally introducing variables that are never actually used. The topic of simplifications is returned to in the concluding section. A proof of the correctness of the translation procedure is given in the appendix.

Theorem 6.2 *For any CTL* formula ϕ, if $\phi \rightsquigarrow \psi$ then* $\{s \mid s \models_{\mathcal{V}} \phi\} = \|\psi\|\mathcal{V}$. □

7 Extended Computation Tree Logic, ECTL*

Several natural extensions of CTL* merit consideration. One direction of pragmatic interest is to add nexttime operators indexed by labels or sets of labels as in Bradfield, Stirling [2]. This direction is pursued in Dam [9]. Another direction of more fundamental interest is to extend the linear-time fragment of CTL* such as to give it the full power of the ω-regular languages. Here we follow the approach of Thomas [28] by adding temporal operators corresponding to Büchi automata on infinite words.

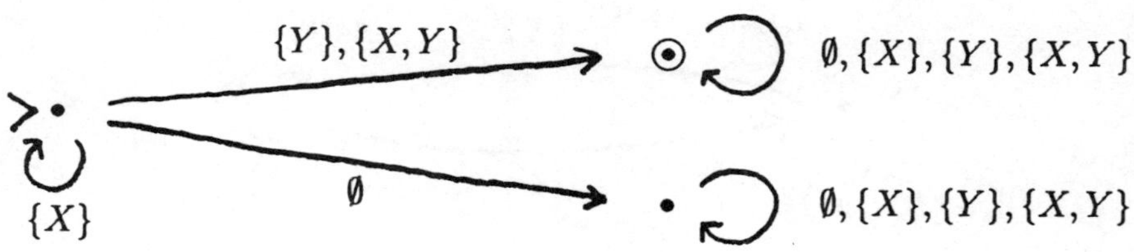

Figure 4: Büchi automaton $\mathcal{A}_1$ for XUY.

A *Büchi automaton* over the finite alphabet Σ is a nondeterministic finite automaton $\mathcal{A} = (Q, q_0, \{\stackrel{a}{\to}\}_{a\in\Sigma}, F)$ with Q the finite set of states, $q_0 \in Q$ the initial state, $\stackrel{a}{\to}\subseteq Q \times Q$ the transition relation for each $a \in \Sigma$, and $F \subseteq Q$ the set of final states. We sometimes write $\mathcal{A}(q_0)$ to emphasize the initial state q_0. A *run* of $\mathcal{A}$ on the ω-word $\alpha \in \Sigma^\omega$ is an ω-word $r \in Q^\omega$ with the property that $r(0) = q_0$ and $r(i) \stackrel{\alpha(i)}{\to} r(i+1)$ for each $i \in \omega$. Then $\mathcal{A}$ *accepts* α, if there is a run r of $\mathcal{A}$ on α and a $q \in F$ s.t. $r(i) = q$ for infinitely many i, and the language *recognised* by $\mathcal{A}$ is $\mathcal{L}(\mathcal{A}) = \{\alpha \in \Sigma^\omega \mid \mathcal{A} \text{ accepts } \alpha\}$.

Formulas of ECTL* are inductively defined as usual and built from propositional variables using boolean connectives and containing the formula $E(\mathcal{A})$ for each Büchi automaton $\mathcal{A}$ over an alphabet $2^{\{\phi_1,\ldots,\phi_n\}}$ where the ϕ_i are ECTL* formulas. Note that all formulas of ECTL* are state-formulas; linear-time dependencies are accounted for by automata. Also the semantics is inductively defined. The clauses for variables and boolean connectives are the usual ones:

$$s \models_{\mathcal{V}} X \text{ iff } s \in \mathcal{V}(X)$$

$$s \models_{\mathcal{V}} \neg\phi \text{ iff } s \not\models_{\mathcal{V}} \phi$$

$$s \models_{\mathcal{V}} \phi_1 \wedge \phi_2 \text{ iff } s \models_{\mathcal{V}} \phi_1 \text{ and } s \models_{\mathcal{V}} \phi_2$$

Let then $\mathcal{A}$ be a Büchi automaton over the alphabet $2^{\{\phi_1,\ldots,\phi_n\}}$. The intuition is that $E(\mathcal{A})$ is true of a state s just in case there is an infinite path ρ originating in s s.t. the ω-word over $2^{\{\phi_1,\ldots,\phi_n\}}$ that encode the holding of $\phi_1, \ldots, \phi_n$ along ρ is in the language recognised by $\mathcal{A}$. More precisely let the word $\alpha(\rho)$ be determined by

$$\alpha(\rho)(i) = \{\phi_j \mid 1 \leq j \leq n,\ \rho(i) \models_{\mathcal{V}} \phi_j\}$$

The satisfaction clause for $E(\mathcal{A})$ is then the following:

$$s \models_{\mathcal{V}} E(\mathcal{A}) \text{ iff } \exists\rho.\ \rho(0) = s,\ \alpha(\rho) \in \mathcal{L}(\mathcal{A})$$

Example 7.1 The ECTL* formula $E(\mathcal{A}_1)$ where $\mathcal{A}_1$ is the Büchi automaton of fig. 4 expresses the CTL* property $E(XUY)$. Similarly the ECTL* formula $E(\mathcal{A}_2)$ expresses $EGFX$ (infinitely often X) where $\mathcal{A}_2$ is the automaton of fig. 5. □

The closure properties of languages recognised by Büchi automata provide mechanisms for deriving various linear-time connectives. Complementation, for

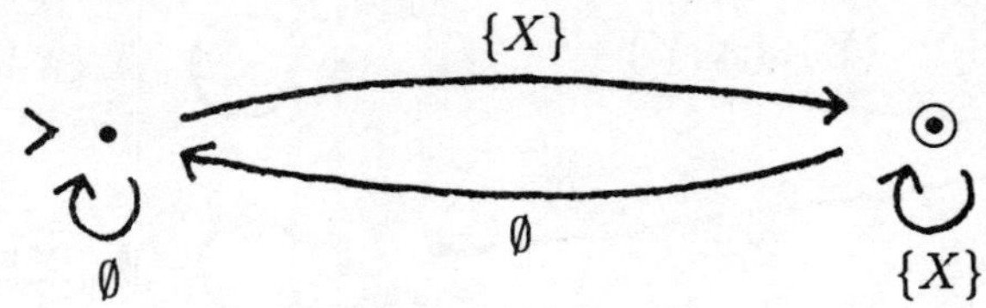

Figure 5: Büchi automaton $\mathcal{A}_2$ for GFX

instance, is derived by complementing the Büchi automaton concerned. In this way it is not too difficult to see that any CTL* formula can be written as an equivalent ECTL* formula.

Note that in particular the standard derivation of the universal path quantifier require complementation of Büchi automata. In this respect the present account sacrifice clarity to some extent. This can be remedied by using for instance deterministic Muller automata as in (Clarke et al [6]) at a cost, however, of a vastly more complicated translation procedure.

8 Translating ECTL*

The use of Büchi automata together with the existential path-quantifier allows attention to be restricted to formulas $E(\mathcal{A})$ in a standard form where $\mathcal{A}$ is an automaton over sets of propositional variables only, and for which F is a singleton set. For let $F = \{q_1, \ldots, q_m\}$ and let each $\mathcal{A}_i$ be obtained from $\mathcal{A}$ by replacing F by $\{q_i\}$. Then in addition to the four rules of section 4 the following rule is validated

$$\frac{E(\mathcal{A}_1) \leadsto_e \psi_1 \quad \cdots \quad E(\mathcal{A}_m) \leadsto_e \psi_m}{E(\mathcal{A}) \leadsto_e \psi_1 \vee \cdots \vee \psi_m}$$

for the ECTL* correlate $\leadsto_e$ of $\leadsto$.

Tableaux are constructed using the following single rule. Let $E(\mathcal{A}(q))$ be in standard form where the alphabet of $\mathcal{A}(q)$ is $\Sigma = 2^{\{Y_1,\ldots,Y_n\}}$. Let $a_1, \ldots, a_m$ list the members of Σ and for each i s.t. $1 \le i \le m$ let $q_{i,1}, \ldots, q_{i,k_i}$ list the q' s.t. $q \xrightarrow{a_i} q'$. Moreover for each $a \in \Sigma$ let $\overline{a}$ abbreviate the formula $\bigwedge a \wedge \bigwedge\{\neg Y \mid Y \notin a\}$. The rule is then the following:

$$\Omega: \quad \frac{E(\mathcal{A}(q))}{E(\mathcal{A}(q_{1,1}))\cdots E(\mathcal{A}(q_{1,k_1}))\cdots E(\mathcal{A}(q_{m,1}))\cdots E(\mathcal{A}(q_{m,k_m}))}$$

where Ω is the operator that takes $X_{1,1}, \ldots, X_{1,k_1}, \ldots, X_{m,1}, \ldots, X_{m,k_m}$ into

$$(\overline{a_1} \wedge \Diamond X_{1,1}) \vee \cdots \vee (\overline{a_1} \wedge \Diamond X_{1,k_1}) \vee \cdots \vee (\overline{a_m} \wedge \Diamond X_{m,1}) \vee \cdots \vee (\overline{a_m} \wedge \Diamond X_{m,k_m}).$$

As we only consider tableau constructed from nodes in standard form, there is at most one node $E(\mathcal{A}(q))$ for which q is an accepting state. The intention is to translate this node as a ν-formula and all other internal nodes as μ-formulas. For this to work, however, we must ensure that all possible ways of "regenerating" q are captured. This can be done by resetting the "visited-table" whenever the accepting state is first encountered.

For the definition of the translation function tr_e assume for each state q a unique variable X_q. The environment $\varepsilon \subseteq Q_{\mathcal{A}}$ keeps track of visited states. First, if $q \in \varepsilon$ then $tr_e(E(\mathcal{A}(q)))\varepsilon = X_q$. If not, let Ω label the rule instance $\frac{E(\mathcal{A}(q))}{E(\mathcal{A}(q_1))\cdots E(\mathcal{A}(q_k))}$. The following schema applies:

$$tr_e(E(\mathcal{A}(q)))\varepsilon = \sigma X_q.\Omega(tr_e(E(\mathcal{A}(q_1)))\varepsilon', \ldots, tr_e(E(\mathcal{A}(q_k)))\varepsilon'). \tag{7}$$

There are two cases: If q is the accepting state then $\sigma = \nu$ and $\varepsilon' = \{q\}$. That is, all previously encountered states are set to "unvisited". If on the other hand q not accepting the obvious strategy applies: $\sigma = \mu$ and $\varepsilon' = \varepsilon \cup \{q\}$. As before we then let $\phi \leadsto_e \psi$ whenever $\psi = tr_e(\phi)\emptyset$. The correctness proof is sketched in the appendix.

Theorem 8.1 *For any ECTL* formula ϕ, if $\phi \leadsto_e \psi$ then $\{s \mid s \models_{\mathcal{V}} \phi\} = \|\psi\|\mathcal{V}$.*
□

Example 8.2 The formula $E(\mathcal{A}_2)$ of example 7.1 is translated into the formula

$$\mu X'.(\neg X \wedge \Diamond X') \vee (X \wedge \Diamond \phi)$$

where ϕ is determined in the following way:

$$\begin{aligned} \phi &= \nu Y'.(\neg X \wedge \Diamond \psi) \vee (X \wedge \Diamond Y') \\ \psi &= \mu X'.(\neg X \wedge \Diamond X') \vee (X \wedge \Diamond Y') \end{aligned}$$

Note that without resetting the "visited-table" ϕ becomes instead

$$\phi = \nu Y'.(\neg X \wedge \Diamond X') \vee (X \wedge \Diamond Y')$$

equivalent to $EFGX$ and inequivalent to $E(\mathcal{A}_2)$.

9 Concluding remarks

As the "standard translation", our translation from CTL* is doubly exponential in the length of the input formula, and the translation from ECTL* is singly exponential. The difference is accounted for by the exponential cost of representing CTL* in ECTL*. This suggests an alternative, also doubly exponential, translation from CTL* in three stages that first translates tableaux into ECTL* using for instance Emerson and Sistla's construction [13], and then translates ECTL* into L_μ. This translation shares, however, with the standard translation the pragmatic but nonetheless important problem that their results are not very intuitive or readable, and indeed best thought of as L_μ encodings of Büchi automata.

The existence of a translation of ECTL* into L_μ is not very surprising. It is well known that ECTL* is strictly less expressive than Rabin's S2S (c.f. Thomas [28]), and Niwinsky [21] shows S2S to be expressively equivalent to a μ-calculus with, effectively, a left and right nexttime operator. This does not, however, give an embedding into L_μ itself. The standard translation, for instance, is easily modified for this purpose, by translating Büchi automata into L_μ via PDL-Δ. In effect our ECTL* translation can be considered a direct version of this algorithm. Note that from the existence of a translation into PDL-Δ, and Niwinsky's result that PDL-Δ is strictly less expressive than L_μ it follows that also ECTL* is strictly less expressive than L_μ.

Although the CTL*-translation of section 6 is doubly exponential in the worst case we hope that its complexity will nonetheless turn out to be manageable in many practical situations. Many optimisations are possible to support this hope. By suitably encoding the conjuncts involved in the translation of internal nodes translated formulas can be represented in size $\mathcal{O}(n2^n)$. Note also that sufficient syntactic criteria for classifying internal nodes as least or greatest fixpoint nodes can easily be found: Suppose Φ contains a formula ϕ of one of the forms $\phi_1 U \phi_2$ or $O(\phi_1 U \phi_2)$, and ϕ is not a subformula of any other $\phi' \in \Phi$. Then ϕ is regenerated along any $\rightarrow$-path $E\Phi_0 \rightarrow \cdots \rightarrow E\Phi_n$ for which $\Phi_0 = \Phi_n = \Phi$. We expect this in particular to cover a large number of applications, and where it applies the complexity can be cut to a single exponential.

An alternative to the use of automata in the syntax of ECTL* is to use a μ-calculus with basic modalities O and E. If fixpoints are restricted such as to allow the formation of $\sigma X.\phi$ only when X does not occur within the scope of E in ϕ yet another version of ECTL* results. This follows by the equivalence of the ω-regular languages with the linear-time μ-calculus (c.f. Park [22]). If the restriction concerning E is lifted the result, the full branching-time μ-calculus (Stirling [23]), is at least as expressive as L_μ. It is open whether the containment is strict.

Acknowledgements: Thanks to Colin Stirling for many valuable discussions and comments.

References

[1] M. Ben-Ari, A. Pnueli and Z. Manna. "The temporal logic of branching time," *Acta Informatica* **20** (1983) 207–226.

[2] J. C. Bradfield and C. P. Stirling. "Verifying temporal properties of processes," *Lecture Notes in Computer Science* **458** (Springer,1990) pp. 115–125. To appear in Theoretical Computer Science.

[3] M. C. Browne, E. M. Clarke, D. L. Dill and B. Mishra. "Automatic verification of sequential circuits using temporal logic," *IEEE Transactions on Computers* **C-35** (1986).

[4] G. Bruns and S. Anderson. "The formalization and analysis of a communications protocol," Tech. rep. ECS-LFCS-91-137, University of Edinburgh (1991).

[5] E. M. Clarke and E.A. Emerson. " Design and synthesis of synchronisation skeletons using branching time temporal logic," *Lecture Notes in Computer Science* **131** (1981) pp. 52–71.

[6] E. M. Clarke, O. Grümberg and R. P. Kurshan. "A synthesis of two approaches for verifying finite state concurrent systems," Manuscript, Carnegie-Mellon University (1987).

[7] E. M. Clarke and B. Mishra. "Automatic verification of asynchronous circuits," *Lecture Notes in Computer Science* **164** (1983) 101–115.

[8] R. Cleaveland, J. Parrow and B. Steffen. "A semantics based verification tool for finite state systems," *Proc. 9th IFIP Symp. on Protocol Specification, Testing, and Verification* North-Holland, 1989.

[9] M. Dam. "Translating CTL* into the modal μ-calculus," Tech. rep. ECS-LFCS-90-123, University of Edinburgh (1990).

[10] E. A. Emerson and J. Halpern. ""Sometimes" and "not never" revisited: On branching versus linear time." *Journal of the ACM* **33** (1986) 151–178.

[11] E. A. Emerson and C. S. Jutla. "The complexity of tree automata and logics of programs," *Proc. 29th Symp. on Foundations of Computer Science* (1988) 328–337.

[12] E. A. Emerson and C. Lei. " Efficient model checking in fragments of the propositional mu-calculus," in *Proc. 1st Ann. Symp. on Logic in Computer Science* (1986) 267–278.

[13] E. A. Emerson and A.P. Sistla. "Deciding full branching time logic," *Information and Control* **61** (1984) pp. 175–201.

[14] M.J. Fischer and R.E. Ladner. " Propositional dynamic logic of regular programs," *Journal of Computer and System Science* **18** pp. 194–211.

[15] D. Gabbay, A. Pnueli, S. Shelah and J. Stavi. "On the temporal analysis of fairness," *Proc. 7th ACM Symp. on Principles of Programming Languages* (1980) 163–173.

[16] D. Gries. "An exercise in proving parallel programs correct," *Communications of the ACM* **20** (1977) pp. 921–930.

[17] M. Hennessy and R. Milner. "Algebraic laws for nondeterminism and concurrency," *Journal of the ACM* **32** (1985) 137–162.

[18] D. Kozen. "Results on the propositional μ-calculus," *Theoretical Computer Science* **27** (North-Holland, 1983) 333–354.

[19] O. Lichtenstein, A. Pnueli and L. Zuck. "The glory of the past," *Lecture Notes in Computer Science* **193** (1985) 97–107.

[20] R. McNaughton. "Testing and generating infinite sequences by a finite automaton," *Information and Control* **9** (1966) 521–530.

[21] D. Niwinsky. "Fixed points vs. infinite generation," in *Proc. 3rd Ann. Symp. on Logic in Computer Science* (1988) 402–409.

[22] D. Park. "Concurrency and automata on infinite sequences," *Lecture Notes in Computer Science* **104** (1981) 167–183.

[23] C. P. Stirling. "Modal and temporal logics," to appear in: *Handbook of Logic in Computer Science* (S. Abramsky, D. Gabbay, T. Maibaum, eds.) Oxford University Press (1991).

[24] C. P. Stirling and D. J. Walker. "Local model checking in the modal mu-calculus," *Lecture Notes in Computer Science* **351** (Springer,1989) pp. 369–383. To appear in Theoretical Computer Science, 1991.

[25] R. S. Streett. "Propositional dynamic logic of looping and converse is elementarily decidable," *Information and Control* **54** (Academic Press, 1982) pp. 121–141.

[26] R.S. Streett and E.A. Emerson. "An automata theoretic decision procedure for the propositional mu-calculus," *Information and Computation* **81** (1989) 249–264.

[27] W. Thomas. "Star-free regular sets of ω-sequences," *Information and Control* **42** (1979) 148–156.

[28] W. Thomas. "Computation tree logic and regular ω-languages," *Lecture Notes in Computer Science* **354** (1988) 690–713.

[29] M. Y. Vardi and P. Wolper. "Yet another process logic," *Lecture Notes in Computer Science* **164** (1984) 501–512.

[30] D. J. Walker. "Automated analysis of mutual exclusion algorithms using CCS," Tech. rep. ECS-LFCS-89-91, University of Edinburgh (1989).

[31] P. Wolper. "A translation from full branching time temporal logic to one letter propositional dynamic logic with looping," unpublished manuscript.

[32] P. Wolper. "Temporal logic can be more expressive," *Information and Control* **56** (1983) 72–99.

[33] P. Wolper, M. Y. Vardi and A. P. Sistla. "Reasoning about infinite computation paths," in: *Proc. 24th IEEE Symp. on Foundations of Computer Science* (1983) 185–194.

10 Appendix

The proofs of the main theorems use the following characterisation of satisfaction for L_μ (c.f. Streett and Emerson [26], Stirling and Walker [24], Bradfield and Stirling [2]). Following [24, 2] we use constants to keep track of the unfolding of fixpoints. However, not to confuse with the tableaux of section 4, the characterisation is presented in terms of choice relations, akin to the choice functions of [26], instead.

Formulas are extended by a denumerable set of *constants*, ranged over by V, that define fixpoint formulas. The *expansion* of ϕ is obtained by recursively replacing all constants in ϕ by their definitions. Our usage of constants ensures this always to be well-defined, and except where constants themselves are concerned we usually do not distinguish between extended formulas and their expansions. Relative to a transition system T, a *choice relation* is a minimal relation $\Rightarrow$ on *sequents* $s \vdash \phi$ s.t. $s \vdash \phi \Rightarrow s' \vdash \phi'$ iff ϕ is neither a propositional variable nor a negated one, and s.t.

$$s \vdash \neg\neg\phi \Rightarrow s \vdash \phi$$

$$s \vdash \phi_1 \wedge \phi_2 \Rightarrow s \vdash \phi_i \text{ for } i = 1 \text{ and } i = 2$$

$$s \vdash \phi_1 \vee \phi_2 \Rightarrow s \vdash \phi_i \text{ for } i = 1 \text{ or } i = 2$$

$$s \vdash \Box\phi \Rightarrow s' \vdash \phi \text{ whenever } sRs'$$

$$s \vdash \Diamond\phi \Rightarrow s' \vdash \phi \text{ for some } s' \text{ s.t. } sRs'$$

$$s \vdash \sigma X.\phi \Rightarrow s \vdash V \text{ where } V \text{ is a fresh constant defining } \sigma X.\phi$$

$$s \vdash V \Rightarrow s \vdash \phi[V/X] \text{ where } V \text{ defines } \sigma X.\phi$$

Rooting $\Rightarrow$ at $s \vdash \phi$ restricts $\Rightarrow$ to $\{s' \vdash \phi' \mid s \vdash \phi \Rightarrow^* s' \vdash \phi'\}$. Let $\Rightarrow$ be rooted at $s \vdash \phi$. Then $\Rightarrow$ *agrees with* $\mathcal{V}$, if whenever $s \vdash \phi \Rightarrow^* s' \vdash (\neg)X$ then s' $(\notin) \in \mathcal{V}(X)$. Regarding fixpoints the crucial issue is to avoid having to regenerate μ-constants infinitely often. A constant V is *regenerated from* s_1 *to* s_2 if $s_1 \vdash V \Rightarrow^+ s_2 \vdash V$, and then $\Rightarrow$ is *well-founded* if the regeneration relation is well-founded for each μ-constant. That is, there is no infinite path $sR^*s_0R^*s_1R^*s_2\cdots$ and no μ-constant V which is regenerated from s_i to s_{i+1} for all $i \in \omega$. A proof of the correctness of the characterisation Theorem 10.1 below can be given along the lines of Bradfield and Stirling [2].

Theorem 10.1 (Streett, Emerson [26], Bradfield, Stirling [2]) *There is a well-founded choice relation* $\Rightarrow$ *from* $s \vdash \phi$ *which agrees with* $\mathcal{V}$ *iff* $s \in \|\phi\|\mathcal{V}$. □

We can then proceed to prove the translations correct.

Theorem 6.2 *For any CTL* formula ϕ, if $\phi \leadsto \psi$ then $\{s \mid s \models_{\mathcal{V}} \phi\} = \|\psi\|\mathcal{V}$.*

PROOF: Let τ be a tableau rooted in $\phi_0 = E\Phi_0$, and let $\phi_0 \leadsto \psi_0$ relative to τ. For simplicity assume ϕ_0 to be in positive form, that is, with $\wedge, \vee, U, \neg U$ primitive and negations applied only to propositional variables. Similarly we also assume ψ_0 to be in positive form. The proof is split into two parts:

(i) If $s_0 \models_{\mathcal{V}} \phi_0$ then $s_0 \vdash \psi_0$ has a successful choice relation, i.e. one which is well-founded and agrees with $\mathcal{V}$.

(ii) If $s_0 \not\models_{\mathcal{V}} \phi_0$ then $s_0 \vdash \neg\psi_0$ has a successful choice relation.

This is sufficient by Theorem 10.1. Both (i) and (ii) are proved by first building a choice relation $\Rightarrow$ agreeing with $\mathcal{V}$, and then showing $\Rightarrow$ to be well-founded. The construction proceed in stages, and is guided by the tableau and the model. Initially we are given the tableau root node ϕ_0 and the sequent $s_0 \vdash (\neg)\psi_0$. At the completion of stage k, having reached tableau node $\phi = E\Phi$ and sequent $s \vdash (\neg)\psi$ the following properties are maintained invariant:

(a) $s \models_{\mathcal{V}} (\neg)\phi$, and

(b) for some ε and Π, ψ is obtained from $(\neg)tr(\Pi \vdash \phi)\varepsilon$ by replacing free occurrences of variables that occur bound in ψ_0 by constants.

We show how to complete stage $k+1$. For leaves the construction of $\Rightarrow$ is complete. Assume then that Ω labels the rule instance $\frac{\phi}{\phi_1,\ldots,\phi_m}$, that ϕ is simple, that ϕ is reachable from one of the nodes $\phi_1, \ldots, \phi_m$, and that $Ev(\Phi) \neq \emptyset$. The proofs where one of these assumptions fail are easy special cases. Depending on Π, $tr(\Pi \vdash \phi)\varepsilon$ is either the variable X_Φ, or the variable $X_{\varepsilon(\Phi),\Phi}$, or else it is

$$tr(\Pi \vdash \phi)\varepsilon = \nu X_\Phi.\bigwedge_{\phi' \in Ev(\Phi)} \mu Y_{\phi',\Phi}.\Omega(tr(\Pi, \phi \vdash \phi_1)\varepsilon[\Phi \mapsto \phi'], \ldots, tr(\Pi, \phi \vdash \phi_m)[\Phi \mapsto \phi'])$$

so one of two cases hold: Either ψ has the form

$$\psi = \nu X_\Phi.\bigwedge_{\phi' \in Ev(\Phi)} \mu Y_{\phi',\Phi}.\Omega(\psi_1, \ldots, \psi_m), \tag{8}$$

or it has the form

$$\psi = \mu Y_{\phi',\Phi}.\Omega(\psi_1, \ldots, \psi_m) \tag{9}$$

for some $\phi' \in Ev(\Phi)$. The important issue is how to resolve choices, and this is dependent on whether we are proving (i) or (ii).

(i). From the assumption that $s \models_{\mathcal{V}} \phi$ the procedure builds a path which validates each member of Φ. The crucial point is to ensure that whenever $\phi_1 U \phi_2$ is a member of Φ, ϕ_2 is eventually validated and until that point ϕ_1 is validated too. This is the purpose of indexing. An index ι assigns a natural number to formulas of the form

$\phi_1 U \phi_2$. The predecessor of ι is the index $pred(\iota)$ defined by $pred(\iota)(\phi_1 U \phi_2) = \iota(\phi_1 U \phi_2) - 1$ when $\iota(\phi_1 U \phi_2) > 0$ and $pred(\iota)(\phi_1 U \phi_2) = 0$ otherwise. Then $\phi[\iota]$ indexes each member of Φ in the following way:

$$((\neg)X)^\iota = (\neg)X,\ (\phi_1 \wedge \phi_2)^\iota = \phi_1^\iota \wedge \phi_2^\iota,\ (\phi_1 \vee \phi_2)^\iota = \phi_1^\iota \vee \phi_2^\iota,$$

$$(O\phi_1)^\iota = O\phi_1^{pred(\iota)},\ (\phi_1 \neg U \phi_2)^\iota = \phi_1 \neg U \phi_2,\ (\phi_1 U \phi_2)^\iota = \phi_1 U^{\iota(\phi_1 U \phi_2)} \phi_2$$

where $\phi_1 U^i \phi_2$ is the obvious approximation, i.e.

$$\begin{aligned} \phi_1 U^0 \phi_2 &= \phi_2 \\ \phi_1 U^{n+1} \phi_2 &= \phi_2 \vee (\phi_1 \wedge O(\phi_1 U^n \phi_2)). \end{aligned}$$

It is clear that if $s \models_{\mathcal{V}} E\Phi$ then there is some index ι appropriate for $E\Phi$ at s—i.e. such that $s \models_{\mathcal{V}} E\Phi[\iota]$. We can use this indexing to guide choices such that whenever the successor $E\Phi'$ of $E\Phi$ is chosen then $E\Phi'$ can be indexed in a way which in the obvious way agrees with the indexing of $E\Phi$ on all formulas of the form $\phi_1 U \phi_2$ that are subformulas of Φ and do not occur within the scope of $\neg U$ in Φ. Using this strategy it is now easy to see how stage $k+1$ is completed.

(ii). Assume that (8) holds so that $\neg\psi$ is a formula of the form

$$\mu X_\Phi . \bigvee_{\phi' \in Ev(\Phi)} \nu Y_{\phi',\Phi} . \neg\Omega(\cdots).$$

If ψ is met for the first time a *scheduler*, f_ψ, for ψ is introduced which picks out a member $f_\psi(\Phi)$ of $Ev(\Phi)$ in a round-robin fashion. Otherwise f_ψ is already defined. Either way we proceed by updating the scheduler, unfold $\neg\psi$, and choose the scheduled disjunct $\psi' = \nu Y_{f_\psi(\Phi),\Phi} . \neg\Omega(\cdots)$. Thus we have reached the negation of a formula as in (9), and we proceed by unfolding ψ'. Stage $k+1$ now completed in the obvious way. In all cases but for $\Omega = \wedge$ is the construction well-determined, and $\Omega = \wedge$ only when one conjunct is a (possibly negated) propositional variable which is chosen whenever possible.

We have thus given strategies for building choice relations $\Rightarrow$ that agree with $\mathcal{V}$. It remains to show that any relation $\Rightarrow$ built using these strategies is well-founded. Assume for a contradiction that it is not. Note that ψ_0 is *well-guarded* in the sense that whenever $\sigma X.\psi$ is a subformula of ψ_0 then each occurrence of X in ψ is in the scope of a modal operator. It then follows that there is an infinite path $\rho \in S^\omega$, a μ-constant V, and an infinite, strictly increasing sequence $i_0, i_1, \ldots$ such that for all $j \in \omega$, V is regenerated from $\rho(i_j)$ to $\rho(i_{j+1})$. The path ρ corresponds to an infinite $\rightarrow$-path $\phi_0, \phi_1, \ldots$ through τ. Assume that each ϕ_i has the form $E\Phi_i$, and that the suffix of ρ corresponding to the $\rightarrow$-path $\phi_i, \phi_{i+1}, \ldots$ is ρ_i. In case (i) the expansion of V is a formula of the form (9), and in case (ii) it is the negation of a formula of the form (8).

(i). Let ι_i be the index assigned to the tableau node ϕ_i during the choice relation construction. An easy induction on the structure of $\phi_i' \in \Phi_i$ then shows that

$\rho_i \models_{\mathcal{V}} \phi_i^{\iota_i}$. For instance for the case $\phi_i' = \gamma_1 U \gamma_2$, as $\rho_i(0) \models_{\mathcal{V}} E\Phi_i[\iota_i]$ by the assumption we obtain a smallest $i' \geq i$ s.t. $\gamma_2 \in \Phi_{i'}$ whence by the induction hypothesis, $\rho_{i'} \models_{\mathcal{V}} \gamma_2$. For all i'' such that $i \leq i'' < i'$, $\gamma_1 \in \Phi_{i''}$, so $\rho_{i''} \models_{\mathcal{V}} \gamma_1$, so indeed $\rho_i \models_{\mathcal{V}} \phi_i^{\iota_i}$. But we are then almost done, for the μ-constant V is regenerated infinitely often along ρ only if we find some infinite $\rightarrowtriangle$-path π relative to the given infinite Π-path through τ which from some point onwards always has one of the forms $\phi_1 U \phi_2$ or $O(\phi_1 U \phi_2)$ for fixed ϕ_1, ϕ_2. But this contradicts the indexing strategy.

(ii). Completing the proof, we show by induction on the size of formulas that $\rho_i \models_{\mathcal{V}} \phi_i$ whenever $\phi_i \in \Phi_i$. The only slightly difficult case is for $\phi_i = \gamma_1 U \gamma_2$. As V defines the negation of a formula of the form (8) it cannot for all $i' \geq i$ be the case that $\gamma_2 \notin \Phi_{i'}$. For otherwise, by Lemma 5.3, for all $i' \geq i$ such that $\Phi_{i'} = \Phi_i$, the eventuality $\gamma_1 U \gamma_2$ would be regenerated along the $\twoheadrightarrow$-derivation from $E\Phi_i$ to $E\Phi_{i'}$. Moreover the scheduling mechanism ensures that the disjunct

$$\nu Y_{\gamma_1 U \gamma_2, \Phi_i}. \neg\Omega(\cdots)$$

is eventually visited for some $i' \geq i$. But then from the point i' onwards, V can never be regenerated. Thus we can find a minimal i' such that $\gamma_2 \in \Phi_{i'}$. By minimality of i' for all $i'' : i \leq i'' < i'$, $\gamma_1 \in \Phi_{i''}$. But then by the induction hypothesis, $\rho_{i'} \models_{\mathcal{V}} \gamma_2$ and $\rho_{i''} \models_{\mathcal{V}} \gamma_1$ whenever $i \leq i'' < i'$, i.e. $\rho_i \models_{\mathcal{V}} \phi_i$. □

Theorem 8.1 *For any ECTL* formula ϕ, if $\phi \rightsquigarrow_e \psi$ then $\{s \mid s \models_{\mathcal{V}} \phi\} = \|\psi\|\mathcal{V}$.*

PROOF: Let a tableau τ for $\phi_0 = E(\mathcal{A}(q_0))$ be given where $\mathcal{A}(q_0)$ is in standard form. Let $\psi_0 = tr_e(\phi_0)\emptyset$. Note that due to the way environments are reset when the accepting state q is first visited by the translation procedure the only ν-subformula of ψ_0 is the formula $tr_e(E(\mathcal{A}(q)))\emptyset$. By Theorem 10.1 it suffices to show that $s_0 \models_{\mathcal{V}} \phi_0$ iff there is a well-founded choice relation $\Rightarrow$ from $s_0 \vdash \psi_0$ which agrees with $\mathcal{V}$.

Corresponding to any choice relation $\Rightarrow$ which agrees with $\mathcal{V}$ there is an infinite path ρ from s_0 and a run r of $\mathcal{A}(q_0)$ on $\alpha(\rho)$. Conversely any run r of $\mathcal{A}(q_0)$ on $\alpha(\rho)$ determines, up to choice of constants, a choice relation $\Rightarrow$ which agrees with $\mathcal{V}$. Fix then a choice relation $\Rightarrow$ which agrees with $\mathcal{V}$. Note that there is exactly one infinite derivation of $\Rightarrow$, say,

$$\Delta = s_0 \vdash \psi_0 \Rightarrow s_1 \vdash \psi_1 \Rightarrow \cdots$$

originating in $s_0 \vdash \psi_0$. The proof is complete when it is shown that the run r corresponding to Δ visits q infinitely often iff $\Rightarrow$ is well-founded. Assume the latter. Then for infinitely many i, ψ_i is the same ν-constant V defining $tr_e(E(\mathcal{A}(q)))\emptyset$, and the result follows. Conversely assume that r visits q infinitely often. Then there is an infinite, strictly increasing sequence $i_0, i_1, \ldots$ such that for all $j \in \omega$ is ψ_{i_j} a constant V_j defining $tr_e(E(\mathcal{A}(q)))\emptyset$. Moreover it is easily seen that in fact V_j is the same constant for all $j \in \omega$, and as a consequence $\Rightarrow$ is well-founded. The proof is thus complete. □

Power Domains
Supporting Recursion and Failure

Reinhold Heckmann

FB 14 – Informatik
Universität des Saarlandes
6600 Saarbrücken
Bundesrepublik Deutschland

e-mail: heckmann@cs.uni-sb.de

December 9, 1991

Abstract

Following the program of Moggi, the semantics of a simple non-deterministic functional language with recursion and failure is described by a monad. We show that this monad cannot be any of the known power domain constructions, because they do not handle non-termination properly. Instead, a novel construction is proposed and investigated. It embodies both non-determinism (choice and failure) and possible non-termination caused by recursion.

1 Introduction

Following the proposals of Moggi [Mog89, Mog91b], functional languages with various notions of *computations* can be denotationally described by means of *monads*. Monads are constructions mapping domains of values into domains of computations for these values. Computations involving destructive assignments, for instance, are handled by the *state transformer monad* [Wad90], whereas computations by non-deterministic choice are handled by *power domain constructions* [Plo76, Smy78, Gun90]. All known power domain constructions and many others are covered by an algebraic theory presented in [Hec90, Hec91].

In this paper, we consider a functional language with non-deterministic choice, failure, and recursion. Surprisingly, none of the known power domain constructions — even those versions that support failure — is suitable to describe the semantics of such a language. The reason is that all constructions described by the theory mentioned above are not well-behaved with respect to non-termination caused by recursion.

Non-determinism and recursion are two independent concepts of computation. Standing alone, non-determinism is properly handled by *Plotkin's power domain construction* (the variant with 0), and recursion and non-termination is described by the *lift monad* that adjoins a bottom element. However, in case of a language where both concepts coexist, neither power domain constructions nor lifting nor any simple combination of both provides an appropriate description of the semantics.

The paper is organized as follows: In section 2, we informally discuss several aspects of non-determinism and recursion. In section 3, we briefly introduce the theoretical background: cpo's and continuity in 3.1, monads and strong monads in 3.2, and algebraic theories and free constructions in 3.3.

In section 4, the (well-known) monads are presented that describe recursion and non-determinism independently. They are implicitly characterized as free constructions w.r.t. suitable theories. This suggests to introduce the novel monad that describes both concepts of computation together as free construction w.r.t. a joint theory. In the subsequent sections, we develop several more explicit representations of the new power domains.

In section 5, the novel construction is decomposed into three steps that introduce recursion, choice, and failure in turn. In section 6, the power domains resulting from the novel construction are decomposed into terminating and non-terminating computations. In section 7, we show that the new power domain construction preserves algebraicity, and present a description of the base in the algebraic case.

2 Non-Determinism and Recursion

In this section, we want to discuss informally several aspects of non-determinism and recursion. In 2.1, a non-deterministic functional language is introduced. The monads for non-determinism and recursion are described in 2.2. In section 2.3, we present an informal semantics of our language, which indicates how a formal semantics should look like.

2.1 A Non-Deterministic Functional Language

In [Hec88], we presented a functional language with powerful patterns. They may match in different ways, thus inducing computations with different values. On the other hand, they may fail to match, which leads to a computation resulting in no value at all. An experimental implementation of this language was used to study the effects of non-determinism.

Syntactically, this language is an extension of a simply typed λ-calculus with base types including `int` and `bool`, pair, list, and function types. Non-determinism is introduced implicitly by overlapping or failing patterns, and also explicitly by the choice operator '`|`' and the constant `fail`. The actual interpreter of this language behaves similar to a Prolog interpreter: it tries to show all results of an expression to the user.

Let us consider some sample functions:

```
elem (H :: T)  =  H
elem (H :: T)  =  elem T
```

where the operator '`::`' denotes list construction. If `elem` is applied to the list `[1,2]`, then both rules in the definition of `elem` are applicable. Application of the first rule immediately produces the value 1, whereas the second rule induces the recursive call `elem[2]`. Again, both rules are applicable; the first rule producing 2, and the second rule leading to the recursive call `elem[]`. In this situation, no rule is applicable, whence the execution fails, i.e., terminates without producing a result. Thus, the interpreter will produce the values 1 and 2, and then terminate. More abstractly, it produces the set of values $\{1, 2\}$.

The same operation can be specified with explicit choice:

```
elem (H :: T)  =  H | elem T
```

It is also possible to define this operation without pattern matching:

```
elem L  =  if  empty L  then  fail
                        else  head L | elem (tail L)
```

Consider some further definitions:

```
loop ()   =  loop ()
small N   =  if  N < 5  then  N  else  fail
from  N   =  N | from (N + 1)
nat   ()  =  from 0
```

The expression `fail` immediately terminates without producing any result. Hence, its semantics is $\emptyset$. The expression `loop()` also produces no result, but it does not terminate. In denotational semantics, non-termination is expressed by '$\perp$', whence the semantics of this expression is $\{\perp\}$. The semantics of `small 4` is $\{4\}$, whereas that of `small 6` is $\emptyset$. The semantics of `nat()` is $\{0, 1, 2, \ldots, \perp\}$. We include $\perp$ in this set, because `nat()` does not terminate; it keeps on producing values forever. The expression `small(nat())` produces the values 0 through 4. Then, it does not terminate, but keeps on computing forever without producing further results. The reason is that the argument `nat()` continuously produces numbers that are all refuted by `small`. Thus, the semantics of `small(nat())` is $\{0, 1, 2, 3, 4, \perp\}$.

2.2 Monads for Recursion and Non-determinism

For the denotational semantics, we follow [Mog89, Mog91b] and distinguish between a domain of values and a domain of computations for every type. The semantics is specified by fixing a *monad*, which is a special kind of domain construction. It is used to map domains of values into domains of computations. The domains of values for the base types are $\mathbf{Z} = \{\ldots, -1, 0, 1, 2, \ldots\}$ and $\mathbf{B} = \{\mathsf{F}, \mathsf{T}\}$ respectively. The domains of computations for these types consist of subsets of $\mathbf{Z} \cup \{\perp\}$ and $\mathbf{B} \cup \{\perp\}$. All other domains may be systematically derived from the base domains and the given monad.

As we have seen above, our language has syntactic means for recursive definitions. Recursion inevitably induces the possibility of non-termination. If recursion is the only concept of computation, then an expression either terminates and results in a value, or it does not terminate. Thus, the appropriate monad is the *lift monad* (section 4.1) which adds a new element $\perp$ to every domain of values.

Non-determinism appears as binary choice and failure. By failure, we understand a computation that terminates without producing a value. Many authors [Plo76, HP79, Smy78] study languages with choice but no failure. Our language however has to support failure because of the possibility of failing patterns. Similarly, most process languages [Abr91, page 172] and Prolog [CC84] support failure. We comprise choice and failure to the notion of non-determinism, since both concepts are closely related: they both affect the number of values of a computation, and failure is the neutral element of choice.

By non-determinism without recursion, every expression results in a finite set of values of its type. Thus, the appropriate monad for non-determinism in absence of recursion seems to be the construction of the set of finite subsets. For cpo's, the *Plotkin power construction* [Plo76, HP79] should be used with an added failure element (section 4.2).

If non-determinism and recursion coexist, the situation becomes much more complex. A computation may terminate resulting in a finite number of values, or yield a finite number of values followed by non-termination, or produce an infinite number of values. Unfortunately, there is no simple combination of the two monads mentioned above that would be appropriate in this case (Theorem 5.1). The aim of this paper is to develop an appropriate monad.

2.3 Observing the Results of an Expression

Let us now consider the language with both recursion and non-determinism in greater detail. Assume we present an expression to the interpreter and observe its results. The interpreter will start to evaluate the expression. Then there are three possibilities: the evaluation does not terminate, the evaluation fails, or the evaluation results in a first value. This value is displayed on the screen, then the evaluation proceeds, and there are again the same three possibilities, etc.

Thus, there are three principal classes of behavior: a finite sequence of values followed by a failure, or a finite sequence of values followed by non-termination, or a potentially infinite sequence of values. For our semantics, we want to abstract from the actual order in which values are presented and from the number of occurrences of a specific value, i.e., we assume that expressions result in sets instead of sequences.

In case of the type `bool` with values T and F, we may observe four terminating sets, namely $\emptyset$, {T}, {F}, and {T, F}, and four non-terminating sets, namely $\{\bot\}$, $\{T, \bot\}$, $\{F, \bot\}$, and $\{T, F, \bot\}$. The terminating sets are the abstractions of the finite sequences ending by failure, whereas the non-terminating sets are abstractions of the remaining sequences. The set {T, F} for instance is produced by the expression `true|false`, whereas $\{T, F, \bot\}$ is produced by `isprime(nat())`, where `nat()` produces all natural numbers (cf. section 2.1), and `isprime` is a predicate testing the primality of natural numbers.

An impatient user will probably hit the interrupt key if an evaluation does not produce a value after a while or seems to keep on producing values forever. In this case, he/she/it cannot know whether the evaluation would really be non-terminating if not interrupted. Thus, the behavior {T} looks like $\{\bot\}$ if interrupted before producing anything. The same behavior looks like $\{T, \bot\}$ if interrupted between the production of T and the final failure. By defining the order $A \leq B$ if B may look like A if prematurely interrupted, we obtain the following poset where arrows denote '$\leq$' relationships:

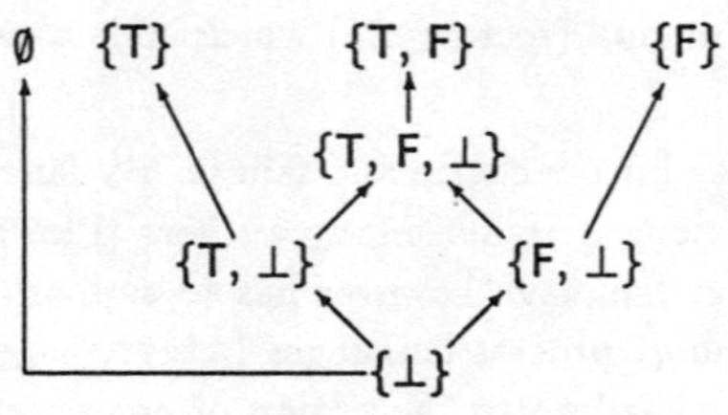

Power domain experts will notice that none of the known power domain constructions is able to produce this domain from the ground domain $\mathbf{B} = \{T, F\}$. The only visible connection to known power domains is that this domain looks like the Plotkin power domain of $\{\bot, T, F\}$ with an empty set artificially adjoined above $\{\bot\}$. This informal observation can indeed be generalized. It leads to the description of the power domain construction presented in section 5.

We may also notice that the power domain consists of four terminating sets (depicted in the top row) and four non-terminating sets below them. This observation leads to the vertical decomposition presented in section 6.

3 Theoretical Background

In this section, we introduce the theoretical background for the remainder of the paper. In 3.1, we briefly recall the definition of cpo's and continuous functions. Then we define monads and strong monads in 3.2. Algebraic theories, algebras, and free constructions are introduced in 3.3.

3.1 Cpo's and Continuity

A *poset* (partially ordered set) is a set P together with a reflexive, antisymmetric, and transitive relation '$\leq$'. We often identify the poset $\mathbf{P} = (P, \leq)$ with its carrier P.

For $A \subseteq \mathbf{P}$, let $\downarrow A$ be the set of all points *below* some point of A, and correspondingly $\uparrow A$ the set of all points *above* some point of A. $A \subseteq \mathbf{P}$ is a *lower set* iff $\downarrow A = A$, and an *upper set* iff $\uparrow A = A$.

We refer to the standard notions of upper bound, least upper bound (join) denoted by '$\bigsqcup$', directed set, and monotonic function. A *cpo* is a poset where every directed set has a join. Notice that in this paper, a cpo need not have a least element. A monotonic function $f : \mathbf{X} \to \mathbf{Y}$ between two cpo's is *continuous* iff it preserves the joins of directed sets. $[\mathbf{X} \to \mathbf{Y}]$ is the cpo of all continuous functions from $\mathbf{X}$ to $\mathbf{Y}$ ordered pointwise.

Every set can be made into a cpo by the definition $a \leq b$ iff $a = b$. Every function from such a cpo to an arbitrary cpo is continuous. Thus, the category SET of sets and arbitrary functions may be considered as a full sub-category of CPO.

A category is *Cartesian closed* if it has a terminal object $\mathbf{1}$, product objects $X \times Y$, and function space objects $[X \to Y]$ satisfying certain requirements [Mac71]. Both SET and CPO are Cartesian closed.

In [LS86, AL91], it is shown that the simply typed λ-calculus can be interpreted in any Cartesian closed category so that types denote objects and λ-expressions denote arrows. In the sequel, we identify λ-expressions and arrows, types and objects. For instance, $\lambda x^X .\, x$ is the identity id_X on object X, and $\lambda x^X .\, g(fx)$ is the composition of $f : X \to Y$ and $g : Y \to Z$. The type superscripts at variables will often be dropped. The fact that simply typed λ-calculus can be interpreted in the category CPO then means that every well-typed closed λ-expression that is built from continuous functions is a continuous function again.

3.2 Monads

There are two equivalent definitions of monads: a definition as a so-called Kleisli triple [Mog91b] and a categorical definition in terms of functors and natural transformations [Mac71, Wad90]. Here, we present the Kleisli triple version because it has fewer operations and axioms.

Definition 3.1 A *monad* in a category C is a triple $(\mathcal{M}, \mathsf{r}, \mathsf{E})$ where

- $\mathcal{M}$ maps objects of C into objects of C,
- r is a family of arrows $\mathsf{r}_X : X \to \mathcal{M}X$ for every object X,
- E maps arrows $X \to \mathcal{M}Y$ into arrows $\mathcal{M}X \to \mathcal{M}Y$ for every two objects X and Y,

(E1) $\mathsf{E}f \circ \mathsf{r}_X = f$ for $f : X \to \mathcal{M}Y$,

(E2) $\mathsf{E}\,\mathsf{r}_X = id_{\mathcal{M}X}$,

(E3) $\mathsf{E}g \circ \mathsf{E}f = \mathsf{E}(\mathsf{E}g \circ f)$ for $f : X \to \mathcal{M}Y$ and $g : Y \to \mathcal{M}Z$.

The construction $\mathcal{M}$ maps domains of values of some type into domains of computations of this type; r maps values v into a trivial computation rv that immediately *results* in v; and E *extends* computation-valued functions defined on values to those defined on computations. An extended function Ef applied to some computation will execute this computation and apply f to the resulting value(s).

As pointed out in [Mog89, Mog91b], one needs ***strong monads*** to model computations in denotational semantics. They are characterized by an additional operation t with five axioms. For Cartesian closed categories, strength of a monad is equivalent to *internality* of E. Internality means E is not just a family of functions between hom-sets, but a family of arrows of second order type $[X \to \mathcal{M}Y] \to [\mathcal{M}X \to \mathcal{M}Y]$. In the category CPO, this means E has to be continuous, whereas in the category SET, it means just nothing, whence all monads in SET are strong.

3.3 Algebraic Theories and Free Constructions

Most of our paper does not deal with monads directly, but with the closely related free constructions w.r.t. algebraic theories.

Usually, an algebraic theory consists of a set of operators with given arity and a set of axioms in form of equations $L = R$ over these operators. Since we want to consider algebraic theories in the category CPO, we also allow inequations $L \leq R$ as axioms.

A *model* of an algebraic theory $\mathcal{T}$ in the category CPO, or shortly a *$\mathcal{T}$-algebra*, is a cpo — the *carrier* — together with a set of *continuous* functions — the *operations* — interpreting the operators and satisfying the axioms. The functions interpreting operators of arity n have type $X^n \to X$ where X is the carrier. A $\mathcal{T}$-algebra homomorphism, or shortly *$\mathcal{T}$-morphism*, is a *continuous* function between (the carriers of) $\mathcal{T}$-algebras preserving all operations.

The *empty theory* $\mathcal{E}$ has neither operators nor axioms, whence $\mathcal{E}$-algebras are just cpo's and $\mathcal{E}$-morphisms are just continuous functions. A theory $\mathcal{S}$ is a subtheory of $\mathcal{T}$ if the set of operators of $\mathcal{S}$ is a subset of that of $\mathcal{T}$, and same for the set of axioms. In this case, all $\mathcal{T}$-algebras are $\mathcal{S}$-algebras, too, and all $\mathcal{T}$-morphisms are $\mathcal{S}$-morphisms, too.

Definition 3.2 (Free constructions) A *free construction* $\mathcal{C} = (\mathcal{C}, c, C)$ from a subtheory $\mathcal{S}$ to a theory $\mathcal{T}$ maps every $\mathcal{S}$-algebra X into a $\mathcal{T}$-algebra $\mathcal{C}X$ by adding the missing operations such that there is a $\mathcal{S}$-morphism $c : X \to \mathcal{C}X$, and for every $\mathcal{T}$-algebra A and every $\mathcal{S}$-morphism $f : X \to A$, there is a unique $\mathcal{T}$-morphism $Cf : \mathcal{C}X \to A$ extending f, i.e., $Cf \circ c = f$. $\mathcal{C}X$ is called the *free $\mathcal{T}$-algebra* over X. The elements cx with x in X are its *generators.*

If the subtheory $\mathcal{S}$ is the empty theory, we shall not explicitly mention it. In this paper, we shall adopt the notational convention to denote the three constituents of a free construction by the same letter in different styles, e.g., $(\mathcal{B}, b, B)$ or $(\mathcal{P}^0, p^0, P^0)$. As short names for these free constructions, $\mathcal{B}$ and $\mathcal{P}^0$ will be used.

Categorically speaking, free constructions from $\mathcal{S}$ to $\mathcal{T}$ are left adjoint to the forgetful functor from $\mathcal{T}$-algebras to $\mathcal{S}$-algebras. Free constructions are uniquely determined up to isomorphism.

In the sequel, we show some properties of free constructions. First of all, they compose:

Proposition 3.3 (Composition of free constructions)
If $\mathcal{C} = (\mathcal{C}, c, C)$ is a free construction from $\mathcal{T}_1$ to $\mathcal{T}_2$, and $\mathcal{D} = (\mathcal{D}, d, D)$ is free from $\mathcal{T}_2$ to $\mathcal{T}_3$, where $\mathcal{T}_1 \subseteq \mathcal{T}_2 \subseteq \mathcal{T}_3$, then $(\mathcal{D} \circ \mathcal{C}, d \circ c, D \circ C)$ is free from $\mathcal{T}_1$ to $\mathcal{T}_3$.

The proof is straightforward. It can be found in [Mac71] for the more general case of adjoints.

Next, we show that free algebras do not have proper sub-algebras containing all generators. Categorically, a *sub-algebra* B of a $\mathcal{T}$-algebra A is a $\mathcal{T}$-algebra such that there is a monic $\mathcal{T}$-morphism $e : B \to A$. Concretely, it is a subset of A closed w.r.t. all operations of $\mathcal{T}$ and directed joins (since we assume cpo's as carriers).

Lemma 3.4 Let $(\mathcal{C}, c, C)$ be a free construction from $\mathcal{S}$ to $\mathcal{T}$, and let X be an $\mathcal{S}$-algebra. Let B be a subset of $\mathcal{C}X$ that is closed w.r.t. all operations of $\mathcal{T}$ and directed joins, and that contains all generators cx. Then B equals $\mathcal{C}X$.

Proof: Since B is closed w.r.t. all $\mathcal{T}$-operations and directed joins, it forms a $\mathcal{T}$-algebra, and the inclusion $i : B \to \mathcal{C}X$ is a $\mathcal{T}$-morphism. Since B contains all generators cx, the $\mathcal{S}$-morphism $c : X \to \mathcal{C}X$ may be co-restricted to a $\mathcal{S}$-morphism $c' : X \to B$ such that $i \circ c' = c$. By freedom of $\mathcal{C}$, this $\mathcal{S}$-morphism can be (uniquely) extended to a $\mathcal{T}$-morphism $Cc' : \mathcal{C}X \to B$. Then, $i \circ Cc'$ is a $\mathcal{T}$-morphism from $\mathcal{C}X$ to itself. $i \circ Cc' \circ c = id \circ c$ holds, whence by the uniqueness statement of freedom, $i \circ Cc' = id$ follows. Thus, i is an isomorphism. □

Every free construction $\mathcal{C}$ from the empty theory induces a monad given by the same triple. Axiom (E1) is immediate, whereas (E2) and (E3) follow from the uniqueness statement of freedom. Using the Cartesian closed structure of CPO, we can show that this monad is strong.

Proposition 3.5 Every free construction to a theory $\mathcal{T}$ induces a strong monad in CPO.

Proof: Since we are in a Cartesian closed category, we use λ-calculus for the proof.

The proof uses the following observation: for every cpo X and $\mathcal{T}$-algebra A, the function space $[X \to A]$ becomes a $\mathcal{T}$-algebra, if the operations op_A on A are raised to operations $op_{[X\to A]}$ on functions by defining $op_{[X\to A]}(f_1, \ldots, f_n) = \lambda x^X.\, op_A(fx_1, \ldots, fx_n)$.

Let the free construction be $(\mathcal{C}, c, \overline{})$, i.e., for this proof, we denote the extension of f by $\overline{f}$. Let X and Y be two fixed cpo's. We have to show that the function that maps f into $\overline{f}$ is continuous. We do so by specifying a closed λ-expression C with $Cf = \overline{f}$ for all functions $f : X \to \mathcal{M}Y$. The simple solution $C \equiv \lambda f.\, \overline{f}$ is illegal, unless we know that extension is continuous. We only know that $\overline{f}$ is continuous whenever f is continuous. Thus, the expression f in $\overline{f}$ must be a *closed* λ-expression, which denotes a continuous function, not a variable.

Consider the closed λ-expression $a \equiv \lambda x^X.\, \lambda f^{[X\to \mathcal{C}Y]}.\, fx$ with type $X \to [[X \to \mathcal{C}Y] \to \mathcal{C}Y]$. By the observation above, $[[X \to \mathcal{C}Y] \to \mathcal{C}Y]$ is a $\mathcal{T}$-algebra since $\mathcal{C}Y$ is a $\mathcal{T}$-algebra. Thus, a has a continuous extension $\overline{a} : \mathcal{C}X \to [[X \to \mathcal{C}Y] \to \mathcal{C}Y]$. By rearranging arguments, we obtain $C \equiv \lambda f^{[X\to\mathcal{C}Y]}.\, \lambda u^{\mathcal{C}X}.\, \overline{a}uf : [X \to \mathcal{C}Y] \to [\mathcal{C}X \to \mathcal{C}Y]$. Then, we have to show $Cf = \overline{f}$ for all $f : X \to Y$. This is done by the uniqueness assertion of freedom. The right hand side is a $\mathcal{T}$-morphism by definition of $\overline{f}$. The left hand side is a $\mathcal{T}$-morphism since for every operation $op_{\mathcal{C}X}$,

$$\begin{aligned}
Cf(op_{\mathcal{C}X}(x_1, \ldots, x_n)) &= \overline{a}\,(op_{\mathcal{C}X}(x_1, \ldots, x_n))f \\
&= op_{[[X\to\mathcal{C}Y]\to\mathcal{C}Y]}(\overline{a}\,x_1, \ldots, \overline{a}\,x_n)f \\
&= op_{\mathcal{C}Y}(\overline{a}\,x_1 f, \ldots, \overline{a}\,x_n f) \\
&= op_{\mathcal{C}Y}(Cf\,x_1, \ldots, Cf\,x_n)
\end{aligned}$$

Here, we used the fact that $\overline{a}$ is a $\mathcal{T}$-morphism as the extension of a. Next, we show that Cf and $\overline{f}$ coincide on generators. $\overline{f}\,(cx)$ yields fx, and

$$Cf(cx) = \overline{a}\,(cx)\,f = a\,x\,f = fx$$

shows that $Cf(cx)$ yields fx, too. □

4 The Monads for Recursion and Non-determinism

In this section, we introduce the well-known monads that model recursion and non-determinism independently. Their implicit characterizations as free constructions w.r.t. some theory suggest the definition of a monad for the combination of both concepts as free construction for a combined theory.

4.1 Recursion

To model recursion, the *fixed point theorem* is employed: every continuous function in a cpo with least element has a unique least fixed point. Thus, our domains of computations should be cpo's with least element $\perp$. This special element denotes non-termination.

As pointed out informally in section 2, recursive computations either result in a proper value or in $\perp$. Hence, this notion of computation can be modeled by the *lift monad* that adds a new least element to each cpo. Formally, let

$$\mathcal{B}X \;=\; X_\perp \;=\; \{\perp\} \cup \{bx \mid x \in X\}$$

ordered by $\perp \leq y$ for all y in $X_\perp$, and $bx \leq bx'$ iff $x \leq x'$. Extension is given by $Bf\perp = \perp$ and $Bf(bx) = fx$. One easily proves that everything is continuous and the monad axioms are satisfied.

The lift monad can also be characterized as the free construction for the $\perp$-theory with one nullary operation $\perp$ and just one axiom $\perp \leq x$ for all x. $\perp$-algebras are then cpo's with least element, and $\perp$-morphisms are strict continuous functions.

4.2 Non-determinism

At first, we want to model non-determinism in the absence of recursion. As described in section 2, non-determinism is introduced in our language by constants for failure and binary choice. Thus, we need domains of computation that contain a special element 0 representing failure and a binary operation '+' representing choice. Since we want to abstract from order and multiplicity of results, '+' should be commutative, associative, and idempotent with neutral element 0. This is the algebraic theory of *commutative idempotent monoids*, or *CI monoids* for short. The morphisms of this theory are the continuous functions f with $f0 = 0$ and $f\,(a+b) = fa + fb$. We call such functions 0-*additive*. The closely related theory of CI semigroups has no operator 0. Its morphisms are called *additive*.

From [HP79], it is known that Plotkin's power construction — defined in [Plo76] for algebraic cpo's — is a free construction $\mathcal{P}$ for CI semigroups. In [Hoo87, Hec91], this construction is shown to exist in the category of all cpo's. This suggests to define the monad for non-determinism with failure and choice as the free construction $\mathcal{P}^0$ for CI monoids. It can be built by composing $\mathcal{P}$ and the free construction $\mathcal{N}$ from CI semigroups to CI monoids.

Proposition 4.1 The free construction $\mathcal{N}$ from CI semigroups to CI monoids is given by

Elements :	$\mathcal{N}Y = \{ny \mid y \in Y\}\ \cup$	$\{0\}$
Order :	$ny \leq ny'$ if $y \leq y'$	$0 \leq 0$
Operations :	$na + nb = n\,(a+b)$	$z + 0 = 0 + z = z$
Extension :	$Nf\,(ny) = fy$	$Nf\,0 = 0$

Thus, for all cpo's X, $\mathcal{P}^0X$ results from $\mathcal{P}X$ by adding a new element 0 incomparable to every other element.

Proof: By case analysis, $\mathcal{N}Y$ is shown to be a CI monoid. Nf as defined above is obviously the only extension of f that preserves 0. Its additivity is shown by case analysis. □

Since 0 is incomparable to every other element, $\mathcal{P}^0 X$ has no least element. This is usually considered a drawback, but notice that there is no need of a least element in the semantic domains in the absence of recursion.

Applied to a set S, the construction $\mathcal{P}^0$ yields the set $\mathcal{P}_{fin} S$ of finite subsets of S. This claim can be proved by showing that $\mathcal{P}_{fin} S$ with binary union and empty set forms the free CI monoid over S. p^0 is the singleton mapping $\lambda x.\{x\}$. Extension P^0 maps a set-valued function defined on elements into a set-valued function defined on sets by $P^0 f A = \bigcup_{a \in A} fa$. By $P^0 f\{x\} = fx$, it is obvious that $P^0 f$ properly extends f.

Remember that our two base types **int** and **bool** are interpreted by cpo's being sets. Because the subcategory SET of CPO is closed w.r.t. product, function space, and the monad $\mathcal{P}^0$ in form of $\mathcal{P}_{fin}$, we never leave this subcategory in modeling non-determinism in the absence of recursion. Thus, the complexity of cpo's and continuous functions is not needed in this case. This corresponds to our informal reasoning in section 2, where we claimed that without recursion, non-deterministic expressions always terminate and yield a finite set of values.

4.3 Recursion and Non-determinism Together

In the two previous sections, we saw how non-determinism and recursion can be independently modeled as free constructions w.r.t. the theory of CI monoids and the $\bot$-theory. These results suggest to model their combined effect by a free construction w.r.t. the combined theory of *CI⊥-monoids.* This theory is given by the following table:

Operators :	$0 : X$	$+ : X \times X \to X$	$\bot : X$
Axioms :	$a + 0 = a$	$a + (b + c) = (a + b) + c$	$\bot \leq a$
	$a + a = a$	$a + b = b + a$	
Morphisms :	$f(0) = 0$	$f(a + b) = fa + fb$	$f(\bot) = \bot$

The similar theory of *CI⊥-semigroups* has no operator 0, and thus no axiom $a + 0 = a$ and no requirement $f(0) = 0$.

The development presented in [Hoo87, Hec91] suffices to show the existence of the free construction $\mathcal{P}^0_\bot$ w.r.t. this theory. This implicit description of $\mathcal{P}^0_\bot$ is not completely satisfactory, because it neither shows the internal structure of the $\mathcal{P}^0_\bot$-powerdomains nor clarifies the relationships to the monads of lifting and $\mathcal{P}^0$. Thus, we develop more explicit representations of $\mathcal{P}^0_\bot X$ in the subsequent sections. With these representations, one can show that $\mathcal{P}^0_\bot\{\mathsf{F}, \mathsf{T}\}$ is indeed the domain depicted in section 2.3 as the result of some informal reasoning.

5 Decomposition into three Free Constructions

In this section, we develop a description of $\mathcal{P}^0_\bot$ by decomposing it into three free constructions to be applied sequentially. It is suggested by the observation that the domain depicted in section 2.3 looks like the Plotkin power domain of $\{\bot, \mathsf{F}, \mathsf{T}\}$ with an empty set adjoined above the least element.

Theorem 5.1 The construction $\mathcal{P}^0_\bot$ can be decomposed into three free constructions to be applied sequentially:

(1) The free construction $\mathcal{B}$ from the empty theory to the $\bot$-theory, which is given by lifting;

(2) The free construction $\mathcal{P}_\bot$ from the $\bot$-theory to the theory of CI⊥-semigroups, which is given by $\mathcal{P}$;

(3) The free construction $\mathcal{N}_\perp$ from CI$\perp$-semigroups to CI$\perp$-monoids, which is given by:

Elements :	$\mathcal{N}_\perp Y = \{n_\perp y \mid y \in Y\}$	$\cup\ \{0\}$
Order :	$n_\perp y \le n_\perp y'$ if $y \le y'$	$n_\perp\perp \le 0 \qquad 0 \le 0$
Operations :	$n_\perp a + n_\perp b = n_\perp(a+b)$	$z + 0 = 0 + z = z$
Extension :	$\mathcal{N}_\perp f(n_\perp y) = fy$	$\mathcal{N}_\perp f\,0 = 0$

The theorem tells that $\mathcal{P}^0_\perp$ is *not* the composition of the lift monad $\mathcal{B}$ and the monad $\mathcal{P}^0 = \mathcal{N} \circ \mathcal{P}$ modeling choice and failure. Instead of $\mathcal{N} \circ \mathcal{P} \circ \mathcal{B}$, it is $\mathcal{N}_\perp \circ \mathcal{P} \circ \mathcal{B}$ where $\mathcal{N}_\perp$ differs from $\mathcal{N}$ by the additional relationship $n_\perp\perp \le 0$.

Proof: Construction (1) was already discussed in section 4.1. For (2), we have to show that the free construction $\mathcal{P}$ from the empty theory to that of CI semigroups is also free from the $\perp$-theory to that of CI$\perp$-semigroups, i.e., $\mathcal{P}$ maps cpo's with bottom into cpo's with bottom, p is strict, and Pf is strict whenever f is strict.

Assume that X has a least element $\perp$. We employ Lemma 3.4 to show that $p\perp$ is the least element of $\mathcal{P}X$. Let $S = \uparrow\{p\perp\}$ be the upper cone of $p\perp$ in $\mathcal{P}X$. Obviously, S is closed w.r.t. directed joins. It is closed w.r.t. addition, since $a, b \ge p\perp$ implies $a + b \ge p\perp + p\perp = p\perp$ by monotonicity and idempotence of addition. It contains all generators because $px \ge p\perp$ by monotonicity of p. Thus, $S = \mathcal{P}X$ follows, whence $\mathcal{P}X$ has a least element and p is strict.

Let X and Y be cpo's with least element, and let $f : X \to \mathcal{P}Y$ be strict and continuous. Then $Pf : \mathcal{P}X \to \mathcal{P}Y$ is strict by $Pf(\perp_{\mathcal{P}X}) = Pf(p\perp_X) = f(\perp_X) = \perp_{\mathcal{P}Y}$.

For construction (3), we have to show that the given construction $\mathcal{N}_\perp$ is free from CI$\perp$-semigroups to CI$\perp$-monoids. This is similar to the proof of Prop. 4.1, where $\mathcal{N}$ is shown to be free from CI-semigroups to CI-monoids. This concludes the proof of Theorem 5.1. □

The decomposition presented in Theorem 5.1 may be used to describe the structure of the power domains a bit more explicitly.

Corollary 5.2 For every cpo X, the power domain $\mathcal{P}^0_\perp X$ results from adjoining a new element 0 to $\mathcal{P}(X_\perp)$ above $p\perp$:

Elements : $\mathcal{P}(X_\perp) \cup \{0\}$

Order : $A \le B$ iff $A \le B$ in $\mathcal{P}(X_\perp)$ or ($A = p\perp$ and $B = 0$)

Employing coalesced sum '$\oplus$', one may also write $\mathcal{P}^0_\perp X = \{0\}_\perp \oplus \mathcal{P}(X_\perp)$.

The representation of $\mathcal{P}^0_\perp X$ given above is closely related to the power construction in [Abr91, page 173], which is defined as $\mathcal{P}_{Abr} = \mathcal{N}_\perp \circ \mathcal{P}$. By comparison with $\mathcal{P}^0_\perp = \mathcal{N}_\perp \circ \mathcal{P} \circ \mathcal{B}$, the relation $\mathcal{P}^0_\perp = \mathcal{P}_{Abr} \circ \mathcal{B}$ follows, whence we obtain $\mathcal{P}^0_\perp X = \mathcal{P}_{Abr}(X_\perp)$ for all domains X. Thus, applying our power domain to X means applying Abramsky's power domain to the lift $X_\perp$. This difference has important implications for the algebraic properties: $\mathcal{P}_{Abr}$ cannot properly extend non-strict functions, whence it is not a monad in the category CPO. It is a monad in the category of cpo's with least element and continuous strict functions, however, because it is a free construction from cpo's with $\perp$ to CI$\perp$-monoids as shown in the proof of Theorem 5.1. In [Abr91], this algebraic property is not explicitly mentioned.

6 Vertical Decomposition

The decomposition of $\mathcal{P}^0_\perp$ in Theorem 5.1 suggests that the failure element 0 be something special. It seems to be added artificially by the third component of the construction. In this section, we present a 'vertical decomposition' of the power domains into terminating sets, which can be found in the upper parts of the power domain, and non-terminating sets, which are located in the lower parts. In this decomposition, 0 does not play a special role.

In 6.1, we introduce an auxiliary algebraic theory. The decomposition theorem is stated and proved in 6.2. In 6.3, it is applied to the case of discrete domains.

6.1 Lower Monoids

In order to state and prove the decomposition, we have to introduce another algebraic theory. A *lower monoid* is a monoid where the neutral element is least: $0 \leq a$ for all a. Equivalently, lower monoids may be described by the axiom $a \leq a + b$. Lower CI monoids are CI⊥-monoids with $0 = \bot$. In the sequel, we show that every CI⊥-monoid contains a lower CI monoid with canonical mappings back and forth.

Let Y be a CI⊥-monoid. The two sets $Y' = \{\bot + y \mid y \in Y\}$ and $\{y \in Y \mid \bot + y = y\}$ coincide by idempotence. Y' is closed w.r.t. directed joins (consider the second representation). Thus, it is a sub-cpo of Y. It is closed w.r.t. addition of Y by $(\bot + y_1) + (\bot + y_2) = \bot + (y_1 + y_2)$. It contains $\bot = \bot + 0$. This is the neutral element of addition *in* Y', because $\bot + (\bot + y) = \bot + y$ by idempotence. Thus, $(Y', +, \bot)$ forms a lower monoid.

Let the function $\iota : Y' \rightarrow Y$ be induced by the subset inclusion of Y' into Y. Because the subset Y' is closed w.r.t. addition, $\bot$, and directed joins of Y, the function ι is additive, strict, and continuous. In general, it does not preserve 0. By the calculations in the previous paragraph, the function $\lambda y^Y.\, \bot + y$ induces a strict, 0-additive, continuous function $\alpha : Y \rightarrow Y'$. The composition $\alpha \circ \iota$ is the identity on Y' because of the representation $Y' = \{y \in Y \mid \bot + y = y\}$ of the subset Y'. Summarizing, we have proved the following:

Proposition 6.1 For every CI⊥-monoid Y, there is a lower CI monoid Y' with:

- $\alpha : Y \rightarrow Y'$ strict, 0-additive, and continuous,
- $\iota : Y' \rightarrow Y$ strict, additive, and continuous,
- $\alpha \circ \iota \;=\; id : Y' \rightarrow Y'$,
- $\iota \circ \alpha \;=\; \lambda y^Y.\, \bot + y \;\leq\; id : Y \rightarrow Y$.

One may further show that $(Y \mapsto Y',\, \alpha,\, f \mapsto f \circ \iota)$ is a free construction from CI⊥-monoids to lower CI monoids. We do not need this additional property in this paper.

6.2 The Vertical Decomposition Theorem

For the decomposition theorem, we need some more notation. As in section 4.2, let $\mathcal{P}^0$ be the free construction to CI monoids. The free construction to lower CI monoids is denoted by $\mathcal{L}^0$. Its variant without 0 is known as *lower* or *Hoare power domain construction.* $\mathcal{L}^0$ has an explicit representation in terms of the cpo of *Scott closed subsets* of the ground domain ordered by inclusion. Scott closed sets are lower sets that are closed w.r.t. directed joins.

The mapping $l^0 : X \rightarrow \mathcal{L}^0 X$ is continuous, and $\mathcal{L}^0 X$ is a CI monoid. Thus, there is a unique 0-additive extension $\ell : \mathcal{P}^0 X \rightarrow \mathcal{L}^0 X$ with $\ell \circ p^0 = l^0$. We use this canonical mapping to compare members of $\mathcal{P}^0 X$ and $\mathcal{L}^0 X$ in the decomposition theorem. If X is a bifinite domain, then $\mathcal{P}^0 X$ is explicitly given by the set of convex Lawson closed subsets of X [Law88]. In this case, ℓ is concretely given by lower closure: $\ell A = {\downarrow} A$.

The decomposition theorem states that $\mathcal{P}^0_\perp X$ consists of an instance of $\mathcal{P}^0 X$ containing the terminating sets, and an instance of $\mathcal{L}^0 X$ containing the non-terminating sets. Two formal symbols, P and L, are used to label the members of the two components.

Theorem 6.2 For every domain X, the power domain $\mathcal{P}^0_\perp X$ is given by

Elements :	$\mathcal{P}^0_\perp X = \{\mathsf{L}A \mid A \in \mathcal{L}^0 X\} \ \cup$	$\{\mathsf{P}A \mid A \in \mathcal{P}^0 X\}$
Order :	$\mathsf{L}A \leq \mathsf{L}B$ iff $A \leq B$	$\mathsf{P}A \leq \mathsf{P}B$ iff $A \leq B$
	$\mathsf{L}A \leq \mathsf{P}B$ iff $A \leq \ell B$	$\mathsf{P}A \leq \mathsf{L}B$ never holds
Constants :	$\perp = \mathsf{L}0$	$0 = \mathsf{P}0$
Addition :	$\mathsf{L}A + \mathsf{L}B = \mathsf{L}(A+B)$	$\mathsf{P}A + \mathsf{P}B = \mathsf{P}(A+B)$
	$\mathsf{L}A + \mathsf{P}B = \mathsf{L}(A+\ell B)$	$\mathsf{P}A + \mathsf{L}B = \mathsf{L}(\ell A + B)$
Generators :	$p^0_\perp x = \mathsf{P}(p^0 x)$	

We use the concepts introduced by Prop. 6.1 to define $P^0_\perp$. For $f : X \to Y$, the extension $P^0_\perp f : \mathcal{P}^0_\perp X \to Y$ is given by

$$P^0_\perp f(\mathsf{P}A) = P^0 f A \qquad P^0_\perp f(\mathsf{L}A) = \iota(L^0(\alpha \circ f)A)$$

Proof: We first show that $\mathcal{P}^0_\perp X$ as described above is a CI$\perp$-monoid. It is obviously a cpo. The least element is L0 since 0 is least in $\mathcal{L}^0 X$. Commutativity and idempotence of addition are inherited from $\mathcal{P}^0 X$ and $\mathcal{L}^0 X$. The neutral element is P0, because

- $\mathsf{P}0 + \mathsf{P}A = \mathsf{P}(0+A) = \mathsf{P}A$
- $\mathsf{P}0 + \mathsf{L}A = \mathsf{L}(\ell 0 + A) = \mathsf{L}(0+A) = \mathsf{L}A$

using the fact that ℓ maps the member 0 of $\mathcal{P}^0 X$ into 0 of $\mathcal{L}^0 X$ by 0-additivity. Associativity of addition is shown by analyzing the obvious 8 cases for choosing 3 elements from $\mathcal{P}^0_\perp X$. For some cases, additivity of ℓ is needed, e.g.,

$$\begin{aligned} \mathsf{L}A + (\mathsf{P}B + \mathsf{P}C) &= \mathsf{L}A + \mathsf{P}(B+C) = \mathsf{L}(A + \ell(B+C)) = \\ \mathsf{L}(A + \ell B + \ell C) &= \mathsf{L}(A+\ell B) + \mathsf{P}C = (\mathsf{L}A + \mathsf{P}B) + \mathsf{P}C \end{aligned}$$

Now, let f be a continuous function from X to some CI$\perp$-monoid Y. Then $\alpha \circ f : X \to Y'$, whence both $P^0 f : \mathcal{P}^0 X \to Y$ and $L^0(\alpha \circ f) : \mathcal{L}^0 X \to Y' \subseteq Y$ are well-defined and continuous. Thus, their combination $P^0_\perp f : \mathcal{P}^0_\perp X \to Y$ is continuous if we succeed in showing that it is monotonic across the border between $\mathcal{L}^0 X$ and $\mathcal{P}^0 X$. We need an auxiliary lemma for this:

- $L^0(\alpha \circ f) \circ \ell = \alpha \circ P^0 f : \mathcal{P}^0 X \to Y'$

The lemma is shown by freedom of $\mathcal{P}^0$. By definition, ℓ is 0-additive from $\mathcal{P}^0 X$ to $\mathcal{L}^0 X$, and $L^0(\alpha \circ f)$ is 0-additive from $\mathcal{L}^0 X$ to Y'. Similarly, $P^0 f$ is 0-additive from $\mathcal{P}^0 X$ to Y, and α is 0-additive from Y to Y' by Prop. 6.1. Thus, both sides are 0-additive. They coincide on the generators:

$$\begin{aligned} \alpha \circ P^0 f \circ p^0 &= \alpha \circ f \\ L^0(\alpha \circ f) \circ \ell \circ p^0 &= L^0(\alpha \circ f) \circ l^0 = \alpha \circ f \end{aligned}$$

This concludes the proof of the auxiliary lemma.

Next, we show that $P^0_\perp f$ is monotonic and properly acts on the operations and generators. We abbreviate $\alpha \circ f$ by f'.

$$\begin{aligned} \leq:&\quad A \leq \ell B \Rightarrow P^0_\perp f(\mathsf{L}A) = \iota(L^0 f' A) \leq \iota(L^0 f'(\ell B)) \stackrel{!}{=} \iota(\alpha(P^0 f B)) \leq P^0_\perp f(\mathsf{P}B) \\ \perp:&\quad P^0_\perp f(\mathsf{L}0) = \iota(L^0 f' 0_{\mathcal{L}^0 X}) = \iota 0_{Y'} = \perp_Y \\ 0:&\quad P^0_\perp f(\mathsf{P}0) = P^0 f\, 0_{\mathcal{P}^0 X} = 0_Y \\ p^0_\perp:&\quad P^0_\perp f(\mathsf{P}(p^0 x)) = P^0 f(p^0 x) = f x \end{aligned}$$

At the place marked by '!', the auxiliary lemma was used. The remaining cases of '$\leq$' are obvious. For additivity, we consider three representative cases. The fourth case follows from commutativity.

$$\begin{aligned}
P^0_\perp f(\mathsf{P}A + \mathsf{P}B) &= P^0 f(A+B) = \\
P^0 fA + P^0 fB &= P^0_\perp f(\mathsf{P}A) + P^0_\perp f(\mathsf{P}B) \\
P^0_\perp f(\mathsf{L}A + \mathsf{L}B) &= \iota(L^0 f'(A+B)) = \\
\iota(L^0 f'A) + \iota(L^0 f'B) &= P^0_\perp f(\mathsf{L}A) + P^0_\perp f(\mathsf{L}B) \\
P^0_\perp f(\mathsf{L}A + \mathsf{P}B) &= \iota(L^0 f'(A+\ell B)) = \iota(L^0 f'A) + \iota(L^0 f'(\ell B)) \stackrel{!}{=} \\
\iota(L^0 f'A) + \perp + P^0 fB &= P^0_\perp f(\mathsf{L}A) + P^0_\perp f(\mathsf{P}B)
\end{aligned}$$

At the place marked by '!', the auxiliary lemma was used. $\iota(L^0 f'A)$ absorbs $\perp$ because it is in the subset Y'.

Finally, we have to show the uniqueness of extended functions. Let $F : \mathcal{P}^0_\perp X \to Y$ be a strict 0-additive continuous function with $F \circ p^0_\perp = f$. We have to show $F = P^0_\perp f$, i.e., $F \circ \mathsf{P} = P^0 f$ and $F \circ \mathsf{L} = \iota \circ L^0(\alpha \circ f)$.

Function $F \circ \mathsf{P}$ maps from $\mathcal{P}^0 X$ to Y. It is 0-additive since P is so by definition of 0 and '+' in $\mathcal{P}^0_\perp X$, and F is 0-additive by assumption. $F \circ \mathsf{P} \circ p^0 = F \circ p^0_\perp = f$ holds by definition of $p^0_\perp$. By freedom of $\mathcal{P}^0$, the claimed equation $F \circ \mathsf{P} = P^0 f$ follows.

Function $\alpha \circ F \circ \mathsf{L}$ maps from $\mathcal{L}^0 X$ to Y'. It is additive and strict as a composition of the additive strict functions L, F, and α. Additive strict functions between lower monoids are 0-additive. Once $\alpha \circ F \circ \mathsf{L} \circ l^0 = \alpha \circ f$ is shown, the equality $\alpha \circ F \circ \mathsf{L} = L^0(\alpha \circ f)$ follows from freedom of $\mathcal{L}^0$.

$$\begin{aligned}
\alpha(F(\mathsf{L}(l^0 x))) &= \alpha(F(\mathsf{L}(\ell(p^0 x)))) \\
&= \alpha(F(\mathsf{L}(0 + \ell(p^0 x)))) \\
&= \alpha(F(\mathsf{L}0 + \mathsf{P}(p^0 x))) \\
&= \alpha(F(\mathsf{L}0)) + \alpha(F(\mathsf{P}(p^0 x))) \\
&= 0_{Y'} + \alpha(F(p^0_\perp x)) \\
&= \alpha(fx)
\end{aligned}$$

holds using additivity of F.

By composing with ι, we obtain $\iota \circ \alpha \circ F \circ \mathsf{L} = \iota \circ L^0(\alpha \circ f)$. By additivity of F, we can show that images of $F \circ \mathsf{L}$ absorb $\perp$:

$$\perp_Y + F(\mathsf{L}A) = F(\mathsf{L}0) + F(\mathsf{L}A) = F(\mathsf{L}A)$$

Thus, $\iota \circ \alpha \circ F \circ \mathsf{L} = F \circ \mathsf{L}$ follows, whence $F \circ \mathsf{L} = \iota \circ L^0(\alpha \circ f)$ as required.

This concludes the proof of Theorem 6.2. □

6.3 The Discrete Case

Theorem 6.2 can be used to compute the power domains $\mathcal{P}^0_\perp X$ for discrete ground domains X. A cpo is *discrete* iff its order is equality: $a \leq b$ iff $a = b$. The base types of our language are modeled by such discrete domains. It is easy to see that the discrete cpo's form a full sub-category of CPO that is isomorphic to SET.

To apply Theorem 6.2, we first have to determine $\mathcal{L}^0 X$ and $\mathcal{P}^0 X$. These power domains are given by the following table:

	$\mathcal{L}^0 X$	$\mathcal{P}^0 X$
Theory :	lower CI monoids	CI monoids
Elements :	all subsets of X	finite subsets of X
Order :	'$\subseteq$'	'$=$'
Constants :	$\bot = 0 = \emptyset$	$0 = \emptyset$
Addition :	union	union
Generators :	$\{x\}$	$\{x\}$

The table can either be derived from the general knowledge about power domain constructions [HP79, Hoo87, Hec90], or it can easily be verified directly. The infinite subsets of X are included in $\mathcal{L}^0 X$, since they can be obtained as directed joins from the finite subsets provided the ordering is subset inclusion. The function ℓ from $\mathcal{P}^0 X$ to $\mathcal{L}^0 X$ operates as an identity on sets.

By Theorem 6.2, the power domain $\mathcal{P}^0_\bot X$ consists of the elements $\mathsf{L}A$ where $A \subseteq X$, and $\mathsf{P}B$ where $B \subseteq_f X$. The situation can be simplified if $\mathsf{P}B$ is replaced by B itself, and $\mathsf{L}A$ is represented by $A \cup \{\bot\}$. Then $\mathcal{P}^0_\bot X$ consists of those subsets of $X \cup \{\bot\}$ that contain $\bot$ or are finite. The proposed representation has the additional advantage that addition in $\mathcal{P}^0_\bot X$ is given by set union. This can be shown by looking at the clauses for addition in Theorem 6.2.
After completely translating Theorem 6.2 into the new representation, we obtain:

Theorem 6.3 For every discrete domain X, the power domain $\mathcal{P}^0_\bot X$ is given by

Elements : $\mathcal{P}^0_\bot X \;=\; \{A \subseteq X \cup \{\bot\} \mid \bot \in A \text{ or } A \text{ is finite}\}$

Order : Case $\bot \in A$: $A \leq B$ iff $A \setminus \{\bot\} \subseteq B$

Case $\bot \notin A$: $A \leq B$ iff $A = B$

Constants : $\bot = \{\bot_X\}$ $\quad 0 = \emptyset$

Addition : union

Generators : $p^0_\bot x = \{x\}$

The theorem shows that $\mathcal{P}^0_\bot\{\mathsf{T}, \mathsf{F}\}$ indeed looks like the picture in section 2.3. The condition that infinite sets have to contain $\bot$ reflects the fact that processes that produce an infinite number of results cannot terminate after finite time. The order given in the theorem above can also be interpreted intuitively: as long there is $\bot$ in the set A, the corresponding process did not yet terminate and may produce further results; once $\bot$ disappears from A, the process has terminated and the set of results cannot increase further.

7 The Base in the Algebraic Case

In this section, we consider the case of an algebraic domain X. We show that $\mathcal{P}^0_\bot X$ is again algebraic, and provide an explicit description of its base.
A cpo X is *algebraic* if it has a *base* X^0, i.e., a subset of its carrier such that

(1) For all a in X^0 and all directed sets D of X, $a \leq \bigsqcup D$ implies $a \in {\downarrow} D$, and

(2) For every x in X, there is a directed set D of X^0 whose join is X.

Every poset P induces an algebraic cpo P^* with base isomorphic to P by *ideal completion*: P^* is the set of directed lower sets (ideals) of P ordered by inclusion. Ideal completion is a free construction from the category of posets to the category of cpo's, since every monotonic function from P to some cpo Y uniquely extends to a continuous function from P^* to Y.
The base of $\mathcal{P}^0_\bot X$ is given by the following theorem:

Theorem 7.1
If X is algebraic with base X^0, then $\mathcal{P}^0_\perp X$ is algebraic with the following base:

Elements :	$\{(\downarrow E, \uparrow E) \mid E \subseteq_f X^0\} \cup \{(\downarrow E, \perp) \mid E \subseteq_f X^0\}$
Order :	$(U, V) \leq (U', V')$ iff $U \subseteq U'$ and ($V \supseteq V'$ or $V = \perp$)
Constants :	$0 = (\emptyset, \emptyset) \qquad \perp = (\emptyset, \perp)$
Addition :	$(U, V) + (U, V') = (U \cup U', V \cup V')$
Generators :	$p^0_\perp x = (\downarrow\{x\}, \uparrow\{x\})$

Here, $\perp$ is a special symbol that is not a set. Union is defined for $\perp$ by $V \cup \perp = \perp \cup V' = \perp$.
Every *monotonic* function $f : X \to Y$ to a CI$\perp$-monoid Y has a unique 0-additive strict *monotonic* extension $F : (\mathcal{P}^0_\perp X)^0 \to Y$ defined by

$$F(\downarrow E, \uparrow E) = \textstyle\sum_{e \in E} fe$$
$$F(\downarrow E, \perp) = \perp + \textstyle\sum_{e \in E} fe$$

Proof: One has to verify that the claimed base B is a poset (not a cpo) with the algebraic structure of a free CI$\perp$-monoid over the poset X^0. This is done by showing that the operations listed in the theorem are well-defined, monotonic, and satisfy the required algebraic laws. Its ideal completion B^* can then be shown to be the free CI$\perp$-monoid over the cpo X. Thus, B is isomorphic to the base of $\mathcal{P}^0_\perp X$. □

The structure of the representation of the base given by the theorem above closely reflects the vertical decomposition of Theorem 6.2: the pairs $(\downarrow E, \perp)$ correspond to the base of $\mathcal{L}^0 X$, which is $\{\downarrow E \mid E \subseteq_f X^0\}$ ordered by inclusion; and the pairs $(\downarrow E, \uparrow E)$ are isomorphic to the base of $\mathcal{P}^0 X$, which is $\{\updownarrow E \mid E \subseteq_f X^0\}$ with the *Egli-Milner order*, where '$\updownarrow$' denotes *convex hull*. The isomorphism is given by $(U, V) \mapsto U \cap V$, i.e., $(\downarrow E, \uparrow E) \mapsto \updownarrow E$, and $K \mapsto (\downarrow K, \uparrow K)$, i.e., $\updownarrow E \mapsto (\downarrow E, \uparrow E)$.

The explicit representation of the base of $\mathcal{P}^0_\perp X$ allows the derivation of further domain-theoretic properties of $\mathcal{P}^0_\perp$. We refrain to formally include the definitions of these properties. They are informally explained in the proof of the following theorem.

Theorem 7.2 The cpo construction $\mathcal{P}^0_\perp$ preserves the following properties of cpo's: algebraicity, ω-algebraicity, continuity, finiteness, bifiniteness, and finite continuity. Bounded completeness and the property to be a Scott domain are not preserved.

Proof: Preservation of algebraicity is given by Theorem 7.1. An algebraic cpo is ω-algebraic if its base is countable. Theorem 7.1 shows that countability of the base is preserved. Domain continuity is preserved, because continuous cpo's are the retracts of algebraic cpo's [Law88], and the retract relationship is preserved by all functors.

Every finite cpo is algebraic and is its own base. The explicit representation of Theorem 7.1 shows that the power domain is finite again. Bifinite cpo's are directed limits of the finite cpo's. Functors whose functional part is continuous (see Prop. 3.5) commute with such directed limits [SP82]. Finitely continuous cpo's are the retracts of the bifinite cpo's.

Bounded completeness is not preserved since $\mathcal{P}^0_\perp$-powerdomains contain Plotkin power domains as sub-domains by Theorem 6.2. The Plotkin power construction is known to destroy bounded completeness [Plo76]. Scott domains are bounded complete algebraic cpo's. □

8 Conclusion

In this paper, we proposed and investigated a novel power domain construction $\mathcal{P}^0_\perp$. Applied to a cpo X, it freely generates a power domain equipped with a binary operation '+' modeling choice, and two constants 0 for failure and $\perp$ for non-termination. This free construction is introduced in section 4.3 and more explicitly described in the subsequent sections. We found a representation as composition of the free introductions of $\perp$, '+', and 0 in this order (Theorem 5.1), where the introduction of 0 is modified by the need to preserve $\perp$. A completely different representation partitions the novel power domains into Plotkin power domains (with 0) and lower power domains (with 0) stacked upon each other (Theorem 6.2). Finally, we described the base in the algebraic case (Theorem 7.1), and investigated the preservation of some domain classes (Theorem 7.2).

We call this construction a power domain construction although it substantially differs from all power domain constructions known so far. All these constructions are covered by a general algebraic theory [Hec90, Hec91] built upon seven axioms of extension. These are the three axioms of a Kleisli triple (see Def. 3.1), two axioms for the 0-additivity of extended functions, and two axioms for the 0-additivity of extension itself. One of these latter axioms would require $P_{\perp}^{0}\,(\lambda x^{X}.\,0)\,A = 0$ for all A in $\mathcal{P}_{\perp}^{0}X$. It is not satisfied, since all extended functions have to be strict, whence $P_{\perp}^{0}\,(\lambda x^{X}.\,0)\perp = \perp$. All other axioms hold.

More abstractly, our paper shows that Moggi's idea to represent concepts of computation by strong monads requires more research. Wadler [Wad90] and Moggi [Mog91b] succeeded in representing a host of concepts of computation by monads — *provided that the considered programming language incorporates exactly one of these concepts.* As soon as several different notions of computations coexist in the language, the situation becomes more complex. The monad $\mathcal{P}_{\perp}^{0}$ modeling non-determinism and non-termination in coexistence is not any simple combination of $\mathcal{P}^{0}$ and the lifting monad. In the extended abstract [Mog91a], Moggi tries to solve the problem of combining monads by raising the level of abstraction: he proposes to describe a concept of computation by a function that transforms monads which already contain some concepts of computation into monads that preserve the old concepts and additionally incorporate the given concept.

The complexity of combining notions of computations seems to disappear on the algebraic level that constitutes the main part of our paper. We modeled notions of computations by algebraic theories, and the theory for non-determinism and non-termination in coexistence is a simple join of the theories for these concepts in isolation (see section 4.3). Thus, it seems worth-while to think about a replacement of monads by free constructions (adjoints) in modeling computations. This shift would not be as big as it sounds, since every free construction induces a monad, and conversely, every monad is a free construction w.r.t. a suitable algebraic theory (more general in structure than the ones occurring here) [Mac71]. Yet the correspondence between monads and free constructions is not one-to-one, whence the proposed shift would not be just an isomorphic change of view.

Acknowledgements

I would like to thank Reinhard Wilhelm, Fritz Müller, Helmut Seidl, and Andreas Hense for many fruitful discussions and careful draft reading.

References

[Abr91] S. Abramsky. A domain equation for bisimulation. *Information and Computation*, 92:161–218, 1991.

[AL91] A. Asperti and G. Longo. *Categories, Types, and Structures.* Foundations of Computing Series. The MIT Press, 1991.

[CC84] W.F. Clocksin and C.S.Mellish. *Programming in Prolog.* Springer-Verlag, 1984.

[Gun90] C.A. Gunter. Relating total and partial correctness interpretations of non-deterministic programs. In P. Hudak, editor, *Principles of Programming Languages (POPL '90)*, pages 306–319. ACM, 1990.

[Hec88] R. Heckmann. A functional language for the specification of complex tree transformations. In H. Ganzinger, editor, *ESOP '88*, pages 175–190. *Lecture Notes in Computer Science 300*, Springer-Verlag, 1988.

[Hec90] R. Heckmann. *Power Domain Constructions.* PhD thesis, Universität des Saarlandes, 1990.

[Hec91] R. Heckmann. Power domain constructions. *Science of Computer Programming*, 1991. to appear.

[Hoo87] R. Hoofman. Powerdomains. Technical Report RUU-CS-87-23, Rijksuniversiteit Utrecht, November 1987.

[HP79] M.C.B Hennessy and G.D. Plotkin. Full abstraction for a simple parallel programming language. In J. Becvar, editor, *Foundations of Computer Science*, pages 108–120. *Lecture Notes in Computer Science 74*, Springer-Verlag, 1979.

[Law88] J.D. Lawson. The versatile continuous order. In Michael G. Main, A. Melton, Michael Mislove, and D. Schmidt, editors, *Mathematical Foundations of Programming Language Semantics (MFPLS '87)*, pages 565–622. *Lecture Notes in Computer Science 298*, Springer-Verlag, 1988.

[LS86] J. Lambek and P. J. Scott. *Introduction to Higher Order Categorical Logic*, volume 7 of *Cambridge Studies in Advanced Mathematics.* Cambridge University Press, 1986.

[Mac71] S. MacLane. *Categories for the Working Mathematician.* Springer-Verlag, 1971.

[Mog89] E. Moggi. Computational lambda-calculus and monads. In *4th LICS Conference.* IEEE, 1989.

[Mog91a] E. Moggi. A modular approach to denotational semantics. In D.H. Pitt, P.-L. Curien, S. Abramsky, A.M. Pitts, A. Poigné, and D.E. Rydeheard, editors, *Category Theory and Computer Science*, pages 138–139. *Lecture Notes in Computer Science 530*, Springer-Verlag, 1991.

[Mog91b] E. Moggi. Notions of computation and monads. *Information and Computation*, 93:55–92, 1991.

[Plo76] G.D. Plotkin. A powerdomain construction. *SIAM Journal on Computing*, 5(3):452–487, 1976.

[Smy78] M.B. Smyth. Power domains. *Journal of Computer and System Sciences*, 16:23–36, 1978.

[SP82] M.B. Smyth and G.D. Plotkin. The category-theoretic solution of recursive domain equations. *SIAM Journal on Computing*, 11:761–783, 1982.

[Wad90] P. Wadler. Comprehending monads. In *Symposium on Lisp and Functional Programming*, pages 61–78. ACM, 1990.

Parallel Contraction of Fibonacci Trees and Prefix Computations on a Family of Interconnection Topologies

W. -J. Hsu, C. V. Page, and J. Liu
Dept. of Computer Science
Michigan State University

Abstract

The computation of prefixes of a given sequence (*prefix computation* [14]) and the fast reduction of a tree to a single node (*tree contraction* [1]) are two useful primitives for many applications on parallel computers. Most previous parallel algorithms have been based on the shared-memory model. We present general parallel algorithms for reducing a class of trees and prefix computations under the distributed-memory model. The new algorithms are shown to be communication-efficient and suitable for a large family of parallel computers. This family of parallel computers are based on a novel interconnection topology called the *p-th order Fibonacci cube* [10] that generalizes the Boolean cube (hypercube) [18] and the (second order) Fibonacci cube [8]. Specifically, the following results are presented:

1. We show that the p-th order Fibonacci tree of size N can be reduced to a single node in $O(\log N)$ steps on a p-th order Fibonacci cube with N nodes (processors).

2. Assume that $O(\log N)$ data items are on each of the N processors. We show that the prefix computation can be done in $O(\log N)$ steps on the p-th order Fibonacci cube.

1 Introduction

Consider a semigroup $(G, *)$, where $*$ denotes an associative binary operator. Let S: $a_0, a_1, ..., a_{N-1}$ be a sequence of N elements from G. The i-th prefix $P(i)$ of S, where $0 \leq i \leq N-1$, is defined to be the "product": $a_0 * a_1 * ... * a_i$. Given a sequence S from $(G, *)$, the *parallel prefix problem* is to compute all N prefixes fast, by using parallel computers [5], [11], [14], [17]. Applications of parallel prefix computations are numerous, mainly those related to linear recurrences of associative operators, e.g., carry lookahead adder/multiplier. computation of nearest dominance, enumeration, ranking, etc. See [2] for many examples.

The *tree contraction problem* is to reduce a rooted tree to its root by a sequence of independent operations to remove its vertices [1], [15]. By *independent*, we mean that two vertices removed in the same time step do not have a parent-child relation and that at most one of a node's children is removed during the same time step. Formally [1], let T denote a tree with vertex set $V(T)$. *A sequence of trees $T_1, T_2, ..., T_k$ is said to be a tree contraction sequence of length k for T if the following conditions are satisfied:*

1. $T_1 = T$; $|V(T_k)| = 1$; $V(T_i) \subseteq V(T_{i-1})$;
2. *(the* independence requirement*) If $v_1, v_2 \in V(T_{i-1})$ have the same parent, then either $v_1 \in V(T_i)$ or $v_2 \in V(T_i)$; moreover. if $v \in V(T_{i-1}) - V(T_i)$, then either v is a leaf of T_{i-1} or v has exactly one child, x, in T_{i-1}, and the parent of v in T_{i-1} is the parent of x in T_i;*

As observed in Abrahamson et al. [1], tree contraction is a general technique for scheduling parallel computations on trees. The independence requirement avoids concurrent read/write operations from/to the same address in the shared-memory model and, in the distributed-memory model, it requires that a processor sends or receives at most one data item during a time step. (The two different models will be described shortly.) Applications of tree contractions include parallel evaluation of mathematical expressions and many algorithms that use a spanning tree to process the gfaph. See [1]. Here we shall consider the abstract tree contraction problem for trees that are both rooted *and* ordered. The following observation is quite obvious, but it will be handy for presenting other results.

Lemma 1 *Let A denote an algorithm that can be applied to a rooted tree T for tree contraction. Then A determines an ordering on T.*

[proof] (Sketch)

Because of the independence requirement, a tree contraction procedure necessarily specifies the order in which a child of a node gets removed, and therefore, implicitly determines an ordering of the tree.

□

Assume that there are N data items, residing in a shared memory which allows concurrent accesses as long as there are no address conflicts. It is rather well known that the prefix computation can be performed in $\Theta(\log N)$ optimal time by using $O(\frac{N}{\log N})$ *ERER* (*Exclusive Read Exclusive Write*) processors. Similarly, assume that the input tree has N vertices and that there are $N/logN$ EREW processors. The contraction of an *arbitrary* tree can be done in $O(logN)$ time. (See [1]). The two problems, therefore, have been pretty much settled under this model.

The class of parallel computers that we will consider belong to the *distributed-memory* model. In this model, as a contrast to the shared-memory model, the communication cost of an algorithm is made explicit. For any processor P, while a data item that resides in the local memory of P is accessible to P in $O(1)$ time, data that reside in other processors must be accessed through a communication network. We will follow the convention that the time required for sending/receiving a message of unit length between a pair of processors is proportional to the number of links lying in between the two communicating processors. Many large-scale parallel computers are more suitably considered based on the distributed-memory model (than the shared-memory model). Under this (stricter) model, it is unlikely that arbitrary trees can be contracted in logarithmic time, unless the processors are completely connected. However, for a large-scale parallel computer, it is simply too expensive to use the complete graph as the interconnection topology. Here we will consider parallel computers that use more practical interconnection topologies, such as the Boolean cube [18] [7] and its generalizations [8]. With these parallel computers, while it is still valid to discuss about general prefix computations, it is feasible to consider only certain types of trees that match the interconnection topology of the computer.

Presently, communication-efficient algorithms for the two problems mentioned (i.e., prefix computation and tree contraction) are still relatively scarce. As one exception, it is known that both prefix computations and contraction of certain trees can be performed optimally in a parallel computer based on the boolean cube (alternatively, hypercube or n-cube) interconnection topology [18], [7]. As pointed out in [7], each Boolean cube embeds a binomial tree, and the contraction of the binomial tree *can* be used to schedule the operations during prefix computations. The independence requirement mentioned earlier is ensured by using the binary code of each node (processor) (cf. Section 2).

Here we will generalize this result to an infinite class of interconnection topologies called the generalized *(p-th order) Fibonacci cube*, which generalizes both the Boolean cube and the Fibonacci cube in [8]. It is known that this family of topologies forms a hierarchy in terms of number of nodes and interconnection density which has apparent implications to fault-tolerance applications. Also, instead of considering each interconnection topology individually, by dealing with a general case, one will be able to obtain results that are generally applicable to an entire family of interconnections.

Specifically, we show that under the same distributed-memory model, both the prefix computations and the contraction of certain trees can be performed in logarithmic time on the generalized Fibonacci cube. Our results suggest that the family of generalized Fibonacci cube are all useful for solving the numerous problems mentioned in [2] and [1]. The following is an outline of our approach.

1. In Lemma 2, we will generalize the observation made in [7] which claims that the contraction of the binomial tree can be applied to the computation of prefixes. In particular, the following lemma is relevant.

   Lemma 2 *Let A denote an algorithm that takes X steps to perform tree contraction on a rooted tree T. Let S denote a sequence of N data items assigned to the nodes of T in an order consistent with the ordering determined by A (cf. Lemma 1). Then the computation of prefixes of S can be performed by using at most $O(X)$ steps.*

   [proof] (Appendix A). □

   This reduction allows us to concentrate on the tree contraction problem.

2. In [8], it has been shown that the Fibonacci cube embeds a Fibonacci tree with perfect dilation and expansion. (The Fibonacci tree is a graph originally used to describe the lineal chart of Fibonacci's original rabbit breeding problem [12]. See Fig. 4.) We will show that the technique employed in reducing the binomial tree can be applied to the reduction of Fibonacci trees. The following general observation is useful.

   Lemma 3 *Let T denote an arbitrary tree and T' a subtree of T. Suppose that A denotes an algorithm that can be applied to perform tree contraction (resp., prefix computation) in X time steps on T. Then the same algorithm A can be applied to perform tree contraction (resp., prefix computation) on T' of T in X steps.*

   [proof] (Appendix B) □

   We will show that the Fibonacci tree is a subtree of the binomial tree, which, by Lemma 3, implies that the tree contraction can be done on the Fibonacci tree in the same number of steps as on the binomial tree. The key idea here is the use of the Fibonacci code [12] (which will be reviewed in Section 2).

3. By following the same approach, we will extend the result to the p-th order Fibonacci cube. We will show that the generalized p-th order Fibonacci tree is a subtree of the binomial tree. Since the generalized p-th order Fibonacci cube [10] embeds the p-th order Fibonacci tree with perfect dilation and expansion, this implies that both the tree contraction and prefix computations can be done optimally on such structures.

This paper is organized as follows. Section 2 reviews two special cases of the general p-th order Fibonacci cube, namely, the Boolean cube and the second order Fibonacci cube. It then presents results about the parallel tree contraction and prefix computation for the second order Fibonacci cube. Section 3 generalizes these results to the p-th order Fibonacci cube. Section 4 briefly summarizes the results.

2 Binomial Tree and Fibonacci Tree

As a starting point, we will first consider two special case of the p-th order Fibonacci cube. The regular Fibonacci cube [8] corresponds to $p = 2$, while the Boolean cube corresponds to $p = \infty$. Section 3 will present the formal definition of the p-th order Fibonacci cube.

2.1 Boolean cube and binomial tree

Both the *Boolean cube* (alternatively, n-cube, (binary) hypercube) [18] and the *binomial tree* are (relatively) well known graphs. Given two n-bit binary-coded numbers i and j. The Hamming distance between two binary numbers i and j is the number of digits where they differ from each other. A Boolean cube of *dimension* n, denoted by B_n, is a graph whose vertices can be labeled exactly by all possible n-bit binary codes, and an edge exists between node i and node j if and only if the binary codes of i and j have a Hamming distance of 1. A binomial tree of rank n (β_n) consists of two binomial trees of degree $n-1$, making the root node from one of the roots of the subtrees. As the basis, β_0 and B_0 are a graph with a single node. See Fig. 1 for illustration.

The following properties of the Boolean cube and Binomial tree are rather well known [7]:

- Both graphs of comparable dimension/rank have the same number of vertices, i.e., β_n and B_n have 2^n vertices.
- $\beta_n \subseteq B_n$ for all $n \geq 0$, i.e., the binomial tree is embedded in a (binary) hypercube. Because of the embedding relation, the nodes of the binomial tree can also be labeled by binary codes. See Fig. 1 for illustration.

In [7], it is shown that by using the binary codes of the Boolean cube, it is possible to contract the binomial tree in logarithmic steps; moreover, the schedule can be applied to compute the prefixes. The tree contraction procedure relies on the binary codes of the nodes (cf. Fig. 2). Based on the least significant bit of its label, each node is scheduled to become inactive (effectively become removed from the tree in the context of tree contraction), or (in the context of prefix computation) to send (resp., receive) a data item to its parent (resp., from one of its children) before becoming inactive. The labels are updated by shifting the bits to the right hand side after each step. Let N denote the number of nodes on the Boolean cube. The operations iterate for $O(\log N)$ times. For example, Fig. 2 shows the process of reducing a binomial tree into a single node. Figures 2 and 3 show that the schedule can be used for prefix computation.

2.2 Second order Fibonacci cube and tree

The *second order Fibonacci cube* (within this section, simply, the Fibonacci cube) can be defined by using the Fibonacci code [8]. We note that the Fibonacci tree considered here is different from the search tree under the same name in [12] and the data structure *Fibonacci heap* in other places. (However, there is a simple relation between the binary Fibonacci tree and the tree presented here.

See [12].) The following briefly reviews the concept of the Fibonacci code. See [12] or [10] for other properties of the code.

- A *second order Fibonacci code of degree* n (or simply, Fibonacci code, if the order and degree are known in the context) is a sequence of $n-2$ bits $b_{n-1}, ..., b_3, b_2$ with no consecutive 1s, i.e.. $b_j \cdot b_{j+1} = \tilde{0}$ for $2 \leq j \leq n-2$. We write $FC_n(i) = b_{n-1}...b_2$ (or $i = (b_{n-1}...b_2)_F$, if n is understood in the context) if $i = \sum_{j=2}^{n-1} b_j \cdot f_j$, where f_k denotes the k-th Fibonacci number, given by $f_0 = 0$. $f_1 = 1$, and $f_k = f_{k-1} + f_{k-2}$ for $k \geq 2$. Notice that in the Fibonacci code. the rightmost bit corresponds to f_2, rather than f_1.
- Let U_n denote the set of all possible n-bit binary numbers. (e.g., $U_1 = \{0,1\}$ and $U_2 = \{00, 01, 10, 11\}$. Let V_n denote the set of degree-n Fibonacci codes, where $n \geq 0$. For instance. $V_3 = \{0,1\}$, $V_4 = \{00, 01, 10\}$. Define $V_0 = \phi$ and $V_1 = V_2 = \{\lambda\}$, where λ denotes the null string. Note that, for $n \geq 0$, the set V_{n+2} (Fibonacci codes) can be obtained from U_n (ordinary n-bit binary codes) by simply discarding binary codes with consecutive 1's. By *Zeckendorf's theorem*[12], any natural number between 0 and $f_n - 1$ can be uniquely represented in the Fibonacci code. which implies that $|V_n| = f_n$, i.e., there are exactly f_n of degree-n Fibonacci codes. For example. here the integers from 0 to 12 ($= f_7$) are given in the Fibonacci codes (of degree 7). $0 = (00000)_F$, $1 = (00001)_F$, $2 = (00010)_F$, $3 = (00100)_F$, $4 = (00101)_F$, $5 = (01000)_F$, $6 = (01001)_F$, $7 = (01010)_F$, $8 = (10000)_F$, $9 = (10001)_F$, $10 = (10010)_F$. $11 = (10100)_F$, $12 = (10101)_F$.

The Fibonacci cube can be defined rigorously by using the Fibonacci code and the Hamming distance. Assume that $n \geq 0$. Let Fibonacci code $FC_n(i)$ and the set of degree-n Fibonacci code V_n be defined as in the preceding paragraphs.

1. The *Fibonacci cube of* dimension n, denoted by Γ_n, is a graph whose vertices can be labeled exactly by V_n such that two vertices i and j are connected if and only if $H(FC_n(i), FC_n(j)) = 1$.

2. The *Fibonacci tree of* rank n, denoted by T_n, is a graph that consists of T_{n-1} and T_{n-2}, where the root of T_{n-2} becomes a child of the root of T_{n-1}. We define T_0 to be an empty graph and T_1 to be a graph with a single node (which is its root).

Example

Fig. 4 shows Γ_n, where $n = 1, 2, .., 7$, respectively. In Γ_6, for example, Node $0 = (0000)_F$ has a link with each of the following nodes: $1 = (0001)_F, 2 = (0010)_F, 3 = (0100)_F, 5 = (1000)_F$.

Fig. 4 also shows T_n, where $n = 1, 2, .., 7$, respectively.

It should be easy to see that for all $n \geq 0$, the graph T_n is indeed a tree. Moreover, it is rather straightforward to verify the following facts [8]:

Lemma 4 *1. The numbers of vertices in both Γ_n and T_n are equal to f_n, the n-th Fibonacci number.*

2. Each Fibonacci cube embeds a Fibonacci tree of comparable rank, i.e., $T_n \subseteq \Gamma_n$ for all $n \geq 0$.

3. The height (highest level of nodes, with the root at level 0 and its adjacent nodes at level 1, and so on) of the tree T_n is $\lceil \frac{n-2}{2} \rceil$.

[proof] ([8]) □

2.3 Relations between Fibonacci tree and binomial tree

The Fibonacci cube and the Fibonacci tree are, respectively, subgraphs of the Boolean cube and the binomial tree [8].

Lemma 5 *Assume that $n \geq 0$.*

1. $\Gamma_{n+2} \subseteq B_n$.

2. $T_{n+2} \subseteq \beta_n$.

[proof]

It is straightforward to see the fact through the codes that are used to label the vertices of the graphs. One needs only observe that V_{n+2} (labels of Γ_{n+2})

are subsets of U_n (the set of labels for B_n). Moreover, since Γ_{n+2} and B_n use the same Hamming distance to determine the edges, so $(i,j) \in \Gamma_{n+2}$ implies $(i,j) \in B_n$, and $\Gamma_{n+2} \subseteq B_n$. The case of Fibonacci tree and binomial tree follows.

□

Example

See Fig. 4. If we delete every node whose label has consecutive 1's in B_4 (resp., β_6), the result becomes the Fibonacci cube Γ_6 (resp., T_6).

Lemma 6 *Let T_n denote the Fibonacci tree of rank n. Then the contraction of T_{n+2} takes n steps.*

[proof]

It is known that tree contraction on β_n can be done in $O(n)$ steps. By Lemma 5. $T_{n+2} \subseteq \beta_n$, so the same schedule can be applied to T_{n+2}.

□

Corollary 1 *Let $(G,*)$ denote a semigroup. Assume that a sequence S of $O(n \cdot f_n)$ data items is taken from $(G,*)$, with $O(n)$ consecutive data items distributed on each node of T_n. Then the prefixes of S can be computed in $O(n)$ time.*

[proof]

We will discuss in two stages.

1. If S contains only f_n data items. By Lemma 2, the tree contraction algorithm for T_{n+2} can be applied to computer the prefixes. So the prefixes of f_n data items can be computed in $O(n)$ steps.

2. With $n \cdot f_n$ data items, each processor will have $O(n)$ data items. The prefixes can be obtained by applying a standard simulation technique: each processor first computes the partial products for the subsequence in its local memory in $O(n)$ steps; consider each subsequence as one element, then uses the algorithm for computing the f_n prefixes in $O(n)$ steps; the

prefixes of the subsequence inside each processor is then updated in $O(n)$ steps. The total number of steps required is still $O(n)$.

Theorem 1 *Let F_n denote the Fibonacci cube of dimension n. Then both the tree contraction and prefix computation can be performed in optimal time.*

Example

Fig. 5 shows the contraction of a Fibonacci tree. Fig. 5 and Fig. 6 show how to apply the schedule to the computation of prefixes. Notice the correspondence between the schedule shown here and the schedule shown in Fig. 2 and 3.

3 Generalization

It is natural to define the generalized Fibonacci cube based on generalized Fibonacci numbers and Fibonacci codes [12]. Let $p \geq 2$ and $n \geq 2$. A *p-th order* Fibonacci Code of rank n is associated with the following recurrence (*p-th order Fibonacci numbers*): $f_n^{[p]} = f_{n-1}^{[p]} + f_{n-2}^{[p]} + \ldots + f_{n-p}^{[p]}$, where $f_0^{[p]} = f_1^{[p]} = \ldots = f_{p-2}^{[p]} = 0$ and $f_{p-1}^{[p]} = 1$. (In other words, $p = 2$ in the Fibonacci code that we have discussed so far.) For $p \geq 3$, the rules for forming the $(n-p)$-bit code of an integer i are analogous:

1. $i = \sum_{j=p}^{n-1} b_j \cdot f_j^{[p]}$

2. $b_j \cdot b_{j+1} \cdot \ldots \cdot b_{j+p-1} = 0$ for $p \leq j \leq n-p$.

The *generalized Zeckendorf's Theorem* states that each positive integer can be uniquely represented by the p-th order Fibonacci numbers (See [12]). Let $V_n^{[p]}$ be the set of all valid p-th order Fibonacci codes for numbers between 0 and $f_n^{[p]} - 1$, where $n \geq p-1$. Define $V_n^{[p]} = \phi$ for $0 \leq n \leq p-2$, and $V_n^{[p]} = \{\lambda\}$ for $n = p-1$. Clearly, by the generalized Zeckendorf's theorem. $|V_n^{[p]}| = f_n^{[p]}$ for all $n \geq 0$ and $p \geq 2$.

Definition

Let $FC_n^{[p]}(i)$ and $V_n^{[p]}$ be defined as in the preceding paragraphs.

1. The *p-th order Fibonacci cube of dimension n* is a graph $\Gamma_n^{[p]}$ whose vertices can be labeled exactly by $V_n^{[p]}$ such that two vertices i and j are connected if and only if $H(FC_n^{[p]}(i), FC_n^{[p]}(j)) = 1$.

2. The *p-th order Fibonacci tree of rank n*, denoted by $T_n^{[p]}$, is a graph that consists of $T_{n-1}^{[p]}, T_{n-2}^{[p]}, ..., T_{n-p}^{[p]}$, where the root of $T_{n-i}^{[p]}$ $(i \geq 2)$ becomes a child of the root of $T_{n-1}^{[p]}$. We define $T_i^{[p]}$ for $0 \leq i < p-1$ to be empty graphs and $T_{p-1}^{[p]}$ to be a graph with a single node (which is its root).

In [10], it is shown that there is a hierarchy among the family of generalized Fibonacci cubes; moreover, each p-th order Fibonacci cube contains a p-th order Fibonacci tree of equal size.

Lemma 7 *1.* $\Gamma_n^{[p]} \subseteq \Gamma_{n+1}^{[p+1]}$.

2. $\Gamma_n^{[p]} \supseteq T_n^{[p]}$. *The embedding has dilation and expansion both equal to* 1.

[proof]

(Sketch. See also [10].)

It is interesting to note that when $p = \infty$, the p-th order Fibonacci cube is reduced to the Boolean cube. As a matter of fact, by using the Zeckendorf's theorem [12], it is not difficult to show that the Fibonacci cube $\Gamma_{n+p}^{[p]}$ (resp.. Fibonacci tree $T_{n+p}^{[p]}$) can be obtained from the Boolean cube B_n (resp.. binomial tree $\mathcal{B}_n$) by deleting nodes that have p consecutive 1's in their labels.

□

With Lemmas 7, 2, and 3, the tree contraction algorithm for the binomial tree can also be applied to the p-th order Fibonacci tree, and that the prefix computation on the p-th order Fibonacci cube can be done in the same time complexity.

Theorem 2 *Let $F_n^{[p]}$ denote the p-th order Fibonacci cube of dimension n, where $p \geq 2$ and $n \geq 0$. Then both the tree contraction and prefix computation on $F_{n+p}^{[p]}$ can be performed in optimal $O(n)$ time.*

4 Concluding Remarks

We have shown that both the prefix computation and tree contraction can be done efficiently on the entire family of generalized Fibonacci cubes. In [8], it is proved that the Fibonacci cube possesses attractive recurrent structures [8], which enable it to efficiently perform some useful communication functions such as node-node send/receive, multi-node send/received, scatter/gather, and total-exchange [8]. The new results have strengthened our belief in the usefulness of the family of interconnection topologies. It would be of great interest to see whether other general operations, such as sorting and/or special permutations, can be performed efficiently on the family of Fibonacci cubes.

References

[1] K. Abrahamson, N. Dadoun, D. G. Kirkpatrick, and T. Przxtycka. A Simple Parallel Tree Contraction Algorithm, J. of Algorithms, Vol. 10, pp. 287-302, 1989.

[2] G. Blelloch, Scans as Primitive Parallel Operations. Proceedings International Parallel Processing Conference, pp. 355-362, 1987.

[3] D. P. Bertsekas and J. N. Tsitsiklis. *Parallel and Distributed Computation: Numerical Methods*. Prentice-Hall. Inc., 1989.

[4] *The Fibonacci Quarterly*: The Official Journal of the Fibonacci Association.

[5] F. E. Fich. New Bounds for Parallel Prefix Circuits. Proceedings ACM Symp. on Theory of Computation. pp. 100-109, 1983.

[6] R. L. Graham, D. E. Knuth, and O. Patashnik, *CONCRETE MATHEMATICS*, Addison-Wesley Publishing Co., 1989 (Chapter 6: Special Numbers).

[7] C. -T. Ho and S. L. Johnsson, Distributed Routing Algorithms for Broadcasting and Personalized Communication in Hypercubes, Proceedings Int'l Conf. on Parallel Processing, 1986.

[8] W. -J. Hsu, Fibonacci Cubes-A New Interconnection Topology, Accepted for publication, IEEE Transactions on Parallel and Distributed Systems, 1991.

[9] W. -J. Hsu and J. Liu, Fibonacci Codes as Formal Languages, Tech. Report CPS-91-05, Michigan State University, May 1991.

[10] W. -J. Hsu, C. V. Page, and J. Liu, Embedding Meshes in the Fibonacci Cubes, submitted for publication, July, 1991.

[11] C. P. Kruskal, L. Rudolph, and M. Snir, The Power of Parallel Prefix, Proceedings International Conference on Parallel Processing, pp. 180-185, 1985.

[12] D. E. Knuth, *THE ART OF COMPUTER PROGRAMMING*, Vol. 1-3, Addison-Wesley, 1973.

[13] J. -S. Liu and W. -J. Hsu, On Embedding Rings and Meshes in Fibonacci Cubes, Tech. Report CPS-91-01, Jan. 1991.

[14] R. E. Ladner and M. J. Fischer, Parallel Prefix Computation, J. ACM, 27(4), pp. 831-838, Oct. 1980.

[15] G. L. Miller and J. H. Reif, Parallel Tree Contraction and Its Application, Proceedings Symp. on Foundations of Comp. Sci., pp. 478-489, Oct. 1985.

[16] M. J. Quinn, *DESIGNING EFFICIENT ALGORITHMS FOR PARALLEL COMPUTERS*, McGraw-Hill, 1987.

[17] J. T. Schwartz, UltraComputers, ACM Trans. on Programming Languages and Systems, 2(4), pp. 484-521, Oct. 1980.

[18] C. L. Seitz, The Cosmic Cube, Comm. ACM, Vol. 28, No. 1, pp. 22-33, 1985.

[19] C. -L. Wu and T. -Y. Feng (eds.) *INTERCONNECTION NETWORKS FOR PARALLEL AND DISTRIBUTED PROCESSING*, IEEE Computer Soc., 1984.

Appendix A -Proof of Lemma 2

[proof]

It is not difficult to see that any tree contraction procedure can be modified to find the total product of all the data items residing in the nodes of the tree; similarly, a value residing in the root can be broadcast to all the nodes by reversing the tree contraction process. We will show that the prefix computation can be done in a similar fashion.

Since A is an algorithm that can be applied to T, a child is always removed before its parent node (therefore, we can arrange to transmit the partial product associated with a subtree to its root). Moreover, because of the independence requirement (cf. *tree contraction*, Section 1), at most one of the children of any internal node will be removed at a time (hence during one time step a node can be arranged to receive at most one partial product from one of its children). The procedure of prefix computation consists of two phases: the Contraction Phase and the Expansion Phase (see Fig. 2 and Fig. 3 for example).

1. In the Contraction Phase, we apply A to send partial products from the leaf nodes to the root node. In a given time step, if a node v_i is scheduled to be removed from T according to A, then we let v_i send its current partial product to its parent node. A node that has sent a data item will cease operation during the rest of this phase. On the other hand, a node that receives a data (from one of its children) will perform a product operation of the data with its partial product, the previous partial product is stored in its stack. By simple induction, it is not difficult to see that the j-th time when a node receives a data item (which must be from its j-th child, because the ordering of T is determined by A), an internal node can obtain a product of all the values in its first i subtrees.

2. In the Expansion Phase, we apply a "reversed" algorithm as follows. If a node v_k received (resp., sends) a data item from v_l in the first (Contraction) phase, then v_k sends to (resp, receives from) v_l. By the nature of A, when node v_k is to send to its jth child, say, v_l, it must have received the partial product $\Pi_{0 \leq i \leq k-1} a_i$ from its parent. Then it performs the following operations:

   (a) multiply the partial product $\Pi_{0 \leq i \leq k-1} a_i$ with a_k to obtain $\Pi_{0 \leq i \leq k} a_i$. This is the final prefix value for this node.

   (b) multiply the partial product $\Pi_{0 \leq i \leq k} a_i$ with $\pi_{k+1 \leq i \leq l-1} a_i$ (which is on the top of stack), to obtain $\Pi_{0 \leq i \leq l-1} a_i$. This value is to be sent to v_l'.

By simple induction, it is not difficult to see the each node will be able to compute the prefix function and the number of steps required is proportional to X. □

Appendix B: Proof of Lemma 3

[proof]

the missing nodes do not participate in the operations and they have no effect on the schedule of the processors in T'. In the case of prefix computation, consider the missing nodes as holding unity elements w.r.t. the operation $*$, then the presence or absence of these nodes makes no difference to the result of the operations.

Note that the argument using unity elements is only for conceptual simplicity. Actually, since the missing nodes never participate in the operations, so the imaginary unity elements never participate in the operations. So the set under consideration needs not be a monoid. □

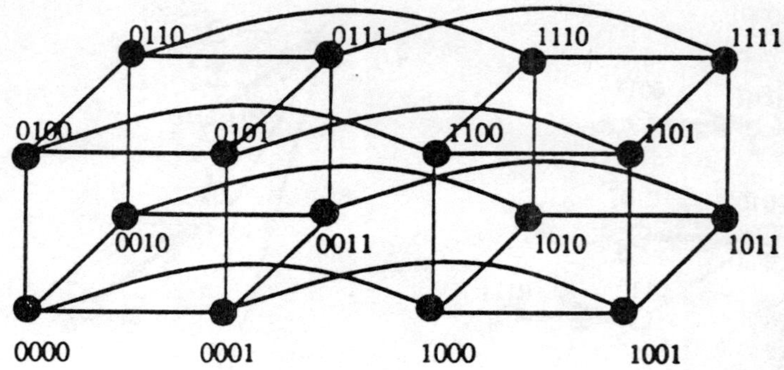

Boolean cube of dimension 4

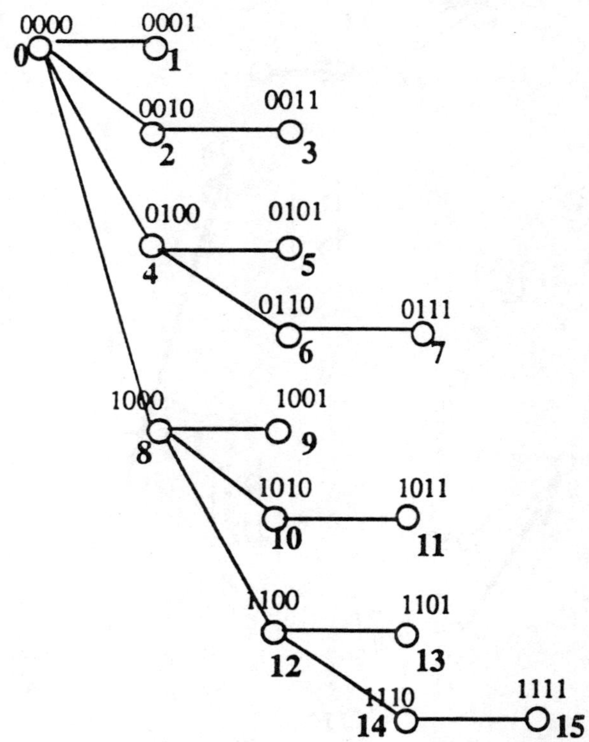

Binomial tree of rank 4.

Fig. 1. Boolean Cube and Binomial Tree

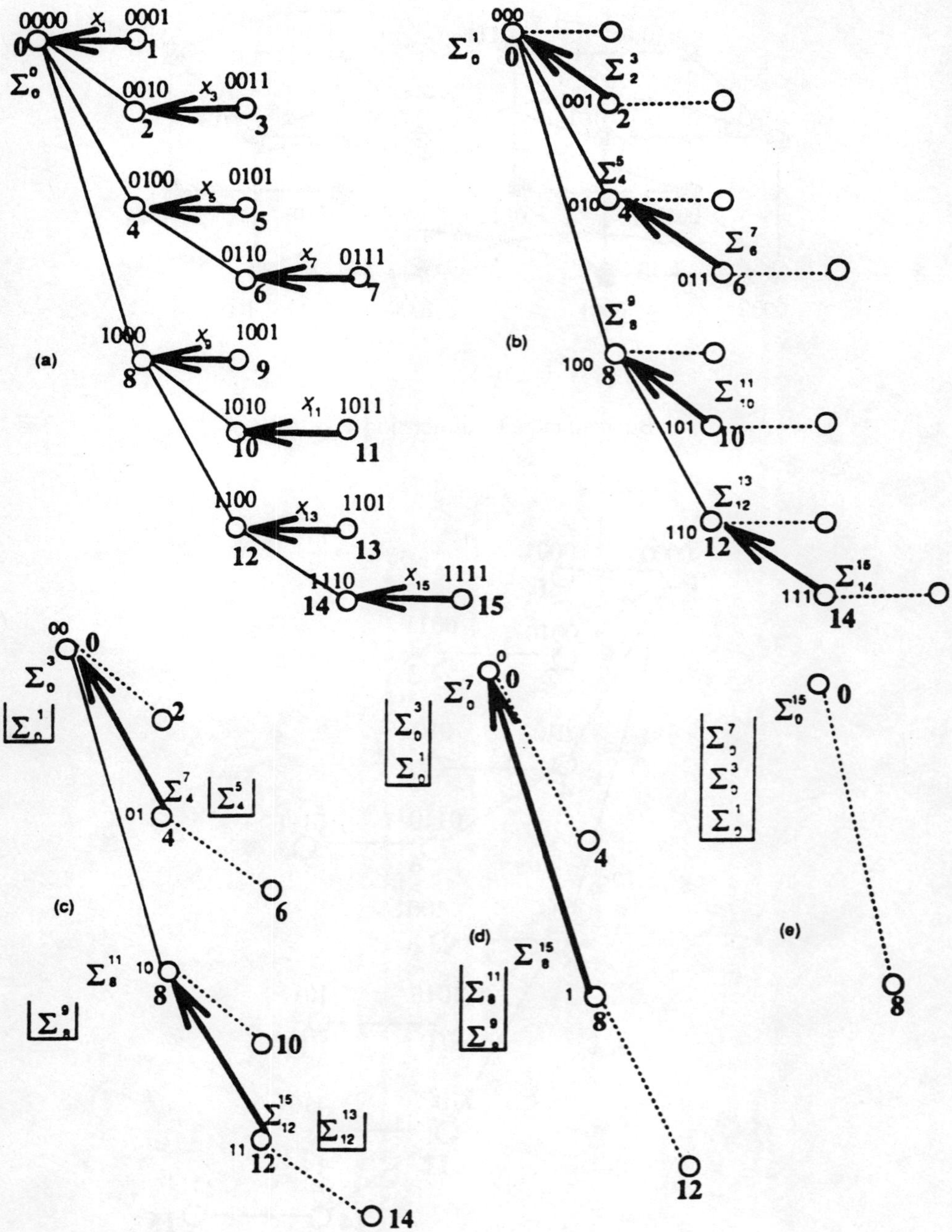

Fig. 2. Contracuon of a Boolean cube

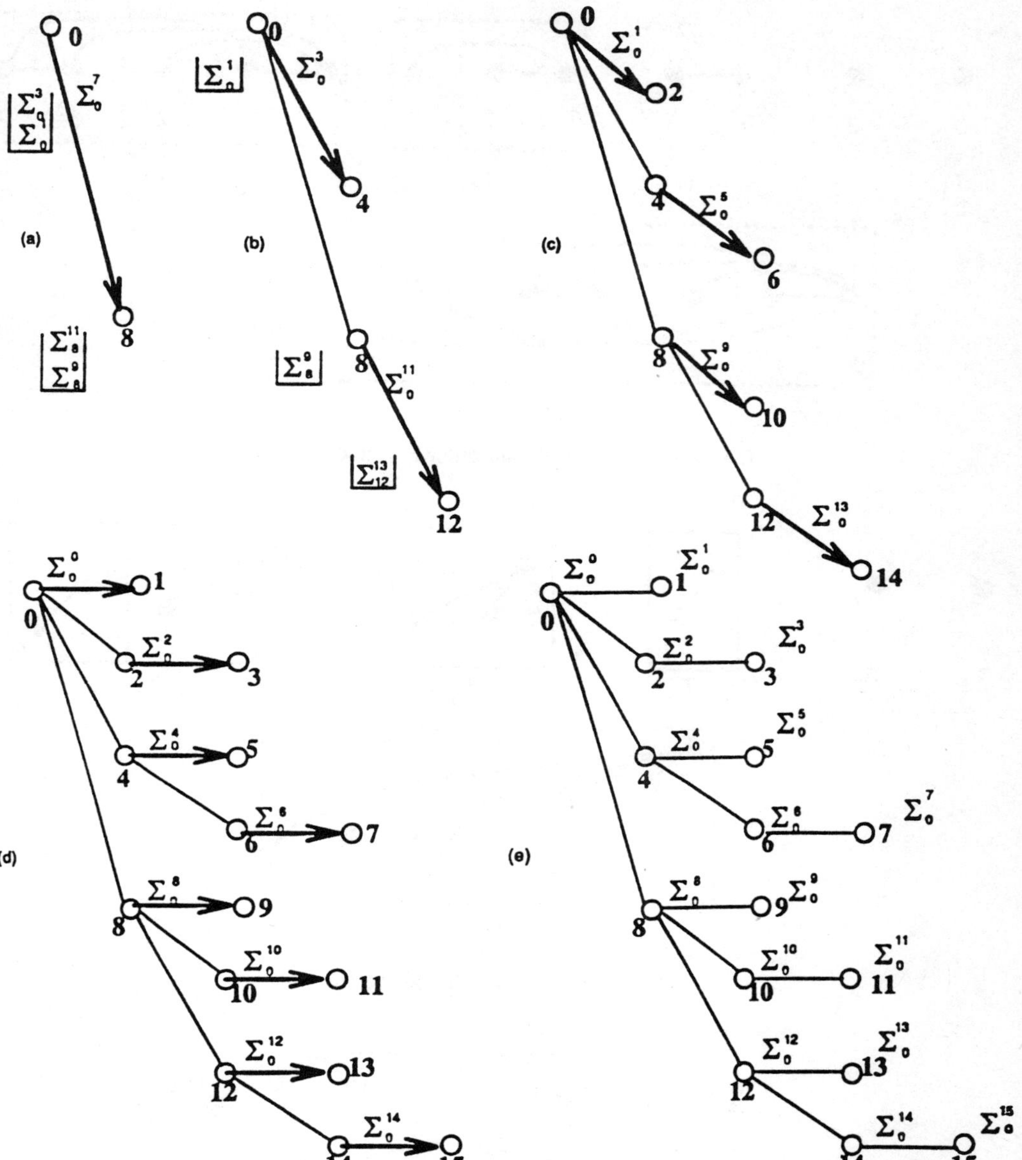

Fig. 3. Expansion on Boolean cube

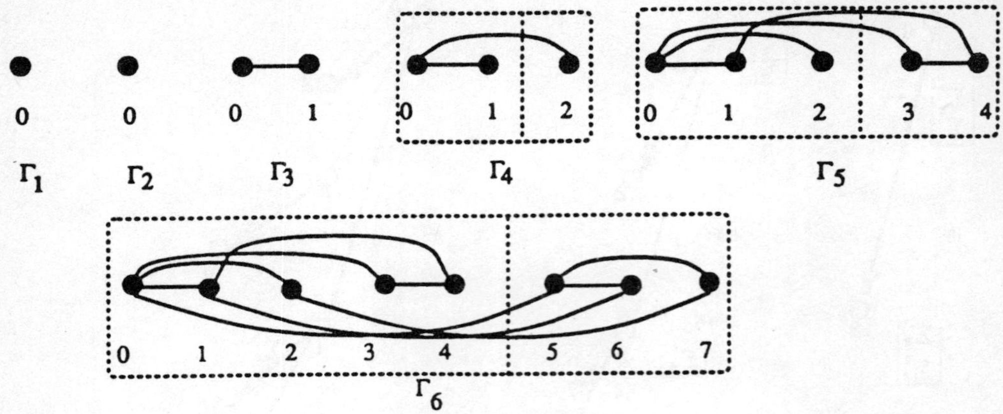

(a). Examples of second order Fibonacci cubes

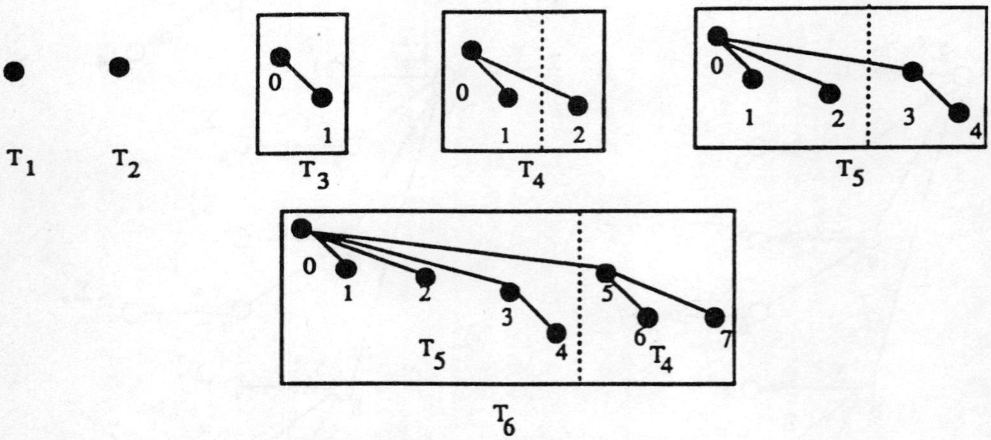

(b). Examples of Fibonacci trees

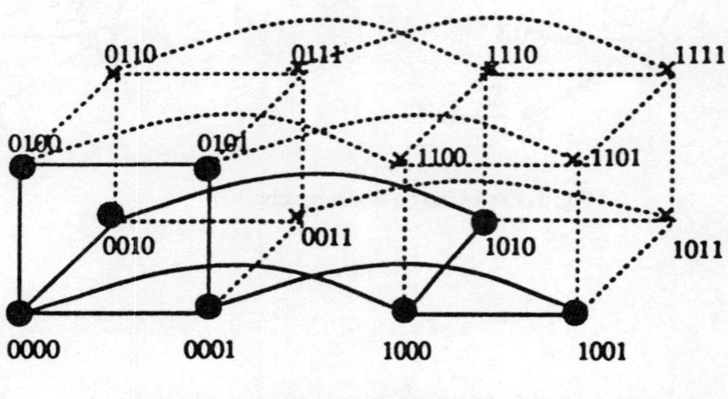

(c). Fibonacci cube as a subgraph of Boolean cube

Fig. 4. Fibonacci Cube and Fibonacci Tree

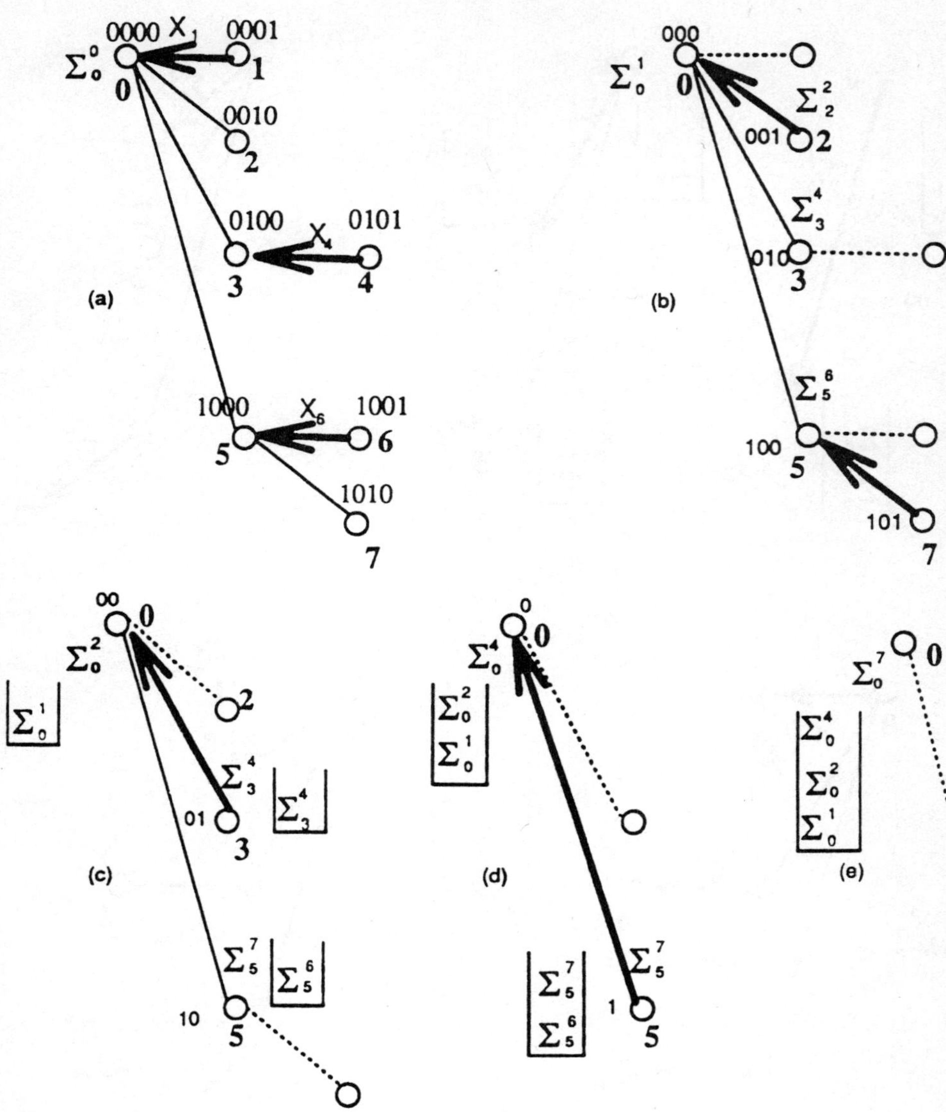

Fig. 5. Contraction of Fibonacci Tree

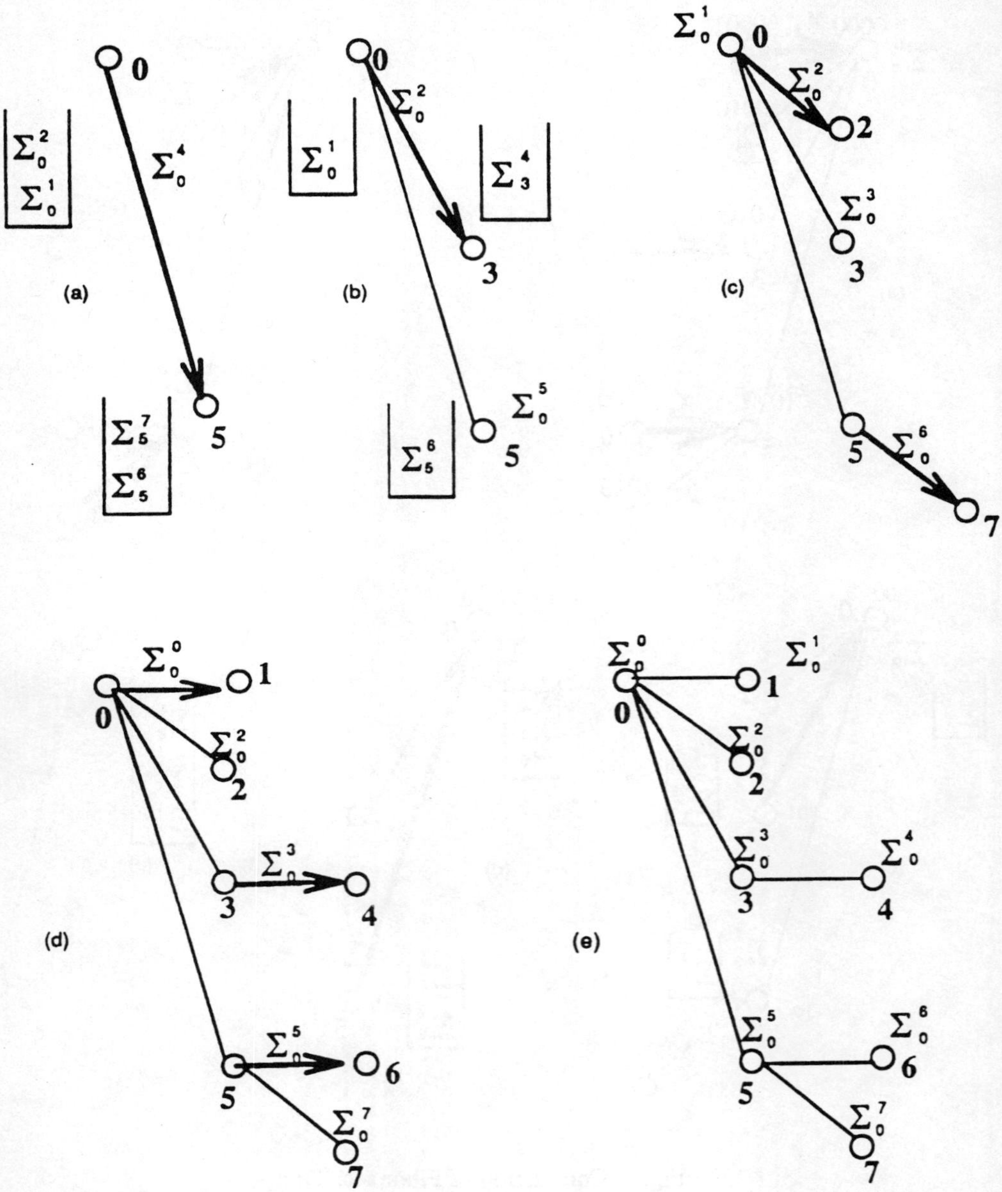

Fig. 6. Expansion of Fibonacci Tree

Must preorder in non-deterministic untyped λ-calculus*

U. de'Liguoro and A. Piperno

Dipartimento di Matematica
Università di Roma "La Sapienza"
Via Salaria 113, 00198 Roma
deliguoro@vaxrma.infn.it
piperno@vaxrma.infn.it

Abstract

This paper studies the interplay between functional application and nondeterministic choice in the context of untyped λ-calculus. We introduce an operational semantics which is based on the idea of *must* preorder, coming from the theory of process algebras. To characterize this relation, we build a model using the classical inverse limit construction, and we prove it fully abstract using a generalization of Böhm trees.

1 Introduction

The study of call-by-name and call-by-value passing mechanisms was tackled, in the framework of untyped λ-calculus, in the pioneering work by Plotkin [18]. More recently, it has been reformulated in a categorical setting by Moggi [16], while lazyness, that is a special case of call-by-name, has been the main issue in the research by Abramsky and Ong [1]. A number of papers has appeared therafter on this topic, which seems to be an area of growing interest.

At the same time, in the field of concurrency theory, the need for a notion of application, and consequently of abstraction, has been recognized (implicitly [15], or explicitly [22]), so that new problems arise, particularly as far as a combination of non-determinism and functional application is concerned.

λ-calculi enriched with non-deterministic operators are not a novelty (see [2, 3]), but studies on a type free calculus are rather rare (see [6, 20, 14]). In Sharma's thesis [20], inspired by the work of Hennessy [10], the problem of finding a correct extension of the notion of λ-theory in the case of a λ-calculus enriched with a choice operator has been connected with the distinction of two value passing mechanisms (i.e. β-rules), which can be

*This work has been partially supported by grants from ESPRIT-BRA 3230.

viewed as restrictions to the choice operator of call-by-name and call-by-value evaluation strategies. The first rule allows unrestricted substitution, in such a way that choices can be multiplied and performed at any moment during evaluation; this is called *run-time-choice* in [10]. The second one forces passed values to be "deterministic", eliminating choices in a term before substituting it for an abstracted variable: this is *call-time-choice* in [10].

Combining methods from classical, type-free λ-calculus [13, 23] with those from the theory of process algebras [9], we investigate on a kind of *must testing* preorder, written $\sqsubseteq_{must}$. Usually the *may* preorder is considered to model parallelism in the functional setting (see [6]), but the must preorder seems to be more deeply connected with correctness problems arising from the value passing mechanism.

However, there is a stronger reason for choosing the idea of must convergency in the λ-calculus: as a matter of fact it turns out to be the right extension of the notion of *solvability*, central in the classical theory, leading to a model and to a theory which nicely includes sensible ones, and precisely which is a conservative extension of $\mathcal{H}^*$, the unique Hilbert-Post complete extension of the λ-theory equating all unsolvable terms (see [4]).

After introducing the reduction relation $\longrightarrow_r$ in section 2, we give a characterization of the operational semantics induced by must preorder, defined in section 3, by means of a model; the model is built in section 4 using a construction based on a powerdomain functor (see [19, 21]) and non deterministic algebras [2, 11]. The main result of the paper is that, for each pair of terms M and N of our calculus,

$$M \sqsubseteq_{must} N \Leftrightarrow [\![M]\!] \sqsubseteq [\![N]\!]$$

where $[\![\cdot]\!]$ is the interpretation map: i.e. a full abstraction theorem. This is proved in section 5 introducing a kind of trees similar to Böhm trees [4], and defining an order relation over them which turns out to be equivalent to those in the main theorem. Finally in section 6 the theory of the model is studied, and it is shown that it conservatively extends $\mathcal{H}^*$. As a byproduct, we prove the consistency of the full theory λ_r, introduced in [20].

We assume familiarity with the classical theory of the λ-calculus and with the powerdomain construction.

2 The non-deterministic λ-calculus

In this section we shortly review two possible ways of adding a choice operator to the type-free λ-calculus, somehow related to *call-by-name* and *call-by-value* reduction strategies.

Definition 1 *(Syntax)*
The syntax of the non-deterministic λ-calculus is defined as follows:

$$M ::= x \mid \lambda x.M \mid MN \mid M \oplus N.$$

Terms, whose set is denoted by $\Lambda_\oplus$, are considered modulo α-congruence; clearly $\Lambda \subset \Lambda_\oplus$.

Following [10, 20], we distinguish two parameter-passing mechanisms, namely two β-rules:

Definition 2 *(Rules)*

(i) *Run-time choice*

(β_r) $(\lambda x.M)N \to M[N/x]$,
where $(M \oplus N)[L/x] \equiv M[L/x] \oplus N[L/x]$;

(i') *Call-time choice*

(β_c) $(\lambda x.M)N \to M[N/x]$ if $N \in \Lambda$;

(ii)
(μ) $N \to N' \Rightarrow MN \to MN'$,
(ν) $M \to M' \Rightarrow MN \to M'N$,
(ξ) $M \to M' \Rightarrow \lambda x.M \to \lambda x.M'$,
(η) $\lambda x.Mx \to M$ *if* $x \notin FV(M)$,

$(\oplus.1)$ $M \to M' \Rightarrow M \oplus N \to M' \oplus N$,
$(\oplus.2)$ $N \to N' \Rightarrow M \oplus N \to M \oplus N'$,
$(\oplus.3)$ $M \oplus N \to M$,
$(\oplus.4)$ $M \oplus N \to N$.

The rules (β_c) and (β_r) yield two different reduction relations, namely $\longrightarrow_c$ and $\longrightarrow_r$. We are interested in the study of the interplay between the functional application and the choice operator, which is fully formalized by the run-time choice reduction; the interest in the aspect of functionality explains also the rule (η). On the other hand, as we will see in the final section, a calculus based on call-time choice is nothing more than a calculus whose objects are finite sets of classical terms.

We shall concentrate our attention on run-time-choice reduction relation. In the following, $\longrightarrow$ will stand for $\longrightarrow_r$.

Despite the lack of the Church-Rosser property, a standardization theorem can be proved. In general one cannot permute β-reductions with $\oplus$-reductions:

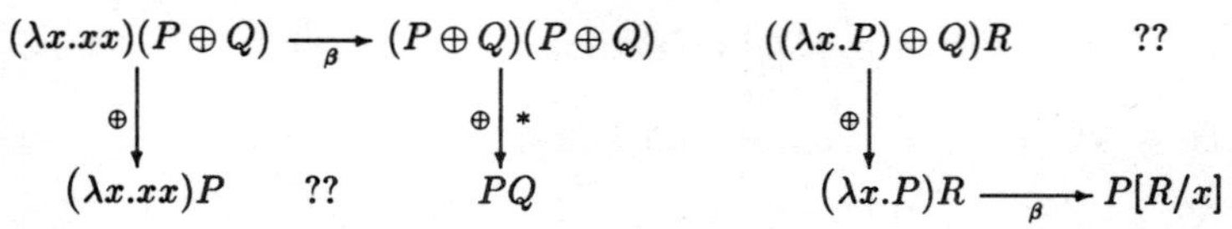

Figure 1: β and $\oplus$-reductions do not always commute

indeed, figure 1 shows that a β-contraction can multiply $\oplus$-redexes (left), hence the number of possible choices, and that $\oplus$-contractions may create new β-redexes (right).

However, if the choice does not delete a β-redex, whose residual[1] is contracted thereafter, then these reduction steps commute. This is the key to prove the following proposition:

Proposition 1 *Let $\mathcal{F} \subseteq M$ be a set of redex occurrences in M, with $\mathcal{F} = \mathcal{F}_\beta \cup \mathcal{F}_\oplus$ where $\mathcal{F}_\beta$ and $\mathcal{F}_\oplus$ are respectively the β- and $\oplus$-redexes in $\mathcal{F}$; then every development of $\mathcal{F}$ is finite; moreover*

[1]For the notions of *residual* and *development*, as well as for the notation, see [4].

$$M \xrightarrow[dev]{\mathcal{F}} N \Rightarrow \exists M'.\, M \xrightarrow[dev]{\mathcal{F}_\beta} M' \xrightarrow[dev]{\mathcal{F}_\oplus} N.$$

The term in which each development ends is in general not unique.

We recall that a reduction is *standard* (STN) iff a residual of a redex whose main operator occurs to the left of the main operator of a contracted redex is never contracted thereafter. Using the previous proposition the following theorem is proved as in the classical case with some minor changes

Theorem 1 *For all* $M, N \in \Lambda_\oplus$. $M \xrightarrow{*} N \Rightarrow M \xrightarrow[STN]{} N$.

The important consequence of this theorem is that any reduction can be transformed into another one consisting of some head reductions followed by internal reductions only.

3 Operational semantics

As it is well known, in the classical λ-calculus a term has no meaning when it doesn't reduce to a head normal form, that is when it is *unsolvable*. In the extension we are interested in, two possible generalizations suggest themselves: the first one says that a term is solvable iff it reduces to a head normal form (we would call it *may convergency*): a study using a similar notion is e.g. [6]. The second one defines a term to be solvable iff it has no infinite head reduction: we call this *must convergency* and write $M\downarrow_{must}$ or simply $M\downarrow$. Beside any other justification for choosing the latter notion as a research topic, we will show that it naturally leads to a conservative extension of the well known sensible theory $\mathcal{H}^*$.

Inspired by the extensional equivalence of Morris [17] and its analogue by Wadsworth [23] and by the idea of testing given by De Nicola and Hennessy [9] for process algebras, we define the following notions (see also [14]):

Definition 3 *For* $M \in \Lambda_\oplus$ *define*

1. $M\downarrow_{must} \Leftrightarrow M$ *has no infinite head reduction,*
2. $M \sqsubseteq_{must} N \Leftrightarrow \forall C[\,].\; C[M]\downarrow_{must} \Rightarrow C[N]\downarrow_{must}$,
3. $M \simeq_{must} N \Leftrightarrow M \sqsubseteq_{must} N \sqsubseteq_{must} M$.

We write $M\uparrow$ *to mean not* $M\downarrow$.

It should be noted that $\sqsubseteq_{must}$ is a preorder, so that, taking the quotient under $\simeq_{must}$, we get an order which is a precongruence.

Furthermore, such order is sensitive to the choice structure of a term, as the following example shows.

Example 1 let $M \equiv \lambda x.x(y \oplus z)$ and $N \equiv (\lambda x.xy) \oplus (\lambda x.xz)$, and consider the context $C[] \equiv (\lambda yz.[\,])H_0H_1\Delta$, with $H_0 \equiv \lambda x.x\mathbf{U}_3^3\Delta$ and $H_1 \equiv \lambda xy.yy$, $\Delta \equiv \lambda x.xx$, $\mathbf{U}_3^3 \equiv \lambda x_1x_2x_3.x_3$; a simple computation shows that $C[M]\uparrow$ while $C[N]\downarrow$; hence $N \not\sqsubseteq_{must} M$: it will be proved that $M \sqsubseteq_{must} N$.

Finally, we note that, if $M \xrightarrow{*} N$ then $M \sqsubseteq_{must} N$, i.e. the order increases under reduction.

4 Denotational semantics

In order to characterize the relation $\sqsubseteq_{must}$, we build a model, which is however of interest on its own. The structure we are looking for is an applicative structure with an extra operator modelling $\oplus$.

Definition 4 *A* semilinear applicative structure *is a triple* $\langle X, \cdot, + \rangle$ *such that*

1. $\langle X, \cdot \rangle$ *is an applicative structure,*

2. $+ : X^2 \to X$ *is an idempotent, commutative and associative operation,*

3. $\forall x, y, z \in X.\ (x + y) \cdot z = (x \cdot z) + (y \cdot z)$.

We call it *semilinear* since we do not allow in general the application to be right distributive too, that is to be linear. This is due to the fact that the application will be used to model functions whose argument are "sets", that is sums, and it is not true in general that the value of these functions is the set of their values on the "elements" of the argument.

To get a fully abstract interpretation of $\Lambda_\oplus$-terms with respect to $\sqsubseteq_{must}$, we have to consider the following issues:

- to build a semilinear applicative structure as an ordered set where the + operation satisfies the Smyth's axiom:
$$x + y \sqsubseteq x;$$
- the structure has not to be linear, i.e.
$$x \cdot (y + z) \neq (x \cdot y) + (x \cdot z);$$
- the stucture has to be extensional, i.e.:
$$(\forall z.\ x \cdot z = y \cdot z) \Rightarrow x = y,$$
since $\simeq_{must}$ validates the equation:
$$\lambda x.Mx = M \quad \text{if } x \notin FV(M).$$

To fulfill the first requirement, we work in the category of Smyth Non-Deterministic Algebras, **SNDA** (see below), which is cartesian closed (see [2]). The second point, however, rules out any solution of the domain equation $D = D \to_{lin} D$, which yields a linear structure. Finally, the extensionality requirement prewents the use of Moggi's construction (see [16]), involving an equation of the form $D = \wp D \to_{cont} \wp D$, to be solved in the category of **CPO**.

We will solve, instead, the equation $D = \wp D \to_{lin} D$ in the category **SNDA**, using the fact that $\wp D \to_{lin} D$ is isomorphic, as a **CPO**, with $D \to_{cont} D$: this satisfies extentionality as well as semilinearity and non-linearity.

4.1 The domain D_*

Our aim is to solve the domain equation

$$D = \wp D \to_{lin} D$$

where $\wp$ is the Smyth powerdomain functor, in the category of **SNDA**. The objects of this category are of the form $\langle D, \sqsubseteq, + \rangle$, where $\langle D, \sqsubseteq \rangle$ is a domain, and $+$ is a binary continuous operation which is idempotent, commutative, associative and such that $x+y \sqsubseteq x$ holds for each $x, y \in D$: we call them *Smyth algebras*. Morphisms are continuous functions preserving $+$; we write $\to_{lin}$ in contrast to $\to_{cont}$, which is referred to continuous funtions.

We recall that, given $\langle D_1, \sqsubseteq_1, +_1 \rangle$ and $\langle D_2, \sqsubseteq_2, +_2 \rangle$, the cartesian product $D_1 \times D_2$ is defined as the product of the domains D_1 and D_2, with the opration $+$ defined:

$$\langle x, y \rangle + \langle x', y' \rangle = \langle x +_1 x', y +_2 y' \rangle,$$

while the exponentiation $D_1 \to_{lin} D_2$ is formed taking the set of linear continuous functions from D_1 to D_2, pointwise ordered, and defining:

$$\forall x \in D_1.\ (f+g)(x) = f(x) +_2 g(x).$$

SNDA can be proved to be cartesian closed.

Finally, we recall that, given any domain D, $\wp D$ is the free Smyth algebra generated by D.

Definition 5 *Take D_0 as any non trivial Smyth algebra (e.g. $\wp\mathbf{2}$), and $D_{n+1} = [\wp D_n \to_{lin} D_n]$; then inductively define $\varphi_n : D_n \to_{lin} D_{n+1}$ and $\psi_n : D_{n+1} \to_{lin} D_n$ as follows:*

1. $\varphi_0(x) = \lambda y.x$, $\psi_0(y) = y(\bot)$,
2. $\varphi_{n+1}(x) = \varphi_n \circ x \circ \wp\psi_n$, $\psi_{n+1}(y) = \psi_n \circ y \circ \wp\varphi_n$.

The $\mathcal{O}$-functoriality of $\wp$ (see e.g. [11]), that is

$$\forall f, g.\ f \sqsubseteq g \Rightarrow \wp f \sqsubseteq \wp g,$$

where $\sqsubseteq$ is the pointwise ordering, ensures that $\langle \varphi_n, \psi_n \rangle$ is an embedding-projection pair, for each n, so that we can take

$$D_* = \varprojlim (D_n, \psi_n).$$

As usual with the inverse limit construction, each D_n embeds into D_*, say by the $\langle \Phi_{n,*}, \Phi_{*,n} \rangle$ embedding-projection pair; setting $x_n = \Phi_{*,n}(x)$ for $x \in D_*$ and $a_n = \wp\Phi_{*,n}(a)$ for $a \in \wp D_*$, we can state

Proposition 2 *The map $F : D_* \to [\wp D_* \to_{lin} D_*]$ defined by*

$$F(x) = \lambda a \in \wp D_*. \bigsqcup_n x_{n+1}(a_n)$$

and the map $G : [\wp D_* \to_{lin} D_*] \to D_*$ defined by

$$G(f) = \bigsqcup_n (\lambda a \in \wp D_n.(f(\wp\Phi_{n,*}(a)))_n)$$

are continuous, linear and mutually inverse.

4.2 A semilinear applicative structure

By proposition 2, the solution of our domain equation is a Smyth algebra, hence it has an operation $+$ which can interpret our $\oplus$. We now introduce the application operation.

Proposition 3 *For any Smyth algebras D and E,*

$$\wp D \rightarrow_{lin} E \simeq D \rightarrow_{cont} E$$

in the category of **CPO**.

Proof. The isomorphism is given by $\_ \circ \{\!| \cdot |\!\}$ and by $(\cdot)^\dagger$, where, for any $f : D \rightarrow_{cont} E$, $f^\dagger$ is the unique linear continuous function such that $f = f^\dagger \circ \{\!| \cdot |\!\}$.

□

Now, setting $\tilde{F} = (\_ \circ \{\!| \cdot |\!\}) \circ F$ and $\tilde{G} = G \circ (\cdot)^\dagger$, we define the application:

$$x \cdot y = \tilde{F}(x)(y) = F(x)\{\!|y|\!\}.$$

We conclude this section listing some basic properties of the structure D_*.

Lemma 1 *For any $x, y, z \in D_*$ and $a \in \wp D_*$,*

1. $(x + y) \cdot z = (x \cdot z) + (y \cdot z)$,
2. $x = \bigsqcup_n x_n$, $a = \bigsqcup_n a_n$,
3. $x_{n+1} \cdot y_n = x_{n+1}(\{\!|y_n|\!\})$,
4. $x_{n+1} \cdot y = x_{n+1} \cdot y_n = (x \cdot y_n)_n$,
5. $x_0 \cdot y = x_0 = (x \cdot \bot)_0$.

Proof. We prove *1*:

$$\begin{array}{rcll}(x+y)\cdot z & = & \tilde{F}(x+y)(z) & \\ & = & F(x+y)(\{\!|z|\!\}) & \\ & = & (F(x)+F(y))(\{\!|z|\!\}) & \text{by linearity of } F \\ & = & F(x)(\{\!|z|\!\}) + F(y)(\{\!|z|\!\}) & \\ & = & (x\cdot z)+(y\cdot z). & \end{array}$$

The other points are almost the same as in the D_∞ model of the λ-calculus; in *3*, we observe that, for any f, $\wp f \circ \{\!| \cdot |\!\} = \{\!| \cdot |\!\} \circ f$; it follows that $\{\!|y|\!\}_n = \{\!|y_n|\!\}$, so that *3* follows from the definition of $\cdot$ and standard properties of the inverse limit constructions.

□

4.3 A fully abstract interpretation of $\Lambda_{\oplus}$

We present a *model*, which actually does not directly interpret the relation $\longrightarrow_r$, but the equivalence relation induced by $\sqsubseteq_{must}$.

Definition 6 *A* syntactical model *is a semilinear applicative structure* $\langle X, \cdot, + \rangle$, *equipped with a map* $[\![\cdot]\!] : \Lambda_{\oplus} \to (Env \to X)$, *such that the triple* $\langle X, \cdot, [\![\cdot]\!] \rangle$ *satisfies the clauses of the classical definition of* syntactical λ-model *of* [12], *and furthermore*

$$[\![M \oplus N]\!]_{\rho} = [\![M]\!]_{\rho} + [\![N]\!]_{\rho},$$

where $\rho \in Env = Var \to X$.

Remark 1 The equation

$$[\![\lambda x.M \oplus N]\!]_{\rho} = [\![\lambda x.M]\!]_{\rho} + [\![\lambda x.N]\!]_{\rho}$$

is easily proved to be valid if the applicative structure is extensional.

Definition 7 *Given the structure* $\langle D_*, \cdot, + \rangle$ *and* $\rho \in Env = Var \to D_*$, *we define the map* $[\![\cdot]\!] : \Lambda_{\oplus} \to (Env \to D_*)$ *as follows:*

1. $[\![x]\!]_{\rho} = \rho(x)$,
2. $[\![MN]\!]_{\rho} = [\![M]\!]_{\rho} \cdot [\![N]\!]_{\rho}$,
3. $[\![\lambda x.M]\!]_{\rho} = \tilde{G}(\lambda d \in D_*.[\![M]\!]_{\rho[d/x]})$,
4. $[\![M \oplus N]\!]_{\rho} = [\![M]\!]_{\rho} + [\![N]\!]_{\rho}$.

This is a good definition, since in *3* the continuity of application, abstraction and + ensures that the function $\lambda d \in D_*.[\![M]\!]_{\rho[d/x]}$ is continuous as well. Now it can be verified that:

Proposition 4 *The quadruple* $\langle D_*, \cdot, +, [\![\cdot]\!] \rangle$ *is a syntactical model, furthermore it is extensional.*

We can now state the main theorem of this paper:

Theorem 2 (Full Abstraction Theorem)
For all $M, N \in \Lambda_{\oplus}$

$$M \sqsubseteq_{must} N \Leftrightarrow \forall \rho.\ [\![M]\!]_{\rho} \sqsubseteq [\![N]\!]_{\rho}.$$

The next section is devoted to the proof of this theorem.

5 Trees for proving full abstraction

In order to represent the functional behaviour of each term, we introduce a kind of unfolding trees, generalizing the notion of Böhm trees of the classical λ-calculus, and a suitable notion of approximation, to be considered as a cut of the tree.

The difficulty here is that, since the Church-Rosser property doesn't hold, we cannot consider our trees as a representation of the directed set of "approximated" reducts of a term: instead, we have to take into account all possible reductions, without making the choices, but simply representing their structure somehow in the tree.

5.1 Non-deterministic Böhm trees and their ordering

As a first step, we introduce a notation to represent approximations.

Definition 8 *We define, by mutual induction, two sets $\mathcal{S}_0$ and $\mathcal{S}_1$:*

1. $\Omega \in \mathcal{S}_0$, *where Ω is a new constant representing divergency,*
2. $M \in \mathcal{S}_0 - \{\Omega\} \Rightarrow \lambda x.M \in \mathcal{S}_0$,
3. $M_1, ..., M_n \in \mathcal{S}_0 \Rightarrow \{M_1, ..., M_n\} \in \mathcal{S}_1$ *for* $n > 0$,
4. $\mathcal{M}_1, ..., \mathcal{M}_m \in \mathcal{S}_1, x \in Var \Rightarrow x\mathcal{M}_1...\mathcal{M}_m \in \mathcal{S}_0$ *for* $m \geq 0$.

For every approximant, there is a term in $\Lambda_\oplus\Omega$ (i.e., $\Lambda_\oplus$ extended with the constant Ω) which corresponds to it in a natural way; we define, by mutual induction, $\vartheta_0 : \mathcal{S}_0 \to \Lambda_\oplus\Omega$ and $\vartheta_1 : \mathcal{S}_1 \to \Lambda_\oplus\Omega$:

$$\vartheta_0(\Omega) = \Omega, \qquad \vartheta_0(\lambda x.M) = \lambda x.\vartheta_0(M),$$
$$\vartheta_0(x\mathcal{M}_1 \ldots \mathcal{M}_m) = x\vartheta_1(\mathcal{M}_1)\ldots\vartheta_1(\mathcal{M}_m);$$
$$\vartheta_1(\{M_1, \ldots, M_n\}) = \vartheta_0(M_1) \oplus \ldots \oplus \vartheta_0(M_n).$$

To simplify the notation, we will identify $\mathcal{M} \in \mathcal{S}_1$ with $\vartheta_1(\mathcal{M}) \in \Lambda_\oplus\Omega$.

Definition 8 allows us to introduce the notion of *Non-deterministic Böhm Tree* (NBT).

Definition 9 *Let $\mathcal{M} \in \mathcal{S}_1$; rather informally, we define:* $\mathrm{NBT}(\mathcal{M}) = \mathrm{NBT}_1(\mathcal{M})$, *where* $\mathrm{NBT}_0(\Omega) = \Omega$ *and:*

$$\mathrm{NBT}_0(\lambda\vec{x}.\xi\mathcal{M}_1...\mathcal{M}_m) = \begin{array}{c} \lambda\vec{x}.\xi \\ \swarrow \quad \searrow \\ \mathrm{NBT}_1(\mathcal{M}_1) \ \cdots \ \mathrm{NBT}_1(\mathcal{M}_m) \end{array} \qquad \mathrm{NBT}_1(\{M_1, ..., M_n\}) = \begin{array}{c} \oplus \\ \swarrow \quad \searrow \\ \mathrm{NBT}_0(M_1) \ \cdots \ \mathrm{NBT}_0(M_n) \end{array}$$

Note that the order of sons of a node labelled by $\lambda\vec{x}.\xi$ is relevant, as well as multiple occurrences of the same subtree; this is not the case for sons of nodes labelled by $\oplus$.

NBT's may be seen as infinite $\mathcal{S}_1$-terms, that is as elements of the completion of $\mathcal{S}_1$ under the order induced on $\mathcal{S}_1$ by the relation freely generated by $\Omega \preceq M$, for all M, on $\mathcal{S}_0$. More precisely, they are the limits of those directed subsets of $\mathcal{S}_1$ generated by terms in $\Lambda_\oplus$ with the following family of maps:

Definition 10 *For each natural number k, we define a map* $\omega^k\colon \Lambda_\oplus \to S_1$ *by:*

1. $\omega^0(M) = \{\Omega\}$,
2. (a) $\omega^{k+1}(M) = \{\Omega\}$, *if M diverges; otherwise:*

   (b) $\omega^{k+1}(M) = \{\lambda\vec{x}.\xi\,\omega^k(M_1)...\omega^k(M_m) \mid \lambda\vec{x}.\xi M_1...M_m$ *is a principal*[2] *head normal form of* $M\}$.

Furthermore, we denote

$$M^{[k]} = \vartheta_1 \circ \omega^k(M).$$

Remark 2 We note that $M^{[k]}$ is always a β-Ω-normal form (see [4]), where each $\oplus$-redex cannot create new β-Ω-redexes. We denote by $\mathrm{N}_\oplus^\Omega$ the set of such terms.

Example 2 Let $M \equiv \lambda x.x(yx) \oplus \lambda x.xz \in \Lambda_\oplus$. Then we have:

$$\begin{array}{rcl} \omega^1(M) & = & \{\lambda x.x\,\omega^0(y\Omega)\ ,\ \lambda x.x\,\omega^0(z)\} = \{\lambda x.x\{\Omega\}\}, \\ \omega^2(M) & = & \{\lambda x.x\,\omega^1(yx)\ ,\ \lambda x.x\,\omega^1(z)\} = \{\lambda x.x\{y\,\omega^0(x)\}\ ,\ \lambda x.x\{z\}\}, \\ & = & \{\lambda x.x\{y\{\Omega\}\}\ ,\ \lambda x.x\{z\}\}, \\ M^{[1]} & = & \lambda x.x\Omega, \\ M^{[2]} & = & \lambda x.x(y\Omega) \oplus \lambda x.xz. \end{array}$$

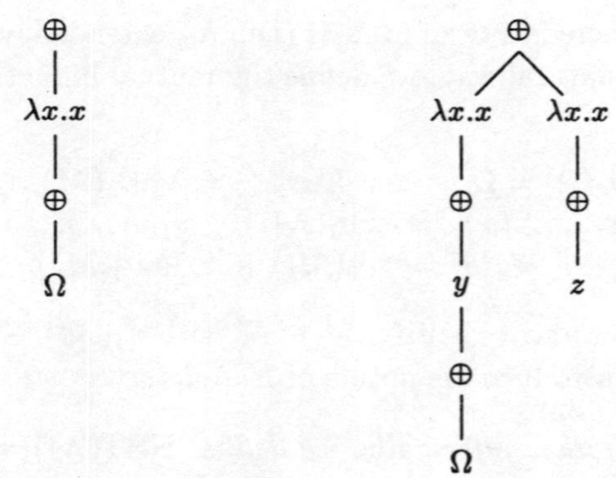

Figure 2: Non-deterministic Böhm trees

The trees $\mathrm{NBT}(\omega^1(M))$ and $\mathrm{NBT}(\omega^2(M))$ are shown in Figure 2.

To compare two terms, that is their trees, simple inclusion doesn't suffice even in the classical λ-calculus: what we need is a generalization of the relation ${}^\eta\sqsubseteq^\eta$ in [4], or, equivalently, of $<_k^s$ in [13]: this will be achieved in several steps.

We first recall the notion of *equivalence* ($\sim$) for head normal forms [5] (called *similarity* in [13]): given two classical hnf's

$$M \equiv \lambda x_1 \ldots x_n.\xi M_1 \ldots M_m \text{ and } N \equiv \lambda x_1 \ldots x_{n'}.\zeta N_1 \ldots N_{m'}$$

[2] i.e. it is reachable by head reductions only.

(where m and m' are called *degrees* of M and N) they are equivalent iff $\xi \equiv \zeta$ and $n - m = n' - m'$.

Since the relation $\sim$ is preserved by η-reduction and expansion, we note that, if $M \sim N$, then we can η-expand M and N in such a way that they have the same degree.

The relation $\sim$ plays an important role in comparing elements of $\Lambda_\oplus$, as shown by the following example.

Example 3 Let $M \equiv \lambda x_1x_2x_3.x_1x_3(x_2x_3) \oplus \lambda x_1x_2.x_1x_2x_2 \oplus \lambda x_1x_2x_3.x_1x_3x_2$ and $N \equiv \lambda x_1x_2.x_1x_1 \oplus \lambda x_1x_2x_3.x_1x_2$.

We have:

$$\begin{aligned}
\omega^2(M) &= \{\lambda x_1x_2x_3.x_1\{x_3\}\{x_2\{\Omega\}\}\ ,\ \lambda x_1x_2.x_1\{x_2\}\{x_2\}\ ,\\
&\quad\ \lambda x_1x_2x_3.x_1\{x_3\}\{x_2\}\};\\
\omega^2(N) &= \{\lambda x_1x_2.x_1\{x_1\}\ ,\ \lambda x_1x_2x_3.x_1\{x_2\}\};\\
M^{[2]} &= \lambda x_1x_2x_3.x_1x_3(x_2\Omega) \oplus \lambda x_1x_2.x_1x_2x_2 \oplus \lambda x_1x_2x_3.x_1x_3x_2;\\
N^{[2]} &= N.
\end{aligned}$$

It comes out that there exists a $\sim$-equivalence class of $\omega^2(M) \cup \omega^2(N)$ which does not contain any element of $\omega^2(M)$. In this case, we can immediately find a context such that $C[M]$ converges while $C[N]$ does not. Indeed, take $C[\,] \equiv [\,](\lambda a_1a_2a_3.a_1)x_2x_3x_4\Omega$, tehn

$$\begin{aligned}
\omega^2(C[M^{[2]}]) &= \{x_4\{x_5\}, x_3\{x_4\}\{x_5\}\},\\
\omega^2(C[N^{[2]}]) &= \{\Omega\}.
\end{aligned}$$

In the general case, however, while comparing two terms, it is necessary to analyze their internal structure.

Definition 11 *Given $\mathcal{M}, \mathcal{N} \in \mathcal{S}_1$, define $\mathsf{Pair}(\mathcal{M},\mathcal{N})$ as the least set such that, if $\mathcal{M}_{/\sim} = \{\mathcal{E}\} \cup \mathcal{M}'$ and $\mathcal{N}_{/\sim} = \{\mathcal{F}\} \cup \mathcal{N}'$, where $\mathcal{E} = \{M^1, \ldots, M^m\}$ and $\mathcal{F} = \{N^1, \ldots, N^n\}$ and $(\mathcal{E} \cup \mathcal{F})_{/\sim}$ is a singleton, assuming*

$$\begin{aligned}
M^i &\equiv \lambda\vec{y}.x\mathcal{M}^i_1 ... \mathcal{M}^i_l, \quad \text{for } 1 \le i \le n,\\
N^j &\equiv \lambda\vec{y}.x\mathcal{N}^j_1 .. \mathcal{N}^j_l, \quad \text{for } 1 \le j \le m,
\end{aligned}$$

then, for each $p \le l$,

$$< \{\mathcal{M}^1_p, ..., \mathcal{M}^n_p\}, \{\mathcal{N}^1_p, ..., \mathcal{N}^m_p\} > \in \mathsf{Pair}(\mathcal{M},\mathcal{N}).$$

Given $\mathcal{M}, \mathcal{N} \in \mathcal{S}_1$, $\mathsf{Pair}(\mathcal{M},\mathcal{N})$ selects the subterms to be compared during the first step of the analysis of the internal structure of $\mathcal{M}$ and $\mathcal{N}$. As in [13], this notion has to be generalized to each level of the tree.

Definition 12 *Given $\mathcal{M}, \mathcal{N} \in \mathcal{S}_1$, define $\mathsf{Pair}_k(\mathcal{M},\mathcal{N})$, for each natural number k, as follows:*

1. $\mathsf{Pair}_1(\mathcal{M},\mathcal{N}) = \mathsf{Pair}(\mathcal{M},\mathcal{N})$.

2. *Let* Pair$(\mathcal{M},\mathcal{N}) = \{<\mathcal{U}_1,\mathcal{V}_1>,\ldots,<\mathcal{U}_n,\mathcal{V}_n>\}$ *and* $\mathcal{U}'_i = \bigcup \mathcal{U}_i$, $\mathcal{V}'_i = \bigcup \mathcal{V}_i$, *where* $1 \leq i \leq n$*: then*

$$\mathsf{Pair}_{k+1}(\mathcal{M},\mathcal{N}) = \{<\mathcal{A},\mathcal{B}>\mid \exists i \leq n.\ <\mathcal{A},\mathcal{B}>\in \mathsf{Pair}_k(\mathcal{U}'_i,\mathcal{V}'_i)\}.$$

Remark 3 Note that in *2*, for $1 \leq i \leq n$, $\mathcal{U}_i$ is a finite non empty set of objects in $\mathcal{S}_1$, hence a family of finite non empty sets of objects in $\mathcal{S}_0$; it follows that its union $\mathcal{U}'_i$ is again an element of $\mathcal{S}_1$.

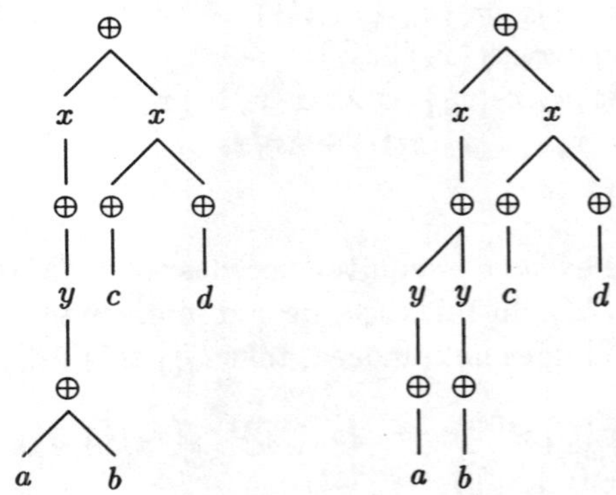

Figure 3: Respectively the trees of $\omega^3(M)$ and $\omega^3(N)$

Example 4 Let $M \equiv x(y(a \oplus b)) \oplus xcd$ and $N \equiv x(ya \oplus yb) \oplus xcd$ (see figure 3); we have

$$\begin{aligned} \omega^3(M) &= \{x\{y\{a,b\}\}\ ,\ x\{c\}\{d\}\} \\ \omega^3(N) &= \{x\{y\{a\},y\{b\}\}\ ,\ x\{c\}\{d\}\}. \end{aligned}$$

From this we compute:

$$\begin{aligned} \mathsf{Pair}_1(\omega^3(M),\omega^3(N)) &= \{\ <\{\{y\{a,b\}\}\},\{\{y\{a\},y\{b\}\}\}>, \\ &\qquad <\{\{c\}\},\{\{c\}\}>\ ,\ <\{\{d\}\},\{\{d\}\}>\ \}; \\ \mathsf{Pair}_2(\omega^3(M),\omega^3(N)) &= \mathsf{Pair}_1(\{y\{a,b\}\},\{y\{a\},y\{b\}\})\cup \\ &\qquad \mathsf{Pair}_1(\{c\},\{c\}) \cup \mathsf{Pair}_1(\{d\},\{d\}) \\ &= \{\ <\{\{a,b\}\},\{\{a\},\{b\}\}>\ \}. \end{aligned}$$

We are now ready to introduce the ordering relation $\leq$ over trees.

Definition 13 *Given* $\mathcal{M},\mathcal{N} \in \mathcal{S}_1$ *we define, for each k, a relation* $\leq_k$ *by:*

$$\begin{aligned} \mathcal{M} \leq_1 \mathcal{N} &\Leftrightarrow \mathcal{M} = \{\Omega\} \vee \forall N \in \mathcal{N}\, \exists M \in \mathcal{M}.\ M \sim N, \\ \mathcal{M} \leq_{k+1} \mathcal{N} &\Leftrightarrow \mathcal{M} \leq_k \mathcal{N} \wedge \\ &\qquad \forall <\mathcal{U},\mathcal{V}>\in \mathsf{Pair}_k(\mathcal{M},\mathcal{N}).\mathcal{U} \sqsubseteq^\sharp \mathcal{V}, \end{aligned}$$

where

$$\mathcal{U} \sqsubseteq^\sharp \mathcal{V} \Leftrightarrow \forall \mathcal{N}_j \in \mathcal{V} \exists \mathcal{M}_i \in \mathcal{U}. \mathcal{M}_i \leq_1 \mathcal{N}_j.$$

From this we can define

$$\mathcal{M} \leq \mathcal{N} \Leftrightarrow \forall k.\ \ \mathcal{M} \leq_k \mathcal{N}.$$

Finally, for any M, $N \in \Lambda_\oplus$,

$$\begin{array}{rcl} M \leq_k N & \Leftrightarrow & \omega^k(M) \leq_k \omega^k(N), \\ M \leq N & \Leftrightarrow & \forall k.\ \ M \leq_k N. \end{array}$$

Let us note that the relation $\sqsubseteq^\sharp$ is the Smyth preorder induced by $\leq_1$.

5.2 The semi-separability theorem

The semi-separability problem has been studied, for finite sets of λ-terms, in [7]. However, these techniques are not sufficient in cases where the relation $\sqsubseteq^\sharp$ is essentially involved, as it will be clear from the proof of the following lemma:

Lemma 2 *For $M, N \in \Lambda_\oplus$,*

$$M \not\leq_2 N \ \Rightarrow\ \exists C[\,].\, C[M]{\downarrow}\ \ \wedge\ C[N]{\uparrow}\ .$$

Proof. (Sketch) By cases. If $M \not\leq_1 N$, then either $\omega^1(N) = \mathcal{N} = \{\Omega\}$ and $\omega^1(M) = \mathcal{M} \neq \{\Omega\}$, so that there is nothing to prove, or there exists $N \in \mathcal{N}$ such that, for all $M \in \mathcal{M}$, $M \not\prec N$: then the problem is solved using the semi-separability techniques described in [7].

We exhibit an example of the case where $M \leq_1 N$ but $M \not\leq_2 N$. Take $M \equiv xy \oplus xz$ and $N \equiv x(y \oplus z)$; now $\omega^2(M) = \{x\{y\}, x\{z\}\}$, while $\omega^2(N) = \{x\{y, z\}\}$; computing $\mathsf{Pair}_1(\omega^2(M), \omega^2(N))$, we get $\{< \{\{y\}, \{z\}\}, \{\{y, z\}\} >\}$ and it can be verified that $\{\{y\}, \{z\}\} \not\sqsubseteq^\sharp \{\{y, z\}\}$. If $\mathbf{1} \equiv \lambda uv.uv$ and $\mathbf{2} \equiv \lambda uv.u(uv)$ are two Church numerals, we take $C_0[\,] \equiv (\lambda xyz.[\,])(\lambda w.aww)\mathbf{1}\,\mathbf{2}$. Simple calculations give us

$$\omega^2(C_0[M]) = \{a\{\mathbf{1}\}\{\mathbf{1}\}, a\{\mathbf{2}\}\{\mathbf{2}\}\}$$

and

$$\omega^2(C_0[N]) = \{a\{\mathbf{1}, \mathbf{2}\}\{\mathbf{1}, \mathbf{2}\}\}.$$

Now, there exists a combinator $\mathbf{H}$ such that, if L is a sum of Church numerals and $\mathbf{n}$ a numeral, then $\mathbf{1} \in \omega^2(\mathbf{H}L\mathbf{n})$ only if $\mathbf{n}$ occurs in the sum L, it is $\{\mathbf{0}\}$ otherwise[3]. Taking

$$C_1[\,] \equiv (\lambda a.[\,])(\lambda uv.\mathbf{P}(\mathbf{H}u\mathbf{1})(\mathbf{H}v\mathbf{2})),$$

where $\mathbf{P}$ λ-defines multiplication, we have

$$\omega^2(C_1[C_0[M]]) = \{\mathbf{0}\} \ \text{ and } \ \omega^2(C_1[C_0[N]]) = \{\mathbf{0}, \mathbf{1}\}.$$

[3] **Basically H is a test for equality for Church numerals, with the property that the first argument is not multiplied.**

Now, taking $C_2[] \equiv [](\mathbf{K}\Omega)\mathbf{I}$, we have

$$\omega^2(C_2[C_1[C_0[M]]]) = \{\mathbf{I}\}$$

while

$$\omega^2(C_2[C_1[C_0[N]]]) = \{\Omega\}.$$

□

The following lemma rephrases, in our context, the Böhm-out lemma of [4].

Lemma 3 *For $M, N \in \Lambda_\oplus$ and $k \geq 2$,*

$$M \not\leq_k N \Rightarrow \exists C[].\, C[M] \not\leq_2 C[N].$$

We are now ready to prove the semi-separability theorem for our calculus.

Theorem 3 *For any M, $N \in \Lambda_\oplus$,*

$$M \sqsubseteq_{must} N \Rightarrow M \leq N.$$

Proof. By contraposition, we prove (see definition 3)

$$\exists k.\, M \not\leq_k N \Rightarrow \exists C[].\, C[M]\downarrow \wedge C[N]\uparrow .$$

Indeed,

$$\begin{aligned} M \not\leq N &\Rightarrow \exists k.\, M \not\leq_k N \\ &\Rightarrow \exists C[].\, C[M] \not\leq_2 C[N] && \text{by lemma 2} \\ &\Rightarrow \exists C[], C'[].\, C'[C[M]]\downarrow \wedge C'[C[N]]\uparrow && \text{by lemma 3.} \end{aligned}$$

□

5.3 Proving the full abstraction theorem

Finally, we can prove the last results leading us to the main theorem.

Theorem 4 *For all $M, N \in \Lambda_\oplus$,*

$$\forall \rho \in Env.\, [\![M]\!]_\rho \sqsubseteq [\![N]\!]_\rho \Rightarrow M \sqsubseteq_{must} N.$$

Proof. (Sketch) Following a pattern similar to that in [13], one shows that, if $L \in \mathrm{N}_\oplus^\Omega$ and $L \leq M$, then $[\![L]\!] \sqsubseteq [\![M]\!]$, and that $[\![M]\!] = \bigsqcup_k [\![M^{[k]}]\!]$; using these facts we have

$$\begin{aligned} M^{[1]} = \Omega &\Leftrightarrow \forall k.\, M^{[k]} = \Omega \\ &\Leftrightarrow \forall k.\, [\![M^{[k]}]\!] = \bot \\ &\Leftrightarrow [\![M]\!] = \bigsqcup_k [\![M^{[k]}]\!] = \bot \end{aligned}$$

since $[\![\Omega]\!] = \bot$; hence

$$\begin{aligned} M \not\sqsubseteq_{must} N &\Rightarrow \exists C[].\, C[M]\downarrow \wedge C[N]\uparrow \\ &\Rightarrow \exists C[].\, \omega^1(C[M]) \neq \{\Omega\} = \omega^1(C[N]) \\ &\Rightarrow \exists C[].\, [\![C[M]]\!] \neq \bot = [\![C[N]]\!] \\ &\Rightarrow [\![M]\!] \not\sqsubseteq [\![N]\!], \end{aligned}$$

being the context operation the composition of abstraction, application and $\uplus$, that is a monotonic function. □

Corollary 1 *For all* $M, N \in \Lambda_\oplus$,

1. $M \le N \Rightarrow [\![M]\!] \sqsubseteq [\![N]\!]$,
2. $M \sqsubseteq_{must} N \Leftrightarrow M \le N \Leftrightarrow [\![M]\!] \sqsubseteq [\![N]\!]$.

Proof. Using the proof of the theorem and the theorem itself, we have

$$\begin{aligned} M \le N &\Rightarrow \forall k.\, M^{[k]} \le M \le N \\ &\Rightarrow \forall k.\, [\![M^{[k]}]\!] \sqsubseteq [\![N]\!] \\ &\Rightarrow [\![M]\!] \sqsubseteq [\![N]\!]. \end{aligned}$$

This establishes *1*; now *2* follows from *1* and theorems 3 and 4. □

6 Non-Deterministic Theories

The convertibility relations generated by $\longrightarrow_r$ $\longrightarrow_c$ are trivially inconsistent;indeed, in both cases:

$$\forall M, N \in \Lambda_\oplus.\ M \longleftarrow M \oplus N \longrightarrow N.$$

However, we have just seen that the equational theory

$$\mathcal{T} = \{M = N \mid M \simeq_{must} N\}$$

has a non trivial model, hence it is consistent. In [20] two extensions of the concept of λ-theory have been proposed: λ_r and λ_c.

Definition 14 *The theory* λ_r *is the equational theory over* $\Lambda_\oplus$ *whose axioms and rules are as follows*

(β_r) $(\lambda x.M)N = M[N/x]$;

(ρ) $M = M$;

(σ) $M = N \Rightarrow N = M$;

(τ) $M = N, N = L \Rightarrow M = L$;

(μ) $M = N \Rightarrow LM = LN$;

(ν) $M = N \Rightarrow ML = NL$;

(ξ) $M = N \Rightarrow \lambda x.M = \lambda x.N$;

(ζ_1) $M \oplus M = M$;

(ζ_2) $M \oplus N = N \oplus M$;

(ζ_3) $(M \oplus N) \oplus L = M \oplus (N \oplus L)$;

(ϵ) $M = N \Rightarrow M \oplus L = N \oplus L$;

(δ) $(M \oplus N)L = ML \oplus NL$;

The theory λ_c is obtained substituting axiom (β_r) by:

$$(\beta_c) \qquad (\lambda x.M)N = M[N/x] \quad \textit{if } N \in \Lambda,$$

and adding the axioms

(θ) $L(M \oplus N) = LM \oplus LN$;

(γ) $\lambda x.M \oplus N = \lambda x.M \oplus \lambda x.N$;

About the theory λ_c we claimed that it is nothing more than a calculus of finite sets of classical terms; more precisely, associating to each term the set of its deterministic behaviours modulo the relation $\longrightarrow_c$, we state the following theorem, whose proof is in [8]:

Theorem 5 *Define* $\mathsf{det}(M) = \{L \in \Lambda \mid M \stackrel{*}{\longrightarrow}_c L\}^+$, *where* $(\cdot)^+$ *means the closure under usual β-conversion, and put $M =_c N$ iff* $\mathsf{det}(M) = \mathsf{det}(N)$; *then, for any $M, N \in \Lambda_\oplus$*

$$\lambda_c \vdash M = N \Rightarrow M =_c N.$$

It follows that λ_c is a conservative extension of λ.

On the other hand, we can show that the theory $\mathcal{T}$ actually includes the theory λ_r, and it is consistent: hence λ_r is consistent too. The consistency of a subtheory of λ_r was established in [20] by orienting the equations from left to right and showing that the relation obtained in this way is Church-Rosser. However, it was not clear how this theory was related with the notion of *choice*. On the contrary $\mathcal{T}$ is strongly related to the reduction relation $\longrightarrow_r$ and its relation with λ_r is comparable to the relation between $\mathcal{H}^*$ and λ; therefore we can prove the consistency of the *full* theory λ_r from the consistency of $\mathcal{T}$. Furthermore $\mathcal{T}$ is a conservative extension of $\mathcal{H}^*$.

This is achieved by means of the following lemma, whose proof is in [8].

Lemma 4 *Let M, $N \in \Lambda_\oplus$. Then*

$$\exists D[\,] \in \Lambda_\oplus[\,].\ D[M]{\downarrow} \wedge D[N]{\uparrow} \Rightarrow \exists C[\,] \in \Lambda[\,].\ C[M]{\downarrow} \wedge C[N]{\uparrow}\,.$$

Concluding we have

Theorem 6 *Let $\mathcal{T} = \{M = N \mid M \simeq_{must} N\}$; then:*

1. *$\lambda_r \subseteq \mathcal{T}$,*

2. *$\mathcal{T}$ is a conservative extension of $\mathcal{H}^*$,*

3. *λ_r and $\mathcal{T}$ are consistent.*

Proof. To prove the first part, we use corollary 1 *2* and the fact that D_* is a model of λ_r. For the second part, let $M, N \in \Lambda$ be such that $\mathcal{T} \not\vdash M = N$; then there is a context $D[\,] \in \Lambda_\oplus[\,]$ such that, say, $D[M]\downarrow$ and $D[N]\uparrow$. By lemma 4, there is a context $C[\,] \in \Lambda[\,]$ such that $C[M]\downarrow$, that is $C[M] \in \mathbf{SOL}$, the set of solvable terms, and $C[N] \notin \mathbf{SOL}$; hence $\mathcal{H}^* \not\vdash M = N$. The third part follows from the first two and the consistency of $\mathcal{H}^*$ (or equivalently of $\mathcal{T}$). □

Acknowledgments

We are greatful to Corrado Böhm, Mariangiola Dezani-Ciancaglini, Gianfranco Mascari and Eugenio Moggi for helpful discussions and suggestions about the topics of this paper.

References

[1] S. Abramsky, C.H.L. Ong, *Full Abstraction in the Lazy Lambda Calculus*, Research Rep., Dept. of Comp., Imperial College 1989.

[2] E.A. Ashcroft, M.C.B. Hennessy, "A mathematical Semantics for a Nondeterministic Typed Lambda Calculus", *TCS* 11, 1980.

[3] E. Astesiano, G. Costa "Distributive Semantics for Nondeterministic Typed λ-calculi", *TCS* 32, 1984.

[4] H.P. Barendregt, *The Lambda-Calculus: Its Syntax and Semantics*, North-Holland, 1984.

[5] C. Böhm, "Alcune proprieta' delle forme β-η-normali nel λ-K-calcolo", Pubblicazioni dell' I.A.C. n. 696, Roma 1968.

[6] G. Boudol, "A Lambda Calculus for Parallel Functions", INRIA Preprint, 1990.

[7] M. Coppo, M. Dezani-Ciancaglini, S. Ronchi della Rocca, "(Semi)-separability of finite sets of terms in Scott's D_∞-models of the λ-calculus", *LNCS* 62, 1978.

[8] U. de'Liguoro, "Non deterministic untyped λ-calculus", Ph.D. Thesis, 1991.

[9] R. De Nicola, M.C.B. Hennessy, "Testing Equivalences for Processes", *TCS* 34, 1983.

[10] M.C.B. Hennessy, "The Semantics of Call-by-value and Call-by-name in a nondeterministic Environment", *SIAM J. Comput.* 9, 1980.

[11] M.C.B. Hennessy, G.D. Plotkin, "Full Abstraction for a Simple Parallel Programming Language", *LNCS* 74, 1979.

[12] J.R. Hindley, G. Longo, "Lambda Calculus Models and Extensionality", *Z. Math. Logik Grundlag. Math.* 26, 1980.

[13] M. Hyland, " A Syntactic Characterization of the Equality in some Models for the Lambda Calculus", *J. of the London Math. Soc.* 12, 1976.

[14] R. Jagadeesan, P. Panangaden, "A Domain-theoretic Model for a Higher-order Process Calculus", *LNCS* 443, 1990.

[15] R. Milner "Functions as Processes", *LNCS* 443, 1990.

[16] E. Moggi, "Notions of Computation and Monads", *Inf. Comp.* 93, 1991.

[17] J.H. Morris, *Lambda Calculus Models of Programming Languages*, Dissertation, M.I.T. 1968.

[18] G.D. Plotkin, "Call-by-name, Call-by-value and the λ-calculus", *TCS* 1, 1975.

[19] G.D. Plotkin, "A Powerdomain Construction", *SIAM J. of Comp.* 5, 1976.

[20] K. Sharma, *Syntactic Aspects of the Non-deterministic Lambda Calculus*, Master's thesis, Washington State University, September 1984. Available as internal report CS-84-127 of the Comp. Sci Dept.

[21] M.B. Smyth, "Power Domains", *J. Comp. Sys. Sci.* 16, 1978.

[22] B. Thomsen, "A Calculus of Higher-Order Communicating Systems", *ACM* 143, 1989.

[23] C.P. Wadsworth, " The relation between computational and denotational properties for Scott's D_∞-models of the lambda-calculus", *SIAM J. of Comp.* 5, 1976.

A PROGRAMMING LANGUAGE FOR DERIVING HYPERGRAPHS [1]

Andrea Maggiolo-Schettini
Dipartimento di Informatica
Università di Pisa
56100 Pisa, Corso Italia 40, Italy

Józef Winkowski
Institute of Computer Science
Polish Academy of Sciences
00-901 Warsaw, PKiN, P.O.Box 22, Poland

Abstract

Transformations of hypergraphs by applying rewriting rules are considered. An idea of programming such transformations and a suitable language with a denotational semantics is presented. It is shown that in this language one can program sequential and parallel processes of rewriting as particular cases.

1 Introduction

The theory of graph-grammars describes how to rewrite graphs according to formal rules called productions, where a rule says that a certain given shape can be replaced by another given shape if it occurs in a graph, and where graphs may be of very general types, including hypergraphs (cf. [CER 79], [ENR 83], [ENRR 87]). Within this theory there are two approaches: a sequential one in which productions are applied without any synchronization, one application after another, and a parallel one in which the possible applications are combined into global steps, each step executed synchronously. Each of these approaches has its own specific and cannot easily be compared with the other. Besides, new applications of graph rewriting methods can be found like that in the style of [CMREL 91] and [CRP 91] to logic programming, where graphs are transformed by applying some complexes of productions rather than single productions. This shows that there is a need of a uniform formalism for describing graph rewriting processes of various types. In this paper we develop a new approach to graph rewriting which is general enough to cover both the sequential and parallel rewriting as special cases and is flexible enough to allow an easy description of complex graph transformations. The essence of this approach relies on applying rewriting rules in a programmed manner. A simple idea of applying productions of a graph-grammar in an ordered manner was presented long ago by Bunke (cf. [B 79]). Some analogues of classical programming constructs were presented in [MW 83] with the intention of defining operations on relational data bases in terms of rewriting rules. Later some modified constructs of this type were studied as means of programming parallel operations on relational structures (cf. [MW 91]). An essential original feature of all these constructs was a possibility of passing data by a mechanism of parameters. However, the offerred proposals were illustrations of half-cooked ideas rather than real solutions. The present paper is an attempt of transforming all these ideas into a more mature formalism.

2 Productions and derivations

Hypergraphs, their morphisms, and rewriting rules (productions) are defined in the standard way.

2.1. Definition. Let C be a fixed set (of *colours*). A *hypergraph* over C is $G = (V, E, \sigma, \tau, \lambda)$, where

(1) V and E are disjoint sets (of *nodes* and *(hyper)edges*, resp.),

[1] This paper has been supported by Consiglio Nazionale delle Ricerche (G.N.I.M.) and by the Institute of Computer Science of the Polish Academy of Sciences

(2) $\sigma, \tau : E \longrightarrow V^*$ are mappings (the *source* and *target function*, resp.),

(3) $\lambda : V \cup E \longrightarrow C$ is a mapping (the *colouring* or *labelling function*).

We denote $V \cup E$ by S and use subscripts, S_G, V_G, E_G, σ_G, τ_G, λ_G, when necessary to avoid a confusion. □

2.2. Definition. A *morphism* from a hypergraph G to a hypergraph H is a triple of the form $f : G \longrightarrow H$, where f is a mapping from S_G to S_H such that $f(V_G) \subseteq V_H$, $f(E_G) \subseteq E_H$, $\sigma_H(f(e)) = f(u_1)...f(u_m)$ whenever $\sigma_G(e) = u_1...u_m$, $\tau_H(f(e)) = f(v_1)...f(v_n)$ whenever $\tau_H(e) = v_1...v_n$, and $\lambda_H(f(s)) = \lambda_G(s)$ for all $s \in S_G$. Sometimes we write such a morphism as $G \xrightarrow{f} H$. By $\mathbf{Hg}_C$ we denote the category of hypergraphs over C and their morphisms. □

It is known that the category $\mathbf{Hg}_C$ has pushouts and that they can be computed componentwise (as a pushout in the category of sets) for nodes and edges (cf. [CRP 91]).

2.3. Example. Let Σ be the many-sorted signature with sorts **word** and **boolean** and operation symbols L of arity **word** $\longrightarrow$ **boolean** and $\bullet$ of arity **word** $\times$ **word** $\longrightarrow$ **word**. Let $C = \{\mathbf{word}, \mathbf{boolean}, L, \bullet\}$. Then $G = (V, E, \sigma, \tau, \lambda)$, where $V = \{u, v, x, y, z\}$, $E = \{A, B, I, J\}$, $\sigma(A) = uv$, $\sigma(B) = vu$, $\sigma(I) = \tau(A) = x$, $\sigma(J) = \tau(B) = y$, $\tau(I) = \tau(J) = z$, $\lambda(u) = \lambda(v) = \lambda(x) = \lambda(y) = \mathbf{word}$, $\lambda(z) = \mathbf{boolean}$, $\lambda(A) = \lambda(B) = \bullet$, and $\lambda(I) = \lambda(J) = L$, is a hypergraph over C (cf. figure 1). Such a hypergraph can be used to represent, in a sense similar to that in [CMREL 91], the fact that a boolean variable z has a value which is the result of evaluating any of the terms $L(u \bullet v)$, $L(v \bullet u)$. □

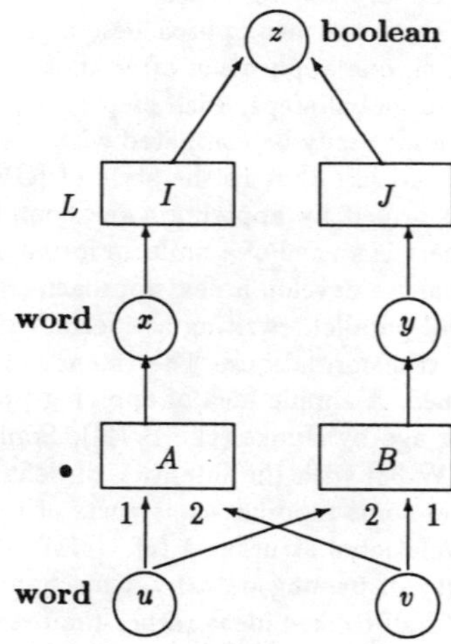

Figure 1

2.4. Definition. A *production* in $\mathbf{Hg}_C$ is a pair of morphisms in $\mathbf{Hg}_C$ of the form $p = (L \xleftarrow{m} K \xrightarrow{n} R)$. We use subscripts, L_p, K_p, R_p, m_p, n_p, when necessary, we call L_p and R_p the *left hand side (lhs)* and the *right hand side (rhs)* of p, respectively, and we call K_p the *gluing hypergraph* of p. □

2.5. Example. A rule for rewriting a concatenation $u \bullet v$ of two words to the concatenation $v \bullet u$ can be represented by a production as the one in figure 2. □

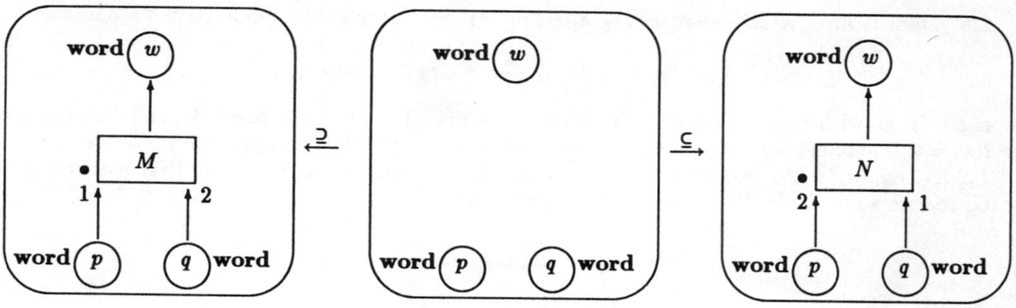

Figure 2

In order to be able to refer to elements (nodes and edges) of productions (which is necessary for enforcing such elements to denote the same objects in different applications of the respective productions) we introduce the concept of parametrized production.

2.6. Definition. Let Ω be a fixed set (of *parameters*). A *parametrized* production is

$$p = (L \xleftarrow{m} K \xrightarrow{n} R, l, r),$$

where $(L \xleftarrow{m} K \xrightarrow{n} R)$ is a production, $\mathbf{pr}_p$, and $l : S_L \longrightarrow \Omega$, $r : S_R \longrightarrow \Omega$ are mappings such that $l(m(x)) = r(n(x))$ for all $x \in S_K$. We use subscripts, L_p, K_p, R_p, m_p, n_p, l_p, r_p, when necessary, and we call l and r *occurrence mappings* of p. The latter ones declare elements (nodes and edges) of L and R to be occurrences of parameters from Ω (when such parameters are the respective images under l or r). By $\mathbf{par}_p$ we denote the set of parameters with occurrences in L or R. By $\mathbf{Pprod}_{C,\Omega}$ we denote the universe of parametrized productions. □

2.7. Example. If we want to declare M and N in the production in figure 2 as occurrences of a parameter Z and p,q,w as occurrences of parameters P,Q,R, respectively, then we choose the occurrence mappings given by $l(M) = r(M) = Z$, $l(p) = r(p) = P$, $l(q) = r(q) = Q$, $l(w) = r(w) = W$ (cf. figure 3). Note that the elements of the gluing part are not considered as occurrences of parameters. □

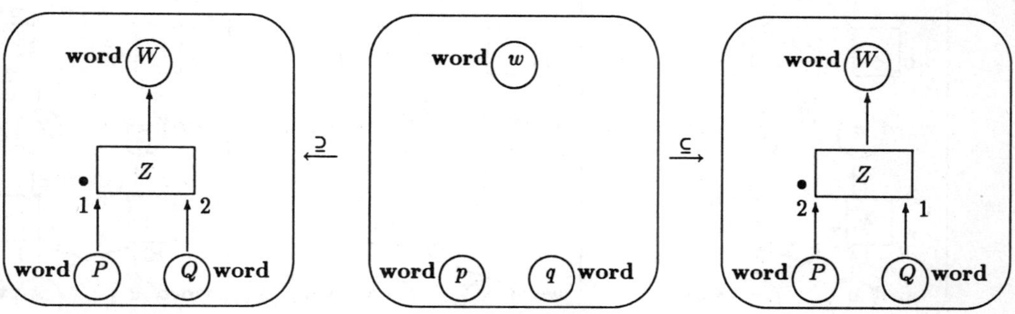

Figure 3

Derivability by applying parametrized productions is defined almost as for the usual productions.

2.8. Definition. A *derivation step* (a *direct derivation*) in $\mathbf{Hg}_C$ via a parametrized production

$$p = (L \xleftarrow{m} K \xrightarrow{n} R, l, r) \in \mathbf{Pprod}_{C,\Omega}$$

is $s = (p, I)$, where I is a diagram as in figure 4 such that (1) and (2) are pushouts, and, for all x, y in L, $l(x) = l(y)$ implies $g(x) = g(y)$, and, for all x, y in R, $r(x) = r(y)$ implies $h(x) = h(y)$. We use subscripts, L_s, K_s, R_s, m_s, n_s, l_s, r_s, G_s, D_s, H_s, g_s, d_s, h_s, b_s, c_s, when necessary, we say that s *derives* H from G, and we write $G \stackrel{s}{\Longrightarrow} H$ and denote p by $\mathbf{prod}_s$. □

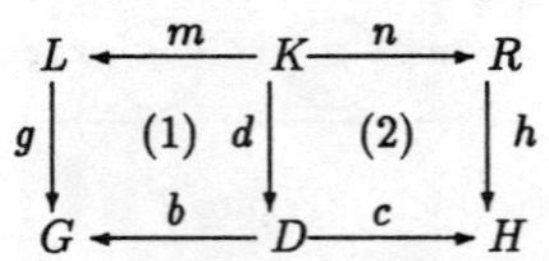

Figure 4

2.9. Example. In figure 5 we show a derivation step via the parametrized production in figure 3. This step derives a hypergraph from the one in figure 1. Note that the concept of a derivation step via a parametrized production differs from the usual concept of a derivation step since we require elements represented by a particular parameter to be identical wherever they occur. □

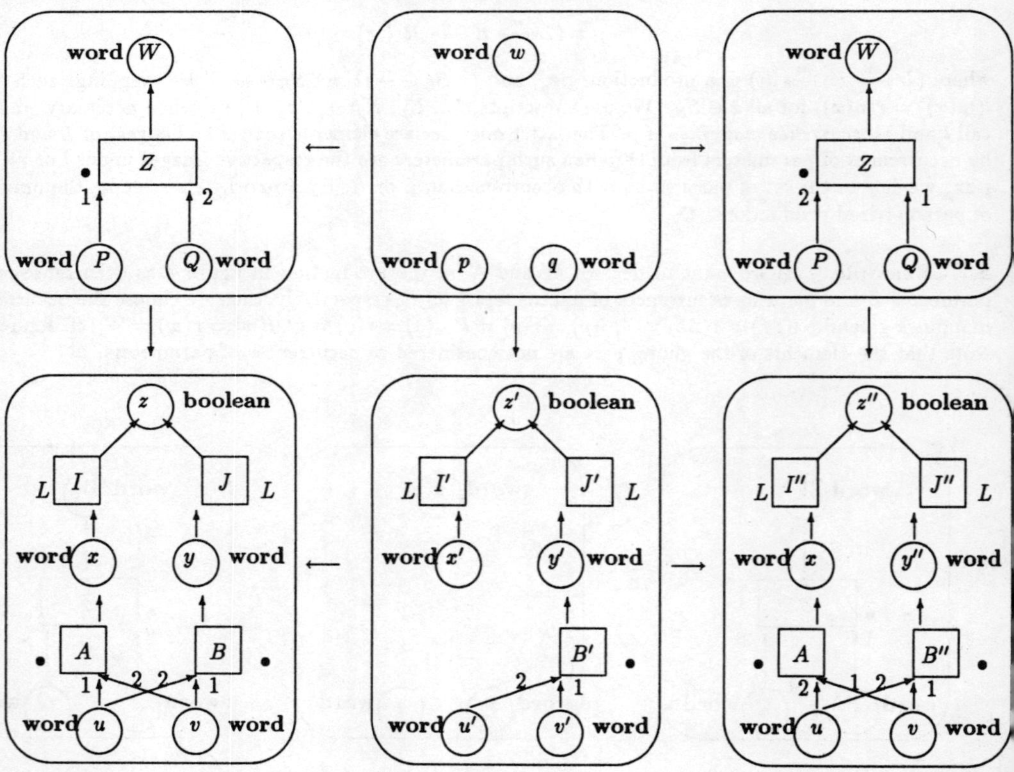

Figure 5

2.10. Definition. Given a set $\Pi \subseteq \mathbf{Pprod}_{C,\Omega}$ of parametrized productions, by a *derivation sequence* (a *derivation*) via productions from Π we mean a finite sequence $s = (G_0 \stackrel{s_1}{\Longrightarrow} G_1 \stackrel{s_2}{\Longrightarrow} G_2 \ldots \stackrel{s_i}{\Longrightarrow} G_i)$ of derivation steps via productions from Π. Given such a sequence s, we say that it *derives* G_i from G_0, write $G_0 \overset{s}{\Longrightarrow} G_i$, and denote G_0 and G_i by **source**(s) and **target**(s), respectively. The empty sequence, ε, is also considered to be a derivation. By $\mathbf{Der}_{C,\Omega,\Pi}$ we denote the universe of derivation sequences via productions from Π. □

2.11. Definition. Given two derivations $s = (G_0 \overset{s_1}{\Longrightarrow} G_1 ... \overset{s_i}{\Longrightarrow} G_i)$ and $t = (H_0 \overset{t_1}{\Longrightarrow} H_1 ... \overset{t_j}{\Longrightarrow} H_j)$ with **target**$(s) =$ **source**$(t) = G$, that is with $G_i = H_0 = G$, a *concatenation* of s and t, written as $s \bullet t$, is the derivation $(G_0 \overset{s_1}{\Longrightarrow} G_1 ... \overset{s_i}{\Longrightarrow} G \overset{t_1}{\Longrightarrow} H_1 ... \overset{t_j}{\Longrightarrow} H_j)$. Given two sets of derivations $A \subseteq \mathbf{Der}_{C,\Omega,\Pi}$ and $B \subseteq \mathbf{Der}_{C,\Omega,\Pi}$, a *concatenation* of A and B, written as $A \bullet B$, is the set $\{s \bullet t : s \in A \text{ and } t \in B\}$. Given a set A of derivations, a derivation $s \in A$ is said to be *terminal* in A iff in A there is no derivation of the form $s \bullet t$ with $t \neq \varepsilon$. Given two sets of derivations $A \subseteq \mathbf{Der}_{C,\Omega,\Pi}$ and $B \subseteq \mathbf{Der}_{C,\Omega,\Pi}$, a *terminal concatenation* of A and B, written as $A \odot B$, is the set $\{s \bullet t : s \text{ terminal in } A \text{ and } t \in B\}$. □

2.12. Definition. Given a set $A \subseteq \mathbf{Der}_{C,\Omega,\Pi}$ of derivations, the relation *represented* by A, written as **rel**(A), is the following binary relation between hypergraphs in $\mathbf{Hg}_C$:

$$(G, H) \in \mathbf{rel}(A) \text{ iff } G = \mathbf{source}(s) \text{ and } H = \mathbf{target}(s) \text{ for some } s \in A.$$

The relation represented by $\mathbf{Der}_{C,\Omega,\Pi}$ is called the *relation of derivability* via productions from Π. Given a set $A \subseteq \mathbf{Der}_{C,\Omega,\Pi}$ of derivations, the *terminal* relation represented by A, written as **trel**(A), is the following binary relation:

$$(G, H) \in \mathbf{trel}(A) \text{ iff } G = \mathbf{source}(s) \text{ and } H = \mathbf{target}(s) \text{ for some } s \text{ terminal in } A.$$

□

2.13. Proposition. The correspondences $A \longmapsto \mathbf{rel}(A)$ and $A \longmapsto \mathbf{trel}(A)$ enjoy the following properties:

(1) $\mathbf{rel}(\emptyset) = \mathbf{trel}(\emptyset) = \emptyset$,

(2) $\mathbf{rel}(\{\varepsilon\}) = \mathbf{trel}(\{\varepsilon\}) = \text{identity}$,

(3) $\mathbf{rel}(\bigcup(A_i : i \in I)) = \bigcup(\mathbf{rel}(A_i) : i \in I)$ and $\mathbf{trel}(\bigcup(A_i : i \in I)) \subseteq \bigcup(\mathbf{trel}(A_i) : i \in I)$,

(4) $\mathbf{rel}(A \bullet B) = \mathbf{rel}(A) \circ \mathbf{rel}(B)$ and $\mathbf{trel}(A \bullet B) \subseteq \mathbf{trel}(A) \circ \mathbf{trel}(B)$,

(5) $\mathbf{rel}(A \odot B) \subseteq \mathbf{rel}(A) \circ \mathbf{rel}(B)$ and $\mathbf{trel}(A \odot B) = \mathbf{trel}(A) \circ \mathbf{trel}(B)$,

where the symbol $\circ$ stands for the usual composition of binary relations. □

A proof is straightforward.

3 Programs

Derivations of hypergraphs can be obtained as executions of programs. Such programs, their executions, and resulting input-output relations can be defined as follows.

3.1. Definition. Given Ω (the set of parameters, or *object variables*), let Γ, where $\Gamma \cap \Omega = \emptyset$, be a fixed set (of *behaviour variables*). Let Δ, where $\Delta \cap \Omega = \emptyset$ and $\Delta \cap \Gamma = \emptyset$, be the set of expressions of the form $f(x_1, ..., x_m)$ (*program forms*), where f is a function symbol from a fixed set and $x_1, ..., x_m$ are elements of Ω. A *program* over C, Ω, Γ, Δ is an expression p with a set **fov**(p) of *free object variables* and a set **fbv**(p) of *free behaviour variables*, where p is constructed inductively as follows:

(1) $p = \mathbf{skip}$ and $\mathbf{fov}(p) = \mathbf{fbv}(p) = \emptyset$,

(2) p is a behaviour variable $X \in \Gamma$ and $\mathbf{fov}(p) = \emptyset$ and $\mathbf{fbv}(p) = \{X\}$,

(3) p is a parametrized production and $\mathbf{fov}(p) = \mathbf{par}_p$ and $\mathbf{fbv}(p) = \emptyset$,

(4) $p = \gamma q$ and $\mathbf{fov}(p) = \gamma(\mathbf{fov}(q))$ and $\mathbf{fbv}(p) = \gamma(\mathbf{fbv}(q))$ for a program q and a substitution γ of object variables or concrete objects for object variables,

(5) $p = q \vee r$ and $\mathbf{fov}(p) = \mathbf{fov}(q) \cup \mathbf{fov}(r)$ and $\mathbf{fbv}(p) = \mathbf{fbv}(q) \cup \mathbf{fbv}(r)$ for some programs q and r,

(6) $p = q; r$ and $\mathbf{fov}(p) = \mathbf{fov}(q) \cup \mathbf{fov}(r)$ and $\mathbf{fbv}(p) = \mathbf{fbv}(q) \cup \mathbf{fbv}(r)$ for a program q with $\mathbf{fbv}(q) = \emptyset$ and r being either a program with $\mathbf{fbv}(r) = \emptyset$ or a behaviour variable,

(7) $p = (\bigvee x)q$ and $\mathbf{fov}(p) = \mathbf{fov}(q) - \{x\}$ and $\mathbf{fbv}(p) = \mathbf{fbv}(q)$ for an object variable x and a program q,

(8) $p = (\mathbf{fix}X)q$ and $\mathbf{fov}(p) = \mathbf{fov}(q)$ and $\mathbf{fbv}(p) = \mathbf{fbv}(q) - \{X\}$ for a behaviour variable X and a program q,

(9) p is an expression of the form

$$\varphi_k(y_{k1}, y_{k2}, ...) \textbf{ where } (\varphi_1(y_{11}, y_{12}, ...) = \psi_1, ..., \varphi_n(y_{n1}, y_{n2}, ...) = \psi_n)$$

and $\mathbf{fov}(p) = \{y_{k1}, y_{k2}, ...\}$ and $\mathbf{fbv}(p) = \emptyset$ with all $\varphi_i(y_{i1}, y_{i2}, ...)$ being program forms, $k \in \{1, ..., n\}$, and all ψ_i being the results of applying to some programs of a substitution of expressions of the form $\varphi_j(\gamma(y_{j1}), \gamma(y_{j2}), ...)$ with γ as in (4) for behaviour variables, such that in each ψ_i occur only variables which are bounded or can be found among $y_{i1}, y_{i2}, ...$. □

The case (8) of this definition and the restriction in (6) on the possible occurrences of behaviour variables in programs lead to a sort of a repetition operator. Roughly speaking, $(\mathbf{fix}X)(p; X)$ defines a program which could be regarded as $p^\star$. The case (9) offers a possibility of writing programs involving a form of recursion. For example, **recolour**(x) **where** (**recolour**$(x) = (\bigvee y)(q(x, y);$ **recolour**$(y) \vee$ **skip**)) in 3.8 is a definition of a recursive program of recolouring properly nodes of a tree.

3.2. Definition. Let $\mathbf{Dersets}_{C,\Omega}$ be the set of sets of derivations via parametrized productions from $\mathbf{Pprod}_{C,\Omega}$. Let $\mathbf{Dval}_{C,\Omega,\Gamma}$ be the set of functions v (*valuations*), where each v consists of a mapping from Ω to the universe of elements (nodes and edges) of hypergraphs from $\mathbf{Hg}_C$ (the *object part* of v) and of a mapping from Γ to $\mathbf{Dersets}_{C,\Omega}$ (the *behaviour part* of v). The *meaning* of a program p over C, Ω, Γ, Δ is a function $[| p |]$ from $\mathbf{Dval}_{C,\Omega,\Gamma}$ to $\mathbf{Dersets}_{C,\Omega}$, where:

(1) $[| \mathbf{skip} |](v) = \{\varepsilon\}$ for each valuation v,

(2) $[| X |](v) = v(X)$ for each $X \in \Gamma$ and each valuation v,

(3) for each parametrized production $p \in \mathbf{Pprod}_{C,\Omega}$ and each valuation v, $[| p |](v)$ is the set of one-step derivations $G \stackrel{s}{\Longrightarrow} H$ with a derivation step s such that $\mathbf{prod}_s = p$, $g_s(x) = v(l_s(x))$ for all x in L_s and $h_s(y) = v(r_s(y))$ for all y in R_s (cf. 2.8),

(4) for each program q, each substitution γ as in (4) of 3.1, and each valuation v, $[| \gamma q |](v) = [| q |](w)$, where $w(x) = v(\gamma(x))$ for $\gamma(x) \in \Omega$ and $w(x) = \gamma(x)$ for $\gamma(x)$ being a concrete object,

(5) $[| q \vee r |](v) = [| q |](v) \cup [| r |](v)$ for all programs q, r and each valuation v,

(6) $[| q; r |](v) = [| q |](v) \bullet [| r |](v)$, the concatenation of $[| q |](v)$ and $[| r |](v)$, for all programs q, r and each valuation v,

(7) for each program q, each object variable (parameter) x, and each valuation v, $[| (\bigvee x)q |](v) = \bigcup([| q |](v_i) : i \in I)$, where I is the set of possible values of valuations for x and v_i is the valuation defined by $v_i(x) = i$ and $v_i(y) = v(y)$ for all $y \neq x$,

(8) for each program q, each behaviour variable X, and each valuation v, $[| (\mathbf{fix}X)q |](v)$ is the least set T of derivations such that $T = [| q |](v_T)$, where v_T is the valuation defined by $v_T(X) = T$ and $v_T(y) = v(y)$ for all $y \neq X$,

(9) for each program p as in (9) of 3.1 and each valuation v, $[| \, p \, |](v)$ is the component $X_{\varphi_k(b_{k1},b_{k2},...)}$ of the least solution of the system of fixed-point equations: $X_{\varphi_i(b_{i1},b_{i2},...)} = \overline{\psi_i}$, where $\overline{\psi_i}$ is the result of replacing in ψ_i each of the object variables $y_{i1}, y_{i2},...$ by $b_{i1} = v(y_{i1})$, $b_{i2} = v(y_{i2})$,..., respectively, and each form φ_j by $X_{\varphi_j(b_{j1},b_{j2},...)}$. □

3.3. Definition. Given a program p over C, Ω, Γ, Δ and a valuation v, the ***input-output relation*** of p for v, written as $[p](v)$, is

$$[p](v) = \mathbf{trel}([| \, p \, |](v)).\square$$

Due to this definition, correspondingly to the function $v \longmapsto [| \, p \, |](v)$, we have a function $v \longmapsto [p](v)$. Unfortunately, as the containment in (3) of 2.13 is in general proper, this function cannot be defined in a compositional way in the style of 3.2. This phenomenon is a consequence of the requirement of terminality of derivations of the first component of terminal concatenation of sets of derivations. On the other hand, such a requirement is necessary in order to guarantee the normal understanding of sequential composition of programs as prescribing execution of one after completing the other.

What we can prove about input-output relations of programs is stated in the following proposition.

3.4. Proposition. The input-output relations of programs over C, Ω, Γ, Δ enjoy the following properties:

(1) $[\mathbf{skip}](v) = $ identity for each valuation v,

(2) $[X](v) = \mathbf{trel}(v(X))$ for each $X \in \Gamma$ and each valuation v,

(3) for each parametrized production $p \in \mathbf{Pprod}_{C,\Omega}$ and each valuation v, $[p](v)$ is the set of pairs (G, H) such that $G \stackrel{s}{\Longrightarrow} H$ with a derivation step s such that $\mathbf{prod}_s = p$, $g_s(x) = v(l_s(x))$ for all x in L_s, and $h_s(y) = v(r_s(y))$ for all y in R_s,

(4) for each program q, each substitution γ as in (4) of 3.1, and each valuation v, $[\gamma q](v) = [q](w)$, where $w(x) = v(\gamma(x))$ for $\gamma(x) \in \Omega$ and $w(x) = \gamma(x)$ for $\gamma(x)$ being a concrete object,

(5) $[q \vee r](v) \subseteq [q](v) \cup [r](v)$ for all programs q, r and each valuation v,

(6) $[q; r](v) = [q](v) \odot [r](v)$, the terminal concatenation of $[q](v)$ and $[r](v)$, for all programs q, r and each valuation v,

(7) for each program q, each object variable (parameter) x, and each valuation v, $[(\bigvee x)q](v) \subseteq \bigcup([q](v_i) \, : \, i \in I)$, where I is the set of possible results of valuations for x and v_i is the valuation defined by $v_i(x) = i$ and $v_i(y) = v(y)$ for all $y \neq x$,

(8) for each program q, each behaviour variable X, and each valuation v, $[(\mathbf{fix}X)q](v)$ is contained in the least binary relation R such that $R = [q](v_R)$, where v_R is the valuation defined by $v_R(X) = R$ and $v_R(y) = v(y)$ for all $y \neq X$,

(9) for each program p as in (9) of 3.1 and each valuation v, $[p](v)$ is contained in the component $X_{\varphi_k(b_{k1},b_{k2},...)}$ of the least solution of the system of fixed-point equations: $X_{\varphi_i(b_{i1},b_{i2},...)} = \tilde{\psi}_i$, where $\tilde{\psi}_i$ is the result of replacing in ψ_i each of the object variables $y_{i1}, y_{i2},...$ by $b_{i1} = v(y_{i1})$, $b_{i2} = v(y_{i2})$,..., respectively, and each form φ_j by $X_{\varphi_j(b_{j1},b_{j2},...)}$. □

A proof by induction on the structure of programs follows from 2.13.

The sequential derivability of hypergraphs is a particular case of a programmed derivability in the sense given by the following theorem.

3.5. Theorem. Let C' be a subset of C. Let $\Pi = \{p_1, ..., p_m\}$ be a finite set of finite parametrized productions in $\mathbf{Pprod}_{C',\Omega}$ (that is of productions p_i with finite L_{p_i}, K_{p_i}, R_{p_i}). There is a program p

without free variables such that, for each valuation v, $[| p |](v)$ is the set of derivations via productions from Π, that is

$$[| p |](v) = \mathbf{Der}_{C,\Omega,\Pi},$$

and $[p](v)$ is the relation of derivability via productions from Π, that is

$$[p](v) = \mathbf{rel}(\mathbf{Der}_{C,\Omega,\Pi}).\Box$$

Proof outline.

The idea is: (1) to transform the given hypergraph to an intermediate form in which to each node an edge is attached having the node as target and empty source, and carrying the colour of the node; this can be done by applying suitable productions, say $q_1, ..., q_i$; (2) to change the colour of each edge from c to $\mathbf{new}(c)$, where c is the original colour (we assume that C is large enough to admit a mapping $\mathbf{new} : C' \longrightarrow C$ such that C' does not contain any colour of the form $\mathbf{new}(c)$); this can be done by suitable productions, say $r_1, ..., r_j$; (3) to modify original productions $p_1, ..., p_m$ $\bar{p_1}, ..., \bar{p_m}$ by replacing the colour of each node, say c, by $\mathbf{new}(c)$, and to introduce special productions $s_1, ..., s_k$ which recolour edges to old colours and delete special edges added in (1); (4) to apply $\bar{p_1}, ..., \bar{p_m}, s_1, ..., s_k$ as long as possible.

The corresponding program can be defined as:

$$\begin{aligned} P \;=\; & (\mathbf{fix}X)(((\bigvee x_1)...(\bigvee x_n))(q_1 \vee ... \vee q_i)); X \vee \mathbf{skip}); \\ & (\mathbf{fix}X)(((\bigvee x_1)...(\bigvee x_n))(r_1 \vee ... \vee r_j)); X \vee \mathbf{skip}); \\ & (\mathbf{fix}X)(((\bigvee x_1)...(\bigvee x_n))(\bar{p}_1 \vee ... \vee \bar{p}_m \vee s_1, ..., s_k)); X \vee \mathbf{skip}), \end{aligned}$$

where $\{x_1, ..., x_n\} = \mathbf{par}_{q_1} \cup ... \cup \mathbf{par}_{r_1} \cup ... \cup \mathbf{par}_{\bar{p}_1} \cup ... \cup \mathbf{par}_{s_1} \cup ....\Box$

A simple (context-free) form of parallel derivability can be introduced as follows.

3.6. Definition. Let C' be a subset of C. Let Π be a finite set of parametrized productions p in $\mathbf{Pprod}_{C',\Omega}$ such that L_p is a one-edge hypergraph, K_p is a hypergraph without edges, and R_p is finite. A *parallel (context-free) derivation step* via productions from Π is a finite set S of derivation steps in the sense of 2.8 via productions from Π such that:

(1) g_s and h_s are surjective for all $s \in S$,

(1) the (componentwise) unions $G = \bigcup(G_s : s \in S)$ and $H = \bigcup(H_s : s \in S)$ are hypergraphs in $\mathbf{Hg}_{C'}$.

We say that such a step *derives* H from G, written as $G \overset{S}{\Longrightarrow}_{\mathbf{par}} H$. The relation defined by

$(G, H) \in \mathbf{parstep}_\Pi$ iff $G \overset{S}{\Longrightarrow}_{\mathbf{par}} H$ for some parallel derivation step via productions from Π

is called the relation of *parallel derivability in one step* via productions from Π. $\Box$

The parallel derivability as in 3.7 is a particular case of programmed derivability in the sense give by the following theorem.

3.7. Theorem For $C' \subseteq C$ as in the definition of parallel derivability let $\mathbf{Finhg}_{C'}$ be the universe of finite hypergraphs in $\mathbf{Hg}_{C'}$. Let Π be a set of parametrized productions in $\mathbf{Pprod}_{C',\Omega}$ as in the definition of parallel derivability. There is a program q without free variables such that, for each valuation v, the restriction of the relation $[q](v)$ to $\mathbf{Finhg}_{C'}$ is precisely the relation of parallel derivability in one step via productions from Π, that is

$$(\mathbf{Finhg}_{C'})^2 \cap [q](v) = \mathbf{parstep}_\Pi.\Box$$

Proof outline.

The idea is: (1) to replace each production p by a production $\bar{p}$ which colours each newly introduced element not with the specified colour c but with a colour $\mathbf{in}(c)$; (2) to apply the obtained productions as long as possible; (3) to define and apply special productions recolouring elements with colours of the form $\mathbf{in}(c)$ to c.

Let $\mathbf{in} : C' \longrightarrow C$ be an injective mapping such that C' does not contain any colour of the form $\mathbf{in}(c)$ (also here we assume that C is large enough to admit such a mapping).

For each $p \in \Pi$ we define a parametrized production $\bar{p}$, where $L_{\bar{p}} = L_p$, $K_{\bar{p}} = K_p$, $R_{\bar{p}} = \bar{G}$, $m_{\bar{p}} = m_p$, $n_{\bar{p}} = n_p$, $l_{\bar{p}} = l_p$, and $r_{\bar{p}} = r_p$, with $\bar{G}$ obtained from $G = R_p$ by changing the colour of each element y which is not of the form $n_p(x)$ for some x in K_p from $\lambda_G(y)$ to $\mathbf{in}(\lambda_G(y))$.

Next, for each element x of $R_{\bar{p}}$ with a colour of the form $\mathbf{in}(c)$ we construct a parametrized production r, written as $\varphi(p, x)$, where L_r is the least hypergraph contained in $R_{\bar{p}}$ which contains all y such that there is a sequence $x = x_0, x_1, ..., x_n, x_{n+1} = y$ with all x_i, x_{i+1} adjacent (that is one being a source or a target of the other) and $x = x_0, x_1, ..., x_n$ having colours of the form $\mathbf{in}(c)$, K_r is the hypergraph contained in L_r and consisting of those elements of L_r which have colours not of the form $\mathbf{in}(c)$ (such elements can be characterized as those of the form $n_p(z)$ for some z in K_p), R_r is the hypergraph obtained from L_r by recolouring each element with a colour of the form $\mathbf{in}(c)$ from $\mathbf{in}(c)$ to c, m_r and n_r are the respective inclusions, and the parametrization is as in $\bar{p}$.

Finally, a program as required can be defined as

$$\begin{aligned} Q \;=\;& (\mathbf{fix}X)(((\bigvee x_1)...(\bigvee x_n))(\bar{p}_1 \vee ... \vee \bar{p}_m)); X \vee \mathbf{skip}); \\ & (\mathbf{fix}X)(((\bigvee x_1)...(\bigvee x_n))(r_1 \vee ... \vee r_k)); X \vee \mathbf{skip}) \end{aligned}$$

where $\{p_1, ..., p_m\} = \Pi$, $\{x_1, ..., x_n\} = \mathbf{par}_{p_1} \cup ... \cup \mathbf{par}_{p_m}$, and $\{r_1, ..., r_k\}$ is the set of productions of the form $\varphi(p, x)$. □

The programs simulating sequential and parallel derivability are very simple and engage only simple mechanisms of our language. However, programs of this kind may be very inefficient because the applications of productions in their executions require full search for the possible loci of application and do not exploit knowledge gained from the previous applications.

The mechanism of parameters allows to program derivations in a more efficient manner. We illustrate it in the following example.

3.8. Example. Suppose that we have a tree with edges of a colour α and nodes of two possible colours β and γ, and that we want to recolour to γ all descendants of nodes with colour γ. In order to avoid technical problems with recolouring nodes which we need as gluing elements, we give the original colour of each node to a special edge having the respective node as target and empty source, and we give the node itself a conventional colour δ (see figure 6).

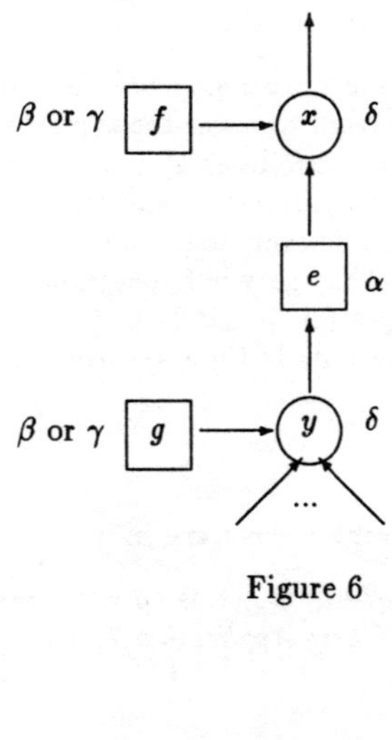

Figure 6

A program to solve the task can be defined as:

$$(\mathbf{fix}X)((\bigvee x)(\bigvee y)(\bigvee e)(\bigvee f)(\bigvee g)p_{\gamma\beta}(x,y,e,f,g);\ X \vee \mathbf{skip}),$$

where $p_{\gamma\beta}(x,y,e,f,g)$ is a parametrized production recolouring the special edge g of a son node y of a father node x from β to γ if the special edge f of x carries the colour γ (see fig.7).

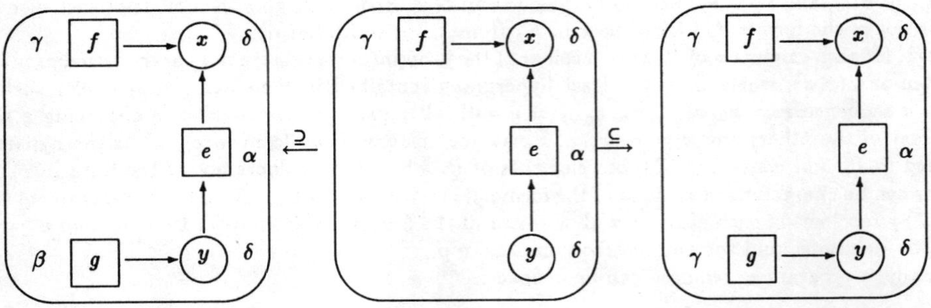

Figure 7

In this program productions apply to the hypergraph in an arbitrary order, each application being a result of a search for a possible locus of application. We may avoid such an arbitrariness by organizing the applications along the paths of the represented tree from root to leaves. A suitable program can be defined as:

$$(\mathbf{fix}X)(\mathbf{recolour}(x)\ \mathbf{where}(\mathbf{recolour}(x){=}\ (\bigvee y)(q(x,y);\mathbf{recolour}(y) \vee \mathbf{skip}));X \vee \mathbf{skip}),$$

where

$$q(x,y) = (\bigvee e)(\bigvee f)(\bigvee g)(p_{\beta\beta}(x,y,e,f,g) \vee p_{\beta\gamma}(x,y,e,f,g) \vee p_{\gamma\beta}(x,y,e,f,g) \vee p_{\gamma\gamma}(x,y,e,f,g))$$

with $p_{\gamma\beta}(x,y,e,f,g)$ as described before, and $p_{\beta\beta}(x,y,e,f,g)$, $p_{\beta\gamma}(x,y,e,f,g)$, $p_{\gamma\gamma}(x,y,e,f,g)$ being the identity productions like $p_{\gamma\beta}(x,y,e,f,g)$ except for the colours of f and g.

In this case terminal derivations consist of consecutive applications of productions $p_{ij}(x,y,e,f,g)$ along the possible paths of the represented tree.

4 Final remarks

We have presented conceptual means for programming processes of deriving hypergraphs by applying productions. These means are flexible enough to cover the typical modes of derivability: the sequential one, and the parallel one. However, their possibilities go much beyond such particular cases due to the powerful mechanisms of communication via parameters and recursion. It is not the aim of this paper to study such possibilities in detail. We would like only to point out that the approach can easily be modified such that it applies not only to the general category of hypergraphs, but to some particular subcategories of this category like the category of jungles (cf. [CRP 91]). To this end it suffices to consider only such derivations the pushouts of which are pushouts in the respective subcategory.

References

[B 79] Bunke, H., *Programmed Graph Grammars*, in [CER 79]

[CER 79] Claus, V., Ehrig, H., Rozenberg, G., (Eds.) *Proceedings of the 1st International Workshop on Graph-Grammars and Their Application to Computer Science and Biology*, Springer LNCS 73, 1979

[CRP 91] Corradini, A., Rossi, F., Parisi-Presicce, F., *Logic Programming as Hypergraph Rewriting*, to appear in the Proceedings of CAAP 91

[EKR 91] Ehrig, H., Kreowski, H.-J., Rozenberg, G., (Eds.) *Proceedings of the 4th International Workshop on Graph-Grammars and Their Application to Computer Science*, to appear in Springer LNCS

[CMREL 91] Corradini, A., Montanari, U., Rossi, F., Ehrig, H., Löwe, M., *Logic Programming and Graph Grammars*, to appear in [EKR 91].

[ENRR 87] Ehrig, H., Nagl, M., Rozenberg, G., Rosenfeld, A., (Eds.) *Proceedings of the 3rd Workshop on Graph-Grammars and Their Application to Computer Science*, Springer LNCS 291, 1987

[MW 83] Maggiolo-Schettini, A., Winkowski, J., *Towards a Programming Language for Manipulating Relational Data Bases*, in: Bjorner, D., (Ed.), Formal Description of Programming Concepts II, North-Holland, 1983

[MW 91] Maggiolo-Schettini, A., Winkowski, J., *Programmed Derivations of Relational Structures*, to appear in [EKR 91]

Graph Grammars as Context-Dependent Rewriting Systems: A Partial Ordering Semantics*

Ugo Montanari and Francesca Rossi

University of Pisa
Computer Science Department
Corso Italia 40, 56100 Pisa, Italy
{ugo,rossi}@dipisa.di.unipi.it

Abstract

Context-dependent rewriting systems allow a higher degree of concurrency w.r.t. context-independent ones, since rewriting rules which apply in intersecting contexts and rewrite different items may be applied concurrently, while this cannot happen with a context-independent specification of the same rules. Context-dependent systems can also be seen as a natural generalization of read/write systems, where several readers of the same items may proceed in parallel. However, all the partial ordering semantics which have been given in the past apply, as far as we know, to context-independent systems. In this paper, instead, we investigate the possibility of giving a partial ordering semantics to graph grammars, which can be seen as elegant and general context-dependent rewriting systems. We accomplish that by associating a deterministic occurrence Petri net to each graph derivation. From such a net, then, a partial ordering relating the applied productions, and expressing the causal dependencies among them, can be obtained. The set of all such partial orderings is then the semantics of the given grammar. We also compare our approach with the classical one for concurrency in graph grammars, and we show that, given a derivation, they generate the same dependencies, although our approach is more abstract than the classical one.

1 Introduction

The possibility of expressing in a formal way the causal dependencies among events of a dynamic system, and thus the fact that some transitions may occur concurrently because they involve independent objects, is of both practical and theoretical interest ([1,5]). Furthermore, when the considered dynamic system is context-sensitive, then such a concurrency analysis is even more interesting and convenient.

Note that throughout this paper by *context-sensitive* (or context-dependent) we mean that a rewrite rule cancels some items and generates some other items only in the presence of a third set of items, called the context (of course the set of items to be cancelled must be present as well). The alternative is that a rewrite rule be *context-independent*, which means that the application of the rule is only dependent on the presence of the set of items to be cancelled.

To see how the context-dependence of the rewriting system can be exploited to gain in concurrency, consider two rewrite rules which rewrite different objects under the presence of the same context. Then they intuitively are not dependent on each other, in the sense that if that context is present, then both of them can be applied at the same time. However, if we can only specify context-independent transitions, then the same two rules now appear to delete objects in common (which are later recreated), and thus they have to be applied sequentially. In other words, context-independent systems may specify only the deletion and the creation of objects, but not the test for their presence. Therefore, it is obvious that context-sensitive rewriting systems allow a higher degree of concurrency than context-independent ones, and thus many

*Research partially supported by the GRAGRA Basic Research Esprit Working Group n.3299 and by Alenia S.p.A.

redundant dependencies, which cannot be avoided in the context-independent specification, are instead not present in the corresponding context-dependent formalization. As far as we know, nobody has defined a partial ordering semantics for a context-dependent formalism. This is what we plan to do in this paper, where we consider graph grammars ([4]) as general and powerful context-dependent rewriting systems.

A graph production rewrites a graph, say L (the left hand side), into another graph, say R (the right hand side), by identifying a certain subgraph, say K, of both L and R. This kind of operation can easily be assimilated to a context-dependent rewrite rule, where $L - K$ is what is being cancelled, $R - K$ is what is being created, and K is the context, i.e. all those objects which have to be present in order for the rule to be applicable but which are not affected by such application. Thus a graph grammar, which consists of a set of graph productions, can be thought of as a context-dependent rewriting system. Therefore, as we noted above for general context-dependent rewriting systems, graph productions whose left hand sides are disjoint but whose contexts intersect may be applied concurrently and therefore they should not be considered to depend on each other.

Note that all graph grammars are context-dependent (in our interpretation of the term), even those that are called *context-free* because (see [6]) their productions rewrite only one arc at a time. In fact, even a production where L contains only one arc (and the connected nodes) can have some items in K (even that same arc in L).

In this paper we propose a semantics for graph grammars which expresses the causal dependencies among productions, and where the above intuitive considerations are matched (i.e., no pair of productions which intersect only in contexts are found to be dependent). The idea is to associate a partial ordering to each graph derivation (i.e., to each sequence of production applications). Such partial ordering relates the production instances (called events) used in the given derivation in such a way that two events are related when the corresponding production applications are dependent on each other. This partial ordering is obtained in two steps: first a non-deterministic occurrence net [14] (where also nodes and arcs, besides events, are present) is obtained from the derivation through an original construction, and then the partial order is straightforwardly obtained from the net by projecting the causal relation of the net over the set of events (i.e., arcs and nodes are "forgotten"). The set of all different partial orderings corresponding to the derivations possible in the given grammar is then the partial ordering semantics of the grammar. In this setting, different derivations which have the same partial ordering are not distinguishable, even though they may involve different production applications which however relate to each other in the same way.

An approach where an observation, in the form of a partial order, is associated to each computation of the considered transition (or rewriting) system, was followed also in [2]. Actually, our formal construction of the occurrence net from each graph derivation reminds the one in [2]. However, in that paper the partial order was obtained directly, and not through the occurrence net. Also, our construction is different in the fundamental way that it exploits the presence of contexts to reduce the causal dependencies.

The issue of concurrency in graph grammars was considered in the fundamental work by Ehrig ([4]), where pairs of production applications were said to be "sequential independent" whenever they intersect only in their contexts. Given a derivation, our approach derives the same dependency information. On the other hand, while derivations which are considered to be equivalent in this framework are also equivalent in ours, i.e. they have the same partial ordering, the opposite is not true. Thus the classical approach is at a more concrete level than ours. An advantage of our approach is that we provide a unique structure (the partial ordering) for each derivation, which explicitely represents all the causal dependencies between the events. In the classical approach, a similar role is played by classes of equivalent derivations and by their standard representatives, called *canonical* derivations. However, no causal dependencies are made explicit in such constructions except for *pairs* of (sequentially dependent) production applications. In some sense, we are able to look at the concurrency in the grammar from a more global level, i.e., the derivation instead of the production level. This goes in the line of being able, eventually, to associate a unique structure (some kind of event structure ([16])) to the whole grammar, which is what we plan to investigate in the near future.

The paper is organized as follows. In Section 2 we give a brief formal definition of graph grammars, then in Section 3 we propose our construction to obtain a deterministic occurrence net from each graph derivation, and in Section 4 we compare our approach for a true-concurrency semantics of graph grammars to the classical one. Section 5 concludes the paper summarizing its results and pointing out some possible future extensions of the proposed approach.

2 (Hyper)Graph Grammars

In this section we will give a brief introduction to graph grammars. In doing that, we will use the classical algebraic approach to define both productions and production applications ([4]). Intuitively, graph grammars can be seen as generalizations of string grammars, where productions rewrite (sub)graphs instead of (sub)strings. Graphs consist of sets of nodes and sets of arcs, where each arc connects two nodes. Hypergraphs are even more general than graphs, since hyperarcs may connect any number of nodes. All the results in this paper hold for hypergraphs and hypergraph grammars, but many times we will call them graphs and graph grammars respectively for simplicity.

Definition 1 ((hyper)graph) *A (hyper)graph $G = (N, A, c, l)$ labelled on $L = (L_N, L_A)$ consists of*

- *a set of nodes N,*
- *a set of (hyper)arcs A,*
- *a connection function $c : A \rightarrow \cup_k N^k$, and*
- *a labelling function $l = (l_N, l_A)$ such that $l_N : N \rightarrow L_N$ and $l_A : A \rightarrow L_A$.*

Given a graph G, we will sometimes write $\mid G \mid$ to denote the set of its nodes and of its (hyper)arcs, i.e., $\mid G \mid = N \cup A$.∎

The connection function returns, for each arc, the ordered set of nodes connected by it, while the labelling function labels each node and each arc with an element from a given set L_N and L_A respectively.

The different setting in which graphs are considered (instead of strings) introduces some complications when defining productions and their applications, since, while it is easy to specify how a string is embedded into another string, this same concept is not so easy for graphs. To solve this problem, the concept of an "interface" or "embedding" graph has been introduced.

Definition 2 (graph production) *A graph production p is a pair of graph morphisms $l : K \rightarrow L$ and $r : K \rightarrow R$, such that both l and r are injective. L, R, and K are called left side, right side, and interface of p, respectively. In the following we will write $p = (L \stackrel{l}{\leftarrow} K \stackrel{r}{\rightarrow} R)$.*∎

In the above definition, given two graphs G and H, a graph morphism f from G to H, written $f : G \rightarrow H$, consists of a pair of functions, mapping nodes and arcs repectively, which are compatible with the connection and labelling functions. Intuitively, a graph production $p = (L \stackrel{l}{\leftarrow} K \stackrel{r}{\rightarrow} R)$ rewrites graph L into graph R, but the subgraph K of L, while being necessary for the application of the production, is not deleted from L and thus will be in R as well. In a view of graph grammars as context-dependent rewriting systems, we may consider a graph production p as a rewriting rule which rewrites $L - l(K)$ into $R - r(K)$ provided that the context $l(K)$ is present.

Definition 3 (direct derivation) *Given a production $p = (L \stackrel{l}{\leftarrow} K \stackrel{r}{\rightarrow} R)$, a graph G, and a graph morphism $g : L \rightarrow G$, called an* occurrence *of L in G, there exists a direct derivation from G to G' iff the diagram in Figure 1 can be built, where both squares are pushouts. In the following we will represent a double pushout construction by the tuple of all the objects involved, i.e., we will write: $PO = \langle p, g, k, h, h_1, h_2, G, H, G' \rangle$, where $p = (L \stackrel{l}{\leftarrow} K \stackrel{r}{\rightarrow} R)$ and the names correspond to those in Figure 1.*∎

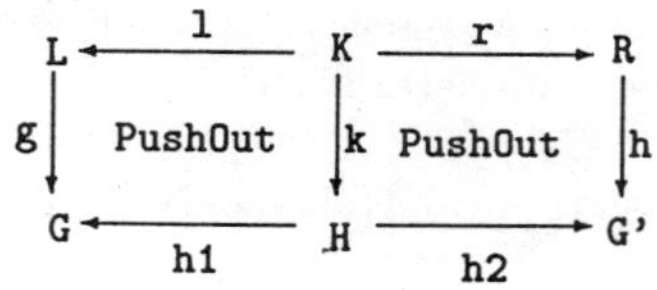

Figure 1: The double pushout construction.

The formal definition of a pushout can be found in [8]. However, we may informally describe the application of a production p to G as follows: in the pushout to the left, the occurrence of L in G identified by g is removed (except for the image of K in L) to produce H; in the pushout to the right, G' is built as the disjoint union of R and H, where the nodes and arcs in $r(K)$ and in $k(K)$ are identified. Thus, while K represents the part of G which is tested but remains unchanged (i.e. the nodes and the arcs which are not deleted), $H - k(K)$ represents the part of G which is not involved at all in the rewriting.

Definition 4 (graph rewriting systems and derivations) *A graph rewriting system $GG = (G_0, PP, V)$ consists of an initial graph G_0, a set of productions PP, and an alphabet V, such that both G_0 and all graphs in the productions in PP are labelled over V. A derivation (of length n) for GG is a finite sequence of double pushout constructions $(PO_1, PO_2, \ldots, PO_n)$, where $PO_i =< p_i, g_i, k_i, h_i, h_{i1}, h_{i2}, G_{i-1}, H_i, G_i >$ (and $p_i = (L_i \stackrel{l_i}{\leftarrow} K_i \stackrel{r_i}{\rightarrow} R_i)$ is in PP), thus such that PO_i is a direct derivation from G_{i-1} to G_i, for $i = 1, \ldots, n$.* ∎

Graph grammars are usually defined as graph rewriting systems where a subset of the alphabet V is considered to be terminal, and the language of the grammar is then the set of all graphs, labelled over the terminal alphabet, which can be derived from the initial graph by using the productions of the grammar. However, being the choice of such terminal alphabet not significant for our purposes, for simplicity in the following of this paper we will always consider graph rewriting systems, and not graph grammars. It is straightforward to see that all our results hold for graph grammars as well without any change. Thus we warn the reader that we may sometimes informally talk about graph grammars when instead the formal treatment deals with graph rewriting systems.

3 A Partial Ordering Semantics

A classical way to give a semantics for a graph rewriting system is to consider the set of all graphs which can be generated by starting from the initial graph and applying the productions. This choice, although it has many convenient uses, does not give any knowledge about the possible parallelism degree in the derivations, even though such information is implicitely contained in them. Since we are instead interested in this kind of information, we propose to associate a suitable deterministic occurrence net (which is the simplest kind of Petri net) to each derivation. This occurrence net relates nodes, arcs, and production applications and represents the causal dependencies among such objects. Then, from such a net, different partial orderings can automatically be derived, depending on what we want to observe. Thus, in this setting, the semantics of a graph rewriting system is a set of partial orderings, which are those induced by the occurrence nets corresponding to all the possible derivations in the graph rewriting system. We will now formally explain how to obtain such a set of partial orderings from a given graph rewriting system.

Note that the formal treatment of the following subsections is an extension of the one presented in [10], where a partial ordering semantics for concurrent constraint programs ([15]) was proposed. Here, we extend it from the class of graph grammars which are sufficient for representing concurrent constraint programs (which is a small subset of the class of all graph grammars) to that of all graph grammars. The extension is not trivial, since the graph grammars corresponding to concurrent constraint programs are such that objects which are tested but not consumed by some production are never deleted. This allows for the simpler treatment of causal dependencies presented in [10].

3.1 Petri Nets, Occurrence Nets, and Related Notions

For a formal and comprehensive treatment of Petri nets and occurrence nets see [14]. Here we will only give the definitions necessary for the rest of the paper.

Definition 5 ((Petri) nets) *A net N is a triple (S,T,F) where*

- *S and T are nonintersecting sets;*
- *$F \subseteq (S \times T) \cup (T \times S)$, called the causal dependency relation (or the flow relation).*■

Definition 6 (pre-set and post-set) *Given a net $N = (S,T,F)$ and an element $x \in S \cup T$, its pre-set if the set $^\bullet x = \{y \mid F(y,x)\}$, and its post-set is the set $x^\bullet = \{y \mid F(x,y)\}$.*■

A traditional interpretation of a net is the following: the elements of S are considered as being "places" or "conditions", and the elements of T are instead "transitions" or "events". A set of conditions, called *case*, represents the global state of the net. If a case c *enables* a transition t, i.e., $^\bullet t \subseteq c$, then *firing* t brings the net from case c to case $(c - {}^\bullet t) \cup t^\bullet$[1]. Note that, by the definition of F, there is no possibility to relate two events or two conditions, but only one event and one condition, or viceversa. This refers to the classical interpretation of nets, which, assuming to move upon a continue time domain, associates a closed interval to each event and an open one to each condition. In this way, a computation is a sequence of closed and open intervals, where two open (or closed) intervals are never adjacent.

Definition 7 ((deterministic) occurrence nets) *A net $N = (S,T,F)$ is an* occurrence *net iff*

- *F^+ (i.e., the transitive closure of F) is irreflexive;*
- *$\forall s \in S$, $\mid {}^\bullet s \mid \leq 1$ and $\mid s^\bullet \mid \leq 1$.*■

That is, an occurrence net is a Petri net without cycles and such that each event can be enabled by (and can enable) at most one condition. That is, an occurrence net can be seen as the unfolding of a Petri net computation, where every choice has already been done.

Theorem 8 (from occurrence nets to partial orderings ([14])) *Given an occurrence net $N = (S,T,F$ then $P(N) = (T,(F^*)_{|T})$, where $(F^*)_{|T}$ is the reflexive and transitive closure of F restricted to T, is a partial ordering.*■

The construction of this partial ordering which relates only events is very common in concurrency theory, since it is important to know when two or more events are independent from each other, and thus can occur concurrently. Intuitively, two different events are considered to be concurrent if none of them causes the other one. The formal definition follows.

Definition 9 (concurrent events) *Given a partial ordering $P(N) = (T,\leq)$, two distinct events e and e' in T are said to be concurrent iff neither $e \leq e'$ nor $e' \leq e$ holds.*■

---

[1]However, if $(c - {}^\bullet t) \cap t^\bullet \neq \emptyset$, then usually t is not considered to be enabled (it is said that we are in a *contact* situation).

3.2 From Derivations to Occurrence Nets

Now that we have given all the necessary notions about occurrence nets and the corresponding partial orderings, we describe how to obtain an occurrence net from each derivation.

Definition 10 (from derivations to occurrence nets) *Given a finite derivation $D = (PO_1, PO_2, \ldots, PO_n)$, where $PO_i =< p_i, g_i, k_i, h_i, h_{i1}, h_{i2}, G_{i-1}, H_i, G_i >$ and $p_i = (L_i \overset{l_i}{\leftarrow} K_i \overset{r_i}{\rightarrow} R_i)$, for $i = 1, \ldots, n$, let us set $E = \{e_1, \ldots, e_n\}$, $B = \{< a, i >, a \in| G_i |\}$, for $i = 0, \ldots, n$, $C_l = \{[\![a, i-1], a \in| K_i |\}$, and $C_r = \{[a, i]\!], a \in| K_i |\}$, where $< x, y >$, $[\![x, y]$ and $[x, y]\!]$ are different pair constructors. Then, let us define the relation F by using the following inference rules (where $i = 1, \ldots, n$ and $\equiv$ is an equivalence relation):*

- $a \in| H_i |$, $a \not\in| k_i(K_i) |$ **implies** $< h_{i1}(a), i-1 > \equiv < h_{i2}(a), i >$;
- $a \in| L_i |$, $a \not\in| l_i(K_i) |$ **implies** $< g_i(a), i-1 > Fe_i$;
- $a \in| K_i |$ **implies**
  - $< h_{i1}(k_i(a)), i-1 > \equiv < h_{i2}(k_i(a)), i >$;
  - $[\![a, i-1]Fe_i$;
  - $e_iF[a, i]\!]$;
  - $bF < h_{i1}(k_i(a)), i-1 >$ **implies** $bF[\![a, i-1]$;
  - $< h_{i2}(k_i(a)), i > Fb$ **implies** $[a, i]\!]Fb$;
- $a \in| R_i |$, $a \not\in| r_i(K_i) |$ **implies** $e_iF < h_i(a), i >$;
- $a \equiv b$ **implies**
  - cFa **implies** cFb;
  - aFc **implies** bFc.

Then, the occurrence net associated to D is $N(D) = (B_{|\equiv} \cup C_l \cup C_r, E, F)$.■

First we will explain informally the above definition, and then we will show that $N(D)$ is indeed an occurrence net.

The above definition describes relation F, which can be interpreted as a causal dependency relation among the arcs and the nodes involved in a derivation and the events representing the applications of the productions. More precisely, the intuitive understanding of aFb is that b depends on a, or, alternatively, that a causes b. However, there are different kinds of elements (nodes and arcs) in a graph which is being rewritten by the application of a production:

- those which are not involved in the production (i.e, all the arcs and nodes a such that $a \in| H_i |$ and $a \not\in| k_i(K_i) |$),
- those which are consumed by the production ($a \in| L_i |$ but $a \not\in| l_i(K_i) |$),
- those which are checked for presence but not consumed ($a \in| K_i |$), and
- those which are generated by the production ($a \in| R_i |$ and $a \not\in r_i(K_i) |$).

Each of these kinds of elements interacts in a different way with the event associated to the applied production. This is the reason why the above definition has one item for each of these four kinds of elements.

The first item ("$a \in| H_i |$, $a \not\in| k_i(K_i) |$ implies $< h_{i1}(a), i-1 > \equiv < h_{i2}(a), i >$") simply states that all those elements of G_{i-1} which are not involved in the application of the production should be identified with the corresponding arcs and nodes of G_i. This means that such elements do not generate any dependency with the event e_i and/or the other elements involved in the production application. Note that, as the last item says, the identification of two elements implies that each of them inherits the dependencies of the other one.

The second item ("$a \in | L_i |$, $a \notin | l_i(K_i) |$ implies $< g_i(a), i-1 > Fe_i$") generates a dependency of the event e_i on all those elements in the left hand side ($a \in | L_i |$) which are consumed by the production ($a \notin | l_i(K_i) |$). In fact, these elements are necessary in order to apply such a production.

The third item concerns all those elements which are checked for presence by the production but are not consumed (since they appear in K_i, and thus they also have to appear both in L_i and in R_i). Intuitively, these elements are necessary for the application of the production (and thus e_i should be dependent on them), but at the same time they should be maintained in G_i (and thus there should be corresponding elements in G_i which are identified with those in G_{i-1}). The identification is accomplished by "$< h_{i1}(k_i(a)), i-1 > \equiv < h_{i2}(k_i(a)), i >$". To model the dependency of the event e_i on such elements, but not on the events which already used them, we consider a fresh copy of the element, called $[a, i-1]$, and we set $[a, i-1]Fe_i$. Such copies are related to the corresponding original by the fact that they depend on the same elements, which is accomplished by "$bF < h_{i1}(k_i(a)), i-1 >$ implies $bF[a, i-1]$". Since event e_i does not consume these items, but later events can, e_i is set to cause an additional copy, written $[a, i]$, of the original element (by "$e_iF[a, i]$"). Copies of the form $[a, i]$ are set to cause the same elements which are caused by their originals (by "$< h_{i2}(k_i(a)), i > Fb$ implies $[a, i]Fb$"). Intuitively, the copies, both of form $[a, i-1]$ and $[a, i]$, represent the particular instance of the element $h_{i1}(k_i(a))$ which is tested but not consumed by the production. Thus we have one original, but as many (pairs of) copies of it as the number of productions testing such an element.

The fourth item ("$a \in | R_i |$, $a \notin | r_i(K_i) |$ implies $e_iF < h_i(a), i >$") means that the event e_i causes all those elements which are in G_i but were not in G_{i-1}. In fact, the presence of such elements in G_i is only due to the application of the production corresponding to e_i.

It is important to notice that the construction of the relation F described by the above definition is really *incremental*. In fact, suppose to have a derivation of length n. Then, after considering the first i steps, we already know all the causal dependencies among elements (arcs, nodes, and events) appearing in such steps, in the sense that no later step can add dependencies involving only elements in previous steps.

Theorem 11 ($N(D)$ is an occurrence net) *Given a finite derivation D, $N(D)$ is an occurrence net.*

Proof: By looking at Definition 10, it is easy to see that $(B_{|\equiv} \cup C) \cap E = \emptyset$, where $C = C_l \cup C_r$, and that $F \subseteq ((B_{|\equiv} \cup C) \times E) \cup (E \times (B_{|\equiv} \cup C))$. Thus $N(D)$ is a net. In order it to be an occurrence net, by Definition 7, we have to prove that F^+ is irreflexive, and also that $\forall s \in (B_{|\equiv} \cup C)$, $| {}^\bullet s | \leq 1$ and $| s^\bullet | \leq 1$.

Proving that F^+ is irreflexive means showing that there is no pair of distinct elements a and b in $(B_{|\equiv} \cup C)$ such that both aF^+b and bF^+a hold. In a topological view of the set $(B_{|\equiv} \cup C)$, elements of the form $< a, i >$ or $[a, i]$ or $[a, i]$ can be considered to be at level i and events e_i can be considered to be between level $i-1$ and level i. Then we will show that, given two elements a and b such that a is in a level with index higher than, or equal to, that of b, aF^+b cannot hold. This is obviously enough to ensure the not-reflexivity of the relation F^+. We will prove the above by induction on the length of the derivation.

As a base case, consider a derivation of length 1. That is, only one production is applied. Then we have only one event, e_1, which is set to depend only on elements of level 0 (by the second and third inference rule) and to cause only elements of level 1 (by the third and fourth rule). Note that propagation of dependencies from original elements to copies (last two items in the third inference rule) does not apply in the case of a single production, as well as the propagation due to the equivalence relation (last inference rule). Thus no element of level 1 is set to cause any element of level 0.

Assume now that that the relation F^+ built in the first $k-1$ steps of a derivation is irreflexive. Then we will show that step k will maintain F irreflexive, that is, that no element in level k will be set to cause any element in any of the levels from 1 to $k-1$. Event e_k is set to depend on elements of level $k-1$ (second inference rule and second item of third inference rule), and to cause elements of level k (third item of third inference rule and fourth rule). Then we have to consider the last two items of the third inference rule, which propagate, both upwards and downwards, the dependencies between the copies and the originals of the elements which are tested but not consumed by the production applied in step k. The first of such items possibly sets elements of level $k-1$ (which are copies of the form $[a, k-1]$) to be caused by elements in levels with lower indexes, while the second one possibly sets elements of level i, with $i \leq k$, to cause elements just created (i.e., elements b of level k). Let us now consider two elements a and b which are set to be equivalent (i.e., $a \equiv b$) by the first or third rule. If a is in level i and b is in level k with $i < k$, and some other rule sets another element c in a level between i and k to cause b (i.e., cFb), then we would also have cFa (by the last rule), which could create problems since c causes an element at a level with lower index. However, it is possible to see that the assumption we started from (that is, $\exists c$ such that cFb) can never occur. In fact, if $a \equiv b$, then one case is that b and a are not involved in the production applications from level i to level k (first inference rule), and thus no event corresponding to any of such applications is ever set to cause b. The other possibility is that they are used but not consumed by some of the productions (third rule). But then, the events corresponding to such productions are set to cause, and to be caused by, the *copies* of a and b and thus do not involve a and b themselves. Similar considerations can convince of the fact that the situation where $a \equiv b$ and $\exists c$ (with c "between" a and b) such that aFc (which implies bFc) can never occur as well. Thus none of the elements of level k is ever set to cause any element of level i with any $i < k$, thereby maintaining F irreflexive.■

We can extract many kinds of information from the above occurrence net $N(D)$. The approach that we will adopt in the rest of this paper is to consider only the events and to forget the nodes and the arcs (and their copies as well). That is, we will consider the partial ordering induced by $N(D)$, i.e., $(E, (F^*)_{|E})$. The following corollary, which follows directly from Theorem 8, states that $(E, (F^*)_{|E})$ is a partial ordering.

Corollary 12 (derivations and associated partial orderings) *Given a finite derivation D and the corresponding occurrence net $N(D) = (B_{|\equiv} \cup C_l \cup C_r, E, F)$, $P(N(D)) = (E, (F^*)_{|E})$ is a partial ordering.*■

In the construction given in Definition 10, both arcs, nodes, and production applications which are involved in the given derivation are related by relation F in order to express their causal dependencies. However, sometimes nodes can be "forgotten" while not loosing any dependency among the events representing the production applications. More precisely, this holds whenever the left hand sides of the productions used in a derivation do not contain isolated nodes. Note that this case is not very restrictive, since in a natural interpretation of graphs in terms of distributed systems, where nodes are channels or variables and arcs are processes, it does not make any sense to have a channel which is not shared by any process. However, our construction of Definition 10 applies to the general case, and thus nodes are taken into consideration as well. The following theorem states formally the result about the possibility of not constructing the node dependencies.

Theorem 13 (sufficiency of arc dependencies) *Given a finite derivation $D = (PO_1, PO_2, \ldots, PO_n)$, where $PO_i = < p_i, g_i, k_i, h_i, h_{i1}, h_{i2}, G_{i-1}, H_i, G_i >$ and $p_i = (L_i \overset{l_i}{\leftarrow} K_i \overset{r_i}{\rightarrow} R_i)$, assume that, for all $i = 1, \ldots, n$, L_i does not contain any isolated node. Let us also call $N'(D)$ the occurrence net which is obtained by using Definition 10 with the interpretation that $\mid G_i \mid$ is the set of all* arcs *of G_i. Then we have that $P(N(D)) = P(N'(D))$.*

Proof: In order for a node x to cause directly an event, say e_i, it must be deleted or tested by production p_i. But since there are no isolated nodes in L_i, there must be an arc a connected to x which is either tested or deleted by p_i. It is easy to see that a must transmit, possibly among others, the same causal links that x would do.■

Example:

Let us now consider a simple example of a derivation and of the corresponding occurrence net and induced partial ordering. Suppose we have two productions, whose graphical description can be seen in Figures 2 and 3. In these pictures, nodes are represented by circles and arcs by lines between the connected nodes, and the graph morphisms are not explicitely drawn but are suggested by the spatial positions of arcs and nodes (i.e., a morphism from G to H maps each element of G into the element of H which has the same position). Neither nodes nor arcs are labeled and arcs are directed from left to right and from top to bottom.

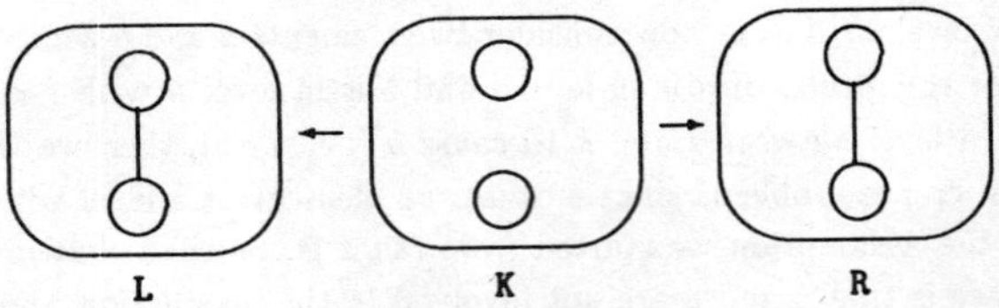

Figure 2: Production p_1.

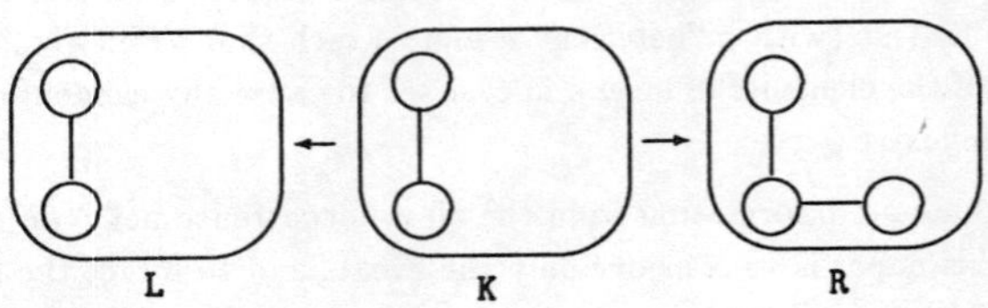

Figure 3: Production p_2.

The derivation we consider consists of the application of production p_1 first, then of p_2, then of p_2 again, and then of p_1. The initial graph contains only one arc connecting two nodes. The graphical representation of the derivation, i.e. of the sequence of double pushouts, can be seen in Figure 4. In this figure, a name is given to each node and arc in every graph, so to use these names for the construction of the occurrence net. Note that different graphs may have elements with the same name (this being not significant), but different elements within the same graph must have a different name.

Since none of p_1 and p_2 has isolated nodes in its left hand side, we will only consider the arcs involved in the derivation while constructing the occurrence net. For the given derivation, we have $E = \{e_1, e_2, e_3, e_4\}$ (i.e., one event for each production application) and the initial graph G_0 consists of the only arc $< a, 0 >$. We recall that the first element of such pairs is the name of the arc, as in Figure 4, while the second element, say i, is the index of the graph G_i which it belongs to. The resulting F relation can be seen in Figure 5, where an arc between objects a and b is intended to mean aFb if a is above b in the picture, and a double arc between a and b stands for $a \equiv b$. The picture is drawn such that, for all $i = 0, \ldots, 4$, all arcs in $| G_i |$ are at the same level. Dependencies inherited via identifications (i.e. via the last rule in Def. 10) are not drawn.

In Figure 5, it is easy to see that the final graph G_4 contains three arcs, which are a, b, and c. Also, event e_4 depends on $[a, 2]$ and on $[a, 3]$, and thus, by closing transitively, on the events e_1, e_2, and e_3. Event e_3, instead, as well as event e_2, depends only on event e_1. Thus events e_2 and e_3 do not depend on each other, even though they both use (but without consuming) the arc generated by e_1. Thus e_2 and e_3 can be considered to be independent, and thus the two applications of production p_2 may be applied concurrently. These informal considerations are formalized in the occurrence net corresponding to the derivation and in the associated partial ordering. Such an occurrence net associated to the above derivation can be seen in Figure 6. As usual in (Petri) nets, places are drawn as circles and transitions as boxes.

The Hasse diagram of the associated partial ordering $(E, (F^*)_{|E})$ is depicted in Figure 7, where it is immediate to see that events e_2 and e_3 are concurrent.∎

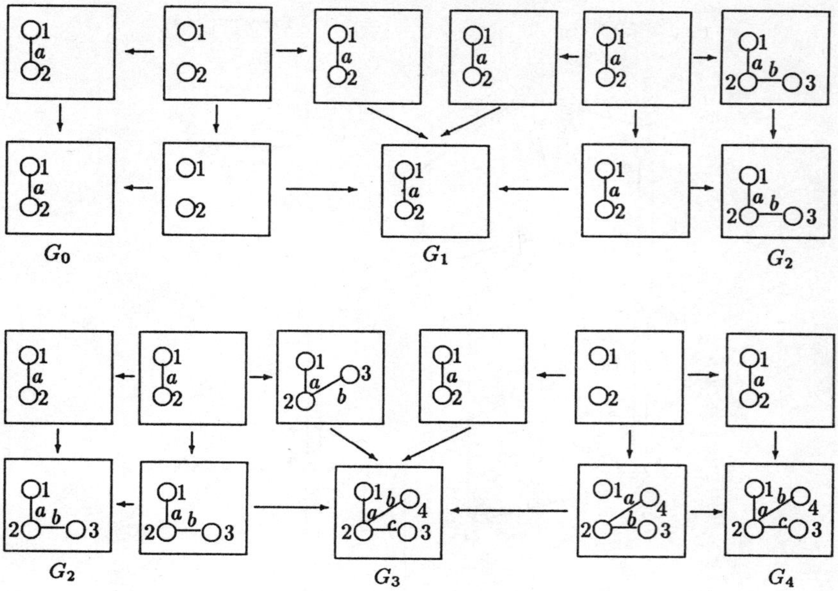

Figure 4: A derivation.

We will now give some notions which will be useful in the next section, where we will compare the causal information obtained in our approach and that obtained in the classical approach to concurrency in graph grammars.

Definition 14 (generation ordering) *Given a (finite) derivation $D = (PO_1, \ldots, PO_n)$, and the associated partial ordering on events $P(N(D)) = (E, \sqsubseteq)$, where $E = \{e_1, \ldots, e_n\}$, its generation ordering is the total ordering $O(D) = (E, \leq)$ on the events in E where $e_i \leq e_j$ if $i \leq j$.*■

Definition 15 (compatibility of total and partial orderings) *Given a total ordering $O = (S, \leq)$ and a partial ordering on the same set $P = (S, \sqsubseteq)$, we say that O is compatible with P whenever $\sqsubseteq$ (as a set) $\subseteq$ $\leq$ (as a set).*■

Theorem 16 (compatibility of generation and partial orderings) *Given a derivation D, consider its associated partial ordering $P(N(D)) = (E, \sqsubseteq)$ and its generation ordering $O(D) = (E, \leq)$. Then we have that $O(D)$ is compatible with $P(N(D))$, i.e., $\sqsubseteq \subseteq \leq$.*

Proof: It is enough to notice that $\leq$ contains exactly all the pairs of the form $< e_i, e_j >$ where $i \leq j$, and that $\sqsubseteq$ cannot contain pairs of the form $< e_i, e_j >$ where $j < i$ (by Definition 10). Thus $\sqsubseteq$ is either smaller than or equal to $\leq$.■

4 Partial Ordering Semantics vs. Parallel and Sequential Independence

The partial ordering defined in Section 3 gives a way to relate the productions applied during a derivation and thus to understand which productions can be applied concurrently. In the classical algebraic description of graph grammars ([4]), this same understanding is obtained through the concepts of parallel and sequential

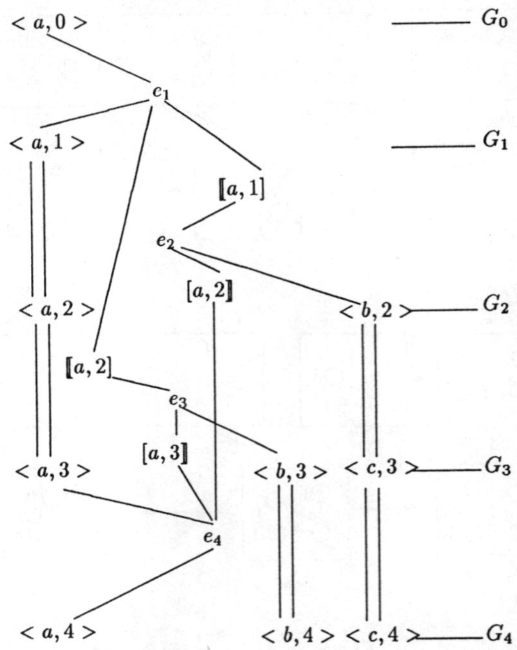

Figure 5: The F relation.

independence. We will now briefly review such notions and then compare the two approaches. This study is an extension of a similar work on a particular class of graph grammars, which was proposed in [11].

In words, two direct derivation steps starting from the same graph are parallel independent if the left hand sides of the corresponding productions intersect only on objects which are not consumed by the productions. In fact, this implies that none of the two productions deletes from the graph something that the other production needs for being applied. The formal definition follows.

Definition 17 (parallel independence, [4]) *Given two productions $p = (L \overset{l}{\leftarrow} K \overset{r}{\rightarrow} R)$ and $p' = (L' \overset{l'}{\leftarrow} K' \overset{r'}{\rightarrow} R')$, two direct derivations, from G to H via p and g, and from G to H' via p' and g' are parallel independent if $g(L) \cap g'(L') = g(l(K)) \cap g'(l'(K'))$.* ■

On the other side, two consecutive direct derivation steps are sequential independent if the left hand side of the second production and the right hand side of the first one intersect only on elements which are maintained by the two productions, i.e. checked for existence but not consumed nor generated. In fact, this assures that the application of the two productions can always be exchanged, since no item needed by the first one is deleted by the second one, and no item needed by the second one is generated by the first one.

Definition 18 (sequential independence, [4]) *Given two productions $p = (L \overset{l}{\leftarrow} K \overset{r}{\rightarrow} R)$ and $p' = (L' \overset{l'}{\leftarrow} K' \overset{r'}{\rightarrow} R')$, two direct derivations, from G to H via p and g, and from H to X via p' and g' are sequential independent if $h(R) \cap g'(L') = h(r(K)) \cap g'(l'(K'))$.* ■

As the intuition tells us, the concepts of parallel and sequential independence are very much related to each other. This relation can be formalized in the following theorems, which informally say that

- if the applications of productions p and p' on a certain graph are parallel independent, then p' can always be applied after p and viceversa and in this case their applications are sequential independent;

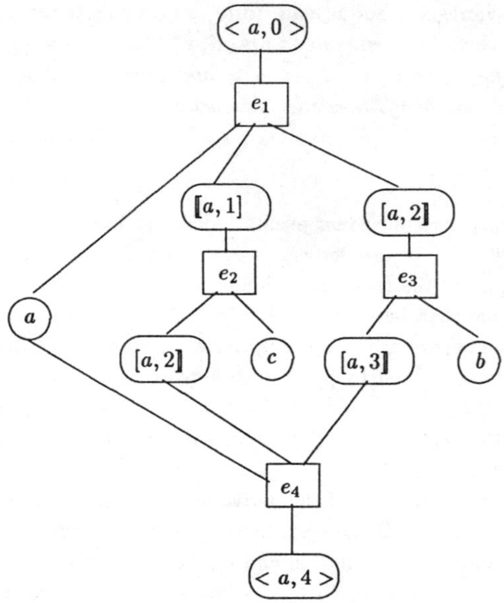

Figure 6: The occurrence net.

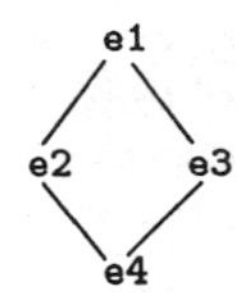

Figure 7: The partial ordering relating events.

- if p can be applied to G returning G' and p' can be applied to G', and such applications are sequential independent, then both p and p' can be applied to G with parallel independent applications.

Theorem 19 (from parallel to sequential independence, [4]) *Given two productions p and p', assume that the two direct derivations, from G to H via p, and from G to H' via p' are parallel independent. Then there is a graph X and two direct derivation steps, from H to X via p', and from H' to X via p, such that the direct derivation steps from G to H via p and from H to X via p' are sequential independent, as well as the direct derivation steps from G to H' via p' and from H' to X via p.*■

Theorem 20 (from sequential to parallel independence, [4]) *Given two productions p and p', assume that the two direct derivations, from G to H via p, and from H to X via p' are sequential independent. Then, there exists two direct derivation steps, from G to H' via p' and from H' to X via p, and they are sequential independent as well. Moreover, the two direct derivation steps, from G to H via p and from G to H' via p' are parallel independent.*■

We will now show that the dependency information which can be obtained by using the above concepts of parallel and sequential independence can also be obtained by the partial ordering associated to derivations as described in the previous section. In particular, we will show that whenever two consecutive events are concurrent, the corresponding derivation steps are sequential independent, and thus may be executed in any order or even concurrently.

Theorem 21 (concurrent events vs. sequential independence) *Given a (finite) derivation* $D = (PO_1, \ldots, PO_n)$, *and the associated partial ordering on events* (E, F^*), *where* $E = \{e_1, \ldots, e_n\}$, *consider two consecutive events* e_i *and* e_{i+1}, *for some* $i = 1, \ldots, n-1$, *and assume that* p_i, g_i, p_{i+1}, *and* g_{i+1} *are the productions and the occurrence morphisms respectively associated to them. Then,* e_i *and* e_{i+1} *are concurrent if and only if the two direct derivation steps, from* G_{i-1} *to* G_i *via* p_i *and* g_i, *and from* G_i *to* G_{i+1} *via* p_{i+1} *and* g_{i+1}, *are sequential independent.*

Proof: Assume that e_i and e_{i+1} are concurrent events. Then, by Definition 9, $e_iF^*e_{i+1}$ cannot hold. We have to prove that steps i and $i+1$ of the derivation are sequential independent, i.e., that the left hand side of (the occurrence of) p_{i+1} and the right hand side of (the occurrence of) p_i intersect, if they do, only on not-consumed items. Assume then by contradiction that the left hand side of (the occurrence of) p_{i+1} and the right hand side of (the occurrence of) p_i do intersect also on some items which are consumed by p_{i+1} (obviously they cannot be consumed by p_i, since otherwise they couldn't be in the left hand side of p_{i+1}). Let us call a one of such objects. Then, by the second inference rule in Definition 10, we would have aF^*e_{i+1}. Now, the only way that e_iF^*a could hold is that a is generated by p_i (see fourth rule) but then the assumption is contradicted.

Let us now assume that steps i and $i+1$ of the derivation are sequential independent, which, we recall, means that the left hand side of p_{i+1} and the right hand side of p_i intersect only on not-consumed items. We will prove then, again by contradiction, that e_i and e_{i+1} are concurrent events. Assume that $e_iF^*e_{i+1}$. Then there must be an object a such that $e_iF^*aF^*e_{i+1}$ holds, since no direct dependency among events is generated by any of the inference rules in Definition 10. Suppose a is not in C. Then, the only possibility for e_iF^*a to hold is that the fourth inference rule is applied, i.e. that a is in the right hand side of p_i without being in its left hand side. This is not possible in the assumption above. If a is one of the copies in C_l, then it means that we have aF^*e_{i+1} (by the third rule) and that a is not consumed by p_{i+1}. Now, the only way that e_iF^*a could hold is that a is newly generated by p_i, which again contradicts the assumption of being not consumed both by p_i and p_{i+1}. If instead a is an element of C_r, then e_iF^*a holds if a is not consumed by p_i (third rule). But aF^*e_{i+1} holds only if p_{i+1} consumes a, which contradicts the assumption.∎

Thus, according to Theorem 20 we can exchange two concurrent events. In terms of derivations, this means that whenever we have a derivation with two concurrent events, we can obtain another derivation of the same graph where the two concurrent events are reverted.

Definition 22 (equivalence of derivations) *Given a derivation* $D_1 = (PO_1, \ldots, PO_n)$, *assume that for some* $i = 1, \ldots, n-1$, PO_i *and* PO_{i+1} *correspond to two sequential independent applications of productions. Then consider the derivation* $D_2 = (PO_1, \ldots, PO_{i-1}, PO_{i+1}, PO_i, \ldots, PO'_n)$. *We will write* $D_1 \Leftrightarrow D_2$. *Let* $\sim = \Leftrightarrow^*$ *be the transitive closure of the relation* $\Leftrightarrow$. *Whenever* $D_1 \sim D_2$, *derivations* D_1 *and* D_2 *are called equivalent (in the sense of [4]).*∎

In terms of the above definition, intuitively Theorem 21 means that concurrency in our framework and sequential independence in graph grammars coincide when we consider equivalent derivations differing only for two consecutive concurrent events. Now we will extend this result to equivalent derivations with any number of concurrent events, thus proving that the partial ordering approach gives exactly the same dependency information as the usual approach to concurrency in graph grammar.

More precisely, our main result can be stated as follows. Given a derivation D, its generation ordering $O(D)$ is compatible with its partial ordering $P(N(D))$ (and thus also with the partial ordering of any derivation D' equivalent to D, since equivalent derivations induce the same partial ordering). And viceversa, any total ordering (on the same set of events) which is compatible with $P(N(D))$ is a generation ordering for some derivation D' equivalent to D. The following theorem proves such a result, and its proof follows the proof of a similar theorem in [3].

Theorem 23 (equivalence of derivations vs. partial ordering) *In a grammar G, consider a derivation D, the associated partial ordering $P(N(D)) \doteq (E, \sqsubseteq)$, and the generation ordering $O(D) = (E, \leq)$. Then*

- *two equivalent derivations have isomorphic associated partial orderings. In symbols: $D \sim D'$ implies $P(N(D)) = P(N(D'))$ (up to isomorphism);*
- *the generation ordering $O(D') = (E, \leq')$ of any derivation D' equivalent to D is compatible with the partial ordering $P(N(D))$. In symbols: $D \sim D'$ implies $\sqsubseteq \subseteq \leq'$;*
- *for any total ordering $\leq''$ on E compatible with $P(N(D))$, there is a derivation D' equivalent to D such that $O(D') = (E, \leq'')$. In symbols, $\sqsubseteq \subseteq \leq''$ implies $\exists D'$, $D \sim D'$, $\leq' = \leq''$.*

Proof: The first two parts are trivial, due to Theorem 21, Definition 22, and Theorem 16.

Consider now a total ordering O on E which is compatible with $P(N(D))$. Then, we have to show that there exists a derivation D' equivalent to D with $O(N(D')) = O$. Take any derivation D_1 equivalent to D. We will construct a sequence $(D_1, D_2, \ldots)$ of derivations equivalent to D, as follows. Assume D_i is a derivation equivalent to D and having $O(D_i) = O_i$ as generation ordering. If $O_i = O$, then $D' = D_i$ and thus the required computation is found. Otherwise, assume that $O = (e_1, \ldots, e_n)$ and that instead $O_i = (e_1, \ldots, e_{j-1}, e'_j, \ldots, e'_{l-1}, e_j, \ldots, e'_n)$. D_i is equivalent to D by assumption, thus e'_{l-1} and e_j must be concurrent, since they appear exchanged in O and O_i. Then there is a derivation D_{i+1} equivalent to D with generation ordering $O_{i+1} = (e_1, \ldots, e_{j-1}, e'_j, \ldots, e'_{l-2}, e_j, e'_{l-1}, \ldots, e'_n)$. By performing $l - j$ exchanges as the above one, we can thus obtain a derivation D_{i+l-j} whose generation ordering has e_j in place j (as in O). By repeating this same exchange as many times as necessary, we may thus obtain the desired derivation D' with generation ordering O.■

Thus we have proved that, given a graph derivation, the dependency information which can be obtained from the classical approach and from our approach coincide. We also have to say that in the usual approach to concurrency in graph grammars, based on the notions of parallel and sequential independence, it is possible to formally construct a new production by a suitable combination of two parallel independent productions, thus expressing their parallel application. However, the usual approach does not associate any partial ordering structure to a sequence of production applications, and thus it does not express the way the various elements involved in a derivation interact. On the contrary, this is possible in the partial ordering approach, which thus can be said to follow more faithfully the true-concurrency line of concurrency theory. Moreover, it is worthwhile to notice that in our case one single derivation is enough to construct the partial ordering, while in the classical approach a complete set of equivalent derivations (possibly very large) is needed to represent the true concurrency actually present.

It is important to notice that our approach is more abstract than the classical one, in the sense that there may be different derivations which have the same partial ordering but which are not equivalent in the sense of Definition 22. Thus, if we say that in our approach two derivations are equivalent whenever they have the same partial ordering, then our equivalence classes may be larger than the ones obtained in the classical approach. However, we believe it is possible to suitably label the occurrence net to obtain exactly the same equivalence classes as in [4]. More precisely, such labelling should be able to capture the minimal amount of information needed to distinguish derivations which consists of the same sequence of productions (and thus would be equivalent in our approach) which are however applied via different occurrence morphisms (and thus are not equivalent in the classical approach). To accomplish that, we argue that it would be enough to label each event with the corresponding production name, and to label instead the dependency arcs connected to such event with names of elements in the left hand side or in the right hand side of the production, so to specify the occurrence morphism which represents its application. In this way, from a labelled occurrence net and a linearization of its events, it should be possible to construct a graph derivation. Furthermore, the class of computations derivable by constructing all possible linearizations should coincide with an equivalence class in the classical approach. We will give a full account of the labelling, together with the proof that it yields the same equivalence classes as in classical approach, in the full version of this paper.

5 Conclusions

We have proposed a new semantics for graph grammars which is able to derive dependency (and thus concurrency) information on the elements and production instances involved in each graph derivation. The study of concurrency in graph grammars is particularly interesting, since in such a formalism it is possible to explicitely express the context which is needed to apply a production and thus to express a higher degree of concurrency (since contexts do not generate dependencies).

We have also considered the classical approach to study concurrency in graph grammars, which makes use of the concepts of parallel and sequential independence, and we have compared such an approach to ours: derivations which are equivalent in the classical sense are also equivalent in our approach, but the viceversa may be not true. Thus, we are at a more abstract level. However, small changes could make our equivalence to coincide with the classical one. Something like encoding in the events and in the dependency arcs of the occurrence net the corresponding production applications should be sufficient.

In our approach a deterministic occurrence net is associated to each derivation. In such a net, transitions correspond to production applications and states to arcs and nodes of the graphs appearing in the derivation. However, these arcs and nodes are treated as a set, i.e., the net does not contain informations on how they are connected to each other. We plan to investigate the possibility of adding such information, so to have a unique structure which describes both the derivation and the concurrency in it.

Since a partial ordering is associated to each derivation, the semantics of a graph grammar is then the set of all partial orderings associated to all derivations possible within the given grammar. However, we believe that it would be worthwhile to study the possibility of having a unique structure which is able to contain the concurrency information in the whole grammar and not in each derivation. In particular, we are considering Winskel's construction, which obtains a non-deterministic occurrence net (and thus an event structure) from each Petri net ([16]), and we plan to apply it instead to graph grammars. In this way, the obtained event structure would express both how different productions in a single derivation relate to each other, and also how different derivations interact.

Acknowledgments

We would like to thank Hartmut Ehrig for many fruitful discussions about concurrency in graph grammars.

References

[1] de Bakker J., de Roever W., Rozenberg G., eds., *Linear time, branching time and partial orders in logics and models for concurrency*, LNCS 354, Springer 1989.

[2] Degano P., De Nicola R., Montanari U., "A Partial Ordering Semantics for CCS", on *TCS 75*, pp. 223-262, 1990.

[3] Degano P., Montanari U., "A Model for Distributed Systems Based on Graph Rewritings", on *Journal of ACM*, Vol.34, n.2, 1987.

[4] Ehrig H., "Introduction to the Algebraic Theory of Graph Grammars", on *Proc. International Workshop on Graph Grammars*, Springer Verlag, LNCS 73, 1978.

[5] Guessarian I., ed., *Semantics of Concurrent Processes*, Springer 1990, LNCS 469.

[6] Habel A., "Hyperedge Replacement: Grammars and Languages", Ph.D. thesis, University of Bremen, 1989.

[7] Hoare C.A.R., "Communicating Sequential Processes", Prentice Hall, 1985.

[8] Mac Lane S., "Categories for the Working Mathematician", Springer Verlag, 1971.

[9] Milner R., "Communication and Concurrency", Prentice Hall, 1989.

[10] Montanari U., Rossi F., "True Concurrency in Concurrent Constraint Programming", on *Proc. ILPS91*, MIT Press, 1991.

[11] Montanari U., Rossi F., "Graph Rewriting for a Partial Ordering Semantics of Concurrent Constraint Programming", will appear on *Teorethical Computer Science*, special issue on graph grammars, Courcelle B. and Rozenberg eds.

[12] Peled D., Pnueli A., "Proving Partial Order Liveness Properties", on *Proc. ICALP90*, Springer-Verlag, LNCS 443, 1990.

[13] Plotkin G., "A structural Approach to Operational Semantics", TR DAIMI FN-19, Aarhus University, CS Department, 1981.

[14] Reisig W., "Petri Nets: An Introduction", EATCS Monographs on Theoretical Computer Science, Springer Verlag, 1985.

[15] Saraswat V. A., "Concurrent Constraint Programming Languages", Ph.D. Thesis, Carnegie-Mellon University, 1989. Also 1989 ACM Dissertation Award, MIT Press.

[16] Winskel G., "Event Structures", on *Petri nets: applications and relationships to other models of concurrency*, Springer-Verlag, LNCS 255.

Empty Stack Pushdown ω-Tree Automata

Wuxu Peng
Department of Computer Science
Southwest Texas State University
San Marcos, TX 78666

S. Purushothaman*
Department of Computer Science
The Pennsylvania State University
University Park, PA 16802

Abstract

In this paper we consider Pushdown automata on infinite trees with empty stack as the accepting condition (ω-EPDTA). We provide the following regarding ω-EPDTA (a) its a relationship to other Pushdown automata on infinite trees, (b) a Kleene-Closure theorem and (c) a single exponential time algorithm for checking emptiness. We also discuss the relevance of the results presented here to model-checking.

1 Introduction

Although hardware advances have made concurrent systems feasible, succinctly specifying and efficiently verifying them remain a major challenge. The recent development [3,4] of automated verification techniques for finite-state systems is one of the most exciting development in verifying concurrent systems.

A number of existing automated verification techniques employ the *model checking* method. Model checking involves expressing the properties of a system to be verified using some logic (such as propositional versions of *temporal logic* or *mu-calculus*) and then invoking a *decision procedure* to test whether the *start state* of the system satisfies the properties. All the existing techniques interpret the logic formulae over *finite Kripke* structures, which can only represent finite-state systems. If a finite Kripke structure is

*Supported in part by NSF CCR-9004121.

unwound, we get a *finite-state automaton* on infinite trees. Formulae in logics such as mu-calculus can also be represented by FSA on infinite trees (ω-FTA's). Therefore the model checking problem for such systems is equivalent to testing whether the intersection of two ω-FTA's on ω-trees is empty (cf. [15]).

It is clear that finite Kripke structures can model the infinite behavior of finite-state systems. It is important to distinguish between finite-state systems and infinite behavior of such systems. Systems like S_1 characterized by regular expression $r = (ab)^\omega$ is finite-state, as we only need a finite number of states to represent the system. The fact that the length of each word in r is infinite reflects the fact that S_1 is *nonterminating*, or has infinite behavior.

There are systems that have unbounded number of states and also exhibit infinite behavior. Consider the system S_2 whose behavior is characterized by the context-free language L^ω where $L = \{a^i b^i | i \geq 0\}$. Like S_1, system S_2 is also nonterminating. In contrast to S_1, however, S_2 cannot be represented by a finite Kripke structure.

Despite some recent success in verifying *finite-state* systems [4], little progress has been made for unbounded systems. Bradfield and Stirling [2] recently proposed a proof system for properties of unbounded concurrent systems expressible in μ-calculus. They showed that their proof system is sound and complete in the sense that any valid property (expressible in μ-calculus) can be verified and that any property proved valid is correct. Clearly, due to the infinite state space, any algorithm implementing their deduction system is not guaranteed to terminate when it is provided an invalid property.

In this paper we propose a new type of automata – *empty stack pushdown automata on infinite trees* (ω-EPDTA for short) which captures a class of unbounded state systems. We show that the class of ω-EPDTA's properly contains the class of ω-FTA's. As a result, EPDTA's can model all systems with finite Kripke structures.

Our notion of ω-EPDTA's is innovative. We show that the emptiness problem of ω-EPTDA's can be decided in single exponential time, which we believe is nearly optimal. Our algorithm for deciding the emptiness problem of ω-EPDTA extends Vardi and Wolper's good subtree techniques for deciding the emptiness problem of ω-FTA's [14]. The basic idea behind our algorithm is a two step reduction – reducing the emptiness problem of ω-EPDTA's to that of a collection of finite EPDTA's, and reducing the latter to emptiness problem of indexed languages. The first reduction is possible due to the Kleene closure property enjoyed by ω-EPDTA's, where by Kleene closure property we mean that the set of trees accepted by a ω-EPDTA is expressible as a ω-Kleene closure of context-free sets of finite trees.

Our definition of finite EPDTA is of independent interests. Finite pushdown tree automata and context-free tree grammars were traditionally studied from an algebraic point view (cf. [6,10]). Our definition is purely automata-theoretic. Yet, as we show later in this paper, our definition is consistent with the traditional algebraic definitions.

The remainder of this paper is organized as follows. In Section 2, we present the necessary basic notations about k-ary finite trees and k-ary ω-trees. Section 3 contains definitions for empty stack pushdown tree automata (EPDTA's), empty stack pushdown automata on ω-trees (ω-EPDTA's), pushdown automata on ω-trees (ω-PDTA's), and finite automata on ω-trees (ω-FTA's). In Section 4, we investigate the relationships among the families of trees accepted by these automata. We show in Section 5 that ω-EPDTA's have the Kleene closure property. Based on the Kleene closure property, in Section 6 we give an exponential algorithm for the emptiness problem of ω-EPDTA's. This result is in sharp contrast with the triple-exponential emptiness algorithm for ω-PDTA's in [11]. Concluding remarks are given in Section 7.

2 Preliminaries

Let N denote the set of non-negative integers, $k > 0$ be some fixed integer constant, and Σ be a finite alphabet. Symbols from Σ will be denoted by lower case letters $a, b, \cdots$. For any set S, $|S|$ denotes the cardinality of S.

Let $[k]$ denote the index set $\{1, 2, \cdots, k\}$. *A k-ary tree t on Σ* is a mapping $dom(t) \longrightarrow \Sigma$ such that $dom(t)$ is a prefix-closed subset of $[k]^*$. Note that

(1) The root of t is λ;
(2) For a node u, its k children are $u1, u2, \cdots, uk$.

A tree t is an ω-tree if every branch of t is infinite. t is a finite tree if every branch of t is finite. For a node u in t, we use $t(u) \in \Sigma$ to denote its label.

$T_k(\Sigma)$ ($T_k^\omega(\Sigma)$, resp.) denotes the set of all finite k-ary trees (the set of all k-ary ω-trees, resp.). All symbols in Σ are assumed to be of arity k. In this paper, we always assume that the only 0-ary symbol is $\perp$ which denotes an empty tree. Furthermore, we always restrict, without loss of generality, the nodes of the tree to either have all of its k children be nonempty trees or all of the children to be empty trees. Thus, we identify a node to be a *leaf node* provided *all of its children are* $\perp$. Note that $\perp$ plays the same role that fr^+ nodes play in the definitions used by Thomas [13] and as such they are not part of the tree.

For a set of variables $X = \{x_1, \cdots, x_n\}$, $T_k(\Sigma, X)$ denotes the set of all finite k-ary trees where some leaf nodes of each tree in it may be labeled by variables from X. For a tree $t \in T_k(\Sigma, X)$, we use $t \backslash X$ to denote the tree $t' \in T_k(\Sigma)$ obtained from t by removing all leaf nodes labeled by variables from X. We use the standard notation $u(t_1, \cdots, t_k)$ to denote a tree rooted at node u with k children $t_1, \cdots, t_k$.

Let t, t' be trees on Σ and u be a node in t then $t(t'/u)$ denotes the tree obtained by substituting t' for the node u in t and is defined by:

(1) $t(t'/u)(uv) = t'(v)$ for all node v in t';
(2) $t(t'/u)(v) = t(v)$ if u is not a left factor of v.

The yield of a finite tree t is a word defined inductively by the homomorphism $yield : T_k(\Sigma) \longrightarrow \Sigma^*$:

(1) $yield(t) = t(u)$, if t is a tree with a single node u;
(2) $yield(u(t_1, \cdots, t_k)) = yield(t_1) \cdots yield(t_k)$.

We say that a tree t_1 is a *prefix* of a tree t_2, notated as $t_1 \leq t_2$, if $dom(t_1) \subseteq dom(t_2)$ and for each node $u \in dom(t_1)$ $t_1(u) = t_2(u)$. Tree t_1 is a *proper prefix* of tree t_2, notated as $t_1 < t_2$, if $dom(t_1) \subset dom(t_2)$ and for each node $u \in dom(t_1)$ $t_1(u) = t_2(u)$. For a set T of finite trees, the *Rabin limit* (cf. [11]) of T is the set of ω-trees defined by

$$Rlim(T) = \{t \mid \exists (t_i)_{0 \leq i \leq \omega} s.t. \forall i \geq 0 : t_i \in T, t_i < t_{i+1}, \text{ and } t_i < t\}.$$

Let $T_i \in T_k(\Sigma, X)$, $0 \leq i \leq n$, be finite trees. We use $T_0.\langle T_1, \cdots, T_n \rangle$ to denote the set of finite trees defined inductively as follows:

(i) If $t = x_i \in T_0$, then $t.\langle T_1, \cdots, T_n \rangle = T_i$;
(ii) If $t = a(t_1, \cdots, t_k) \in T_0$, then $t.\langle T_1, \cdots, T_n \rangle = a(t_1.\langle T_1, \cdots, T_n \rangle, \cdots, t_k.\langle T_1, \cdots, T_n \rangle)$;
(iii) $T_0.\langle T_1, \cdots, T_n \rangle = \cup_{t \in T_0} t.\langle T_1, \cdots, T_n \rangle$.

Define $T_0.\langle T_1, \cdots, T_n \rangle^m = (T_0.\langle T_1, \cdots, T_n \rangle^{m-1}).\langle T_1, \cdots, T_n \rangle$, where $T_0.\langle T_1, \cdots, T_n \rangle^0 = T_0$. We further define $T_0.\langle T_1, \cdots, T_n \rangle^\omega = \{t \in T_k^\omega(\Sigma) \mid \exists (t_i)_{0 \leq i \leq \omega}$ s.t. $t_0 \in T_0$, $t_i \in t_{i-1}.\langle T_1, \cdots, T_n \rangle$, and $t \in Rlim\{t_i \backslash X : 0 \leq i \leq \omega\}\}$. We say that a set T of ω-trees is the *ω-Kleene closure* of a collection of finite tree sets $T_0, T_1, \cdots, T_n$ if $T = T_0.\langle T_1, \cdots, T_n \rangle^\omega$.

3 EPDTA's and ω-EPDTA's

Definition 3.1 (Empty Stack Pushdown Tree Automaton) An empty stack pushdown tree automaton (EPDTA for short) is a 6-tuple $M = (Q, \Sigma, \Gamma, q_0, Z_0, \delta)$, where Q is a finite set of states, Σ is the input alphabet, Γ is the stack alphabet, $q_0 \in Q$ is the initial state, $Z_0 \in \Gamma$ is the initial stack symbol. Without loss of generality, we assume that any stack symbol (including the initial stack symbol Z_0) that can appear at the bottom of the stack can never appear on top of any other stack symbol in the pushdown store. The transition function δ is a mapping:

$$\delta : Q \times (\Sigma \cup \{\varepsilon\}) \times \Gamma \longrightarrow 2^{(Q \times \Gamma^*)^k} \cup 2^{Q \times \Gamma^*}$$

A transition rule of the form $(q, \gamma) \in \delta(q', \varepsilon, Z)$ is called an ε-rule, while a transition of the form $(q_1, \gamma_1) \cdots (q_k, \gamma_k) \in \delta(q, a, Z)$ is called a read rule. A configuration (at a particular node of a tree) is a tuple $\langle q, s \rangle$, where $q \in Q$ is the current state and $s = Zs' \in \Gamma^*$ is the stack contents with Z as the top stack symbol. An ε-path e of a configuration $\langle q_1, s_1 \rangle$ is a sequence of ε moves starting at $\langle q_1, s_1 \rangle$, i.e. $e = (\langle q_1, s_1 \rangle, \cdots, \langle q_l, s_l \rangle)$ where

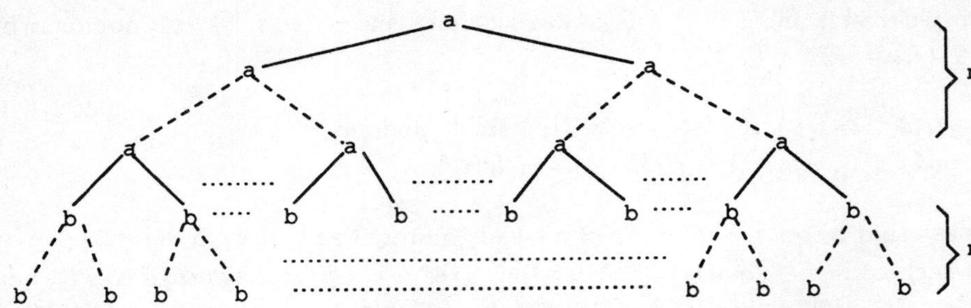

Figure 1: 2-ary trees accepted by EPDTA M in Example 1

for $2 \leq i \leq l$, if $s_{i-1} = Zs'$, then $(q_i, \gamma) \in \delta(q_{i-1}, \varepsilon, Z)$, and $s_i = \gamma s'$. $E(q, s)$ denotes the set of all ε-paths starting at $\langle q, s \rangle$.

For a k-ary finite tree $t : [k]^* \longrightarrow \Sigma$, a *run* of M on t is a tree $c : [k]^* \longrightarrow (Q \times \Gamma^*)^+$ inductively defined by

(1) $c(\lambda) = (\langle q_0, Z_0 \rangle, \langle q_1, s_1 \rangle, \cdots, \langle q_l, s_l \rangle) \in E(q_0, Z_0)$;

(2) If $c(u) = (\langle q_1, s_1 \rangle, \cdots, \langle q_l, s_l \rangle) \in E(q_1, s_1)$, where $s_l = z\gamma$, and $(q_1^1, s_1^1) \cdots (q_1^k, s_1^k) \in \delta(q_l, t(u), z)$, and node u has children, then for $1 \leq i \leq k$,

$$c(ui) = (\langle q_1^i, s_1^i \gamma \rangle, \cdots, \langle q_{n_i}^i, s_{n_i}^i \gamma \rangle) \in E(q_1^i, s_1^i \gamma).$$

A run c is *accepting* if each leaf node u of c is labeled by an ε-path $(\langle q_1, Z \rangle, \cdots, \langle q_l, Z \rangle)$ where Z_0 is a symbol that can appear only at the bottom of the stack, and there exists $(q^1, \varepsilon) \cdots (q^k, \varepsilon) \in \delta(q_l, t(u), Z_0)$. □

An EPDTA M accepts a tree t if M has an accepting run on t. $T(M)$, the set of finite k-ary trees accepted by M, is defined by

$$T(M) = \{t \in T_k(\Sigma) | M \text{ has an accepting run on } t\}$$

Example 1. Consider a 2-ary EPDTA $M = (Q, \Sigma, \Gamma, q_0, Z_0, \delta)$ where $Q = \{q_0, q_1\}$, $\Sigma = \{a, b, c\}$, $\Gamma = \{Z_0, A, B\}$, and the transition function δ is defined by:

(1) $\delta(q_0, \varepsilon, Z_0) = \{(q_0, BZ_0), (q_0, AZ_0)\}$; (2) $\delta(q_0, \varepsilon, B) = \{(q_0, BB), (q_0, AB)\}$;
(3) $\delta(q_0, \varepsilon, A) = \{(q_0, AA), (q_1, A)\}$; (4) $\delta(q_1, a, A) = \{(q_1, \varepsilon)(q_1, \varepsilon)\}$;
(5) $\delta(q_1, b, B) = \{(q_1, \varepsilon)(q_1, \varepsilon)\}$; (6) $\delta(q_1, b, Z_0) = \{(q_1, \varepsilon)(q_1, \varepsilon)\}$.

Then $T(M)$ is the set of trees shown in Fig. 1, where $n, m > 0$. □

Definition 3.2 (Empty Stack ω-Pushdown Tree Automata) An empty stack ω-pushdown k-ary tree automaton (ω-EPDTA for short) is a 6-tuple $M = (Q, \Sigma, \Gamma, q_0, Y, \delta)$, where

Q, Σ, Γ, q_0, and δ are defined the same as EPDTA's, and $Y \in \Gamma$ is a special initial stack symbol that can only be at the bottom of the stack.

For an ω-tree $t: [k]^* \longrightarrow \Sigma$, a *run* of M on t is an ω-tree $c: [k]^* \longrightarrow (Q \times \Gamma^*)^+$ and is defined similar to the run on a finite tree, except that now a computation is on an infinite tree.

Each infinite branch starting at the root λ in a run c is called an ω-path. A run $c: [k]^* \longrightarrow (Q \times \Gamma^*)^+$ is *accepting* if the stack symbol Y becomes the top stack symbol infinitely many times along each ω-path. □

An ω-EPDTA M accepts an ω-tree t if M has an accepting run on t. $T(M)$ is the set of ω-trees on each of which M has an accepting run.

Example 2. Consider a 2-ary ω-EPDTA $M_1 = (Q, \Sigma, \Gamma, q_0, Y, \delta)$ where $Q = \{q_0, q_1\}$, $\Sigma = \{a, b, c\}$, $\Gamma = \{Y, Z_0, A, B\}$, and the transition function δ is defined by:

(1) $\delta(q_0, \varepsilon, Y) = \{(q_0, Z_0Y)\}$; (2) $\delta(q_0, \varepsilon, Z_0) = \{(q_0, BZ_0), (q_0, AZ_0)\}$;
(3) $\delta(q_0, \varepsilon, B) = \{(q_0, BB), (q_0, AB)\}$; (4) $\delta(q_0, \varepsilon, A) = \{(q_0, AA), (q_1, A)\}$;
(5) $\delta(q_1, a, A) = \{(q_1, \varepsilon)(q_1, \varepsilon)\}$; (6) $\delta(q_1, b, B) = \{(q_1, \varepsilon)(q_1, \varepsilon)\}$;
(7) $\delta(q_1, \varepsilon, Y) = \{(q_0, Y)\}$.

Call a finite 2-ary tree t an (n, m)-tree if t is accepted by M in Example 1 with $n > 0$ levels of a's and $m > 0$ levels of b's. $T(M_1)$ is the set of 2-ary ω-trees t such that there is an (n, m)-tree t_1 that is a prefix of t. Each leaf node of t_1 is root of another (n_1, m_1)-tree, and so on. □

Definition 3.3 (ω-Pushdown Tree Automata) An ω-pushdown k-ary tree automaton (ω-PDTA for short) is a 7-tuple $M = (Q, \Sigma, \Gamma, q_0, Z_0, \delta, F)$, where Q, Σ, Γ, q_0, and δ are defined as in ω-EPDTA's, Z_0 is the initial stack symbol, and $F \subseteq Q$ is the designated set of final states.

For an ω-path $r = \Pi_{i=0}^{\omega} u_i$, $c(r) = \Pi_{i=0}^{\omega} c(u_i)$ denotes the infinite sequence obtained by concatenating ε-paths found on each node along r. Define the *state trace* τ as a mapping: $[k]^* \longrightarrow Q^*$. For each node u in a run c, $\tau(u) = q_1 \cdots q_l$, where $(\langle q_1, s_1\rangle, \cdots, \langle q_l, s_l\rangle) = c(u)$. We extend τ as a mapping: $([k]^*)^\omega \longrightarrow (Q^*)^\omega$ such that for an ω-path $r = \Pi_{i=0}^{\omega} u_i$ in c, $\tau(r) = \Pi_{i=0}^{\omega} \tau(u_i)$.

Let r be a ω-path such that $\tau(r) = q_0 q_1 \ldots q_i \ldots$. path r induces a mapping $f_r : N \longrightarrow Q$ where $f_r(i) = q_i$. Define $inf(r) = \{q \mid |f_r^{-1}(q)| = \omega\}$. A run $c: [k]^* \longrightarrow (Q \times \Gamma^*)^+$ is *accepting* iff $F \cap inf(r) \neq \emptyset$ for each ω-path r. □

$T(M)$, the set of ω-trees accepted by an ω-PDTA M is defined similarly. An EPDTA (or ω-EPDTA, or ω-PDTA) M is *deterministic* if (1) $|\delta(q, a, z)| \leq 1$, where $a \in \Sigma \cup \{\varepsilon\}$; and (2) if $|\delta(q, \varepsilon, z)| = 1$ then $|\delta(q, a, z)| = 0$ for all $a \in \Sigma$. If the stack is removed from ω-PDTA's definition, we obtain the finite k-ary ω-tree automata (ω-FTA for short, cf. [15]). If $k = 1$ then we get Pushdown automata on infinite strings (ω-PDA) [5].

Definition 3.4 (Context-Free Tree Grammar, [6]) An k-ary context-free tree grammar (CFTG) G is a 4-tuple (V_N, Σ, P, S_0), where (1) $V_N = \{S_0, S_1, \cdots, S_{m-1}\}$ is the set of finite ranked nonterminal symbols. For $S \in V_N$, $r(S)$ denotes its rank; (2) Σ is the set of finite ranked terminal symbols; (3) $S_0 \in V_N$ is the initial nonterminal of rank 0; (4) P is the set of productions of the form $S_i(x_1, \cdots, x_{r(S_i)}) \to t_i^j$, where for $i = 0, \cdots, m-1$, $j = 1, \cdots, n_i$, $t_i^j \in T_k(V_N \cup \Sigma, \{x_1, \cdots, x_{r(S_i)}\})$.

A tree t *derives* t', written as $t \Rightarrow t'$, iff there exists a prefix $\underline{t}$ of t, a production $S_i(x_1, \cdots, x_s) \to t_i^j \in P$, some node u of t labeled by S_i, subtrees $t_1, \cdots, t_s$ of t such that $t = \underline{t}(S_i(t_1, \cdots, t_s)/u)$ and $t' = \underline{t}(t_i^j(t_1, \cdots, t_s)/u)$. $t \Rightarrow t'$ means that, a node u in tree t labeled by S_i, which has children nodes $t_1, \cdots, t_s$, is replaced by $t_i^j(t_1, \cdots, t_s)$. □

The transitive closure $\stackrel{*}{\Rightarrow}$ of one-step derivation $\Rightarrow$ is defined in the usual way. $T(G)$, the set of trees generated by G, is defined by

$$T(G) \;=\; \{t \mid t \in T_k(\Sigma) \;\&\; S \stackrel{*}{\Rightarrow} t\}.$$

Example 3. Consider the CFTG $G = (V_N, \Sigma, P, S_0)$, where $V_N = \{S_0, A_0, A_1, B_0, B_1, R\}$, $\Sigma = \{a, b, c\}$, P contains productions: (1) $S_0 \to B_0(R) \mid A_0(R)$; (2) $B_0(x) \to B_0(B_1(x))$; (3) $B_0(x) \to A_0(B_1(x))$; (4) $A_0(x) \to A_0(A_1(x))$; (5) $A_0(x) \to A_1(x)$; (6) $A_1(x) \to a(x,x)$; (7) $B_1(x) \to b(x,x)$; (8) $R \to b$.

$T(G) = T(M)$, where M is the EPDTA in Example 1 in Section 2. For instance, the tree $a(b(b,b), b(b,b))$ is generated by the derivations: $S_0 \Rightarrow B_0(R) \Rightarrow A_0(B_1(R)) \Rightarrow A_1(B_1(R)) \Rightarrow a(B_1(R), B_1(R)) \Rightarrow a(b(R,R), B_1(R)) \Rightarrow a(b(b,R), B_1(R)) \Rightarrow a(b(b,b), B_1(R$ $\Rightarrow a(b(b,b), b(R,R)) \Rightarrow a(b(b,b), b(b,R)) \Rightarrow a(b(b,b), b(b,b))$ □

A CFTG G is regular if for all $S \in V_N$, $r(S) = 0$, i.e. all nonterminals are parameterless in the productions.

We will use $\mathcal{FT}$ to denote the family of trees accepted by a Buchi tree automaton, or equivalenty generated by regular tree grammars. The family of trees accepted by (or generated by, as appropriate) ω-PDA, ω-FTA's, ω-PDTA's, ω-EPDTA's, EPDTA's, and CFTG's are denoted by $\mathcal{PD}_\omega$, $\mathcal{FT}_\omega$, $\mathcal{PDT}_\omega$, $\mathcal{EPDT}_\omega$, $\mathcal{EPDT}$, and $\mathcal{CFT}$ respectively.

4 $\mathcal{FT}_\omega \subset \mathcal{EPDT}_\omega \subset \mathcal{PDT}_\omega$

In this section we investigate the relationships among $\mathcal{PDT}_\omega$, $\mathcal{EPDT}_\omega$, and $\mathcal{FT}_\omega$. We show that $\mathcal{FT}_\omega$, the class of trees accepted by Büchi automata, is properly contained in $\mathcal{EPDT}_\omega$ and $\mathcal{EPDT}_\omega$ in turn is properly contained in $\mathcal{PDT}_\omega$.

Theorem 4.1 $\mathcal{FT}_\omega \subset \mathcal{EPDT}_\omega$. □

Proof: Given any ω-FTA $A = (Q, \Sigma, \delta, q_0, F)$, we can construct an ω-EPDTA $M = (Q', \Sigma, \Gamma, q_0', Y, \delta')$ such that $T(A) = T(M)$ as follows. $Q' = Q \cup \{p\}$, where $p \notin Q$.

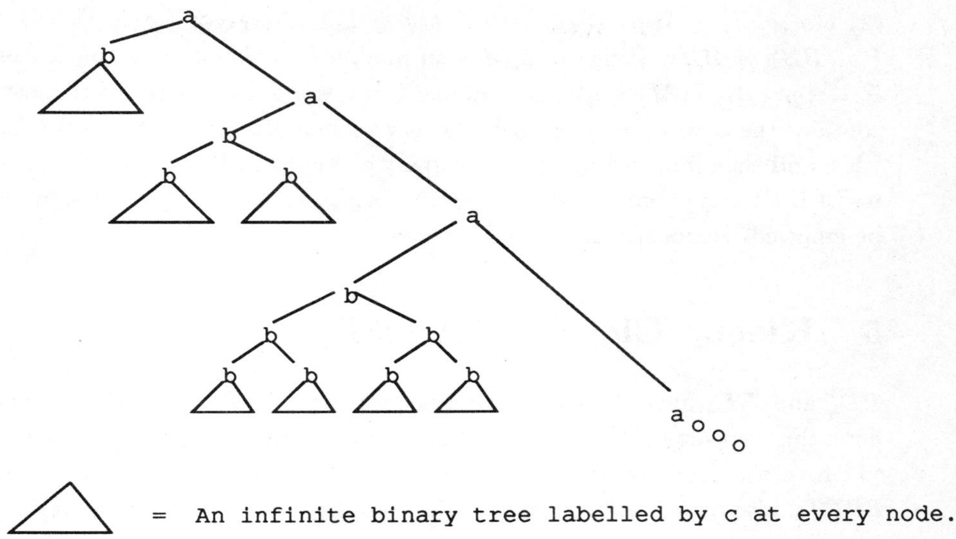

Figure 2: A infinite tree showing $\mathcal{EPDT}_\omega \subset \mathcal{PDT}_\omega$

$\Gamma = \{Z, Y\}$. M essentially puts ZY onto the stack and then simulates A's moves. Every time A enters a state $q \in F$, M will enter the special state p and pop Z (thus exposing symbol Y). It then pushes back Z onto the stack and return to state q to resume the simulation. It is clear to see that for any tree t, M has an accepting run on t iff A has one. Thus $\mathcal{FT}_\omega \subseteq \mathcal{EPDT}_\omega$ holds.

To see that the inclusion is proper, consider the ω-EPDTA M_1 in Example 2 in Section 3. We claim that there is no ω-FTA A such that $T(A) = T(M_1)$. To justify this, we observe that any tree t accepted by M_1 consists of a prefix t_0 of t that is an (n,m)-tree rooted at λ. Each of t_0's leaf nodes are the root of another (n,m)-tree, and so on. There are no FTA's that accept only (n,m)-trees. Hence there are no ω-FTA's that accept trees accepted by M_1. □

Theorem 4.2 $\mathcal{EPDT}_\omega \subset \mathcal{PDT}_\omega$. □

Proof:

Let $M = (Q, \Sigma, \Gamma, q_0, Y, \delta)$ be an ω-EPDTA. We can construct an ω-PDTA $M' = (Q', \Sigma, \Gamma, q_0, Y, \delta', F)$ such that $T(M) = T(M')$ as follows. Define $\overline{Q} = \{\overline{q} | q \in Q\}$. $Q' = Q \cup \overline{Q}$; $F = \overline{Q}$; $\delta \subseteq \delta'$. In addition, δ' also contains rules $(\overline{q}, Y) \in \delta'(q, \varepsilon, Y)$ and $(q, Y) \in \delta'(\overline{q}, \varepsilon, Y)$, for each $q \in Q$. Intuitively, M' simulates M until Y is exposed in M. M' then can enter a state $\overline{q} \in F$, and come back to state q from state $\overline{q}$. It then continues the normal simulation of M. It is easy to see that $T(M) = T(M')$.

To show that the inclusion is proper, let us consider the ω-PDTA $M = (Q, \Sigma, \Gamma, q_0, Z_0, \delta, F)$, where $Q = \{q_0, q_1, q_2\}$, $\Gamma = \{B, Z_0\}$, and δ is defined by (1) $\delta(q_0, a, Z_0) = \{(q_1, BZ_0)(q_2, BZ_0)\}$;

(2) $\delta(q_1, b, B) = \{(q_1, \varepsilon)(q_1, \varepsilon)\}$; (3) $\delta(q_1, c, Z_0) = \{(q_1, Z_0)(q_1, Z_0)\}$; (4) $\delta(q_2, a, B) = \{(q_1, BB)(q_2, BB)\}$ (this example is an modified version of Example 1 from [11]). Let $F = \{q_1, q_2\}$. $T(M)$ contains only one 2-ary tree t where the right most branch of t contains the ω-word a^ω, and each of other branches begins with $i(> 0)$ a's, followed by i b's, and then followed by infinitely many c's (refer to Figure 2). It is easy to see that no EPDTA can accept $T(M)$, because the stack along the right most branch can never be emptied. Hence the inclusion is proper. □

5 Kleene Closure of $\mathcal{EPDT}_\omega$

$\mathcal{PD}_\omega$ and $\mathcal{FT}_\omega$ have the Kleene closure property. $\mathcal{PDT}_\omega$, on the other hand, does not have this property [11]. Kleene closure is important in that it provides a handy tool to prove the decidability of the emptiness problem [9]. In this section we show that $\mathcal{EPDT}_\omega$ also have Kleene closures. We begin by recalling one of the results in [11].

Theorem 5.1 (Nivat and Saoudi [11]) For a set T of ω-trees, the following conditions are equivalent:

(1) T is the ω-Kleene closure of $\mathcal{FT}$;
(2) T is accepted by a nondeterministic FTA. □

Saoudi showed in [11] that $\mathcal{PDT}_\omega$ is not equal to the ω-Kleene closure of $\mathcal{CFT}$. We show here that $\mathcal{EPDT}_\omega$ is equal to the ω-Kleene closure of $\mathcal{EPDT}$.

Let $M = (Q, \Sigma, \Gamma, q_0, Y, \delta)$ be an ω-EPDTA. Consider an ω-tree t and an accepting run c of M on t. Because c is an accepting run, Y is reached infinitely often along each ω-path of c. Therefore each branch starting from the root node λ of c will reach, infinitely often, a node u labeled by an ε-path $(\langle q_1, s_1\rangle, \cdots, \langle q_l, s_l\rangle)$, where for some $1 \le i \le l$, $s_i = Y$. Call such a node u as a *periodic node*, and the configuration $\langle q_i, Y\rangle$ the *periodic configuration*. Starting from the root λ, c will reach a periodic node along each of its branches for the first time in a finite number of steps. It is easy to see that each subtree t_λ rooted at λ with all these periodic nodes as the leaf nodes is a finite k-ary tree that can be accepted by an EPDTA. Starting from any leaf node u of t_λ, M will continue to grow the stack and ultimately reach a periodic node along each of its branches for the first time in a finite number of steps. The subtree t_u rooted at u with these periodic nodes as leaf nodes is again a finite k-ary tree accepted by an EPDTA. The same arguments can be applied to the leaf nodes of the subtree t_u and so on.

On the other hand, assume that $T = T_0.\langle T_1, \cdots, T_n\rangle^\omega$, where $T_i = T(M_i)$, M_i is an EPDTA. Let $t \in T$. T_0 has a run on a prefix t_0 of t. All the leaf nodes are labeled by variables $x_j \in X$ and the stack of M_0 is emptied. From each leaf node x_j, T_j has a run on a portion of t and then eventually empties the stack at all its leaf nodes. Therefore it appears that we can construct an ω-EPDTA that accepts t. The following theorem makes these ideas precise.

Theorem 5.2 For a set T of ω-trees, the following conditions are equivalent:

(1) T is the ω-Kleene closure of $\mathcal{EPDT}$;
(2) T is accepted by an ω-EPDTA. □

Proof: (1) $\Rightarrow$ (2). Assume that T is the ω-Kleene closure of the set of trees $T_0, T_1, \cdots, T_n \in \mathcal{EPDT}$, i.e. $T = T_0.\langle T_1, \cdots, T_n\rangle^\omega$. Let $M_i = (Q_i, \Sigma \cup X, \Gamma_i, q_0^i, Z_0^i, \delta_i)$, $0 \le i \le n$, be the EPDTA s.t. $T_i = T(M_i)$ (recall that $X = \{x_1, \cdots, x_n\}$). Assume that $Q_i \cap Q_j = \emptyset$ and $\Gamma_i \cap \Gamma_j = \emptyset$, when $i \neq j$. We construct, from M_i, $0 \le i \le n$, an ω-EPDTA $M = (Q, \Sigma, \Gamma, q_0, Y, \delta)$, s.t. $T(M) = T$. Specifically we have $Q = \cup_{i=0}^n Q_i \cup \{q^j : 1 \le j \le n\} \cup \{q_0\}$ ($q_0, q^j \notin \cup_{i=0}^n Q_i$), $\Gamma = \cup_{i=0}^n \Gamma_i \cup \{Y\}$ ($Y \notin \cup_{i=0}^n \Gamma_i$). The transition function δ includes all transition rules in δ_i ($0 \le i \le n$), except those rules of the form $\delta_i(q, x_j, Z)$, where $x_j \in X$. In addition, δ also contains the following two types of rules: (a) $\delta(q_0, \varepsilon, Y) = \{(q_0^0, Z_0^0 Y)\}$; (b) If $(q_1^i, \varepsilon) \cdots (q_k^i, \varepsilon) \in \delta_i(q, x_j, Z)$, then $(q_0^j, \varepsilon) \in \delta(q, \varepsilon, Z)$, and $(q_0^j, Z_0^j Y) \in \delta(q_0^j, \varepsilon, Y)$.

Intuitively, at initial state q_0, M puts Z_0^0 onto the stack and starts to simulate M_0. If $(q_1^i, \varepsilon) \cdots (q_k^i, \varepsilon) \in \delta_i(q, x_j, Z)$, then at configuration $\langle q, ZY\rangle$ M will nondeterministically transfer to configuration $\langle q_0^j, Y\rangle$. At configuration $\langle q_0^j, Y\rangle$, M has to enter configuration $\langle q_0^j, Z_0^j Y\rangle$, hence starting to simulate M_j. If M gets into configuration $\langle q', Z'Y\rangle$ where $(q_1^j, \varepsilon) \cdots (q_k^j, \varepsilon) \in \delta_j(q', x_l, Z')$, then M can nondeterministically transfer to configuration $\langle q_0^l, Z_0^l Y\rangle$, hence starting to simulate M_l, $1 \le j, l \le n$.

(2) $\Rightarrow$ (1). Assume that there exists an ω-EPDTA $M = (Q, \Sigma, \Gamma, q_0, Y, \delta)$, s.t. $T = T(M)$. Define $trans(M) = \{(q, \gamma) \mid \exists (q, \gamma) \in \delta(q', \varepsilon, Z)\} \cup \{(q_i, \gamma_i) : 1 \le i \le k \mid \exists a \in \Sigma, (q_1, \gamma_1) \cdots (q_k, \gamma_k) \in \delta(q, a, Z)\}$.

We construct, from M, a collection of EPDTA's $M_i = (Q_i, \Sigma \cup X, \Gamma_i, q_0^i, Y, \delta_i)$, $0 \le i \le n$, s.t. $T = T(M_0).\langle T(M_1), \cdots, T(M_n)\rangle^\omega$, where $n = |trans(M)|$. We assume that the tuples in $trans(M)$ is ordered and a function $\rho : trans(M) \longrightarrow \{1, \cdots, n\}$ such that for each tuple $(q, \gamma) \in trans(M)$ if $\rho(q, \gamma) = i$ then (q, γ) is the ith tuple in $trans(M)$. Intuitively, each tuple (q, γ) corresponds to the machine M_j, where $\rho(q, \gamma) = j$, $1 \le j \le n$.

Let us call rules of the form $(q_1, \gamma_1 Y) \cdots (q_k, \gamma_k Y) \in \delta(q, a, Y)$ type (a) rule, and rules of the form $(q, \gamma Y) \in \delta(q', \varepsilon, Y)$ type (b) rules. Note that these rules are needed to continue after the bottom-of-the-stack symbol Y has been exposed.

M_i ($0 \le i \le n$) is defined as follows. $Q_0 = Q, q_0^0 = q_0$, $Q_j = Q \cup \{q_0^j\}$ ($1 \le j \le n$), where $q_0^j \notin Q$. Define $\Gamma_i = \Gamma \cup \{Z_{\rho(q,\gamma)} : (q, \gamma) \in trans(M)\}$. Finally, δ_i includes all the rules in δ except those rules involving $\delta(q, \theta, Y)$, where $\theta \in \Sigma \cup \{\varepsilon\}$. δ_i also contains the following two types of rules:

- For each type (a) rule $(q_1, \gamma_1 Y) \cdots (q_k, \gamma_k Y) \in \delta(q, a, Y)$ we should have
$$(q_1, Z_{\rho(q_1,\gamma_1 Y)}) \cdots (q_k, Z_{\rho(q_k,\gamma_k Y)}) \in \delta_i(q, a, Y)$$
and $(q_i, \varepsilon) \cdots (q_i, \varepsilon) \in \delta_i(q_i, x_{\rho(q_i,\gamma_i Y)}, Z_{\rho(q_i,\gamma_i Y)})$.
- For each type (b) rule $(q, \gamma Y) \in \delta(q', \varepsilon, Y)$, we should add the transition $(q, \varepsilon) \cdots (q, \varepsilon) \in \delta_i(q', x_{\rho(q,\gamma Y)}, Y)$ to machine M_i.

In addition to all of these transitions, we need rules to start any machine M_j with the appropriate stack symbols. Consequently, we add the transition $\delta_j(q_0^j, \varepsilon, Y) = \{(q, \gamma Y)\}$, where $\rho(q, \gamma Y) = j$, to M_j.

M_0 starts with configuration $\langle q_0, Y\rangle$ (which is also M's initial configuration), while M_j $(1 \leq j \leq n)$ starts with configuration $\langle q_0^j, Y\rangle$ and then immediately transfers to configuration $\langle q, \gamma Y\rangle$,where $\rho(q, \gamma Y) = j$. After that, M_i $(0 \leq i \leq n)$ will simulate M until a type (a) or (b) rule is to be used by M. In case of type (a) rule, M_i acts according to the rule $(q_1, Z_{\rho(q_1,\gamma_1 Y)}) \cdots (q_k, Z_{\rho(q_k,\gamma_k Y)}) \in \delta_i(q, a, Y)$, then follows the rule $(q_j, \varepsilon) \cdots (q_j, \varepsilon) \in \delta_i(q_j, x_{\rho(q_j,\gamma_j Y)}, Z_{\rho(q_j,\gamma_j Y)})$. Therefore every time M finds the symbol Y on top of the stack and is poised to enter the configuration $\langle q_j, \gamma_j Y\rangle$ at its jth child node, M_i simply accepts $x_{\rho(q_j,\gamma_j Y)}$ and empties the stack. If $\rho(q_j, \gamma_j Y) = l$, then M_l will start to grow the tree from configuration $\langle q_j, \gamma_j Y\rangle$. □

6 Emptiness Problem of ω-EPDTA's

In this section, using the Kleene closure property of last section, we give an exponential algorithm for the emptiness problem of ω-EPDTA's. This result is in sharp contrast to the triple-exponential algorithm for ω-PDTA's in [7].

By Theorem 5.2, each set $T(M)$ of ω-trees accepted by an ω-EPDTA M is the ω-Kleene closure of a collection of finite trees $T(M_0), \cdots, T(M_n)$ accepted by EPDTA $M_0, \cdots, M_n$ respectively. The emptiness of $T(M)$ can be decided based on the emptiness of the $T(M_i)$'s. We first show that for each EPDTA M there exists a CFTG G such that $T(M) = T(G)$. To test whether $T(G)$ is empty, we observe the fact that the set of yields of trees accepted by a CFTG G is an indexed language. This observation allows us to use the exponential time algorithm in [12] to test the emptiness of CFTG's.

Lemma 6.1 $\mathcal{EPDT} \subseteq \mathcal{CFT}$. □

Proof: The construction follows that of [6] and is repeated as it is critical to the rest of the paper. Let $M = (Q, \Sigma, \Gamma, q_0, Z_0, \delta)$ be a EPDTA where $Q = \{q_0, q_1, \cdots, q_{m-1}\}$. Let $I = \{0, 1, \cdots, m-1\}$ and $X = \{x\}$. We construct a CFTG $G = (V_N, \Sigma, P, S_0)$ as follows. $V_N = \{Z^i | 0 \leq i \leq m-1, Z \in \Gamma\}$. Each nonterminal $Z^i \in V_N$ has rank $m \times r(Z^i)$, where $r(Z)$=0 if Z can appear at the bottom of the stack and 1 otherwise. Define $X^I = \{x^i | i \in I\}$. Define a mapping $\sigma : Q \times (\Gamma^* X \cup \Gamma^*) \longrightarrow T(V_N, X^I)$ inductively:

(1) $\sigma(q_i, s) = s^i$, if s is a variable or s is a bottom stack letter;
(2) $\sigma(q_i, \varepsilon) = \perp$;
(3) $\sigma(q_i, Zt)) = Z^i(\sigma(q_0, t), \sigma(q_1, t), \cdots, \sigma(q_{m-1}, t))$.

The start nonterminal $S_0 = \delta(q_0, Z_0) = Z_0^0$, and the set of productions P is defined by:

a) For each ε-rule $(q', \gamma) \in \delta(q, \varepsilon, Z_0)$, we have a production of the form:

$$\sigma(q, Z_0) \rightarrow \sigma(q', \gamma);$$

b) For each ε-rule $(q', \gamma) \in \delta(q, \varepsilon, Z)$, $Z \neq Z_0$, we have a production of the form:

$$\sigma(q, Zx) \rightarrow \sigma(q', \gamma x);$$

c) For each read rule $(q_1, \pi_1) \cdots (q_k, \pi_k) \in \delta(q, a, Z_0)$, we have a production of the form:

$$\sigma(q, Z_0) \rightarrow a(\sigma(q_1, \pi_1), \cdots, \sigma(q_k, \pi_k));$$

d) For each read rule $(q_1, \pi_1) \cdots (q_k, \pi_k) \in \delta(q, a, Z)$, $Z \neq Z_0$, we have a production of the form:

$$\sigma(q, Zx) \rightarrow a(\sigma(q_1, \pi_1 x), \cdots, \sigma(q_k, \pi_k x))'$$

Notice that in case (c), if $\pi_i = \varepsilon$, $1 \leq i \leq k$, then $\sigma(q_i, \pi_i) = \perp$, and hence $a(\sigma(q_1, \varepsilon), \cdots, \sigma(q_k, \varepsilon)) = a$. Following an argument analogous to that in [6], it can be easily shown that $T(M) = T(G)$. □

Example 4. For the EPDTA M in Example 1, we can construct an equivalent CFTG $G = (V_N, \Sigma, P, Z^0)$ using Lemma 6.1. $V_N = \{Z_0^0, Z_0^1, A^0, A^1, B^0, B^1\}$, where $r(Z_0^0) = r(Z_0^1) = 0$, $r(A^0) = r(A^1) = r(B^0) = r(B^1) = 2$, and the productions are

$Z_0^0 \rightarrow B^0(Z_0^0, Z_0^1) \mid A^0(Z_0^0, Z_0^1)$;
$B^0(x^0, x^1) \rightarrow B^0(B^0(x^0, x^1), B^1(x^0, x^1))$;
$B^0(x^0, x^1) \rightarrow A^0(B^0(x^0, x^1), B^1(x^0, x^1))$;
$A^0(x^0, x^1) \rightarrow A^0(A^0(x^0, x^1), A^1(x^0, x^1))$;
$A^0(x^0, x^1) \rightarrow A^1(x^0, x^1)$;
$A^1(x^0, x^1) \rightarrow a(x^1, x^1)$;
$B^1(x^0, x^1) \rightarrow b(x^1, x^1)$;
$Z_0^1 \rightarrow b$;

For instance, the tree $a(b(b, b), b(b, b))$ can be derived by

$Z_0^0 \Rightarrow B^0(Z_0^0, Z_0^1) \Rightarrow A^0(B^0(Z_0^0, Z_0^1), B^1(Z_0^0, Z_0^1)) \Rightarrow A^1(B^0(Z_0^0, Z_0^1), B^1(Z_0^0, Z_0^1)) \Rightarrow$
$a(B^1(Z_0^0, Z_0^1), B^1(Z_0^0, Z_0^1)) \Rightarrow a(b(Z_0^1, Z_0^1), B^1(Z_0^0, Z_0^1)) \Rightarrow a(b(b, Z_0^1), B^1(Z_0^0, Z_0^1)) \Rightarrow$
$a(b(b, b), B^1(Z_0^0, Z_0^1)) \Rightarrow a(b(b, b), b(Z_0^1, Z_0^1)) \Rightarrow a(b(b, b), b(b, Z_0^1)) \Rightarrow a(b(b, b), b(b, b))$.

□

A CFTG G is in *Quasi-Chomsky normal form* (QCNF) if each production in G is in one of the following forms:

(1) $A(x_1, \cdots, x_n) \to a(C_1(x_1, \cdots, x_n), \cdots C_m(x_1, \cdots, x_n))$;
(2) $A(x_1, \cdots, x_n) \to B(C_1(x_1, \cdots, x_n), \cdots C_m(x_1, \cdots, x_n))$;
(3) $A(x_1, \cdots, x_n) \to a(x_1, \cdots, x_n)$;
(4) $A(x_1, \cdots, x_n) \to x_i$

Recall (from Theorem 5.2) that for an ω-EPDTA M *trans*(M) is defined as the set of all tuples of the form (q, γ) s.t. (q, γ) appears in some transition rule of M. Let $\eta(M) = max(|\gamma| : (q, \gamma) \in trans(M))$, and *rule*$(M)$ be the number of transition rules in M.

Lemma 6.2 Let $M = (Q, \Sigma, \Gamma, q_0, Z_0, \delta)$ be an EPDTA and $G = (V_N, \Sigma, P, S_0)$ be the CFTG constructed from M by Lemma 6.1. If $\eta(M) \leq 2$ then G is in QCNF. □

Proof: Let $(q, \gamma) \in trans(M)$, such that $|\gamma| \leq 2$. Let $q_i \in Q$ and consider two cases:

Case 1: $\gamma = Z$. $\sigma(q_i, \gamma x) = \sigma(q_i, Zx) = Z^i(\sigma(q_0, x), \cdots, \sigma(q_{m-1}, x)) = Z^i(x^0, \cdots,, x^{m-1})$. Therefore $\sigma(q_i, \gamma x)$ meets the requirement of QCNF regardless whether it will appear on right hand side or left hand side of a production.

Case 2. $\gamma = Z_2 Z_1$. $\sigma(q_i, \gamma x) = \sigma(q_i, Z_2 Z_1 x) = Z_2^i(\sigma(q_0, Z_1 x), \cdots, \sigma(q_{m-1}, Z_1 x))$ $= Z_2^i(Z_1^0(x^0, \cdots, x^{m-1}), \cdots, Z_1^{m-1}(x^0, \cdots, x^{m-1}))$. Notice that here $\sigma(q_i, \gamma x)$ can only appear at the right hand side of productions. Again it is easy to see that $\sigma(q_i, \gamma x)$ meets the requirement of QCNF. □

It was well known that the set of yields of trees accepted by an CFTG G, *yield*(G), is an indexed language [10]. Furthermore, if G is already in QCNF, then testing whether *yield*$(G) = \emptyset$ can be done in exponential time (cf. [12]). Because $T(G) = \emptyset$ iff *yield*$(G) = \emptyset$, we have the following theorem regarding the emptiness problem of EPDTA's.

Theorem 6.1 Given an EPDTA M with $\eta(M) \leq 2$, the problem whether $T(M)$ is empty can be solved in exponential time.

Theorem 6.2 Let M be an ω-EPDTA with $\eta(M) \leq 2$. Let H be the time needed to solve the emptiness problem of CFTG's. Then the problem of whether $T(M)$ is empty can be solved in time $O(n^2(n + H))$, where $n = |trans(M)|$. □

Proof: Let $M = (Q, \Sigma, \Gamma, q_0, Y, \delta)$ be the given ω-EPDTA. Consider the Algorithm EMPTINESS shown in Table 1, where M_i, $0 \leq i \leq n$, are defined in Theorem 5.2.

Claim: $T(M) \neq \emptyset$ iff $M_0 \in C_{new}$ at the end of Algorithm EMPTINESS.

Proof of the claim: $\Rightarrow$ Assume that $T(M) \neq \emptyset$. Let $t \in T(M)$ and c be an accepting run of M on t. Let u_i, $1 \leq i \leq n_1$ be the collection of first periodic nodes from the root λ of ω-tree c and let $\langle q^i, Y\rangle$ be the periodic configuration associated with u_i. There are two cases to consider, depending upon if the periodic configuration is the last configuration in the ε-path of $c(u_i)$. We consider the case where the periodic configuration is the last one (the other case is simpler). Assume that $(q_1, \gamma_1 Y)\cdots(q_k, \gamma_k Y) \in \delta(q^i, a, Y)$. Then δ_0 has the rules $(q_1, Z_{\rho(q_1,\gamma_1 Y)})\cdots(q_k, Z_{\rho(q_k,\gamma_k Y)}) \in \delta_0(q^i, a, Y)$ and $(q_i, \varepsilon)\cdots(q_i, \varepsilon) \in \delta_0(q_i, x_{\rho(q_i,\gamma_i Y)}, Z_{\rho(q_i,\gamma_i Y)})$. If $T(M_{\rho(q_i,\gamma_i)}) = \emptyset$, for some i, then $t \notin T(M)$, because t would have a finite branch. Therefore all $M_{\rho(q_i,\gamma_i)}$, $1 \leq i \leq n_1$, are still in C_{new} after the algorithm. Hence $T(M_0) \neq \emptyset$ at the end of the algorithm, which implies that $M_0 \in C_{new}$.

$\Leftarrow$ Assume that $M_0 \in C_{new}$ at the end of Algorithm EMPTINESS. Let $t_\lambda \in T(M_0)$ and c_λ be a run of M_0 on t_λ. Let $u_1, u_2, \cdots, u_{n_1}$ be the leaf nodes of c_λ and $\langle q_i, Z_{(q_i,\gamma_i)}\rangle$ be the last configuration of $c_\lambda(u_i)$. Each $\langle q_i, Z_{(q_i,\gamma_i)}\rangle$ corresponds to an emptying action $(q_i, \varepsilon)\cdots(q_i, \varepsilon) \in \delta_0(q_i, x_{(q_i,\gamma_i)}, Z_{(q_i,\gamma_i)})$. Because these emptying actions are still in M_0, we can conclude that $M_{\rho(q_i,\gamma_i)}$ is still in C_{new} at the end of the algorithm (cf. line 10, 11). Hence $T(M_{\rho(q_i,\gamma_i)}) \neq \emptyset$, $1 \leq i \leq n_1$. Now we can apply the same argument to $M_{\rho(q_i,\gamma_i)}$. The leaf nodes of any tree u_i accepted by $M_{\rho(q_i,\gamma_i)}$ again will refer to a collection of periodic nodes and configurations associated with emptying actions. Continuing the argument we can obtain an infinite sequence of trees $(t_i)_{0\leq i\leq\omega}$, such that $t_i \in t_{i-1}.\langle T_1, \cdots, T_n\rangle$. Therefore there exists $t = \mathit{Rlim}((t_i)_{0\leq i\leq\omega})$, hence $T(M) \neq \emptyset$.

Each iteration of the **while** loop will remove at least one EPDTA $M_{(q,\gamma)}$ from $c(new)$. Line 5 will be executed $O(n^2)$ times. Because $\eta(M) \leq 2$, each EPDTA M_i can be transformed to a CFTG G_i. By Theorem 6.1, testing the emptiness of each of these CFTG's takes time $O(H)$. The **for** loop at lines 9, 10, 11 takes $O(n^3)$. All together the algorithm takes time $O(n^2(n+H))$. □

Theorem 6.2 is correct when $\eta(M) \leq 2$. Although most ω-EPDTA's do satisfy this requirement, to be complete we should also consider the case where $\eta(M) > 2$. The following theorem says that given any ω-EPDTA M with $\eta(M) > 2$, we can create another ω-EPDTA M_1, such that $\eta(M_1) \leq 2$, with a comparable number of states and transition rules.

Theorem 6.3 For each ω-EPDTA $M = (Q, \Sigma, \Gamma, q_0, Y, \delta)$ with $\eta(M) = m > 2$, we can construct another ω-EPDTA $M_1 = (Q_1, \Sigma, \Gamma, q_0, Y, \delta_1)$ equivalent to M such that $\eta(M_1) = 2$, and $|Q_1| = O(nm|Q|)$, where $n = |\mathit{trans}(M)|$, and $\mathit{rule}(M_1) \leq m \times \mathit{rule}(M)$. □

Proof: Let $M = (Q, \Sigma, \Gamma, q_0, Y, \delta)$ be an ω-EPDTA such that $\eta(M) = m > 2$. We construct another ω-EPDTA $M_1 = (Q_1, \Sigma, \Gamma_1, q_0, Y, \delta_1)$ such that $T(M) = T(M_1)$ and $\eta(M_1) = 2$ as follows. $Q_1 = Q \cup Q'$, where $Q' = \{[q, \gamma] \mid (q, \gamma\gamma' Z Z') \in \mathit{trans}(M)$ where $Z, Z' \in \Gamma$, $\gamma, \gamma' \in \Gamma^*$ and $|\gamma| > 0\}$. It is clear that $|Q'| \leq nm|Q|$ where $n = |\mathit{trans}(M)|$. δ_1 contains all the rules in δ except those rules that involve tuples (q, γ) where $|\gamma| > 2$.

```
Algorithm EMPTINESS
C_new := {M_0} ∪ {M_j | (q,γ) ∈ trans(M) & ρ(q,γ) = j};
C_old := ∅;
while (C_new ≠ C_old) and (M_0 ∈ C_new) do
        C_old := C_new;
        Let E := {M_ρ(q,γ) | M_ρ(q,γ) ∈ C_new & M_ρ(q,γ) = ∅};
        if E = ∅ then
           exit;
        endif;
        C_new := C_new − {E};
        for each M_ρ(q,γ) ∈ C_new do
           Let D := {δ_ρ(q,γ)(q_i, x_ρ(q_i,γ_i), Z_ρ(q_i,γ_i)) : M_ρ(q_i,γ_i) ∈ E};
           δ_ρ(q,γ) = δ_ρ(q,γ) − D;
        endfor;
endwhile;
```

Table 1: Algorithm EMPTINESS

Each ε-rule $(q,\gamma) \in \delta(q',\varepsilon,Z)$, where $\gamma = Z_{i_j} \cdots Z_{i_1}$, $j > 2$, is decomposed into $j-1$ ε-rules: $([q, Z_{i_j} \cdots Z_{i_3}], Z_{i_2}Z_{i_1}) \in \delta(q',\varepsilon,Z)$, $([q, Z_{i_j} \cdots Z_{i_{l+1}}], Z_{i_l}Z_{i_{l-1}}) \in \delta([q, Z_{i_j} \cdots Z_{i_l}], \varepsilon, Z_{i_{l-1}}$ $3 \le l \le j-1$, and $(q, Z_{i_j}Z_{i_{j-1}}) \in \delta([q, Z_{i_j}], \varepsilon, Z_{i_{j-1}})$.

Each read rule $(q_1,\gamma_1)\cdots(q_k,\gamma_k) \in \delta(q,a,Z)$, where some $|\gamma_i| > 2$, is decomposed into the one read rule and a collection of ε-rules as follows. If $|\gamma_i| > 2$, write $\gamma_i = \beta_i\gamma_i'$, where $|\gamma_i'| = 2$. The read rule is: $\alpha_1 \cdots \alpha_k \in \delta(q,a,Z)$, where $\alpha_i = (q_i,\gamma_i)$ if $|\gamma_i| \le 2$, and $\alpha_i = ([q_i,\beta_i],\gamma_i')$ if $|\gamma_i| > 2$. For each $([q_i,\beta_i],\gamma_i')$, where $\beta_i = Z_{i_j} \cdots Z_{i_1}$, $j > 0$, and $\gamma_i' = Z\gamma_i''$, we have the following ε-rules, depending upon the value of j. If $j = 1$, then we have only one ε-rule: $(q_i, Z_{i_1}Z) \in \delta([q_i, Z_{i_1}], \varepsilon, Z)$. If $j > 1$, we have j corresponding ε-rules: $([q_i, Z_{i_j} \cdots Z_{i_2}], Z_{i_1}Z) \in \delta(q_i,\varepsilon,Z)$, $([q_i, Z_{i_j} \cdots Z_{i_{l+1}}], Z_{i_l}Z_{i_{l-1}}) \in \delta([q_i, Z_{i_j} \cdots Z_{i_l}], \varepsilon, Z_{i_{l-1}})$, $2 \le l \le j-1$, $(q_i, Z_{i_j}Z_{i_{j-1}}) \in \delta([q_i, Z_{i_j}], \varepsilon, Z_{i_{j-1}})$.

It is straightforward to show that $T(M) = T(M_1)$. Moreover $rule(M_1) \le \eta(M) \times rule(M)$. Hence the conclusion holds. □

Combining Theorem 6.2 and 6.3, we have our main theorem.

Theorem 6.4 The emptiness problem for ω-EPDTAs can be solved in time exponential to their size. □

7 Discussion

We have introduced the notion of ω-EPDTA that accepts an infinite tree provided the bottom-of-the-stack symbol is exposed infinitely often in some run of the tree. We have established its relation to pushdown automata on infinite trees that accept by distinguished set of final states infinitely often. More importantly, we have shown that trees accepted by ω-EPDTA are expressible as ω-Kleene closure of a finite number of context-free term languages. We have shown that the emptiness problem for ω-EPDTA is solvable in single exponential time, which is probably optimal.

The practical motivation for considering ω-EPDTA is that they can be used to specify a class of unbounded state space systems. For example, we can capture the behavior of a counter which counts but which should count down to zero infinitely often, by the following ω-EPDTA $M = (Q, \Sigma, \Gamma, q_0, Z_0, \delta)$:

- $Q = \{q_0\}$, Σ={inc, dec}, and $\Gamma = \{Z_0, Z\}$.
- $\delta(q_0,\ \text{inc}, Z_0) = \{(q_0, ZZ_0)(q_0, ZZ_0)\}$
  $\delta(q_0,\ \text{inc}, Z) = \{(q_0, ZZ)(q_0, ZZ)\}$
  $\delta(q_0,\ \text{dec}, Z) = \{(q_0, \varepsilon)(q_0, \varepsilon)\}$

Clearly ω-EPDTA can be used to capture systems that have a context-free behavior. There has been a lot of interest lately [1,8] on context-free processes. We conjecture that the behavior of normed context-free processes, as discussed in [8], can be captured as trees accepted by a ω-EPDTA.

Acknowledgements: We would like to thank the referees for their constructive comments.

References

[1] J. C. M. Baeten, J. A. Bergstra, J. W. Klop. Decidability of Bisimulation Equivalence for Processes Generating Context-Free Languages. In *LNCS 259*, pp: 93–114. Springer-Verlag, 1987.

[2] J. Bradfield and C. Stirling, Local Model Checking for Infinite State Spaces. To appear in *Theoretical Comp. Sci.*.

[3] E. M. Clarke, E. A. Emerson, A. P. Sistla, Automatic Verification of Finite-State Concurrent Systems Using Temporal Logic Specifications: a Practical Approach. *Proc. of the 10th ACM Symp. on Principles of Prog. Lang.*, 1983, pp.117–126.

[4] R. Cleaveland, Tableau-Based Model Checking in the Propositional Mu-Calculus. *Acta Informatica*, Vol.27, 1990, pp.725–747.

[5] R. S. Cohen and A. Y. Gold, Theory of ω-Languages I: Characterizations of ω-Context-Free Languages. *J. of Comp. and Sys. Sci.*, Vol. 15, 1977, pp.169–184.

[6] I. Guessarian, Pushdown Tree Automata. *Math. Sys. Theory*, Vol. 16, 1983, pp.237–263.

[7] D. Harel and D. Raz, Deciding Properties of Nonregular Programs. *IEEE 31st Symp. on Found. of Comp. Sci.*, 1990, pp.652-661.

[8] H. Hüttel and C. Stirling, Actions Speak Louder Than Words: Proving Bisimilarity for Context-Free Processes. *Report ECS-LFCS-91-145*, Dept. of Comp. Sci., Univ. of Edinburgh, April 1991. Also in *Proc. of 6th Symp. on Logic in Comp. Sci.*, 1991.

[9] M. Linna, On ω-Sets Associated with Context-Free Languages. *Information and Control*, Vol. 31, 1976, pp.272–293.

[10] T. S. E. Maibaum, Pumping Lemmas for Term Languages. *J. of Comp. and Sys. Sci.*, Vol. 17, 1978, pp.319–330.

[11] A. Saoudi, Pushdown Automata on Infinite Trees and Omega-Kleene Closure of Context-Free Tree Sets. *Proc. of Math. Found. of Comp. Sci., LNCS 379*, Springer-Verlag, 1989.

[12] S. Tanaka and T. Kasai, The Emptiness Problem for Indexed Language is Exponential-Time Complete. *Sys. and Comp. in Japan*, Vol. 17(9), 1986, pp.29–37.

[13] W. Thomas. Automata on Infinite Objects. In *Handbook of Theoretical Computer Science, Vol B.* (ed) J. van Leeuwen, pp:133-192, MIT Press, 1990.

[14] M. Y. Vardi and P. Wolper, Automata-Theoretic Techniques for Modal Logics of Programs. *J. of Comp. and Sys. Sci.*, Vol. 32, 1986, pp.183–221.

[15] M. Y. Vardi and P. Wolper, An Automata-Theoretic Approach to Automatic Program Verification. *Proc. of 1st Symp. on Logic in Comp. Sci.*, 1986, pp.332–344.

Modulo counting quantifiers over finite trees *

Andreas Potthoff
Institut für Informatik und Praktische Mathematik
Christian-Albrechts-Universität Kiel
Olshausenstr. 40, D 2300 Kiel 1
e-mail: apo@informatik.uni-kiel.dbp.de

Abstract

This paper studies logical definability of tree languages (sets of finite trees). The logical systems we consider are located between first-order logic and monadic second-order logic. We obtain results which clarify the expressive power of first-order logic extended by "modulo counting quantifiers".

1 Introduction

The regular tree languages coincide with the tree languages definable in monadic second-order logic [2],[18]. Fragments of monadic second-order logic were considered in [17]. There set quantifiers were restricted to range over special subsets of nodes of a tree, for example over antichains, i.e. sets of nodes which are incomparable w.r.t. the partial order of a tree. This extension of first-order logic FO is called antichain logic and denoted by FO+ACh. In the present paper a logic "FO+MOD" is considered which is closer to first-order logic. We allow quantifiers $\exists^{r,q}x\varphi(x)$ which express "there are r mod q many nodes x such that $\varphi(x)$". A standard property expressible in this logic is the existence of an even number of nodes with a certain fixed label.

For regular word languages, the "absence of modulo counting" characterizes the expressive power of first-order logic. This follows from results of McNaughton [8] and Schützenberger [14] which say that for regular word languages first-order definability, star-freeness, and the "noncounting property" are equivalent. (A language L is called *noncounting*, or *aperiodic*, if for sufficiently large n and any words x,y,z: $xy^nz \in L$ iff $xy^{n+1}z \in L$.) Straubing, Thérien and Thomas [15] showed that for word languages first-order logic with modulo counting quantifiers is located in expressive power strictly between first-order logic and monadic second-order logic.

The notions of aperiodicity and star-freeness have been transferred to tree languages but most of the results mentioned above fail for tree languages. From Thomas [17] we

*The present work was supported by EBRA Working Group 3166 "Algebraic and Syntactic Methods in Computer Science (ASMICS)".

know that star-freeness corresponds to FO+ACh and that the class of first-order definable tree languages is strictly included in the class of star-free languages. Every first-order definable tree language is aperiodic but Heuter [6] showed that the converse direction fails for regular tree languages. As Niwiński [12] has shown, the expressive power of FO+MOD is covered by FO+ACh.

Our first result states that FO+MOD is *properly* included in antichain logic. Moreover our example tree language is aperiodic and hence shows in which way the strength of antichain logic can be exploited without referring to modulo counting. Thus we obtain also an interesting supplement to Niwiński's result. As a tool in our proof we introduce a version of the Ehrenfeucht-Fraïssé-game which characterizes FO+MOD. The used example tree language also serves to show limitations in the approach of Nivat and Podelski [11] to classify tree languages by syntactic monoids associated with tree languages. We show that first-order definability cannot be characterized by the syntactic monoid.

Concerning the comparison of FO+MOD with FO, it is known that the strict inclusion FO $\subsetneq$ FO+MOD in the case of word languages extends to the case of trees using tree languages which code word languages (say on the leftmost branch of trees). Languages obtained in this way which prove strictness are "counting". Our second result states that this inclusion is strict also for aperiodic tree languages. Thus modulo-counting quantifiers increase the power of first-order logic even within the class of aperiodic tree languages.

The remainder of the paper has five sections. After technical preliminaries (Section 2) we will introduce in Section 3 an Ehrenfeucht-Fraïssé game and sketch the proof that it characterizes FO+MOD. We will use this game in Sections 4 and 5 in order to show that FO+MOD is more powerful than FO but less powerful than FO+ACh, (in both cases with respect to aperiodic tree languages). In Section 6 we will give an outline of future work and open questions.

I would like to thank W.Thomas for introducing me to the subject and his support in this research. I also thank D.Niwiński for fruitful discussions.

2 Technical preliminaries

For simplicity of notation we consider only binary trees. Let $\Sigma = \Sigma_0 \cup \Sigma_2$ be a finite ranked alphabet. By T_Σ we denote the set of all trees built up from Σ in the usual way. We consider a tree $t \in T_\Sigma$ also as a function $t : dom(t) \to \Sigma$ where $dom(t) \subset \{1,2\}^*$ is a prefix closed set of words (called nodes) with the additional property: $k1 \in dom(t) \iff k2 \in dom(t)$ and $t(k) \in \Sigma_0 \iff k$ has no successors in $dom(t)$. If k is a node in $dom(t)$ we denote by $t^{[k}$ the subtree of t with root k, i.e. $dom(t^{[k}) = \{r \mid kr \in dom(t)\}$ and $t^{[k}(r) = t(kr)$ for all $r \in dom(t^{[k})$. $|t|_a$ denotes the number of nodes labelled a in t.

Let $c \notin \Sigma$ be a 0-ary symbol. We denote by S_Σ the set of all trees over $\Sigma \cup \{c\}$ with exactly one occurrence of c. Trees in S_Σ are called special. We use special trees in order to introduce concatenation of trees. $s \cdot s'$ denotes the tree which results from s by substituting s' for c. Hence $s \cdot s'$ is a special tree iff s' is a special tree. This concatenation serves to extend the notion of syntactic congruence and aperiodicity from word languages to tree languages. Trees $s, t \in S_\Sigma$ are congruent with respect to $T \subseteq T_\Sigma$ iff $\forall u \in S_\Sigma\ \forall v \in T_\Sigma \quad u \cdot s \cdot v \in T \iff u \cdot t \cdot v \in T$. A tree language is called aperiodic iff $\exists n \in \mathbb{N} \quad \forall u, s \in S_\Sigma \, \forall v \in T_\Sigma \quad u \cdot s^n \cdot v \in T \iff u \cdot s^{n+1} \cdot v \in T$.

We turn now to the description of tree languages in terms of mathematical logic. We identify each tree t with a relational structure also denoted t: $t = (dom(t), <, S_1, S_2, (P_a)_{a \in \Sigma})$. S_1 and S_2 denote the successor relations (with $x\, S_i\, y$ iff $y = xi$) and $<$ the proper partial prefix ordering on $dom(t)$. P_a denotes the set of all nodes labelled a in t.

Monadic second-order formulas are built up from variables $x, y, \ldots$ ranging over nodes, variables $X, Y, \ldots$ ranging over sets of nodes, the boolean connectives $\neg$, $\wedge$ and $\vee$, the quantifiers $\exists$, $\forall$ for both kind of variables and the symbols $<$, $=$, S_1, S_2, P_a (for $a \in \Sigma$). We write $\varphi(X_1, \ldots, X_m, x_1, \ldots, x_n)$ to indicate that at most $X_1, \ldots, X_m, x_1, \ldots, x_n$ occur free in φ. The satisfaction relation $(t, K_1, \ldots, K_m, k_1, \ldots, k_n) \models \varphi(X_1, \ldots, X_m, x_1, \ldots, x_n)$ for $K_1, \ldots, K_m \subseteq dom(t)$ and $k_1, \ldots, k_n \in dom(t)$ is defined in the natural way. Formulas without quantification over sets are called first-order formulas.

Thomas defined in [17] the following restriction of second-order quantification. An antichain is a set of nodes such that any two distinct nodes in the set are incomparable w.r.t. $<$. Antichain formulas are monadic second-order formulas where set variables range only over antichains.

Modulo counting quantifiers $\exists^{i,q}$ have been introduced in [15]. For $q \geq 2$, $0 \leq i < q$ and $k_1, \ldots, k_n \in dom(t)$ we define: $(t, k_1, \ldots, k_n) \models \exists^{i,q} x\, \varphi(x_1, \ldots, x_n, x)$ iff the number of nodes k with $(t, k_1, \ldots, k_n, k) \models \varphi(x_1, \ldots, x_n, x)$ is congruent i modulo q.

We call FO (resp. FO+MOD, FO+ACh) the set of formulas in first-order logic (resp. first-order logic with modulo counting quantifiers, first-order logic extended by set quantifiers ranging over antichains). Every sentence, i.e. a formula without free variables, defines a tree language $T(\varphi) = \{\, t \mid t \models \varphi \,\}$. We call *FO* (resp. *FO+MOD* , *FO+ACh*) the set of tree languages definable by formulas in FO (resp. FO+MOD, FO+ACh).

The quantifier-depth of a formula φ in FO+MOD (written qd(φ)) is the maximum number of nested quantifiers in φ where we count both kind of quantifiers. For $q \geq 2$ we call FO+MOD(q) the set of formulas in FO+MOD where only modulo counting quantifiers $\exists^{i,q}$ are allowed. These formulas define a normal form in the following sense:

Lemma 2.1 Every formula of FO+MOD is equivalent to a formula in FO+MOD(q) for some q.

Proof Define q to be the least common multiple m of all r such that there exists a subformula $\exists^{i,r} x\, \varphi(\bar{x}, x)$. Then replace each subformula of this kind by the following equivalent formula where k is defined by $q = k \cdot r$: $\exists^{i,q} x\, \varphi(\bar{x}, x) \vee \ldots \vee \exists^{i+(k-1)\cdot r, q} x\, \varphi(\bar{x}, x)$.
□

Theorem 2.2 states known results concerning the expressive power of these logics over trees:

Theorem 2.2
$FO \subsetneq FO{+}ACh$ [17]
$FO{+}MOD \subseteq FO{+}ACh$ [12]
$FO \subsetneq FO{+}ACh$ even for aperiodic tree languages [6]

3 An Ehrenfeucht-Fraïssé-game characterizing FO+MOD

In this section we define two equivalence relations on trees. The first relation distinguishes two trees if there exists a formula in FO+MOD(q) of a fixed quantifier-depth that distinguishes these trees. The other relation is defined by an Ehrenfeucht-Fraïssé-game. This game is played by two players on two trees. The aim of player II is to show that the given trees are "similar". Trees are taken to be equivalent if the second player has a winning strategy. The rules of the game reflect the underlying set of logical formulas whereas the number of moves corresponds to the quantifier-depth under consideration. The main theorem of this section states that game-equivalence and formula-equivalence coincide. A detailed treatment of an Ehrenfeucht-Fraïssé-game characterizing FO can be found in [6].

Let $q \geq 2$ be fixed in the sequel and let $\bar{k} = k_1, \ldots, k_m \in dom(s)$ and $\bar{k}' = k'_1, \ldots, k'_m \in dom(t)$ be two sequences of nodes of length m in trees s and t. A play of the game $G^q_n((s,\bar{k}),(t,\bar{k}'))$ consists of n moves. Player I can decide to do either a FO-move or a MOD(q)-move. In a FO-move player I chooses a node in s or t. Player II reacts by choosing a node in the other tree. A MOD(q)-move consists of two steps. In the first step player I marks a set of nodes in s or t. Now player II marks a set of nodes of the same size modulo q in the other tree. In the second step player I chooses a node in s or t either marked (by himself or by player II) or not marked. Player II has to choose a node in the other tree which has to be marked if and only if the node chosen by player I is marked. The move is finished by deleting all markings. We call k_{m+i} (resp. k'_{m+i}) the node of s (resp. t) chosen in the i-th move of the game. Player II wins the game if $k_1, \ldots, k_{m+n}, k'_1, \ldots, k'_{m+n}$ fulfil the following conditions for all $i, j \leq m+n$:

$$(\star) \quad \begin{array}{llll} \text{(a)}\; k_i = k_j & \iff & k'_i = k'_j & \\ \text{(b)}\; k_i < k_j & \iff & k'_i < k'_j & \\ \text{(c)}\; k_i S_l k_j & \iff & k'_i S_l k'_j & l = 1,2 \\ \text{(d)}\; P_a k_i & \iff & P_a k'_i & \forall a \in \Sigma \end{array}$$

We denote by $G_n((s,\bar{k}),(t,\bar{k}'))$ the game where only FO-moves are allowed. If no nodes are specified in s and t we write $G^q_n(s,t)$ ($G_n(s,t)$ respectively).

Definition 3.1 Let $\bar{x} = x_1, \ldots, x_m$ and let $\bar{k} = k_1, \ldots, k_m \in dom(s)$ and $\bar{k}' = k'_1, \ldots, k'_m \in dom(t)$ be sequences of nodes in trees s and t.

(formula-equivalence)

$(s,\bar{k}) \equiv^q_n (t,\bar{k}')$ iff $\forall \varphi(\bar{x}) \in$ FO+MOD(q), qd$(\varphi(\bar{x})) \leq n$
$(s,\bar{k}) \models \varphi(\bar{x}) \iff (t,\bar{k}') \models \varphi(\bar{x})$

$(s,\bar{k}) \equiv_n (t,\bar{k}')$ iff $\forall \varphi(\bar{x}) \in$ FO, qd$(\varphi(\bar{x})) \leq n$ $\quad (s,\bar{k}) \models \varphi(\bar{x}) \iff (t,\bar{k}') \models \varphi(\bar{x})$

(game-equivalence)

$(s,\bar{k}) \approx^q_n (t,\bar{k}')$ iff player II has a winning strategy for the game $G^q_n((s,\bar{k}),(t,\bar{k}'))$

$(s,\bar{k}) \approx_n (t,\bar{k}')$ iff player II has a winning strategy for the game $G_n((s,\bar{k}),(t,\bar{k}'))$

Remark 3.2 The relations $\equiv_n^q$, $\equiv_n$, $\approx_n^q$ and $\approx_n$ are equivalence relations.

Proof $\equiv_n^q$ and $\equiv_n$ are equivalence relations by definition. For $\approx_n^q$ and $\approx_n$ it suffices to treat transitivity. Let us suppose that player II has winning strategies for the games $G_n^q((s,\bar{k}),(t,\bar{k}'))$ and $G_n^q((t,\bar{k}'),(u,\bar{k}''))$. Then player II uses $(t,\bar{k}')$ to construct a winning strategy for the game $G_n^q((s,\bar{k}),(u,\bar{k}''))$. After player I has made his choice w.l.o.g in s player II reacts on t according to his winning strategy in the game $G_n^q((s,\bar{k}),(t,\bar{k}'))$. Then he makes his choice on u according to his own move on t and his winning strategy in the game $G_n^q((t,\bar{k}'),(u,\bar{k}''))$. □

Example 3.3 Let $q = 2$,

$s =$ 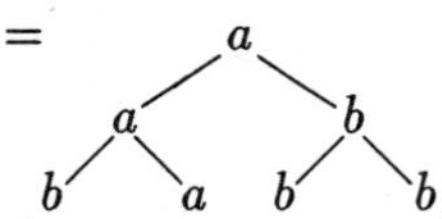

$t =$ 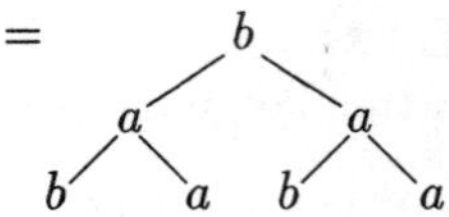

We shall explain that $s \not\approx_1^2 t$. Player I starts marking all nodes labelled a in s. Now player II has to mark an odd number of nodes in t. If he marks a node labelled b player I chooses this node in the second step of this MOD(2)-move. Now player II is obliged to choose a marked node in s. These nodes are labelled a, hence player I wins because the chosen nodes violate condition (d) of ($\star$). Hence player II has to mark an odd number of nodes labelled a in t. Therefore at least one node labelled a remains unmarked in t. Player I chooses one of these nodes in the second step and player II has to choose an unmarked node in s. But these nodes are labelled b and so player I wins again. A formula of quantifier-depth 1 that distinguishes s and t (which exists by Theorem 3.7 below) looks as follows: $\exists^{0,2}x\, P_a x$.

The remainder of this section is devoted to the proof that game-equivalence and formula-equivalence coincide. The techniques used in [7], [10, Chapter 26] and [13] for games characterizing FO can be used also for FO+MOD(q). We reformulate the main lemmata according to FO-MOD(q) but omit some proofs.

Definition 3.4 Let $m > 0$ be fixed. We denote by T_Σ^m the set of all trees $(s, k_1, \ldots, k_m)$ in T_Σ with a sequence of m specified nodes. Each equivalence relation $\approx_n^q$ (resp. $\approx_n$) defines a partition of T_Σ^m. We denote by $C_{m,n}^q$ the set of all $\approx_n^q$-classes of T_Σ^m.

The following Lemma reduces $\approx_{n+1}^{(q)}$-equivalence to $\approx_n^{(q)}$-equivalence.

Lemma 3.5

$$(s,\bar{k}) \approx_{n+1}^q (t,\bar{k}')$$

$$\Longleftrightarrow$$

$$\forall C \in C_{m+1,n}^q$$

$$\begin{array}{lllll}(& [\ \exists\, k \in dom(s)\ (s,\bar{k},k) \in C & \Longleftrightarrow & \exists\, k' \in dom(t)\ (t,\bar{k}',k') \in C &] \\ \wedge & [\ |\{k \in dom(s) \mid (s,\bar{k},k) \in C\}| & \equiv & |\{k' \in dom(t) \mid (t,\bar{k}',k') \in C\}|\ (\mathrm{mod}\ q)\ ] &)\end{array}$$

Lemma 3.10
Let $n \geq 1$ and $(s, \bar{k}), (t, \bar{k}') \in T^m_{\Sigma\cup\{c\}}$ be $\approx^q_n$-equivalent trees where all leaves are labelled c and let $u_1, \ldots, u_n \in T_\Sigma$ be $\approx^q_n$-equivalent trees. Then $(s', \bar{k}) \approx^q_n (t', \bar{k}')$ where s' and t' result from s and t by replacing all leaves by $u_1, \ldots, u_n$ in an arbitrary way. □

4 *FO+MOD* $\subsetneqq$ *FO+ACh*, even for aperiodic tree languages

In this section we show that the set T_1 of trees corresponding to boolean expressions with value 1 (over the constants 0 and 1 and the boolean connectives $\wedge$ and $\vee$) is aperiodic and antichain definable, but not definable using MOD-quantifiers. First we construct a formula of FO+ACh defining T_1. Then we show using the Ehrenfeucht-Fraïssé-game of section 3 that this language is not definable in FO+MOD.

Definition 4.1 Let $\Sigma = \{\wedge, \vee, 0, 1\}$ where $\Sigma_0 = \{0,1\}$ and $\Sigma_2 = \{\wedge, \vee\}$. Every tree in $T_{\{\wedge,\vee,0,1\}}$ corresponds to a boolean expression. We define T_1 to be the set of trees in $T_{\{\wedge,\vee,0,1\}}$ where the value of the corresponding expression is 1.

Theorem 4.2 The tree language T_1 is aperiodic, definable in FO+ACh, but not definable in FO+MOD.

We first show aperiodicity of T_1.

Lemma 4.3 T_1 is aperiodic.

Proof Every special tree $s \in S_\Sigma$ represents a function $f_s : \{0,1\} \to \{0,1\}$ and in this sense concatenation of special trees corresponds to composition of functions. $\wedge$ and $\vee$ are monotone functions. Therefore we have $f_s = (f_s)^2$ for all special trees s, and $\forall u, s \in S_\Sigma\ \forall t \in T_\Sigma \quad u \cdot s \cdot t \in T_1$ iff $u \cdot s^2 \cdot t \in T_1$. Special trees are syntactically congruent with respect to T_1 if they represent the same function. Thus the syntactic semigroup consists of only three elements, the identity and the constant functions **1** and **0**. □

The following remark shows that FO-definability of regular tree languages cannot be decided by inspecting only the syntactic semigroup.

Remark 4.4 There is a first-order definable tree language whose syntactic semigroup is isomorphic to that of T_1.

Proof Let $\Sigma' = \Sigma'_0 = \Sigma'_2 = \{0, 1, x\}$. We define $T \subseteq T_{\Sigma'}$ to be set of all trees such that the labelling of the leftmost branch written down from root to frontier yields a word in $x^* \cdot 1 \cdot \Sigma'^* \cup x^*$. Then the syntactic semigroups of T and T_1 are isomorphic and T is first-order definable. We omit the details. □

Now we turn to the proof that T_1 is definable in FO+ACh. The following Lemma describes a tree-like structure of nodes in all trees belonging to T_1. It is built up from root to frontier and collects those nodes which determine the value to be 1.

$$(s,\bar{k}) \approx_{n+1} (t,\bar{k}') \iff \begin{array}{ll} \forall k \in dom(s)\, \exists k' \in dom(t) & (s,\bar{k},k) \approx_n (t,\bar{k}',k') \\ \wedge \forall k' \in dom(t) \exists k \in dom(s) & (s,\bar{k},k) \approx_n (t,\bar{k}',k') \end{array}$$

Lemma 3.6 The index of $\approx_n^q$ in T_Σ^m is finite for all $m, n \in \mathbb{N}$.

Proof The proof works by induction on n. The $\approx_0^q$-equivalence class of a tree $(s,\bar{k})$ with m specified nodes is determined by the labelling of these nodes and by relations $<, S_1, S_2, =$ that hold between each pair of these nodes. There are only finitely many possibilities for fixed m, and therefore the index of $\approx_0^q$ in T_Σ^m is finite.

For the induction step we assume that the index of $\approx_n^q$ in T_Σ^m is finite for all $m \in \mathbb{N}$. Let $C_1, \ldots, C_l$ be an enumeration of all $\approx_n^q$-classes in T_Σ^{m+1}. By Lemma 3.5 the $\approx_{n+1}^q$-class of $(s,\bar{k}) \in T_\Sigma^m$ is determined by the number modulo q of nodes k in s such that $(s,\bar{k},k)$ belongs to class C_i and whether or not a node k in s exists such that $(s,\bar{k},k)$ belongs to class C_i. Thus we have finitely many possibilities for each class $C_i (i = 1, \ldots, l)$ and therefore only finitely many $\approx_{n+1}^q$-classes in T_Σ^m. □

Theorem 3.7

$$\forall (s,\bar{k}),(t,\bar{k}') \in T_\Sigma^m \qquad \begin{array}{l} (s,\bar{k}) \equiv_n^q (t,\bar{k}') \iff (s,\bar{k}) \approx_n^q (t,\bar{k}') \\ (s,\bar{k}) \equiv_n (t,\bar{k}') \iff (s,\bar{k}) \approx_n (t,\bar{k}') \end{array}$$

Proof For the direction from left to right we show that for all C in $C_{m,n}^q$ there exists a formula $\varphi_C(x_1, \ldots, x_m)$ such that for all $(s, k_1, \ldots, k_m) \in T_\Sigma^m$:

$(s, k_1, \ldots, k_m) \in C \iff (s, k_1, \ldots, k_m) \models \varphi_C(x_1, \ldots, x_m)$.

The proof works by induction and uses Lemma 3.5.

For the reverse direction it can be shown that every formula of quantifier-depth n with m free variables is equivalent to a finite disjunction of formulas φ_C with C in $C_{m,n}^q$. □

We apply this theorem in the following way to prove that a given tree language is not definable in FO or FO+MOD(q).

Remark 3.8

$T \notin FO$ iff for all $n \in \mathbb{N}$ there exist trees s_n and t_n such that: $s_n \in T$, $t_n \notin T$ but $s_n \approx_n t_n$.

$T \notin FO + MOD(q)$ iff for all $n \in \mathbb{N}$ there exist trees s_n^q and t_n^q such that: $s_n^q \in T$, $t_n^q \notin T$ but $s_n^q \approx_n^q t_n^q$. □

The construction of trees s_n^q and t_n^q as in Remark 3.8 will proceed by induction. We will construct $\approx_{n+1}^q$-equivalent trees using several $\approx_n^q$-equivalent ones. Lemma 3.9 and Lemma 3.10 will be used to deduce $\approx_{n+1}^q$-equivalence of trees from $\approx_n^q$-equivalence of certain subtrees of these trees.

Lemma 3.9 (Composition Lemma)

$((s,k) \approx_n^q (t,k') \wedge (s^{[k} = t^{[k'})) \Rightarrow (s,kr) \approx_n^q (t,k'r)$ for all nodes of form kr in $dom(s)$.

$((s,k) \approx_n (t,k') \wedge (s^{[k} = t^{[k'})) \Rightarrow (s,kr) \approx_n (t,k'r)$ for all nodes of form kr in $dom(s)$. □

Lemma 4.5 . A tree t is in T_1 iff there exists a set $K \subseteq dom(t)$ with the following properties:

(a) the root of t belongs to K

(b) if $t(k) = \wedge$ and k is in K then both successors of k are in K

(c) if $t(k) = \vee$ and k is in K then at least one successor of k is in K

(d) if k is a leaf and k is in K then $t(k) = 1$

(e) if k is in K and $k' < k$ then k' is in K

Proof First we show the direction from right to left. Conditions (b-d) imply that all subtrees corresponding to nodes in K have value 1. Together with condition (a) we obtain that t belongs to T_1. For the reverse direction define K to be the set of all nodes k such that the subtrees corresponding to k and all ancestors of k have value 1. □

Condition (e) of Lemma 4.5 is not necessary, but it implies that the set K of nodes is determined by the set of leaves in K. We use this fact in the following formula of FO+ACh where we describe the existence of a set X of leaves such that the set K of nodes, defined by $x \in K \iff \exists y'\ Xy' \wedge x \leq y' (= \varphi(x))$ fulfils conditions (a-d) of Lemma 4.5. In this case condition (c) is fulfilled automatically and condition (a) can be replaced by the requirement that X is not empty.

$$\begin{array}{lr} \exists X (\ \exists x\, Xx & \text{(a)} \\ \quad \wedge \forall x \{(P_\wedge x \wedge \varphi(x)) \rightarrow (\exists y\ [\, xS_1 y \wedge \varphi(y)] \wedge \exists y\ [\, xS_2 y \wedge \varphi(y)])\} & \text{(b)} \\ \quad \wedge \forall x\, (Xx \rightarrow P_1 x)) & \text{(d)} \end{array}$$

In the current and the next section we will use the following trees in order to build $\approx^q_{n+1}$-equivalent trees from $\approx^q_n$-equivalent ones.

$u_0 = c$ $\qquad\qquad$ $u_m =$

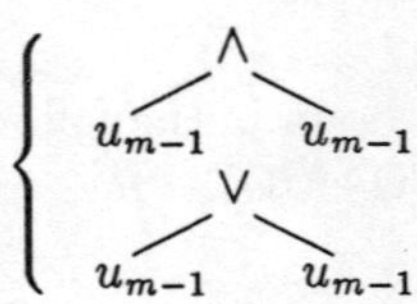

m even

m odd

Lemma 4.6 Let $m \geq 2$ and let l, l' be two leaves in u_m which are not neighbours. Then we can label all leaves of u_m with 0 and 1 in two different ways such that the resulting trees v_m and w_m have the following properties:

- $v_m(k) = w_m(k)$ for all leaves except l and l'
- $v_m(l) = w_m(l') = 1$
- $v_m(l') = w_m(l) = 0$
- $v_m \in T_1$ and $w_m \notin T_1$

Proof of Theorem 4.2

We have to show that $T_1 \notin FO+MOD(q)$ for all $q \geq 2$. Let $q \geq 2$ be fixed in the sequel. Following Remark 3.8 we have to construct trees s_n^q and t_n^q for $n \in \mathbb{N}$ such that: $s_n^q \in T_1$, $t_n^q \notin T_1$ and $s_n^q \approx_n^q t_n^q$. We define these trees by induction on n.

For $n = 1$ we define

$s_1^q =$ 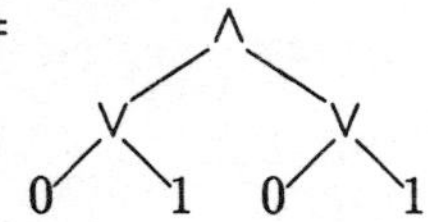

and $t_1^q =$ 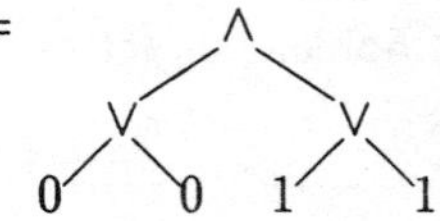

We have $s_1^q \approx_1^q t_1^q$ because each letter occurs in both trees in the same number (cf. Example 3.3).

For the induction step we assume that s_n^q and t_n^q are given with the required properties. Because of the finite index of $\approx_n^q$ there exist $m \geq 2$ and two leaves l and l' in u_m which are not neighbours such that $(u_m, l) \approx_n^q (u_m, l')$. Applying Lemma 4.6 we get trees v_m and w_m. We construct s_{n+1}^q (t_{n+1}^q) by replacing in v_m (w_m respectively) each 1 by s_n^q and each 0 by t_n^q. Thus we have $s_{n+1}^q \in T_1$ and $t_{n+1}^q \notin T_1$. It remains to show that s_{n+1}^q and t_{n+1}^q are $\approx_{n+1}^q$-equivalent. Both trees have the same set of nodes and differ only in the subtrees below nodes l and l'. We show that there exists a bijective mapping $h : dom(s_{n+1}^q) \rightarrow dom(t_{n+1}^q)$ such that:

$$\forall k \in dom(s_{n+1}^q) \quad (s_{n+1}^q, k) \approx_n^q (t_{n+1}^q, h(k)) \quad (\star).$$

This mapping yields a winning strategy for the second player (cf. Lemma 3.5). Whatever player I chooses in the first move, player II can answer in a correct way choosing $h(k)$ when player I chooses a node k in s_{n+1}^q or $h^{-1}(k)$ if player I plays in t_{n+1}^q.

The mapping h is defined by: $h(k) = \begin{cases} k & : \quad \neg l \leq k \wedge \neg l' \leq k \\ lr & : \quad k = l'r \\ l'r & : \quad k = lr \end{cases}$

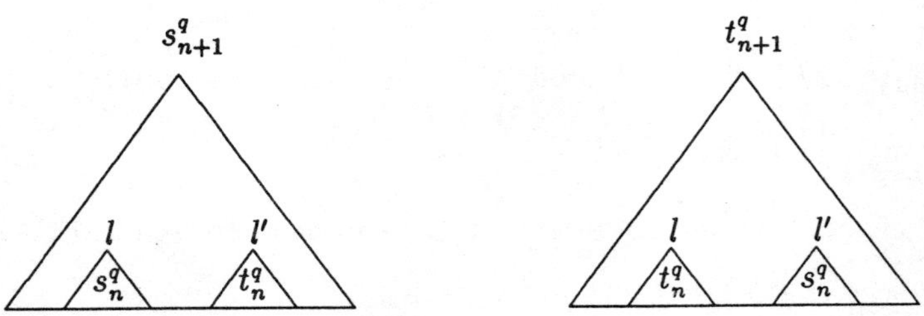

Lemma 3.10 applied to $(u_m, l) \approx_n^q (u_m, l')$ and $s_n^q \approx_n^q t_n^q$ yields $(s_{n+1}^q, l) \approx_n^q (t_{n+1}^q, l')$ and $(s_{n+1}^q, l') \approx_n^q (t_{n+1}^q, l)$. The Composition Lemma 3.9 together with $s_{n+1}^q{}^{[l} = t_{n+1}^q{}^{[l'} = s_n^q$ and $s_{n+1}^q{}^{[l'} = t_{n+1}^q{}^{[l} = t_n^q$ shows that $(\star)$ holds for all nodes below or equal to l and l'. For nodes in $dom(u_m)$ or in subtrees s_n^q, t_n^q not below l and l' we achieve $(\star)$ directly by an application of Lemma 3.10. $\square$

5 *FO* $\subsetneq$ *FO+MOD*, even for aperiodic tree languages

In this section we prove that even for aperiodic tree languages modulo counting quantifiers give additional power to first-order formulas. In a first step we prove that the language T_2 defined below belongs to *FO+MOD*(2).

Definition 5.1 Let $\Sigma' = \{\bar\wedge, \bar\vee, 0, 1\}$ where $\Sigma'_0 = \{0,1\}$ and $\Sigma'_2 = \{\bar\wedge, \bar\vee\}$. $\bar\wedge$ and $\bar\vee$ denote partial boolean functions defined by the following tables:

$\bar\wedge$	0	1	$\perp$
0	$\perp$	0	$\perp$
1	0	1	$\perp$
$\perp$	$\perp$	$\perp$	$\perp$

$\bar\vee$	0	1	$\perp$
0	0	1	$\perp$
1	1	$\perp$	$\perp$
$\perp$	$\perp$	$\perp$	$\perp$

We denote by $\mathrm{val}(t) \in \{0, 1, \perp\}$ the value of the expression corresponding to t. T_2 consists of all trees over Σ' with value 1.

Remark 5.2 T_2 is aperiodic.

Proof The syntactic monoid of T_2 consists of six elements. By inspecting the multiplication table we get: $\forall u, s \in S_\Sigma \ \forall t \in T_\Sigma \quad u \cdot s^2 \cdot t \in T_2$ iff $u \cdot s^3 \cdot t \in T_2$. □

The following Lemma states a relation between the value of a tree and the number of nodes labelled $\bar\wedge$ and 1 respectively.

Lemma 5.3
Let $t \in T_{\{\bar\wedge,\vee,0,1\}}$
$$\begin{aligned} \mathrm{val}(t) = 1 &\quad\Rightarrow\quad |\,t\,|_1 = |\,t\,|_{\bar\wedge} + 1 \\ \mathrm{val}(t) = 0 &\quad\Rightarrow\quad |\,t\,|_1 = |\,t\,|_{\bar\wedge} \end{aligned}$$

Proof The proof works by a simultaneous induction on both implications. □

We will use Lemma 5.3 in a slightly different but equivalent form.

Lemma 5.4
Let $t \in T_{\{\bar\wedge,\vee,0,1\}}$
$$\begin{aligned} |\,t\,|_1 \equiv |\,t\,|_{\bar\wedge} + 1 \,(\mathrm{mod}\,2) \ \wedge\ \mathrm{val}(t) \neq \perp &\iff \mathrm{val}(t) = 1 \\ |\,t\,|_1 \equiv |\,t\,|_{\bar\wedge} \quad (\mathrm{mod}\,2) \ \wedge\ \mathrm{val}(t) \neq \perp &\iff \mathrm{val}(t) = 0 \end{aligned}$$

The first part of each conjunction of Lemma 5.4 can be expressed in FO+MOD by

$$\varphi_i(y) = \exists^{i,2} y' \; y < y' \wedge (P_{\bar\wedge} y' \vee P_1 y') \quad \text{for } i = 0, 1.$$

Let us now consider a tree t with value $\perp$. Then there is a $<$-maximal node k where this value occurs first. Suppose $t(k) = \bar\wedge$. Then the value of the subtrees corresponding to both successors of k must be 0. Because the value of these trees is not $\perp$ we can apply Lemma 5.4 once more. So we come up with the following formulas.

$$\begin{aligned} v(t) \neq \perp \iff t \models \psi \text{ where } \psi = \neg\exists x \exists x_1 \exists x_2\ (\ & x S_1 x_1 \wedge x S_2 x_2 \\ & \wedge [\{P_{\bar{\wedge}} x \wedge \varphi_0(x_1) \wedge \varphi_0(x_2)\} \\ & \vee \{P_{\bar{\vee}} x \wedge \varphi_1(x_1) \wedge \varphi_1(x_2)\}]) \end{aligned}$$

$$v(t) = 1 \iff t \models \psi \wedge \exists x\ \varphi_1(x) \wedge \forall x_1\ x \leq x_1$$

This shows that T_2 is definable in FO+MOD. In the remainder of this section we show that T_2 is not first-order definable. The proof proceeds like the one of Theorem 4.2. In a first step we prove that another labelling of leaves of u_m suitable to this problem exists. Then we use this labelling to construct $\equiv_{n+1}$-equivalent trees from $\equiv_n$-equivalent ones.

Lemma 5.5 Let l be a leaf in u_m ($m \geq 2$). Then we can label the leaves of u_m with 0 and 1 in two different ways such that the resulting trees v_m and w_m have the following properties:

- $v_m(k) = w_m(k)$ for all leaves except l
- $v_m(l) = 1$ and $w_m(l) = 0$
- $\text{val}(v_m) = 1$ and $\text{val}(w_m) = 0$
- every subtree of height ≥ 2 has at least one leaf labelled with 0 and one leaf labelled with 1

Proof $\bar{\wedge}$ and $\bar{\vee}$ are commutative functions. Therefore subtrees corresponding to direct successors of a node can be exchanged without altering the value of the tree. Hence we may assume that l is the leftmost leaf of u_m. The construction of v_m and w_m proceeds by induction on $m \geq 2$. v_2 and w_2 look as follows:

For the induction step we define v_m and w_m in the following way:

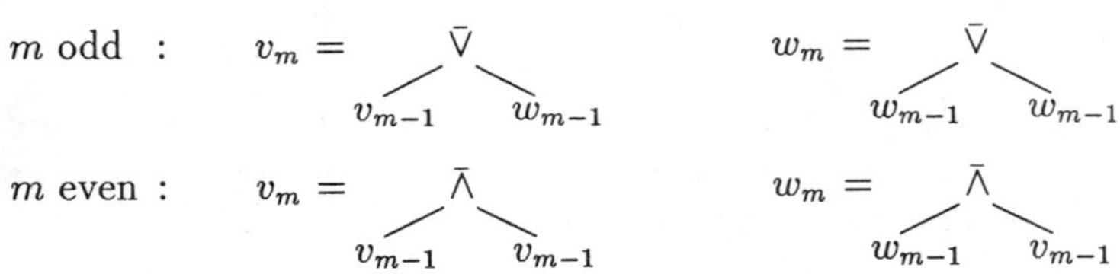

□

Lemma 5.6 Let l, l', l'' be three leaves in u_m ($m > 3$) such that each of them belongs to a different subtree of height 2. Then we can label the leaves of u_m with 0 and 1 in two different ways such that the resulting trees v_m and w_m have the following properties:

- $v_m(k) = w_m(k)$ for all leaves except l
- $v_m(l) = 1$, $w_m(l) = 0$
- $\text{val}(v_m) = 1$ and $\text{val}(w_m) = 0$
- $v_m(l') = w_m(l') = 1$
- $v_m(l'') = w_m(l'') = 0$

Proof The trees v_m and w_m of Lemma 5.5 fulfil the first three conditions. Every subtree of height 2 has at least one leaf labelled by 0 and 1 respectively. By interchanging the nodes in those subtrees of height 2 to which l' and l'' belong we achieve the remaining properties. □

Theorem 5.7 T_2 is not first-order definable.

Proof Following Remark 3.8 we have to construct two sequences of trees (s_n) and (t_n) with $s_n \equiv_n t_n$, $\text{val}(s_n) = 1$, $\text{val}(t_n) = 0$. We will also ensure that s_n and t_n differ only in the labelling of a single leaf.

For $n = 1$ we take as s_1 and t_1 the trees v_2 and w_2 of Lemma 5.5. s_1 and t_1 are $\equiv_1$-equivalent because all letters occur in both trees.

For the induction step we assume that s_n and t_n with the desired properties are given. Because the index of $\equiv_n$ is finite we may assume $u_m (m > 3)$ and leaves l, l', l'' with $(u_m, l) \equiv_n (u_m, l') \equiv_n (u_m, l'')$ and all three leaves belong to different subtrees of height 2. Let v_m and w_m be the trees guaranteed by Lemma 5.6. We construct s_{n+1} and t_{n+1} by replacing each leaf labelled 1 (resp. 0) in v_m and w_m by s_n (resp. t_n).

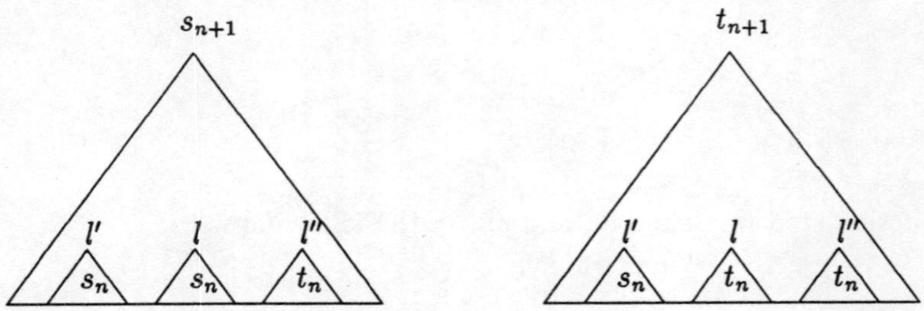

Hence $\text{val}(s_{n+1}) = 1$ and $\text{val}(t_{n+1}) = 0$. Since v_m and w_m differ only at leaf l, s_{n+1} and t_{n+1} differ only in one leaf in the corresponding subtrees s_n and t_n. In order to define a winning strategy for player II we have to distinguish two cases.

- If player I chooses any node k not below node l in s_{n+1} or t_{n+1}, then player II reacts choosing the same node in the other tree. $(s_{n+1}, k) \equiv_n (t_{n+1}, k)$ follows directly from Lemma 3.10.

- If player I chooses a node lr in s_{n+1}, then player II chooses the node $l'r$ in t_{n+1}. Applying Lemma 3.10 to $(u_m, l) \equiv_n (u_m, l')$ and $s_n \equiv_n t_n$ we obtain $(s_{n+1}, l) \equiv_n (t_{n+1}, l')$ and together with $s_{n+1}^{[l} = t_{n+1}^{[l'} = t_n$ and the Composition Lemma 3.9 we conclude that $(s_{n+1}, lr) \equiv_n (t_{n+1}, l'r)$.

  If player I chooses a node lr in t_{n+1}, then player II chooses the node $l''r$ in s_{n+1} and we deduce $\equiv_n$-equivalence of $(s_{n+1}, l''r)$ and (t_{n+1}, lr) in the same way.

□

6 Conclusion

In this paper we have studied modulo counting logics over finite trees. We have shown that FO+MOD is located in expressive power strictly between FO and FO+ACh and that these results still hold for the class of aperiodic tree languages. Our ongoing work is concerned with techniques that allow to deduce (non-)first-order definability of one language from (non-)first-order definability of another language; the simplicity of the example language T_1 and T_2 is of special interest in this approach. Without proof we state here that these methods allow to obtain example languages as in Theorem 4.2 and Theorem 5.7 over a one letter alphabet.
The main open questions we consider are the following:

- to find an effectively decidable characterization of first-order definability and
- to settle the status of *FO+ACh*, i.e. whether or not it exhausts the class of regular tree languages.

References

[1] J.R.Büchi, Weak second-order arithmetik and finite automata, Z. math. Logik Grundlagen Math., 6, 1960, pp. 66-92.

[2] J.Doner, Tree acceptors and some of their applications, J. of Comp. and System Sci., 4, 1970, pp. 406-451.

[3] A.Ehrenfeucht, An application of games to the completeness problem for formalized theories, Fund. Math., 49, 1961, pp. 129-141.

[4] C.C.Elgot, Decision problems of finite automata design and related arithmetics, Trans. Amer. Math. Soc., 98, 1961, pp. 21-52.

[5] F.Gecség and M.Steinby, "Tree Automata ", Akadémiai Kiadó, Budapest, 1984.

[6] U.Heuter, First-order properties of trees, star-free expressions and aperiodicity, RAIRO Informatique Théor. Appl., 25, 1991 , pp. 125-145.

[7] U.Heuter, Zur Klassifizierung regulärer Baumsprachen, Dissertation, RWTH Aachen, 1989.

[8] R.McNaughton and S.Papert, "Counter-free Automata", M.I.T.-Press, Cambridge, Mass., 1971.

[9] A.R.Meyer, A note on star-free events, J. Assoc. Comput. Mach., 16, 1969, pp. 220-225.

[10] J.D.Monk, "Mathematical Logic", Springer Verlag, New York Heidelberg Berlin.

[11] M.Nivat and A.Podelski, Tree monoids and recognizability of sets of finite trees, LITP Report 87-43, Université Paris VII, 1987.

[12] D.Niwiński, Modular quantifiers in antichain logic of trees, manuscript, 1990.

[13] J.G.Rosenstein, "Linear orderings", Academic Press, New York, 1982.

[14] M.P.Schützenberger, On monoids having only trivial subgroups, Inform. Contr., 8, 1965, pp. 190-194.

[15] H.Straubing, D.Thérien and W.Thomas, Regular languages defined with generalized quantifiers, Proc. 15th ICALP, T.Lepistö, A.Salomaa Eds., LNCS 317, 1988, pp. 561-575.

[16] W.Thomas, Classifying regular events in symbolic logic, J. of Comp. and System Sci., 25, 1982, pp. 360-376.

[17] W.Thomas, Logical aspects in the study of tree languages, Ninth Colloquium on Trees in Algebra and Programming, B.Courcelle Ed., Cambridge Univ. Press, 1984, pp. 31-51.

[18] J.W.Thatcher and J.B.Wright, Generalized finite automata with an application to a decision problem of second-order logic, Math. Syst. Theory, 2, 1968, pp.57-82.

Finite Tree Automata

with Cost Functions

Helmut Seidl

Fachbereich Informatik
Universität des Saarlandes
Im Stadtwald
D-6600 Saarbrücken 11
Federal Republic of Germany

ABSTRACT

Cost functions for tree automata are mappings from transitions to (tuples of) polynomials over some semiring. We consider four semirings, namely **N** the semiring of nonnegative integers, **A** the "arctical semiring", **T** the tropical semiring and **F** the semiring of finite subsets of nonnegative integers. We show: for semirings **N** and **A** it is decidable in polynomial time whether or not the costs of accepting computations is bounded; for **F** it is decidable in polynomial time whether or not the *cardinality* of occurring cost sets is bounded. In all three cases we derive explicit upper bounds. For semiring **T** we are able to derive similar results at least in case of polynomials of degree at most 1.
For **N** and **A** we extend our results to multi-dimensional cost functions.

0. Introduction

Finite tree automata are finite state devices which operate on labeled ordered trees. *Cost functions* c for tree automata map transitions to (tuples of) polynomials over some semiring **R** such that every computation obtains a *cost* c(ϕ) in **R** (resp. $\mathbf{R}^d$ in the multi-dimensional case). A pair of a finite tree automaton and a cost function is called cost automaton. There are two reasons why we are interested in finite tree automata with cost functions.
First, finite tree automata are an important tool of compiler generating systems like OPTRAN where they are applied for generating code selectors from descriptions of target machine assembly languages [GieSch88, WeiWi88]. A generated tree automaton A is meant to traverse the abstract syntax tree of an input program. The different accepting computations of A correspond to different possibilities of target machine code generation. From these the "cheapest" one is selected according to some suitable cost measure. In fact, these measures are of a type similar to the cost functions we consider here.
The second reason why we are interested in cost automata is of a more theoretical nature. In [CouMo90] Courcelle and Mosbah investigated MS (i.e. *M*onadic *S*econd-Order) evaluations

on graphs and came up with a general method to translate these to evaluations of graph expressions over suitable semirings. Their method allows to derive polynomial algorithms for a huge class of problems on families of graphs like series parallel graphs, graphs definable by contextfree hyperedge replacement grammars, etc.. To be more specific consider, e.g., the family SP(Σ) of *series parallel graphs* with edge labels from Σ. It consists of acyclic digraphs with one source and one sink whose edges are labeled by elements from Σ. SP(Σ) inductively can be defined as follows:

(1) A single directed edge e labeled by some $a \in \Sigma$ is in SP(Σ);

(2) If $G_1, G_2 \in$ SP(Σ) then both the series and the parallel composition of G_1 and G_2 are elements from SP(Σ). The series composition is obtained from G_1 and G_2 by pasting the sink of G_1 with the source of G_2 whereas the parallel composition is obtained by pasting the two sources as well as the two sinks.

Every series parallel graph can be represented by a graph expression, i.e. some tree over the ranked alphabet $\Sigma \cup \{\|, \cdot\}$ where symbols $a \in \Sigma$ represent edges labeled by a, $\cdot$ and $\|$ have rank 2 and denote series and parallel composition respectively.

Let G denote the graph represented by the graph expression g (the binary operators written in infix notation):

$$g = a \,\|\, ((a \cdot d) \,\|\, b) \cdot c)$$

If we are interested in the *number* of paths from the source to the sink of G we use an evaluation of g over the semiring **N** of naturals. Namely, the leaves of the expression tree (i.e. the edges of G) are counted 1; whereas $\|$ and $\cdot$ are viewed as the polynomials $x_1 + x_2$ and $x_1\, x_2$. Evaluating g, we obtain 3 as a result.

To compute the *length* of the shortest path from the source to the sink of G we employ the *tropical* semiring **T** where addition is $\sqcap$ and multiplication is +. We attach cost one to the leaves; to $\|$ and $\cdot$ we attach the polynomials $x_1 \sqcap x_2$ and $x_1 + x_2$ respectively. The result is 1.

The maximal *breadth* of G is computed over the "arctical" semiring **A**. Here, addition is $\sqcup$ instead of $\sqcap$ whereas multiplication is again +. As above, cost one is attached to the leaves of the expression, to $\|$ we now attach the polynomial $x_1 + x_2$, and to $\cdot$ the polynomial $x_1 \sqcup x_2$. Thus, evaluation of g yields 3.

Finally, to compute the *set of path lengthes* of G we need semiring **F**. **F** consists of all finite subsets of $\mathbb{N}_0$ where addition is set union and multiplication is addition of numbers extended to sets. We attach cost $\{1\}$ to the leaves of the expression. $\|$ is interpreted as the polynomial $x_1 \cup x_2$, and $\cdot$ as the polynomial $x_1 + x_2$. The resulting set is $\{1, 2, 3\}$.

We are interested in decision problems like this:

- "Is there a global bound to the breadth of graphs described by graph expressions from some tree language L?"
- "Is there a global bound to the length of the shortest path in graphs described by graph expressions from some tree language L?"

Provided the tree language L is the language accepted by some finite tree automaton A the evaluation functions in question turn out to be cost functions for A over a suitable semiring **R**. Thus, decision problems of the above type correspond to boundedness problems for tree automata with cost functions over **R**. In [HaKre89] decidability was proven for the case of cost functions over **N** or **A**. We improve their results by giving *polynomial time* algorithms for boundedness in these cases. Our algorithms are based on *syntactic* properties which are easy to test but which (at least for "parameter-reduced" automata) precisely characterize boundedness. We furthermore consider semirings **T** and **F**. In case of **T** we are able to decide boundedness - provided the polynomials occurring in the cost function are of degree at most 1. For this, we introduce a new technique to pump up different (even overlapping) subparts of a computation simultaneously. In case of **F** we show that it can be decided in polynomial time whether or not the *cardinalities* of cost sets of accepting computations are bounded or not.

The paper is organized as follows. In Section 1, we introduce our basic notation concerning trees and tree automata. In Section 2, we introduce semirings, our notation concerning polynomials over semirings and cost functions. We give a general method how to parameter-reduce **R**-cost automata (Theorem 1). In Section 3, we consider the case of 1-dimensional cost functions for each of the semirings **N**, **A**, **T** and **F** (Theorems 2, 3, 4 and 5). We derive polynomial time algorithms deciding boundedness for each of these semirings - in case of **T** however, only provided the polynomials occurring in the cost function have degree at most 1. Also, we provide explicit upper bounds depending only on structural parameters of the automata and cost functions in question. Section 4 extends the results of Section 2 and 3 to multidimensional cost functions for the semirings **N** and **A** (Theorems 6, 7 and 8). Section 5 concludes with open problems.

1. Basics

A *ranked alphabet* or *signature* is a pair (Σ,ρ) where Σ is a finite alphabet and $\rho\colon \Sigma \to \mathbb{N}_0$ is a function mapping symbols to their rank. Usually, if ρ is understood we write Σ for short and define $\Sigma_j = \rho^{-1}(j)$. The maximal j such that $\Sigma_j \neq \emptyset$ is called the *rank* of Σ.

T_Σ denotes the free Σ-algebra of (finite ordered Σ-labeled) *trees*, i.e. T_Σ is the smallest set T satisfying (i) $\Sigma_0 \subseteq T$, and (ii) if $a \in \Sigma_m$ and $t_1,\ldots,t_m \in T$, then $a(t_1,\ldots,t_m) \in T$. Note: (i) can be viewed as the subcase of (ii) where m = 0.

The set of *nodes* of t , O(t) is the subset of $\mathbb{N}^*$ defined by $O(t) = \{\varepsilon\}\cup\bigcup_{j=1}^{m} j\cdot O(t_j)$ where $t = a(t_1,\ldots,t_m)$ for some $a \in \Sigma_m$, $m \geq 0$. The *size* $|t|$ of t is defined as the cardinality of O(t). For nodes r, r' we write $r < r'$ to denote that r is a proper prefix of r'. If neither $r < r'$, $r' < r$ nor $r = r$ then we call r and r' *incomparable* and write $r \not\lessgtr r'$.

t defines maps $t(\_)\colon O(t) \to \Sigma$ and $t/\_\colon O(t) \to T_\Sigma$ mapping the nodes o of t to their labels or the subtree of t with root o, respectively. We have

$$t(o) = \begin{cases} a & \text{if } o=\varepsilon \\ t_j(o') & \text{if } o=j\cdot o' \end{cases} \quad \text{and} \quad t/o = \begin{cases} t & \text{if } o=\varepsilon \\ t_j/o' & \text{if } o=j\cdot o' \end{cases}$$

Let X denote a set of variables of rank 0. Define $T_\Sigma(X) = T_{\Sigma\cup X}$. We use this different notation in order to indicate which variables are to be substituted. (Clearly, $T_\Sigma \subseteq T_\Sigma(X)$.) Assume $t \in T_\Sigma(X)$. t is called X-*proper* iff every $x \in X$ occurs in t exactly once. If $X = \{x\}$ we write x-proper instead of $\{x\}$-proper, and if X is understood we skip the prefix X.

Every map $\theta\colon X \to T_\Sigma(X)$ can be extended to a map $\theta\colon T_\Sigma(X) \to T_\Sigma(X)$ by $t\theta = a(t_1\theta,\ldots,t_m\theta)$ whenever $t = a(t_1,\ldots,t_m)$. θ is called X-*substitution* or simply substitution if X is understood. If $X = \{x_1,\ldots,x_m\}$ and $x_i\theta = t_i$, we denote $t\theta$ also by $t[t_1,\ldots,t_m]$. Of special importance is the case where the set X of variables which are to be substituted consists of just one element x.

Assume $x\theta = t_2$ and $t_1 \in T_\Sigma(x) = T_\Sigma(\{x\})$. Then we write $t_1\theta = t_1t_2$. The set $T_\Sigma(x)$ is a monoid w.r.t. x-substitution. (The neutral element is x).
For $t \in T_\Sigma(X)$ we define the k-th power t^k of t by $t^1 = t$ and for $k > 1$, $t^k = t\theta$ where $x\theta = t^{k-1}$ for every $x \in X$. Observe that even if t was proper t^k does not need to be proper as well.

A *finite tree automaton* (FTA for short) is a 4-tuple $A = (Q,\Sigma,\delta,Q_F)$ where Q is a finite set of *states*, $Q_F \subseteq Q$ is the set of *final* states, Σ is the signature of *input trees*, and $\delta \subseteq \bigcup_{m\geq 0} Q\times\Sigma_m\times Q^m$ is the set of *transitions* of A; the transitions in $\delta\cap\bigcup_{m\geq 0}\{q\}\times\Sigma_m\times Q^m$ are also called q-*transitions*.
For Sections 1, 2 and 3 let X denote the set of variables $\{x_j \mid j \in \mathbb{N}\}$, and X_k the set of variables $\{x_j \mid j \in [1,k]\}$ for $k \in \mathbb{N}$. Let $t = a(t_1,...,t_m) \in T_\Sigma(X_k)$ and $q, q_1,..., q_k \in Q$. A $(q,q_1...q_k)$-*computation* ϕ of A for t starts at variables x_j in states q_j and consists of $(p_j,q_1...q_k)$-computations of A for the subtrees t_j, $j = 1,...,m$, together with a transition $(q,a,p_1...p_m) \in \delta$ for the root. We write the state at the root to the left of the states at the variable leaves. This convention is chosen in accordance with our prefix notation of trees and the left-to-right order of substitutions. Formally, we represent ϕ as a tree over signature δ and set of variables X_k as follows. If $t = x_j$ and $q = q_j$ then $\phi = x_j$. If $t = a(t_1,...,t_m)$ then $\phi = \tau(\phi_1,...,\phi_m)$ where $\tau = (q,a,p_1...p_m) \in \delta$ for suitable states $p_1,...,p_m \in Q$ and ϕ_j is a $(p_j,q_1...q_k)$-computation for t_j, $j = 1,...,m$.
The set of all $(q,q_1...q_k)$-computations is denoted by $\Phi^{(q,q_1...q_k)}$.
Assume $t \in T_\Sigma(X_k)$ and $t = t_0[t_1,...,t_k]$. Assume ϕ_0 is a $(q,p_1...p_k)$-computation for t_0, and ϕ_i are $(p_i,q_1...q_m)$-computations for t_i, $i = 1,...,k$. Then $\phi_0[\phi_1,...,\phi_k]$ is a $(q,q_1...q_m)$-computation ϕ of A for t. Conversely, if t_0 contains exactly one occurrence of any x_j, $j = 1,...,k$ (i.e. is X_k-proper), then every $(q,q_1...q_m)$-computation ϕ for t uniquely can be decomposed into a $(q,p_1...p_k)$-computation ϕ_0 for t_0, and $(p_i,q_1...q_m)$-computations ϕ_i for t_i (for suitable states p_i) such that $\phi = \phi_0[\phi_1,...,\phi_k]$. ϕ_i is called *subcomputation* of ϕ on t_i.
A (q,ε)-computation is also called q-computation. A q-computation is called *accepting*, iff $q\in Q_F$. $L(A) = \{t \in T_\Sigma \mid$ there is an accepting computation of A for t$\}$ is the *language* accepted by A. The *size* of A, $|A|$, is defined by $|A| = \sum_{(q,a,q_1...q_m)\in\delta} (m+2)$. For estimating the complexity of our algorithms we always assume that the input signature Σ is *fixed*. Only the sets of states and transitions vary. Thus especially, the rank of Σ is viewed as a *constant*.
The algorithms for tree automata we consider mainly run on a data structure called *trace graph*. For FTA $A = (Q,\Sigma,\delta,Q_F)$ the *trace graph* of A is the edge-labeled digraph $G(A) = (V,E)$ where the set of vertices V equals Q, and the set of edges E consists of all triples $(q,<\tau,j>,q')$ where $\tau = (q,a,q_1...q_m)$ is a q-transition in δ with $q_j = q'$.

Call a state $q \in Q$ *useless* if there is no accepting computation in which there occurs a q-transition, and *useful* otherwise. An FTA A is called *reduced* iff A has no useless states. Useless states can be removed without changing the "behavior" of A. We have:

Proposition 1
For every FTA $A = (Q,\Sigma,\delta,Q_F)$ there is an FTA $A_r = (Q_r,\Sigma,\delta_r,Q_{r,F})$ with $L(A) = L(A_r)$ such that

- $Q_r \subseteq Q$, $\delta_r \subseteq \delta$ and $Q_{r,F} \subseteq Q_F$;
- A_r is reduced; and

A_r can be constructed from A in polynomial time. □

2. Cost Automata

In this section we consider polynomials over semirings and introduce cost automata. A (commutative) *semiring* **R** (with 0 and 1) is a 5-tuple **R** = (R,+,·,0,1) where (R,+,0) and (R,·,1) are commutative monoids with neutral elements 0 and 1 respectively such that

$$0 \cdot a = 0 \quad \text{and} \quad a \cdot (b + c) = (a \cdot b) + (a \cdot c)$$

for all a, b, c ∈ R. R is also called the *carrier* of **R**. As usual, we also write r ∈ **R** iff r is an element of the carrier of **R**. Especially, we consider the following four semirings.

(1) The *naturals* **N** = ($\mathbb{N}_0$,+,·,0,1) with usual addition and multiplication;

(2) The *arctical semiring* **A** with carrier $\mathbb{N}_0 \cup \{-\infty\}$ where addition is $\sqcup$ and multiplication is + on integers extended by $x + -\infty = -\infty + x = -\infty$;

(3) The *tropical semiring* **T** with carrier $\mathbb{N}_0 \cup \{\infty\}$ where addition is $\sqcap$ and multiplication is + on integers extended by $x + \infty = \infty + x = \infty$;

(4) The semiring **F** whose carrier consists of all finite subsets of nonnegative integers where addition is set union, and multiplication is addition extended to sets i.e. $A + B = \{a+b \mid a \in A, b \in B\}$.

Observe that all four semirings have a natural (in case of **F** partial) ordering which in case of N, **T** and **A** is derived from the ordering $-\infty < 0 < 1 < 2 < \ldots < n < \ldots < \infty$. The ordering of **F** is given by set inclusion. For these orderings all finite least upper bounds exist. In **N**, **A** and T, we denote the least upper bound of an unbounded set of semiring elements by ∞. For **F**, the least upper bound of a finite number of semiring elements is their union. A least upper bound of an infinite number of elements from **F** is defined as their union as well - although it may no longer be an element of **F**.

The set of polynomials over **R** with variables from X is denoted by **R**[X]. A *monomial* m is a polynomial of the form $h \cdot x_1^{\varepsilon_1} \cdot \ldots \cdot x_k^{\varepsilon_k}$. h is called the *coefficient*, and $\varepsilon_1 + \ldots + \varepsilon_k$ the *degree* of m. The *size* of m, |m| is defined as $|m| = 1 + \#\{j \mid \varepsilon_j \neq 0\}$. The latter definition refers to the intuition that both every semiring element and every exponent can be stored in one storage cell of a Random Access Machine (with uniform cost measure). For simplicity we assume that such a machine can execute comparisons and semiring operations of two elements r, r' ∈ **R** in one step. Thus, a polynomial algorithm (say, for a Turing machine) is only obtained from a polynomial algorithm for such a RAM if each involved comparison and semiring operation can be executed in polynomial time.

For our purposes we assume that a polynomial p ∈ **R**[X_m] always is given as a sum of monomials where no monomial has a coefficient 0. The degree of p is the maximal degree of a monomial in p whereas we choose the *size* of p as the sum of the sizes of the monomials in p. Variable x_j *occurs* in p, or p *depends* on x_j iff p contains a monomial $h \cdot x_1^{\varepsilon_1} \cdot \ldots \cdot x_k^{\varepsilon_k}$ with $\varepsilon_j \neq 0$.

As for substitutions, a map θ: X → **R**[X] can be extended to a map **R**[X] → **R**[X] which is denoted by θ as well. For f ∈ **R**[X], fθ is defined by function composition: fθ is the function obtained from f by first applying the functions xθ and then applying f to the results. As for trees, we call θ a *X-substitution* or substitution, if X is understood. If $X = \{x_1,...,x_m\}$ and $x_i\theta = f_i$ we denote $f\theta$ by $f[f_1,...,f_m]$ and also write $f\ f_1$ for $f[f_1]$.

Fact 0

Assume $\mathbf{R} \in \{\mathbf{N}, \mathbf{A}, \mathbf{F}\}$ and p is a polynomial in $\mathbf{R}[x] = \mathbf{R}[\{x\}]$. Then the following holds:

(1) If $b_1, b_2 \in \mathbf{R}$ and $b_1 \leq b_2$ then $p[b_1] \leq p[b_2]$.

(2) Assume x occurs in p and $b \in \mathbf{R}$.

- If $\mathbf{R} \in \{\mathbf{N}, \mathbf{A}\}$, then $p(b) \geq b$.
- If $\mathbf{R} = \mathbf{F}$ then $\#p(b) \geq \#b$. □

Assume $A = (Q,\Sigma,\delta,Q_F)$ is an FTA and $\mathbf{R} \in \{\mathbf{N}, \mathbf{T}, \mathbf{A}, \mathbf{F}\}$. A $\mathbf{R}$-*cost function* for A is a mapping c: $\delta \rightarrow \mathbf{R}[X]$ where $c(\tau) \in \mathbf{R}[X_m]$ provided $\tau = (q,a,q_1...q_m)$.
c(_) is extended to computations ϕ in the natural way. If $\phi = x_j$ then $c(\phi) = x_j$. If $\phi = \tau(\phi_1,...,\phi_m)$ for some $\tau \in \delta$ then $c(\phi) = c(\tau)[c(\phi_1),...,c(\phi_m)]$. A $\mathbf{R}$-*cost automaton* M is a pair M = (A,c) where A is the FTA *underlying* M and c: $\delta \rightarrow \mathbf{R}[X]$ is a $\mathbf{R}$-cost function for A.
The *size* of M consists of the size of A together with the space to represent c. Hence we define $|M| = |A| + \sum_{\tau\in\delta} |c(\tau)|$.
The set of costs of A w.r.t. c, c(A), is defined by

$$c(A) = \{c(\phi) \mid \phi \text{ accepting computation of } A\}$$

In case $\mathbf{R} \in \{\mathbf{N}, \mathbf{A}, \mathbf{N}\}$, we are interested in whether the least upper bound of costs $\sqcup M = \sqcup\ c(A)$ is finite. In case $\mathbf{R} = \mathbf{F}$ we are interested in whether the least upper bound of cost cardinalities $\#M = \sqcup\ \{\#B \mid B \in c(A)\}$ is finite. If so, we say that the costs of M are *bounded*, or shorter: M ist bounded.
We would like to eliminate costs of subcomputations which do not contribute to the final cost. Consider, e.g., semiring **N**. A subcomputation may not contribute to the final cost if its cost is multiplied by 0. It turns out that we can decide "online" whether or not a given subcomputation has cost 0 (or, if we like, 1). In order to have a machinery general enough to cope with semirings **A** and **F** as well we introduce the notion of *faithful* subsets of semirings.
Assume H: $\mathbf{R} \rightarrow \mathbf{R'}$ is a surjective homomorphism of semirings where $\mathbf{R'}$ is finite. Subset E $\subseteq \mathbf{R}$ is called faithful (via H) iff $E \subseteq \{r \in \mathbf{R} \mid H^{-1}(H(r)) = \{r\}\}$.

Examples: For every $m \in \mathbb{N}$,

(1) $[0,m-1]$ is a faithful subset of **N**;

(2) $\{-\infty\} \cup [0,m-1]$ is a faithful subset of **A**;

(3) $[0,m-1] \cup \{\infty\}$ is a faithful subset of **T**; and

(4) $2^{[0,m-1]}$ is a faithful subset of **F**.

In all these four cases of faithful subsets $E \subseteq \mathbf{R}$, the subset E is faithful via some homomorphism H_m: $\mathbf{R} \rightarrow \mathbf{R}_m$ where $\mathbf{R}_m$ is a finite semiring obtained from **R** by an appropriate "truncation".

(1) N_m is the semiring with carrier $[0,m]$ where addition $+_m$ and multiplication $\cdot_m$ are defined by $x +_m y = m \sqcap (x + y)$ and $x \cdot_m y = m \sqcap (x \cdot y)$; such that $H_m(x) = x \sqcap m$.

(2) A_m is the semiring with carrier $\{-\infty\} \cup [0,m]$ ordered by $-\infty < 0 < 1 < \ldots < m$. As for **A**, addition is $\sqcup$ and multiplication is $+_m$ defined by $x +_m y = m \sqcap (x + y)$ where "+" here is ordinary addition extended by $-\infty + x = x + -\infty = x$. Again, $H_m(x) = x \sqcap m$.

(3) Analogously to $\mathbf{A}_m$, $\mathbf{T}_m$ is the semiring with carrier $[0,m] \cup \{\infty\}$ ordered by $0 < 1 < \ldots < m < \infty$. Addition is now $\sqcap$ and multiplication is $+_m$ defined by: $x +_m y = m \sqcap (x + y)$ where "+" here is ordinary addition extended by $\infty + x = x + \infty = \infty$. Now, $H_m(x) = \infty$ if $x = \infty$ and $H_m(x) = x \sqcap m$ otherwise.

(4) Finally, $\mathbf{F}_m$ is the semiring with carrier $2^{[0,m-1]} \cup \{u\}$ for some new symbol u. Addition in $\mathbf{F}_m$ is set union extended by $x \cup u = u \cup x = u$, whereas multiplication $+_m$ is defined by

$$A +_m B = \begin{cases} \{a + b \mid a \in A, b \in B\} & \text{if } a + b < m \text{ for all } a \in A, b \in B \\ u & \text{otherwise} \end{cases}$$

Now, $H_m(B) = B$ if $B \subseteq [0,m-1]$ and $H_m(B) = u$ otherwise.

Since all the semirings $\mathbf{R}_m$ are finite we can incorporate the evaluation of cost functions $H_m\, c$ into the computation of the tree automaton itself. Assume $M = (A,c)$ is a **R**-cost automaton where A is reduced and $E \subseteq R$ is faithful where $0 \in E$. M is called E-*reduced* iff there are sets $U_r(A,c)$, $r \in E$, such that a q-computation has cost r iff $q \in U_r(A,c)$.

We would like to use information about costs of subcomputations to "simplify" the polynomials involved. We call M E-*parameter-reduced* iff M is E-reduced and the following holds:

(1) For every $r \in E \setminus \{0\}$, $p \in U_r(A,c)$, $\tau = (q,a,q_1 \ldots q_k) \in \delta$ and $j \in [1,k]$, $p \neq q_j$.

(2) If $\tau \in \delta$ is a q-transition with $q \in U_r(A,c)$ then $c(\tau) = r$.

(3) If $\tau = (q,a,q_1 \ldots q_k) \in \delta$ and x_j does not occur in $c(\tau)$ then $q_j \in U_0(A,c)$.

For our characterizations of bounded costs we only will refer to E-parameter-reduced **R**-cost automata where $E = \{0, 1\}$. For simplicity, we skip the prefix "E-" in this case.

Before we explain the corresponding results we first convince ourselves that we w.l.o.g. always may assume that the cost automata in question are parameter-reduced. For this we prove Theorem 1:

Theorem 1

Assume $\mathbf{R} \in \{\mathbf{N}, \mathbf{T}, \mathbf{A}, \mathbf{F}\}$, and $E \subseteq \mathbf{R}$ is faithful via H_m: $\mathbf{R} \to \mathbf{R}_m$ with $0 \in E$.

(1) For every **R**-cost automaton $M = (A,c)$ there is an E-reduced **R**-cost automaton $M_E = (A_E,c_E)$ such that

- $L(A) = L(A_E)$ and $c(A) = c_E(A_E)$;
- if A has n states then A_E has at most $(\#\mathbf{R}_m) \cdot n$ states and $|M_E| \leq |M| \cdot (\#\mathbf{R}_m)^L$;
- M_E can be constructed by a RAM in time polynomial in $|M|$ and $\#\mathbf{R}_m$.

(2) For every E-reduced **R**-cost automaton $M = (A,c)$ there is an E-parameter-reduced **R**-cost automaton $M_{E,r} = (A_{E,r},c_{E,r})$ such that

- $L(A) = L(A_E)$ and $c(A) = c_{E,r}(A_{E,r})$;
- if A has n states then $A_{E,r}$ has at most 3·n states and $|M_{E,r}| \le |M| \cdot 3^L$
- $M_{E,r}$ can be constructed by a RAM in polynomial time. □

As a corollary we obtain:

Corollary 1

(1)

- Assume $\mathbf{R} \in \{\mathbf{N}, \mathbf{T}, \mathbf{A}\}$. It can be decided in polynomial time for a given **R**-cost automaton M = (A,c) and $m \in \mathbb{N}$, whether or not $\sqcup M < m$.
- Assume $m \in \mathbb{N}$ is fixed. Then it can be decided in polynomial time for a given **F**-cost automaton M = (A,c), whether or not $c(A) \subseteq 2^{[0,m-1]}$.

(2) Let $\mathbf{R} \in \{\mathbf{N}, \mathbf{T}, \mathbf{A}, \mathbf{F}\}$. For every **R**-cost automaton M = (A,c), a parameter-reduced **R**-cost automaton $M_r = (A_r, c_r)$ can be constructed in polynomial time with $L(A) = L(A_r)$ and $c(A) = c_r(A_r)$. □

3. Upper Bounds for Bounded Costs

In the next four subsections we successively consider semirings **N**, **A**, **T** and **F**. In case of the semirings **N**, **A** and **T** (here at least for cost functions of degree at most 1) we compute upper bounds for bounded costs and give polynomial time decision procedures for boundedness. In case of semiring **F** we derive an upper bound for the cardinality of occurring cost sets provided it is finite and prove that it also can be decided in polynomial time whether or not it is finite.

3.1. The Semiring *N*

In this section we consider costs in the semiring **N**.

Fact 1

Assume $p \in \mathbf{N}[x]$ and $b \notin \{0,1\}$. Then either $p[b] > b$ or $p \in \mathbf{N} \cup \{x\}$. □

The **N**-cost automaton M = (A,c) has Property (N) iff

(N) If $(q,\langle\tau,j\rangle,q')$ is an edge of a strong component of the trace graph G(A), then $c(\tau) \in \{0,x_j\}$.

Obviously, it can be decided in polynomial time whether or not M has Property (N). We have:

Theorem 2

For a parameter-reduced **N**-cost automaton M = (A,c) the following three statements are equivalent:

(1) M is bounded;

(2) M has Property (N);

$$\text{(3)} \qquad \sqcup M \leq \begin{cases} [(L+1)\cdot H]^{n} & \text{if } k = 1 \\ [(L+1)^{k}\cdot H]^{k^{n}} & \text{if } k > 1 \end{cases}$$

where n is the number of states of A; L is the rank of the input signature; H and k are upper bounds for the coefficients and degrees resp. of polynomials occurring in c.
It can be decided in polynomial time whether or not M is bounded.

Proof: Assume M does not have Property (N). Then there is an accepting computation $\phi = \psi_1\psi_2\psi_3$ for proper (f,q)-computation ψ_1, proper (q,q)-computation ψ_2 and q-computation ψ_3 such that $c(\psi_2) \notin N$ and $c(\psi_2) \neq x_1$. Especially, it contains variable x_1. It follows that $c(\psi_3) \notin \{0,1\}$ since M is parameter-reduced. Hence by Fact 1 for every $k > 1$, $c(\psi_2^k\psi_3) = c(\psi_2)^k c(\psi_3) > k-1 + c(\psi_3) > k$. Since M is parameter-reduced, $c(\psi_1) \notin N$. Hence by Fact 0 (2), $c(\psi_1\psi_2^k\psi_3) = c(\psi_1)c(\psi_2)^k c(\psi_3) > k$; and the costs of M cannot be bounded. Therefore, (1) implies (2).
Since statement (3) trivially implies (1) it remains to show that (2) implies the upper bounds given in (3). Assume ϕ is an accepting computation of A. Define a *recursive decomposition* D of $\phi = \phi_\varepsilon$ by

$$\phi_o = \psi_o\tau_o(\phi_{o1},\ldots,\phi_{om_o}),\ o \in O(v)\ ,$$

for some $v \in T_\Sigma$ such that for every $o \in O(v)$:

(D1) $\tau_o \in \delta$;

(D2) ψ_o is a proper (q_o,q_o)-computation for some state $q_o \in Q$ which differs from every state $q_{o'}$ where o' is a proper prefix of o.

If M has Property (N) then for all $o \in O(v)$, $c(\psi_o) \in \{0, x_1\}$. Since M is parameter-reduced, this implies that for every $o \in O(v)$,

$$c(\phi_o) = c(\tau_o)[c(\phi_{o1}),\ldots,c(\phi_{om_o})].$$

By (D2), the depth of v is at most n-1. Since every polynomial $c(\tau_o)$ is a sum of monomials $h\cdot x_1^{\varepsilon_1}\cdot\ldots\cdot x_m^{\varepsilon_m}$ with $h \leq H$ and $\sum_{j=1}^{m}\varepsilon_j \leq k$, the upper bounds in statement (3) of the Theorem follow.

□

3.2. The Semiring *A*

Next, we consider costs in the semiring **A**.

Fact 2

Assume $p \in A[x]$ and $b \notin \{-\infty,0\}$. Then either $p^k[b] > k$ for all $k > 0$ or, p has one of the forms $p = a$ or $p = a \sqcup x$ for some $a \in A$. □

The A-cost automaton M = (A,c) has Property (A) iff

(A) If $(q,\langle\tau,j\rangle,q')$ is an edge of a strong component of the trace graph G(A), then $c(\tau) \in A[X \setminus \{x_j\}]$ or $c(\tau) = p \sqcup x_j$ where $p \in A[X \setminus \{x_j\}]$.

Obviously, it can be decided in polynomial time whether or not M has Property (A). We have:

Theorem 3
Assume M = (A,c) is a parameter-reduced A-cost automaton. The following three statements are equivalent:

(1) M is bounded;

(2) M has Property (A);

(3) $\sqcup M \leq \begin{cases} n \cdot H & \text{if } k = 1 \\ 2 \cdot H \cdot k^n & \text{if } k > 1 \end{cases}$

where n is the number of states of A; L is the rank of the input signature; H and k are upper bounds for the coefficients and degrees resp. of polynomials occurring in c.
It can be decided in polynomial time whether or not M is bounded.

Proof: The proof of implication (1)=>(2) is analogous to the proof of the corresponding implication of the last theorem. Assume M does not have Property (A). Then there is an accepting computation $\phi = \psi_1\psi_2\psi_3$ for proper (f,q)-computation ψ_1, proper (q,q)-computation ψ_2 and q-computation ψ_3 such that $c(\psi_2)$ neither is in **A** nor in $\mathbf{A}\sqcup x_1$. Especially, it contains an occurrence of x_1. Since M is parameter-reduced $c(\phi_3) \notin \{-\infty,0\}$. Hence by Fact 2 for every k > 1, $c(\psi_2^k\psi_3) = c(\psi_2)^k c(\psi_3) > k$. Also since M is parameter-reduced, x_1 occurs in $c(\psi_1)$. Hence by Fact 0 (2), $c(\psi_1\psi_2^k\psi_3) = c(\psi_1)c(\psi_2)^k c(\psi_3) > k$ and the costs of M cannot be bounded. Therefore, (1) implies (2).
Since implication (3)=>(1) is again trivial it only remains to deal with implication (2)=>(3). Assume ϕ is an accepting computation of A. As in the proof of Theorem 2, we consider recursive decompositions of ϕ. By Property (A) there exists such a recursive decomposition of $\phi = \phi_\varepsilon$, $\phi_o = \psi_o\tau_o(\phi_{o1},\ldots,\phi_{om_o})$, $o \in O(v)$, together with monomials m_o in $c(\tau_o)$, $o \in O(v)$, for some tree $v \in T_\Sigma$ of depth at most n-1 such that for all $o \in O(v)$:

$$c(\phi_o) = m_o[c(\phi_{o1}),\ldots,c(\phi_{om_o})]$$

Since every occurring monomial is of the form $m = h + \sum_{j=1}^{L}\varepsilon_j \cdot x_j$ with $h \leq H$ and $\sum_{j=1}^{L}\varepsilon_j \leq k$ we obtain the desired upper bounds. □

3.3. The Semiring *T*

In this subsection we consider costs in the semiring **T**. So, let M = (A,c) be a **T**-cost automaton where $A = (Q,\Sigma,\delta,Q_F)$. Here, we do not have such a simple characterization for bounded costs as in the two former cases. We consider only polynomials $p \in \mathbf{T}[X]$ of degree at most 1, i.e. polynomials of the form $p = h_0 \sqcap \prod_{j=1}^{m}(h_j+x_j)$ for some $h_j \in \mathbf{T}$. The set of these polynomials is denoted by $\mathbf{T}^{(1)}[X]$.

Assume ϕ is an accepting computation of A and $c\phi(o) = h_{o,0} \sqcap \prod_{j=1}^{m_o} h_{o,j}+x_j$. The *cost of a node* $o \in O(\phi)$ (in ϕ w.r.t. **c**) consists of the cost of o itself together with the costs along the path in ϕ from the root of ϕ to r, i.e. $c(o) = h_{o,0} + \sum_{o'j \leq o} h_{o',j}$. We have:

$$c(\phi) = \prod_{o \in O(\phi)} c(o)$$

Clearly, we are only interested in nodes o where c(o) < ∞. These nodes are called *∞-free*.
A node $o \in O(\phi)$ has a *costly cycle* iff $o = o_1o_2o_3$ such that both $\phi(o_1)$ and $\phi(o_1o_2)$ are p-transitions for some $p \in Q$, and there is a prefix o'j of o_2 such that $h_{o_1o',j} > 0$. The main result of this subsection is:

Theorem 4
Assume M = (A,c) is a T-cost automaton where the polynomials in **c** have degree at most 1. Then the following statements are equivalent:

(1) M is bounded;

(2) For every accepting computation ϕ there is a ∞-free node r which has no costly cycle;

(3) $\sqcup M \leq H \cdot n$

where n is the number of states of A, and H is an upper bound of the coefficients of the polynomials in **c**.
It is decidable in polynomial time whether or not M is bounded.

Proof: Certainly, (2) implies (3) and (3) implies (1). Also, provided the upper bound (3) holds we can by Corollary 1 decide in polynomial time whether or not M is bounded. Hence, it only remains to prove that (1) implies (2). The idea of the proof is the following. Assume (2) does not hold. Then there exists an accepting computation ϕ such that every minimal ∞-free node contains a costly cycle. We pump up all these cycles simultaneously to obtain an accepting computation of arbitrarily high costs. We interrupt the proof in order to introduce some machinery to treat *simultaneous pumping*. Note that some care has to be taken since pumping in one place may introduce new places where pumping has to be performed. To study this formally, we introduce the notion of *residual decompositions*.

Assume $\phi \in \Phi^{(p,\varepsilon)}$. A decomposition f of ϕ is given by proper computations $\phi_0 \in \Phi^{(p,q)}$, $\psi \in \Phi^{(q,q..q)}$ and $\phi_1,\ldots,\phi_d \in \Phi^{(q,\varepsilon)}$ such that $\phi = \phi_0\psi[\phi_1,\ldots,\phi_d]$.
Equivalently, the decomposition f of ϕ may be described by a pair <r,R> where $r \in O(\phi_0)$ is the leaf in u labeled by x_1 and R is the set of leaves of ψ labeled by a variable x_j. r is also called *root* of f.
A node o of ϕ is *factored* by f = <r,R>, iff o = rr'o' for some r' ∈ R.
Assume k ≥ 0. Pumping ϕ up k-times w.r.t. f, we obtain computation $\phi^{f,k} = \phi_0\psi^k[\phi_1,\ldots,\phi_d]$.
For ϕ and decomposition f = <r,R> of ϕ define $r_ж$ as the set of nodes o of ϕ of which r is *not* a prefix; R_0 is the set of proper prefixes of elements in R; R_1 is the set of nodes in ϕ/r which are incomparable to every node in R; and R_2 is the set of nodes o in ϕ/r which have a prefix in R.
Consider as an example $\phi = a(bc, a(a(c, c), c)) = \phi_0\psi[\phi_1,\phi_2]$ where $\phi_0 = a(bc, x_1)$; $\psi = a(a(x_1, c), x_2)$; $\phi_1 = c$ and $\phi_2 = c$. Then this decomposition can be written f = <r,R> with r = 2 and R = {1·1, 2}.
We have $r_ж$ = {ε, 1, 1·1}; R_0 = {ε, 1}; R_1 = {1·2}; and R_2 = {1·1, 2}.

Using these definitions we can partition the nodes of ϕ as follows:

$$O(\phi) = r_ж \cup r{\cdot}R_0 \cup r{\cdot}R_1 \cup r{\cdot}R_2$$

Accordingly, the set of nodes of the k-th pump $\phi^{f,k}$ of ϕ is partitioned:

$$O(\phi^{f,k}) = r_{\not\approx} \cup r{\cdot}R^{\leq k-1}{\cdot}R_0 \cup r{\cdot}R^{\leq k-1}{\cdot}R_1 \cup r{\cdot}R^{k}{\cdot}R_2$$

where $R^{\leq k-1} = \bigcup\{R^j \mid j \in [0,k-1]\}$.

Thus, every node $o \in O(\phi)$ gives rise to a set $O_o \subseteq O(\phi^{f,k})$, namely

$$O_o = \begin{cases} o & \text{if } o \in r_{\not\approx} \\ rR^{\leq k-1}o_1 & \text{if } o = ro_1 \text{ with } o_1 \in R_0 \\ rR^{\leq k-1}o_1 & \text{if } o = ro_1 \text{ with } o_1 \in R_1 \\ rR^{k-1}o_1 & \text{if } o = ro_1 \text{ with } o_1 \in R_2 \end{cases}$$

such that $O(\phi^{f,k}) = \bigcup\{O_o \mid o \in O(\phi)\}$.

For our application we are not interested in nodes o_1 in O_o which have proper prefixes in O_o. Therefore, we define the set $RES_{f,k}(o)$ of *residuals* of o as the set of *minimal* elements in O_o, i.e.

$$RES_{f,k}(o) = \begin{cases} o & \text{if } o \in r_{\not\approx} \\ ro_1 & \text{if } o = ro_1 \text{ with } o_1 \in R_0 \\ rR^{\leq k-1}o_1 & \text{if } o = ro_1 \text{ with } o_1 \in R_1 \\ rR^{k-1}o_1 & \text{if } o = ro_1 \text{ with } o_1 \in R_2 \end{cases}$$

Note that the definition of $RES_{f,k}(o)$ differs from O_o only in the second line. We find:

Proposition 2

(1) Assume $o, o' \in O(\phi)$.
If $o < o'$ then

$$\forall o_2 \in RES_{f,k}(o')\ \exists o_1 \in RES_{f,k}(o) : o_1 < o_2$$

If $o \not\approx o'$ then

$$\forall o_2 \in RES_{f,k}(o')\ \forall o_1 \in RES_{f,k}(o) : o_1 \not\approx o_2$$

(2) If o is ∞-free then $RES_{f,k}(o)$ consists also of ∞-free nodes.

(3) Every minimal ∞-free node of $\phi^{f,k}$ is the residual of some minimal ∞-free node of ϕ.
□

Besides decomposition $f = <r,R>$ consider a second decomposition $f' = <r',R'>$ of ϕ. f' gives rise to a set $RES_{f,k}(f')$ of *residual decompositions*, short: *residuals*. This set of decompositions of $\phi^{f,k}$ is determined in two steps. First, we compute the sets

$$S_0 = RES_{f,k}(r') \text{ and } S_1 = RES_{f,k}(r'R') = \bigcup_{o \in r'R'} RES_{f,k}(o)$$

The set S_0 gives the set of roots of the residual decompositions. By Proposition 2 (1), the nodes in S_1 can be partitioned into sets $S_{1,w}$, $w \in S_0$, where $S_{1,w}$ contains all nodes from S_1 of which w is a prefix. Define $R_w = \{o_1 \mid wo_1 \in S_{1,w}\}$. Finally, put $RES_{f,k}(f') = \{<w,R_w> \mid w \in S_0\}$.

We make the following simple observations:

- If $r' \not\asymp r$ then $RES_{f,k}(f') = \{f'\}$.
- If r' is a prefix of r then $RES_{f,k}(f') = \{<r',R''>\}$ for some set of nodes R''.
- $RES_{f,k}(f) = \{<r,R^k>\}$;
- If $r' = ro_1 \in rR_2$ then $RES_{f,k}(f') = \{<o,R'> \mid o \in rR^{k-1}o_1\}$.

Proposition 3 follows from the above definition and Proposition 2 (1).

Proposition 3
If node o of ϕ is factored by f' then every $\overline{o} \in RES_{f,k}(o)$ is factored by some $g \in RES_{f,k}(f')$.
□

Assume $c: \delta \rightarrow T^{(1)}[X]$ is a cost function, and $\phi \in \Phi^{(q,\varepsilon)}$. A decomposition $f = <r,R>$ of ϕ has *cost* at least k, iff $\sum_{o \lhd r'} c(\phi(ro)) \geq k$ for every $r' \in R$.
Assume $F = \{f_1,...,f_m\}$ is a set of decompositions f_μ of ϕ. F is called *complete* (for ϕ w.r.t. c) iff every ∞-free node o of ϕ is factored by some decomposition f_μ in F. If furthermore every f_μ has cost at least k, then F is called *k-complete*. Observe that if ϕ admits a k-complete set F of decompositions then $c(\phi) \geq k$. From Propositions 2 and 3 we deduce:

Proposition 4

(1) If F is complete then $RES_{f,k}(F) = \bigcup_{f' \in F} RES_{f,k}(f')$ is complete as well.

(2) If f' has cost at least h then every decomposition in $RES_{f,k}(f')$ also has cost at least h.
□

Proposition 5
Assume the accepting computation ϕ has a 1-complete set of decompositions. Then for every $k > 1$, an accepting computation ϕ' exists having a k-complete set of decompositions.

Proposition 5 can be applied to obtain a proof of Theorem 4.

Proof of Theorem 4 (continued): Assume statement (2) does not hold. Then there exists an accepting computation ϕ having a 1-complete set decompositions. By Proposition 5, this implies that for every k, there is a computation ϕ_k having a k-complete set of decompositions. Since $c(\phi_k) \geq k$, M cannot be bounded. □

The rest of this subsection is concerned with a proof of Proposition 5.

Proof of Proposition 5: Assume the 1-complete set of decompositions of ϕ is $F = \{f_1,...,f_m\}$ where r_μ is the root of f_μ. W.l.o.g. we assume that

(*) If $\mu < \mu'$ then r_μ is *not* a prefix of $r_{\mu'}$.

For h = 0,...,m, we inductively define computations ϕ_h with corresponding sets of decompositions F_h.

For h = 0, we set $\phi_0 = \phi$ and $F_0 = F$. $\phi_1 = \phi_0^{f_1,k}$, i.e. ϕ_1 is obtained from ϕ_0 by pumping up ϕ k times w.r.t. f_1. Accordingly, $F_1 = RES_{f_1,k}(F_0)$. By assumption (∗), the sets of residual decompositions of $f_2,...,f_m$ consist of just single elements, say $f_{1,2},...,f_{1,m}$ respectively, where the roots of $f_{1,\mu}$ and f_μ coincide. We can proceed with pumping up ϕ_1 k times w.r.t. $f_{1,2}$ to obtain ϕ_2 where $F_2 = RES_{f_{1,2},k}(F_1)$.

In general, assume ϕ_{h-1} and F_{h-1} are already computed and $f_{h-1,h},...,f_{h-1,m}$ are the decompositions in F_{h-1} with roots $r_h,...,r_m$. Then we define $\phi_h = \phi_{h-1}^{f,k}$ and $F_h = RES_{f,k}(F_{h-1})$ with $f = f_{h-1,h}$.

We claim that ϕ_m has a k-complete set of decompositions.

For a proof of this claim call a set F of decompositions of ϕ k-*complete up to* F' ⊆ F iff F is complete and (1) and (2) holds:

(1) Every decomposition f ∈ F \ F' has cost at least k.

(2) Every decomposition f ∈ F' has cost at least 1.

We prove:

- For h = 0...,m, F_h is k-complete for ϕ_h up to $\{f_{h,h+1},...,f_{h,m}\}$.

Proposition 5 is the special instance of this statement where h = m . It is proved in three steps: For every h ∈ {0,...,m},

- F_h is complete;
- Every decomposition in F_h has cost at least 1;
- Every decomposition in $F_h \setminus \{f_{h,h+1},...,f_{h,m}\}$ has cost at least k.

By assumption, $F_0 = F$ is 1-complete. Therefore, the first two statements follow from Proposition 4 (1) and (2) by induction.

The third statement is also proved by induction on h. For h = 0, it trivially holds. Assume the assertion holds for h-1. Then the inductive step "h-1 → h" follows from Proposition 4 (1) and the the fact that if decomposition f has cost at least 1 then the residual decomposition in $RES_{f,k}(f)$ has cost at least k. □

3.4. The Semiring *F*

Finally, we consider costs in the semiring **F**. Again, we would like to concentrate on the form of costs occurring in cycles of the trace graph. However, now there are several possibilities how the cardinality of costs may increase. We have:

Fact 3:

Assume p ∈ **F**[x] and b ∉ {∅, {0}}. Then $\#(p^k[b]) > k$ for every k ∈ ℕ or $\#(p^k[b]) = \#(p[b])$ and one of the following statements hold:

- p = a or p = a ∪ x for some a ∈ **F**;
- p = a + j·x where #a = 1 and j = 1;
- p = a + j·x where #a = 1, j > 1 and #b = 1. □

Assume $M = (A,c)$ is a F-cost automaton with $A = (Q,\Sigma,\delta,Q_F)$. For $q \in Q$, define M_q as the F-cost automaton obtained from M by replacing the set Q_F of accepting states with $\{q\}$. M has Property (F) iff

(F) Every strong component Q' of G(A) is of one of the following three types:
Type I: $Q' \subseteq \{q \in Q \mid \#M_q \leq 1\}$.
Type II: For every edge $<q,(\tau,j),q_j>$ in Q' with $\tau = (q,a,q_1...q_m)$, $c(\tau) = x_j \cup p$ for some polynomial p in which x_j does not occur and where $\#(c(A_{q_i})) < \infty$ for every x_i occurring in p.
Type III: For every edge $<q,(\tau,j),q_j>$ in Q' with $\tau = (q,a,q_1...q_m)$, $c(\tau) = x_j + p$ where $p = H+\sum_{i=1}^{m}\varepsilon_i \cdot x_i$ with $\#H = 1$, $\varepsilon_j = 0$ and $\#M_{q_i} \leq 1$ for every x_i occurring in p.

Opposed to Properties (N) and (A), it is not at all clear that Property (F) can be decided in polynomial time.

Theorem 5
For a parameter-reduced F-cost automaton $M = (A,c)$ the following three statements are equivalent:

(1) M is bounded;

(2) M has Property (F);

(3) $\#M \leq \begin{cases} [(L+1)\cdot n\cdot(Hn+1)]^n & \text{if } k = 1 \\ [(L+1)^k\cdot 2H\cdot n\cdot k^n]^{k^n} & \text{if } k > 1 \end{cases}$

where n is the number of states of A; L is the rank of the input signature; H and k are upper bounds for the cardinalities of the coefficients and degrees resp. of polynomials occurring in c. It can be decided in polynomial time whether or not M is bounded.

Proof: (3) trivially implies (1). To prove that (1) implies (2) we build on Fact 3. Consider for example $\tau = (q,a,q_1...q_m) \in \delta$ and an edge $<q,(\tau,j),q_j>$ in a strong component which contradicts *type II*, i.e. for which $c(\tau) = x_j \cup p$ for some polynomial p in which x_j does not occur but in which some x_i occurs with $\#c(A_{q_i}) = \infty$. It follows that we can find a sequence $\psi_1,..,\psi_r,..$ of q_i-computations such that $c(\psi_r)$ contains some $x \geq r$. Since M is parameter-reduced there exist

- a proper (f,q)-computation ϕ_1 for some $f \in Q_F$ such that $c(\phi_1)$ depends on x_1;
- a proper $(q,q_i q)$-computation ϕ_2 such that $c(\phi_2) = p_1 \cup p_2$ where x_1 occurs only in p_1, and x_2 occurs only in p_2;
- a q-computation ϕ_3 such that $c(\phi_3) \notin \{\emptyset, \{0\}\}$.

For every $k > 0$, we construct an accepting computation $\phi^{(k)}$ by iterating ϕ_2 k times and inserting computations ψ_i into the different instances of ϕ_2. Precisely, define $\phi^{(k)} = \phi_1\tilde{\phi}^{(k)}$ where $\tilde{\phi}^{(0)} = \phi_3$ and for $i > 0$, $\tilde{\phi}^{(i)} = \phi_2[\psi_r,\tilde{\phi}^{(i-1)}]$ where r is larger than the maximal element in $p_2c(\tilde{\phi}^{(i-1)})$. Since p_1 depends on x_1, $p_1c(\psi_r)$ also contains an element $x \geq r$ which therefore is not in $p_2(\tilde{\phi}^{(i-1)})$. Hence, we have $\# c(\tilde{\phi}^{(0)}) > 0$, and for $i > 0$,

$$\begin{aligned} \# c(\tilde{\phi}^{(i)}) &= \# c(\phi_2[\psi_r, \tilde{\phi}^{(i-1)}]) \\ &= \# [p_1(c(\phi_r)) \cup p_2(c(\tilde{\phi}^{(i-1)}))] \end{aligned}$$

$$\geq 1 + \#\, p_2(c(\tilde{\phi}^{(i-1)}))$$
$$\geq 1 + \#\, c(\tilde{\phi}^{(i-1)}) > 1 + (i-1) = i.$$

Since x_1 occurs in $c(\phi_1)$ we conclude that for all $k > 0$,

$$\#\, c(\phi^{(k)}) = \#\, [c(\phi_1)\, c(\tilde{\phi}^{(k)})] > k$$

in contradiction to $\#M < \infty$.
It remains to show that (2) implies the upper bound for #M given by statement (3). For this observe that $\#(c(A_q)) < \infty$ implies that $\#M_q \leq Hn + 1$ in case $k = 1$ and $\#M_q \leq 2 \cdot H \cdot k^n$ otherwise.
Secondly, observe that $\#(A \cup B) \leq \#A + \#B$ and $\#(A + B) \leq \#A \cdot \#B$. These observations allow similar calculations as in the proof of Theorem 2 which gives the desired result.
In order to prove that it can be decided in polynomial time whether or not $\#M < \infty$ it remains to show that Property (F) can be decided in polynomial time. Property (F) in turn can be decided in polynomial time if we succeed to decide in polynomial time for every $q \in Q$, whether or not $\#(c(A_q)) < \infty$ as well as whether or not $\#M_q \leq 1$. This is the contents of subsequent Propositions 6 and 7 respectively. □

Proposition 6
It can be decided in polynomial time for a **F**-cost automaton $M = (A,\mathbf{c})$ whether or not $\#(\mathbf{c}(A)) < \infty$.

Proof: There is a semiring morphism π: $\mathbf{F} \to \mathbf{A}$ given by: $\pi(B) = \bigsqcup_{b \in B} b$. Define $M_\pi = (A, \mathbf{c}_\pi)$ as the **A**-cost automaton where $\mathbf{c}_\pi = \pi\, \mathbf{c}$. We have:
$\#(\mathbf{c}(A)) < \infty$ iff $\#\bigcup\{\mathbf{c}(\phi) \mid \phi \text{ accepting}\} < \infty$ iff $\bigsqcup\{\pi\, \mathbf{c}(\phi) \mid \phi \text{ accepting}\} < \infty$ iff $\bigsqcup M_\pi < \infty$.
Since the latter can be decided in polynomial time by Theorem 3, we are done. □

Proposition 7
It can be decided in polynomial time for a given parameter-reduced **F**-cost automaton M, whether or not $\#M \leq 1$.

The method we apply here to prove Proposition 7 is inspired by techniques used in [Sei90] when dealing with single-valued transducers. Especially, we learn from [Sei90] that we may find a simple syntactical characterization of $\#M \leq 1$ provided M is in a special normal form.
A state $q \in Q$ is called *constant* iff $\mathbf{c}(\phi) = \mathbf{c}(\phi')$ for every two q-computations ϕ and ϕ'. Let Const(A,c) denote the set of all constant states, and define a function $\mathbf{c}$: Const(A,c) $\to$ **F** by $\mathbf{c}(q) = B$ iff $\mathbf{c}(\phi) = B$ for some q-computation ϕ. A state $q \in Q$ is called *1-constant* iff q is constant and $\#\mathbf{c}(q) \leq 1$. The set of all 1-constant states of A is denoted by $\mathrm{Const}_1(A,c)$. M = (A,c) is called *1-strongly reduced* iff M is parameter-reduced and $\mathrm{Const}_1(M) \cap [Q \setminus Q_F] \subseteq U_\varnothing(M)$. At least the set of 1-constant states can be computed in polynomial time. This gives rise to the following proposition.

Proposition 8
For every parameter-reduced **F**-cost automaton $M = (A,\mathbf{c})$ exists a 1-strongly reduced **F**-cost

automaton $M_s = (A_s, c_s)$ such that $L(A) = L(A_s)$ and $c(A) = c_s(A_s)$. M_s can be computed in polynomial time.

Proof: First, we compute the 1-constant states. The algorithm doing so is a special instance of grammar flow analysis as introduced in [MöWi82].
Let $A = (Q,\Sigma,\delta,Q_F)$. W.l.o.g. assume M is already parameter-reduced and $f \in Q_F$ implies $f \neq q_j$ for every $(q,a,q_1,...,q_m) \in \delta$. Assume **R** is the ordered semiring with carrier $\{\perp, ERR, \emptyset\} \cup \{\{i\} \mid i \in \mathbb{N}_0\}$ where the ordering is given by $\perp < \emptyset < ERR$ and $\perp < \{i\} < ERR$ for $i \in \mathbb{N}_0$; addition is $\cup$ defined by $\perp \cup x = x \cup \perp = \perp$; $\emptyset \cup x = x \cup \emptyset = x$; $x \cup x = x$; and $\{x\} \cup \{y\} = ERR$ provided $x \neq y$. Multiplication is defined by: $\emptyset + x = x + \emptyset = \emptyset$; $\perp + x = x + \perp = \perp$ whenever $x \neq \emptyset$; $ERR + x = x + ERR = ERR$ whenever $x \notin \{\emptyset, \perp\}$; $\{x\} + \{y\} = \{x+y\}$. There is a semiring morphism $\tilde{(\_)}$: $\mathbf{F} \to \mathbf{R}$ defined by $\tilde{A} = A$ if $\#A \leq 1$ and $\tilde{A} = ERR$ otherwise.
Consider the trace graph $G(A) = (V,E)$ and define a map OUT: $V \to \mathbf{R}$ as the least upper bound of mappings OUT_i, $i \in \mathbb{N}_0$, where

$$OUT_0(q) = \perp; \text{ and}$$

$$OUT_i(q) = \bigsqcup_{(q,a,q_1...q_m)\in\delta} \tilde{c}(\tau)[OUT_{i-1}(q_1),...,OUT_{i-1}(q_m)] \text{ for } i > 0.$$

We have:

(1) $q \in Q$ is 1-constant iff $OUT(q) \neq ERR$.

(2) $OUT(q) = c(q)$ whenever $q \in Const_1(M)$.

The map OUT(_) can be computed from M by a RAM in polynomial time which can perform additions and multiplications in $\mathbb{N}_0$ constant time. The values of OUT(_) different from ERR or $\emptyset$ are bounded by $2 \cdot H \cdot k^n$ where k is the maximal degree of a polynomial $c(\tau)$ and H is the maximal occurring coefficient in $\mathbb{N}_0$. Hence, the lengthes of the values are polynomial in the input size, and the algorithm runs in polynomial time.
Now, define $A_s = A$ and c_s as follows. Assume $\tau = (q,a,q_1...q_m) \in \delta$. If $q \in Q_F \cap Const_1(M)$ then $c_s(\tau) = c(q)$. If $q \in Const_1(M) \setminus Q_F$ then $c_s(q) = \emptyset$. Otherwise, $c_s(\tau) = c(\tau)[s_1,...,s_m]$

$$\text{where } s_j = \begin{cases} c(q_j) & \text{if } q_j \in Const_1(M) \\ x_j & \text{otherwise} \end{cases} \quad . \square$$

Proof of Proposition 7: Assume $M = (A,c)$ is parameter-reduced. M has Property (U1) iff

(U1) For every $\tau = (q,a,q_1...q_m) \in \delta$, $c(\tau) = \emptyset$ or $c(\tau) = \{h\} + \sum_{j=1}^{m} \varepsilon_j \cdot x_j$ for some $h \in \mathbb{N}_0$ and $\varepsilon_j \in \mathbb{N}_0$.

Clearly, it can be decided in polynomial time whether or not M has Property (U1). We show:

(*) If M is 1-strongly reduced then $\#M \leq 1$ iff M has Property (U1).

By Proposition 8, we w.l.o.g. may assume that M is 1-strongly reduced. Therefore, statement (*) implies Proposition 7. It remains to prove statement (*). If M has Property (U1) then clearly $\#M \leq 1$. For the converse implication we need the following observation about polynomials in $\mathbb{N}_0[X]$ of degree at most one.

(**) Assume for i = 1, 2, $p_i = h_i+\sum_{j=1}^{m}\varepsilon_{i,j}\cdot x_j$ for some $h_i \in \mathbb{N}_0$ and $\varepsilon_{i,j} \in \mathbb{N}_0$. Furthermore, $a_{1,j} \neq a_{2,j}$ for $j \in [1,m]$. If $p_1[a_{\mu(1),1},\ldots,a_{\mu(m),m}] = p_2[a_{\mu(1),1},\ldots,a_{\mu(m),m}]$ for all μ: $[1,m] \rightarrow \{1, 2\}$ then $p_1 = p_2$.

Assume #M ≤ 1 and all coefficients occurring in the image of δ have cardinality at most 1. Thus (by ignoring set brackets) we can view the occurring monomials as polynomials from N[X] of degree at most 1. For a contradiction assume some $\tau = (q,a,q_1...q_m)$ δ exists such that $c(\tau) = p_1 \cup ... \cup p_r$ for monomials p_i where, e.g., $p_1 \neq p_2$ (as functions). Consider a variable x_j occurring either in p_1 or p_2. Since M is 1-strongly reduced and #M ≤ 1 by assumption there are q_j-computations $\phi_{1,j}$ and $\phi_{2,j}$ such that $c(\phi_{1,j}) \neq c(\phi_{2,j})$. Thus, observation (**) implies that some computation $\phi = \tau(\phi_1,\ldots,\phi_m)$ exists with $p_1[c(\phi_1),\ldots,c(\phi_m)] \neq p_2[c(\phi_1),\ldots,c(\phi_m)]$ and hence, $\#c(\phi) > 1$. By parameter-reducedness of M and Fact 0 (2), this contradicts #M ≤ 1. We conclude that M has Property (U1) whenever #M ≤ 1. □

4. Multi-Dimensional Cost Automata

Although cost functions as considered so far may suffice for a lot of interesting cases (see, e.g., the examples in the introduction), MS-evaluations in general give rise to *multi-dimensional* cost functions [CouMo90]. Therefore in this section, we extend our methods to the multi-dimensional case. We succeed to prove results concerning boundedness at least in case of the semirings **N** and **A**.

For the following, we fix a dimension $d \in \mathbb{N}$. Let now X denote the *doubly indexed* set of variables $\{x_{i,j} \mid i \in \mathbb{N}, j \in [1,d]\}$, and $X_k = \{x_{i,j} \mid i \in [1,k], j \in [1,d]\}$ for every $k \in \mathbb{N}$. Assume $A = (Q,\Sigma,\delta,Q_F)$ is an FTA and **R** denotes a semiring. An d-*dimensional* **R**-*cost function* for A is a mapping $\mathbf{c}$: $\delta \rightarrow \mathbf{R}[X]^d$ where $\mathbf{c}(\tau) \in \mathbf{R}[X_k]^d$ provided $\tau = (q,a,q_1...q_k)$.

c(_) is extended to computations φ in the natural way. If $\phi = x_j$ then $\mathbf{c}(\phi)_\mu = x_{j,\mu}$ for all $\mu \in [1,d]$. (As usual, we write the μ-th component of c(_) as $c(\_)_\mu$.) If $\phi = \tau(\phi_1,\ldots,\phi_m)$ for some $\tau \in \delta$ then $\mathbf{c}(\phi) = \mathbf{c}(\tau)[\mathbf{c}(\phi_1),\ldots,\mathbf{c}(\phi_m)]$ where substitution is extended to tuples in the natural way.

A **R**-*cost automaton* M or dimension d is a pair M = (A,**c**) where A is the FTA underlying M, and **c**: $\delta \rightarrow \mathbf{R}[X]^d$ is an d-dimensional **R**-cost function for A.

The *size* of M again consists of the size of A together with the space to represent **c**. Hence we define $|M| = |A| + \sum_{\tau\in\delta} |\mathbf{c}(\tau)|$.

In case **R** ∈ {**N**, **T**, **A**, **F**}, we may define the set of **R**-costs of M, **c**(A), by

$$\mathbf{c}(A) = \{\mathbf{c}(\phi)_1 \mid \phi \text{ accepting computation of } A\}$$

Accordingly for **R** ∈ {**N**, **A**, **N**}, ⊔M = ⊔ **c**(A) is the least upper bound for **R**-costs of M. The notions of E-reducedness and E-parameter-reducedness can be extended to d-dimensional cost automata in a straight forward way. Especially, instead of sets of states $U_r(M)$ we need sets of states $U_{<r_1,\ldots,r_d>}(M)$ for every d-tuple $<r_1,\ldots,r_d> \in (E\cup\{\perp\})^d$ where symbol ⊥ denotes a cost ∉ E.

Theorem 6

Assume **R** ∈ {**N**, **T**, **A**, **F**} and E ⊆ **R** is faithful via H_m: $\mathbf{R} \rightarrow \mathbf{R}_m$ with 0 ∈ E. Then the following holds:

(1) For every d-dimensional **R**-cost automaton $M = (A,\mathbf{c})$ with n states there is an E-reduced **R**-cost automaton $M_E = (A_E, \mathbf{c}_E)$ such that

- $L(A) = L(A_E)$ and $\mathbf{c}(A) = \mathbf{c}_E(A_E)$;
- A_E has at most $(\#R_m)^d \cdot n$ states and $|M_E| \leq |M| \cdot (\#R_m)^{dL}$;
- M_E can be constructed by a RAM in time polynomial in $|M|$ and $\#R_m$.

(2) For every E-reduced **R**-cost automaton $M = (A,\mathbf{c})$ with n states there is an E-parameter-reduced **R**-cost automaton $M_{E,r} = (A_{E,r}, \mathbf{c}_{E,r})$ such that

- $L(A) = L(A_{E,r})$ and **c** sub E,r (A) $= \mathbf{c}_{E,r}(A_{E,r})$;
- $A_{E,r}$ has at most $3^d \cdot n$ states and $|M_{E,r}| \leq |M| \cdot 3^{dL}$;
- If d is fixed, $M_{E,r}$ can be constructed by a RAM in polynomial time. □

From Theorem 6 we deduce:

Corollary 2

(1)

- Assume $\mathbf{R} \in \{\mathbf{N}, \mathbf{T}, \mathbf{A}\}$. It can be decided in polynomial time for $m \in \mathbb{N}$ and a given d-dimensional **R**-cost automaton $M = (A,\mathbf{c})$, whether or not $\sqcup M < m$.
- Assume $m \in \mathbb{N}$ is fixed. Then it can be decided in polynomial time for a given d-dimensional **F**-cost automaton $M = (A,\mathbf{c})$, whether or not $\mathbf{c}(A) \subseteq 2^{[0,m-1]}$.

(2) Let $\mathbf{R} \in \{\mathbf{N}, \mathbf{T}, \mathbf{A}, \mathbf{F}\}$. For every **R**-cost automaton $M = (A,\mathbf{c})$, a parameter-reduced **R**-cost automaton $M_r = (A_r, \mathbf{c}_r)$ can be constructed in polynomial time with $L(A) = L(A_r)$ and $\mathbf{c}(A) = \mathbf{c}_r(A_r)$. □

We extend Property (N) of Section 3 to the multi-dimensional case.

The d-dimensional **N**-cost automaton $M = (A,\mathbf{c})$ has Property (N) iff

(N) If $(q,\langle\tau,j\rangle,q')$ is an edge of a strong component of the trace graph G(A), then either $\mathbf{c}(\tau)_\mu = 0$ or $\mathbf{c}(\tau)_\mu = x_{j,\nu}$ for some $\nu \in [1,d]$.

Obviously, it can be decided in polynomial time whether or not M has Property (N). We have:

Theorem 7

For a parameter-reduced **N**-cost automaton $M = (A,\mathbf{c})$ of dimension d the following three statements are equivalent:

(1) M is bounded;

(2) M has Property (N);

(3) $$\sqcup M \leq \begin{cases} [(L+1)\cdot H]^n & \text{if } k = 1 \\ [(L+1)^k \cdot H]^{k^n} & \text{if } k > 1 \end{cases}$$

where n is the number of states of A; L is the rank of the input signature; H and k are upper bounds to the coefficients and degrees resp. of polynomials occurring in **c**.

It can be decided in polynomial time whether or not M is bounded. □

Note that the characterization given in Theorem 7 can be viewed as a stronger version of the non-ramification lemma as described in [Sei89, Sei91] which gives a characterization of finitely ambiguous FTAs.

A syntactical characterization of bounded costs is also possible for parameter-reduced d-dimensional **A**-cost automata.

The d-dimensional **A**-cost automaton M = (A,**c**) has Property (A) iff

(A) If (q,<τ,j>,q') is an edge of a strong component of the trace graph G(A), then for every $i \in [1,d]$, $\mathbf{c}(\tau)_i$ has the form $p \sqcup \bigsqcup_{\mu \in J} x_{j,\mu}$ for some $J \subseteq [1,d]$ where p does not contain variables $x_{j,\nu}$ for any ν.

Clearly, it can be decided in polynomial time whether or not M has Property (A). We have:

Theorem 8

For a parameter-reduced **A**-cost automaton M = (A,**c**) of dimension d the following three statements are equivalent:

(1) M is bounded;

(2) M has Property (A);

(3) $$\bigsqcup M \leq \begin{cases} n \cdot H & \text{if } k = 1 \\ 2 \cdot H \cdot k^n & \text{if } k > 1 \end{cases}$$

where n is the number of states of A; L is the rank of the input signature; H and k are upper bounds to the coefficients and degrees resp. of polynomials occurring in **c**.

It can be decided in polynomial time whether or not M is bounded. □

Theorems 7 and 8 give efficient versions of the result of [HaKre89] proving that boundedness of costs is decidable. Note that Habel et al. prove a somewhat stronger result by allowing not only polynomials over **N** or **A** but also polynomials where all three operations ⊔, + and · occur. In fact, our methods allow to derive a polynomial decision procedure for boundedness of costs also in this slightly more general situation. It was for descriptional clearity only that we omitted to include a corresponding result.

5. Conclusion

We considered cost automata with cost in several semirings, derived upper bounds for bounded costs and gave polynomial time algorithms to decide boundedness. Not for all semirings in {**N**, **T**, **A**, **F**} we could prove results in full generality. Especially, it remains open whether an upper bound can be derived for costs in **T** when either the degree of the occurring polynomials or the dimension is > 1. Also, it is rather unclear how our result on boundedness in **F** can be extended to the multi-dimensional case.

References

[CouMo90] B. Courcelle, M. Mosbah: Monadic second-order evaluations on tree-decomposable graphs. Tech. Report LaBRI No. 90-110, Bordeaux, 1990

[GeSt84] F. Gecseg, M. Steinby: Tree automata. Akademiai Kiado, Budapest, 1984

[GiSch88] R. Giegerich, K. Schmal: Code selection techniques: pattern matching, tree parsing and inversion of derivors. Proc. of ESOP 1988, LNCS 300 pp. 245-268

[HaKre89] A. Habel, H.-J. Kreowski, W. Vogler: Decidable boundedness problems for hyperedge-replacement grammars. Proc. TAPSOFT '89 vol. 1, LNCS 352, pp. 275-289; long version to appear in TCS

[MöWi82] U.Möncke, R. Wilhelm: Iterative algorithms on grammar graphs. Proc. 8th Conf. on Graphtheoretic Concepts in Computer Science, Hanser Verlag 1982, pp. 177-194

[Paul78] W. Paul: Komplexitätstheorie. B.G. Teubner Verlag Stuttgart 1978

[Sei89] H. Seidl: On the finite degree of ambiguity of finite tree automata. Acta Inf. 26, pp. 527-542 (1989)

[Sei90] H. Seidl: Single-valuedness of tree transducers is decidable in polynomial time. To appear in: TCS, special issue of CAAP 90

[Sei91] H. Seidl: Ambiguity and Valuedness. To appear in: M. Nivat, A. Podelski (eds.): "Definability and Recognizability of Sets of Trees". Elsevier Amsterdam

[WeiWi88] Two tree pattern matchers for code selection. Proc. 2nd CCHSC Workshop 1988, LNCS 371, pp. 215-229

Partial Type Assignment in Left Linear Applicative Term Rewriting Systems*

Theory, Applications and Implementation

Steffen van Bakel[1†] Sjaak Smetsers[1] Simon Brock[2]

[1] Department of Informatics, Faculty of Mathematics and Informatics, University of Nijmegen, Toernooiveld 1, 6525 ED Nijmegen, The Netherlands.

[2] School of Information Systems, University of East Anglia, Norwich NR4 7TJ, United Kingdom.

Abstract

This paper introduces a notion of partial type assignment on left linear applicative term rewriting systems that is based on the extension defined by Mycroft of Curry's type assignment system. The left linear applicative TRS we consider are extensions to those suggested by most functional programming languages in that they do not discriminate against the varieties of function symbols that can be used in patterns. As such there is no distinction between function symbols (such as append and plus) and constructor symbols (such as cons and succ). Terms and rewrite rules will be written as trees, and type assignment will consist of assigning types to function symbols, nodes and edges between nodes. The only constraints on this system are imposed by the relation between the type assigned to a node and those assigned to its incoming and out-going edges. We will show that every typeable term has a principal type, and formulate a needed and sufficient condition typeable rewrite rules should satisfy in order to gain preservance of types under rewriting. As an example we will show that the optimisation function performed after bracket abstraction is typeable. Finally we will present a type check algorithm that checks if rewrite rules are correctly typed, and finds the principal pair for typeable terms.

---

*Supported by the Esprit Basic Research Action 3074 "Semagraph".

†Partially supported by the Netherlands Organisation for the advancement of pure research (N.W.O.).

Introduction

In the recent years several paradigms have been investigated for the implementation of functional programming languages. Not only the lambda calculus [Bar84], but also term rewriting systems [Klo90] and graph rewriting systems [BvEG$^+$87] are topics of research. Lambda calculus (or rather combinator systems) forms the underlying model for the functional programming language Miranda [Tur85], term rewriting systems are used in the underlying model for the language OBJ [FGJM85], and graph rewriting systems is the model for the language Clean [BvEvLP87, NSvEP91].

There exists a well understood and well defined notion of type assignment on lambda terms, known as the Curry type assignment system [CF58]. This type assignment system is the basis for many type checkers and inferers used in functional programming languages. For example the type assignment system for the language ML [Mil78], as defined by R. Milner forms in fact an extension of Curry's system. The type inference algorithm for the functional programming language Miranda works in roughly the same way as the one for ML. A real difference between these languages lies in the fact that Miranda also contains a type check algorithm, which is based on the type assignment system defined by A. Mycroft, an extension of Milner's type assignment system [Myc84, KTU88].

To provide a formal type system for all languages that use pattern matching this paper presents a formal notion of type assignment on left linear applicative term rewriting systems. As shown in this paper type assignment in term rewriting systems in general does not satisfy the subject reduction property: i.e. types are not preserved under rewriting. The main result of this paper, the formulation of a needed and sufficient condition on rewrite rules to obtain subject reduction, could be used to prove that all rewrite rules that can be defined in a language like Miranda are safe in that respect. Also if at first sight one could think that the generalization of type assignments from functional programming languages to term rewriting systems would be straightforward, this is not true, as is shown from the conditions given to guarantee preservance of types under rewriting.

It is our aim to extend the notion presented in this paper to a notion of type assignment for term graph rewriting systems, and, possibly, general graph rewriting systems.

The type assignment system we present in this paper is a partial system in the sense of [Pfe85], because we not only define how terms and rewrite rules can be typed, but also provide a type for each function symbol. There are several reasons to do so.

For symbols for which there is a rewrite rule (called defined symbols), and for symbols for which such a rule does not exist (called constants), there must be some way of determining what type can be used for an occurrence. Instead of for defined symbols investigating their rule every time the symbol is encountered, we can store the type of the symbol in a mapping from symbols to types, and use this mapping instead. Of course it makes no difference to assume the existence from the start of such a mapping from symbols to types, and to define type assignment using that mapping. This mapping is also convenient to make sure that types assigned to different occurrences of constants do not conflict.

In fact, the approach we take here is very much the same as the one taken by Hindley in [Hin69], where he defines the principal type scheme of an object in Combinatory Logic. Even his notion of type assignment could be regarded as a partial one. Moreover, since combinator systems can easily be translated into left linear applicative term rewriting systems, the results of this paper, when restricting the allowed rewrite rules to those that correspond to combinators, are the same as in [Hin69].

In section 1 we define the left linear applicative term rewriting systems, as the subclass of term rewriting systems that contain a predefined symbol *Ap*, and in which all rewrite rules are left linear. The definition of applicative term rewriting systems is not the one normally used, but more general: in the systems we consider, *Ap* is not the only function symbol.

The notion of type assignment on left linear applicative term rewriting systems as defined in subsection 3.2 is in fact defined on the tree representation of terms and rewrite rules, defined in section 2, by assigning in a consistent way types (as defined in subsection 3.1) to nodes and edges. The only constraints on this system are imposed by the relation between the type assigned to a node and those assigned to its incoming and out-going edges. It is based on the Mycroft type assignment system as used in Miranda.

In subsection 3.3 we will show that for every basis B, term M, type σ and substitution S: if $B \vdash M{:}\sigma$ (i.e. M is typeable by σ starting from the set B of typed term variables), then also $S\,(B) \vdash M{:}S\,(\sigma)$. In that subsection we will also show that for every typeable term M, there is a principal pair $<P, \pi>$ for M, i.e. for every pair $<B, \sigma>$ such that $B \vdash M{:}\sigma$ there is a substitution S such that $S\,(<P, \pi>) = <B, \sigma>$.

Another result presented in that subsection is that if $<B, \sigma>$ is the principal pair for M, and M' is obtained from M by replacing (in a consistent way) term variables by terms, and M' is typeable by τ, then there is a substitution S such that: $S\,(\sigma) = \tau$, and for every $x{:}\rho$ occurring in B, the replacement of x is typeable by $S\,(\rho)$.

In subsection 4.1 we show that if type assignment is done in the most obvious, straight-forward way, there are rewrite rules that are typeable, that match a term M typeable with σ, but for which the result of the application of the rewrite rule on M is not typeable with σ. In subsection 4.2 we formulate a condition that typeable rewrite rules should satisfy in order to guarantee preservance of types under rewriting. In that subsection we prove this condition to be needed and sufficient.

In section 5 we show that the usually defined optimisation algorithm after bracket abstraction (a translation of lambda terms to combinator expressions) is typeable in our system. In the appendix we present a type check algorithm, that checks if rewrite rules are correctly typed, and finds the principal pair for typeable terms.

1 Left linear applicative term rewriting systems

In this paper we study left linear applicative term rewriting systems (LLATRS), which are a subclass of term rewriting systems, as defined in [Klo90]. LLATRS's are defined as the class of term rewriting systems that (can) contain a special binary operator *Ap*, and in which all rewrite rules are left linear. To distinguish them from the term rewriting systems that have *only* the function symbol *Ap*, we call the latter the *pure* applicative term rewriting systems.

The motivation for the use of applicative term rewriting systems instead of the general term rewriting systems can be illustrated by the following example: If we would want to translate Combinatory Logic (CL)

$$S\ x\ y\ z = x\ z\ (y\ z)$$

$$\begin{array}{ll} K\,x\,y & = x \\ I\,x & = x \end{array}$$

into a term rewriting system, then it could look like (making the implicit application explicit):

$$\begin{array}{ll} Ap\,(Ap\,(Ap\,(S,x),y),z) & \Rightarrow\ Ap\,(Ap\,(x,z),Ap\,(y,z)) \\ Ap\,(Ap\,(K,x),y) & \Rightarrow\ x \\ Ap\,(I,x) & \Rightarrow\ x \end{array}$$

However, we prefer to see the symbols S, K and I as functions, with 3, 2 and 1 operands respectively. If we try to capture that view in our translation, we would need to define also the Curried versions of those symbol:

$$\begin{array}{ll} S\,(x,y,z) & \Rightarrow\ Ap\,(Ap\,(x,z),Ap\,(y,z)) \\ Ap\,(S_2\,(x,y),z) & \Rightarrow\ S\,(x,y,z) \\ Ap\,(S_1\,(x),y) & \Rightarrow\ S_2\,(x,y) \\ Ap\,(S_0,x) & \Rightarrow\ S_1\,(x) \\ K\,(x,y) & \Rightarrow\ x \\ Ap\,(K_1\,(x),y) & \Rightarrow\ K\,(x,y) \\ Ap\,(K_0,x) & \Rightarrow\ K_1\,(x) \\ I\,(x) & \Rightarrow\ x \\ Ap\,(I_0,x) & \Rightarrow\ I\,(x) \end{array}$$

We consider the applicative rewriting systems, because they are far more general than the subclass of systems in which there exists only the function symbol *Ap*. Since the pure left linear applicative term rewriting systems are a subclass of the left linear applicative term rewriting systems, all results obtained in this paper are also valid for that subclass.

We take the view that in a rewrite rule a certain symbol is defined, and it is clear that the rules added to obtain the Curried versions of symbols in the translation of CL into a rewriting system are not intended as definitions for *Ap*, which is more or less a 'predefined function', but as definitions for the Curried versions.

However, in general term rewriting systems are not sensitive for the names used for functions symbols. So the rewriting system given above is in fact the same as the one obtained by replacing all *Ap*'s by F, and then all rewrite rules starting with F could be seen as rules that define F. In order to avoid this problem, we regard those rewriting systems that have a 'predefined' binary function, called *Ap*, which then cannot be renamed. The symbol *Ap* is neglected when we are looking for the symbol that is defined in a rewrite rule.

In the lambda calculus there is a clear difference between free and bound variables of a term. In term rewriting systems a term variable x that occurs in the left hand side of a rewrite rule can be seen as the binding occurrence of x, binding the occurrences of x in the right hand side. However, in general x can occur more than once in the left hand side, making the notion of *the* binding occurrence obscure. In this paper we consider left linear rewriting systems, that contain only rewrite rules for which the left hand side is linear (term variables occur only once), because for those rules the binding occurrence of a term variable is unique.

The following definitions are based on definitions given in [Klo90]. Definition 1.1 defines

LLATRS's, in the same way as the definition given by Klop for term rewriting systems, extended with part (i.c) to express the existence of the predefined symbol *Ap*. Definition 1.2 defines a notion of rewriting on LLATRS's, in the same way as the definition of rewriting given by Klop for term rewriting systems, extended with part (ii.a.2) to express the left linearity of rewrite rules, part (ii.a.4) to express that the possible use of the symbol *Ap* in the left hand side is restricted, and part (iii) to define the notion of defined symbol of a rewrite rule. In fact, parts (ii.a.4) and (iii) are related.

We introduce in some parts a different notation, because some of the symbols or definitions normally used are also used in papers on type assignment, but with a different meaning. For example we use the word 'replacement' for the operation that replaces term variables by terms, instead of the word 'substitution', which will be used for operations that replace type variables by types.

Substitution and replacement are also operations defined in [CF58]. Both operations are there defined as operations on terms, where substitution is defined as the operation that replaces term variables by terms, and replacement is defined as the operation that replaces subterms by terms. Note that our definition therefore differs from the one given in [CF58].

To denote a replacement, we use capital characters like 'R', instead of greek symbols like 'σ', which are used to denote types. We use the symbol '$\Rightarrow$' for the rewriting symbol, instead of '$\rightarrow$' which is used as a type constructor. We use the notion 'constant symbol' for a symbol that cannot be rewritten, instead of for a function symbol with arity 0.

Definition 1.1 A *Left Linear Applicative Term Rewriting System* (LLATRS) is a pair (Σ, **R**) of an *alphabet* or *signature* Σ and a set of *rewrite rules* **R**.

i) The alphabet Σ consists of:
   a) A countable infinite set of variables $x_1, x_2, x_3, \ldots$ (or $x, y, z, x', y', \ldots$).
   b) A non empty set Σ_0 of *function symbols* or *operator symbols* $F, G, \ldots$, each equipped with an 'arity' (a natural number), i.e. the number of 'arguments' it is supposed to have. We have 0-ary, unary, binary, ternary etc function symbols.
   c) A special binary operator, called *application* (*Ap*).
ii) The set of *terms* (or *expressions*) 'over' Σ is *Ter* (Σ) and is defined inductively:
   a) $x, y, z, \ldots \in$ *Ter* (Σ).
   b) If $F \in \Sigma_0 \cup \{Ap\}$ is an n-ary symbol, and $T_1, \ldots, T_n \in$ *Ter* (Σ) ($n \geq 0$), then
      $F(T_1, \ldots, T_n) \in$ *Ter* (Σ).
   The T_i ($i = 1, \ldots, n$) are the arguments of the last term.
iii) Terms in which no variable occurs twice or more, are called *linear*.

Definition 1.2 Let (Σ, **R**) be a LLATRS.

i) A *replacement* R is a map from *Ter* (Σ) to *Ter* (Σ) satisfying
   $$\mathrm{R}(F(T_1, \ldots, T_n)) = F(\mathrm{R}(T_1), \ldots, \mathrm{R}(T_n))$$
   for every n-ary function symbol F (here $n \geq 0$). So, R is determined by its restriction to the set of variables. We also write T^{R} instead of R (T).
ii) a) A *rewrite rule* $\in$ **R** is a pair (*Lhs*, *Rhs*) of terms $\in$ *Ter* (Σ). Often a rewrite rule will get a name, e.g. **r**, and we write **r** : $Lhs \Rightarrow Rhs$. Four conditions will be imposed:

1) *Lhs* is not a variable.
2) *Lhs* is linear.
3) The variables occurring in *Rhs* are contained in *Lhs*.
4) For every *Ap* in *Lhs*, the left hand argument is not a variable.

b) A rewrite rule $\mathbf{r} : Lhs \Rightarrow Rhs$ determines a set of *rewrites* $Lhs^{\mathrm{R}} \Rightarrow Rhs^{\mathrm{R}}$ for all replacements R. The left hand side Lhs^{R} is called a *redex*; it may be replaced by its '*contractum*' Rhs^{R} inside a context C[ ]; this gives rise to *rewrite steps*:

$$\mathrm{C}[\, Lhs^{\mathrm{R}} \,] \Rightarrow_{\mathbf{r}} \mathrm{C}[\, Rhs^{\mathrm{R}} \,].$$

c) We call $\Rightarrow_{\mathbf{r}}$ the *one-step rewrite relation* generated by **r**. Concatenating rewrite steps we have (possibly infinite) *rewrite sequences* $T_0 \Rightarrow T_1 \Rightarrow T_2 \Rightarrow \cdots$ or *rewrites* for short. If $T_0 \Rightarrow \cdots \Rightarrow T_n$ we also write $T_0 \twoheadrightarrow T_n$, and T_n is a *rewrite* of T_0.

iii) a) In a rewrite rule, the leftmost, outermost symbol in the left hand side that is not an *Ap*, is called *the defined symbol* of that rule.
b) If the symbol F is the defined symbol of **r**, then **r** *defines* F.
c) F is *a defined symbol*, if there is a rewrite rule that defines F.
d) $A \in \Sigma_0$ is called a *constant symbol* if A is not a defined symbol.

Part (ii.a.4) of definition 1.2 is added in order to avoid rewrite rules with left hand sides like $Ap\,(x, y)$, because such a rule would not have a defined symbol.

Proposition 1.3 Let F be the defined symbol of the rewrite rule $\mathbf{r} : Lhs \Rightarrow Rhs$. Then there are $n \geq j \geq 0$, and $A_1, \ldots, A_n$ such that:

$$Lhs = Ap\,(Ap\,(\ldots Ap\,(F(A_1, \ldots, A_j), A_{j+1}), \ldots), A_n).$$

and $A_1, \ldots, A_n$ are called the *patterns* of **r**.

Proof: Easy. ■

We will consider rewriting systems that are *Curry-closed*, i.e. for every rewrite rule that defines the symbol F with arity $n \geq 0$, we will assume that there are n additional rewrite rules that define the function symbols F_0 upto F_{n-1} as follows:

$$\begin{array}{ll}
Ap(F_{n-1}(x_1, \ldots, x_{n-1}), x_n) & \Rightarrow F(x_1, \ldots, x_n) \\
Ap(F_{n-2}(x_1, \ldots, x_{n-2}), x_{n-1}) & \Rightarrow F_{n-1}(x_1, \ldots, x_{n-1}) \\
\vdots & \\
Ap(F_1(x_1), x_2) & \Rightarrow F_2(x_1, x_2) \\
Ap(F_0, x_1) & \Rightarrow F_1(x_1)
\end{array}$$

The added rules with $F_{n-1}, \ldots, F_1, F_0$, etc. give in fact the 'Curried'-versions of F.

We could have defined a closure operation on LLATRS's, by adding rules and extending the alphabet Σ, but it is easier to assume that every LLATRS is Curry-closed. When presenting a rewrite system however, we will only show the rules that are essential: we do not show the rules that define the Curried-versions.

2 Tree representation of terms and rewrite rules

Definition 2.1 i) The tree representation of terms and rewrite rules is obtained in a straightforward way, by representing a term $F(A_1, \ldots, A_n)$ by:

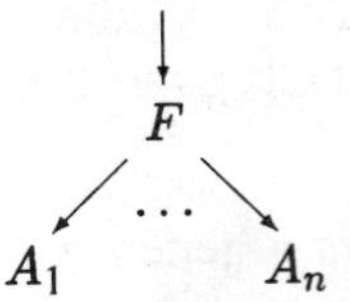

ii) The *spine* of a tree is defined as usual, i.e.: the root node of the tree is on the spine, and if a node is on the spine, then its left most descendant is on the spine.

iii) In the tree representation of a rewrite rule, the first node on the spine of the left hand side, starting from the root node, that does not contain an *Ap*, is called the *defining node* of that rule. (Notice that if F is the defined symbol of a rewrite rule, then it occurs in the defining node of the tree representation of that rule.)

Example 2.2 We give some of the rewrite rules of CL in tree representation:

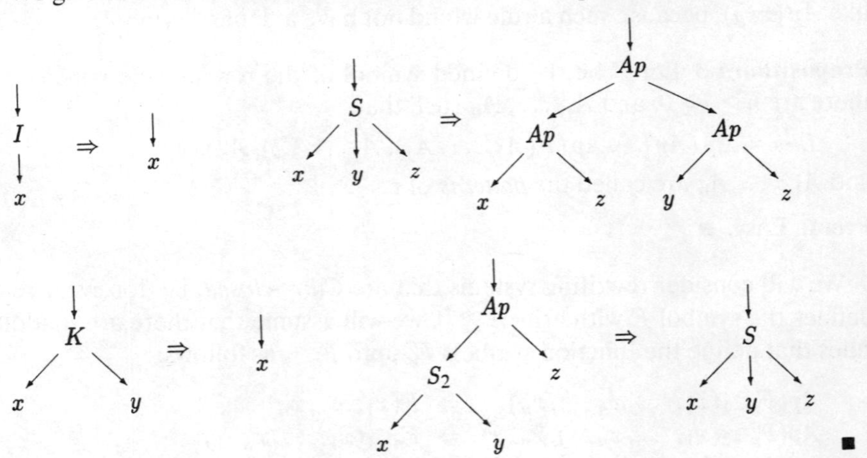

■

Example 2.3 Rewrite rules can of course be more complicated than illustrated above by the rules for CL. In general, if the left hand side of a rewrite rule is $F(T_1, \ldots, T_n)$, then the T_i need not be simple variables but can be terms as well, as for example in the rewrite rule $M\,(S_2\,(x,y)) \Rightarrow S_2\,(I_0, y)$. In tree representation, this rule looks like:

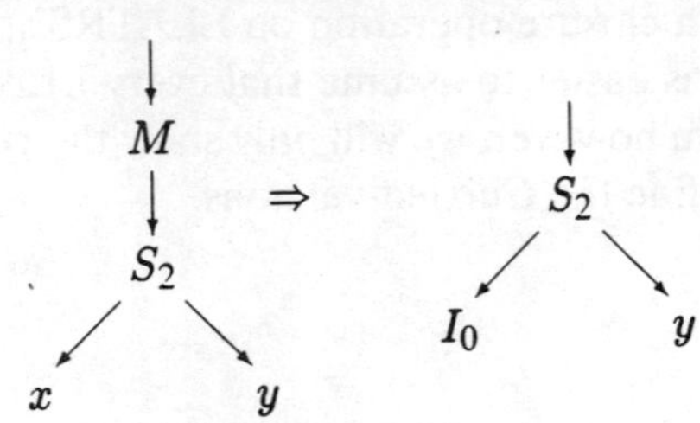

■

3 Type assignment in LLATRS's

In this section we present a notion of partial type assignment on LLATRS's, based on the Mycroft type assignment system [Myc84, KTU88]. Assigning types to a LLATRS will consist of labelling the nodes and edges in the tree representation of terms and rewrite rules with type information. Types are assigned to nodes to capture the notion of 'type of a function', 'type of a constant' or 'type of a variable', and are assigned to edges to capture the notion of 'type of a subterm' (or tree). The edge pointing to the the root of a term is called the *root edge*.

The difference between Milner's and Mycroft's type assignment system lies in the way they handle recursion. Would we have used Milner's system, then we would have demanded that all occurrences of recursively defined objects are, within their definition, typed with the same type. Mycroft's approach is a more general one. Using his system the only requirement for recursive definitions would be to demand that the separate occurrences of the object within the definition are typed with types that are substitution instances of the type of the object.

There is one major difference between the notion of type assignment we introduce in this paper and Curry's type assignment system. In that system a basis is usually defined as a mapping from term variables to types, or, equivalently, as a set of statements with distinct term variables as subjects. The bases allowed in the system we present however can contain several different statements for the same term variable. This in fact corresponds to the definition of ML-type assignment as given in [Dam85], and is used there for dealing with the let-construct. It could also be compared with using intersection types [BCD83] on free variables of terms. Unlike in lambda calculus, in term rewriting systems this causes no difficulties, since there is no notion of 'abstraction' in this world. Moreover, condition (i.b) of definition 3.2.3 deals with this apparent anomaly. So in the system we present, it is possible to assign a type to the term $Ap(x, x)$.

3.1 Types

The type system we define in this subsection is based on the Curry type system, extended with type constants.

Definition 3.1.1 i) $\mathcal{T}_C$, the set of Curry types is inductively defined by:

a) All type variables $\varphi_0, \varphi_1, \ldots \in \mathcal{T}_C$.

b) All type constants $c_0, c_1, \ldots \in \mathcal{T}_C$.

c) If $\sigma, \tau \in \mathcal{T}_C$, then $\sigma \rightarrow \tau \in \mathcal{T}_C$.

ii) A *statement* is an expression of the form $M{:}\sigma$, where $M \in \mathit{Ter}(\Sigma)$ and $\sigma \in \mathcal{T}_C$. M is the *subject* and σ the *predicate* of $M{:}\sigma$.

iii) A *basis* B is a set of statements with term variables, not necessarily distinct, as subjects. If a basis is denoted as $\{x_1{:}\rho_1, \ldots, x_n{:}\rho_n\}$, the x_i are distinct.

In the notation of types, often outermost and rightmost brackets are omitted. We will use the symbol φ to denote a type variable and all other greek characters to denote arbitrary types. Also, instead of φ indexed by a number, we will write the number.

Definition 3.1.2 i) A *substitution* $S : \mathcal{T}_C \rightarrow \mathcal{T}_C$ is as usual inductively defined by:

a) The substitution $(\varphi := \alpha)$, where φ is a type variable and $\rho \in \mathcal{T}_C$, is defined by:

1) $(\varphi := \alpha)(\varphi) = \rho$.
2) $(\varphi := \alpha)(\varphi_0) = \varphi_0$, if $\varphi \neq \varphi_0$.
3) $(\varphi := \alpha)(c_i) = c_i$.
4) $(\varphi := \alpha)(\sigma \rightarrow \tau) = (\varphi := \alpha)(\sigma) \rightarrow (\varphi := \alpha)(\tau)$.

b) If S_1 and S_2 are substitutions, then so is $S_1 \circ S_2$, where $S_1 \circ S_2(\sigma) = S_1(S_2(\sigma))$.

ii) If for σ, τ there is a substitution S such that $S(\sigma) = \tau$, then τ is called a *(substitution) instance* of σ.

iii) If σ is an instance of τ, and τ is an instance of σ, then σ is called a *trivial variant* of τ. We identify types that are trivial variants of each other.

iv) $S(B) = \{x{:}S(\rho) \mid x{:}\rho \in B\}$.

v) $S(<B, \sigma>) = <S(B), S(\sigma)>$.

3.2 Type assignment

Type assignment on a LLATRS (Σ, R) is defined as the labelling of nodes and edges in the tree representation of terms and rewrite rules with types. If a node or edge is labelled with a type σ, we say that it is *typed* with σ, and σ is *assigned* to it.

In this labelling, we use that there is a mapping that provides a type in $\mathcal{T}_C$ for every $F \in \Sigma_0 \cup \{Ap\}$. Such a mapping is called an environment.

Definition 3.2.1 Let $(\Sigma, \mathbf{R})$ be a LLATRS. A mapping $\mathcal{E} : \Sigma_0 \cup \{Ap\} \rightarrow \mathcal{T}_C$ is called an *environment* if $\mathcal{E}(Ap) = (1 \rightarrow 2) \rightarrow 1 \rightarrow 2$, and for every $F \in \Sigma_0$ with arity n, $\mathcal{E}(F) = \mathcal{E}(F_{n-1}) = \cdots = \mathcal{E}(F_0)$.

Definition 3.2.2 Let $(\Sigma, \mathbf{R})$ be a LLATRS.

i) We say that $M \in Ter(\Sigma)$ *is typeable by* $\sigma \in \mathcal{T}$ *with respect to* $\mathcal{E}$, if there exists an assignment of types to edges and nodes that satisfies the following constraints:

a) The root edge of M is typed with σ.

b) If a node contains a symbol $F \in \Sigma_0 \cup \{Ap\}$ that has arity n ($n \geq 0$), then there are $\sigma_1, \ldots, \sigma_n$ and σ, such that this node is typed with $\sigma_1 \rightarrow \cdots \rightarrow \sigma_n \rightarrow \sigma$, the n out-going edges are from left to right typed with σ_1 up to σ_n, and the in-going edge is typed with σ.

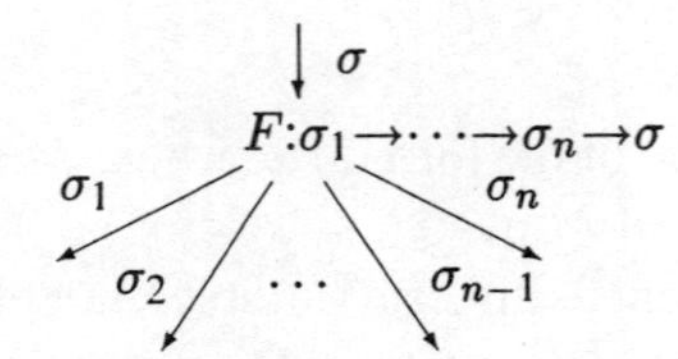

c) If a node containing a symbol $F \in \Sigma_0 \cup \{Ap\}$ is typed with σ, then there is a substitution S, such that $S(\mathcal{E}(F)) = \sigma$.

ii) Let $M \in Ter(\Sigma)$ be typeable by σ with respect to $\mathcal{E}$. If B is a basis containing all statements with variables as subjects that appear in the typed tree for $M{:}\sigma$, we write $B \vdash_{\mathcal{E}} M{:}\sigma$.

Notice that if $B \vdash_{\mathcal{E}} M{:}\sigma$, then B can contain more statements than needed to obtain $M{:}\sigma$.

Definition 3.2.3 Let $(\Sigma, \mathbf{R})$ be a LLATRS.

i) We say that **r**: $Lhs \Rightarrow Rhs \in \mathbf{R}$ with defined symbol F *is naively typeable with respect to* $\mathcal{E}$, if the following constraints hold:
   a) There are $\sigma \in \mathcal{T}_C$ and basis B such that $B \vdash_{\mathcal{E}} Lhs{:}\sigma$ and $B \vdash_{\mathcal{E}} Rhs{:}\sigma$.
   b) All nodes within **r** containing the same term variable x, are typed with the same type.
   c) The defining node of **r**, containing F, is typed with $\mathcal{E}(F)$.
ii) We say that $(\Sigma, \mathbf{R})$ *is naively typeable with respect to* $\mathcal{E}$, if for every $\mathbf{r} \in \mathbf{R}$: **r** is naively typeable with respect to $\mathcal{E}$.

Condition (i.c) is in fact added to make sure that the type provided by the environment for a function symbol F is not in conflict with the rewrite rules that define F. By restricting the type that can be assigned to the defining node to the type provided by the environment, we are sure that the rewrite rule is typed using that type, and not using a substitution instance.

In the rest of this paper, we will assume the environment to be fixed, so we omit the subscript on $\vdash_{\mathcal{E}}$. Also, instead of saying '(naively) typeable with respect to $\mathcal{E}$', we just say 'typeable'.

It is easy to check that if F is a function symbol with artity n, and all rewrite rules that define F are typeable, then there are $\gamma_1, \ldots, \gamma_n, \gamma$ such that $\mathcal{E}(F) = \gamma_1 \rightarrow \cdots \rightarrow \gamma_n \rightarrow \gamma$.

The use of an environment corresponds to the use of 'axiom-schemes', and part (i.c) of definition 3.2.2 to the use of 'axioms' as in [Hin69].

A typical example for part (i.b) of definition 3.2.2 is the function symbol *Ap*, which has the type $(1\rightarrow 2)\rightarrow 1\rightarrow 2$. So for every occurrence of *Ap* in a tree, there are σ and τ such that the following is part of the tree.

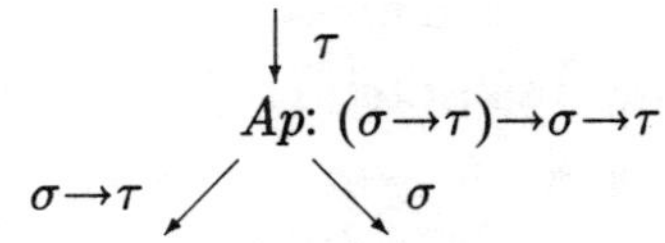

3.3 The principal pair for a term

In this subsection we define the principal pair for a typeable term M with respect to $\mathcal{E}$, consisting of basis B and type σ, by defining the notion $pp(M)$ using Robinsons unification algorithm $unify_R$ [Rob65]. (Notice that, from a formal point of view, we would have to define $pp_{\mathcal{E}}(M)$, but that again we are omitting the subscript $\mathcal{E}$.) In the following we show that for every typeable term, this is a legal pair and is indeed the most general one.

We recall the following well known property of $unify_R$.

Property 3.3.1 [Rob65] If two types have an instance in common, they have a highest common instance which is returned by $unify_R$, so for all σ, τ: if $S_1 = unify_R\,(\sigma, \tau)$ and S_2 is a substitution such that $S_2\,(\sigma) = S_2\,(\tau)$, then there is a substitution S_3 such that $S_2\,(\sigma) = S_3 \circ S_1\,(\sigma) = S_3 \circ S_1\,(\tau) = S_2\,(\tau)$. ■

Definition 3.3.2 We define, for every term M the notion $pp(M) = <P, \pi>$ inductively by:

i) For all x, φ: $pp(x) = <\{x{:}\varphi\}, \varphi>$.

ii) If for every $1 \leq i \leq n$: $pp(A_i) = <P_i, \pi_i>$, $\mathcal{E}\,(F) = \sigma_1 \rightarrow \cdots \rightarrow \sigma_n \rightarrow \sigma$, (we choose if necessary trivial variants such that the $<P_i, \pi_i>$ are pairwise disjoint and these pairs share no type variables with $\sigma_1 \rightarrow \cdots \rightarrow \sigma_n \rightarrow \sigma$), and

$$S = unify_R\,(\sigma_1 \rightarrow \cdots \rightarrow \sigma_n \rightarrow \sigma, \pi_1 \rightarrow \cdots \rightarrow \pi_n \rightarrow \varphi),$$

where φ does not occur in any of the pairs $<P_i, \pi_i>$, nor in $\sigma_1 \rightarrow \cdots \rightarrow \sigma_n \rightarrow \sigma$, then:

$$pp(F(A_1, \ldots, A_n)) = <S\,(P_1 \cup \cdots \cup P_n), S\,(\sigma)>.$$

The following theorem shows that substitution is a sound operation on trees. As illustrated in section 3.5, we cannot show such a result for rewrite rules.

Theorem 3.3.3 Soundness of substitution. If $B \vdash M{:}\sigma$, then for every substitution S: $S\,(B) \vdash M{:}S\,(\sigma)$.

Proof: By easy induction on the structure of M. ■

By induction on the definition of $pp(M)$, using theorem 3.3.3 it is easy to verify that $pp(M) = <P, \pi>$ implies $P \vdash M{:}\pi$.

In the following theorem we show that the operation of substitution is complete.

Theorem 3.3.4 Completeness of substitution. If $B \vdash M{:}\sigma$, then there are P, π, and a substitution S such that: $pp(M) = <P, \pi>$, and $S\,(P) \subseteq B$, $S\,(\pi) = \sigma$.

Proof: By induction on the structure of M.

i) $M \equiv x$. Then $\{x{:}\sigma\} \subseteq B$. Then there is a φ such that $pp(x) = <\{x{:}\varphi\}, \varphi>$. Take $S = (\varphi := \sigma)$.

ii) $M \equiv F(A_1, \ldots, A_n)$. Then there are $\sigma_1, \ldots, \sigma_n$ such that

$$F \text{ is typed with } \sigma_1 \rightarrow \cdots \rightarrow \sigma_n \rightarrow \sigma, \text{ and for every } 1 \leq i \leq n\text{: } B \vdash A_i{:}\sigma_i.$$

Also there are $\gamma_1, \ldots, \gamma_n, \gamma$, and a substitution S_0 such that

$$\mathcal{E}\,(F) = \gamma_1 \rightarrow \cdots \rightarrow \gamma_n \rightarrow \gamma, \text{ and } \sigma_1 \rightarrow \cdots \rightarrow \sigma_n \rightarrow \sigma = S_0\,(\gamma_1 \rightarrow \cdots \rightarrow \gamma_n \rightarrow \gamma).$$

By induction for every $1 \leq i \leq n$ there are $<P_i, \pi_i>$, (pairwise disjoint) and a substitution S_i, such that

$$S_i\,(P_i) \subseteq B, S_i\,(\pi_i) = \sigma_i, \text{ and } pp(A_i) = <P_i, \pi_i>.$$

Assume, without loss of generality, that none of the type variables of the types $\gamma_1, \ldots, \gamma_n, \gamma$ occur in any pair $<P_i, \pi_i>$. Take $S' = S_n \circ \cdots \circ S_0$, then:

$$S'\,(\gamma) = \sigma, S'\,(P_1 \cup \cdots \cup P_n) \subseteq B, \text{ and for every } 1 \leq i \leq n\text{: } S'\,(\gamma_i) = S'\,(\pi_i) = \sigma_i.$$

Let φ be a type variable not occurring in any other type. Since $\sigma_1 \rightarrow \cdots \rightarrow \sigma_n \rightarrow \sigma$ is a common instance of both $\gamma_1 \rightarrow \cdots \rightarrow \gamma_n \rightarrow \gamma$ and $\pi_1 \rightarrow \cdots \rightarrow \pi_n \rightarrow \varphi$, by property 3.3.1 there are substitutions S_g and S such that:

$S_g = unify_{\mathrm{R}}\,(\gamma_1{\rightarrow}\cdots{\rightarrow}\gamma_n{\rightarrow}\gamma,\ \pi_1{\rightarrow}\cdots{\rightarrow}\pi_n{\rightarrow}\varphi)$ and

$\sigma_1{\rightarrow}\cdots{\rightarrow}\sigma_n{\rightarrow}\sigma = S{\circ}S_g\,(\gamma_1{\rightarrow}\cdots{\rightarrow}\gamma_n{\rightarrow}\gamma) = S{\circ}S_g\,(\pi_1{\rightarrow}\cdots{\rightarrow}\pi_n{\rightarrow}\varphi)$.

We can assume without loss of generality, that $S'\,(\beta) = S{\circ}S_g\,(\beta)$ for all β. By 3.3.2(ii):

$pp(F(A_1,\ldots,A_n)) = \langle S_g\,(P_1\cup\cdots\cup P_n),\ S_g\,(\gamma)\rangle$.

and $S'\,(P_1\cup\cdots\cup P_n) = S{\circ}S_g\,(P_1\cup\cdots\cup P_n)$, and $S'\,(\gamma) = S{\circ}S_g\,(\gamma)$. ■

In the following lemma we show that if F is the defined symbol of a rewrite rule, then the type $\mathcal{E}\,(F)$ dictates not only the type for the left and right hand side of that rule, but also the principal type for the left hand side.

Lemma 3.3.5 If F is the defined symbol of the typeable rewrite rule $\mathbf{r} : Lhs \Rightarrow Rhs$, then there are P, B, $\sigma_1, \ldots, \sigma_n$, and σ such that

$$\mathcal{E}(F) = \sigma_1{\rightarrow}\cdots{\rightarrow}\sigma_n{\rightarrow}\sigma,\ pp(Lhs) = \langle P, \sigma\rangle,\ B \vdash Lhs{:}\sigma \text{ and } B \vdash Rhs{:}\sigma.$$

Proof: Easy, using 3.3.4, 1.3 and the fact that if τ is a substitution instance of σ, and σ a substitution instance of τ, then $\sigma = \tau$. ■

The following lemma plays an important part in the proof that the condition, as defined in definition 4.2.1, imposed on typeable rewrite rules is needed and sufficient, as given in theorem 4.2.3 and formulates the relation between replacements performed on a term and possible type assignments for that term.

Lemma 3.3.6 i) If $pp(M) = \langle P, \pi\rangle$, and for the replacement R there are B and σ such that $B \vdash M^{\mathrm{R}}{:}\sigma$, then there is a substitution S, such that $S\,(\pi) = \sigma$, and for every statement $x{:}\rho \in P$: $B \vdash x^{\mathrm{R}}{:}S\,(\rho)$.

ii) If $B \vdash M{:}\sigma$, and R is a replacement and B' a basis such that for every statement $x{:}\rho \in B$: $B' \vdash x^{\mathrm{R}}{:}\rho$, then $B' \vdash M^{\mathrm{R}}{:}\sigma$.

Proof: By induction on the structure of M.

i) The proof is very much the same as the one for theorem 3.3.4.

ii) Easy. ■

3.4 Examples

Example 3.4.1 Typed variants of some of the rewrite rules given in example 2.2. We have only inserted those types that are not immediately clear. Notice that we have assumed that

$\mathcal{E}\,(S) = (1{\rightarrow}2{\rightarrow}3){\rightarrow}(1{\rightarrow}2){\rightarrow}1{\rightarrow}3$,
$\mathcal{E}\,(K) = 1{\rightarrow}2{\rightarrow}1$, and
$\mathcal{E}(I) = 1{\rightarrow}1$.

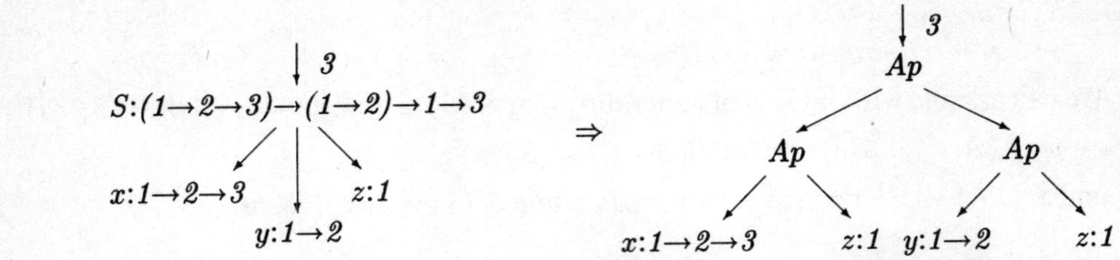

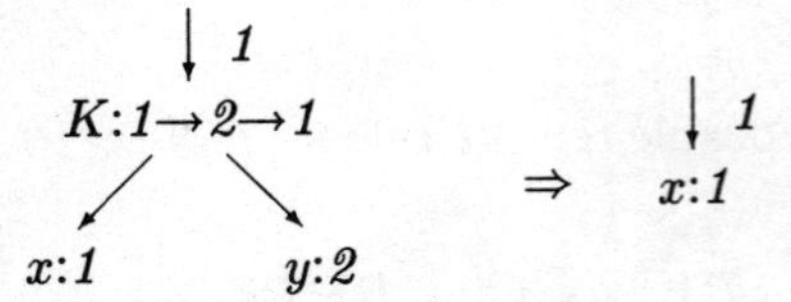

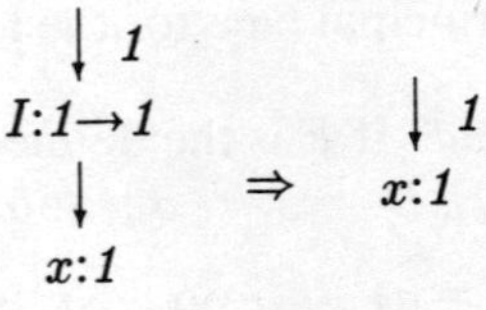

■

Example 3.4.2 Using

$\mathcal{E}(M) = ((1\to 2)\to 3)\to(1\to 2)\to 2,$
$\mathcal{E}(S) = (1\to 2\to 3)\to(1\to 2)\to 1\to 3,$ and
$\mathcal{E}(I) = 1\to 1$

the rule of example 2.3 can be typed as follows:

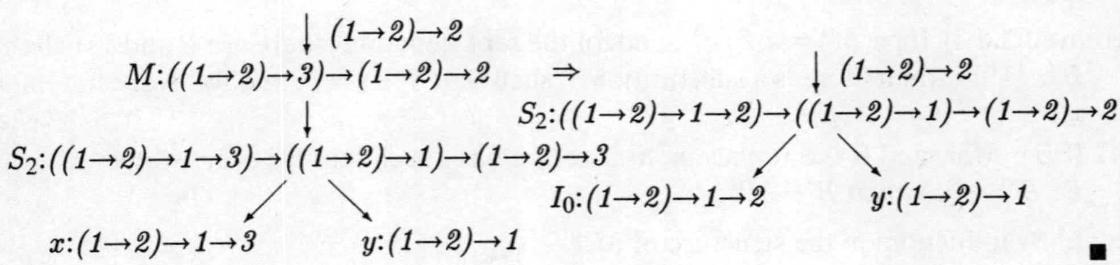

■

3.5 About recursion

The rule $R(x, y) \Rightarrow R(R(y, K_0), x)$ can be typed using $\mathcal{E}(R) = 1\to 2\to 3$:

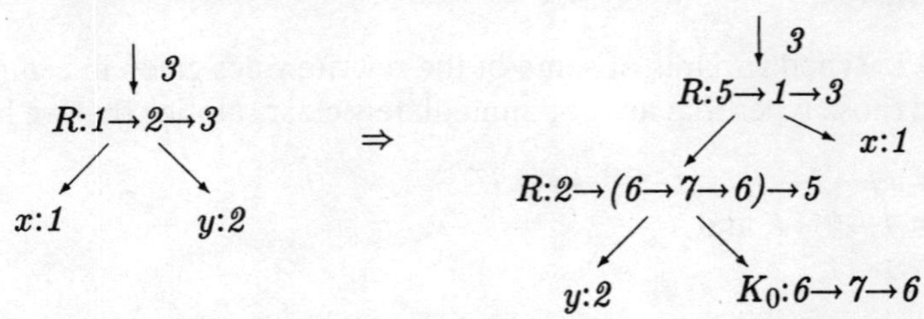

Notice that because of definition 3.2.2(i.c) the types assigned to the nodes containing R in the right hand side need only be instances of $1\to 2\to 3$.

Not every substitution instance of the type $1\to 2\to 3$ can be proven to be a correct type for R. For example when using $\mathcal{E}(R) = 1\to 1\to 2$, this rule cannot be typed. If first and second argument of R should have the same type, then the only types possible for R are the substitution instances of $(1\to 2\to 1)\to(1\to 2\to 1)\to 1\to 2\to 1$.

However, by definition 3.2.2(i.c) it is possible that R occurs in a term with type $1\to 1\to 2$. This means of course that although we allow all substitutions on the environment types of defined symbols, we cannot prove that all the types that are obtained in this way, are correct types for the rewrite rule.

This means in fact that the Mycroft approach is not very well suited for type assignment in term rewriting systems. If instead of Mycroft's approach we would use Milner's, which would require that all occurrences of the defined symbol F of a rule within that rule are typed with $\mathcal{E}(F)$, it is easy to verify that soundness of substitution can even be shown for rewrite rules.

4 Safe type assignment

In this section we show that the naive type assignment is not safe: there are typeable rewrite rules that match a term M typeable with σ, for which the result of the application of the rewrite rule on M is not typeable with σ. We will formulate a condition typeable rewrite rules should satisfy in order to obtain preservance of types under rewriting. We will show that this condition is needed and sufficient.

4.1 Patterns cause problems

Definitions 3.2.1, 3.2.2 and 3.2.3 define what a type assignment should be, just using the strategy as used in languages like for example Miranda. It is called *naive*, because it not sufficient to guarantee preservance of types under rewriting. (This is also called the 'subject reduction property'.) Not even typeability is kept under rewriting.

Take for example the definition of M as in example 2.3, which can be typed as shown in example 3.4.2. If we take the term $M\,(S_2\,(K_0, I_0))$ then it is easy to see that the rewrite is allowed, and that this term will be rewritten to: $S_2\,(I_0, I_0)$.

Although the first term is typeable in the following way:

$$\downarrow\ (4\to 5)\to 5$$

$$M{:}((4\to 5)\to 4\to 5)\to(4\to 5)\to 5$$

$$\downarrow$$

$$S_2{:}((4\to 5)\to(4\to 5)\to 4\to 5)\to((4\to 5)\to 4\to 5)\to(4\to 5)\to 4\to 5$$

$$\swarrow \qquad\qquad \searrow$$

$$K_0{:}(4\to 5)\to(4\to 5)\to 4\to 5 \qquad\qquad I_0{:}(4\to 5)\to 4\to 5$$

the term $S_2\,(I_0, I_0)$ is not typeable with the type $(4\to 5)\to 5$. In fact, it is not typeable at all.

4.2 A needed and sufficient condition for preservance of types under rewriting

By definition 1.2, if a term M is rewritten to the term M' using the rewrite rule $Lhs \Rightarrow Rhs$, there is a subterm M_0 of M, and a replacement R, such that $Lhs^{\mathrm{R}} = M_0$. M' is obtained by replacing M_0 by Rhs^{R}. To guarantee the subject reduction property, we should accept only those rewrite rules $Lhs \Rightarrow Rhs$, that satisfy:

For all replacements R, bases B and types σ: if $B \vdash Lhs^{\mathrm{R}}{:}\sigma$, then $B \vdash Rhs^{\mathrm{R}}{:}\sigma$.

because then we are sure that all possible rewrites are safe.

In the notion of type assignment as presented in this paper, it is easy to formulate a condition that rewrite rules should satisfy in order to be accepted.

Definition 4.2.1 i) We call a rewrite rule $Lhs \Rightarrow Rhs$ *safe* if:

If $pp(Lhs) = <P, \pi>$, then $P \vdash Rhs{:}\pi$.

ii) The definition of a *safe type assignment with respect to* $\mathcal{E}$ is the same as the one for a naive type assignment, by replacing in definition 3.2.3 condition (i.a) and (i.b) by:

If $pp(Lhs) = <P, \pi>$, then $P \vdash Rhs{:}\pi$.

Notice that the notion $pp(M)$ is defined independently from the definition of typeable rewrite rules.

As an example of a rule that is not safe, take the typed rewrite rule in the next example: the types assigned to the nodes containing x and y are not the most general ones needed to find the type for the left hand side of the rewrite rule.

Example 4.2.2 Take the definition of M as in example 2.3. To obtain $pp(M\,(S_2\,(x,y)))$, we assign types to nodes in the tree in the following way:

$$\downarrow (1\to 2)\to 2$$

$$M{:}((1\to 2)\to 3)\to (1\to 2)\to 2$$

$$\downarrow$$

$$S_2{:}((1\to 2)\to 4\to 3)\to ((1\to 2)\to 4)\to (1\to 2)\to 3$$

$$\swarrow \qquad \searrow$$

$$x{:}(1\to 2)\to 4\to 3 \qquad\qquad y{:}(1\to 2)\to 4$$

If the right hand side should be typed with $(1\to 2)\to 2$, the type needed for the node containing y is $(1\to 2)\to 1$.

$$\downarrow (1\to 2)\to 2$$

$$S_2{:}((1\to 2)\to 1\to 2)\to ((1\to 2)\to 1)\to (1\to 2)\to 2$$

$$\swarrow \qquad \searrow$$

$$I_0{:}(1\to 2)\to 1\to 2 \qquad\qquad y{:}(1\to 2)\to 1$$

So this rule is not safe, and should therefore be rejected. ∎

In the following theorem, we prove that our solution is correct. The structure of the first proof depends greatly on the fact that for every type σ we can trivially find an $A \in \Sigma_0$, such that $\mathcal{E}\,(A) = \sigma$: we just pick a constant A, not already used. We do not require in the proof that for every symbol A there is a rewrite rule that defines A.

Theorem 4.2.3 i) **The condition is needed.** Let *Lhs*, *Rhs* $\in$ *Ter* (Σ), and **r** : *Lhs* $\Rightarrow$ *Rhs* be a typeable rewrite rule that is not safe. Then there there exists a replacement R, and a type μ, such that $\vdash Lhs^{\mathrm{R}}{:}\mu \ \& \ \neg \vdash Rhs^{\mathrm{R}}{:}\mu$.

ii) **The condition is sufficient.** Let *Lhs*, *Rhs* $\in$ *Ter* (Σ), and **r** : *Lhs* $\Rightarrow$ *Rhs* be a safe rewrite rule. Then for every replacement R, basis B and a type μ: $B \vdash Lhs^{\mathrm{R}}{:}\mu \Rightarrow B \vdash Rhs^{\mathrm{R}}{:}\mu$.

Proof: i) Since **r** is typeable and left linear, we know that there are $\beta_1, \ldots, \beta_n, \tau$, and distinct $x_1, \ldots, x_n$, such that:

$$\{x_1{:}\beta_1, \ldots, x_n{:}\beta_n\} \vdash Lhs{:}\tau \ \& \ \{x_1{:}\beta_1, \ldots, x_n{:}\beta_n\} \vdash Rhs{:}\tau.$$

Then by theorem 3.3.4, and lemma 3.3.5 we know that there are bases P_l, P_r, types $\alpha_1, \ldots, \alpha_n$, δ and a substitution S_0, such that:

$$pp(Lhs) = <P_l, \tau> \ \& \ pp(Rhs) = <P_r, \delta> \ \& \ P_l = \{x_1{:}\rho_1, \ldots, x_n{:}\rho_n\} \ \&$$
$$S_0(\tau) = S_0(\delta) = \tau \ \& \ S_0(P_l) = S_0(P_r) = \{x_1{:}\beta_1, \ldots, x_n{:}\beta_n\}.$$

Let S_1 be the substitution such that for every i: $S_1(\varphi_i) = c_i$ (the i-th type constant), μ be a type such that $S_1(\tau) = \mu$, $A_1, \ldots, A_n$ be constants such that for every $1 \leq i \leq n$, $\mathcal{E}(A_i) = S_1(\rho_i)$, and R be the replacement such that for every $1 \leq i \leq n$: $x_i^{\mathrm{R}} = A_i$. Then by lemma 3.3.6(ii): $\vdash Lhs^{\mathrm{R}}{:}\mu$. (Notice that Lhs^{R} does not contain term variables.) Since **r** is not safe, we know that

$$\neg \{x_1{:}\rho_1, \ldots, x_n{:}\rho_n\} \vdash Rhs{:}\tau.$$

Suppose towards a contradiction that $\vdash Rhs^{\mathrm{R}}{:}\mu$.
Then by lemma 3.3.6(i) there is a substitution S_2 such that

$$S_2(\delta) = \mu \text{ and for every } x{:}\gamma \in P_r{:}\ \vdash x^{\mathrm{R}}{:}S_2(\gamma).$$

By definition 1.2(ii.a.3) for every $x{:}\gamma \in P_r$ there is a $1 \leq i \leq n$ such that $x = x_i$. Since S_1 replaces type variables by type constants, the type assigned to A_i can only be $S_1(\rho_i)$. This implies that for every $x{:}\gamma \in P_r$ there is a $1 \leq i \leq n$ such that $x = x_i$ and $S_2(\gamma) = S_1(\rho_i)$. It is straightforward to verify that, since S_1 replaces type variables by type constants, there is a substitution S_3 such that $S_2 = S_1 \circ S_3$. So for every $x{:}\gamma \in P_r$ there is a $1 \leq i \leq n$ such that: $x = x_i$ and $\rho_i = S_3(\gamma)$. But then by lemma 3.3.3:

$$\{x_1{:}\rho_1, \ldots, x_n{:}\rho_n\} \vdash Rhs{:}S_3(\delta).$$

Moreover, $\mu = S_1(\tau) = S_2(\delta) = S_1 \circ S_3(\delta)$, so $\tau = S_3(\delta)$.

ii) Since **r** is safe, there are P, π such that: if $pp(Lhs) = <P, \pi>$, then $P \vdash Rhs{:}\pi$
Suppose $pp(Lhs) = <P, \pi>$, and R is a replacement such that there are basis B and type μ such that $B \vdash Lhs^{\mathrm{R}}{:}\mu$, then by lemma 3.3.6(i) there is a substitution S such that

$$S(\pi) = \mu \ \& \ \forall\, x{:}\rho \in P\ [\ B \vdash x^{\mathrm{R}}{:}S(\rho)\ ].$$

But then by lemma 3.3.3:

$$S(P) \vdash Rhs{:}S(\pi) \ \& \ \forall\, x{:}\rho \in P\ [\ B \vdash x^{\mathrm{R}}{:}S(\rho)\ ].$$

So by lemma 3.3.6(ii): $B \vdash Rhs^{\mathrm{R}}{:}\mu$. ∎

Notice that although the proof of part (i) uses explicitly the presence of type constants, the problem of loss of subject reduction also arises if type constants are not in the type system. However, we do not believe that it is possible to prove that the condition is also needed in that case. (See also conjecture 5.1).

5 Optimisation after bracket abstraction

Bracket abstraction algorithms are used to translate lambda expressions to combinators. With some accompanying optimization rules they provide an interesting example. If in the bracket abstraction we would use the following combinator set:

$$\begin{array}{ll} I\ x & = x \\ K\ x\ y & = x \\ B\ x\ y\ z & = x\ (y\ z) \\ C\ x\ y\ z & = x\ z\ y \\ S\ x\ y\ z & = x\ z\ (y\ z) \end{array}$$

then we could define, as Curry did in [CF58], the following optimizations:

$$\begin{array}{ll} S\ (K\ x)\ (K\ y) & = K\ (x\ y) \\ S\ (K\ x)\ I & = x \\ S\ (K\ x)\ y & = B\ x\ y \\ S\ x\ (K\ y) & = C\ x\ y \end{array}$$

We can see that these rules work on combinators that have not yet been applied to all their arguments. When using the environment:

$$\begin{array}{ll} \mathcal{E}\ (Opt) & = (1 \rightarrow 2) \rightarrow 1 \rightarrow 2, \\ \mathcal{E}\ (I) & = 1 \rightarrow 1, \\ \mathcal{E}\ (K) & = 1 \rightarrow 2 \rightarrow 1, \\ \mathcal{E}\ (B) & = (1 \rightarrow 2) \rightarrow (3 \rightarrow 1) \rightarrow 3 \rightarrow 2, \\ \mathcal{E}\ (C) & = (1 \rightarrow 2 \rightarrow 3) \rightarrow 2 \rightarrow 1 \rightarrow 3, \\ \mathcal{E}\ (S) & = (1 \rightarrow 2 \rightarrow 3) \rightarrow (1 \rightarrow 2) \rightarrow 1 \rightarrow 3 \end{array}$$

the rewrite rules for I, K, B, C, and S and their Curried versions, and rewrite rules for a function *Opt* as below (where the rules that are not safe are preceded by '•'), can be typed. These rules for *Opt* are only typeable using Mycroft's approach, not using Milner's.

$$\begin{array}{lll} \bullet Opt\ (S_2\ (K_1\ (x), K_1\ (y))) & \Rightarrow & K_1\ (Ap\ (Opt\ (x), Opt\ (y))) \\ Opt\ (S_2\ (K_1\ (x), I_0)) & \Rightarrow & Opt\ (x) \\ Opt\ (S_2\ (K_1\ (x), y)) & \Rightarrow & B_2\ (Opt\ (x), Opt\ (y)) \\ \bullet Opt\ (S_2\ (x, K_1\ (y))) & \Rightarrow & C_2\ (Opt\ (x), Opt\ (y)) \end{array}$$

(The rules for *Opt* are not intended to be complete.) They can now be used in combination with the previous rules for bracket abstraction to produce simplified combinator expressions. For example, the combinator expression that would be produced for $\lambda x.\lambda y.x$ (i.e. $S\ (K\ K)\ I$) will be evaluated as below:

$$Opt(Ap\ (Ap\ (S_0, Ap\ (K_0, K_0)), I_0)) \twoheadrightarrow K_0$$

This is what we would expect for the above lambda expression.

Conjecture 5.1 As indicated above, some of the rewrite rules for *Opt* are not safe. By theorem 4.2.3(i) we can give a term M, typeable by σ such that one of the unsafe rewrite rules matches M, but the result of rewriting M with this rule is not typeable with σ. However, in this construction we use that the type system contains also type constants. If we would use a type system without type constants, we conjecture that the safeness condition can be formulated in such a way that the rewrite rules for *Opt* are all safe. ■

Future work

Although we could very well motivate that for type assignment with Curry types the LLATRS's are the best equipped, it seems natural to generalize our notion of type assignment to the non-left linear systems, since in a number of functional programming languages it is possible to have non-left linear rewrite rules. The only property that is lost in this generalization is the neededness of the condition on rewrite rules, since only in that proof the left linearity of rewrite rules is used. Another approach to this problem could be to apply our notion of type assignment to conditional term rewriting systems.

It seems straightforward to use our notion of type assignment in term graph rewriting systems. However, some accuracy will very likely be lost, and it seems necessary to base such a notion on a (restriction of) the intersection type assignment system. At the moment a paper on partial intersection type assignment of Rank 2 is in preparation. This system also seems promising for the definition of functions in functional programming languages that have internal polymorphism and for overloaded definitions.

Jan Willem Klop asked us if we could characterize the kind of rewrite rules that are typeable in our system. At this moment we have no direct answer to that question, but it will be interesting to explore this.

We are looking for good examples of areas where our notion of type assignment can be useful. It is probably not very interesting in an executable system, because by allowing arbitrary function symbols in patterns we loose the Church-Rosser property. Their main use could be providing type checking (and eventually type inference) for people who are writing specifications in the style of the rewrite systems we deal with. One of the main areas could be in program transformation and semantics.

Acknowledgement

The main problem solved in this paper (as given in section 4.1) was first brought to our attention by M. Coppo and M. Dezani-Ciancaglini of the university of Turin, Italy. The construction used in the proof of theorem 4.2.3(i) is partly due to M. van Eekelen, of the university of Nijmegen, the Netherlands.

Appendix: A type check algorithm for LLATRS's

In this section we present a type check algorithm that, when applied to a LLATRS and a environment determines whether this LLATRS is safely typeable with respect to the environment. The algorithm is specified in a notation based on the programming language Clean.

A.1 Representing LLATRS's and Curry types

Since type assignment is syntax directed, it is convenient to make the structure of an LLATRS explicit, for such a structure enables us to use pattern matching to distinguish the different syntactical parts. In Clean new data structures are defined by means of algebraic type definitions, and Clean uses square brackets (i.e. '[' and ']') to denote list types.

The algebraic type definitions for LLATRS's that we use are the following:

```
TYPE
:: TRS      → [Rule]                                               ;
:: Rule     → (Term, Term)                                         ;
:: Term     → Var Variable | Symb Symbol [Term] | DefSymb Symbol [Term] ;
:: Variable → x | ...                                              ;
:: Symbol   → Ap | ...                                             ;
```

The last alternative for Term (defining the constructor DefSymb) is used to indicate that the corresponding (sub)term starts with the defined symbol (definition 1.2(iii.a)). So, using DefSymb makes only sense when specifying the left hand side of a rewrite rule. Note that it is very well possible to determine the defining node of a certain left hand side of a rewrite rule. This however would make the algorithm somewhat more complicated and therefore less clear.

A basis (definition 3.1.1(iii)) is a set of statements with term variables as subjects. Since there are no sets in Clean we use lists instead. Hence, the representation of bases becomes:

```
TYPE
:: Statement → (Variable, CurryType) ;
:: Basis     → [Statement]           ;
```

A.2 The type check algorithm

The goal of the type check algorithm presented below is to determine whether a safe type assignment can be constructed such that all the conditions of definitions 3.2.2 and 3.2.3 are satisfied. The main function of the algorithm, called TypeTRS, expects a LLATRS as well as a environment as parameters. It returns a boolean that indicates whether the construction of the type assignment was successful.

It is easy to prove that the algorithm presented here is correct and complete:

Theorem A.2.1 i) If M is typeable with respect to the environment $\mathcal{E}$, then TypeTerm M $\mathcal{E}$ returns $pp(M)$.

ii) If TypeTerm M $\mathcal{E}$ returns the pair $<B, \sigma>$, then $pp(M) = <B, \sigma>$.

iii) There is a safe type assignment with respect to $\mathcal{E}$ for the LLATRS TRS, if and only if TypeTRS TRS $\mathcal{E}$ returns TRUE.

Proof: By straightforward induction on the structure of terms and rewrite rules. ■

The algorithm does not perform any consistency check on its input so it assumes the input to be correct according to definitions 1.1 and 1.2. Moreover, all possible error messages and error handling cases are omitted, and the algorithm returns only TRUE for rewrite systems that are safely typeable. It could easily be extended to an algorithm that accepts unsafe rewrite rules.

The algorithm as presented here is not purely functional. The 0-ary function FreshVariable (used amongst others by TypeSymb and TypeVar) is supposed to return a new, unused type variable. It is obvious that such a function is not referential transparent, but for the sake of readability, we prefer not to be explicit on the handling of typevariables.

```
:: TypeTRS TRS Environment  → BOOL                                    ;
   TypeTRS [ ] ℰ             → TRUE                                    |
   TypeTRS [r | rules] ℰ     → And (TypeRule r ℰ) (TypeTRS rules ℰ)   ;
```

Constraint 3.2.2(i.b) describes that for every term variable occurring in a rewrite rule, all the nodes containing this variable in the bases for both the left and the right hand side should contain equal predicates. This is provided in TypeRule by unifying all predicates for each subject occurring in the bases after a rule has been type checked. These unifications are performed by the function UnifyBasis. TypeRule also takes care of checking the safeness constraint as given in definition 4.2.1(ii), by checking, using EqualBases, if the unification of left and right hand sides of a rewrite rule has changed the left hand side basis.

```
:: TypeRule Rule Environment  → BOOL                              ;
   TypeRule (Lhs, Rhs) ℰ       → EqualBases (S₂ (S₁ (Bₗ))) Bₗ
       S₂: UnifyBasis (S₁ (Bₗ) ∪ S₁ (Bᵣ)),
       S₁: UnifyTypes σ τ,
       (Bₗ, σ): TypeTerm Lhs ℰ,
       (Bᵣ, τ): TypeTerm Rhs ℰ                                    ;
```

The type of a symbol is either an instance of the type for that symbol given by the environment (in case of a Symb) or that type itself (in case of a DefSymb). The distinction between the two is determined by the function TypeTerm. The defining node of a rewrite rule can only be typed with *one* type, so any substitution resulting from a unification is forbidden to change this type. This is solved by the unification algorithm UnifyTypes, an extension of Robinsons unification algorithm; it is capable of deciding whether or not a type variable is special (so it appears in some environment type) and it refuses to substitute this variable by other types.

```
:: TypeTerm Term Environment      → (Basis, CurryType)                      ;
   TypeTerm (Var x) ℰ              → TypeVar x                               |
   TypeTerm (Symb F args) ℰ        → TypeSymb (Instance (ℰ(F))) args ℰ       |
   TypeTerm (DefSymb F args) ℰ     → TypeSymb (ℰ (F)) args ℰ                 ;
```

The function TypeSymb verifies the constraints 3.2.2(i.b) by the means of the method indicated by definition 3.3.2.

```
:: TypeSymb CurryType [Term] Environment → (Basis, CurryType) ;
   TypeSymb σ [ ] ℰ                       → (B, σ)             |
   TypeSymb σ terms ℰ                     → (S (B), S (φ)),
       S: UnifyTypes τ σ,
       (B, τ): TypeArguments terms φ ℰ,
       φ: FreshVariable                                        ;
```

TypeArguments is an auxiliary function that derives the types for all arguments of a node and constructs an arrow type out of these types. Note that this function expects the last type of the arrow type that is constructed as a parameter: the type variable φ is passed to the function TypeArguments to make sure that the type $\sigma_1 \rightarrow \cdots \rightarrow \sigma_n \rightarrow \varphi$ is created, instead of $(\sigma_1 \rightarrow \cdots \rightarrow \sigma_n) \rightarrow \varphi$. Besides the adjusted basis, this arrow type is delivered as a result.

```
::TypeArguments [Term] CurryType Environment → (Basis, CurryType) ;
TypeArguments [ ] σ ℰ                        → (∅, σ)            |
TypeArguments [M | terms] σ ℰ                → (B, σ1→σ2),
     B: B1 ∪ B2,
     (B1, σ1): TypeTerm M ℰ,
     (B2, σ2): TypeArguments terms σ ℰ                            ;
```

TypeVar assigns a new type variable φ to a term variable x.

```
:: TypeVar Variable → (Basis, CurryType) ;
   TypeVar x        → ([(x, φ)], φ),
      φ: FreshVariable                   ;
```

References

[Bar84] H. Barendregt. *The lambda calculus: its syntax and semantics*. North-Holland, Amsterdam, revised edition, 1984.

[BCD83] H. Barendregt, M. Coppo, and M. Dezani-Ciancaglini. A filter lambda model and the completeness of type assignment. *The Journal of Symbolic Logic*, 48(4):931–940, 1983.

[BvEG+87] H.P. Barendregt, M.C.J.D. van Eekelen, J.R.W. Glauert, J.R. Kennaway, M.J. Plasmeijer, and M.R. Sleep. Term graph rewriting. In *Proceedings of PARLE, Parallel Architectures and Languages Europe, Eindhoven, The Netherlands*, volume 259-II of *Lecture Notes in Computer Science*, pages 141–158. Springer-Verlag, 1987.

[BvEvLP87] T. Brus, M.C.J.D. van Eekelen, M.O. van Leer, and M.J. Plasmeijer. Clean - A Language for Functional Graph Rewriting. In *Proceedings of the Third International Conference on Functional Programming Languages and Computer Architecture, Portland, Oregon, USA*, volume 274 of *Lecture Notes in Computer Science*, pages 364–368. Springer-Verlag, 1987.

[CF58] H.B. Curry and R. Feys. *Combinatory Logic*, volume 1. North-Holland, Amsterdam, 1958.

[Dam85] L.M.M. Damas. *Type Assignment in Programming Languages*. PhD thesis, University of Edinburgh, Department of Computer Science, Edinburgh, 1985. Thesis CST-33-85.

[FGJM85] K. Futatsugi, J. Goguen, J.P. Jouannaud, and J. Meseguer. Principles of OBJ2. In *Proceedings 12th ACM Symposium on Principles of Programming Languages*, pages 52–66, 1985.

[Hin69] J.R. Hindley. The principal type scheme of an object in combinatory logic. *Transactions of the American Mathematical Society*, 146:29–60, 1969.

[Klo90] J.W. Klop. Term Rewriting Systems. Report CS-R9073, Centre for Mathematics and Computer Science, Amsterdam, 1990.

[KTU88] A.J. Kfoury, J. Tiuryn, and P. Urzyczyn. A proper extension of ML with an effective type-assignment. In *Proceedings of the Fifteenth Annual ACM SIGACT-SIGPLAN Symposium on Principles of Programming Languages*, pages 58–69, San Diego, California, 1988.

[Mil78] R. Milner. A theory of type polymorphism in programming. *Journal of Computer and System Sciences*, 17:348–375, 1978.

[Myc84] A. Mycroft. Polymorphic type schemes and recursive definitions. In *Proceedings of the International Symposium on Programming, Toulouse*, volume 167 of *Lecture Notes Computer Science*, pages 217–239. Springer-Verlag, 1984.

[NSvEP91] E.G.J.M.H. Nöcker, J.E.W. Smetsers, M.C.J.D. van Eekelen, and M.J. Plasmeijer. Concurrent Clean. In *Proceedings of PARLE '91, Parallel Architectures and Languages Europe, Eindhoven, The Netherlands*, volume 506-II of *Lecture Notes in Computer Science*, pages 202–219. Springer-Verlag, 1991.

[Pfe85] F. Pfenning. Partial Polymorphic Type Inference and Higher-Order Unification. In *Proceedings of the conference on Functional Programming Languages and Computer Architecture*, volume 201 of *Lecture Notes in Computer Science*, pages 1–16. Springer-Verlag, 1985.

[Rob65] J.A. Robinson. A machine-oriented logic based on the resolution principle. *Journal of the ACM*, 12(1):23–41, 1965.

[Tur85] D.A. Turner. Miranda: A non-strict functional language with polymorphic types. In *Proceedings of the conference on Functional Programming Languages and Computer Architecture*, volume 201 of *Lecture Notes in Computer Science*, pages 1–16. Springer-Verlag, 1985.

A linear algorithm for solving fixed-point equations on transition systems

Bart Vergauwen and Johan Lewi
Department of Computer Science, KU Leuven
Celestijnenlaan 200A
B-3001 Leuven, Belgium

E-mail: bartv@cs.kuleuven.ac.be

Abstract. In this paper we present an algorithm for effectively computing extremal fixed-points of a system of mutually recursive equations over a finite transition system. The proposed algorithm runs in time linear in the size of the transition system and linear in the size of the system of equations, thereby improving on [AC].

Keywords. model checking, modal logics, transition systems

Introduction

Finite transition systems (also called finite-state systems) play a central role as formal models for reactive and concurrent systems. A very promising technique for *automatically* verifying transition systems is *model checking*. In the model-theoretic approach we mechanically determine whether a given transition system TS meets a specification S (expressed as a formula of some temporal logic) by checking whether TS is a model for S.
In [CES] model checking algorithms are described for the branching-time temporal logic CTL. The algorithms from [CES] run in time linear in the size of the transition system and formula to be checked.
In [D] system properties are expressed as least fixed-points of a set of mutually recursive equations. In this case model checking amounts to effectively computing these least fixed-points. This is clearly related to the μ-calculus [K], more precisely to formulas of alternation-depth 1 [EL].

[D] and [EL] describe algorithms for computing least fixed-points of systems of equations, running in time quadratic in the size of the transition system. An improved algorithm is given in [AC]. The algorithm of [AC] runs in time linear in the size of the transition system, but still quadratic in the size of the system of equations.
In this paper we describe an algorithm for computing extremal fixed-points of a recursive system of equations. Our algorithm improves upon [AC] as it runs in time linear in the size of the transition system and linear in the size of the system of equations.
Furthermore our algorithm is well suited to be implemented on parallel architectures, thereby allowing for a further reduction of the execution time.
Finally the proposed algorithm can easily be modified to obtain a linear-time *local* model checking algorithm.

The paper is organized as follows: after the preliminaries (section 1) we discuss in section 2 the key ideas behind our model checking algorithm. The algorithm itself is given in section 3. In section 4 we examine the correctness and the time complexity of the proposed algorithm. In section 5 we touch upon some implementation considerations. The final section contains the conclusions.

1. Preliminaries

Transition systems. A (finite) transition system TS is a tuple [ST, TR] with ST a finite, non empty set and TR $\subseteq$ ST^2. ST represents the set of all possible system states whereas elements of TR represent possible state transitions.
The size |TS| of a transition system TS = [ST, TR] is defined in the obvious way: |TS| = max(#ST, #TR).

The signature SIG. Let C_σ and C_τ be two finite, disjoint sets (of constants). We define the two sorted signature SIG_{C_σ,C_τ} as follows:

signature SIG_{C_σ,C_τ}
  sorts σ, τ;
  operations
   -- constants
    $\_: C_\sigma \to \sigma$;
    $\_: C_\tau \to \tau$;
   -- boolean operators
    $\wedge_\sigma: \sigma * \sigma \to \sigma$;
    $\vee_\sigma: \sigma * \sigma \to \sigma$;
    $\neg_\sigma: \sigma \to \sigma$;
    $\wedge_\tau: \tau * \tau \to \tau$;
    $\vee_\tau: \tau * \tau \to \tau$;

$\neg_\tau: \tau \rightarrow \tau;$

-- modal operator and selectors

$\_[]\_: \sigma * \sigma \rightarrow \tau;$

Source: $\tau \rightarrow \sigma;$

Target: $\tau \rightarrow \sigma;$

end signature SIG_{C_σ,C_τ};

Let X be a finite set of (state) variables of sort σ and Y be a finite set of (transition) variables of sort τ. We assume X and Y disjoint. We define $T^\sigma_{C_\sigma,C_\tau}(X, Y)$ resp. $T^\tau_{C_\sigma,C_\tau}(X, Y)$ to be the set of all terms of sort σ resp. sort τ over $SIG_{C_\sigma,C_\tau} \cup X \cup Y$.

Interpretation of terms w.r.t. a transition system. Let TS = [ST, TR] be a transition system. Assume interpretation functions $\delta_\sigma: C_\sigma \rightarrow \mathbb{P}(ST)$ and $\delta_\tau: C_\tau \rightarrow \mathbb{P}(TR)$ for the constants of C_σ and C_τ.

Terms of sort σ are interpreted as subsets of ST i.e. elements of $\mathbb{P}(ST)$ whereas terms of sort τ are interpreted as subsets of TR i.e. elements of $\mathbb{P}(TR)$.

As terms may contain free variables, their interpretation will be relative w.r.t. an environment ρ, providing meaning for all variables of X and Y. Hence an environment ρ is an element from RHO:

$$RHO \triangleq [X \rightarrow \mathbb{P}(ST)] * [Y \rightarrow \mathbb{P}(TR)]$$

We now introduce semantic functions $[[\_]]_\sigma$ and $[[\_]]_\tau$:

$$[[\_]]_\sigma \_ : T^\sigma_{C_\sigma,C_\tau}(X, Y) \rightarrow RHO \rightarrow \mathbb{P}(ST)$$
$$[[\_]]_\tau \_ : T^\tau_{C_\sigma,C_\tau}(X, Y) \rightarrow RHO \rightarrow \mathbb{P}(TR)$$

$[[t_\sigma]]_\sigma \rho$ resp. $[[t_\tau]]_\tau \rho$ denotes the meaning of term t_σ resp. t_τ when evaluated in context ρ. The denotation functions $[[\_]]_\sigma$ and $[[\_]]_\tau$ are defined by structural induction:

$[[c_\sigma]]_\sigma \rho = \delta_\sigma(c_\sigma)$ for $c_\sigma \in C_\sigma$

$[[c_\tau]]_\tau \rho = \delta_\tau(c_\tau)$ for $c_\tau \in C_\tau$

$[[x]]_\sigma (\rho_\sigma,\rho_\tau) = \rho_\sigma(x)$ for $x \in X$

$[[y]]_\tau (\rho_\sigma,\rho_\tau) = \rho_\tau(x)$ for $y \in Y$

$[[term^1_\sigma \wedge_\sigma term^2_\sigma]]_\sigma \rho = [[term^1_\sigma]]_\sigma \rho \cap [[term^1_\sigma]]_\sigma \rho$

$[[term^1_\sigma \vee_\sigma term^2_\sigma]]_\sigma \rho = [[term^1_\sigma]]_\sigma \rho \cup [[term^1_\sigma]]_\sigma \rho$

$[[\neg_\sigma term_\sigma]]_\sigma \rho = ST - [[term_\sigma]]_\sigma \rho$

$[[term^1_\tau \wedge_\tau term^2_\tau]]_\tau \rho = [[term^1_\tau]]_\tau \rho \cap [[term^1_\tau]]_\tau \rho$

$[[term^1_\tau \vee_\tau term^2_\tau]]_\tau \rho = [[term^1_\tau]]_\tau \rho \cup [[term^1_\tau]]_\tau \rho$

$[[\neg_\tau term_\tau]]_\tau \rho = TR - [[term_\tau]]_\tau \rho$

$[[term^1_\sigma [] term^2_\sigma]]_\tau \rho = \{ (st_1,st_2) \in TR \mid st_1 \in [[term^1_\sigma]]_\sigma \rho$ and $st_2 \in [[term^2_\sigma]]_\sigma \rho \}$

$[[Source(term_\tau)]]_\sigma \rho = \{ st_1 \in ST \mid \exists\, st_2$ such that $(st_1, st_2) \in [[term_\tau]]_\tau \rho \};$

$[[Target(term_\tau)]]_\sigma \rho = \{ st_2 \in ST \mid \exists\, st_1$ such that $(st_1, st_2) \in [[term_\tau]]_\tau \rho \};$

Systems of equations. Let X and Y be finite and disjoint sets. Let C_σ and C_τ be finite and disjoint sets.
A system Σ of equations over X,Y,C_σ,C_τ is a pair (Σ_σ, Σ_τ) of sets with:

$$\Sigma_\sigma = \{ x = \text{term}_\sigma \mid x \in X \text{ and } \text{term}_\sigma \in T^\sigma_{C_\sigma,C_\tau}(X, Y) \}$$

$$\Sigma_\tau = \{ y = \text{term}_\tau \mid y \in Y \text{ and } \text{term}_\tau \in T^\sigma_{C_\sigma,C_\tau}(X, Y) \}$$

Note that we will assume that exactly one equation is associated with every variable.
We define the size $|\Sigma|$ of a system of equations Σ as the number of occurrences of elements from SIG_{C_σ,C_τ}.

Function associated with a system of equations. Let TS = [ST, TR] be a transition system and $\Sigma = (\Sigma_\sigma, \Sigma_\tau)$ be a system of equations over X,Y,C_σ,C_τ with $\Sigma_\sigma = \{ x^i = \text{term}^i_\sigma \mid i = 1..n \}$ and $\Sigma_\tau = \{ y^j = \text{term}^j_\tau \mid j = 1..m \}$. Assume interpretation functions δ_σ and δ_τ for the constants of C_σ and C_τ.
We now define a function f_Σ from ($\mathbb{P}$(ST $)^n$ * $\mathbb{P}$(TR $)^m$) into itself as follows:

$$f_\Sigma(sp^1, ..., sp^n, tp^1, ..., tp^m)$$
$$= ([[\text{term}^1_\sigma]]_\sigma\, \rho, ..., [[\text{term}^n_\sigma]]_\sigma\, \rho, [[\text{term}^1_\tau]]_\tau\, \rho, ..., [[\text{term}^m_\tau]]_\tau\, \rho)$$

with $\rho = (\rho_\sigma, \rho_\tau)$, $\rho_\sigma(x^i) = sp^i$ for i=1..n and $\rho_\tau(y^j) = tp^j$ for j=1..m

Interpretation of a system of equations w.r.t. a transition system. Let TS = [ST, TR] be a transition system and $\Sigma = (\Sigma_\sigma, \Sigma_\tau)$ be a system of equations over X,Y,C_σ,C_τ with $\Sigma_\sigma = \{ x^i = \text{term}^i_\sigma \mid i = 1..n \}$ and $\Sigma_\tau = \{ y^j = \text{term}^j_\tau \mid j = 1..m \}$. Assume interpretation functions δ_σ and δ_τ for the constants of C_σ and C_τ.
Assume that each occurrence of a variable in the right hand sides of Σ occurs within an even number of negations. Under this syntactic restriction, it can be proved that f_Σ is a monotonic mapping (with point-wise set-inclusion as the ordering relation). Hence, according to the Tarski [T] fixed-point theorem, f_Σ has a unique least fixed-point (notation μf_Σ) as well as a greatest fixed-point (notation νf_Σ).
For the rest of this paper we only consider systems of equations satisfying the above syntactic monotonicity requirement.

Normal form for systems of equations. A system Σ of equations over X,Y,C_σ,C_τ is in normal form if and only if every equation of Σ is in one of the following forms (with x, x_1, $x_2 \in$ X and y $\in$ Y):

- $x = c_\sigma$ where $c_\sigma \in C_\sigma$
- $x = \bigvee X'$ with $X' \subseteq X$ and $\#X' \geq 2$
- $x = \bigwedge X'$ with $X' \subseteq X$ and $\#X' \geq 2$

- $x = \text{Source}(y)$
- $x = \text{Target}(y)$
- $x = \tilde{\text{Source}}(y)$
- $x = \tilde{\text{Target}}(y)$
- $y = c_\tau$ where $c_\tau \in C_\tau$
- $y = \bigvee Y'$ with $Y' \subseteq Y$ and $\#Y' \geq 2$
- $y = \bigwedge Y'$ with $Y' \subseteq Y$ and $\#Y' \geq 2$
- $y = x_1 \,[]\, x_2$

Remark: in the above the following abbreviations were used: $\tilde{\text{Source}}$ ($\tilde{\text{Target}}$) is the dual of Source (Target) i.e. $\tilde{\text{Source}}(y) = \neg_\sigma \text{Source}(\neg_\tau y)$ and $\tilde{\text{Target}}(y) = \neg_\sigma \text{Target}(\neg_\tau y)$, $\bigvee X' = (x_1 \vee_\sigma \dots \vee_\sigma x'_n)$ and $\bigwedge X' = (x'_1 \wedge_\sigma \dots \wedge_\sigma x'_n)$ with $X' = \{ x'_1, \dots, x'_n \}$, $\bigvee Y' = (y'_1 \vee_\tau \dots \vee_\tau y'_n)$ and $\bigwedge Y' = (y'_1 \wedge_\tau \dots \wedge_\tau y'_n)$ with $Y' = \{ y'_1, \dots, y'_n \}$.
We now have the following theorem.

Theorem. Let Σ be a system of equations, satisfying the syntactic monotonicity requirement. Σ may be transformed, in linear time, into a system Σ', which is in normal form, such that μf_Σ is a subvector of $\mu f_{\Sigma'}$ and νf_Σ is a subvector of $\nu f_{\Sigma'}$. Moreover, $|\Sigma'| = O(|\Sigma|)$.

In the rest of this paper we propose an algorithm (CompSIGMA) for computing μf_Σ and νf_Σ, when TS, X, Y, C_σ, C_τ, δ_σ and δ_τ are given. The proposed algorithm will run in time $O(|TS| \,.\, |\Sigma|)$.
Because of the above theorem we may restrict ourselves to systems in normal form.

2. Computing μf_Σ and νf_Σ

To compute μf_Σ and νf_Σ, with Σ in normal form, we follow a two step procedure. First we transform Σ into an equivalent boolean system (section 2.1). Next we propose a method to compute the extremal fixed-points of boolean systems (section 2.2).

2.1 Transformation to boolean systems

In this section we describe how a system Σ in normal form may be transformed into an equivalent boolean system Δ involving only boolean variables and the boolean connectives $\wedge$ and $\vee$.

Let TS = [ST, TR] be a transition system and let $\Sigma = (\Sigma_\sigma, \Sigma_\tau)$ be a normal system of equations over X, Y, C_σ, C_τ. We assume interpretation functions δ_σ and δ_τ for the constants of C_σ and C_τ.
An equivalent boolean system Δ may be obtained in the following way:

Variables of Δ. The system Δ has the following set Var(Δ) of variables:

- for each state variable $x \in X$ and each state $st \in ST$ we introduce a boolean variable *st.x*
- for each transition variable $y \in Y$ and each transition $tr \in TR$ we introduce a boolean variable *tr.y*

We have: Degree(Δ) = #Var(Δ) = #ST.#X + #TR.#Y.

Equations of Δ. The system Δ has the following set Eq(Δ) of equations:

- for each equation $(x = c_\sigma) \in \Sigma_\sigma$ and each state $st \in ST$ we introduce a boolean equation:

  $st.x = \bigwedge\varnothing$[1] if $st \in \delta_\sigma(c_\sigma)$
  $st.x = \bigvee\varnothing$ if $st \notin \delta_\sigma(c_\sigma)$

- for each equation $(x = \bigvee X') \in \Sigma_\sigma$ and each state $st \in ST$ we introduce a boolean equation:

  $st.x = \bigvee \{ st.x' \mid x' \in X' \}$

- for each equation $(x = \bigwedge X') \in \Sigma_\sigma$ and each state $st \in ST$ we introduce a boolean equation:

  $st.x = \bigwedge \{ st.x' \mid x' \in X' \}$

- for each equation (x = Source(y)) $\in \Sigma_\sigma$ and each state $st \in ST$ we introduce a boolean equation:

  $st.x = \bigvee \{$ tr.y | tr is a transition leaving st $\}$

- for each equation (x = Target(y)) $\in \Sigma_\sigma$ and each state $st \in ST$ we introduce a boolean equation:

  $st.x = \bigvee \{$ tr.y | tr is a transition arriving at st $\}$

---

1. Note that $\bigwedge\varnothing$ = true whereas $\bigvee\varnothing$ = false

- for each equation (x = Soūrce(y)) $\in \Sigma_\sigma$ and each state st $\in$ ST we introduce a boolean equation:

  st.x = $\bigwedge$ { tr.y | tr is a transition leaving st }

- for each equation (x = Tarḡet(y)) $\in \Sigma_\sigma$ and each state st $\in$ ST we introduce a boolean equation:

  st.x = $\bigwedge$ { tr.y | tr is a transition arriving at st }

- for each equation (y = c_τ) $\in \Sigma_\tau$ and each transition tr $\in$ TR we introduce a boolean equation:

  tr.x = $\bigwedge \varnothing$ if tr $\in \delta_\tau(c_\tau)$
  tr.x = $\bigvee \varnothing$ if tr $\notin \delta_\tau(c_\tau)$

- for each equation (y = $\bigvee Y'$) $\in \Sigma_\tau$ and each transition tr $\in$ TR we introduce a boolean equation:

  tr.y = $\bigvee$ { tr.y' | y' $\in$ Y' }

- for each equation (y = $\bigwedge Y'$) $\in \Sigma_\tau$ and each transition tr $\in$ TR we introduce a boolean equation:

  tr.y = $\bigwedge$ { tr.y' | y' $\in$ Y' }

- for each equation (y = x_1 [] x_2) $\in \Sigma_\tau$ and each transition tr $\in$ TR with tr = (source, target) we introduce a boolean equation:

  tr.y = source.x_1 $\bigwedge$ target.x_2

The constructed boolean system Δ is equivalent to the original system Σ in the following way:

- for all st $\in$ ST and x $\in$ X we have: the st.x component of μf_Δ is true iff st $\in$ (the x component of μf_Σ)

- for all tr $\in$ TR and y $\in$ Y we have: the tr.y component of μf_Δ is true iff tr $\in$ (the y component of μf_Σ).

The same equivalence holds for the greatest fixed-point.
An inspection of the boolean system Δ reveals that all right hand sides of Δ are of one of the following two forms:

- $\bigvee$ { b_1, ..., b_k } (with $k \geq 0$)

- $\bigwedge$ { b_1, ..., b_k } (with $k \geq 0$)

Hence the algorithm for computing least and greatest fixed-points of boolean systems need only apply to systems having the above form.

2.2 Calculation of μf_Δ and νf_Δ for boolean systems

We now describe a method for computing greatest and least fixed-points of a boolean system $\Delta = \{ b_i = term_i \mid i = 1..N \}$ with right hand sides of the form:

- $\bigvee B$ (with $B \subseteq Var(\Delta)$)
- $\bigwedge B$ (with $B \subseteq Var(\Delta)$)

where $Var(\Delta) = \{ b_1, ..., b_N \}$.
Let $\mu f_\Delta = (\mu b_1, ..., \mu b_N)$ and $\nu f_\Delta = (\nu b_1, ..., \nu b_N)$. The key idea is to compute μf_Δ and νf_Δ by applying a number of transformations on Δ. These transformations all yield equivalent boolean systems (thereby preserving extremal fixed-points).
First put $\Delta^1 = \Delta$. In order to solve Δ^1 we will transform Δ^1 into an equivalent boolean system. The transformation rule is based on the following observation: suppose that Δ^1 contains an equation ($b_i = term_i$) such that $term_i$ is variable-free (i.e. $term_i$ is of the form $\bigvee\emptyset$ or $\bigwedge\emptyset$). In this case we can partially evaluate all other right hand side terms $term_j$ (with $j \neq i$) of Δ^1 by replacing every occurrence of b_i with its known fixed-point value (= $term_i$).
In this way the system Δ^1 has been split into two independent systems $\Delta^{1'}$ and $\Delta^{1''}$:

$$\Delta^1 = \Delta^{1'} + \Delta^{1''}$$

with: $\Delta^{1'} = \{ b_i = term_i \}$

$$\Delta^{1''} = \{ b_j = term_j[b_i \leftarrow term_i] \mid j = 1, ..., i\text{-}1, i\text{+}1, ..., N \}$$

with:

$$(\bigvee \{ b'_1, ..., b'_k \})[b_i \leftarrow \bigwedge\emptyset] = \bigwedge\emptyset \qquad \text{if } b_i \in \{ b'_1, ..., b'_k \}$$
$$(\bigvee \{ b'_1, ..., b'_k \})[b_i \leftarrow \bigwedge\emptyset] = \bigvee \{ b'_1, ..., b'_k \} \qquad \text{if } b_i \notin \{ b'_1, ..., b'_k \}$$

$$(\bigvee \{ b'_1, ..., b'_k \})[b_i \leftarrow \bigvee\emptyset] = \bigvee (\{ b'_1, ..., b'_k \} - \{ b_i \}) \qquad \text{if } b_i \in \{ b'_1, ..., b'_k \}$$
$$(\bigvee \{ b'_1, ..., b'_k \})[b_i \leftarrow \bigvee\emptyset] = \bigvee \{ b'_1, ..., b'_k \} \qquad \text{if } b_i \notin \{ b'_1, ..., b'_k \}$$

$$(\bigwedge \{ b'_1, ..., b'_k \})[b_i \leftarrow \bigwedge\emptyset] = \bigwedge (\{ b'_1, ..., b'_k \} - \{ b_i \}) \qquad \text{if } b_i \in \{ b'_1, ..., b'_k \}$$
$$(\bigwedge \{ b'_1, ..., b'_k \})[b_i \leftarrow \bigwedge\emptyset] = \bigwedge \{ b'_1, ..., b'_k \} \qquad \text{if } b_i \notin \{ b'_1, ..., b'_k \}$$

$$(\bigwedge \{ b'_1, ..., b'_k \})[b_i \leftarrow \bigvee\emptyset] = \bigvee\emptyset \qquad \text{if } b_i \in \{ b'_1, ..., b'_k \}$$
$$(\bigwedge \{ b'_1, ..., b'_k \})[b_i \leftarrow \bigvee\emptyset] = \bigwedge \{ b'_1, ..., b'_k \} \qquad \text{if } b_i \notin \{ b'_1, ..., b'_k \}$$

After application of the above transformation the initial problem (solve Δ^1) has been reduced to two subproblems: solve $\Delta^{1'}$ and solve $\Delta^{1''}$. As $Var(\Delta^{1'}) = \{ b_i \}$ and $Var(\Delta^{1''}) = Var(\Delta) - \{ b_i \}$ the two resulting systems are independent (i.e. $Var(\Delta^{1'}) \cap Var(\Delta^{1''}) =$

$\emptyset$). Therefore it suffices to solve both systems independently and combine their solutions to get the solutions for system Δ^1.
The system $\Delta^{1'}$ has exactly one solution which is immediate from the definition of $\Delta^{1'}$. Hence $\mu_{f_{\Delta^{1'}}} = \nu_{f_{\Delta^{1'}}}$ = true (if term$_i \equiv \bigwedge\emptyset$) and $\mu_{f_{\Delta^{1'}}} = \nu_{f_{\Delta^{1'}}}$ = false (if term$_i \equiv \bigvee\emptyset$). It remains to solve $\Delta^{1''}$.
The system $\Delta^{1''}$ is of a lower degree than the system Δ^1. So we put $\Delta^2 = \Delta^{1''}$ and start the whole procedure all over again for Δ^2 etc.
Finally we will obtain a system $\Delta^n = \Delta^{n'} + \Delta^{n''}$ such that no further transformation can be applied to $\Delta^{n''}$ (because no term of $\Delta^{n''}$ is variable-free). In this case there are two possibilities:

- either we have: Degree($\Delta^{n''}$) = 0: in this case the original system Δ has exactly one solution (hence $\mu f_\Delta = \nu f_\Delta$) which is immediate from the definitions of $\Delta^{j'}$ for j = 1..N.
- or Degree($\Delta^{n''}$) > 0:
  - as the operators $\bigvee$ { b'_1, ..., b'_k } and $\bigwedge$ { b'_1, ..., b'_k } are false-strict for k>0 it follows that all components of $\mu f_{\Delta^{n''}}$ are false; (remark: the fact that k>0 for all right hand sides of $\Delta^{n''}$ follows from the fact that no right hand side of $\Delta^{n''}$ is variable-free).
  - as the operators $\bigvee$ { b'_1, ..., b'_k } and $\bigwedge$ { b'_1, ..., b'_k } are true-strict for k>0 it follows that all components of $\nu f_{\Delta^{n''}}$ are true;

3. The algorithm

Following the ideas of section 2 we now describe an algorithm CompSIGMA to compute the least fixed-point of a system of equations (for the greatest fixed-point there is, mutatis mutandis, a similar algorithm).

```
procedure CompSIGMA( in TS, Σ; out value_Σ )
-- input parameters:
--   TS represents a finite transition system: TS = [ ST, TR ]
--   Σ represents a system (in normal form) of equations over X,Y,C_σ,C_τ
--   we assume that C_σ and C_τ are given a fixed interpretation w.r.t. TS
-- output parameters:
--   value_Σ represents a pair ( value_σ, value_τ ) with:
--      value_σ: X → IP( ST ) and value_τ: Y → IP( TR )
--   value_σ and value_τ have the following meaning:
--      value_σ( x ) = μf_Σ^x where μf_Σ^x is the x-component of μf_Σ
--      value_τ( y ) = μf_Σ^y where μf_Σ^y is the y-component of μf_Σ
begin
  step 1. Transform Σ into an equivalent boolean system Δ (see section 2.1)
  step 2. Compute the least fixed-point of Δ: CompDELTA( Δ, value_Δ )
  step 3. Calculate value_Σ from value_Δ:
          value_σ := λx.∅; value_τ := λy.∅;
          for every b ∈ Var( Δ ) with value_Δ( b ) = true do
             if b is of the form st.x then add st to value_σ( x )
             else add tr to value_τ( y ) endif;
          endfor;
          value_Σ := ( value_σ, value_τ );
end;
```

Procedure CompDELTA implements the ideas of section 2.2. A direct (but naïve) implementation of CompDELTA is given below. It makes use of the following data structures:

- to encode the current system of equations (Δ_{curr}), we associate with every variable b $\in$ Var(Δ) an attribute, denoted by *b.currterm*, containing the current right hand side of the equation associated with b. So at any moment the current system Δ_{curr} is given by Δ_{curr} = { b = b.currterm | b $\in$ Var(Δ) }. If b.currterm equals $\bigvee\emptyset$ or $\bigwedge\emptyset$ we have: μf_Δ^b = b.currterm where μf_Δ^b is the b-component of μf_Δ.

- a set *Fix* of variables containing all variables that have already been eliminated from Δ_{curr}.

Now let Arg($\bigvee B$) = B and Arg($\bigwedge B$) = B. The following invariant relations hold between Fix and Δ_{curr}:

- for all b $\in$ Fix we have: Arg(b.currterm) = $\emptyset$

- for all b ∈ Fix and b' ∈ Var(Δ) we have: b ∉ Arg(b'.currterm)

```
  -- direct implementation of CompDELTA
procedure CompDELTA( in Δ; out valueΔ )
  -- input parameters:
  --   Δ is a boolean system with rhs of the form ⋁B or ⋀B with B ⊆ Var( Δ )
  -- output parameters:
  --   valueΔ is a function of the form:
  --     valueΔ: Var( Δ ) → Bool;
  --   valueΔ has the following meaning:
  --     valueΔ( b ) = μf^b_Δ where μf^b_Δ is the b-component of μfΔ
begin
   -- initialization of Δcurr and Fix
   for each ( b = term ) ∈ Eq( Δ ) do b.currterm := term endfor;
   Fix := ∅;
   -- main loop
   while { b1 ∈ Var( Δ ) | Arg( b1.currterm ) = ∅ and b1 ∉ Fix } ≠ ∅ do
       select a variable b1 such that Arg( b1.currterm ) = ∅ and b1 ∉ Fix;
       add b1 to Fix;
       -- partially evaluate Δcurr w.r.t. b1
       for each variable b2 ∈ Var( Δ ) do
           b2.currterm := b2.currterm[ b1 ← b1.currterm ];
       endfor;
   endwhile;
   for each variable b ∈ Var( Δ ) do valueΔ( b ) := ( b.currterm ≡ ⋀∅ ) endfor;
end;
```

The naïve implementation for CompDELTA uses a miminal number of data structures but runs in time cubic in |TS|.|Σ|.

We will now optimise the above code to arrive at a linear time implementation for CompDELTA. The decrease in time-complexity is obtained by introducing some extra additional data structures.

As a first improvement, note that the set $\{ b_1 \in Var(\Delta) \mid Arg(b_1.currterm) = \emptyset \text{ and } b_1 \notin Fix \}$ need not be recomputed on each iteration step. Instead we may continuously keep track of this set by introducing an extra data structure *Eval.* The set Eval will contain all variables that are not yet eliminated from the current system Δ_{curr} of equations but whose least fixed-point values are already known. More formally, we have the following invariant relation between Eval, Δ_{curr} and Fix:

- $Eval = \{ b_1 \in Var(\Delta) \mid Arg(b_1.currterm) = \emptyset \text{ and } b_1 \notin Fix \}$

Secondly, note that, when partially evaluating Δ_{curr} w.r.t. a variable b, it is only necessary to handle the right hand sides of Δ_{curr} that actually depend upon b. Hence we define dep(b) as the set of variables currently depending upon b. More precisely:

$$\forall b_1 \in Var(\Delta): dep(b_1) \stackrel{\Delta}{=} \{ b_2 \in Var(\Delta) \mid b_1 \in Arg(b_2.currterm) \}.$$

Using the above observations we arrive at the following improved implementation for CompDELTA:

```
-- improved implementation of CompDELTA
procedure CompDELTA( in Δ; out value_Δ )
begin
  -- initialization of Δ_curr, Fix and Eval
  for each ( b = term ) ∈ Eq( Δ ) do b.currterm := term endfor;
  Fix := ∅;
  Eval := { b ∈ Var( Δ ) | ( b = term ) ∈ Eq( Δ ) with Arg( term ) = ∅ };
  -- main loop
  while Eval ≠ ∅ do
     remove a variable from Eval, say b1; add b1 to Fix;
     -- partially evaluate Δ_curr w.r.t. b1
     calculate dep( b1 );
     for each variable b2 ∈ dep( b2 ) do
        b2.currterm := b2.currterm[ b1 ← b1.currterm ];
        if Arg( b2.currterm ) = ∅ then add b2 to Eval endif;
     endfor;
  endwhile;
  for each variable b ∈ Var( Δ ) do value_Δ( b ) := ( b.currterm ≡ ∧∅ ) endfor;
end;
```

As dep(b_1) may be calculated in linear time, the above improved version of CompDELTA runs in time quadratic in $|TS|.|\Sigma|$.

It is clear that, in order to obtain a linear time algorithm for CompDELTA, it is vital to develop an efficient computation schema for dep(b_1). The set dep(b_1) is dynamic as it may change each time a variable is eliminated from Δ_{curr}. Therefore, to efficiently compute dep(b_1), we will try to relate dep(b_1) to its initial value.

Let's define the (static) set $dep_\Delta(b_1)$ as follows:

$$\forall b_1 \in Var(\Delta): dep_\Delta(b_1) \stackrel{\Delta}{=} \{ b_2 \in Var(\Delta) \mid (b_2 = term) \in Eq(\Delta) \text{ with } b_1 \in Arg(term) \}$$

The static set $dep_\Delta(b_1)$ is related to the initial system of equations Δ, whereas the (dynamic) set dep(b_1) is related to the current system Δ_{curr}. We obviously have: dep(b_1) $\subseteq dep_\Delta(b_1)$. Furthermore one can easily observe that as long as variable b_1 has not been eliminated from Δ_{curr}, we have for every variable $b_2 \in dep_\Delta(b_1)$: $b_2 \notin dep(b_1)$ iff b_2 has already reached its fixed-point value. More precisley, dep(b_1) may be characterised in terms of $dep_{\Delta}(b_1)$ as follows:

$$dep(b_1) = \{ b_2 \in dep_{\Delta}(b_1) \mid b_2 \notin (Fix \cup Eval) \}$$

Hence to efficiently compute dep(b_1), it suffices to develop an efficient computation schema for $dep_{\Delta}(b_1)$.
Because of the particular form of the equations of Σ (and Δ), a variable st.x of Δ may only effect variables related to the same state st and variables of the form tr.y where tr is a transition arriving at st or leaving from st. For the same reason a variable tr.y of Δ may only effect variables related to the same transition tr and variables of the form st.x where st is the source or the target of tr. More precisely, the set $dep_{\Delta}(b_1)$ obeys the following rules (we distinguish between the two possible forms for b_1 namely *st.x* and *tr.y*):

Table 1: rules for $dep_{\Delta}(b_1)$
$dep_{\Delta}(st.x) = \{ st.x' \mid x' \in dep_{\Sigma_\sigma}(x) \}$
$\cup \{ tr'.y' \mid y' \in dep^{+}_{\Sigma_\tau}(x)$ with tr' a transition leaving st $\}$
$\cup \{ tr'.y' \mid y' \in dep^{-}_{\Sigma_\tau}(x)$ with tr' a transition arriving at st $\}$
$dep_{\Delta}(tr.y) = \{ tr.y' \mid y' \in dep_{\Sigma_\tau}(y) \}$
$\cup \{ st'.x' \mid x' \in dep^{+}_{\Sigma_\sigma}(y)$ with st' being the source of tr $\}$
$\cup \{ st.x' \mid x' \in dep^{-}_{\Sigma_\sigma}(y)$ with st' being the target of tr $\}$
with:
$x' \in dep_{\Sigma_\sigma}(x)$ **iff** $(x' = term) \in \Sigma_\sigma$ with term of the form $\bigwedge X'$ or $\bigvee X'$ with $x \in X'$
$y' \in dep^{+}_{\Sigma_\tau}(x)$ **iff** $(y' = x \,[]\, x_2) \in \Sigma_\tau$ for some x_2
$y' \in dep^{-}_{\Sigma_\tau}(x)$ **iff** $(y' = x_1 \,[]\, x) \in \Sigma_\tau$ for some x_1
$y' \in dep_{\Sigma_\tau}(y)$ **iff** $(y' = term) \in \Sigma_\tau$ with term of the form $\bigwedge Y'$ or $\bigvee Y'$ with $y \in Y'$
$x' \in dep^{+}_{\Sigma_\sigma}(y)$ **iff** $(x' = term) \in \Sigma_\sigma$ with term of the form Source(y) or $\widetilde{Source}$(y)
$x' \in dep^{-}_{\Sigma_\sigma}(y)$ **iff** $(x' = term) \in \Sigma_\sigma$ with term of the form Target(y) or $\widetilde{Target}$(y)

Now note that the sets $dep_{\Sigma_\sigma}(x)$, $dep^{+}_{\Sigma_\tau}(x)$, $dep^{-}_{\Sigma_\tau}(x)$, $dep_{\Sigma_\tau}(y)$, $dep^{+}_{\Sigma_\sigma}(y)$ and $dep^{-}_{\Sigma_\sigma}(y)$ may be *precalculated*[2] for all $x \in X$ and $y \in Y$. Using appropriate data structures (for example pointer structures), we may assume that, given a state $st \in ST$, we have direct

2. This precalculation can be done during the initialisation phase of procedure CompSIGMA and can be performed in time $O(|\Sigma|)$.

access to the transitions leaving from and arriving at st, and given any transition tr $\in$ TR we have direct access to the source and target of tr. Hence by directly applying the rules of table 1, we arrive at an efficient (actually linear, see further) computation schema for $dep_\Delta(b_1)$.
Hence we propose the following final implementation for CompDELTA:

```
procedure CompDELTA( in Δ; out value_Δ )
  -- input parameters:
  --   Δ is a boolean system with rhs of the form ⋁B or ⋀B with B ⊆ Var( Δ )
  -- output parameters:
  --   value_Δ is a function of the form:
  --     value_Δ: Var( Δ ) → Bool;
  --   value_Δ has the following meaning:
  --     value_Δ( b ) = μf_Δ^b where μf_Δ^b is the b-component of μf_Δ
begin
   -- initialization of Δ_curr, Fix and Eval
   for each ( b = term ) ∈ Eq( Δ ) do b.currterm := term endfor;
   Eval := { b ∈ Var( Δ ) | ( b = term ) ∈ Eq( Δ ) with Arg( term ) = ∅ };
   Fix := ∅;
   -- main loop
   while Eval ≠ ∅ do
      remove a variable from Eval, say b1;
      add b1 to Fix;
      PartEval( b1 )
   endwhile;
   for each variable b ∈ Var( Δ ) do
      value_Δ( b ) := ( b.currterm ≡ ⋀∅ )
   endfor;
end;
```

```
procedure PartEval( in b1 )
-- effect
-- PartEval(b1) partially evaluates all rhs of the current system Δcurr w.r.t. variable b1;
-- furthermore all variables whose least fixed-point value became known during this
-- partial evaluation are added to Eval

begin
  calculate depΔ( b1 ) using table 1;
  for each variable b2 ∈ depΔ( b1 ) such that b2 ∉ ( Fix ∪ Eval ) do
    case b2.currterm of
      ⋁{ b1 }, ⋀{ b1 }: insert b2 in Eval; b2.currterm := b1.currterm;
      ⋀( { b1 } ∪ B ) with B ≠ ∅ and b1 ∉ B:
          if b1.currterm ≡ ⋀∅ then
            b2.currterm := ⋀B;
          else { b1.currterm ≡ ⋁∅ }
            insert b2 in Eval; b2.currterm := ⋁∅;
          endif;
      ⋁( { b1 } ∪ B ) with B ≠ ∅ and b1 ∉ B:
          if b1.currterm ≡ ⋁∅ then
            b2.currterm := ⋁B;
          else { b1.currterm ≡ ⋀∅ }
            insert b2 in Eval; b2.currterm := ⋀∅;
          endif;
    endcase;
  endfor;
end;
```

4. Correctness and time complexity

Theorem (correctness): procedure CompSIGMA is correct.

Proof: (sketch) Partial correctness of procedure CompSIGMA follows immediately from the fact that we basically perform transformations on systems of equations. The transformations are based on the substitution of variables with their already computed fixed-point values. Hence these transformations yield equivalent systems, hence preserving extremal fixed-points.

Termination of the method is guaranteed because each transformation reduces the degree of the resulting system to be solved. ■

We now prove that algorithm CompSIGMA(TS, Σ, _) may be executed in linear time.

Theorem (time complexity): algorithm CompSIGMA(TS, Σ, _) may be executed in time O(|TS| . |Σ|).

Proof: Denote by ExecTime the time needed to execute procedure CompSIGMA. We obviously have: ExecTime = $T_1 + T_2 + T_3$ where T_i (i=1..3) is the time needed to execute step i. It is not hard to see that T_1 = O(|TS| . |Σ|). Furthermore T_3 = O(#Var(Δ)). As #Var(Δ) = #X . #ST + #Y . #TR we have: T_3 = O(|TS| . |Σ|). It remains to prove that T_2 (i.e. the time needed to execute procedure CompDELTA) may be executed in linear time.
We obviously have: $T_2 = T_{init} + T_{while} + T_{foreach}$. The initialisation time (T_{init}) of procedure CompDELTA and the time to execute the for-each loop of CompDELTA may obviously be executed in time O(|TS| . |Σ|).
It remains to show that T_{while} (i.e. the time needed to execute the while-loop of procedure CompDELTA) may be executed in linear time. To do so we note that the body of the while loop is executed at most once for every variable of Δ. Hence:

$$T_{while} \leq (c_1 \, . \#Var(\Delta)) + (\sum_{b_1 \in Var(\Delta)} T_{PE}(b_1))$$

where c_1 is a constant (not depending on |TS| or |Σ|) and $T_{PE}(b_1)$ denotes the maximum time needed to execute PartEval(b_1).
Note that the body of the for-each-loop of procedure PartEval is only concerned with a few term manipulations. Using appropriate data structures (for Δ_{curr}), it can be executed in constant time. Hence:

$$T_{PE}(b_1) \leq T_{\Delta}(b_1) + c_2 \, . \#dep_{\Delta}(b_1)$$

where c_2 is a constant (not depending on |TS| or |Σ|) and $T_{\Delta}(b_1)$ denotes the maximum time needed to calculate $dep_{\Delta}(b_1)$.
Hence:

$$T_{while} \leq (c_1 \, . \#Var(\Delta)) + (c_2 \, . \sum_{b_1 \in Var(\Delta)} \#dep_{\Delta}(b_1)) + (\sum_{b_1 \in Var(\Delta)} T_{\Delta}(b_1))$$

The sets $dep_{\Sigma_\sigma}(x)$, $dep^+_{\Sigma_\tau}(x)$, $dep^-_{\Sigma_\tau}(x)$, $dep_{\Sigma_\tau}(y)$, $dep^+_{\Sigma_\sigma}(y)$ and $dep^-_{\Sigma_\sigma}(y)$ may be *precalculated*[3] for all x ∈ X and y ∈ Y. Using appropriate data structures (for example pointer-structures), we may assume that, given a state st ∈ ST, we have direct access to the transitions leaving from and arriving at st, and given any transition tr ∈ TR we have direct access to the source and target of tr. Hence by directly applying the rules of table 1, the set $dep_{\Delta}(b_1)$ may indeed be calculated in time proportional to $\#dep_{\Delta}(b_1)$. Hence:

3. This precalculation can be done during the initialisation phase of procedure CompSIGMA and can be performed in time O(|Σ|).

$$T_{while} \leq c_1 \,.\, \#Var(\Delta) + c_3 \,.\, \sum_{b_1 \in Var(\Delta)} \#dep_\Delta(b_1)$$

for some constants c_1 and c_3.
Now let's determine $\sum_{b_1 \in Var(\Delta)} \#dep_\Delta(b_1)$. We have:

$$\sum_{b_1 \in Var(\Delta)} \#dep_\Delta(b_1)$$

$$= \sum_{st \in ST} \sum_{x \in X} \#dep_\Delta(st.x) + \sum_{tr \in TR} \sum_{y \in Y} \#dep_\Delta(tr.y)$$

$$= \sum_{st \in ST} \sum_{x \in X} \#dep_{\Sigma_\sigma}(x) + \sum_{st \in ST} \sum_{x \in X} (\#succs^4(st) \,.\, \#dep^+_{\Sigma_\tau}(x))$$

$$+ \sum_{st \in ST} \sum_{x \in X} (\#preds^5(st) \,.\, \#dep^-_{\Sigma_\tau}(x)) + \sum_{tr \in TR} \sum_{y \in Y} \#dep_{\Sigma_\tau}(y)$$

$$+ \sum_{tr \in TR} \sum_{y \in Y} \#dep^+_{\Sigma_\sigma}(y) + \sum_{tr \in TR} \sum_{y \in Y} \#dep^-_{\Sigma_\sigma}(y)$$

From table 1 we immediately deduce the following inequalities:

$$\sum_{st \in ST} \sum_{x \in X} \#dep_{\Sigma_\sigma}(x) \leq \sum_{st \in ST} |\Sigma_\sigma| \leq |ST| \,.\, |\Sigma_\sigma|$$

$$\sum_{st \in ST} \sum_{x \in X} (\#succs(st) \,.\, \#dep^+_{\Sigma_\tau}(x))$$
$$\leq \sum_{st \in ST} [\#succs(st) \,.\, \sum_{x \in X} \#dep^+_{\Sigma_\tau}(x)]$$
$$\leq \sum_{st \in ST} [\#succs(st) \,.\, |\Sigma_\tau|] \leq |\Sigma_\tau| \,.\, \sum_{st \in ST} \#succs(st) \leq |TR| \,.\, |\Sigma_\tau|$$

$$\sum_{st \in ST} \sum_{x \in X} (\#preds(st) \,.\, \#dep^-_{\Sigma_\tau}(x))$$
$$\leq \sum_{st \in ST} [\#preds(st) \,.\, \sum_{x \in X} \#dep^-_{\Sigma_\tau}(x)]$$
$$\leq \sum_{st \in ST} [\#preds(st) \,.\, |\Sigma_\tau|] \leq |\Sigma_\tau| \,.\, \sum_{st \in ST} \#preds(st) \leq |TR| \,.\, |\Sigma_\tau|$$

$$\sum_{tr \in TR} \sum_{y \in Y} \#dep_{\Sigma_\tau}(y) \leq \sum_{tr \in TR} |\Sigma_\tau| \leq |TR| \,.\, |\Sigma_\tau|$$

$$\sum_{tr \in TR} \sum_{y \in Y} \#dep^+_{\Sigma_\sigma}(y) \leq \sum_{tr \in TR} |\Sigma_\sigma| \leq |TR| \,.\, |\Sigma_\sigma|$$

$$\sum_{tr \in TR} \sum_{y \in Y} \#dep^-_{\Sigma_\sigma}(y) \leq \sum_{tr \in TR} |\Sigma_\sigma| \leq |TR| \,.\, |\Sigma_\sigma|$$

Hence we readily conclude that $\sum_{b_1 \in Var(\Delta)} \#dep_\Delta(b_1) \leq c_4 \,.\, |TR| \,.\, |\Sigma|$ for some constant c_4.

---

4. succs(st) represents the set of successor states of st i.e. succs(st) = { st' ∈ ST | (st, st') ∈ TR }.
5. preds(st) represents the set of predecessor states of st i.e. preds(st) = { st' ∈ ST | (st', st) ∈ TR }.

Consequently: $T_{while} \leq (\#Var(\Delta) . c_1) + (c_3 . \sum_{b_1 \in Var(\Delta)} \#dep_\Delta(b_1)) \leq C . |TR| . |\Sigma|$ for some constant C, not depending upon |TR| and |Σ|.
Combining the above results we finally obtain the desired result: ExecTime = O(|TS| . |Σ|).
■

5. Implementation considerations

Reducing the average execution time. The *average* execution time of procedure CompDELTA may be reduced based upon the following observation: to compute the least fixed-point of the boolean system Δ we only need to eliminate a variable b_1 on condition that b_1.currterm $\equiv \bigwedge\emptyset$. Mutatis mutandis, to compute the greatest fixed-point of the boolean system Δ we only need to eliminate a variable b_1 on condition that b_1.currterm $\equiv \bigvee\emptyset$.
To incorporate the above observation we give the following new meaning to variable Eval of procedure CompDELTA: set Eval contains all variables that are not yet eliminated from the current system Δ_{curr} but whose least fixed-point values are already known and equal $\bigwedge\emptyset$. The only code that must be changed in procedure CompDELTA is the initialisation code for set Eval which now becomes:

```
-- initialization of Eval
Eval := { b ∈ Var( Δ ) | ( b = ⋀∅ ) ∈ Eq( Δ ) }
```

Because we only eliminate a variable if its least fixed-point value equals $\bigwedge\emptyset$, the body of procedure PartEval can be substantially simplified and now becomes:

```
-- body of PartEval
begin
   calculate depΔ( b1 ) using table 1;
   for each variable b2 ∈ depΔ( b1 ) such that b2 ∉ ( Fix ∪ Eval ) do
      case b2.currterm of
         ⋀{ b1 }, ⋁B: insert b2 in Eval; b2.currterm := ⋀∅;
         ⋀( { b1 } ∪ B ) with B ≠ ∅ and b1 ∉ B: b2.currterm := ⋀B;
      endcase;
   endfor;
end;
```

Remark that although the above optimisation will decrease the *average* execution time of procedure CompDELTA, it will not improve its worst case behaviour (corresponding to a system Δ where all least fixed-point components are true).

Storage requirements. We now discuss an efficient representation for the system Δ_{curr}. The choice of an adequate representation is of uttermost importance w.r.t. the memory (storage) space needed.

Choosing a representation for Δ_{curr} boils down to choosing a representation for the *currterm* attributes. These attributes are of the form $\bigvee B$ or $\bigwedge B$ with $B \subseteq Var(\Delta)$. A straightforward (but naïve) implementation would represent such an attribute by a pair (tag, B) with tag $\in \{ \bigvee, \bigwedge \}$ (i.e. tag is a boolean variable) and B simply being a set of variables. However, a closer inspection of procedures CompDELTA and PartEval reveals that, when using the above technique for reducing the average execution time, the only information we need about such an attribute is its tag together with the *cardinality* of B in case the attribute is of the form $\bigwedge B$. The cardinality of B is within the range $0..max_{card}$ with $max_{card} = max(d^+, d^-, 2, \#X, \#Y)$ where d^+ (d^-) is the maximum number of transitions leaving from (arriving at) any state of the transition system. Hence we can implement the *currterm* attributes as elements from $\{ \bigvee, \bigwedge_0, ..., \bigwedge_{max_{card}} \}$ using the following correspondence: $\bigvee \leftrightarrow \bigvee B$ and $\bigwedge_i \leftrightarrow \bigwedge B$ with $\#B = i$. This corresponds to a storage need of $\log_2(max_{card} + 2)$ bits per attribute.
Note that, in [AC] and [CS], the cardinality information is represented by means of 'counter' variables. Hence from the above discussion it is clear that these counter variables aren't but one possible way to implement the currterm attributes; they by no means form the theoretical basis of the algorithm.

6. Conclusions

We have presented an algorithm for computing the extremal fixed-points of a system of recursive equations over a transition system. The proposed algorithm runs in time $O(|TS|.|\Sigma|)$ thereby improving upon [AC].
The proposed algorithm may be classified as a *global* model cheking algorithm as it checks for all system states whether or not some recursive formula is valid. The algorithm may however easily be modified to obtain a linear-time *local* model checking agorithm. In local model checking, one is only interested in the validity of a formula w.r.t. a particular state (typically the initial system-state). To decide whether or not μf_Δ^b is true for some variable b, procedure CompDELTA may be modified as follows: in a first step we change the initialisation code for Eval such that only variables that may effect μf_Δ^b are included. In a second step the (modified) initialisation code of Eval is merged with the main loop of CompDELTA, i.e. as soon as an element of Eval is detected, it is eliminated from Δ_{curr}. If μf_Δ^b is set to true, the local model checker may terminate. Local model checking algorithms (for the full μ-calculus) are given in [C], [SW] and [W]. However, in none of these papers a complexity analysis is given. To the best of our knowledge, linear-time local model checking algorithms have not been reported in the literature thus far.
The proposed algorithm may also be used as a cornerstone for a (global) model checking algorithm for the full μ-calculus running in time $O((|TS|.|\Sigma|)^{ad(\Sigma)}$ where $ad(\Sigma)$ is the alternation-depth of Σ, as defined in [EL]. This result is important as it improves upon the $O((|TS|.|\Sigma|)^{ad(\Sigma)+1}$ time complexity of [EL], the best known algorithm for model checking

the μ-calculus known thus far.
The [AC] algorithm has also been improved independently by Cleaveland and Steffen [CS]: they discuss a linear model-checking algorithm for a fragment of the modal mu-calculus. Their algorithm, like ours, exploits the fact that upon modification of a variable b, only variables that are actually depending upon b need recomputation. To compute these variables, they use a data structure similar to the dep_{Δ}-function of table 1. Furthermore they extend the use of counters (see [AC]) to boolean equations of the form 'b = $\bigwedge$B' (in case of least fixed-points) and 'b = $\bigvee$B' (in case of greatest fixed-points). In contrast with [AC] and [CS], we did not a priori make use of counter variables. On the contrary, our algorithm has been obtained by stepwise optimisation of the straightforward (cubic) least fixed-point algorithm. The counter variables from [AC] and [CS] turned out to be implementation details, not the theoretical basis of the algorithm.

References

[AC], Arnold, A., Crubille, P.: *A linear algorithm to solve fixed-points equations on transition systems*, Information Processing Letters, vol.29, 57-66, 1988

[CES] Clarke, E.M., Emerson, E.A., Sistla, A.P.: *Automatic verification of finite-state concurrent systems using temporal logic specifications*, ACM Transactions on Progr. Languages and Systems, Vol.8, No. 2, pp. 244-263, April 1986

[C], Cleaveland, R.: *Tableau-based model checking in the propositional μcalculus*, Acta Informatica, 1990

[CS], Cleaveland, R., Steffen, B.: *Computing Behavioural Relations, Logically*, ICALP 91, pp. 127-138, LNCS 510

[D], Dicky, A.: *An algebraic and algorithmic method of analysing transition systems*, TCS, 46, 285-303, 1986

[EL], Emerson, E.A., Lei, C.-L.: *Efficient model checking in fragments of the propositional μ-calculus*, LICS, 267-278, 1986

[K], Kozen, D.: *Results on the propositional μ-calculus*, TCS, 27, 333-354, 1983

[SW], Stirling, C., Walker, D.: *Local model checking in the modal mu-calculus*, CAAP 1989, pp. 369-383, LNCS 351

[T], Tarski, A.: *A lattice-theoretic fixpoint theorem and its applications*, Pacific Journal of Mathematics, vol 5, 1955

[W], Winskel, G.: *On the compositional checking of validity*, LNCS 458, 481-501, CONCUR'90

BEYOND CONDITIONAL EQUATIONS
Quasi-Initial Semantics for Parametric Algebraic Specifications *

Uwe Wolter, Michael Löwe

FB Informatik, Technische Universität Berlin
Sekr. FR 6-1, Franklinstr. 28/29, D-1000 Berlin 10

E-mail: wolter@cs.tu-berlin.de

Abstract

Inspired by the work of S. Kaplan about positive/negative conditional rewriting, we investigate initial semantics for algebraic specifications with Gentzen-formulas. Since the standard initial approach is limited to conditional equations (i.e. positive Horn-formulas), the notion of semi-initial and quasi-initial algebras is introduced and it is shown that all specifications with (positive) Gentzen-formulas admit quasi-initial models.

The whole approach is generalized to the parametric case where quasi-initiality generalizes to quasi-freeness. Since quasi-free objects need not be isomorphic, the persistency requirement is added to obtain a *unique* semantics for many interesting practical examples. Unique persistent quasi-free semantics can be described as a free construction when the parameter category is restricted to injective homomorphisms.

An example which does not admit a correct initial semantics but a correct unique persistent quasi-initial semantics demonstrates that the concepts introduced in this paper might be of some importance w.r.t. practical applications.

1 Introduction

Algebraic specifications have been proposed as a formal method for software specification in the early seventies [Zil74, Gut75, GTW76]. Since then, algebraic specification techniques have been further developed in order to provide precise formal notions for concepts like implementation, generic data types, modularity and semantical compositionality, interfaces, and others.

Among the various research lines, there are two main streams centered around *loose* resp. *initial* semantics[1] [Gut75, BDP*79] resp. [GTW76, EM85]. While the former approach assigns a class of non-isomorphic models to an algebraic specification on the semantical level, the latter chooses the most typical model in this class as semantics, i.e. the initial model. It has been shown that the initial model exists as long as the axioms which are used in the specification are restricted to (positive) conditional equations [MM82, Wec88, Mal73]. Hence, initial algebra semantics is tied to a specific subclass of algebraic specifications, while

*This work has been partly supported by the German Ministry of Research and Technology (BMFT) as part of the compound project "KORSO – Korrekte Software".

[1] The behavioural specification approaches [Rei81, Wir86] can be seen as a separate framework. We subsume them under loose semantics here.

the notions of loose semantics work well even if the whole repertoire of first order logic is used [Wir89].

In this paper, we try to bring both approaches closer together. This is done by extending the concept of initiality to specifications with general Gentzen-formulas[2]. With this extension, we loose the uniqueness of the semantics but we avoid to assign the whole class of possible models by picking out again the most typical models which, in the case of Gentzen-formulas, need not be isomorphic. These models are called *quasi-initial* resp. in the case of parametric specifications *quasi-free*.

For parametric specifications, we discuss the special case that all consistent quasi-free models are isomorphic, which allows to speak of *the* quasi-free semantics of a parametric specification. If *the quasi-free semantics* is additionally complete, we can characterize it as a free construction w.r.t. a parameter category whose morphism set is appropriately restricted. Complete quasi-free semantics seems to be the only natural way to generalize initial resp. free semantics for data type contructors to Gentzen-specifications. Syntactical criteria are provided which allow to prove the correctness of parametric Gentzen-specifications w.r.t. a pre-given data type constructor. Correctness means that the specification has quasi-free semantics which coincides on the object part with the data type constructor.

The paper is organized as follows: Section 2 presents a data type constructor which cannot be specified by algebraic specifications with initial semantics[3]. It is the *array* resp. *finite functions* constructor over a pair of index and attribute resp. domain and codomain sets. Since this constructor is typical for practical applications, the results of section 2 show that the restriction to initial semantics might not be adequate in practice. If, however, Gentzen-formulas are allowed as axioms, small, very ellegant, and correct (first order) specifications can be written for this type of constructor. The rest of the paper aims at providing precise foundations for this concept of correctness.

The key notion in this respect is *quasi-initiality* which is introduced and investigated in section 3. The pre-ordering concepts of minimal (maximal) elements and minimal coverings (floorings)[4] are specialized to categories which naturally leads to the notions of quasi-initial object and *initial covering*. These concepts can be generalized to *quasi-free extensions* and *free coverings* by considering appropriate comma categories. The concept of an *initial covering* preserves the idea of the initial approach that only most typical models should be chosen as semantics of specification texts: all objects in an initial covering are *incomparable* (i.e. there are no homomorphisms between different objects in an initial covering) and each other object in the category is a *unique specialization* of at least one model in the covering (i.e. there is a unique homomorphism from at least one member of the initial covering to any other object in the category).

Section 4 is devoted to the proof that a sub-category of all SIG-algebras which is specified by an arbitrary set of Gentzen-formulas G always admits a free covering w.r.t. the inclusion functor $\subseteq$: Alg(SIG,G) $\to$ Alg(SIG).

The work presented in sections 3 and 4 has been very much inspired by a paper of Kaplan

[2]Gentzen-formulas are implications with a finite conjunction of equations in the premise and a finite disjunction of equations in the conclusion. A Gentzen-formula is positive if its conclusion is not empty. A conditional equation resp. positive Horn-formula is a Gentzen-formula whose conclusion has length one. A negative Horn- or Gentzen-formula is a Gentzen-type formula whose conclusion is empty. Equations are positive Horn-formulas with empty premise (compare section 4 for precise definitions).

[3]By specification, we always mean specifications with first order formulas. Hence we do not consider any constraints like generation or hierarchy requirements [EM90].

[4]Compare [Gog88].

[Kap88] about positive/negative conditional term rewriting. It contains a proof that each model class specified by Gentzen-formulas contains quasi-initial objects. The idea for our proof in section 4 is due to Kaplan, his notion of quasi-initiality, however, must be adjusted as it is done in section 3 in order to properly evaluate the suggested proof idea.

Section 5 investigates the criteria under which the construction of a free covering on objects can be extended to homomorphisms. The aim is to present a functor semantics for parametric Gentzen-specifications which is based on quasi-free constructions. It turns out that the ambiguity within free coverings prevents any general functor semantics. But adding the requirement that the semantics should be persistent leads to *unique persistent quasi-free constructions* which can be modeled as a free construction between categories whose morphism sets are restricted to injective ones.

Choosing unique persistent quasi-free constructions as the appropriate semantical model for parametric Gentzen-specifications, section 6 provides (syntactical) criteria for its existence and correctness proofs.

Section 7 contains some concluding remarks. Firstly, we apply the theory introduced in this paper to show the correctness of the Gentzen-specification for the array constructor presented in section 2. Secondly, some open questions for future research are addressed.

We presuppose some familiarity with concepts from category theory [HS73, Mac71] and universal algebra [Mal73, EM85]. Our notation follows [EM85].

2 A Data Type Constructor without Initial Specification

There are data type constructors which cannot be specified correctly using initial resp. free semantics. One very typical member of this group is the *array* resp. *finite functions* constructor, which is defined below:

Let the following two signatures PAR and FinFUNC be given.

PAR =
  SORTS dom, cod
  OPNS $\perp$: $\rightarrow$ cod
FinFUNC = PAR +
  SORTS func
  OPNS Ω: $\rightarrow$ func
    chg: dom, cod, func $\rightarrow$ func
    val: func, dom $\rightarrow$ cod

The finite functions data type constructor F: $|\text{Alg(PAR)}| \rightarrow |\text{Alg(FinFUNC)}|$[5] is defined for each algebra $A \in |\text{Alg(PAR)}|$ by:[6]

$F(A)_{\mathsf{dom}} = A_{\mathsf{dom}}$, $F(A)_{\mathsf{cod}} = A_{\mathsf{cod}}$, $F(A)_{\mathsf{func}} = [F(A)_{\mathsf{dom}} \rightarrow F(A)_{\mathsf{cod}}]^{fin}$

$\perp^{F(A)} = \perp^{A}$,

$\Omega^{F(A)} \in F(A)_{\mathsf{func}}$ is the function defined by: $\Omega^{F(A)}(x) = \perp^{F(A)}$,

[5] Alg(SIG) denotes the category of all SIG-algebras together with all homomophisms between them. |Alg(SIG)| denotes the associated class of objects.

[6] We use the following notation: If A and B are sets and $\perp \in B$, a function $f : A \rightarrow B$ is an element of the set of *finite functions* $[A \rightarrow B]^{fin}$ if the set $\{x \mid f(x) \neq \perp\}$ is finite.

$\mathsf{chg}^{F(A)} : F(A)_{\mathsf{dom}} \times F(A)_{\mathsf{cod}} \times F(A)_{\mathsf{func}} \to F(A)_{\mathsf{func}}$ provides the behaviour:

$$\mathsf{chg}^{F(A)}(x,y,f)(x') = \begin{cases} y & : \; x = x' \\ f(x') & : \; x \neq x' \end{cases},$$

$$\mathsf{val}^{F(A)} : F(A)_{\mathsf{func}} \times F(A)_{\mathsf{dom}} \to F(A)_{\mathsf{cod}} ::= \mathsf{val}^{F(A)}(f,x) = f(x)$$

Note that the constructor F is *strongly persistent*, i.e. we have for each PAR-algebra A, $[F(A)]_{\mathsf{PAR}} = A$. This means that the parameter of the constructor can be embedded into the constructed result by the identity morphism.[7]

The data type constructor F does not possess a correct specification with initial resp. free semantics. In order to prove this result, we need a preliminary notion for this type of correctness (precise definitions can be found in section 4).

Definition 2.1 (Initial Correctness of Specifications) Let signatures PSIG and BSIG be given such that PSIG⊆BSIG

1. A BSIG-*extension* (B,b) of a PSIG-algebra A is a BSIG-algebra B together with a PSIG-homomorphism $b : A \to [B]_{\mathsf{PSIG}}$.[8]
2. A *data type constructor* $F : |\mathrm{Alg(PSIG)}| \to |\mathrm{Alg(BSIG)}|$ assigns to every PSIG-algebra A a BSIG-extension of A.
3. A *specification* of F is a set CE of conditional equations w.r.t. BSIG.
4. A specification CE is *correct* w.r.t. F if for each PSIG-algebra A, $\mathrm{FREE}(A) \cong F(A)$, where FREE : Alg(PSIG) → Alg(BSIG, CE) is the free construction w.r.t. the specification inclusion (PSIG, $\emptyset$) ⊆ (BSIG, CE).

In order to prove that the finite functions constructor F: |Alg(PAR) | → |Alg(FinFUNC)| has no correct initial specification, we show that F cannot be extended to a functor. Essential for this proof is the following technical lemma:

Lemma 2.2 (**FinFunc-Homomorphisms**) *For each homomorphism* $f : F(A) \to F(B)$ *in Alg(*FinFUNC*),* f_{dom} *not being injective implies* $f_{\mathsf{cod}}(x) = \bot^{F(B)}$ *for all* $x \in F(A)_{\mathsf{cod}}$.

Proof. If f_{dom} is not injective, there are two elements $a, b \in F(A)_{\mathsf{dom}}$ such that $a \neq b$ and $f(a) = f(b)$. Since $a \neq b$, for all $x \in F(A)_{\mathsf{dom}}$:

$$\mathsf{chg}^{F(A)}(a,x,\mathsf{chg}^{F(A)}(b,\bot^{F(A)},\Omega^{F(A)})) = \mathsf{chg}^{F(A)}(b,\bot^{F(A)},\mathsf{chg}^{F(A)}(a,x,\Omega^{F(A)}))$$

f being homomorphism provides:

$$f(\mathsf{chg}^{F(A)}(a,x,\mathsf{chg}^{F(A)}(b,\bot^{F(A)},\Omega^{F(A)}))) = \mathsf{chg}^{F(B)}(f(a),f(x),f(\mathsf{chg}^{F(A)}(b,\bot^{F(A)},\Omega^{F(A)})))$$

and

$$f(\mathsf{chg}^{F(A)}(b,\bot^{F(A)},\mathsf{chg}^{F(A)}(a,x,\Omega^{F(A)}))) = \mathsf{chg}^{F(B)}(f(b),\bot^{F(B)},f(\mathsf{chg}^{F(A)}(a,x,\Omega^{F(A)})))$$

---

[7] The notion $[A]_{\mathsf{SIG}}$ denotes the restriction of an algebra A to a smaller signature by the forgetful functor associated to signature inclusions.

[8] Note that signature enlargements as they are used for example in [EM85] lead to an equivalent notion of extension.

Since $f(a) = f(b)$, the definition of chg and the intermediate results above allow to conclude $f(x) = \bot^{F(B)}$. □

Proposition 2.3 (Extension to Homomorphisms) *The finite functions constructor cannot be extended to a functor.*

Proof. Consider the following PAR-homomorphisms $h : A \to B$ and $k : B \to A$, as defined below:

$A ::= A_{\mathsf{dom}} = \{0,1\},\ A_{\mathsf{cod}} = \{a, \bot\},\ \bot^A = \bot$

$B ::= B_{\mathsf{dom}} = \{0\},\ B_{\mathsf{cod}} = \{a, \bot\},\ \bot^B = \bot$

$h : A \to B ::= h_{\mathsf{dom}}(x) = 0$ for all $x \in A_{\mathsf{dom}}$ and $h_{\mathsf{cod}} = \mathrm{ID}_{\{a,\bot\}}$

$k : B \to A ::= k_{\mathsf{dom}}(0) = 0$ and $k_{\mathsf{cod}} = \mathrm{ID}_{\{a,\bot\}}$

Note that $h \circ k = \mathrm{ID}_B$. If there were an extension of F to homomorphisms, it would be $F(h \circ k) = \mathrm{ID}_{F(B)}$. But $F(B)_{\mathsf{dom}} = B_{\mathsf{dom}} \subset A_{\mathsf{dom}} = F(A)_{\mathsf{dom}}$[9] and therefore $F(h)_{\mathsf{dom}}$ is not injective. Lemma 2.2 provides now for all $x \in F(A)_{\mathsf{cod}} = A_{\mathsf{cod}}$ that $F(h)_{\mathsf{cod}}(x) = \bot^{F(B)}$ and $F(h \circ k)_{\mathsf{cod}}(x) = F(h)_{\mathsf{cod}} \circ F(k)_{\mathsf{cod}}(x) = \bot^{F(B)} = \bot^B$. Thus, $F(h \circ k)_{\mathsf{cod}} \neq \mathrm{ID}_{\{a,\bot\}}$ which is a contradiction to the assumption that there is a functor extension of F. □

Theorem 2.4 (Missing Correct Initial Specification) *The finite functions constructor F as defined above has no correct initial specification.*

Proof. Definition 2.1 requires for a correct specification that F coincides (up to isomorphism) with a free construction on objects. But each free construction can be extended to a functor. With proposition 2.3, it can be concluded that F has no correct free specification.[10] □

The theorem demonstrates that free semantics, which is tied to conditional equations [MM82], is not sufficient if practical important data type constructors, like arrays, must be specified. We do not follow some approaches like [EM90] which introduce constraints to handle these cases. With constraints being second order tools, we loose, to some extend, syntactical access to the specifications which is crucial for evaluating tools, like interpreter and compiler, and for syntactical proof methods, like structural induction (compare section 7). By contrast, we propose to use axioms that go *beyond conditional equations.* If also *inequations* about parameter parts are allowed in the premises of conditional axioms, very ellegant and simple, first order specifications for such complex data type constructors like arrays can be written:

PAR =
  SORTS dom, cod
  OPNS $\bot$: $\to$ cod
FinFUNC-Spec = PAR +

[9] $\subset$ means *proper subset*, i.e. $\subseteq$ and $\neq$.

[10] With the same techniques, it is also possible to show that free semantics is not able to provide a correct specification for F even if *hidden sorts and operations* are allowed in the parameter and/or the 'body' part of the specification.

SORTS func
OPNS Ω: $\rightarrow$ func
chg: dom, cod, func $\rightarrow$ func
val: func, dom $\rightarrow$ cod
AXIOMS
(a1) $\text{chg}(x,y,\text{chg}(x,y',f)) = \text{chg}(x,y,f)$
(a2) $x \neq x' \Longrightarrow \text{chg}(x,y,\text{chg}(x',y',f)) = \text{chg}(x',y',\text{chg}(x,y,f))$
(a3) $\text{chg}(x,\perp,\Omega) = \Omega$
(a4) $\text{val}(\text{chg}(x,y,f),x) = y$

From the intuitive point of view, this specification seems to describe exactly and correctly the array data type constructor F. On the other hand, we loose the standard free semantics due to axiom a2 which is not a conditional equation. Therefore we need a new mathematical foundation for our intuition, which is systematically developed in the following sections by means of *quasi-initial* resp. *quasi-free* semantics. On this basis, it is easy to show formally that the specification above is correct w.r.t. F (compare section 7).

3 Quasi-Initiality and Initial Coverings

Starting from pre-order concepts, this section develops the notion of quasi-initial objects in arbitrary categories. Quasi-initial objects inherit one aspect from initial objects: if they can be related to other objects in the category by a homomorphism, this homomorphism is uniquely determined. The other aspect of initiality, namely the existence of a homomorphism to any other object in the category, which makes the initial object "the least one" of the category, is replaced by a minimality requirement. We begin the discussion by explaining this sort of minimality.

Let $(C, \leq)$ be a pre-ordered set in the following, i.e. a set C equipped with a transitive and reflexive relation $\leq$. The pre-order $\leq$ defines an equivalence $\equiv$ on C by letting $x \equiv y$ if $x \leq y$ and $y \leq x$. The relation $\leq$ can be lifted to the quotient $C_{/\equiv}$ by defining $[x] \leq_{/\equiv} [y]$ if $x \leq y$. The lifted relation $\leq_{/\equiv}$ is a partial order. Hence all concepts for partial orderings like *lower* and *upper bound*, *minimal*, *maximal*, *least*, and *greatest element*, *chain*, etc. carry over to pre-orders if we define that an element or a subset of $(C, \leq)$ has the property if and only if the corresponding equivalence class or set of equivalence classes in $(C_{/\equiv}, \leq_{/\equiv})$ satisfies the property. This means for minimal elements that m is minimal w.r.t. a pre-order $(C, \leq)$ if for all $c \in C$, $c \leq m$ implies $m \leq c$, i.e. $c \equiv m$ or $[c] = [m]$ In this setting, we obtain immediately:

Proposition 3.1 (Equivalence and Minimality) *Any element x in a pre-order $(C, \leq)$ equivalent to a minimal element y is minimal as well.*

Proof. All concepts for pre-orderings are defined up to equivalence. □

In the following, we are interested in the question under which conditions a pre-order can be "covered" by its set of minimal elements. (The next definition is due to [Gog88].)

Definition 3.2 (Covering) A *covering* of a pre-ordered set $(C, \leq)$ is a subset $F \subseteq C$ such that for each $c \in C$ there is $f \in F$ with $f \leq c$. A *minimal covering* is a covering such that none of its proper subsets is a covering.

Lemma 3.3 (Coverings and Minimal Elements) *A covering F contains up to equivalence all minimal elements.*

Proof. Let m be minimal. Since F is a covering, there is $f \in F$ with $f \leq m$. Minimality of m provides $m \equiv f$. Hence f is equivalent to m and minimal itself by proposition 3.1. □

Minimal coverings possess two additional properties as expressed in the following lemma.

Lemma 3.4 (Minimal Coverings and Minimal Elements)

1. *A minimal covering contains only minimal elements.*
2. *A covering is minimal if and only if its elements are incomparable.*

Proof. Let F be a minimal covering of $(C, \leq)$ containing f which is not minimal in C, i.e. there is some $c \in C$ with $c \leq f$ and $f \not\leq c$. Since F is a covering, we obtain $g \in F$ with $g \leq c \leq f$ and $f \neq g$. Thus $F - \{f\}$ is a covering contradicting the minimality of F.

For the second part of the statement, assume $f, g \in F$, $f \neq g$ but $g \leq f$. Again $F - \{f\}$ is a covering which is a contradiction. Now let F be a covering with incomparable elements and assume for some $f \in F$, $F - \{f\}$ is a covering. Then there is $g \in F$ with $g \leq f$ and by the incomparability of F, $g = f$; another contradiction. □

Zorn's lemma provides a sufficient condition for pre-ordered sets to possess a minimal covering.

Proposition 3.5 (Sufficient Condition for Minimal Coverings) *A non-empty pre-order $(C, \leq)$ has a minimal covering if each chain has a lower bound.*

Proof. Zorn's lemma states that C contains minimal elements. Let M be the (non-empty) set of all these elements and $M_{/\equiv}$ the corresponding set of equivalence classes w.r.t. the equivalence relation induced by $\leq$. Build the minimal covering F by choosing one element from each set in $M_{/\equiv}$.

Obviously all elements in F are incomparable. It remains to be shown that F is a covering, compare lemma 3.4(2). So let $c \in C$ be given. Define $c^{\leq} = \{d \in C \mid d \leq c\}$. $c^{\leq}$ inherits the property from C that each chain has a lower bound. Hence, $c^{\leq}$ contains a minimal element m which must be also minimal in C. Therefore, there is $f \in F$ with $f \equiv m \leq c$. Thus $f \leq c$. □

The notions minimal element and minimal covering can be adopted to arbitrary categories where they naturally lead to the concepts of quasi-initial object resp. quasi-initial covering.

Definition 3.6 (Category Pre-Ordering) Each category $\mathcal{C}$ induces a pre-ordering $\leq$ on its class of objects $|\mathcal{C}|$: for all $C, D \in \mathcal{C}$, $C \leq D$ if there is a homomorphism $f : C \to D$ in $\mathcal{C}$.

Note that initial objects in a category are least objects w.r.t. $\leq$. Vice versa, however, being the least object w.r.t. $\leq$ does not imply initiality. There is a second property required for initiality, namely that initial objects relate uniquely to any other object in the category, i.e. there is a unique homomorphism to each other object.

For the notion of quasi-initial object, we carefully weaken both properties. We substitute the requirement to be the least object by minimality and the unique relationship requirement is only demanded if there exists a relationship at all.

Definition 3.7 (Semi- and Quasi-Initiality) Let $\mathcal{C}$ be a category and $\leq$ the induced pre-order on its objects.

1. An object $S \in \mathcal{C}$ is *semi-initial* in $\mathcal{C}$ if for each $A \in \mathcal{C}$ there is at most one morphism $h : S \to A$.

2. An object $Q \in C$ is said to be *quasi-initial* in C if it is semi-initial and minimal w.r.t. $\leq$.

Quasi-initiality is more general than initiality. In categories which admit initial objects, however, both notions coincide.

Corollary 3.8 (Initiality and Quasi-Initiality) *If a category has an initial object, all its quasi-initial objects are initial as well.*

Proof. Let I be initial in C and Q be quasi-initial. Hence, there are morphisms $f : I \to Q$ and (due to the minimality requirement for Q and $I \leq Q$) $g : Q \to I$. Since I and Q are both semi-initial, the identity is their only automorphism. Thus, $g \circ f = \mathrm{ID}_I$ and $f \circ g = \mathrm{ID}_Q$ which implies $I \cong Q$ and initiality of Q. □

Note that the set $\{I\}$ is a minimal covering for a category C with initial object I. We define more generally:

Definition 3.9 (Initial Covering) An *initial covering* for a category C is a minimal covering containing only semi-initial objects.

The results obtained above for minimal coverings immediately imply:

Corollary 3.10 (Properties of Initial Coverings)

1. *An initial covering G for a category C coincides up to isomorphism with the class of all quasi-initial objects in C, i.e. G contains only quasi-initial objects and for each quasi-initial object $Q \in C$ there is a unique $P \in G$ such that $Q \cong P$.*
2. *Two initial coverings G, H for the same category C are "isomorphic" in the sense that for each object $Q \in G$ there is a unique $P \in H$ such that $Q \cong P$.*

Proof. (1) Due to lemma 3.4(1), G contains only minimal objects. Since all objects in G are semi-initial, they are quasi-initial. If $Q \in C$ is quasi-initial, there is a morphism $f : P \to Q$ for some $P \in G$ and $g : Q \to P$, since Q is minimal. Semi-initiality of P and Q immediately provides $P \cong Q$. Uniqueness of P follows from lemma 3.4(2).

(2) can be proved by an analogous argument. □

The rest of the paper investigates categories of SIG-algebras for which we obtain the following general results concerning quasi-initiality. Note, that an algebra is said to be *generated* if it has no proper subalgebra.

Lemma 3.11 (Quasi-Initiality in Algebraic Categories) *Let $\mathcal{A}$ be a category of* SIG-*algebras closed w.r.t. subalgebras and inclusion homomorphisms.*

1. *The generated subalgebra of a minimal algebra in $\mathcal{A}$ is quasi-initial in $\mathcal{A}$.*
2. *Each quasi-initial algebra in $\mathcal{A}$ is generated.*

Proof. (1) Let M be minimal in $\mathcal{A}$ and N its generated subalgebra. This provides us with two homomorphisms, namely the inclusion $i : N \to M$ and $f : M \to N$ due to minimality of M. With proposition 3.1, N is minimal itself. Since all generated algebras are semi-initial in Alg(SIG) and thus in $\mathcal{A}$, N is quasi-initial.

(2) If M is quasi-initial, it is especially semi-initial. Thus the morphisms i and f above are isomorphisms which means that M is isomorphic to its generated subalgebra and ,thereby, generated itself. □

If a category of SIG-algebras is closed w.r.t. subalgebras, the set of generated algebras becomes a covering. Hence, lemma 3.11 guarantees that any initial covering for the whole category must be found in the subcategory of generated algebras.

Proposition 3.12 (Initial Coverings and Generated Algebras) *Let $\mathcal{A}$ be a category of SIG-algebras closed w.r.t. subalgebras and inclusion homomorphisms. Then G is an initial covering for $\mathcal{A}$ if and only if it is a minimal covering for the subcategory $\mathcal{B} \subseteq \mathcal{A}$ of generated algebras.*

Proof. If G is an initial covering for $\mathcal{A}$, all its elements are quasi-initial by corollary 3.10(1) and, thereby, generated by lemma 3.11(2). G is obviously a covering of $\mathcal{B}$ and the incomparability property is invariant under the restriction to a subcategory. Vice versa, if G minimally covers $\mathcal{B}$, it is also a minimal covering for $\mathcal{A}$ since each algebra in $\mathcal{A}$ is greater than its generated subalgebra, which is in $\mathcal{B}$.

Since each algebra in G is generated it is semi-initial. Thus, G is an initial covering for $\mathcal{A}$. □

Another way to obtain an initial covering is the lifting of any minimal covering.

Proposition 3.13 (Minimal Covering Lifting) *In a category of SIG-algebras which is closed under subalgebras and inclusion homomorphisms, the class of the generated subalgebras G of a minimal covering F is an initial covering.*

Proof. Obviously, G is a covering. Lemma 3.11(1) guarantees that each algebra in G is quasi-initial. Now suppose, we have $A, B \in G$ such that $A \neq B$ but there is a homomorphism $f : A \to B$. Let A^* and B^* be the algebras in F from which A and B have been constructed. This provides inclusions $a : A \to A^*$ and $b : B \to B^*$. Since F is a covering, there is $X \in F$ and a morphism $x : X \to A$. Since $a \circ x : X \to A^*$ is a morphism, it can be concluded $X = A^*$ by the minimality of F. But now the homomorphism $b \circ f \circ x$ "compares" A^* and B^* which implies $A^* = B^*$ in contradiction to the assumption that the generated subalgebras of A^* and B^* are different. Hence all members of G are incomparable and G is minimal itself by lemma 3.4(2). □

4 Quasi-Free Semantics for Gentzen-Specifications

The central issue of this section is the proof that the inclusion functor I : Alg(SIG,G) $\to$ Alg(SIG), which embeds the SIG-algebras satisfying a set of Gentzen-formulas G into the class of all SIG-algebras, admits a free covering of I-extensions for each SIG-algebra. For this purpose, we define the concept of U-extension for arbitrary functors $U : \mathcal{K} \to \mathcal{H}$ which generalizes the notion of extension given in definition 2.1. *Quasi-free extensions* are going to be defined as quasi-initial extensions in the comma category of all extensions. We immediately focus on free coverings in order to be prepared to introduce a general semantical concept for *parametric* Gentzen-specifications.

Definition 4.1 (Extension and Free Covering) If $U : \mathcal{K} \to \mathcal{H}$ is a functor and $H \in |\mathcal{H}|$, a *U-extension*[11] of H is an object $K \in |\mathcal{K}|$ together with an $\mathcal{H}$-morphism $k : H \to U(K)$.

An extension $(K, k : H \to U(K))$ is *consistent*, *complete*, resp. *persistent* if k is a mono-, epi-, or isomorphism respectively.

[11]We also speak of *$\mathcal{K}$-extensions* if the underlying functor is obvious from the context

A morphism $e : (K_1, k_1) \rightarrow (K_2, k_2)$ between U-extensions of the same object is a $\mathcal{K}$-morphism $e : K_1 \rightarrow K_2$ satisfying $U(e) \circ k_1 = k_2$.
A U-extension of H is *free* resp. *quasi-free* over H if it is initial resp. quasi-initial in the comma category $(H \downarrow U)$[12] of all U-extensions and extension morphisms for H. An initial covering in $(H \downarrow U)$ is also called *free U-covering* for H.

Note that in case $\mathcal{H}$ is equal to a trivial one object category $(*, \mathrm{ID}_*)$, e.g. Alg($\emptyset$), we have $(* \downarrow U) \cong \mathcal{K}$. Thus the notion of initiality resp. quasi-initiality is covered by this definition.

The next definition formalizes the notions Gentzen-formula and -specification and the correspondent concepts of satisfaction and model class (compare [HK89]).

Definition 4.2 (Gentzen-Specification) A *Gentzen-type formula* g w.r.t. a signature SIG has the form $g = (\forall X : r_1 = s_1, \ldots, r_n = s_n \Longrightarrow t_1 = u_1, \ldots, t_m = u_m)$ where X is a finite set of variables, n,m are natural numbers ≥ 0, and for $i = 1 \ldots n$ and $j = 1 \ldots m$, $r_i, s_i, t_j, u_j \in T_{\mathrm{SIG}}(X)$. A formula is said to be *negative* if $m = 0$, it is a *Horn-type formula* if $m = 1$ (also called *conditional equation*), and it is an *equation* if it is a Horn-formula with empty premise.

A SIG-algebra A *satisfies* a Gentzen-formula g, written $A \models g$, if for each variable assignment $h : X \rightarrow A$ the induced unique SIG-homomorphism $h^* : T_{\mathrm{SIG}}(X) \rightarrow A$ provides $h^*(t_1) = h^*(u_1)$ or $\ldots$ or $h^*(t_m) = h^*(u_m)$ if $h^*(r_1) = h^*(s_1)$ and $\ldots$ and $h^*(r_n) = h^*(s_n)$.[13]

A *Gentzen-specification* GSPEC = (SIG, G) is a signature SIG together with a set G of Gentzen-formulas over SIG. Alg(SIG,G) is the full subcategory of all SIG-algebras satisfying every $g \in G$.

To show the existence of free coverings in the extension categories w.r.t. the inclusion functor I : Alg(SIG,G) $\rightarrow$ Alg(SIG), we use Zorn's lemma and the technique of minimal covering lifting introduced in proposition 3.13. As a technical requirement for this procedure, the following well-known result is needed:

Lemma 4.3 (Closure w.r.t. Subalgebras) *Each category* Alg(SIG,G) *specified by Gentzen-fomulas G is closed w.r.t. subalgebras.*

Proof. Direct consequence of the fact that all $g \in G$ are universally quantified, compare [Mal73]. □

Lemma 4.4 (Covering for Extensions) *If I :* Alg(SIG,G) $\rightarrow$ Alg(SIG) *is the inclusion functor associated to a Gentzen specification and $A \in$* Alg(SIG), *each (non-empty) chain in the category $(A \downarrow I)$ has a lower bound w.r.t. the induced pre-order $\leq$ (compare definition 3.6).*

Proof. A chain $\mathcal{A}$ in $(A \downarrow I)$ consists of a family $|\mathcal{A}| = (A_j, a_j)_{j \in J}$ of extensions of A for a totally ordered index set J and a family of extension morphisms $(f_{jk} : (A_j, a_j) \rightarrow (A_k, a_k))_{j \leq k \in J}$ which means

$$I(f_{jk}) \circ a_j = f_{jk} \circ a_j = a_k \text{ for all } j \leq k \in J \qquad \text{(e1)}$$

[12] For comma category constructions compare [Mac71, HS73].

[13] Note that this means for negative formulas that no assignment is allowed to satisfy the premise, i.e. if $m = 0$, $A \models g$ if for all $h : X \rightarrow A$, $h^*(r_1) \neq h^*(s_1)$ or $\ldots$ or $h^*(r_n) \neq h^*(s_n)$. In such a way negative Gentzen-formulas coincide with disjunctions of inequalities.

since I is an inclusion functor in this case. The lower bound is constructed as follows:

First build the product $(\prod |\mathcal{A}|, (p_j : \prod |\mathcal{A}| \to A_j)_{j\in J})$ in Alg(SIG) for all extensions in the chain. The family $(p_j)_{j\in J}$ represents the product projections. The universal property of the product provides a unique homomorphism $\pi : A \to \prod |\mathcal{A}|$ such that

$$p_j \circ \pi = a_j \text{ for all } j \in J \qquad \text{(e2)}$$

Second construct the epi-mono-factorization of π, i.e. decompose π into an epimorphism $\pi^e : A \to L$ and a monomorphism $\pi^m : L \to \prod |\mathcal{A}|$ such that

$$\pi^m \circ \pi^e = \pi \qquad \text{(e3)}$$

The pair (L, π^e) is the required lower bound!

We have to show (i) that there is an extension morphism l_j from (L, π^e) to (A_j, a_j) for each $j \in J$ and (ii) that $L \models G$.

(i) The required morphism is $l_j = p_j \circ \pi^m$. Due to (e2) and (e3), it satisfies $p_j \circ \pi^m \circ \pi^e = p_j \circ \pi = a_j$. Furthermore with (e1), we obtain $f_{jk} \circ p_j \circ \pi^m \circ \pi^e = f_{jk} \circ a_j = a_k = p_k \circ \pi^m \circ \pi^e$. Since π^e is epi, we get moreover that $((L, \pi^e), (l_j)_{j\in J})$ is a cone of $\mathcal{A}$ in $(A \downarrow I)$, i.e.:

$$f_{jk} \circ l_j = f_{jk} \circ p_j \circ \pi^m = p_k \circ \pi^m = l_k \text{ for all } j \leq k \in J \qquad \text{(e4)}$$

(ii) Let $g = (\forall X : r_1 = s_1, \ldots, r_n = s_n \Longrightarrow t_1 = u_1, \ldots, t_m = u_m) \in G$ and $h : X \to L$ be an assignment satisfying $h^*(r_p) = h^*(s_p)$ for all $p = 1 \ldots n$. This induces assignments $h_j = p_j \circ \pi^m \circ h : X \to A_j$ for all $j \in J$. They satisfy for all $p = 1 \ldots n$:

$$h_j^*(r_p) = (p_j \circ \pi^m \circ h)^*(r_p) = p_j \circ \pi^m \circ h^*(r_p) = p_j \circ \pi^m \circ h^*(s_p) = h_j^*(s_p)$$

Since all algebras in the chain satisfy g, there must be for every $j \in J$ at least one index $q \in \{1, \ldots, m\}$ such that $h_j^*(t_q) = h_j^*(u_q)$. Thus, for all $j \in J$, the sets $E_j = \{q \in \{1, \ldots, m\} | \, h_j^*(t_q) = h_j^*(u_q)\}$ are all not empty. With (e4) it can be concluded that $f_{jk} \circ h_j^* = f_{jk} \circ p_j \circ \pi^m \circ h^* = p_k \circ \pi^m \circ h^* = h_k^*$ and, thereby, $E_j \subseteq E_k$ for all $j \leq k \in J$. Gentzen-formulas have only a finite number of equations in the conclusion. Hence, $\bigcap(E_j)_{j\in J} \neq \emptyset$. Let $y \in \bigcap(E_j)_{j\in J}$. It provides

$$h_j^*(t_y) = h_j^*(u_y) \text{ for all } j \in J \qquad \text{(e5)}$$

Since elements of the cartesian product are equal if all projections coincide and $h_j^* = p_j \circ \pi^m \circ h^*$, equation (e5) entails $\pi^m \circ h^*(t_y) = \pi^m \circ h^*(u_y)$ which leads to $h^*(t_y) = h^*(u_y)$ due to π^m being monomorphism. Hence $L \models g$. □

Theorem 4.5 (First Main Result) *For a Gentzen-specification* (SIG, G) *and a* SIG-*algebra* A, *the category of all* I-*extensions of* A *w.r.t. the inclusion functor* I : Alg(SIG,G) $\to$ Alg(SIG), *i.e.* $(A \downarrow I)$, *is either empty or has a free covering.*

Proof. Let $(A \downarrow I) \neq \emptyset$. With lemma 4.4 and proposition 3.5, we obtain a minimal covering of $(A \downarrow I)$. Let this covering be $(M_q, m_q : A \to M_q)_{q\in Q}$. Since Alg(SIG,$G$) is closed under subalgebras, compare lemma 4.3, the epi-mono-factorization of all these extension morphisms, i.e. their decomposition into an epimorphism $m_q^e : A \to F_q$ and a monomorphism $m_q^m : F_q \to M_q$ yields another covering $(F_q, m_q^e : A \to F_q)_{q\in Q}$ which contains only semi-initial objects since the morphisms are epi. With the argument of proposition 3.13 the incomparability property of $(M_q, m_q : A \to M_q)_{q\in Q}$ carries over to $(F_q, m_q^e : A \to F_q)_{q\in Q}$. Hence it is a free covering by lemma 3.4(2). □

Corollary 4.6 (Quasi-Free Construction) *If* (SIG, G) *is a Gentzen-specification without negative formulas, the inclusion functor* I : Alg(SIG,G) $\rightarrow$ Alg(SIG) *comes equipped with a quasi-free construction, which assigns to each* $A \in$ Alg(SIG) *the free covering of all* I*-extensions of* A.

Proof. In the case of positive Gentzen-formulas, the trivial or terminal algebra $\perp^{\mathsf{SIG}}$ in Alg(SIG) is also in Alg(SIG,G). Thus $(\perp^{\mathsf{SIG}}, \perp : A \rightarrow \perp^{\mathsf{SIG}})$,with $\perp$ being the terminal homomorphism, is an I-extension for each $A \in$ Alg(SIG). Hence $(A \downarrow I) \neq \emptyset$ for all $A \in$ Alg(SIG) which means by theorem 4.5 that it contains a free covering. □

Note that the initiality of T_{SIG} in Alg(SIG) entails $(T_{\mathsf{SIG}} \downarrow I) \cong$ Alg(SIG, G). Thus the free covering of all I-extensions of T_{SIG} provides the initial covering of Alg(SIG, G).

Quasi-free constructions can be used to assign semantics to arbitrary parametric Gentzen-specifications, which is done in the rest of this section.

Definition 4.7 (Parametric Gentzen-Specification) A *parametric Gentzen-specification* ((PSIG,G_P),(BSIG,G_B)) is a pair of Gentzen-specifications such that PSIG$\subseteq$BSIG and $G_P \subseteq G_B$. The component (PSIG,G_P) is called *formal parameter* and (BSIG,G_B) constitutes the *body* of the parametric specification.

Since there are free constructions for each forgetful functor U : Alg(BSIG) $\rightarrow$ Alg(PSIG), associated to a signature inclusion (compare [EM85]), and quasi-free constructions for each inclusion functor I : Alg(BSIG,G_B) $\rightarrow$ Alg(BSIG), the following lemma about composition of quasi-free and free constructions guarantees that quasi-free semantics can be assigned to each parametric Gentzen-specification with positive formulas.

Lemma 4.8 (Composition of Quasi-Free Constructions) *If* $V : \mathcal{K} \rightarrow \mathcal{H}$ *and* $U : \mathcal{H} \rightarrow \mathcal{G}$ *are functors such that* U *has free* $\mathcal{H}$*-extensions and* V *admits free* $\mathcal{K}$*-coverings, the functor* $U \circ V$ *has free* $\mathcal{K}$*-coverings for each* $G \in \mathcal{G}$.

Proof. Let $G \in \mathcal{G}$, $(H, h : G \rightarrow U(H))$ the free U-extension of G, and $\mathcal{Q}$ the free V-covering over H. The class $\mathcal{Q}' = \{(K, U(k) \circ h : G \rightarrow U \circ V(K)) | (K, k : H \rightarrow V(K)) \in \mathcal{Q}\}$ is a free covering of $U \circ V$-extensions over G.

Each element in $\mathcal{Q}'$ is semi-initial since the assumption of two $\mathcal{K}$-morphisms $x, y : K \rightarrow X$ such that $(U \circ V)(x) \circ U(k) \circ h = (U \circ V)(y) \circ U(k) \circ h$ provides $U(V(x) \circ k) \circ h = U(V(y) \circ k) \circ h$, $V(x) \circ k = V(y) \circ k$ due to (H, h) being free extension, and $x = y$ since (K, k) is a semi-initial extension.

Any $(U \circ V)$-extension $(Z, z : G \rightarrow U \circ V(Z))$ is covered by $\mathcal{Q}'$: (H, h) as a free extension provides a morphism $z^* : H \rightarrow V(Z)$ such that $U(z^*) \circ h = z$. The pair (Z, z^*) constitutes a V-extension of H. Hence there is $(K, k : H \rightarrow V(K)) \in \mathcal{Q}$ such that there is a $\mathcal{K}$-morphism $z^{**} : K \rightarrow Z$ with $V(z^{**}) \circ k = z^*$. By construction $(K, U(k) \circ h : G \rightarrow U \circ V(K)) \in \mathcal{Q}'$. It covers (Z, z) since the morphism z^{**} satisfies $(U \circ V)(z^{**}) \circ U(k) \circ h = U(V(z^{**}) \circ k) \circ h = U(z^*) \circ h = z$.

Finally, we have to show that all elements in $\mathcal{Q}'$ are incomparable: Having $(K_1, U(k_1) \circ h) \neq (K_2, U(k_2) \circ h) \in \mathcal{Q}'$ and $f : K_1 \rightarrow K_2$ with $(U \circ V)(f) \circ U(k_1) \circ h = U(k_2) \circ h$, the universal property of h provides $V(f) \circ k_1 = k_2$ which finally leads to $(K_1, k_1) = (K_2, k_2)$ since $\mathcal{Q}$ is a free covering and contains incomparable elements only. □

Note that the opposite composition, namely first applying a free covering constructor and afterwards a free construction to each member of the covering, does not always yield a free covering.

Example 4.9 (Missing Compositionallity) Consider the signature $\mathsf{SIG} = (\text{SORTS S};$ OPNS a,b,c:→ S) and the axioms: $(a1) \quad a = b \vee b = c$ and $(a2) \quad a = b \Rightarrow b = c$.

We obtain inclusion functors $I_1 : \text{Alg}(\mathsf{SIG},\{a1, a2\}) \to \text{Alg}(\mathsf{SIG},\{a1\})$ and $I_2 : \text{Alg}(\mathsf{SIG},\{a1\}) \to \text{Alg}(\mathsf{SIG})$. I_2 has free coverings by corollary 4.6 and I_1 has a left-adjoint since $(a2)$ is a conditional equation.

The quasi-free extensions of T_{SIG} are isomorphic to the algebras $A^1 ::= A^1_S = \{[a, b], c\}$ and $A^2 ::= A^2_S = \{a, [b, c]\}$ with the obvious assignment of the constants. The free I_1-extension of A^1 is the algebra A^3 uniquly defined by the S-carrier $\{[a, b, c]\}$ and the free I_1-extension of A^2 is A^2 itself. If the involved free and quasi-free constructors are composed, it yields the covering $\{A^3, A^2\}$ which is not a free $(I_2 \circ I_1)$-covering due to the existence of the terminal morphism $\perp : A^2 \to A^3$. □

Theorem 4.10 (Quasi-Free Semantics) *For each parametric positive Gentzen-specification* $((\mathsf{PSIG},G_P),(\mathsf{BSIG},G_B))$, *the associated forgetful functor* $U : \text{Alg}(\mathsf{BSIG},G_B) \to \text{Alg}(\mathsf{PSIG},G_P)$ *allows to assign free* (BSIG,G_B)*-coverings to each* $A \in \text{Alg}(\mathsf{PSIG},G_P)$. *This assignment denotes the semantics of the specification.*

Proof. Direct consequence of corollary 4.6 and lemma 4.8 using the inclusion functor $V' : \text{Alg}(\mathsf{BSIG},G_B) \to \text{Alg}(\mathsf{BSIG})$ and the forgetful functor $U' : \text{Alg}(\mathsf{BSIG}) \to \text{Alg}(\mathsf{PSIG})$. □

The next sections are going to investigate this type of quasi-free semantics for parametric positive Gentzen-specifications and the conditions under which it can be extended to a left-adjoint functor on suitably adjusted categories.

5 Functor Semantics for Quasi-Free Constructions

Quasi-free constructions for parametric Gentzen-specifications which assign to each actual parameter algebra the free covering of its body extensions are a compromise between initial and loose semantics. Since Gentzen-formulas do not admit a single simplest model, a class of models constitutes the semantics which, however, represents the whole category in the simplest way: each other extension in the category is a unique specialization of at least one member of the free covering and the free covering is the smallest ensemble with this property, i.e. removing an object from the covering makes the representation of the category (in the above sense) incomplete.

Thus as far as objects are concerned, the semantical concepts introduced in the previous section are satisfactory. The question which is addressed in this section is how or under which conditions this object assignment can be extended to homomorphisms. The ultimate goal is to interpret quasi-free constructions as left-adjoint functors on suitably adjusted categories. This seems to be a necessary prerequisite if we want to apply the theory for parameter passing, extension, and amalgamation [EM85] to Gentzen-specifications.

Since left-adjoint functors require (up to isomorphism) unique object assignments and the concept of quasi-free constructions is inherently ambiguous, the essential question in this respect is which additional requirements are suitable to distinguish "the best quasi-free extension".

That this selection of a best extension is necessary shows the following intuitive approach to map homomorphisms. It tries to handle the ambiguity on objects but fails to provide the functor properties on homomorphisms.

Definition 5.1 (Intuitive Extension to Homomorphisms) Let $U : \mathcal{K} \to \mathcal{H}$ be a functor which has free coverings, $f : A \to B$, $g : B \to C$ be $\mathcal{H}$-morphisms, and $Q(A), Q(B)$, and $Q(C)$ be the free U-coverings for A, B, C resp. The set

$$Q(f) = \{f^* : Q_A \to Q_B | (Q_A, u_A) \in Q(A), (Q_B, u_B) \in Q(B) \text{ and } u_B \circ f = U(f^*) \circ u_A\}$$

of homomorphisms between quasi-free extensions in $Q(A)$ and $Q(B)$ is said to be the *intuitive free covering morphism* for f w.r.t. U, $Q(f) : Q(A) \to Q(B)$ in symbols.

Composition $Q(g) \circ Q(f) : Q(A) \to Q(C)$ is defined by:

$$Q(g) \circ Q(f) = \{g^* \circ f^* | (f^* : Q_A \to Q_B) \in Q(f), (g^* : Q_B \to Q_C) \in Q(g)\}$$

Proposition 5.2 (Intuitive Extension) *There are Gentzen-specifications* (PSPEC, BSPEC) *for which the free-covering semantics together with the intuitive extension to homomorphisms does not provide a functor.*

Proof. Consider the Gentzen-specifications below:

PAR =
  SORTS S
  OPNS a,b,c: → S
BOD = PAR +
  OPNS x: → S
  AXIOMS
    (a1) x = b ∨ x = c
    (a2) a = b ⟹ x = b

Choose the following PAR-algebras and homomorphisms:

$$A ::= A_S = \{a, b, c\},\ a^A = a,\ b^A = b,\ c^A = c$$

$$B ::= B_S = \{[a, b], c\},\ a^B = [a, b],\ b^B = [a, b],\ c^B = c$$

$$C ::= C_S = \{[a, b, c]\},\ a^C = b^C = c^C = [a, b, c]$$

$$f : A \to B ::= a \mapsto [a, b],\ b \mapsto [a, b],\ c \mapsto c$$

$$g : B \to C ::= [a, b] \mapsto [a, b, c],\ c \mapsto [a, b, c]$$

The free BOD-covering for A consists of two BOD-algebras, i.e.:

$$A1 ::= A1_S = \{a, [b, x], c\},\ a^{A1} = a,\ b^{A1} = [b, x],\ c^{A1} = c,\ x^{A1} = [b, x] \text{ and}$$

$$A2 ::= A2_S = \{a, b, [c, x]\},\ a^{A2} = a,\ b^{A2} = b,\ c^{A2} = [c, x],\ x^{A2} = [c, x]$$

There is only one quasi-free BOD-extension in $Q(B)$ and $Q(C)$ for B and C:

$$B1 ::= B1_S = \{[a, b, x], c\},\ a^{B1} = b^{B1} = x^{B1} = [a, b, x],\ c^{B1} = c \quad \text{resp.}$$

$$C1 ::= C1_S = \{[a, b, c, x]\},\ a^{C1} = b^{C1} = c^{C1} = x^{C1} = [a, b, c, x]$$

The extension morphisms are the natural homomorphisms. The crucial point is that there are morphisms $(g \circ f)_1^* : A1 \to C1$, $(g \circ f)_2^* : A2 \to C1$, $f^* : A1 \to B1$, $g^* : B1 \to C1$ and that there are no other morphisms. Especially there is no homomorphism between $A2$ and $B1$. Hence $Q(g \circ f) = \{(g \circ f)_1^*, (g \circ f)_2^*\} \neq Q(g) \circ Q(f) = \{g^* \circ f^*\}$. □

Note that the example in the proof is of the same type as example 4.9. There seems to be no chance to extend quasi-free constructions naturally to homomorphisms unless we get rid of the ambiguity of quasi-free extensions.

The direct way to achieve this uniqueness, namely to require for "reasonable specifications" that all free coverings are singleton sets is not very useful. Free coverings as singleton sets imply that there is an initial extension. Hence we are back to ordinary free semantics which is tied to specifications with conditional equations [MM82, Wec88]. Therefore, this notion of "reasonable specification" is equivalent to specification with conditional equations. The example in section 2 demonstrates that this might not be sufficient for practical needs.

And a second look at the introductory example can give an important hint what the right tool for achieving uniqueness can be: The example specification does not use arbitrary Gentzen-formulas. What is actually used is inequations concerning parameter components in the premise of 'conditional equations'.

The intuitive background of this demand for inequations is that the specification task concerns the data type constructor *not* the parameter. Each actual parameter is pre-given and might be inspected w.r.t. equality *as well as* inequality. The idea is that we specify the constructor *on top of* the parameter. A similar concept for the introduction of negative knowledge is known from logic and logic programming under the name *stratification* [ABW87, BF89].

But this concept of *hierarchical* specification immediately implies that the result, i.e. the constructed data type, should not destroy its basis, i.e. the actual parameter. This means that not only the set of equations valid in the actual parameter should also be valid in the constructed result, which is guaranteed since each extension comes equipped with an extension homomorphism transporting equations. It also means that all inequations satisfied by the parameter shall also be true in the constructed data type. This conception is exactly reflected if we require reasonable extensions to be consistent.

Furthermore, if we require complete knowledge about equality *and* inequality of all parameter algebras, the homomorphism concept between parameter objects immediately reduces to injective ones. It is exactly this class of homomorphisms which respects and transports not only equality but also inequality.

The statements and arguments above motivate the following definition.

Definition 5.3 (Unique Quasi-Free Semantics) A functor $U : \mathcal{K} \to \mathcal{H}$ has a *unique quasi-free semantics* if for each object $H \in |\mathcal{H}|$, the free U-covering for H contains exactly one consistent extension.

Note that the uniqueness property for consistent quasi-free extensions entails that some Gentzen-specifications do not possess semantics in this sense. It might be due to two reasons: (1) for some parameters, there is no consistent quasi-free extension at all and (2) some parameters admit several consistent extensions. Let us shortly discuss both aspects:

In the case of free-functor-semantics [EM85, Rei87], it is possible to assign semantics even to inconsistent specifications. The theory, however, and the languages based on this theory can only be developed for consistent specifications (compare [EM85, EM90, ECB*89]). Hence consistence either built-in in semantics or required as a prerequisite for theoretical and practical results seems unavoidable if algebraic specifications are put to practice.

On the other hand, it does not seem to be harmful if ambiguous specifications do not get semantics. The process of specification is always specification of data types or data type constructors in the sense of definition 2.1. Since they are unique resp. functorial, correct semantics for their specifications should have the same property.

That unique quasi-free semantics goes beyond free-functor semantics is demonstrated in section 7 by showing the specification FinFUNC-Spec correct w.r.t. the array constructor F, both defined in section 2.

Proposition 5.4 (Extension to Homomorphisms) *If $U : \mathcal{K} \to \mathcal{H}$ is a functor with unique quasi-free semantics, the object assignment $H \mapsto (K, k : H \to U(K))$, which assigns to each $H \in |\mathcal{H}|$ the consistent quasi-free U-extension K, can be extended to all monomorphisms in $\mathcal{H}$, i.e. for each monomorphism $m : H_1 \to H_2$ in $\mathcal{H}$, there is a unique $\mathcal{K}$-morphism $m^* : K_1 \to K_2$ such that $U(m^*) \circ k_1 = k_2 \circ m$ where (K_1, k_1) resp. (K_2, k_2) is the unique extension of H_1 resp. H_2.*

Proof. Consider the U-extension $(K_2, k_2 \circ m : H_1 \to U(K_2))$. Since U admits a free $\mathcal{K}$-covering for H, there must be a quasi-free extension $(X, x : H_1 \to U(X))$ in this covering such that there exists a $\mathcal{K}$-morphism $y : X \to K_2$ such that $U(y) \circ x = k_2 \circ m$. The morphisms m and k_2 are monomorph implying that x is monomorph. Hence $(X, x : H \to U(X))$ is a consistent quasi-free extension of H. But this extension is unique up to isomorphism, i.e. $X \cong K_1$ and $U(\cong) \circ k_1 = x$. Let $m^* = y \circ \cong : K_1 \to K_2$. It satisfies $U(m^*) \circ k_1 = U(y \circ \cong) \circ k_1 = U(y) \circ U(\cong) \circ k_1 = U(y) \circ x = k_2 \circ m$. The uniqueness of m^* follows directly from the semi-initiality of the extension (K_1, k_1). □

With the result of proposition 5.4, it seems promising to investigate if the unique quasi-free semantics w.r.t. a functor $U : \mathcal{K} \to \mathcal{H}$ can be turned into a left-adjoint of U if $\mathcal{H}$ and $\mathcal{K}$ are suitably restricted to monomorphisms.

Definition 5.5 (Functor Restriction to Monomorphisms) If $U : \mathcal{K} \to \mathcal{H}$ is a functor and $\mathcal{H}_{|m}$ the subcategory of $\mathcal{H}$ containing all and only the monomorphisms of $\mathcal{H}$, let $\mathcal{K}_{|m}$ be the preimage of $\mathcal{H}_{|m}$ w.r.t. U and let $U_{|m} : \mathcal{K}_{|m} \to \mathcal{H}_{|m}$ be the corresponding *restriction of U to $\mathcal{H}$-monomorphisms.*

The following example shows that unique quasi-free semantics of a functor U is in general not sufficient for the existence of a left-adjoint functor for $U_{|m}$.

Example 5.6 (Incomplete Specifications) Consider the parametric Gentzen-specification below:

PAR =
  SORTS S1, S2
BOD = PAR +
  OPNS a,b: $\to$ S1
  AXIOMS $\forall x, y \in$S2: $x \neq y \Longrightarrow$ a = b

Obviously the specification allows exactly one consistent quasi-free BOD-extension for each PAR-algebra. So let the following PAR-homomorphism $f : A \to B$ be given:

$$A ::= A_{S1} = \emptyset,\ A_{S2} = \{*\};\quad B ::= B_{S1} = \emptyset,\ B_{S2} = \{*, +\};\quad f ::= f_{S1} = \emptyset,\ f_{S2} = \subseteq$$

The morphism f is monomorph. i.e. $f \in \mathrm{Alg(PAR)}_{|m}$. The quasi-free extensions of A and B are isomorphic to A^* and B^* resp.:

$$A^* ::= A^*_{S1} = \{a, b\},\ A^*_{S2} = \{*\},\ a^{A^*} = a,\ b^{A^*} = b$$

$$B^* ::= B^*_{S1} = \{[a, b]\},\ B^*_{S2} = \{*, +\},\ a^{B^*} = b^{B^*} = [a, b]$$

The extension $f^* : A^* \to B^*$ is defined as follows:

$f^*_{S1} ::= a \mapsto [a,b], b \mapsto [a,b]; \; f^*_{S2} ::= * \mapsto *$

Since $[f^*]_{\mathsf{PAR}} = f^*$ as a mapping,$[f^*]_{\mathsf{PAR}}$ is not monomorph and, thereby, $f^* \notin \mathrm{Alg}(\mathsf{BOD})_{|m}$. Thus the unique quasi-free semantics for this example fails to map homomorphisms into the desired target category and the restricted forgetful functor together with the quasi-free semantics do not constitute a pair of adjoints. □

In order to obtain a suitable adjoint situation for unique quasi-free semantics, we need additional requirements. One very natural property to demand is the completeness of the semantics, which is actually sufficient for quasi-free semantics to be turned into a free functor.

Theorem 5.7 (Second Main Result) *If $U : \mathcal{K} \to \mathcal{H}$ is a functor whose unique quasi-free semantics is* persistent, *its restriction to monomorphisms, i.e. $U_{|m} : \mathcal{K}_{|m} \to \mathcal{H}_{|m}$, has a left-adjoint functor, i.e. the quasi-free semantics.*

Proof. Proposition 5.4 guarantees that the unique object assignment of the quasi-free semantics can be extended to monomorphisms. It remains to show that the morphisms of $\mathcal{H}_{|m}$ are actually mapped into $\mathcal{K}_{|m}$. This means we have to prove that for each morphism $f : A \to B \in \mathcal{H}_{|m}$ its extension $f^* : A^* \to B^*$ to $\mathcal{K}$ satisfies $U(f^*) \in \mathcal{H}_{|m}$. Let $a : A \to U(A^*)$ and $b : B \to U(B^*)$ be the extension morphisms which are isomorphisms since the quasi-free semantics is persistent. Proposition 5.4 guarantees $U(f^*) \circ a = b \circ f$. Since $b \circ f$ is monomorph and a is an isomorphism, $U(f^*)$ must be monomorph, i.e. $U(f^*) \in \mathcal{H}_{|m}$. □

To summarize: Quasi-free semantics can be turned into a free construction on the parameter category restricted to monomorphisms, if the free covering contains exactly one consistent extension for each parameter algebra which is additionally complete.

6 On the Existence of Unique Quasi-Free Semantics

The remarks in section 5 concerning definition 5.3 pointed out that Gentzen-specifications are not guaranteed to possess unique quasi-free semantics. This section provides first criteria for its existence which are sufficient to evaluate the sample specification FinFUNC-Spec in section 2. The most powerful tools are provided for *hierarchical* specifications. Their axioms can be interpreted as implications with a single equation in the conclusion. The premise consists of a finite number of equations and a finite number of *inequations on parameter sorts.*

Definition 6.1 (Extension Theory) Let $\mathsf{PSIG} \subseteq \mathsf{BSIG}$ be two signatures, $U : \mathrm{Alg}(\mathsf{BSIG}) \to \mathrm{Alg}(\mathsf{PSIG})$ the associated forgetful functor, and $A \in \mathrm{Alg}(\mathsf{PSIG})$. If $\mathcal{K}$ is a subcategory of $(A \downarrow U)$, the *$\mathcal{K}$-theory* $\equiv^{\mathcal{K}}$ for A is the following set of equations:

$$\equiv^{\mathcal{K}} = \{(t = t') \mid t, t' \in T_{\mathsf{BSIG}}(|A|) \text{ and for all } (K,k) \in \mathcal{K} : k^*(t) = k^*(t')\}$$

where $k^* : T_{\mathsf{BSIG}}(|A|) \to K$ is the unique evaluation of terms satisfying $U(k^*) \circ \subseteq = k$ with $\subseteq : |A| \to |U(T_{\mathsf{BSIG}}(|A|))|$ being the obvious inclusion.

We have the following well-known result about the relationship between free extensions in a category $\mathcal{K}$ and the associated theory $\equiv^{\mathcal{K}}$.

Proposition 6.2 (Representation of Free Extensions) *Let $U : \mathrm{Alg}(\mathsf{BSIG}) \to \mathrm{Alg}(\mathsf{PSIG})$ be a forgetful functor associated to a signature inclusion and $A \in \mathrm{Alg}(\mathsf{PSIG})$.*

1. *If a (isomorphism closed) category* $\mathcal{K} \subseteq (A \downarrow U)$ *has a free extension* $(F, f : A \to U(F))$, *then* $F \cong T_{\mathsf{BSIG}}(|A|)_{/\equiv^{\mathcal{K}}}$ *and* $(U(\cong) \circ f) = (U(\equiv^{\mathcal{K}}) \circ \subseteq)$.
2. *If the* BSIG*-extension* $(T_{\mathsf{BSIG}}(|A|)_{/\equiv^{\mathcal{K}}}, (U(\equiv^{\mathcal{K}}) \circ \subseteq) : A \to U(T_{\mathsf{BSIG}}(|A|)_{/\equiv^{\mathcal{K}}}))$ *is in* $\mathcal{K}$, *it is initial in* $\mathcal{K}$.

Note that $\equiv^{\mathcal{K}}$ contains the ground theory of A. Thus the mapping $(U(\equiv^{\mathcal{K}}) \circ \subseteq)$ above actually becomes a PSIG-homomorphism.

Corollary 6.3 (Existence Criterion) *A Gentzen-specification* $((\mathsf{PSIG}, G_P), (\mathsf{BSIG}, G_B))$ *has a unique quasi-free semantics if and only if for each parameter algebra* A, $T_{\mathsf{BSIG}}(|A|)_{/\equiv^{\mathcal{K}}}$ *is a consistent* (BSIG, G_B)*-extension of* A *where* $\mathcal{K}$ *is the category of all consistent* (BSIG, G_B)*-extensions of* A.

Proof. Direct consequence of proposition 6.2 and the observation that definition 5.3 and proposition 5.4 state that there is unique quasi-free semantics if and only if all consistent extensions have an initial object. □

On the basis of corollary 6.3, the existence of a persistent unique quasi-free semantics can be characterized as follows.

Corollary 6.4 (Persistent Semantics) *A Gentzen-specification* $((\mathsf{PSIG}, G_P), (\mathsf{BSIG}, G_B))$ *has a persistent unique quasi-free semantics if and only if for each parameter algebra* A

1. *there is a consistent* (BSIG, G_B)*-extension of* A,
2. $T_{\mathsf{BSIG}}(|A|)_{/\equiv^{\mathcal{K}}} \models G_B$, *and*
3. *for every parameter sort* S *and term* $t \in T_{\mathsf{BSIG}}(|A|)_S$, *there is a* $a \in A_S$ *such that* $(a = t) \in \equiv^{\mathcal{K}}$

where $\mathcal{K}$ *is the category of all consistent extensions of* A.

Proof. (1) and (2) simply reformulate corollary 6.3 and (3) is the standard characterization of completeness in terms of the associated theory, compare [EM85]. □

A careful analysis of these three conditions shows that the crucial point is condition (2). The first requirement is almost trivial if a persistent data type constructor is pre-given as in the example in section 2: it just has to satisfy the body axioms. The third condition can be proved using structural induction on terms, a sound deduction system for first order logic with equation [HK89], and as ground facts the instances of the body axioms, the ground-equality of the parameter, and its *ground-inequalities*.

Hence in a last step, we want to get rid of the second condition, which actually works for *hierarchical* parametric specifications.

Definition 6.5 (Hierarchical Positive Gentzen-Specifications) A parametric Gentzen-specification $((\mathsf{PSIG}, G_P), (\mathsf{BSIG}, G_B))$ is said to be *hierarchical* if every formula $g \in G_B$ looks like:

$$g = (\forall X : r_1 = s_1, \ldots, r_n = s_n, t_1 \neq u_1, \ldots, t_m \neq u_m \Longrightarrow t = u)$$

with $n, m \geq 0$ such that for $i = 1 \ldots m$, t_i, u_i are terms of a parameter sort.

Theorem 6.6 (Third Main Result) *A hierarchical specification* $((\mathsf{PSIG}, G_P), (\mathsf{BSIG}, G_B))$ *has a persistent unique quasi-free semantics if and only if for each parameter algebra* A *the following conditions are satisfied:*

1. *There is a consistent* (BSIG, G_B)*-extension of* A *and*

2. *for every parameter sort* S *and term* $t \in T_{\mathsf{BSIG}}(|A|)_S$*, there is* $a \in A_S$ *such that* $(a = t) \in \equiv^{\mathcal{K}}$

Proof. It remains to show that for hierarchical specifications (1) and (2) above imply $T_{\mathsf{BSIG}}(|A|)_{/\equiv^{\mathcal{K}}} \models G_B$ for $\mathcal{K}$ being the category of all consistent extensions of A. (1) and (2) entail that $(U(\equiv^{\mathcal{K}}) \circ \subseteq)$ is isomorphic. Thus for every consistent (BSIG, G_B)-extension (K, k) of A the PSIG-part $U(h)$ of the unique extension morphism $h : T_{\mathsf{BSIG}}(|A|)_{/\equiv^{\mathcal{K}}} \rightarrow K$ becomes monomorphic. But this means that any ground inequation (and equation) on parameter sorts is valid in $T_{\mathsf{BSIG}}(|A|)_{/\equiv^{\mathcal{K}}}$ if and only if it is valid in all consistent extensions of A. In such a way a variable assignment satisfying the premise of an implication in G_B has to satisfy the conclusion as well according to the construction $\equiv^{\mathcal{K}}$. □

7 Concluding Remarks

Motivated by a data type constructor which cannot be specified correctly using initial resp. free semantics, we have introduced and developed the theory of Gentzen-specifications and their quasi-free semantics. The aim to model unique quasi-free semantics as an adjoint situation has naturally led to an algebraic analogon to stratification, namely the requirement for a *unique consistent* quasi-free extension, compare section 5. In the previous section, we have discussed first criteria for the existence of unique quasi-free semantics which allow to evaluate the finite functions example of section 2.

It can be shown that the specification FinFUNC-Spec is correct w.r.t. the data type constructor F (both defined in section 2) in the sense that

- the specification *has* a unique quasi-free semantics which is persistent and
- the semantics coincides up to isomorphism with the constructor F.

For the first point, we only have to prove the two sufficient conditions of theorem 6.6, since the specification is hierarchical. (1) The constructor F is persistent itself and it is easy to check that $F(A)$ satisfies the axioms (a1) –(a4) of the specification FinFUNC-Spec for every PAR-algebra A. Hence there is a consistent FinFUNC-Spec-extension for all parameters. (2) Completeness of the specification requires a proof by structural induction that each term t of sort func is equivalent to a term chg(a,x,f) for any given (parameter) element $\mathsf{a} \in A_{\mathsf{cod}}$. With this lemma, it is easy to show that the val-operation is completely specified.

The second issue, namely the coincidence of the semantics with F, can be proved by standard techniques using representation systems of terms, compare [EM85].

Thus, quasi-free semantics for hierarchical Gentzen-specifications, as it has been developed in this paper, is able to provide short, readable, correct first-order specifications for important data type constructors which fail to have a correct specification with free semantics. Correctness proofs for this type of semantics can use the same technique as already known for initial semantics, compare [Kap88]. In order to better evaluate the impact of this new approach w.r.t. practical applications and theoretical results

- some more and bigger examples should be modeled by quasi-free semantics,
- the relationship to specifications with constraints should be investigated, and
- a theory of parameter passing, amalgamation, and extension should be provided.

These issues are left to future research.

References

[ABW87] K. Apt, H. Blair, and A. Walker. Towards a theory of declarative knowledge. In J. Minker, editor, *Foundations of Deductive Databases and Logic Programming,* Morgan Kaufmann, Los Altos, 1987.

[BDP*79] M. Broy, W. Dosch, H. Partsch, P. Pepper, and M. Wirsing. Existential quantifiers in abstract data types. In H. A. Maurer, editor, *Sixth International Colloquium on Automata, Languages, and Programming,* pages 73 – 87, Springer Lecture Notes on Computer Science 71, Berlin, 1979.

[BF89] S. Bratella and G. File. *A completeness result for SLDNF resolution.* Technical Report Rapporto Interno Dip 9, Dipartimento di Mathematica, Universita di Padova, 1989.

[ECB*89] H. Ehrig, I. Claßen, P. Boehm, W. Fey, M. Korff, and M. Löwe. Algebraic concepts for software development in ACT ONE, ACT TWO, and LOTOS. In *GI Tagung Softwareentwicklung,* pages 201 – 224, Springer Informatik Fachberichte 212, Berlin, 1989.

[EM85] H. Ehrig and B. Mahr. *Fundamentals of Algebraic Specifications 1. Monographs in Computer Science,* Springer, Berlin, 1985.

[EM90] H. Ehrig and B. Mahr. *Fundamentals of Algebraic Specifications 2. Monographs in Computer Science,* Springer, Berlin, 1990.

[Gog88] J. A. Goguen. *What is unification? A categorical view of substitution, equation, and solution.* Technical Report CSLI-88-124, Center for the Study of Languages and Information, 1988.

[GTW76] J. A. Goguen, J. W. Thatcher, and E. G. Wagner. *An Initial Algebra Approach to the Specification, Correctness, and Implementation of Abstract Data Types.* Research Report RC 6487, IBM T. J. Watson Research Center, Yorktown Heights, 1976. Also in: Current Trends in Programming IV: Data Structuring (ed. R.Yeh), Prentice Hall, 80–149 (1978).

[Gut75] J. V. Guttag. *The specification and application to programming of abstract data types.* PhD thesis, University of Toronto, 1975.

[HK89] D. Hofbauer and R. Kutsche. *Grundlagen des machinellen Beweisens.* Vieweg, Braunschweig/Wiesbaden, 1989.

[HS73] H. Herrlich and G. Strecker. *Category Theory.* Allyn and Bacon, Rockleigh, New Jersey, 1973.

[Kap88] S. Kaplan. Positive/negative conditional rewriting. In S. Kaplan and J. P. Jouannaud, editors, *Conditional Term Rewriting Systems,* pages 129 – 143, Springer Lecture Notes in Computer Science 308, Berlin, 1988.

[Mac71] S. MacLane. *Categories for the Working Mathematician.* Springer, Berlin, 1971.

[Mal73] A. I. Mal'cev. *Algebraic Systems.* Springer, Berlin, 1973. translated from the original edition 1970.

[MM82] B. Mahr and J.A. Makowski. *Characterizing specification languages which admit initial semantics.* Technical Report 232, Technion Haifa, 1982. Also in Theoretical Computer Science, 31:49–59, 1984.

[Rei81] H. Reichel. Behavioural equivalence – a unifying concept for initial and final specification methods. In *Third Hungarian Computer Science Conference,* pages 27 – 39, 1981.

[Rei87] H. Reichel. *Initial Computability, Algebraic Specifications, and Partial Algebras.* Akademie-Verlag, Berlin, 1987.

[Wec88] W. Wechler. *Universal algebra for computer scientists.* Technical Report, Technische Universität Dresden, Sektion Mathematik, 1988. To be published as a book by Springer.

[Wir86] M. Wirsing. Structured algebraic apecification: a kernel language. *Theoretical Computer Science,* 43:123 – 250, 1986.

[Wir89] M. Wirsing. *Algebraic Specification.* Research Report MIP-8914, University of Passau, 1989. Updated version also in "Handbook of Theor. Comp. Sci. Vol. B, Elsevier, Amsterdam,1990.

[Wol91] U. Wolter. Deduction in partial equational Horn theories. *Journal of Information Processing and Cybernetics (EIK),* 27(2):85 – 128, 1991.

[Zil74] S. N. Zilles. *Algebraic specification of data types.* Technical Report, MIT, Project MAC Progress Report 11, pages 28 – 52, 1974.

Lecture Notes in Computer Science

For information about Vols. 1–491
please contact your bookseller or Springer-Verlag

Vol. 492: D. Sriram, R. Logcher, S. Fukuda (Eds.), Computer-Aided Cooperative Product Development. Proceedings, 1989 VII, 630 pages. 1991.

Vol. 493: S. Abramsky, T. S. E. Maibaum (Eds.), TAPSOFT '91. Volume 1. Proceedings, 1991. VIII, 455 pages. 1991.

Vol. 494: S. Abramsky, T. S. E. Maibaum (Eds.), TAPSOFT '91. Volume 2. Proceedings, 1991. VIII, 482 pages. 1991.

Vol. 495: 9. Thalheim, J. Demetrovics, H.-D. Gerhardt (Eds.), MFDBS '91. Proceedings, 1991. VI, 395 pages. 1991.

Vol. 496: H.-P. Schwefel, R. Männer (Eds.), Parallel Problem Solving from Nature. Proceedings, 1990. XI, 485 pages. 1991.

Vol. 497: F. Dehne, F. Fiala. W.W. Koczkodaj (Eds.), Advances in Computing and Information - ICCI '91. Proceedings, 1991. VIII, 745 pages. 1991.

Vol. 498: R. Andersen, J. A. Bubenko jr., A. Sølvberg (Eds.), Advanced Information Systems Engineering. Proceedings, 1991. VI, 579 pages. 1991.

Vol. 499: D. Christodoulakis (Ed.), Ada: The Choice for '92. Proceedings, 1991. VI, 411 pages. 1991.

Vol. 500: M. Held, On the Computational Geometry of Pocket Machining. XII, 179 pages. 1991.

Vol. 501: M. Bidoit, H.-J. Kreowski, P. Lescanne, F. Orejas, D. Sannella (Eds.), Algebraic System Specification and Development. VIII, 98 pages. 1991.

Vol. 502: J. Bārzdiņž, D. Bjørner (Eds.), Baltic Computer Science. X, 619 pages. 1991.

Vol. 503: P. America (Ed.), Parallel Database Systems. Proceedings, 1990. VIII, 433 pages. 1991.

Vol. 504: J. W. Schmidt, A. A. Stogny (Eds.), Next Generation Information System Technology. Proceedings, 1990. IX, 450 pages. 1991.

Vol. 505: E. H. L. Aarts, J. van Leeuwen, M. Rem (Eds.), PARLE '91. Parallel Architectures and Languages Europe, Volume I. Proceedings, 1991. XV, 423 pages. 1991.

Vol. 506: E. H. L. Aarts, J. van Leeuwen, M. Rem (Eds.), PARLE '91. Parallel Architectures and Languages Europe, Volume II. Proceedings, 1991. XV, 489 pages. 1991.

Vol. 507: N. A. Sherwani, E. de Doncker, J. A. Kapenga (Eds.), Computing in the 90's. Proceedings, 1989. XIII, 441 pages. 1991.

Vol. 508: S. Sakata (Ed.), Applied Algebra, Algebraic Algorithms and Error-Correcting Codes. Proceedings, 1990. IX, 390 pages. 1991.

Vol. 509: A. Endres, H. Weber (Eds.), Software Development Environments and CASE Technology. Proceedings, 1991. VIII, 286 pages. 1991.

Vol. 510: J. Leach Albert, B. Monien, M. Rodríguez (Eds.), Automata, Languages and Programming. Proceedings, 1991. XII, 763 pages. 1991.

Vol. 511: A. C. F. Colchester, D. J. Hawkes (Eds.), Information Processing in Medical Imaging. Proceedings, 1991. XI, 512 pages. 1991.

Vol. 512: P. America (Ed.), ECOOP '91. European Conference on Object-Oriented Programming. Proceedings, 1991. X, 396 pages. 1991.

Vol. 513: N. M. Mattos, An Approach to Knowledge Base Management. IX, 247 pages. 1991. (Subseries LNAI).

Vol. 514: G. Cohen, P. Charpin (Eds.), EUROCODE '90. Proceedings, 1990. XI, 392 pages. 1991.

Vol. 515: J. P. Martins, M. Reinfrank (Eds.), Truth Maintenance Systems. Proceedings, 1990. VII, 177 pages. 1991. (Subseries LNAI).

Vol. 516: S. Kaplan, M. Okada (Eds.), Conditional and Typed Rewriting Systems. Proceedings, 1990. IX, 461 pages. 1991.

Vol. 517: K. Nökel, Temporally Distributed Symptoms in Technical Diagnosis. IX, 164 pages. 1991. (Subseries LNAI).

Vol. 518: J. G. Williams, Instantiation Theory. VIII, 133 pages. 1991. (Subseries LNAI).

Vol. 519: F. Dehne, J.-R. Sack, N. Santoro (Eds.), Algorithms and Data Structures. Proceedings, 1991. X, 496 pages. 1991.

Vol. 520: A. Tarlecki (Ed.), Mathematical Foundations of Computer Science 1991. Proceedings, 1991. XI, 435 pages. 1991.

Vol. 521: B. Bouchon-Meunier, R. R. Yager, L. A. Zadek (Eds.), Uncertainty in Knowledge-Bases. Proceedings, 1990. X, 609 pages. 1991.

Vol. 522: J. Hertzberg (Ed.), European Workshop on Planning. Proceedings, 1991. VII, 121 pages. 1991. (Subseries LNAI).

Vol. 523: J. Hughes (Ed.), Functional Programming Languages and Computer Architecture. Proceedings, 1991. VIII, 666 pages. 1991.

Vol. 524: G. Rozenberg (Ed.), Advances in Petri Nets 1991. VIII, 572 pages. 1991.

Vol. 525: O. Günther, H.-J. Schek (Eds.), Advances in Spatial Databases. Proceedings, 1991. XI, 471 pages. 1991.

Vol. 526: T. Ito, A. R. Meyer (Eds.), Theoretical Aspects of Computer Software. Proceedings, 1991. X, 772 pages. 1991.

Vol. 527: J.C.M. Baeten, J. F. Groote (Eds.), CONCUR '91. Proceedings, 1991. VIII, 541 pages. 1991.

Vol. 528: J. Maluszynski, M. Wirsing (Eds.), Programming Language Implementation and Logic Programming. Proceedings, 1991. XI, 433 pages. 1991.

Vol. 529: L. Budach (Ed.), Fundamentals of Computation Theory. Proceedings, 1991. XII, 426 pages. 1991.

Vol. 530: D. H. Pitt, P.-L. Curien, S. Abramsky, A. M. Pitts, A. Poigné, D. E. Rydeheard (Eds.), Category Theory and Computer Science. Proceedings, 1991. VII, 301 pages. 1991.

Vol. 531: E. M. Clarke, R. P. Kurshan (Eds.), Computer-Aided Verification. Proceedings, 1990. XIII, 372 pages. 1991.

Vol. 532: H. Ehrig, H.-J. Kreowski, G. Rozenberg (Eds.), Graph Grammars and Their Application to Computer Science. Proceedings, 1990. X, 703 pages. 1991.

Vol. 533: E. Börger, H. Kleine Büning, M. M. Richter, W. Schönfeld (Eds.), Computer Science Logic. Proceedings, 1990. VIII, 399 pages. 1991.

Vol. 534: H. Ehrig, K. P. Jantke, F. Orejas, H. Reichel (Eds.), Recent Trends in Data Type Specification. Proceedings, 1990. VIII, 379 pages. 1991.

Vol. 535: P. Jorrand, J. Kelemen (Eds.), Fundamentals of Artificial Intelligence Research. Proceedings, 1991. VIII, 255 pages. 1991. (Subseries LNAI).

Vol. 536: J. E. Tomayko, Software Engineering Education. Proceedings, 1991. VIII, 296 pages. 1991.

Vol. 537: A. J. Menezes, S. A. Vanstone (Eds.), Advances in Cryptology – CRYPTO '90. Proceedings. XIII, 644 pages. 1991.

Vol. 538: M. Kojima, N. Megiddo, T. Noma, A. Yoshise, A Unified Approach to Interior Point Algorithms for Linear Complementarity Problems. VIII, 108 pages. 1991.

Vol. 539: H. F. Mattson, T. Mora, T. R. N. Rao (Eds.), Applied Algebra, Algebraic Algorithms and Error-Correcting Codes. Proceedings, 1991. XI, 489 pages. 1991.

Vol. 540: A. Prieto (Ed.), Artificial Neural Networks. Proceedings, 1991. XIII, 476 pages. 1991.

Vol. 541: P. Barahona, L. Moniz Pereira, A. Porto (Eds.), EPIA '91. Proceedings, 1991. VIII, 292 pages. 1991. (Subseries LNAI).

Vol. 543: J. Dix, K. P. Jantke, P. H. Schmitt (Eds.), Nonmonotonic and Inductive Logic. Proceedings, 1990. X, 243 pages. 1991. (Subseries LNAI).

Vol. 544: M. Broy, M. Wirsing (Eds.), Methods of Programming. XII, 268 pages. 1991.

Vol. 545: H. Alblas, B. Melichar (Eds.), Attribute Grammars, Applications and Systems. Proceedings, 1991. IX, 513 pages. 1991.

Vol. 547: D. W. Davies (Ed.), Advances in Cryptology – EUROCRYPT '91. Proceedings, 1991. XII, 556 pages. 1991.

Vol. 548: R. Kruse, P. Siegel (Eds.), Symbolic and Quantitative Approaches to Uncertainty. Proceedings, 1991. XI, 362 pages. 1991.

Vol. 550: A. van Lamsweerde, A. Fugetta (Eds.), ESEC '91. Proceedings, 1991. XII, 515 pages. 1991.

Vol. 551:S. Prehn, W. J. Toetenel (Eds.), VDM '91. Formal Software Development Methods. Volume 1. Proceedings, 1991. XIII, 699 pages. 1991.

Vol. 552: S. Prehn, W. J. Toetenel (Eds.), VDM '91. Formal Software Development Methods. Volume 2. Proceedings, 1991. XIV, 430 pages. 1991.

Vol. 553: H. Bieri, H. Noltemeier (Eds.), Computational Geometry - Methods, Algorithms and Applications '91. Proceedings, 1991. VIII, 320 pages. 1991.

Vol. 554: G. Grahne, The Problem of Incomplete Information in Relational Databases. VIII, 156 pages. 1991.

Vol. 555: H. Maurer (Ed.), New Results and New Trends in Computer Science. Proceedings, 1991. VIII, 403 pages. 1991.

Vol. 556: J.-M. Jacquet, Conclog: A Methodological Approach to Concurrent Logic Programming. XII, 781 pages. 1991.

Vol. 557: W. L. Hsu, R. C. T. Lee (Eds.), ISA '91 Algorithms. Proceedings, 1991. X, 396 pages. 1991.

Vol. 558: J. Hooman, Specification and Compositional Verification of Real-Time Systems. VIII, 235 pages. 1991.

Vol. 559: G. Butler, Fundamental Algorithms for Permutation Groups. XII, 238 pages. 1991.

Vol. 560: S. Biswas, K. V. Nori (Eds.), Foundations of Software Technology and Theoretical Computer Science. Proceedings, 1991. X, 420 pages. 1991.

Vol. 561: C. Ding, G. Xiao, W. Shan, The Stability Theory of Stream Ciphers. IX, 187 pages. 1991.

Vol. 562: R. Breu, Algebraic Specification Techniques in Object Oriented Programming Environments. XI, 228 pages. 1991.

Vol. 563: A. Karshmer, J. Nehmer (Eds.), Operating Systems of the 90s and Beyond. Proceedings, 1991. X, 285 pages. 1991.

Vol. 564: I. Herman, The Use of Projective Geometry in Computer Graphics. VIII, 146 pages. 1992.

Vol. 565: J. D. Becker, I. Eisele, F. W. Mündemann (Eds.), Parallelism, Learning, Evolution. Proceedings, 1989. VIII, 525 pages. 1991. (Subseries LNAI).

Vol. 566: C. Delobel, M. Kifer, Y. Masunaga (Eds.), Deductive and Object-Oriented Databases. Proceedings, 1991. XV, 581 pages. 1991.

Vol. 567: H. Boley, M. M. Richter (Eds.), Processing Declarative Kowledge. Proceedings, 1991. XII, 427 pages. 1991. (Subseries LNAI).

Vol. 568: H.-J. Bürckert, A Resolution Principle for a Logic with Restricted Quantifiers. X, 116 pages. 1991. (Subseries LNAI).

Vol. 569: A. Beaumont, G. Gupta (Eds.), Parallel Execution of Logic Programs. Proceedings, 1991. VII, 195 pages. 1991.

Vol. 570: R. Berghammer, G. Schmidt (Eds.), Graph-Theoretic Concepts in Computer Science. Proceedings, 1991. VIII, 253 pages. 1992.

Vol. 571: J. Vytopil (Ed.), Formal Techniques in Real-Time and Fault-Tolerant Systems. Proceedings, 1992. IX, 620 pages. 1991.

Vol. 572: K. U. Schulz (Ed.), Word Equations and Related Topics. Proceedings, 1990. VII, 256 pages. 1992.

Vol. 573: G. Cohen, S. N. Litsyn, A. Lobstein, G. Zémor (Eds.), Algebraic Coding. Proceedings, 1991. X, 158 pages. 1992.

Vol. 574: J. P. Banâtre, D. Le Métayer (Eds.), Research Directions in High-Level Parallel Programming Languages. Proceedings, 1991. VIII, 387 pages. 1992.

Vol. 575: K. G. Larsen, A. Skou (Eds.), Computer Aided Verification. Proceedings, 1991. X, 487 pages. 1992.

Vol. 576: J. Feigenbaum (Ed.), Advances in Cryptology - CRYPTO '91. Proceedings. X, 485 pages. 1992.

Vol. 577: A. Finkel, M. Jantzen (Eds.), STACS 92. Proceedings, 1992. XIV, 621 pages. 1992.

Vol. 578: Th. Beth, M. Frisch, G. J. Simmons (Eds.), Public-Key Cryptography: State of the Art and Future Directions. XI, 97 pages. 1992.

Vol. 579: S. Toueg, P. G. Spirakis, L. Kirousis (Eds.), Distributed Algorithms. Proceedings, 1991. X, 319 pages. 1992.

Vol. 581: J.-C. Raoult (Ed.), CAAP '92. Proceedings. VIII, 361 pages. 1992.